CANDIDA YEAST INFECTION

The "Silent Killer"

A PRACTICAL HANDBOOK ON THE CAUSE AND CURE

OF DEGENERATIVE DISEASE.

FOR

THE PHYSICIAN,

THE STUDENT,
and
THE VICTIM.

By RUPERT BEEBE.
Scientific Nutritional Consultant.

HEALTHOLOGY
ASSN. CANADA.
"The SCIENCE of Health"

6024 -- 180A St.
Surrey, B.C., V3S 6W6.
Canada.

Candida Yeast Infection, "The Silent Killer", is published by the Healthology Assn. (Canada), 6024 -- 180 A St. Surrey (Vancouver) B.C. Canada, V3S 6W6.

ISBN 0-9693588-0-6

Printed and Bound in Canada
By
Hignell Printing Ltd.
Winnipeg, Manitoba.
Canada.

This Book.

This book is written for the Doctor or other Health Professional, for the student, and for all victims of ill health.

This book is written in simple language, and in general terms, to show that all forms of ill health are based in Candida Yeast Infection, or that they have a Candida Yeast component. Specific information on reducing Candida Yeast infection has been included as a guide for both the professional and the afflicted.

This book is written as educational material, with important points repeated several times in different ways to ensure that the general concepts are grasped and remembered.

All material in this book has been drawn from apparently reliable sources and every effort has been made to keep everything scientifically correct in all respects. A list of the principal reference materials is provided.

This book is written for information only. This book should not be construed as being diagnostic or prescriptive. In all Provinces of Canada and in all States of the U.S.A. your Medical Doctor has the sole right to diagnose and prescribe.

The final purpose and intent of this book is to bring new practical information to you, to your Doctor, and to other Health Professionals, and thereby improve Health Technology: with wide benefits to all.

****

CANDIDA YEAST INFECTION
"THE SILENT KILLER".

by

Rupert Beebe.

Scientific Nutritional Consultant.

DEDICATION ----

The ill, the sick, and the weary,-- it is to these people that this book is dedicated,--- for these are the people without hope.

These are the people that medicine has abandoned, through lack of learning, and through lack of using, the knowledge that mankind has gained.

To the ill, the sick, and the weary,-- in the hope that they can better understand, and help their hapless state;-- and with the further hope that they will gain a little more of the medical attention that they so sorely deserve.

This book is also dedicated to the many intelligent doctors who have contributed so greatly to our knowledge of Candida Yeast, and who have struggled in vain to convince their colleagues of the many hidden dangers from this ubiquitous common infective.

In this dedication I must also express my deep appreciation to my wife Edna, who has not only tolerated the inevitable disruption associated with the writing of such a large book, but who has also struggled many long hours with an Xerox Memorywriter to produce each of the finished camera ready pages for the printing of this book. To Edna my thanks and my love.

Rupert Beebe.

CANDIDA YEAST INFECTION

"THE SILENT KILLER".

CONTENTS.

Page.

Ch. 1. **OVERVIEW**.. 1.

Ch. 2. **SEEKING THE SHADOWY AGENT OF DEATH**.... 20.

Ch. 3. **CHRONIC INFECTION**..................................... 27.
    CANDIDA YEAST INFECTION,"THE SILENT KILLER". 27.
    CANDIDA UPDATE,----by DR. BUSCHER................... 27.
    MEDICAL PAPERS ON CANDIDA YEAST INFECTION. 31.
    SOURCES OF INFECTION... 31.
    MEDICAL PAPERS ON CANDIDA YEAST IN NATURE. 32.
    MEDICAL PAPERS ON CANDIDA YEAST SPECIES..... 32.
    OTHER INFECTIVES ASSOCIATED WITH CANDIDA. .. 32.
    SUBSTANCES SYNTHESIZED BY CANDIDA YEAST..... 32.
    MEDICAL PAPERS ON CANDIDAL DISEASES............. 35.
    INCREASE OF CANDIDA INFECTION......................... 37.
    CANDIDA IN THE MEDICAL ESTABLISHMENT.......... 38.
    ANTIFUNGALS AND INHIBITING FACTORS. .... 39.
    CANDIDA IN THE MEDICAL LIBRARY. .... 42.
    FATAL FUNGAL INFECTIONS.................................. 42.
    TOTAL CHRONIC INFECTION................................. 44.
    ENDOTOXEMIA IN ATYPICAL CANDIDIASIS. .... 45.
    CLINICAL INDICATIONS OF YEAST INFECTION........ 56.
    MINERAL TESTS. .... 57.
    LAB.TESTS.. 59.
    ANTIGEN SKIN TESTS. .... 59.
    CANDIDAL CAPACITY TEST...................................... 60.
    BLOOD TESTS. .... 60.
    FINGERNAILS. .... 60..
    TOENAILS. .... 61.
    "BURNING FEET".. 62.
    NOSE AND SINUSES.. 62.
    MOUTH AND CANKER SORES.................................... 62.
    ESOPHAGUS AND HIATUS HERNIA. .... 62.
    DIGESTIVE. .... 62.
    COLON AND ANUS.. 63.
    SEXUAL.. 63.
    BLUE AND RED SPOTS AND COLD AREAS. .... 64.
    ENDOTHALMITIS AND DISSEMINATED CANDIDA..... 64.
    URINARY.. 65.
    LUNGS AND AIR TRACT... 65.
    PROBABILITY FACTORS... 65.
    ASSESSING CANDIDA YEAST INFECTION................. 66.

CONTENTS (cont.)

Page.

THE INFECTIVE CALLUS MATRIX............................... 66.
TOXINS AND THEIR ROLE IN METABOLIC PROCESSES. 71.
YEAST PEOPLE... 76.
TRANSMISSION OF YEAST INFECTION........................ 79.
Ch.4. **REDUCING CANDIDA YEAST INFECTION**................. 81.
YOUR DOCTOR AND YOU...................................... 81.
CANDIDA YEAST SPECIES..................................... 83.
EUKARYOTIC CELLS.. 87.
MODERN FACTORS IN CANDIDA YEAST INFECTION.. 89.
REDUCING CANDIDA YEAST INFECTION.................... 92.
MINERAL TESTS WITH NUTRITIONAL EVALUATION.... 96.
THE PERILS OF AMALGAM TOOTH FILLINGS.............. 98.
MERCURY POISONING AND CANDIDA INFECTION... 100.
MERCURY AND ARSENIC CHELATION...................... 101.
MERCURY AND THE THYROID................................ 102.
CADMIUM.. 102.
HIGH ALUMINUM.. 102.
HIGH IRON... 102.
LOW IRON.. 103.
HIGH COPPER.. 103.
SODIUM & POTASSIUM....................................... 103.
SODIUM & POTASSIUM SUPPLEMENTS...................... 105.
SODIUM/POTASSIUM ASCORBATE........................... 106.
OTHER PRINCIPAL ADRENAL/IMMUNE NUTRIENTS... 106.
LITHIUM-SODIUM BALANCE.................................. 106.
LITHIUM.. 106.
ZINC... 106.
CALCIUM/MAGNESIUM....................................... 107.
NUTRITIONAL CHELATORS.................................. 108.
BLOOD TESTS.. 108.
BLOOD MICROSCOPY.. 108.
BLOOD PRESSURE... 110.
THE FAITHFUL LIVER... 112.
LIVER TESTS... 113.
LIVER INJECTIONS.. 113.
THE LIVER AND FEELING COLD AND CHILLY............. 113.
AMINO-ACID TESTS.. 113.
CITRIC ACID-ASPARTIC ACID SUPPLEMENTATION.... 113.
THE SPERMINE TEST.. 114.
GETTING BETTER.. 116.
THE REAL YOU AND YOUR INFECTIVES.................... 118.
THE DEGENERATIVE PROCESS................................ 119.
THE REAL YOU... 121.
DOING EVERYTHING.. 122.
DIET... 122.
CAFFEINE, TOBACCO AND STIMULANTS.................... 123.

CONTENTS (CONT.)

	Page.
CAFFEINE THERAPY	124.
CAFFEINE ENEMAS	124.
ADRENAL DEPLETION	124.
VITAMIN C. (ASCORBATE)	126.
BIOFLAVINOIDS & VITAMIN C	126.
CANDIDA & VITAMIN C	126.
VITAMIN C & THE ACID/ALKALINE BALANCE	127.
CHOLESTEROL & VITAMIN C	128.
ASCORBIC ACID ULTRA-FINE POWDER	128.
VITAMIN C & THE COLON	131.
ASCORBATE RETENTION ENEMA	132.
UNDERSTANDING VITAMIN C	133.
POTASSIUM & SODIUM	135.
HI KC FIZZ	136.
SALT	137.
CALCIUM & PROTEIN	138.
CALCIUM MAGNESIUM & CALCINOSIS	139.
PERNICIOUS ANEMIA & B12 INJECTIONS	142.
WATER	143.
FREE RADICALS & SOD, DMSO, ETC	143.
VITAMIN B15.(Pangamic Acid)	144.
VITAMIN B13.(Orotic Acid)	144.
LOW THYROID FUNCTION (Hypothyroidism.)	144.
THYROID FUNCTION TEST	146.
LITHIUM and the THYROID	146.
THYROID SUPPLEMENTS	147.
CYSTEINE. The PERILS of not EATING EGGS	148.
LOW PARATHYROID (Hypoparathyroidism)	150.
LYMPHATIC INFECTIONS	151.
MUCUS & MUCOUS MEMBRANE	152.
STRESS & MUCOUS MEMBRANES	153.
INTESTINAL FLORA, CAPRYLIC (Octonic) ACID	154.
CHANGING THE INTESTINAL FLORA	156.
HERBS & THE MUCOUS MEMBRANE	156.
OXYGEN	157.
OXYGEN THERAPY	157.
SLEEP	158.
SLEEPING PROBLEMS	159.
NEUROSIS, PSYCHOSIS & DEPRESSION	166.
ANTI-INFECTIVE FUNCTION	167.
TOPICAL & SYSTEMIC ANTI-INFECTIVES	168.
ANTIBIOTICS, ANTI-MYCOTICS & DISINFECTANTS	170.
CHRONIC INFECTION CHEMOTHERAPY	171.
TOXIC SIDE EFFECTS	172.
SKIN DIALYSIS SALTZ BATH	173.
ANTI-FUNGALS (ANTI-MYCOTICS.)	173.

CONTENTS (CONT.)   Page.

ANTI-INFECTIVES AGAINST CANDIDA INFECTION...... 174.
MEDICAL LITERATURE ON KETOCONAZOLE............. 177.
KETOCONAZOLE, SULFAMETHOXIZOLE & COPIAMYCIN. 178.
TOXICITY, LIVER PROBLEMS............................... 179.
TOXICITY, VITAMIN D, CALCIUM & PROTEINS........... 179.
NIACIN-KETOCONAZOLE THERAPY......................... 182.
RESTECLIN (MYSTECLIN)................................. 183.
MICONAZOLE.(MONISTAT, MICATIN)..................... 184.
HYDROGEN PEROXIDE.................................... 184.
NYSTATIN (MYCOSTATIN)............................... 185.
THE PERILS OF NYSTATIN.............................. 186.
2% PHENOL in GLYCERINE.............................. 187.
MAGNESIUM HYDROXIDE.(MILK of MAGNESIA).......... 187.
PHENOL ALKALIZER.................................... 188.
DMSO.(DIMETHYLSUPHOXIDE)........................... 188.
CHLOROPHYL.. 188.
GARLIC... 189.
CAPRYSTATIN.. 189.
CAPRICIN... 191.
SORBIC ACID.(ORITHRUSH,POLYSORBATE).............. 191.
ECONAZOLE (ECOSTATIN).............................. 192.
NaEDTA.(CALCIUM CHELATOR).......................... 192.
CANDIDA EXTRACT.................................... 193.
AUTOGENOUS VACCINE................................. 193.
ANTIBIOTICS & ANTI-FUNGALS......................... 194.
CANDIDA INFECTIONS throughout the BODY............ 202.
THE SEXUAL INTERCONNECTIONS...................... 203.
CANDIDA INFECTIONS of the FEET.................... 205.
ALTERNATE HEALTH THERAPIES....................... 212.
SUPPORTIVE THERAPIES.............................. 215.
CHIROPRACTIC....................................... 215.
NERVCITE THERAPY.................................. 216.
NEURSAGE... 219.
WHOLE BODY REFLEXOLOGY........................... 219.
AURICULAR THERAPY................................. 221.
CALCIUM CHELATION THERAPY........................ 227.
THE PERILS of NIACIN............................... 229.
IRIDOLOGY... 230.
GLAND & ORGAN SUPPLEMENTS........................ 231.
SPECIAL FOODS...................................... 232.
BODY WEIGHT.. 233.
GRAPEFRUIT & EGG DIET.............................. 234.
THE T-J MIRACLE SOUP DIET.(ONION & CABBAGE)... 235.
COMBINATION DIET................................... 237.
BODY TYPE DIETS.................................... 238.

CONTENT (CONT.)

	Page.
CH.5. CANDIDA YEAST INFECTION THERAPY	241.
THE ROOTS of DEGENERATIVE DISEASE	241.
THE PANCREAS as a SHOCK ORGAN	242.
BASIC ROOT CAUSES of DEGENERATIVE DISEASE	246.
ANTI-CANDIDA COCKTAIL	246.
HIGH BLOOD SUGAR	249.
FREE SUGARS	251.
YEAST ALLERGIES	252.
OTHER ALLERGIES	254.
DIGESTION	256.
ALLERGIES & METABOLITES	257.
TOXIC FOOD GROUPS	260.
CANDIDA YEAST & SEXUAL TISSUES	261.
ANTI-FUNGALS & ANTIBIOTICS	262.
SLOW KETOCONAZOLE THERAPY	263.
HIGH KETOCONAZOLE THERAPY	267.
INFECTION in BODY CAVITIES	268.
THE CANDIDA PROGRAM CHECK LIST	268.
CH.6. SPECIFIC CANDIDA INFECTIONS	271.
CANDIDA INFECTION in SEXUAL TISSUES	271.
CANDIDA INFECTION & the LOSS of HAIR	271.
ENDOTHALMITIS & CANDIDA INFECTION of the EYES.	273.
CANDIDA INFECTION of the EARS	274.
CANDIDA INFECTION of the NOSE & SINUSES	276.
CANDIDA INFECTION of the MOUTH	280.
CANDIDA INFECTION of the THROAT	282.
CANDIDA INFECTION of the ESOPHAGUS	282.
HIATUS HERNIA	282.
CANDIDA INFECTION of the STOMACH & INTESTINES.	284.
HALITOSIS.(BAD BREATH)	290.
ULCERS	290.
CANDIDA INFECTION of the COLON	292.
CONSTIPATION & COLONICS	294.
DIARRHEA & VOMITING	296.
COPING with GAS & CRAMPS	300.
COPING with DINNERS & PARTIES	303.
CANDIDA YEAST INFECTION of the FEET	304.
CANDIDA YEAST INFECTION of the FINGERNAILS	309.
SEXUAL CANDIDA YEAST INFECTIONS	310.
FEMALE SEXUALITY	312.
NORMAL SEXUAL LEVELS.(HISTAMINE LEVELS)	315.
DETERMINATION of SEX	315.
MALE SEXUALITY	316.
THE MALE MENOPAUSE	318.
CONJUGAL BLISS	318.
SEXUAL DEVIATION	320.

CONTENTS (CONT.)

Page.

REVIVING CONJUGAL BLISS............................ 330.
MAINTAINING SEXUAL HAPPINESS........................ 335.
APHRODISIACS.. 338.
VASECTOMIES... 339.
FEMALE SEXUAL PROBLEMS.............................. 340.
VAGINAL CANDIDA INFECTION........................... 342.
  (CANDIDOSIS, CANDIDIASIS, MONILIASIS)............. 342.
PELVIC INFLAMMATORY DISEASE.(PID)................... 345.
FEMALE SEXUAL THERAPY............................... 345.
FEMALE ORGASMIC FAILURE. (FRIGIDITY)................ 346.
REVIVING FEMALE SEXUAL FUNCTION..................... 348.
MALE SEXUAL CANDIDA INFECTIONS...................... 352.
ENLARGED PROSTATE................................... 353.
VARICOCELES, (HYDROCELES,SPERMATOCELES)............. 354.
CANDIDA INFECTION OF THE TESTICLES.................. 355.
REVIVING MALE SEXUAL FUNCTION....................... 358.
CH.7. DEGENERATIVE DISEASES......................... 364.
DEGENERATIVE DISEASE................................ 364.
THE ROOTS of DEGENERATIVE DISEASE................... 365.
CANDIDA YEAST INFECTION............................. 369.
THE FOCAL POINT in DEGENERATIVE DISEASE............. 369.
METABOLIC DEGENERATION BY CANDIDA................... 370.
ACETALDEHYDE & ALCOHOL DAMAGE....................... 372.
DIABETES, HYPOGLYCEMIA & ATHEROSCLEROSIS............ 376.
ALLERGIES... 380.
ARTHRITIS... 382.
FALSE ARTHRITIS (TRAVELLING ARTHRITIS).............. 385.
BURSITIS.. 386.
BELL'S PALSY.(and other PALSIES).................... 386.
NEURALGIA... 386.
HEART & BLOOD CIRCULATION........................... 386.
ANGINA & CORONARY OCCLUSION (HEART ATTACK). 391.
CORONARY BY-PASS.................................... 392.
THE VINEBERG HEART OPERATION........................ 393.
CORONARY OCCLUSION.................................. 395.
CALCIFIED HEART VALVES.............................. 396.
HEART PALPITATIONS.................................. 396.
BLOOD PRESSURE...................................... 397.
CATARACTS.(SCURVY of the EYES)...................... 399.
KIDNEY DISEASE.(NEPHRITIS, NEPHROSIS, PYELITIS). 399.
OSTEOPOROSIS.. 401.
ALZHEIMERS DISEASE.................................. 402.
MYOSITIS, SYNOVITIS, & FIBROSITIS................... 403.
BRONCHITIS & EMPHYSEMA.............................. 403.
SLIPPED DISC.. 406.
SCIATICA.. 407.

CONTENTS (CONT.)

	Page.
HANDS & CARPAL TUNNEL SYNDROME	407.
BROWN "AGE SPOTS"	408.
PSORIASIS & SKIN PROBLEMS	408.
SCHIZOPHRENIA, NEUROSIS, PSYCHOSIS & DEPRESSION	409.
MULTIPLE SCLEROSIS	411.
PARTIAL PARALYSIS	413.
CANCER	413.
HYDRAZINE SULPHATE	415.
LAETRILE	416.
CURING CANCER	418.
CHEMOTHERAPY	421.
PREVENTING CANCER	422.
OTHER DEGENERATIVE DISEASES	423.
CANDIDA YEAST in DEGENERATIVE DISEASE	424.
HEALTH RENEWAL PROGRAM	428.
CANDIDA INFECTION PROGRAM PROBLEMS	433.
CH.8. VIRAL INFECTIONS & OTHER HEALTH PROBLEMS.	**436.**
HERPES VIRUS INFECTIONS	436.
HERPES ZOSTER (CHICKEN POX & SHINGLES)	436.
HERPES E.B. (MONONUCLEOSIS)	437.
HERPES SIMPLEX (COLD SORES) (GENITAL HERPES)	438.
LARYNGITIS	438.
AIDS	438.
WARTS (VERRUCA)	440.
CAFFEINE DISEASE. (DEHYDRATION)	441.
PHOBIAS. (IMAGINED FEARS)	441.
NAUSEA & VOMITING	442.
BIRTHMARKS & MOLES	442.
ULCERS & OPEN SORES	443.
BAD BREATH & BODY ODOR (B.O.)	444.
SCIATICA, NEURITIS, NEURALGIA & SHINGLES	444.
DISABILITIES, & MENTAL RETARDATION	445.
STUTTERING & DISLEXIA	447.
DEEP ACHES,(BONE ACHES)	447.
ALCOHOLISM	447.
JAPANESE DRUNKEN DISEASE. (MEITEI-SHO)	463.
DRUG ADDICTION	464.
CH.9. THE BRAVE NEW WORLD	**465.**
NEW CONCEPTS for BETTER HEALTH	465.
THE ULTIMATE CONTRACEPTIVE	465.
IMPROVING BLOOD CIRCULATION	466.
CANDIDA INFECTION & the NEW BORN CHILD	468.
HELPING ALL of THOSE PROBLEM CHILDREN	470.
PRESCRIPTION DRUGS & ANTI-INFECTIVES	471.
ANTIFUNGALS, OLD & NEW	472.
PANDORA'S HOPE for a BRAVE NEW WORLD	474.

CONTENTS (CONT.)

Page.

ADDENDUM UPDATE.

CHRONIC INFECTION. .... 477.

    Primaxin. .... 477.

    Vitek. .... 477.

CHELATION THERAPY. .... 478.

    Blood Cleansing With Intravenous Chelation. .... 478.

ALZHEIMERS DISEASE AND CANDIDA. .... 479.

PROTEIN ALLERGIES AND CANDIDA. .... 481.

COENZYME Q-10 AND CANDIDA. .... 482.

AMINO ACID THERAPY. .... 482.

    VITAMINS AND AMINO ACIDS. .... 484.

    AMINO ACIDS IN HEALTH AND DISEASE. .... 484.

    AMINO ACID INTERACTIONS. .... 485.

    AMINO ACID THERAPY. .... 485.

    L-CYSTEINE AND CANDIDA. .... 486.

    TYROSINE, ADRENAL DEPLETION AND DEPRESSION. 487.

    TAURINE AND CANDIDA. .... 488.

    THE ROOTS OF DEGENERATIVE DISEASE. .... 489.

        Free Radicals. .... 489.

    CALCIUM CHELATION THERAPY. .... 491.

    FREE RADICALS AND CHOLESTEROL PROBLEMS. .. 492.

    FREE RADICALS AND HARDENING OF TISSUES. .... 494.

    REDUCING FREE RADICALS. .... 496.

CANDIDA YEAST,-- THE LIVING AGENT OF DEATH. ... 498.

* * * * * * * * * * * * * *

CHAPTER 1.

OVERVIEW.

"Oh childhood days of Zest and Glee,
What made'st thou flee so rapidly?
So full of bloom, so full of Life,
To romp and play from morn' till night,
In boistrous noise, and child delight!
Why hast thou gone? --
    Why? -- Why? ---

Oh Yes! The wonderful exhuberance of Youth! Now gone forever. But Why? Why hast thou gone? Where hast thou gone? When didst thou depart?

Remember when you used to run? You ran because the high metabolic rate of childhood made you overloaded with energy. You ran because life was full, life was exciting, and you just could not wait! You had to run! You felt like shouting, and you shouted! You felt like singing, -- singing like the birds; -full, strong, loud and clear! Where now is the exhuberance of youth? What has happened to it? Why do you no longer slide down the bannister? Where did the "joy of life" go? Why did it depart?

Oh Yes! You are older now! You are aging! But why should age affect the spring in your step? Why? -- But, you say, you are like an old car, and everything is worn, and shabby, and shaken. General debility, they call it, -- and yet, -- now there is Joe. Joe is much older than you, yet he seems to be much younger! And really now, your body is not like an old car. The body rebuilds itself continuously, so why should it wear out? So where did the "general debility come from? And then, just look at Gwen! She must be in her sixties, yet when strangers see her with her daughter they think that they are sisters! So what has happened? Why did Gwen and Joe escape the debilitation of old age, while others, who abide more carefully by the rules of health, fall by the wayside at a much too early age? When, then, did Youth start to depart? Why? And can the clock be turned back, -- even just a little?

Diet! It is all in the diet, you say? You are what you eat! But are you? Much has been written about diet, about protein, about sugar, about white flour, about vegetarianism, even about living on air! Much has been written on the perils of coffee, tea, chocolate and cola. Much has been written about tobacco and alcohol, and the clean colon, and stress, and late nights; and indeed all of these things certainly are detrimental to health, but remember Sam,- Sam, that rotten old so and so,--always quarreling with his neighbours, always fighting with his wife,always going out on weekend binges, smokes like a chimney, chews, gobbles candy, drinks coffee by the gallon, and lives on nice white baking powder biscuits with lots of syrup; does everything wrong and nothing right, yet the dirty old guy is never ill and can outwork any man half his age! Why? Why should he be different? Heredity,you say? But his parents died young, and so did his brothers and sisters.So why is he so totally immune to ill health? "Biological individuality ?" Yes! Yes! Now we have the answer! But are his stomach acids different? Are his arteries different? Does his hair have a different composition? Do the cells in his body metabolize sugar differently? If so, why is he not like a cow, and require a different diet? Yet somehow he is different, somehow he is healthier even without vitamins and minerals,or protein powder, or other supplements.

Unquestionably many people are indeed much healthier with vitamins and minerals, and health foods. Some people feel much better with four or five grams of vitamin C every day."Biological Dependance" they call it. But these same people felt well in their youth without the extra vitamin C, so it must be "developed dependance". And iron:Many people have a high need for iron, yet again, in youth the extra iron was not needed. Why? Why? Adelle Davis too, mentions that some people have a high requirement for pantothentic acid. Again one must ask why? Are these people really different? Does their liver, or their pancreas, or their bladder really have a different function? And so it goes. Low selenium, low chromium, low manganese, low zinc! Poor soils you say? Perhaps, but others in the same household and eating the same foods have normal levels! Then, poor assimilation! Perhaps, but why then the poor assimilation? Or is there a tapeworm, or something assimilating the nutrients and starving the host? Who knows? And why are these things not known? All of which brings us to Technology.

It is Technology that keeps our clocks on time.It is technology that keeps our cars on the roads and our planes in the skies.It is technology that grows our corn and our cattle. Medical technology is excellent in obstetrics. It is excellent in surgery. It is excellent in diagnosis. Function of nutrients is known, function of biological systems is known, methods for improving many functions are known. Then medical technology faulters, fails, withers, and dies, and therefore many people also fail, wither and die. The medical technology fails, not so much because of the technology itself,(although knowledge in many areas is lacking,) but because the medical technology is bungled and the knowledge is not applied and used. Much of the medical technology is supressed and immobilized by imperious government regulations, and by decadent medical associations that prevent its use, or harass those who try to make use of the hard won knowledge. Medical technology is also degraded and deformed by the drug companies, who twist facts for corporate profit, and apply extreme pressure to continue the use of drugs,-drugs that try to cure by interfering with natural biological function,-drugs that consequently produce many weird and dangerous side effects of which the hapless victim is seldom forewarned. Further, the advance of medical technology is almost completely stalled by insistance on "management"of disease. Management? Yes, management, as if disease was a natural consequence of living, as if disease was inevitable, as if disease was certain. No mention of cure. Just mangement. Everything is dedicated to management,-so everything is dedicated to the certain continuing return of the patient to the doctor,-even unto death.

During the great depression, survival depended upon "management". Boots were patched with tire patch, holes in pots were plugged with rivets, bearings in cars were renewed with leather, radiater leaks were stopped with oatmeal, coal oil was used for antifreeze and cork was put into worn gear boxes to reduce noise. Anything was done to 'get by'.It was very poor technology indeed, and it rapidly sent many cars to an early grave. Unfortunately, many people receive similar treatment from their physicians even today. Treatment with insulin, with aspirin, with diuretics, with laxatives, with barbiturates, with cortisone, with cocaine, and with many other drugs, is even worse technology because it depletes the rest of the body to provide a few fleeting moments of doubtful relief.

Where has technology and the medical profession been for these many years, while people have unwittingly been poisoning themselves into senility with aluminum from aluminum pots, aluminum foil,baking powder, and etc.?

What has medical technology(?) done to millions of women by giving them oral contraceptives that may destroy the liver, increase copper levels to insanity,and invariably sets the stage for a Candida yeast infection?

Yes, Candida yeast infection. Medical technology, and educational technology, is so poor that you probably have never heard of it before. But it is not a stranger. Your dentist knows it well. Your mother knew of it as monilia, and it was also called Trench foot and Trench mouth. So it is not a stranger to you, or to your mother. In fact, Candida yeast infection is endemic in man. It is present in all humans. You were infected by it at birth, when you passed through the birth canal, and three days after birth you had "thrush" as your immune system developed antigens against it. Ever since your first breath the yeast has been waiting,- waiting for your immune system to falter, so that it can invade and devour you. Yes, Candida yeast infection, one of your worst enemies; lives inside you, lives on you, and lives off you and your nutrients, and gives you all of its toxins and wastes, and yet medical technology is so poor that you have never heard of it! So how could you know that every time you take antibiotics of any kind you increase the risk of invasive Candida yeast infection, and if you have taken tetracyline, invasive infection is almost certain.

And aspirin. Aspirin shows the state of technology. Aspirin is the effective agent in corn salve. Aspirin is very invasive and will make holes in the stomach and intestines,- holes where Candida yeast can invade and colonize. Then the yeast colony will use your nutrients to give you large quantities of gas and toxins,- while your doctor technology continues to give you more aspirin, and then both you and your doctor wonder why you are getting worse! So where is the technology?

And the corns and callouses, and athlete's foot, and junk from the nose and ears? What technology can accept these as "natural"or"nothing".And how can hemorrhoids be innocuous? The fact is that all of these can be associated with yeast infection. If your doctor reads his own literature, he will soon find that the fact is that Candida yeast infection impairs the immune system, so each infected area increases the ability of the infective to colonize other areas. Then the infective, with its toxins and metabolites, can affect any body system, or, if the yeast reaches the bloodstream through ulcers, surgery, abrasion, or accident, the yeast infection may become disseminated throughout the body, where it may colonize and infect and affect any part, hair, ears, eyes, mind, nose, mouth, chest, heart, blood, lungs, stomach, glands, organs, sexual system, lymphatic system, circulatory system, knees, joints, ankles, feet, right down to the big toe. Yes! Candida yeast can infect and affect any part of you from the hair on your head to the tip of your big toe, and you have probably never heard of it before! Why? It is there in the medical books. It is there in the medical journals! The knowledge is there,- but it is largely unused. So where is the Technology? And what about the many other infective organisms, like the 1400 different strains of salmonella (including cholera,typhus,and paratyphoid) or like Herpes Zoster, that starts as chicken pox in the young, then lives in and on the nervous system and re-appears several decades later as shingles. And what about Progenitor Cryptocides,(always present in Cancer) and all of the other actinomycetales? Why is so little done with these infectives? Where is our Technology?

Many universities and other "learned"(?)"reseach" groups spend billions of dollars yearly on medical research, with rats and guinea pigs, and other animals that do not have the same infectious organisms as man; or the research may be with "normal" human subjects that are not even tested or asked if they have had measles or tuberculosis, or any other infection. Then the results are published as "scientific". Scientific? When they disinfect for bacteria while the fungii thrive? Is this science, or is it simple stupidity? Has Pasteur been entirely forgotten?

Also many drugs are tested on "normal" subjects, and the results are presented as scientific fact. But what is "normal"? Did the "normal" people have dandruff? Did they have digestive problems? Breathing problems? Did they all have "normal" minerals? If so, what level of minerals is "normal"? Are mineral levels affected by infectives? If so, is anyone "normal"? Obviously, until these questions are answered the results of all such learned "scientific" research must be suspect, because the reseach is less than scientific, and the results are therefore less than useful.

Now of course there are a few individuals in the health field who have made a significant discovery, but frequently, because they have found a way to help some people, they think that their discovery will apply equally to all. There is the exercise man, the molasses man, the cod liver oil man. There are the vitamin A doctors, the vitamin B doctors, the vitamin C doctors, the vitamin E doctors, the vitamin B6 doctors, the niacin doctors, the zinc doctors, the methionine doctors, the juice doctors, the "fasting"doctors, the "cleansing" doctors, the diet doctors, the massage people, the reflexologists, and many, many more, earnest, dedicated people. Most of these people have a good history of success. But alas, most are so narrowly dedicated to THEIR way, that they refuse to recognize the value of any of the others. They then usually try to make their specialty fit everyone that is ill, while their successes come only from those in need of their specialty.Then, although their successes are limited, their successes are real. Real, except that they are usually treating a symptom, instead of a cause, and the improvement usually flees, with time.

Where then is the technology? Why do these health practit- ioners fail to recognize the value of each other? Why do they not ask the inevitable final questions;--Why should there be a severe shortage of Vitamins A-B-C-D-E? Why a shortage of methionine? What is there to be "cleansed"? What does the fast actually do? What is the factual action of the homeopathic remedy? Why does calcium build up in the blood-vessels and joints? Why are the muscles spasmed? Is it not poor technology indeed that fails to ask the basic final "Why"? Is in fact the vitamin shortage due to poor nutrition,due to poor digestion, or due to poor absorption, or is it in fact due to some infective organism stealing the nutrients before the body can use them? Does the fast clear out some unknown mythical toxins, or does the fast simply starve both the host and his infectives? Strong coffee enemas ars effectively used for cancer and other afflictions, but what does the coffee actually do? It is said that the coffee is rapidly absorbed and that it induces the liver to cleanse the intestinal tract with bile. Cleanse the intestines of what? Animal intestines have been and still are used to make sausage.Animal intestines have never been very difficult to cleanse. "The cleansing" coffee enemas are frequently used for two weeks or more. Fourteen days of "coffee cleansing" is far more cleansing than sausage skins have ever had,yet the coffee enemas are very effective,so what in fact do they do? Where is the Technology? Coffee is a potent poison. One drop of pure caffiene will kill a mouse. So is the coffee killing somethimg? Is the coffee killing a virus, or bacteria, or yeasts? Who knows? Why does someone not know? Where are all of the microscopes? Where is the technology?

And then there is vitamin C. Vitamin C has been effective against many diseases, including cancer. Large amounts are used. But why? What exactly does it do? "To fight the toxins from the cancer", they say. But cancer cells are normal cells growing out of control,- they produce no more toxins than the other cells. The vitamin C is certainly effective and necessary, what is it detoxifying? Toxins from a virus? Toxins from bacteria? Toxins from fungii? What? Who knows? Where are the research funds? What are they being used for? Where, oh where is the technology? You cannot build bridges, and aircraft, and microwave ovens without technology, so how can you have health without technology?

Emulsified vitamin A has also been proven to be effective against cancer. Dr. Manner explains that it is picked up by the lymphatic system, and will triple the lymphocytes that fight the cancer. Excellent technology! Absolutely excellent.

Now we are getting somewhere! Or are we? Rest assured that the emulsified vitamin A does increase the ability of the body to fight infection. Excellent! Then why is it not being used to fight infections other than cancer? Where has everyone been? A new biologically effective method of aiding the body to fight any and all infection, yet it is heralded only as a cancer break-through! Did you read about it in the newspaper? In "Alive"? In "Lets Live"? Or in "Bestways"? Do you see it in the health food store or in the drug store? Do the "popular" writers write about it? One very popular "health book" author has written over twenty books without even mentioning the lymphatic system. Does he not know, and do his readers not know that the lymphatic system is more extensive and far more complex than the vascular system, and is equally important! Yet few authors even mention the lymphatic system, and therefore do not mention emulsified vitamin A. So where is the medical technology? Where is the Orthomolecular technology? Where is the health food technology? What is there about cancer that responds to improvement in lymphatic function? Existing technology states that the cancer cells are not destroyed by lymphocytes because they are body cells and the immune system does recognize them as being foreign. Does then the emulsified vitamin A improve the memory of the immune system? Does it suddenly make the immune system capable of discerning, recognizing, and destroying the cancer cells? If so, the emulsified vitamin A must induce production of new and different lymphocytes with greatly enhanced capabilities, So where is the microscope? Who knows? But the emulsified vitamin A is in fact effective. So if the extra lymphocytes are true to form (which seems certain) just what are those extra lymphocytes doing? Are they gobbling up some infectious agent associated with the cancer? If so,(which seems likely) is the cancer actually the result of the toxins from the infection? If the cancer is the ultimate result of toxins from infectives, what are the infectives, and who among us has such an infection waiting for a so-called "carcinogen" to trigger the waiting cancerous condition? Who knows? But we do know that cancer seems to strike the "health nuts" almost as frequently as those who eat and drink anything.

Among the effective cancer remedies there are the digestive and anti-neoplastic pancreatic enzymes. The anti-neoplastic enzymes will certainly help to clear up the cancer, and the digestive enzymes will help the digestion and thereby the entire body. Good!- Good? Now just a minute. What is the cause of the pancreatic failure? If we clean up the cancer, will the pancreas again fail and the cancer return? Pancreatic failure usually results from excess sugar, but some people eat large amounts of sugar for a complete lifetime without trouble, so is the pancreatic failure the direct result of the excess sugar, or is it that the sugar feeds bacteria and yeasts which produce toxins that interfere with pancreatic function? Or again, is the pancreatic failure due to allergy. What is allergy? Dr.Philpott shows that it is produced by pancreatic failure, with pancreatic failure produced by lack of amino acids, while the lack of amino acids is a result of digestive failure caused by pancreatic failure;-a vicious cycle that can be broken only with predigested protein and pancreatic enzymes. Predigested protein and pancreatic enzymes? Are they not the essential part of one of the successful slimming programs? Is overweight and obesity then linked to pancreatic failure, and therefore linked to cancer? And that predigested protein and enzyme program, is it not also what skinny people need to put on weight? So just maybe, and perhaps, skinny people too, are potential cancer victims? Who knows how much pancreatic failure produces cancer? Where is the technology?

Now also there is the anti-cancer diet:- No refined sugars or starches, no dairy products, no salt, no saturated fats, no eggs, no alcohol. Why? This is the heart and circulatory problem diet, so why is it necessary for cancer? If the pancreas is working properly, why are "naked" calories eliminated? What can be wrong with dairy products? The saturated fats and eggs may raise the blood levels of cholesterol and triglycerides, with potential heart problems, but many victims of cancer do not have heart and circulatory problems. Yet the diet is an essential part of effective cancer therapy, so what does it in fact do? Who has taken the trouble to investigate? How can we hope to correct a health problem without finding the actual, factual, cause? We do know that hard fats and cholesteral coat the stomach and intestines, and slow down the rate of digestion and absorption. We also know that bacteria and yeasts feed rapidly on refined carbohydrates and the lactose in milk. So if the grease locks the fermenting mass within the intestinal tract, what will the body do for food? What will the body finally do with all of the toxins from the infectives? Can such toxins be the root cause of cancer? Can such toxins also induce all of the other degenerative diseases? What about alcohol? What is the role of alcohol in cancer? Alcohol is one of the few disinfectants that you can drink. Does it kill off the bacterial infectives and increase yeast infection, or does it trigger an allergy. Who knows? Is alcohol an allergen? Just what is an allergen?

The allergists glibly speak about allergens,- and say that tomatoes, or tobacco, or hair, etc; and etc; are allergens, and this glib explanation is accepted by the scientific community and by the public, and the different allergens are wisely discussed by the learned scientific community. Scientific? Shades of snake oil! What can be less scientific than to say that someone is allergic to dust, or to tobacco smoke, or to hair, or to anything else that is complex and variable? To say that someone is allergic to something in the dust or tomatoes is correct. But what is the something? Again, it is an almost total lack of technology on the part of the allergist. It must be obviously dumb to test for allergic reactions to complex substances, without seeking the specific part of the substance that produced the allergy. It has certainly been known for years that the allergy is produced by the reaction of the immune system. It is therefore obvious that the body detects an infective or something that is particularly poisonous in the so-called allergen. It should be logical and obvious that the immune system is already overloaded with some toxic substance, and the allergen simply overloads an already overloaded system. Thus if present technology was used to determine the specific allergic entity, one would look for a similar toxic substance, or similar organism, in the body. If the true allergen was a fungus, one would look for a fungal infection, like athlete's foot, actively growing somewhere in the body. Incredible! Foot problems causing running nose and red eyes? Impossible! Yet in the medical books, when you read the fine print, you find that the basic cause of hives is always chronic infection somewhere, usually Candida yeast, and Canidida yeast is one of the common infectives in athlete's foot. So usually it is not knowledge that fails,it is technology that fails. What greater folly than for the learned allergist to be looking outside of the body for the cause of the allergy, when the obvious cause is inside the body! This is not only stupid, but it is dumb! The public would not pay a graduate mechanic to test a tire for leaks, accept the fact that the tire was leaking, and then have the graduate mechanic "manage" the problem by continuing to put air in the still leaky tire, when quite obviously the graduate mechanic should patch the hole. Would you pay such a mechanic? Yet you pay your allergist, and you pay him well.

Allergies and arthritis, aching bones, heart problems, and cancer. These are the burdens of the aging body.

" Oh Youth! Where hast thou gone? When? Why?"

Degenerative disease is always a nasty condition because it creeps up slowly as the years pass.Thus the true point of the start of degeneration cannot be definitely pinpointed, and, because the changes are so slow, it is even more difficult to pinpoint the exact cause of the changes. But in youth, most people are healthy, with everything fully functional. What then, can go wrong?

Technically ill health must start somewhere, someway, at some specific time. Genetic or inherited abnormalities can be a cause, but only in a few. Loss of organ or glandular function can be a cause, but only in a few. Mechanical injury can be a cause, but only in a few. Toxic substances in the air or food (tobacco, coffee, etc;) can be a cause, but many people who strictly avoid them, still fall ill. Lack of nutrients could be a cause, but good health may be present for ten, twenty, thirty, or forty years on the same diet, only to be followed by disaster.

The only other possibility then is chronic infection. If full health was present at any time, for any length of time, then the change in health must be caused by an exterior force, an exterior "something" that enters and alters the stable metabolic state. After all, the body is a highly complex fully mobile, electro-chemical-mechanical heat machine.Technically, if such a machine is operating smoothly, and if it is encased to prevent contaminants from entering, and if it is fed uncontaminated materials, and if the wastes are taken away, it will continue to function almost forever. The youth is indeed just such a machine, fully enclosed, and operating smoothly. The change in health must then logically come from the exterior,-from exterior contaminants that penetrate the enclosure, or from the growth of contaminants already in the enclosure in such small amounts that they do not interfere with the mechanism. Thus chronic infection, some place somewhere must be the true cause of changes in health. In short, Pasteur was right, and is still right.

The average person, along with many health professionals, have little concept of the true nature of the environment in which we live. The thin oxygen-rich skin that surrounds our world,-our atmosphere,-is filled with billions of different organisms, most of which are feeding on each other, and all are multiplying as rapidly as possible. Man is the only creature that consciously limits his rate of reproduction. All other living organisms multiply according to natural limitation,-usually the food supply. Every breath of air we inhale is filled with living organisms. Every drop of water we drink is filled with living organisms.Yeasts and moulds and other fungii, viruses, bacteria, mites, and many other organisms, much too small to be seen by the naked eye, some so small or transparent that they escape the microscope, but nonetheless countless creeping, crawling, swimming, floating organisms, all living, all seeking food, and all multiplying to the full extent of the available food supply. Further, these organisms are different than man. Man takes many years to grow, and must be nurtured

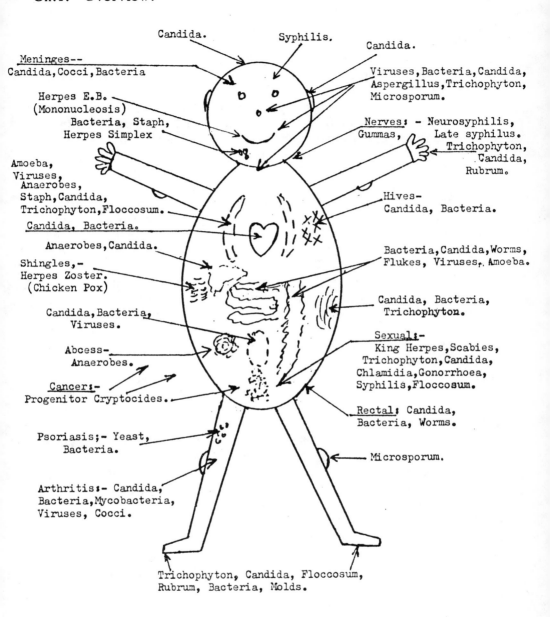

FIG. 1. MAN AND HIS VERY INTIMATE COMPANIONS.
Man is never alone. The real YOU is you and all of your infectives. There are a great many more infectives than the ones shown. Toxins and metabolites from each of the infectives alters body function.

and cared for, for several years of early life. But the simple organisms do not have to care for the young,--they simply grow, divide, and grow,--sometimes doubling the population in only a few seconds,so the total rate of multiplication may be very rapid.

These organisms are all around us. They are in our food and drink, on our skin, in our eyes and nostrils, in our intestines and throughout the digestive tract, in the bladder and kidneys and throughout the entire urinary and sexual tracts, and in the lungs and throughout the entire air tract. They are even in the air we breathe, for the air will contain airborne dust, and many particles of dust will be occupied by dust mites, and the mites in turn may be infected with bacteria or fungii, which in turn may be infected with viruses or viros. Eat and be eaten is the rule of Nature,and man is not exempt from nature's rules.

We have prepared a smiling little person, called Fig.1, just to make everyone feel better, and to reassure everyone that man does follow Nature's Rules;-- that man is never alone in the world because he always has very intimate company. Just look at Fig.1.,and intoduce yourself to a few of your most intimate guests;---guests that you may not have noticed before; guests that you may not have heard of before; yet all closely attached and intimate guests that really deserve your consideration and your attention. Just look at them, and these are only a few;--there are many, many more!

There can be nothing more beautiful in life than the event of the first-born, healthy, baby child. The proud Father; the tender young Mother, and the helpless little bundle itself. The New Life is beautiful and wondrous;--wondrous because it is the renewing of life;--life with a fresh clean start. Like the first tender shoots of grass in spring, a new life has started. Everything is new, everything is clean, everything is beautiful,--and yet,--everything is hopeful. Yes hopeful, for even the newborn babe is not alone. Even in the moments before birth the many, many, organisms that live with man;--the bacteria, the yeasts, the molds and the cocci, had already joined the new host, some for the better, and yet some for the worse. One of the first and one of the worst, was Candida yeast, so with the very beginning of the new life also began the very first chronic infection;-- Candida yeast, which is endemic in man and is present in all humans. Candida yeast, lying as always on the mucous lining of the birth canal, was picked up by the new-born babe, and even before the first breath was drawn the yeast was already starting to invade the tender skin, and colonize someplace, somewhere. Then,even before the babe's very first cry, the immune defences were already started on the lifelong struggle between the unwanted yeast and the unwilling host, with the outcome of the struggle largely determining the final capabilities and sometimes the total life of the newborn baby child.

Pasteur pointed out many years ago that infectives were the only thing that could interfere with normally operating biological processes, and logically therefore, infectives were the basic cause of disease. Pasteur was ridiculed, then vindicated, but even today the same voices of ridicule continue to refuse to look at, and to recognize, the role of infection in degenerative disease.

The rule of nature is eat and be eaten. All around us, in the streams, in the forests, in the fields, and even in the skies and under the ground, biology is at work;- eat and be eaten. Most plants, plankton, algae etc; are basic food producers that live on chemicals extracted from soil, water and air, and from then on it is eat, and be eaten, dead or alive. The farmer knows it well. Manure and compost grow good crops;- if the mice or robins do not get them. And if the deer, or the cutworms, or the grasshoppers do not get his crops, the mold, smut, or blight will. If chickens, turkeys or pigs become ill, they are killed before "whatever it is" spreads to the others. Huge herds of cattle are destroyed to eradicade brucellosis or T.B..The farmer uses forty different sprays and seed treatments, and the orchardist uses another forty different sprays and treatments.Coyotes and wolves are poisoned, and guns boom to scare off birds.

Eat and be eaten is the obvious order of biology, yet the obvious and the scientific stops at Man. With all other living things, if health is impaired either the nutrition is wrong, or something is eating at it, but with man "we do not know why", while the voices of ridicule refuse to listen to the new "Pasteurs", to Dr.Orion Truss (Candida Yeast), to Dr. Virginna Livingston, (progenitor and cancer), to Dr.Phillpot (pancreatic failure), to Dr. Pfieffer (minerals). Even Dr. Linus Pauling, with a Nobel prize for vitamin C, is "officially" ignored.

Yet the total implications of nutrition are so obvious. No living thing, no plant, bird, animal, insect or bacteria, can ever be healthy without adequate nutrients. With man too, then, all disease must spring from indequate nutrition, or from infection. Infection of somekind, someplace, somewhere. Not just chronic infection, but infection, because any infection can become chronic. Childhood chicken-pox comes and goes, yet half a lifetime or more later the Herpes Zoster virus that .caused the chicken-pox may re-appear as shingles, the virus living somewhere in the nervous system during those many long years.So what during that time had the virus also been doing? What other aches, pains, and ill health had it caused? We will never know, but we do know that mumps and rubella also sequester themselves in the tissues, and may appear many years later as arthritis. Further, in storms and in other catastrophies where mass death occurs, the dead must be buried, for if they are not, typhus, or diptheria, or cholera, or other deadly contagious disease will break out. Why? Because someway, somehow thriving active members of these highly infective organisms have been living sequestered somewhere within the body, living and multiplying in the host, yet neatly contained by the immune system. With death, the infective is no longer contained and multiplies rapidly in the dying flesh, and immediately then becomes a threat to the living.

So man's infectives are waiting for him when he is born, live in and on him, and eat both him and his food constantly during life, and die only after he has already expired. Man is never alone. He is like a composite organism. He is the net product of himself and his infectives. He is not what he eats, he is what he and his infectives eat.His physical capability is not his alone, for it is tempered by his chronic infectives, good and bad. Even his thinking is not his alone, for it is altered and changed by foods and toxins processed by his many constant infectives.

The chronic and transient infectives continuously living in the body number into the thousands. Some are acidic, others alkaline, so even the pH of the blood, lymph, digestive tract, sexual tract, and the entire body is constantly being altered and changed by the changing quantities and kinds, of infectives in the various parts of the body. Who knows what specific changes come from the various cumulative effects? We do know from Adelle Davis that some infectives change the amino acid histadine into the neurotransmitter histamine, with allergies and sexual effects. We do know, according to the chinese, that two infectives can combine to produce nitrosamines and cancer. We do know that progenitor cryptocides produces human chorionic gonadatrophin, and accellerates cancer. We do know that acidophilus manufactures B vitamins in the intestinal tract, much to our benefit. We do know the E. Coli (of coliform fame) is ever present in the colon, where it manufactures ATP, proteins, and lipids, again to our benefit. We also know that the same E. Coli can invade the urinary system and cause colitis, which is very painful and not to our benefit.

In all, there are about 75 infective organisms normally present in the birth canal, about 75 in the colon, and over one hundred in the digestive and air tract. Some are good, some are neutral, some are bad. There are hundreds of different bacteria, hundreds of different viruses, hundreds of different yeasts and molds and other fungi, hundreds of cocci, and viros, etc; that infect and affect man. Eat, and be eaten is the rule of nature. Defend or be eaten is the only rule for man.

Then let there be no question; If caffeine, heavy metals, and other poisons are eliminated; and if nutrition is adequate, then all other health factors and all health problems must be centered in chronic infection. This is the crux of Health, the very nub of all health problems; - Chronic infection; - chronic infection someplace, somewhere, determines the real being, determines the real state of health, determines the real you. Here then, is the truth. A simple truth, an obvious truth. Yet a truth that few doctors recognize, and a truth that few people wish to accept. Comes the old refrain: - "Who? Me? Nonsense! I do not have all of those nasty little bugs in me!" Then comes the old reply. "Perhaps not, so just take aspirin (or valium) and perhaps the arthritis will go away." A stupid palliative measure that accomplishes less than nothing, because the underlying infection continues to flourish.

The problem is not only that neither the doctor nor the patient want to recognize the basic chronic infection, but also that both the doctor and the patient are seeking only palliative measures. Hence the folly of the long, long list of palliative drugs.

The 'natural' health practioner does little better. Their creed also ignores the role of chronic infection. "Natural is Good". So both the herbalist and the afflicted seek a palliative herb, that in fact masks the real problem and allows the basic infection to proceed relentlessly on. Now of course there will be many successes, particularly if nutritional or anti-infective herbs are used, but in general the many advertised herbal concoctions are designed only to relieve symptoms. Hence the folly of many herbs, many of which are simply drugs in natural form.

The naturopaths, to their credit, have developed many methods for improving health, with emphasis on colon function, complete with colored pictures of healthy and unhealthy stools. The naturopaths have also discovered and used to good effect many raw glandulars and similar tissue extracts. Most certainly glandulars should be used to improve body functions, but they should not be used year after year without asking the obvious question:

"What infective is actively preventing the gland from working properly?"

The nutritionists of course select this food, that mineral, and these vitamins to bolster the lagging physical function, and this is certainly better than drugs or herbs, yet it is really only palliative, because no one asked the obvious question as to why the extra nutrients should be needed when the diet was already adequate. Man is never what he eats. He is never alone. Man is what he and his infectives eat, and when his nutrition is improved he will improve, and feel better, but with improved nutrition his infectives will also improve and multiply, and they will then again overtake him, after which he will again feel worse. Supernutrition is better than drugs, and sometimes it does help the body sufficiently that it will overtake and destroy a persistent infection, but usually it is only palliative, and without taking other measures against the infectives it is near folly to try to conquer ill health with nutrition alone.

The chiropractors select the back, the reflexologists select the feet, and the masseurs, the yoga-ists, and the body builders etc; work over the entire body,pushing, pulling, heating, cooling, bending, and rubbing the various tissues to "improve circulation", to "improve lymph flow", to "improve adrenal function", and etc; to make people feel better. People do feel better. People do see great improvements, and the improvements are real, yet because the improvements are only palliative, with the basic chronic infection ignored, the improvement keeps slipping away, with the whole thing repeated over and over again, week after week, month after month, year after year.

Then there are the specialists. The Vitamin A doctor, the Vitamin E doctor, the mineral specialist, Mr.Cod Liver Oil, and the specialists in hypoglycemia, diabetis, allergies, schizsophrenia, and etc. These are usually good, honest,conscientious near sighted people. Near sighted because they usually fail to seek and remove the chronic infection that caused the glands and organs to fail.

Even the controversial Chelation therapy, that removes plaques and restores flow in hardened arteries is only palliative, because these plaques are really a form of tumor, caused by the proliferation of a single displaced cell from the middle lining of the blood vessel, displaced and made tumorous by the effects of some infective, someway, somehow.

Most doctors, and other health practioners, do recognize that fulminating infection of any kind alters the function of organs and glands, and forces toxins on the body with many weird effects. Such rampant infections are usually promptly subdued with anti-biotics or similar agents, but where infectives are not life threatening they are constantly being disregarded, overlooked, and ignored, even while they are slowly but certainly bringing their victim to his doom.

From the moment of birth, until after death our infectives are constantly with us. Some are helping us live, while many others are helping us die. We cannot get away from them, not even for one fraction of a second. We can only constantly and relentlessly fight them. Fight them with nutrition, fight them with exercise, fight them with antibiotics, fight them with anti-fungals, fight them with disfectants, fight them with heat and light, and above all fight them with vaccines that raise the competence of the immune system, for until our end it is the effectiveness of the immune system that constantly stands guard for us. It is the immune system that finally determines our resistance to the invaders. It is the effectiveness of the immune system that determines the rate of life;- and the rate of death!

So it is the body that is the Hero. It is the immune system,- with it's various types of cells that engulf and destroy any foreign organisms that manage to enter the tissues or bloodstream, that saves us from being eaten. It is the body that is the Hero, and any who doubt should read "The Body is the Hero", by Ronald J. Glasser M.D.(Random House) who tells us how life, partial life, and death, depend upon the immune system. He tells us how it functions, he tells us why, he tells us that indeed it is not the physician that heals, he tells us that everything depends upon the body,- and the immune system. A wonderful half-book! Yes, a Half-book, for Dr. Glasser tells us how our life and health depend upon the immune system, but there is not one word on how we can nurture and maintain the immune system. Not one word on it's nutrients. Not one word! So why was the half-book written? Where is the Technology? What a shame!

The start of degenerative disease must therefore lie in immune system failure, or in an overwhelming episode of infection, or both. Or is there more? If there was a massive infection, which the immune system valiantly cleaned up, the body must still take care of the toxins from the infective, and the toxins from the dead bodies of the infective. If the body cannot clean up these toxins, what happens to them? Are they deposited in the joints to produce arthritis? Are they deposited in the arteries to join the plaques we call arteriosclerosis? Which diseases do they produce? Health, then, also depends upon a fully functioning detoxification system, namely the liver and the detoxification nutrients,- the principal nutrient being ascorbate, commonly known as vitamin C.Vitamin C is also used by the adrenals as a nerve nutrient to combat stress, and, if the supply is adequate it is also used by the body to "harden" the collagen and provide strengh to the tissues. Here now is perhaps one of man's greatest handicaps. Man lacks the genetic coding to make the enzymes necessary for his own production of ascorbate. Only the hominids,(including man), the guinea pig, and some fruit eating bats are genetically impaired. Unlike most of the other mammals, man is therefore entirely dependent upon food for his ascorbate, and the natural ascorbate intake usually falls far short of his minimum requirements, even in times of health.If an infection invades, ascorbate is needed for detoxification, while the stress from the infection increases the ascorbate requirement of the adrenals. If ascorbate is not supplemented and becomes depleted, the toxins build up (somewhere), the adrenals become depleted, (frequently resulting in muscle spasm somewhere) and, if the trauma continues, the tissues are deprived of adequate ascorbate. The tissues then lose their strength, become scurvous, and are more easily invaded and consumed by the infective.

Chronic continuous infections then, even when they may be labelled "mild" or "innocuous" are actually a grave threat to health because of the constant stress, the constant unrelenting drain on the immune system, and the constant continuing requirement for ascorbate and other nutrients. Thus mouth and nasal infections, a touch of sinus infection, a constant slight cough, mild indigestion, constipation, hemorrhoids, athlete's foot, acne, or perhaps even dandruff should not be considered innocuous. Each little bit of infection contributes to the total stress on the adrenals. Each little bit of infection adds to the drain on the immune system. Each little bit of infection creates a finite waste of nutrients.

Consider this (i.s.) as being the total capability of the immune system when fully supplied with nutrients. If a chronic infection is steadily drawing on this total capability the effective capability would be reduced to (i.s.)). Then if the chronic infection spread and increased, the feeling of health might not be impaired, but the effective capability of the immune system would be reduced to (i.s.)). If then a cold or the flu was contracted the apparently well person would suddenly become ill, and the chronic infection, - the innocuous infection, - would run wild and unchecked.

Now consider this same situation where nutrients, and

18

particularly ascorbate, are undersupplied. The total immune system capability would then be reduced, the chronic infection would further reduce the capability, the reserve would be reduced, and disaster would follow with the first slight cold.

Fortunately for us this representation is oversimplified. The immune system is highly complex, and each infective organism may be destroyed in several different ways. But we do in fact see apparently healthy people suddenly become severly ill, and we do in fact see many people with very high requirements for ascorbate, or for pantothenic acid, so there is little question that chronic infection, however slight, does greatly affect the total health.

Linus Pauling, and many other nutritionists have been telling us about ascorbate for many years, and we must praise them for it. For many years many people have been feeling much better by increasing their ascorbate intake, some using 15 or 20 grams per day. Yet is this not similar to putting diabetics on insulin instead of re-activating the defective pancreas? If the ascorbate buffs improved their technology, even just a little, would they not be looking for the reason for the high requirement for ascorbate? The value of the ascorbate is real. The need for the ascorbate is real. But they would probably have to look no further than the calluses on the feet or the colitis in the colon to find the real cause of the high need for ascorbate.

" Oh Joys of Youth, Where hast Thou gone? Where did ye go? When did ye leave?"Ah, yes the bacteria, and the viruses, and the yeasts, and the molds destroyed you, starting slowly from the moment of birth, and gradually increasing until Youth has faded into rickety old bones, "sans teeth, sans eyes, sans ears, sans sex, - sans Everything!"

CHAPTER. 2.

SEEKING THE SHADOWY AGENT OF DEATH.

Life is Wonderful and Life is Beautiful,- for all who can maintain their Health. Man, like the flowers and trees, starts life as a tender replica of the parent;- grows, blooms, reproduces, and dies. Everyone understands that this is the life cycle of man and of all other creatures. But why should one person have a healthy life, and another an unhealthy life? Why should one person have a short life, and another person have a life three times as long? We all start the same. Most of us start as a pure wholesome baby, yet our health and life span may differ greatly. All babies are biologically very similar. Logically, the difference in health and life span does not come from within, the difference therefore must come from without. The difference must then come from the combined effects of infectives from outside the body that materially alter the normal body processes, with the altered metabolic state leading to degenerative disease and early death.

Just look back at Fig.1. We are certainly not alone. We do have many unwanted guests living on, living within, and living off us, and making us carry away their garbage. We cannot see these devilish little creatures, and perhaps that is just as well, because it would certainly give us an abhorrent feeling in the pit of the stomach if we could actually watch these little devils devouring our body cells, and spitting and excreting their wastes into our tissues and into our bloodstream. Little wonder then that the nutritionists, and the yoga-ists, and the joggers, and all of the other purists pretend that these infective little devils are not there. So the purists insist that we are alone. Man is far above such nasty things! Let all else in nature eat and be eaten,- except man! Besides, just to think of all of those nasty infectives chomping away is enough to turn the strongest stomach,- - and to see them would be worse, no, no, they cannot be there. Man is Godly, man is above all of the creatures, man must be alone,-and yet,-yes,flu and colds do come, and so does T.B., and so also does V.D. Yet even the thought turns the stomach,so many tiny, tiny bits of life,- and all so voracious, and so grotesque, and so different,- all fighting and eating each other, and you,- all eating at your nerves, nibbling at your organs and your glands, floating along in the lymph and the blood, and chewing at your body cells, all of the little devils consuming your foods and your liquids, all dividing and multiplying, and all spitting and spewing their sewage into your food,-so your poor body knows not which is food and which is poison.The very thought does turn the stomach,-- and when the stomach turns, the scene is little changed, for there they are, all of those devilish little organisms, the bacteria, the coccii, the yeasts, the molds, the viruses, and the viros, along with millions of bits and pieces of metabolic material broken off by digestion, and broken down by the billions of active organisms. All of the organisms are there, they are there because they were in and on our good and natural food.

These creatures came home with the nice fresh celery, they came with the fresh pressed carrot juice, they came with the sprouts, and they came with the fish and the fowl. They came because they are part of nature. They came because the law of nature is eat and be eaten. They came to eat,-- and perhaps be eaten. Some friendly, some indifferent, some potential death. They are here and man is here. Man is not alone, and man can never be alone. So man must fight off the infectives that endanger him, and how well he battles his perilous foe determines his life;-or his death. So contrary to the doctors, and the nutritionists, and the vitamin addicts, and the other health nuts, it is happenstance and battle that largely determines the health, and death, of man. The happenstance is the number and kind of perilous infectives, and the battle is the body's total defences. The battle is the strength of the salivary and digestive juices; the amount and strength of the alkalizing fluids; the amount and strength of the friendly bacteria; the capacity and capability of the liver and detoxification system; and the total strength and capacity of the immune system; while opposed to all of these,the battle is the number and kind and strength of the perilous infectives. The outcome of the battle is your walking, talking, state of health. The outcome of the battle is your date of death. Yes, Yes! The battle will be influenced by vitamins and minerals and fresh air, and jogging, and yoga, and dancercise, and by, sleep and rest, just as the faddists say. The battle will be influenced by caffeine and drugs and alcohol and heavy metals and foul air just as the purists say. The battle will be influenced by cleanliness and sanitation and food preservatives just as we have been taught; and the battle will be influenced by good wholesome food, as we all must know. Yet finally,moment by moment the real battle will be by happenstance; by the total strength of the immune system opposed by the strength and number and kind of perilous infectives that happen to be present. That is the real battle. That is the real test. That is the real health, and that is the real death. That also is the very real challenge;for man in fact is different than all of the other creatures. Whether by chance, circumstance, evolution, or Devine design, only man has reached the point of intelligence whereby he can effectively alter his environment and thus escape the otherwise inevitable. Man can find ways to reduce the effects of his attackers. He can find ways to locate, isolate and destroy even the smallest perilous infective. In fact he is doing that now, and he has been doing it for years! So why are there allergies, and arthritis, and degenerative diseases? Quite obviously degenerative disease is still with us because we are missing something; we are missing the devil infective; we are somehow overlooking or not recognizing the little monster. There must be some ubiquitous common infective that is worse than all others, some infective that somehow shelters the other infectives, or sequesters itself someplace somewhere in some way so that it avoids the immune system. There must be some such infective, but which one? Which one is the real devil infective? Which one is the Shadowy Agent of Death, and slow death? Which one?

In seeking the shadowy agent of death; the real devil infective, we can assume that this infective will have certain characteristics:

1. It will be endemic in man, and it will affect all people.
2. It will be very common in other creatures, and elsewhere in nature.
3. It will be commonly considered as only a nuisance, and of little consequence.
4. It will be very resistant to most disinfectants, and will be difficult or impossible to eradicate.
5. It will impair the immune system, and thus reduce the resistance to it's growth.
6. It will produce a large number of toxins and metabolites that will alter and affect all body functions.
7. It will join with other infectives, and other infectives will mix with it.
8. It will have some means or function by which it protects itself from disinfectants, and from the body's defences.
9. It will be very tenacious, and it therefore will probably be a fungus.

The one infective that has all of these characteristics, is the lowly Candida Yeast (monilia) that is always present in the birth canal, and infects each one of us from the moment of birth, even until after death. Candida yeast, the lowly infective of calluses and finger nails, -this is the real shadowy agent of death,- this is the real devil infective,- that is always lying on the surfaces of the mucosa, some where,- anywhere,- waiting, always waiting for some chance to invade and colonize, and slowly start to devour the host.Candida yeast, the common infective in vaginitis, the common infective in digestive problems,— considered only a nuisance,— this is the devil infective that slowly destroys man with it's toxins. Candida yeast, the shadowy agent of death, always on us, always in us, always eating at us, and always eating our food.

The truth is that at present the medical profession (in general) seems little concerned about minor infections, like athlete's foot or chronic nose and throat problems. They consider them to be "minor irritations". Indeed they are minor irritations compared to cholera or scarlet fever. This attitude of the physicians is quite understandable when one considers that it is only about sixty years ago that epidemics of major infective diseases swept many parts of North America, swept away the lives of many people, and left many other people half dead, badly damaged, and highly susceptible to re-infection by other organisms. These health problems of not-so-long-ago were frequently increased by tissue damage from frostbite (usually hands, feet, or nose) and were greatly increased by poor nutrition due to lack of fresh vegetables in winter, and lack of fresh meat, or perhaps the use of half-spoiled meat, in summer, together with poor sanitation and poor water supplies, with the water frequently contaminated by excrement, ground water, toxic materials, or alkali. Only sixty years,- therefore many of the readers of this book will well remember these unhealthy conditions, and perhaps the remembering of past illness may help them find the probable location of present infections.

Only sixty years,-so the doctors cannot really be too much blamed if they consider apparently small infections as "minor irritants", but it is still poor technology and it certainly is not helpful to you. Further the attitude precludes even considering these apparently small infections as a health problem. The attitude closes the door, and leaves you to struggle with your problems,- without help. But really, do none of these physicians (?) ever wonder why so many iron tablets are sold? Do none of them ever wonder why so many aspirins are sold? Do they never wonder why so many laxatives are sold? Oh Yes! They make a urine test, but is it tested for infection? Is the stool examined for size, color, quantity, water-content or infection? Of course not! But why not?

The obvious place to start looking for infection is in the intestinal tract. After all, all food is contaminated with living organisms, and if each and every one of the many infectives is not destroyed by digestive juices, or by the alkalinity phase of digestion, it will pass into the intestines alive and capable of growing. If the infective is Candida yeast, it will invade and colonize any area that is not protected by mucosa. As previously pointed out, any infectious disease may leave tissues damaged, and therefore subject to re-infection. Also, the salicylic acid in every aspirin tablet that may be taken, is highly invasive to all tissues (it is the active agent in corn salve,-just look and see) so aspirin too may help any infective become your permanent unwelcome guest. The oral antibiotics are very effective in killing bacteria, but the yeasts are immune to the antibiotics, so yeasts frequently colonize an area of previous bacterial infection, then, after the antibiotics are gone, the invasive yeasts are joined by bacteria and other infectives in a large multicultural infective commumity, all living off your nutrients and forcing you to take away their sewage. Then you and your physician wonder why you have arthritis, or allergies, or headache, so he tells you to take more aspirin! It is poor technology to (perhaps) relieve the symptoms and aggravate the cause! It is even worse technology not to wonder, even a little, just what the aspirin does? Adelle Davis, many years ago pointed out that the aspirin is so toxic that it gives the adrenals "a kick in the seat of the pants", which persuades the already tired adrenals to produce just a little more cortisone, and it is the cortisone that clears the headache. Aspirin is also invasive to all tissues, so the aspirin may also help the headache by killing off some of the infectives, and thus momentarily reduce the toxins, while the tissue damage will enable the infective to increase the size of the infective village to a whole city of unwelcome guests, with much more sewage, so that the next headache will be a real dilly!

Now let us add sugar, nice sweet sugar, to this scene. Bread, of course, is made with yeast, and yeasts love sugar, so when you make bread you add about two teaspoons of sugar to the mix, "to activate the yeast". Then you let the bread rise for about an hour at room temperature before baking. If too much sugar is added, the bread will rise too rapidly. If the room is too hot (above 80º) the bread will rise so rapidly it will be full of holes and will overflow the pans, and of course it will keep on rising if you do not bake it quickly enough to kill the yeast. Now let us suppose that aspirin, or tetracycline, or "the pill" has induced an intestinal Candida yeast infection, and you then have tea, with two teaspoons of sugar, along with some nice sweet cake. You did not feed yourself, you fed the yeast! Would you then not expect your stomach to rise like a loaf of bread? You gave the yeast sugar from the tea. and you gave it more sugar and white flour with the cake, and then you incubated it at a full 98º! Of course there was gas, gas, and more gas, along with many toxins. Yet the registered nurse, giving a lecture on digestion and following her nurses training, says, " a little gas is natural". Natural?

Ch.2. Seeking the Shadowy Agent of Death.

Gas is a natural result from fermentation, but however common, is fermentation in the digestive tract natural? Certainly many people are bothered by gas, yet others are not, so the fermentation and gas, however common, cannot be natural. The difference must be in the amount of chronic yeast infection present. So does the training of the nurse actually reflect the view that most people, unknowingly, do have a little intestinal yeast infection somewhere along the digestive tract?

One may indeed think that intestinal yeast is an uncommon minor irritation. But one must remember that Candida yeast is found many places in nature, including the skins of fruit. One should also remember that an invasive overgrowth of Candida yeast is a form of soft callus, with the infectives mixed with the cells of the host, and, although the Candida is the invasive infective that creates the overgrowth, other infectives invariably join the infectious colony. Now it is never pleasant to touch upon distasteful facts of life, but Health is Health, and fact is fact. Adelle Davis has pointed to the fact that if digestion is functioning properly smelly gas will be absent, the bowels will move regularly and quickly, and with ease, and the stool will be almost odorless. Yet who, except a healthy child, has such excellent function? A trip to any busy public washroom, with the many grunts and groans and the many different foul odors should convince anyone that constipation with intestinal infections of many kinds, are present in almost the entire human population. You too then can be assured that you are probably also a victim of unwelcome intestinal guests that must also be part of any afflictions that you may have.

The point is that if any one infective agent invades the body anywhere, all other organisms will join in according to their opportunity. Thus each multiple infectious congregation is different, and each set of multiple toxins is different, and each individual odor is different, while added to the total toxic load may be toxins from other sites of infection, from tonsils, or sinuses, or acne, or psoriasis, or athlete's foot, or whatever. So the total toxin mix,-the toxins that the body must continuously respond to and cope with,- will also be individual and will affect each of the separate body parts for which the toxins have a chemical affinity, thus producing each of the many degenerative diseases, which are then named for the body part that is affected, irregardless of the simple fact that they all share a common infective and toxic cause.

The role of infections and toxins in degenerative disease is also greatly increased by inflammation from the immune

25

response to the infectives, while the stagnant fluids from the continuous inflammation slowly promotes calcinosis and solidification of the inflamed tissues, resulting in the hardened muscles, high blood pressure, and poor circulation that so commomly progresses with age.

Candida yeast, the real devil infective, the real Silent Killer, is the basic infective that induces and maintains chronic infection. We cannot escape it; so to live, we must deal with it with intelligence and persistance, and with all of the help that we can find.

Candida Yeast Infection, the Silent Killer, is not new to man. Hippocrates described it in ancient Greece, and it has certainly been observed and described by the medical profession ever since. Everything from candidal arthritis and candidal anemia to urticuria and endocarditis is adequately shown in the medical books, yet the vast amount of candida infection is either overlooked, or ignored. So let us look at the extent of some of the medical literature, and let us also examine the infective matrix, and the role of toxins in metabolism and disease.

Chapter.3

CHRONIC INFECTION. .

CANDIDA YEAST INFECTION, "THE SILENT KILLER."

Although all chronic infectives contribute greatly to all forms of ill health, Candida yeast is the one single infective that has the greatest influence on health and illness because:

!. Candida yeast is an opportunistic organism. It is continuously present, waiting for an opportunity to invade and colonize.

2. If tissues are damaged anywhere, by physical abrasion, aspirin, drugs, laxatives, transient infection, or any other cause, Candida can invade and start a colony. The Candida yeast then uses magnesium from the damaged cells to form an osmoresistant layer (water resistant skin) over the yeast colony, which gives the yeast infection a secluded and protected home where it can grow and multiply largely unaffected by body defences, and virtually immune to any disinfectants that are applied to it.

3. Other infectives then join the Candida colony, where they too can grow and multiply largely unaffected by the immune system and other body forces.

4. The Candida colony (with its associated infectives) then uses up and ties up lithium, selenium, chromium, and other minerals and nutrients, which alters thyroid function and slowly impairs the immune system, and thereby further reduces the ability of the body to combat the mixed chronic infectives.

The following excerpt from Allergy Alert, P.O.Box 15181.Seattle, Washington, 98115., by Sally Rockwell, author of "The Rotation Game" gives a greatly simplified indication of the extent of the Candida problem and how it affects the lives of so many people.

CANDIDA UPDATE,---- by DR. BUSCHER

Written by Sally Rockwell.

Dr. David Buscher, a local family practitioner in Kent, spoke at our March meeting, giving a thorough overview of the problem of yeast (Candida) infections. After several years of traditional family practice, seeing up to 60 patients a day and prescribing lots of drugs, he became discouraged and depressed over this mode of treatment. He began to investigate the efficacy of a nutritional approach to many of the problems his patients were presenting him with. He spent a year with Theron Randolph in his clinical ecology unit in Chicago and became aware of the vast amount of suffering that is caused by food and chemical sensitivities.

Ch.3. Chronic Infection.

The bulk of his practice for several years now has been diagnosing and treating people who are food and chemically sensitive. (Chemical sensitivity he defined as being very susceptible to the "normal" levels pf pollution found in our environment.) A complicating factor in very many of the people he sees has proven to be yeast (Candida) infections.

Yeast infections are not new to the human species. Hippocratos noted that people with white patches on their tongues (yeast overgrowth) were people who would soon die. In modern times the physician who has done the most to bring the problem of yeast infections to the fore has been Dr. C. Orian Truss, an Alabama Internist whose establishment credentials are impeccable: Cornell medical School, Chief Resident in Internal Medicine at Bellevue Hospital in New York. Dr. Truss has done much of the work of discovering how Candida infects people.

Candida is found in all (99+%) people. It is considered to be part of the normal bowel flora: organisms that coexist with us in our lower digestive tract. However, Candida also coexists there with many species of bacteria in a competitive balance that keeps them in check unless that balance is upset.

Unfortunately, there are a number of factors endemic to life in our times that can upset the balance and allow the yeast to overgrow, causing major problems. Antibiotics are the chief culprit in upsetting the balance, leading to overgrowth of Candida by destroying the bacterial component of the normal flora that keeps them in check. (Antibiotics kill only bacteria- both beneficial and harmless ones- they do not directly affect yeasts or viruses.) Steroid hormones such as cortisone, birth control pills (which contain progesterone, a female sex hormone) and sugar can also cause or maintain massive overgrowth.

Once Candida overgrowth occurs, the effects are many:

1. The organisms can spread out from the lower bowel to colonize the entire digestive tract, including up through the stomach (esp.in cases of low or no stomach acid) into the throat, mouth and nasal passages and down into the lungs.

2. The bowel wall itself is normally a very sturdy, protective membrane that keeps toxic products of digestion out of the bloodstream. In Candida overgrowth, the yeast colonies dig deep into the wall with such a tenacious grasp that they damage the bowel wall itself. This phenomenon has given rise to the "leaky bowel" theory in which it is hypothesized that the toxic by products of digestion leak into the blood where they cause a myriad of different systemic (allergic) reactions at distant sites such as joints, lungs, and especially, the brain.

28

3. In addition, 79 different toxic products (antigens) of the yeast itself have so far been identified in the human species. This in itself is a tremendous load on the immune system (IS) and could contribute to lowered reactivity to other infections or antigens.

4. Candida infection also appears to attack the IS itself. It causes suppressor cell disease, in which there are not enough of the cells, which slows down the production of antibodies by the B-cells. The IS goes overboard, producing antibodies to everything at the slightest provocation. This may explain why so many patients are allergic to so many things. In particular, many people with Candida infection are extremely susceptible to all sorts of chemicals. They have a hard time living (as opposed to existing) in the late 20th century.

Incidence.

Dr. Buscher estimates that approximately 50% of his patients have Candidal overgrowth to th extent that it is causing symptoms. Dr. Randolph, the famed clinical ecologist, says that 90% of the people they see in his unit have it.

Risk.

Women are more likely to get infected than men.This is related to the female sex hormone progesterone which rises in the body during the last half of the menstrual cycle (followimg ovulation). Progesterone increases the amount of glycogen (animal starch, easily converted to sugar) in the vaginal tissues and provides an ideal growth medium for the yeast. Dr. Buscher believes this is the major reason why his practise is predominated by women patients. It may also shed light on why so many women's health goes downhill (esp. allergies) during pregnancy, due to the elevated progesterone levels that are found then.

Men are affected less frequently but are by no means invulnerable to yeast infections. In particular, a course of antibiotic or steroid therapy can give the yeast the foothold it needs. And sugar in the diet keeps it fed.

In children, yeast infection is seen as thrush or severe diaper rash. The yeast can be transferred from mother to child at birth.

****

As we shall see, there is of course much, much more, to Candida infections than Sally Rockwell's very commendable but simplistic review. Candida infections are never pure. Candida yeast is simply the harboring infective. It is the infective that harbors and shelters other infectives, some of which are also fungii. Fungal infections usually infect the skin, and these infections are medically called superficial mycoses, internal fungal infections are called deep mycoses.

Ch.3. Chronic Infection.

In 1970 Ajello presented a medical paper that likened the mycoses to an iceberg with "it's vast bulk ------ submerged in a murky sea of ignorance." You see, there are a very large number of mycotic infections that plague man, particularly in Africa, Asia, and South America, and anyone holidaying in these countries most certainly can return with a mycotic infection as a more or less permanent souvenir. The extent of the problem in North America is less, but ringworm alone in the U.S. costs over thirty-five million dollars per year for treatments. Only a few of the fungal infections are reportable diseases, so the total number of mycotic infections can not even be guessed.

One might wonder why a problem of such great proportions and with such far reaching consequences as Candida infection has remained so submerged and so obscure for so many years. The truth is that it has not been obscure. It is really only a matter of time and perspective.

Man has lived on earth a great many years, and has survived many changes. Fifteen thousand years ago, at the end of the Great Ice Age, man was killing and consuming so many mammoths along the Dnepr River just north of the BLack Sea,that he built his houses from mammoth bones and burned mammoth bones for fuel. During almost all of the ensuing fifteen thousand years health and illness were largely a matter of happenstance, sometimes mitigated and sometimes aggravated by the efforts of the Medicine Man, who was less than scientific, and therefore usually less than useful.Proof of even the presence of micro-organisms had to await the development of the microscope, and the identification of infectives on and in man had to await Louis Pasteur, who died less than a century ago; who died less than a hundred years ago; just before the authors still healthy oldest brother, was born! True science, in health and disease has therefore been with man for really only a few years, scant time for the Medicine Man to change from chant and ritual to science and disinfectants. World War 1, when the author was born, brought iodine, anaesthetics, and surgery, but during the author's school days tuberculosis and other diseases were still in the milk; can type outside toilets were still in use in the towns; water came from a poorly sealed town pump; the schools were sometimes closed for diptheria and other diseases;and quarantine signs were still frequently seen on the doors of houses. Tuberculosis, was still a very dread disease until antibiotics arrived with World War 2, only about forty years ago. During only this short time the medicine men have been learning to become scientists and doctors.

Certainly, more could have been done to combat fungal infections, but the medicine man syndrome still remains. The medicine man did not seek a cure. He sought only mitigation of the ailment. He sought, and still seeks only relief from the symptoms. He seeks only to "manage" the disease. Indeed, with drugs and antibiotics, many ailments are "managed" quite well, and people do live longer, with much less pain and trauma, than they used to have. But the antibiotics, and many other medical measures have increased the fungal infections, and, although fungii are in fact very primitive plants, they are composed of highly complex eukaryotic cells that have highly complex metabolic processes so similar to mammalian tissues that until very recently it has been almost impossible to find or to develop a substance that would selectively kill the fungus without also destroying the host.Therefore the fungal problem was known, but the extent of the problem was not investigated because so little could be done about it. In general, since Candida infection could not be effectively arrested, the medical people have had to simply do what they still have to do with many diseases; they have had to watch the infection run its course. Still, to their great credit, many of the doctors have not been idle.

MEDICAL PAPERS ON CANDIDA YEAST INFECTION.

The continuing extensive role of Candida yeast infection in human disease is seldom fully recognized. We find that yeast infection is always a part of illness, and very frequently it is at the very core of the health problem.

The Healthology Association, 195 Peveril ave; Vancouver Canada, has a list of over 2,300 titles of medical papers on Candida yeast and other fungal infections. The following lists are arranged roughly by indicated subject. Some of the titles are very revealing. Note that this is only a list, subject to inaccuracies from confusion between title and content.

SOURCES OF INFECTION.

Candida yeast is always present in the birth canal of the human mother. It normally lives on the surface of the mucosa, and does no harm unless the tissues are damaged so that it can invade and colonize. Candida in the birth canal is passed on to the newborn at birth. The amount of initial infection in the newborn is determined by the tissue injury to the baby during the delivery, the length of the delivery, the amount of infection present in the birth canal, and the state of health of the newborn. Highly infected mothers commonly have low health and consequently weaker babies and longer more difficult delivery, with high infection passed on through the females to succeeding generations. It can sometimes be seen in the great-grandmother, grandmother, mother, and children, with none of the people fully healthy. In one case the last child was hyperactive,- born covered with yeast (thrush) which was wiped off and cleaned up with nystatin cream. Cleaned on the outside, yes, but infected perhaps in the eyes, ears, nose, mouth, lungs, digestive tract, sexual tract, etc; etc.

Candida infection is therefore a family affair, passed back and forth by sexual contact, and passed around to the rest of the family on the floors, in the bathroom, in the kitchen, and in the dining room.

Further, Candida yeast is all around us, in nature. We cannot escape from it. It is everywhere, even in our chickens and on our apples and fruit.

MEDICAL PAPERS ON CANDIDA YEAST FOUND IN NATURE.
Airborne spread of Candida.
Endemic fungal area, soil, Brazilian soil, composted sewage.
Fowl, Chickens,(loss of feathers),chicks,crop mycosis in chicks.
Turkeys,(blackhead), Geese, Pigeons.
Birds, Gulls and Terns, Partridge.
Animal diseases, Animals in New Zealand, Cattle,(4 papers), Bovine abortion, Swine, Bush pig, goat mastitis, Black tongue, Central African hedge-hog, rabbits, Dogs, Rats,(4 papers),Mice,(5 papers), Simian primates, Baboons, Hippopotamus.
Fruit canners disease, damietta cheese, Corn, Farmers lung.

MEDICAL PAPERS ON CANDIDA YEAST SPECIES.
This list shows that there are a number of Candida infectives, each with different characteristics,and therefore each with different toxins and metabolites.

Candida Albicans, Y and K.   Parapsilosis.
Mycotorula albicans.   Guilliermondii.
Tropicalus, psuedotropicalus,   Stellatoidea.
Krusei,Parakrusei.   Aloofii.
Claussenii.   Viswanathil.
Bogoriensis.
Transformation by Actinomycetales into many different strains.

MEDICAL PAPERS SHOWING OTHER INFECTIVES ASSOC-IATED WITH CANDIDA YEAST.
Candida is never alone.It is invasive,and it will intermingle with body cells to form hard or soft calluses, which become a perfect home for other infectives.Indeed, some viral infections are maintained by the virus infecting both the Candida yeast

and the host. One paper "Magnesium Stimulated Re-synthesis of Asmoresistant Layer by Candida Yeast", shows how the yeast protects itself,(and it's associated infectives) from anti-fungal agents.

Note that these are only the infectives mentioned in the titles of the papers.There are many more that join the infective matrix. Note the Actinomycetales,-Nocardia Asteroides, and the different Torula yeasts, that may have a distinctive role in cancer.

Tinea Pedis
Tinea Cruris.
Trichophyton.
Trichophyton montagrophytes.
Histomonas Meleagrides.
Aspergillus fumigatus.
Alternaria.
Trichomoas vaginalis.
Fusarium solani.
Bacterical infection.
Cryptococcus neoformans.
Cryptococcus albidus.
Sporobolomyces salmonicolor.
Saccharomyces coroviglao.
Kluyveromyona lactic.
Listoria monocytonene
Glabratta.
Rubra.
Fungaemia and funguria.
Renal Torulopsis.
Mycobacterium Tuberculosis.
Virus-Like Particles in Yeast Cells.
Interaction of malignant cells with Yeast.

Streptomyces.
Enteric Bacilli.
Lactobacillus casei.
F oxysporum.
Mycoplasma.
Asbestos.
N.gonorrhoeae.
Homophilus vaginalis.
Tropicalis guilliermondii.
Salmonella tyhimurium.
Nocardia asteroides.
Coccidioidos imitis.
psoudomonas aoruginosa.
Brettanomyces,
Blastomycetes.
Torulopsis.
Rhodotorula.
Pityrosporum ovale.
Non-pathogenic yeast.
Torulopsis granulomatous

METABOLIC SUBSTANCES SYTHESIZED by CANDIDA YEAST.

This list should not be a surprise because many of our commercial chemicals, and human biological chemicals, are manufactured by extracting the desired subances from yeast grown on a substrate of suitable material. Chromium and selenium supplements, and many of the vitamins are good examples.

Note the production of Vitamin B2,which means that a high yeast infection would steal nutrients to make B2, and the excess B2 would then upset the famous "Balanced Bs" so recommended by avid nutritionists. It would be fair then, to ask the question,"Is the beri-beri seen in alcoholics,in fact, due to excess B2, instead of a shortage of B1?"It is also then fair to wonder if all alcoholics are victims of yeast infection? Does the yeast follow alcoholism, or does yeast infection create alcoholism? When will we know? The experience of Healthology is that all alcoholics do have a high yeast infection, which will only aggravate the alcoholism by producing alcohols and sterols and serotoin, with weird effects on the mind.

Note the NADPH, and the enzymes and the many other metabolic substances that can alter body function.

Note also the production of lactic acid, that increases the retention of water and leads to calcinosis.

This list is taken from the titles of the papers only. How many more substances are shown in the papers? How many more are produced that have not been discovered? How many more substances are produced by the infectives associated with the Candida infection? What are their combined total physical and mental effects? With so very many possibilities the combined toxins and altered metabolism may easily be the very root cause of every illness.

It is little wonder, then, that Candida yeast infects and or affects every body part and every life process from the hair on the head to the tip of the big toenail.

Metbolites of Pathogenic Fungi.   Aerial Hyphae.
Sythesis of Seleno-amino acids.   Sterols.
Sterol Biosynthesis.   NADPH-enoye CO-AReductase.
Soluble Polysaccharides.   Glycoprotein.
Hydroxyptamine.   Methionine.
Sulphur Amino Acids.   Enzymes.
Anti bacterical Compounds.   Oxidative Enzymes.
Soluble Polysaocharides.   Seratonin.
Phenylethyl Alcohol.   Candida precipitins.
Phenethyl Alcohol and Tryptophol.   2-phenethyl alcohol.
Synthesis of nucleic acid and proteins.   2-phenylacetic acid.
Transformation to Actinomycetales.   Beta indole ethanol.
Beta indolelactic acid.   Ethanol and Lactic acid.
Vitamin,B2.(Riboflavin).
Coversion of glycogen of vagina into lactic acid.
Production of Hydrolytic Enzymes and Toxins.
Transformation of C18, C!9, and C21, steroids.
Synthesis of nucleic acids and proteins.
Fungal toxins and their role in fungal infections.
Psuedomycelium in asporogenous yeasts.
Glycoprotein Acid Phosphatase.   RNA Synthesis.
Mast cell sentitizing antibodies.   Thiomethyladenosine.
Proteolytic Enzymes.   Hemolysin.
Enzyme secretion.   Cytochrome.C.
Mannan.   N-Acetyl-alanine, N-Acetylglycine.

MEDICAL PAPERS ON CANDIDAL DISEASES

This list shows that indeed all body parts are affected and that Candida infection can be part of every degenerative disease in man. The numbers indicate the number of medical papers on the specific affliction.

Eyes,20.	Heart,19.	Feet,3.
Ears,4.	Endocrine,8.	Calcinosis,3.
Skin,16.	Papillary.	Keratin.
Hair, Follicles.	Pulmonary,9.	Urinary,18.
Kidney.7.	Visceral.	Leg ulcers,3.
Colon and Diarrhea,6.	Esophagus,9.	Stomach.
Diverticulosis.	Ulcers,2.	Sinusitis.
Maxillary.	Infant.	Geotrichosis.
Endocarditis,91 cases.	Mouth,15.	Hair Growth.
Saliva and Sputum,7.	Dental,3.	Immune System,13.
Inflammation.	Thymus.	Displasia.
Conversion.	Tongue.	Stool of Children.
Hypothyroid.	Thyroid.	Adrenal Cortex.
Hyperparathyroid,6.	Liver,2.	Hyoparathyroid.
Throat,3.	Larynx,2.	Calculus Pyonephrosis.
Tonsils,5.	Lymphomas	Lupus Erythematosis.
Nails,2.	Sprue,2.	Asthma,4.
Burns,7.	Bones,2.	Skeletal muscles.
Groin.	Mastoid.	Leukoplakia.
Fenestran Cavities.	Costchondral.	Otology.
Osteomyelitis,5.	Endothalmitis,5.	Within Leukocytes.
Intestines,8.	Anemia,2.	Leucorrhoea.
Otitis.	Septicaemia.	Granulomas,3.
Leukocyte Chemotaxis.	Disseminated.	Fulminating.
Otomycosis,2.	Tuberculosis.	Phlebitis.
Cystic Fibrosis.	Erysipelas.	Paronychia.
Steatorhoea.	Pemphigus.	Glossodinia.
Cheilosis.	Anuria.	Colpitis.
Amyloidosis.	Pyarthrosis.	Onychomycosis.
Bursa Follicles.	Pyrogenicity.	Ependymitis.
Aqueductal Occlusion.	Femoral Emboli.	Lichen Planus.
Phenyl Oligophrenia.	Dysuria.	Fever.
Erythema Annulare.	Protoplasts.	Hypovitaminosis.
Cushings Syndrome.	Cushings Syndrome.	Glycogen Levels.
FATAL,5.		

ARTHRITIS,7. Rheumatoid, neonatal, spine, knee,3. Arthritis is known to sometimes be caused by Candida infection.(Candidal Arthritis).

The multiple effects of pain and pressure also should not be ignored.
ALLERGIES,6. Allergies affect the entire body including, particularly, digestion, the immune and lymphatic system, and the mind.
BRAIN,8. Any thought, function, or life process can be altered by the yeast. Brain calcification, iron deposits, and tonic-clonic convulsions.Central nervous system,2. Cerebral Spinal Fluid,2. Meningitis,3.
BLOOD. Filaments and Hyphae in Blood. Energy and Plasma Inhibitor, Anemia, Serum and Aglutinins,7. Clumping Factor.Probably the real cause of circulatory problems. In known cases of high Candida infection the blood, under the microscope, will show damaged cells, clumping, jellied bodies, filaments, L forms etc; Intravenous Chelation with NaEDTA will usally relieve tension, headache, toxic episodes, and psychosis, showing that either infectives in the bloodstream are being killed, or the NaEDTA has altered toxins. The total "junk" in the bloodstre4am is reduced by chelation. Although calcium is definitely removed from the blood-vessel plaques,the instrument- proven increased blood flow following chelation therapy may actually come mostly from the breakdown and removal of foreign material from the bloodstream. Most certainly, high amounts of foreign material in the bloodstream would thicken the blood, leading to poor circulation, and high blood pressure.
CANCER,9.Leukemia,7. Malignancy, Collagen Disease, and Myasthenia Gravis. Hodgkins,2.
Immune system failure is always present in cancer. Candida yeast impairs the B and T lymphocytes and sets the stage for cancer. Candida infection may also foster the fulmination of Progenitor Cryptocides, which is always present in cancer. Note that Malignancy, Collagen Disease, and Myasthenia Gravis are all lumped together in a paper.236.
DIABETES,6. Pancreas Islet Cells. Glucose Metabolism. Diabetes is always associated with poor circulation and damage to bodysystems.(Dr. Phillpot.) The diabetic condition also alters blood-sugar levels, which affects the mind, and can lead to mental problems, addictions, and criminal behavior.
SEXUAL. Genital, 3. Female,-breast, lacrymal sacs, ovaries, Chorion,2. Cervix,2. Vaginal,220. Conversion of Glycogen of Vagina to lactic acid- childbirth, familial, congenital, premature, infant, 25.
Blood changes and fertility, sexual transmissions,-5. Male,-8.
Candida yeast infection is commonly thought of as solely a vaginal infection. It certainly infects and affects the entire

female reproductive system as seen by the many papers, but it also infects the male. Dr.Pilar has now found Candida yeast in spermatic fluid taken from a spermatocelle. It is known that yeast causes clumping of seminal fluid. Yeast infection is therefore the probable cause of the thick curdled spermatic fluid present in about 60% of males over 45 years old. It is also the probable cause of hydrocelles, tender testicles, and enlarged prostate. #328 "Induction of Mycelial Form of Albicans by Hydrolysates of Peptides from Seminal Plasma" re-inforces this probability, and also shows that intercourse greatly increases candidal vaginitis.

OTHER TITLES. The other titles largely speak for themselves. This medical literature definitely proves that Candida yeast infection can, and does, infect and affect all life systems from the hair on the top of the head to the tip of the large toenail. Athlete's foot is not a minor nuisance, because the usual infection is Candida yeast, and Candida yeast, can be, and sometimes is,-fatal.

A review of this mass of medical literature should impress every medical doctor, and it should inspire each and every doctor to look for Candida infection as a first possibility in every and all cases of ill health. It should be obvious to all, to the victim and to the medical specialist alike,--that in all cases of ill health Candida can be the cause,---and if Candida is the cause,the health problem, however treated,will remain until the Candida infection is reduced.

INCREASE OF CANDIDA INFECTION.

Dr. Orion Truss has pointed out that the social drug craze started in North America at approximately the same time as the first antibiotics appeared. It is known that antibiotics, and particularly tetracycline, increase yeast and fungal infections because the yeasts move in on the tissues injured by the other infectives. (Many health professionals have discovered that the reverse is equally true;-that bacterial infections may increase with the use of anti-fungals.) Dr. Truss attributes the increased use of social drugs to reduced health levels from the increased chronic fungal infections.The "pill", steroids,and increased sexual activity with multiple partners has also greatly increased the incidence of Candidal infections,to the point that almost every female has had episodes of vaginitis,and therefore almost every male is also infected.The increase in infections also comes from the high resistance of the yeast to most disinfectants,including alcohol. Note that one paper is titled,"Survival of Gram Negative Bacilli and Candida Albicans in Hexachlorophane Preparations and Other Disinfectants".

Ch.3. Chronic Infection.

The factors that increase Candida infection, shown in the titles of the medical papers, are:- Antibiotics,- Chlorpromazine,- Corticosteroids,- Tranquilizers,- Anti-lymphocyte serum,- Lysozyme,- Thorazine,- Diabetes,- Glucose,- Vitamins,- Tampons,- methionine mutants,- hand creams,- the "pill".

"Induction of Mycelial Form of Albicans by Hydrolysates of Peptides From Seminal Plasma".

MEDICAL PAPERS ON CANDIDA IN THE MEDICAL ESTABLISHMENT.

You can also have your Candida infection regenerated or increased by either your doctor or your hospital, all without your consent and without your knowledge, and obviously without the knowledge of the hospital or the physican. Again the entire problem is that Candida infection is known, most of the medical information is here, but most medical doctors do not read the papers prepared by their more scientific colleages,they do not make themselves aware of their own information,- and therefore they usually do not USE it. Nonetheless we must certainly applaud the oft-ignored efforts of the many doctors who have contributed to the knowledge of Candida yeast infection. Without them we would not have the many anti-fungals shown in list 8.

HOSPITALS.

Eradicating thrush from hospital nurseries.

Survival of gram negative bacilli and Candida Albicans in hexachlorophene prepartions and other dieinfectants.

Fatal candidiasis following colonic sterilization.

Candida in hyperalimentation solutions.

Parenteral feeding.

Renal transplant.

Candida in a skin disease hospital.

Maternity hospitaL.

Hospital inpatients.

Venous catheters.

Hospital infection.

Thrush in premature nursey.

Surgical patients.

Hospital patients.

PHYSICIAN INDUCED.

Hippocrates (377 B.C.)"Epidemics".

Iatrogenic oral candidosis.

Chorionitis and I.U.D.s.

Steroids.

Contraceptive Pill.

Candida Albicans Endothalmitis due to catheter tip sepsis.

List 8 -.ANTI FUNGALS and INHIBITING FACTORS.

The recently developed anti-fungal Ketoconazole (Nizeral), is not shown on the list. Ketoconazole is the first wide range systemic oral anti-fungal. It is specific against fungus, and it is highly effective, with the only side effects coming from the dead bodies of the killed infective.

Gentian Violet, the old army standby, is on the list but the other old army standby,- Potassium permanganate (still highly effective) appears to have been forgotten. Other old anti-fungals not on the list are hydrogen peroxide, and phenol (usually 2% phenol in glycerine).

ANTI-FUNGALS and INHIBITING FACTORS.

Sodium N-alkylsalicylate.
Sodium azide.
Triamcinolone acetonide.
Heptaene.
Chlorhexidine.
Fungilin.
Polyenic antibiotics.
Lactobacillus.
Ultraviolet radiation.
Candicidin
Sorbic acid.
S-fluorocytosine.
Iron.
Natamycin.
Haloprogin.
Thiabendazole.
Clotrimazole.
Fluvomycin.
Providone iodine.
Pimaricin.
1-4-napthoquinones.
Dithiothretol.
Benzalkonium chloride.
Hydrolytic enzymes.
Pyrrolnitrin.
Amphotericin B.
L-phenylethinidazole.
Butyl Hydrogen Peroxide.
Chlorhexidine.
Pimafusin (natamycin).
Trichomycin.
Polmethylene.

Crystal violet.
Arthrobacter.
Copper sulphate.
Sulfamethoxazole.
Gentian violet.
Trimonil.
Polynoxylin.
Iron unsaturated lactoferrin.
Myeloperoxidase.
1040 Topical anaesthetics.
NaN-succinylperimycin.
Econazole.
Copiamycin.
Phenanthroline.
Cu-oxine complex.
PDDB.
Minocycline.
Formic acid.
Bromopyruvic acid.
Trifluoromethylhomocysteine.
Beclomethasone dipropionate.
Benlate.
Sodium propionate.
Nitrofurylene.
Heptaene macrolide.
Chlorantoin.
Tricetin.
Filipin
Hamycin (Hindustan).
Levorin.
Tennectin.
Polyfungin (Poland).

Garlic.
Brilliant green aerosol.
Nalidixic acid.
Nifuratel.
Lactocyd.
Amidomycin.
Anti fungal agents.
Aerosol chemotherapy.
Bladder instillations.
Blood.
Hyperbaric oxygen.
Bordetella pertussis vaccine.
E.Coli.
Antibiotics and drugs on Candida.
End products of intestinal bacteria.
Ethylene-diamine-di-hydro-iodide.

Asterol.
Cetylpyridinium chloride.
Polynoxalin.
Methyl patricin.
Tolnaftate.
Boride.
Intravitreal antibiotics.
Lymphocyte transfusions.
Foetal thymus.
Immume therapy.
Mannitol.
Prostatic fluid.
B.Complex.

OTHER MEDICAL PAPERS.   The total list of medical papers on fungal infections contains approximately 1200 more titles that are more complex and have not as yet been assigned numbers.The list continues to grow.

TYPICAL MEDICAL REFERENCES on FUNGAL DISEASES.

Abbreviations of journal titles conform to ISO standards.

Clinical experience with Canestencream(Bay b5097) against dermatophytes in Egypt. Mykosen 16,369-71. 1973.

Monilial infection of the umbilical cord. Obstet. Gynecol. 27,845-9.1966.

Candida Albicans endophthalmitis due to catheter tip sepis.Del.Med.J.48,121-6. 1976.

A method for quantitative estimation of yeast species in sputum.Sabouraudia 3,185-94. 1964.

A new antibiotic for treatment of moniliasis. West.Med.5,62-3. 1964. The importance of CANDIDA as an infectious agent.Surg.Gynecol. Obstet.140,65-8. 1975.

Life history of experimentally induced acute oral candidiasis in the rat.J.Dent.REs.50,643-4.1971.

Evaluation of a modified Wickerham medium for identifying medically important yeasts. Am.J.Med. Technol. 40,377-88. 1974.

Effects of sodium caprylate on CANDIDA ALBICANS. 1.Influence of concentration on ultrastructure. J.Bacteriol.86,548-57.1963.

Candidal osteomyelitis and arthritis in a neonate. Am.J.Dis.Child.123,595-6.1972.

Experimental moniliasis in mice.Am.J.Pathol.31,859-73. 1955.

Mycotic corneal ulcers. Br.J.Ophthalmol. 47, 109-15. 1963.

Speciation and densities of yeasts in human urine specimens. Sabouraudia 5, 110-19. 1966.

Use of shaken cultures in the assimillaton test for yeast identification. J.Bacteriol. 79,369-71. 1960.

Synergism between ultrasonic waves and hydrogen peroxide in the killing of micro-organisms. J.Appl. Bacteriol. 39,31-40. 1975.

Fungal flora of the conjunctival sac in healthy and disceased eyes. Br.J.Ophtalmol. 49,505-15. 1965.

The effect of tubercle bacillus concentration procedures on fungii causing pulmonary mycoses. J.Lab. Clin, Med.38, 486-91. 1951.

The biology of intestinal moniliasis. J.Fac. Med. Baghdad 2,63-9. 1960.

Use of a hyperbaric solution for administration of intrathecal amphotericin B.New Engl. J. Med. 290,641-6. 1974.

CANDIDA ALBICANS infection of the placenta and fetus. Report of a case. Obstet.Gynecol.30, 838-41.1967.

Oral amphotericin B.in the management of cutaneous and mucosal candidiasis in infants. Curr. Ther.Res. 14, 158-61.1972.

Amphotericin B.oral suspension in the treatment of thrush. Curr. Ther.Res.12, 479-84. 1970.

Pathogenicity in mice of strains of CANDIDA ALBICANS (Robin) Berk.isolated from burn patients. Mycopathol. Mycol. Appl. 49,283-8. 1973.

Renal failure following prostatovesiculectomy related to methoxyflurane anesthesia and tetracycline- complicated by CANDIDA infection.J.Urol. 106, 348-50. 1971.

CANDIDA endocarditis of the tricuspid valve. Report of a case. J.Am.Med.Assoc.224, 517-18.1973.

Studies on the pathogenicity of CANDIDA ALBICANS isolated from baboon. Can. J. Microbiol.14, 443-8. 1968.

An immune factor in baboon anti-CANDIDA serum. Sabouraudia 8, 41-7. 1970.

Scrum protein patterns in experimental candidiasis. Indian J.Exp. Biol.8, 289-92. 1970.

Comparative observations of ultrastructure of five species of CANDIDA. Mycopathol. Mycol. Appl.44,355-67. 1971.

Thrush bowel infection: existence, incidence, prevention and treatment, particularly by a LACTOBACILLUS ACIDOPHILUS preparation. Curr. Med. Drugs 8,3-11. 1967.

Allergy in the gastrointestinal tract. Lancet2,1264. 1975.

Miconazole (R14889) in the treatment of vaginal candidosis. Amulticentric trial in gynecological practice.Eur.J. Obstet.Gynecol.2,65-70. 1972.

Transformation of lymphocytes of normal and hospitalized adults by CANDIDA ALBICANS extract.Proc. Soc. Exp. Biol. Med. 144, 826-9. 1973.

CANDIDA IN THE MEDICAL LIBRARY.

Many victims of Candida infection have never even heard about it, yet it is very well known in the Medical Library. The following list is taken from the Index of Scientific American Medical Library. (Ref.1.). If your doctor does not have a good knowledge of Candida infection, and its many consequences, he certainly should have the knowledge. So if you have any of the afflictions shown on this list, or shown on the preceeding pages, discuss the possibility of Candida being a major factor with your doctor, and have him help you with your anti-Candida program.

Candida, 2:VII:1, 3, 6; 7:X:12, 13
  addict-associated endocarditis caused by, 7:XVIII:9
  balanitis caused by, 7:XXII:15
  diarrhea caused by, 4:III:9–10
  5-fluorocytosine–amphotericin B synergism and, 7:XIV:7
  fungal arthritis caused by, 7:XV:7
  immunosuppressed host and, 7:X:6
  infective endocarditis caused by, 7:XVIII:1, 3
  miconazole in treating, 7:X:21
  mycetomas caused by, 7:X:12
  peritonitis caused by, 7:XXI:2
  pneumonia and, 7:XX:5
  prosthetic valve endocarditis caused by, 7:XVIII:10
  T lymphocyte function and, 7:X:1
  tetracycline therapy and, 2:I:5
  in upper respiratory tract, 7:XIX:2
  vaginitis caused by, 7:XXII:13
Candida antigen, in evaluating cell-mediated immunity, 6:XIV:4
Candida antigen skin test, 2:X:3
Candida guilliermondii, 7:X:12
Candida osteomyelitis, 7:XVI:2

Candida parapsilosis, 7:X:12
  infective endocarditis caused by, 7:XVIII:3
Candida tropicalis, 7:X:12, 13
Candidiasis, 2:VII:1, 2, 4
  antibiotic therapy causing, 7:XIV:18
  chronic,
    immune status of patient with, 6:XII:10
    therapy for, 6:XIII:4
  chronic mucocutaneous, 7:X:14
  cutaneous, 7:X:14
  diarrhea caused by, 4:III:9–10
  disseminated, 7:X:15–17
  immunosuppressed host and, 7:X:12–17
  lesions of, 2:VII:5
  membranous pharyngitis caused by, 7:IV:5
  mucosal, 7:X:14
  nonspecific vaginitis and, 7:XXII:14
  ocular toxoplasmosis differentiated from, 7:XXXIV:2
  oral, beclomethasone treatment and, 6:IX:7
  tetracycline therapy and, 2:I:5
  treatment of, 2:VII:7
  urinary tract, 7:X:15
  vaginal, diabetics and, 7:X:2
Candidosis, see Candidiasis

FATAL FUNGAL INFECTIONS IN THE NEWBORN.

Sex hormones oppose Candida yeast. Male babies develop testicles while in the womb, and they are already producing testosterone at birth, which increases their ability to combat Candida when they are first exposed during childbirth. Female babies, however, may be at risk if the birth is difficult or prolonged, and if Candida infection in the mother is high, because female babies do not start to produce estrogen until about a year after birth. Unfortunately and all too frequently, female babies will be overwhelmed by a massive Candida infection, that may take their life, or, if they do survive, that will result in poor health throughout their entire life.

FATAL FUNGAL INFECTIONS.

Most medical doctors, when confronted with vaginitis, will prescribe nystatin cream to reduce the discomfort, and when confronted with calluses on the feet they will dismiss the problem as being of very little consequence. Yet the Candida yeast infection that is usually involved, can be and sometimes is fatal, as we have seen.

We say that Candida yeast is "sometimes" fatal because no one knows how often it is the true immediate cause of death, and no one knows how often it is the underlying cause of death. It is certainly known that a high chronic yeast infection impairs the immune system, and that many diseases, including cancer and AIDS, are associated with or result from, the immune suppressed condition. It is also known that when the immune system is suppressed Candida infection can fulminate, and result in death in only a few hours. Yet commonly no one ever hears of direct death from yeast infection, and since most people that die from "natural causes" are not autopsied after death, we cannot know how many people die directly from yeast infection, and we certainly cannot know how many people die from diseases that result from, or are complicated by, chronic yeast infection.

The truth is that Health is a private matter, and therefore health is governed by the Provinces.(In the U.S.,each State), and the Provinces (and States) have abrogated their specific duty to govern health, and without the legal authority to do so, they have transferred their right to govern health to the Provincial Medical Association, who may, or may not, govern health matters to the best interests of the citizens.

In all cases,the true cause of death can be established only by autopsy, and even by autopsy Candida infections can easily be missed unless it is specifically being sought. Statistics on autopsy are meager, but the autopsy rate in Canada is thought to be even lower than the U.S.A. Scientific American, March, 1983, shows that in the U.S. the rate of autopsy has declined from about 50% of deaths in 1946 to about 15% of deaths today. Further, in the few cases autopsied, the medical diagnosis made before death was in fact wrong in about 40% of the people autopsied,while in about 40% of the death certificates the information recorded was inaccurate. Thus the factual cause of death is recorded in only 1 or 2% of the total deaths. Also, Yeast infection is not on the list of common causes of death, so the possible death rate from Candida infection cannot even be guessed.

This almost total absence of factual statistical information on the actual causes of death is a sad, sad comment on the effectiveness of a socialistic HiTech computer aided society!---- "Oh TECHNOLOGY! Where art thou? Where hast thou gone? And who took thee away?"

TOTAL CHRONIC INFECTION.
From the list of infectives associated with Candida infection it can readily be seen that Candida yeast infection is never a simple infection of Candida alone. Instead it is invariably a mixed infection, with the Candida sheltering itself and harbouring the other infectives within the Candida callus matrix.
Note now the substances synthesized by Candida yeast. Some of these, like (vitamin B2),may be "good" for you, while others like (phenylethyl alcohol) may be highly toxic to you. Now consider that this list is only the list of substances syntheized by Candida yeast. Each of the infectives associated with the basic Candida infection will also have its own list of substances that it synthesizes, again some good, and some bad, yet with many of these substances having a profound effect on the normal body processes, frequently with devastating effects on total health.
Perhaps the greatest problem with chronic infection is the attitude of most of the medical profession, who do not attempt to cure, but try only to "manage" the health problems. Thus if infection is great, and visible, and easily identified, the doctor will usually attempt to reduce it. But if the infection appears to be small, or if it is well hidden, the doctor may simply dismiss it as being of very little consequence without considering that it may be greater than it appears, or that several small infections can produce more toxins and can have a greater affect on total health than a much larger, single, obvious infection. Usually therefore the doctor will respond to a visible infection, either adequately with every anti-fungal and antibiotic at his command, or more commonly today, inadequately with cortisone or other "management" drugs that do very little to reverse the basic cause.
Most Candida infections however are not easily identified typical infections that neatly fit the medical literature. Instead, they are "non typical" or atypical infections that are well hidden, and usually are spread between all of the cutaneous and muco-cutaneous tissues. Thus the typical Candida infections are usually recognised by the doctor, but severe cases of atypical candidiasis are frequently missed, mis-diagnosed, or ignored.
To assist the general reader, and particularly to assist the medical doctors and other health professionals in understanding the plight of the atypical Candida victim, the following paper is presented. This paper is included through the courtesy of Ecological Formulas, 1061 Shary Circle, Concord Ca. 94518; who have developed Caprystatin, Orithrush, and other antifungals. The content of this paper is excellent, but the over-use of medical jargon is unfortunate.

Note however, that the victim of atypical Candida infection is usually neither sick nor well,with many complaints and many health problems, yet without sufficient definitive symptoms to make a definite diagnosis.

CHRONIC ENDOTOXEMIA in ATYPICAL CANDIDIASIS.
  A Hypothesis by Robert A. Da Prato.M.D.
  (Re-printed by permissiom from Ecological Formulas.
    1061 B. Shary Circle, Concord Ca. 94518).

Classically described systemic or mucocutaneous Candidiasis requires s demonstration of overgrowth or parenchymal invasion of Candida albicans. "Atypical" Candidiasis, however, is a hypothesis for a wide variety of symptom complexes which usually have in common certain medical history patterns and clinical improvement following therapeutic trials of specific anti-fungal medications along with a variety of "anti-Candida" environmental and dietary modifications. Demonstration of systemic or mucocutaneous candida infection is not pre-requisite for this diagnosis. Confirmatory diagnostic laboratory tests are lacking.

Any useful hypothesis of the pathogensis of atypical Candidiasis must explain the characteristic medical history and clinical signs and symptoms of this illness as well as predict as yet undiscovered relationships. Finally, therapies based on this hypothesis should result in clinical improvement.

The medical history of the atypical Candidiasis patient frequently includes repeated therapy with antibiotics, oral contraceptives, or other steroid medications. Prolonged peroids of psychological stress may be reported. Symptoms are chronic, persisting for months or years. Symptom complexes may vary widely both between patients and for each individual patient over time. The usual common denominator symptoms are:

1. Central Nervous System, (fatigue, mental confusion, dizziness, anxiety).
2. Gastrointestinal (belching, fullness, heartburn, abdominal distention, nausea, constipation, diarrhea, abdominal burning sensation).
3. Immunologic (sensitivity to foods, chemicals, other inhalents).
4. Endocrinologic (immune dysregulation affecting various endocrine glandsthe Candida "Polyendocrineopathy syndrome").
5. Metabolic (Evidence of hypometabolism: lowered body temperature, bradycardia, low blood pressure,chronic fatigue).

The sequence of events leading to this clinical picture are hypothesized to be as follows:

1. Psychological stress or oral antibiotic use disturbes normal intestinal microflora.
2. Increased mucosal permeability together with an increased

load of endotoxin and other antigens transiently paralyse the reticuloendothelial system (RES) and the level of circulation endotoxin increases.

3. Endotoxin acting on certain brain loci causes increased adrenergic outflow to splanchnic vessels and intestinal musculature causing relative ischemia of liver and intestines, and disordered gut motility.

4. Ischemia further compromises mucosal integrity and RES function.

5. The decreased ability of hydrolytic enzymes in the RES lysosomes to properly degrade self and non-self antigens initiates maladaptive immune responses (auto-immunity, immune paralysis, tolerance) which may in their own complex circuits be self perpetuating.

The vicious circle described above can be entered and perpetuated at many points, intestinal microflora being one. In a series of classic experiments Dubos (2) (3) showed that compared with genetically similar controls, mice with an intestinal flora free of pathogenic and potentially pathogenic organisms and with an abundance of lactobacilla resisted contamination by pathogenic bacteria, gained weight and thrived on a variety of diets considered deficient for normal mice and showed "extraordinary" resistance to the lethal effects of very large doses of endotoxin. Such mice also showed great resistance to developing adverse effects from high doses of cortisone and radiation. All these effects were abolished with a change in bacteria flora. Dubos found that the fecal flora of these mice could be altered rapidly, profoundly, and lastingly by--

1. Changing the diet.

2. Treating the animals with microbial drugs.

3 " Psychologically" stressing them in various ways.

4. Intestinal motility is the major non-immunological factor regulating intestinal microflora. Reciprocally, anaerobic bacteria function to maintain intestinal tone and peristalsis.

5. Production of short and medium chain fatty acids by intestinal anaerobes may be of particular importance in preserving indigenous flora.

6. Such fatty acids are strongly fungistatic and fungicidal in low concentrations against Candida albicans and other fungi.

7. Bacteria in close association with intestinal epithelial cells are more significant to the host than those located intralumenally.

8. Competition for mucosal receptors may be one additional mechanism by which indigenous organisms protect against pathogens. As an example, Liljemark and Gibbons found that the indigenous oral flora inhibits the adherence of Candida albicans.

Ch.3. Chronic Infection.

Since indigenous intestinal microbes create the conditions for their dominance, a decrease in their number weakens their ability to do so. This potential for a vicious cycle may explain changes in intestinal flora which are profound and, more significantly, lasting.

It is hypothesized that loss of these protective mechanisms by a disturbed intestinal flora leads to a transient depression of RES function and elevated levels of circulating endotoxin by one or more of the following events:

1. Pathogenic bacteria may damage intestinal mucosa. Wadstrom, (9) for example, showed that some acid and alcohol metabolites of certain strains of E.COLI are toxic to the intestinal epithelium.

2. Candida albicans is postulated to affect mucosal integrity and lead to a "leaky mucosa".

3. While endotoxin physiologically stimulates RES function as well as immune parameters (10), overgrowth of endotoxin producing bacterial species could substantially increase the amount of endotoxin presented to RES, especially when the normal barrier function is compromised (11).

4. Alcohol has a specific depressant effect on reticuloendothelial function (12). Candida albicans can produce alcohol by fermentation, some strains quite dramatically. It is possible that long term exposure of the liver to low levels of alcohol produced by Candida albicans might affect RES function. MacDougall etal (13) reported that in acute alcoholic hepatitis colloid liver scans (an index of RES function) showed markedly reduced activity although selenomethionine scans (an index of hepatocyte uptake) were normal.

If circulating endotoxin is not promptly removed from the circulation it binds to glycolipids in the plasmaling absorption of larger molecules, including endotoxin.

If circulating endotoxin is not promptly removed from the circulation it binds to glycolipids in the plasma membrane of cells in many tissues and causes a shift of calcium ions into the cells and an increased output of cell products. Critical body response to endotoxin is mediated through certain loci within the central nervous system. Endotoxin causes CNS norepinephrine discharge which leads to generalized arteriolar spasm critically affecting the splanchnic area, especially intestine and liver. Reduced hepatic blood flow compromises the RES ability to detoxify endotoxin (and other antigens);relative intestinal ischemia further compromises mucosal function. This cycle may be self sustaining. Atypical Candidiasis, then is viewed as one varient of chronic, low grade endotoxemia.

The main symptoms and signs of atypical Candidiasis may be explained by the above cycle.

GENERAL METABOLIC LEVEL:
Body core temperature has been a neglected but potentially useful diagnostic and therapeutic tool for the atypical Candida patient. Many such patients, especially the sub-group manifesting the chemical hypersensitivity syndrome, show a definite and sometimes striking decrease in core temperature. This finding is frequently accompanied by other signs of "hypometabolism" such as slow pulse, decreased blood pressure, increased muscle relaxation time, and fatigue. Endotoxin injected into a variety of animals causes hypothermia probably secondary to its release of norepinephrine. Administration of norepinephrine into the lateral ventricles or hypothalamus produces hypothermia in a wide variety of species. Muscle fibrils in venules become disoriented secondary to endotoxin membrane effects and blood pools in them and in capillary beds leading to a decline in venous return and cardiac output. Experimental endotoxic injections in laboratory animals causes decreased blood pressure, cardiac output, body temperature and arterial pCO_2.

The relationship between RES function and endotoxin sensitivity also involves glucoregulatory and insulin-regulatory disturbances. After experimental reticuloendothelial system blockade or injection of endotoxin there is a profound hypoglycemia with increased glucose tolerance (more rapid disappearance of a i.v. glucose load), decreased insulin tolerance (deeper glucose nadir after insulin injection), increased glycogenolysis and glucose oxidation, increased serum insulin after glucose challange, and decreased gluconeogenesis. If the central hypothesis of this paper is correct, then one would expect atypical Candidiasis patients to demonstrate these abnormalities in a milder form. Low grade persistent or intermittent endotoxemia occurs in a variety of depleting illnesses: its detection in atypical Candida patients would support this hypothesis.

CNS SYMPTOMS:
In addition to fatigue, patients report a variety of CNS effects such as depression, mental confusion, dizziness, anxiety and numbness. Focal and generalized CNS neurologic symptoms can result from a lowered arterial concentration of carbon dioxide. Injection of endotoxin induces hyperventilation probably secondary to CNS effects as well as decreased metabolic rate with a consequent lowering of CO_2 production. This combination of decreased production and increased respiratory "blow off" causes depressed arterial carbon dioxide levels. Since the concentration of arterial carbon dioxide is the major determinant of cerebral blood flow, neurologic signs of atypical Candidiasis may be caused partially by this mechanism. The rapid and dramatic effectiveness of bicarbonate and carbonate salts in

relieving CNS symptoms in these patients may be partially due to carbon dioxide supplementation. Rapid onset of symptoms, negative neurological examination and complete reversibility argue for this mechanism. The effects of circulating dietary psychoactive peptides and depressed metabolic rate are two other factors which may also profoundly influence CNS function.

GASTROINTESTINAL:

One or more of the following symptoms usually occur in atypical Candidiasis: repeated belching, uncomfortable full feeling after a normal sized meal, abdominal distention, burning in the upper abdomen, burning discomfort in the chest, nausea, and rarely, vomiting. Johnson and Jenkins proposed the hypothesis of a tiered symptom complex (symptoms not on a line representing increased severity, but rather occurring in blocks or tiers and the progression in jumps) and postulated that all symptoms could be produced by a motility disorder affecting different parts of the gastro-intestinal tract to varying degrees. For example, belching and fullness may be produced by abnormal stomach wall tone with delayed emptying with some pyloric spasm; abdominal burning may be caused by pyloric regurgitation; and abdominal distention a result of abnormal smooth muscle relaxation of the small and large intestine. As noted above, the composition of intestinal flora is a determinant of intestinal tone and peristalsis, but central nervous system mechanisms share control. Adrenergic hyperactivity secondary to endotoxin excess may effect intestinal motility, as could focal hypocapnia induced cerebral vasospasm.

IMMUNOLOGIC:

Phagocytosis and enzymatic degradation of self and non-self antigens by macrophage lysosomes are essential steps in generating immune responses. Mehta postulates that each species contains the enzymes necessary to completely degrade self antigens. Non-self antigens may or may not be completely degraded. Partial degradation of antigens leads to production of fragments of high immunogenicity. Incompletely degraded antigens trigger immune responses. If self antigens are processed by enzymes partially inactivated by low temperatures or toxins from the intestine, and complete degradation is inhibited, auto antibodies could be formed. On the other hand, total inability to degrade specific antigens (such as Candida) would result in immune paralysis. The health of this "enzyme surveillance"system would, like other aspects of RES function seem to be primarily dependent on hepatic blood flow (oxygenation of tissues with effective ATP production) and temperature.(Since many enzymes lose significant activity within one or two degrees Centigrade below their optimal temperature).

Severly stressed animals (endotoxin injection, hemorrhagic shock, etc;)treated by perfusing the liver with blood from healthy donors survived, as did animals with prophylactic denervation of the liver (to abolish sympathetic vasospasm); all control animals died. The unpredictable immune dysregulation of atypical Candidiasis with auto-antibody formation, apparent immune tolerance, and bizarre reactions to foods and chemicals may be caused by initial damage to RES function and depression of enzyme function.

The major active component of endotoxin is a lipopolysaccharide which is an excellent adjuvant when injected together with antigen but which can inhibit immune responses as well. Under certain conditions in vitro, endotoxin stimulates T suppressor cell generation.Many such substances with adjuvant activity can be shown to be inhibitory by the proper manipulation of dose, timing and accompanying antigen.

THERAPY:

A standard of care fot the atypical Candida patient is evolving, with excellent lay and professional publications outlining treatment. Based on the hypothesis presented above, the following therapies would seem to have a rational basis for inclusion in the necessary complex therapy of this illness.

RESTORING NORMAL FLORA.

The current pharmaceutical therapy of atypical Candidiasis consists primarily of the polyene antibiotics, nystatin and amphotericin B, and imidazoles such as Ketoconazole. All function to lower the concentration of viable Candida organism. If an endotoxic process is involved, then imidazoles would have an additional justification for use because of the posited protective role of imidazoles in endotoxic states. Use of these agents is well described although the benefit of synergistic therapy has not been adequately explored. Beggs tested weakly fungistatic concentrations of ketoconazole in combination with a subinhibitory level of sulphamethoxizole against different strains of Candida albicans in vitro. The combined drug activity markedly surpassed that seen with ketoconazole alone. Uno et al. found copiamycin, a macrocyclic lactone antifungal antibiotic, to potentiate the antifungal effect of imidazole compounds both in vivo and in vitro. A marked reduction in the minimum inhibitory and minimal fungicidal concentrations was noted when the drugs were used in combination. Both studies suggested increased effectiveness of these agents can be coupled with decreased toxicity by exploring their synergistic effects.

The clinical use of saturated fatty acids supplementation is worthy of further study because of their physiological production by normal intestinal bacteria and posited homeostatic role as anti-fungal agents.

Exogenous administration of fatty acids such as caprylic acid has been shown to be effective clinically against entering Candidiasis and has some justification in the treatment of atypical Candidiasis. Endogenous synthesis of fatty acids by the intestinal bacteria can be fostered by specific dietary fiber.

Elemental sulfur demonstrates potent anti fungal effects in vitro and topically. It is a strong antioxidant, and protect animals from experimental enterotoxemia. In its flowers of sulfur form it is essentially non-absorbable from the intestine.

The oral administration of activated charcoal in the treatment of digestive tract infections and adsorption of bacterial toxins was extensively studied in the first three decades of this century. Its use in endotoxic shock was recently rediscovered by Kopp who noted disappearance of small and large bowel distention along with other clinical improvements, and commented on adsorption of toxic degradation products within the intestinal lumen following oral activated charcoal use.

Preoccupation with Candida albicans may cause one to neglect the pathogenic effects of other microflora. Disordered small intestinal motility can lead to overgrowth of pathogenic bacteria which interfere with absorption of fats, amino acids, and vitamins. Patients presenting with steatorrhea, macrocytic anemia secondary to B12 depressed absorption, amino acid malabsorption and carbohydrate intolerance may be suffering from the Contaminated Small Bowel syndrome. Antibiotics effective against anaerobes would be indicated in this condition along with appropriate antifungal medication.

MAINTAINING EUTHERMIA.

All known infective agents are temperature sensitive in terms of production of toxins and virulence factors.The clinical expression of many fungal diseases is dramatically affected by temperature. CANDIDA ALBICANS' favored ecological niche seems to be below 37°C. Host defences are temperature sensitive and temperature gradients can modulate the pathogenesis and clinical presentation of metabolic and autoimmune disease. The marked effect of relatively small temperature changes on enzyme kinetics may be a major explanation for these effects. Supporting this hypothesis is the observation by numerous environmentally ill atypical Candidiasis patients that on the rare occasions they experience a fever there is a striking, sometimes complete remission of their symptom complexes which lasts only for the duration of the fever. The physiologic processes responsible for temperature elevation may be more important than that of the temperature itself since passive elevation of temperature (e.g. sauna, hot tub) in these patients, while occasionally beneficial, is more frequently ennervating and does not produce the dramatic clear cut symptom relief found with temperature elevation of apparently central nervous system origin. Nevertheless, cool weather stress should be avoided in these patients. In experimental endotoxemia, maintainence of euthermia by ambient temperature modulation resulted in a protective effect equal to that of cortisone use. Raising or lowering the core temperature abolished the protective effect of cortisone. Cortisone has a recognized euthermic effect,raising hypothermic temperatures and exhibiting potent fever lowering capabilities. Cortisone, however, is a short term adaptogen with chronic disease consequences when elevated levels are prolonged, and its use is not recommended. Numerous pharmacological therapies exist which may effect euthermia and which deserve further study:e.g. thyroid supplementation (see below), Lithium (Lieb reported on rapid reversal of persistent hypothermia following electric shock by the use of a short course of lithium carbonate), phenytoin (Dilantin).

HYPERADRENERGIC OUTFLOW:

This model postulates chronic excess adrenergic CNS outflow to splanchnic circulation with an ineffective compensatory attempt by the parasympathetic system to counter-act. Phenytoin(Dilantin) has been shown by Karmazyn et al. to inhibit the pressor response to norepinephrine in isolated rat mesenteric vascular bed preparations as well as protect against the effects of reduced tissue oxygenation in vivo and in vitro. It is mentioned only as an example of a pharmaceutical capable of interrupting several vicious cycles posited by this hypothesis.

HYPOCAPNIA:

Increasing the metabolic rate and decreasing hyperventilation are the goals of therapy in this regard. Acute treatment would consist of oral carbonate and bicarbonate use (in between meals to avoid interfering with digestive acid and enzymes).Oxygen with carbon dioxide might also benefit. Various relaxation techniques (massage, biofeedback, guided imagery, etc;) might assist not only in decreasing the hyperadrenergic state but also compensate partially for the social and physical isolation that many atypical Candida patients experience.

THYROID SUPPLEMENTATION:

"Rational" (i.e. laboratory guided) thyroid therapy is difficult since many modifiers in the pathway from T4 to the inner cell are not commonly measured or measured at all. T3, free T3, free T4, reverse T3, anti T3, anti T4 antibodies and receptor density and affinity all affect the final metabolic expression.

T4 competitively inhibits T3 and in patients with difficulty converting T4 into the active form (T3) a T4 supplement can actually reduce brain metabolism. T3 (Cytomel) or a combination T4/T3 agent (Armour,Euthyroid) would seem preferable to T4 administration in certain cases. Abundant magnesium must be supplied since cellular uptake of this ion is enhanced by increased metabolic rate. Uncoupling of oxidative phosphorylation occurs when magnesium is insufficient to balance increased ATP production. Organic magnesium compounds such as orotates and aspartates are claimed to be more effectively absorbed. The risks of thyroid therapy may be minimized by starting with a low dose with a slow, gradual increase. Since the relaxation phase of muscle action is ATP dependend, one would expect to find increased relaxation times for the Achilles tendon reflex in hypometabolic patients. One would also expect prolonged systole and disturbed relaxation (delayed repolarization) as EKG findings in this state- a possible means of diagnosis and monitoring thyroid therapy. Magnesium and thyroid function as physiologic calcium channel blockers and may offer protection against the pathological calcium influx caused by endotoxin.

OPTIMIZING RETICULOENDOTHELIAL FUNCTION:

RES function requires abundant cellular energy production. Mitochondrial ATP generation is essential to the active macrophage. Substantial amounts of superoxides and peroxides are formed in the processing of antigens and if antigen load is increased antioxidant protection must be adequate to prevent free radical disruption of mitochondrial membranes. In an excellent review article McCarty outlines the RES stimulant and protective effects of Coenzyme Q(Ubiquinone), selenium, manganese and vitamin E on mitochondrial function. In normal conditions the level of peroxide oxidation of lipids and the ability to form hydroperoxides capable of destroying cell membranes are limited by the body's antioxidant system. In a stress state,following depletion of cellular energy (e.g. by decreased hepatic blood flow) peroxide oxidation of lipids increased with damage to lysosomal membranes. Abnormal lysosomal processing of antigens may occur. Antioxidant supplementation is a logical therapeutic adjunct. There is some controversy of the use of large doses of Vitamin C. Meerson demonstrated the use of iron and ascorbic acid as a non-enzymatic method of inducing lipid peroxidation, ascorbic acid being a potent free radical generator. This iv vivo "pro-oxidant" aspect of vitamin C has received little emphasis but certainly deserves more in view of widespread use of pharmacologic doses of ascorbic acid for both acute and chronic symptom relief in this illness.

DIET:

Elimination and rotation diets have been a mainstay treatment for the atypical Candidiasis patient. While these approaches may decrease symptoms, they are tiresome and socially difficult. They do not seem to substantially affect the underlying disorder and must be maintained with varying rigor. A novel approach to dietary cycling has been described by Erlander who claims that specific dietary cycling regimens based on generation times of supressor and helper cell induction can effectively break the vicious immune circuit of food, chemical and inhalent allergies. A safely testable hypothseis such as this should never be ignored.

SUMMARY:

Atypical Candidiasis is considered a variant of a chronic, low grade endotoxemic process, in which many pathologic effects are secondary to direct toxicity of and/or immunologic hypersensitivity to Candida albicans cell substances. It is hypothesized that a more primary pathological mechanism involves disturbed intestinal microflora with increased production of endotoxin and decreased ability of the body to safely process this bacterial lipopolysaccharide. Secondary effects of excess endotoxin on general metabolic processes and immune function disturb the normal commensal relationship between the host and Candida albicans. Therapy of such patients must extend beyond specific anti-Candida measures since an aberrant response to this organism is only one aspect of a more basic pathologic process.

Therapy of this illness is necessarily complex and must encompass biochemical, physiological and ecologic concepts. Biochemically, the stress related decline in cellular energy production with attendant lipid peroidation and calcium influx may be countered with natural and man made antioxidants and "anti-calcium" agents.

Physiologically, self-perpetuating vicious cycles such as CNS hyperadrenergic effects on splanchnic circulation and gut motility may be identified and interruped. "Retraining" programs for immune surveillance mechanisms should be explored. Ecologically, not only should external stressors be minimized, but the internal ecology of the intestine must favor the recolonization of indigenous flora. Diet selection, the use of saturated fatty acids, normalization of intestinal motility, specific and non-specific antibacterical and antifungal agents and direct introduction of desired flora are steps towards this goal.

****

Ch.3. Chronic Infection.

Further to the foregoing paper it should be pointed out that one of the other medical papers shows that some of the actinomycetales (like tuberculosis) can transform Candida albicans into about forty different strains, each strain distinctly different from the others, and therefore each strain would have its own list of toxins and metabolites to further complicate both symptoms and therapy.

The question follows then, that if actinomycetales transforms Candida albicans into different strains, does actinomycetales also transform Candida krusei, or Candida parapsilosis, or other Candida species into many different strains each with different toxins? If actinomycetales transforms Candida species into many different transformants, do other mycobacteria or other micro-organisms also transform Candida species into different strains? Quite obviously, when everything is considered, the total number of different toxins and other bits of biological material that may be produced by a mixed chronic infection is astronomical, and many weird and peculiar symptoms become a certainty.

Excellent as this paper is, we should also consider that the paper concentrates on atypical Candidiasis of the G.I.tract, while atypical Candida infection usually encompasses all of the sexual tissues, specifically ears, sinuses, hands, feet, nails, mouth, G.I.tract, anus, genitals and gonads. With each local infection contributing to further infection the total infection weakens the immune system, and other body systems,sometimes to the point of death, yet the death of course will result from pneumonia or other condition that has advanced while the body defences were impaired.

Now from all of the foregoing medical papers every health practitioner and every victim of ill health must surely realize that in every case of ill health the possibility that Candida infection is a contributing or causitive factor should always be considered, and the Candida status should therefore be determined with the ketoconazole challange test. After all, good health cannot return if Candida infection is part of the problem, and if the Candida remains unrecognized.

At this point we now have a special request. We would like to urge all doctors and other health professionals to make copies of the foregoing and foist them upon your unbelieving colleagues, and we would like to urge all Candida victims, and particularly "yeast people"(whom Candida has handicapped since birth), to make copies of the foregoing and force them upon your doctor, so that your doctor will fully understand your plight, and so that your doctor will fully understand what you need and expect from him.

Ch.3. Chronic Infection.

Although the foregoing paper on atypical Candida infection shows the complexity of mixed infections, the paper still deals with only part of the whole problem where atypical infection is present along with typical infection, and where many years of chronic infection and ill health have chronically altered the size, shape, and function of the many glands and organs, the endocrine system, the vascular and lymphatic systems, the immune system, the hands, feet, limbs, and sometimes the entire body. Undoubtedly you will read about this or that quick "cure" for Candida infection, but if the so-called cure fails to adequately cover all of the many factors outlined in the foregoing paper,- along with much, much more,-then the "cure" must be invalid and misleading because even when everything possible is done it still takes a long time to kill out yeast, fungus, and other infectives when they are mixed and mingled with live body cells in living body tissues; it takes a long time to re-build damaged and altered glands and organs;it takes a long time to restore altered nerve, adrenal, endocrine, and hormone function; it takes a long time to restore vascular and lymphatic flow and to raise immune function; it takes a long time to reduce the inevitable calcinosis and to rebuild atrophied tissues;- and it takes a much longer time when all of the foregoing are interdependent and each improvement can go forward only after other systems have improved. We would suggest that the following paper should be reread and referred to as the various topics,-and more,are covered in the following pages.

CLINICAL INDICATIONS of YEAST INFECTION.

Among the medical paper-titles, there were a number of papers on the identification of specific fungal infectives, but few papers were devoted to clinical indicators that could assist in diagnosis.

Broadly, as may be seen from the medical papers, that if there is a serious health problem, there is always a yeast component, or the problem will be based directly in yeast infection. A simple test would be the judicious use of Ketoconazole, starting with 1/8 tablet per day, with morning meal, and increasing by 1/8 tablet per day until toxic symptoms (like the flu) or other indicators appear. Most "apparently healthy" people (like all of the "apparently healthy" people so frequently used as a scientific standard in medical research) will usually show signs of toxicity with only 1 or $1\frac{1}{4}$ tablets. The toxic symptoms do not come from the Ketoconazole, which only affects plants, the symptoms come from the dead bodies of the killed infectives,(the Herxheimers reaction).Thus the relative amount of active infection can be judged by the amount of Ketoconazole required to show toxic symptoms.

Unfortunately, in Canada the "authorities" who regulate food and drugs seem to be functionally impaired, and are unable to distinguish between foods, drugs, and anti-infectives. They are so intent upon "protecting" the public from everything except caffiene, alcohol, and aspirin, that until January, 1985 they were denying Canadians the benefits of Ketoconazole. Ketoconazole is now available on prescription at a cost of about $1.50 per tablet.

MINERAL TESTS:

Mineral tests (by hair analysis) may also indicate possible yeast infection, because the yeast will use up and metabolically tie up iron, zinc, manganese, chromium, and selenium.

The following form -form A, has been used by the Healthology Association. When mineral tests showed four of these five minerals were deficient, the member was alerted to the possibility of serious yeast infection. The indication was always later confirmed; with a rapid decline in all health problems as the infection was reduced.

This form does not mention lead and cadmium, but yeast infected tissue shows abnormally high levels of lead and cadmium, which may indicate that the yeast induces the body to accept and store these toxic metals.

Note that in the usual use of mineral tests the test is used to show abnormal minerals, and these levels are then reduced or supplemented without seeking the cause of the abnormal levels. If yeast infection is present and is using up the minerals normally supplied by the diet, increasing the minerals will certainly help the body and will improve the health, but if the yeast is not reduced the improved nutrition will also feed the yeast, and with time the increased infection will again overtake the host.

Mercury retention may also result from yeast infection but the possible pathway is not clear. High toxic levels of copper may also be linked to yeast infection through the effects of the yeast on sex hormones. Iron siderosis (toxic iron) may also be entwined with yeast infection, as high yeast levels are frequently found in these cases.

Toxic levels of lead, cadmium, mercury, copper, or iron, affect the mind, and may induce violence, psychosis, or other mental problems. Conversely then psychosis and mental problems may indicate yeast infection.

In reviewing about 250 mineral tests, lithium was always approximately the same. It was always low, or just above low. This suggests that the tests are not sensitive enough, and the standards may be incorrect. However, in all known cases of

The HEALTHOLOGY Assn.
195 Peveril Ave.
Vancouver   V5Y 2L5

Re. Mineral Test with Nutritional Evaluation.

        In addition to the enclosed computer Printout you may wish to consider
the following;
        Where toxic minerals are high, other mineral levels will be affected
and ill health will remain until the toxic minerals are reduced. The most
effective method is with chelation therapy. Details are available to
Healthology members.
        High nutritional mineral levels may indicate that the minerals are
being sequestered in the tissues, and blood levels may be very low. Blood
levels should be checked. High tissue levels of minerals may be associated
with chronic infection.
        If mineral levels are low, the general health will improve with
supplements, and this will mask the true cause of the health problems. The
true cause of the low minerals must therefore be sought. Where nutrition
is adequate the true cause must be;
1. . Poor digestion.
2.   Poor assimilation.
3. Chronic infection, which can produce poor digestion and poor assimilation.
Chronic infection can assimilate the minerals and thus deprive the host. The
most common such infective is Candida Yeast, which can also impair the B and
T lymphocytes in the immune system, with lowered resistance to the Candida
and increased risk of other diseases.
        Other indications of Candida Yeast infection are: (Check them), Callouses ___
canker sores ___, indigestion ___, gas and flatulence ___, acid colon ___,
constipation ___, hiatus hernia ___, sinus infection ___, allergies ___,
arthritis ___, vaginitis ___, balanitis (irritation of the tip of the penis) ___,
impotence ___, sexual failure ___, fridgidity ___, adrenal exhaustion ___.
        High or low sodium and/or potassium may be indicative of adrenal
exhaustion. Low iron may be linked to loss of intrinsic factor and a
requiremnet for B$_{12}$ by injection only.
        For purposes of determining low minerals indicative of Candida Yeast
infection , mineral supplements must be deducted from the levels shown for
the significant minerals. On this basis your low mineral levels would be:-
Iron ___ , Manganese ___ , Zinc ___ , Chromium ___ , Selenium ___ .
        We would therefore suggest that you consider the possibility that you
have Candida Yeast infection. Your doctor can help you with Nystatin, Resteclin,
Miconazole and Ketoconazole. Further information and suggestions are available
to Healthology Members.

Comments ___

Form A.- - Used by the Healthology Assn. to alert members
to possible Candida infection. Where four out of the five minerals
were low, along with altered levels of sodium or potassium,
high Candida infection was invariably found. Candida may also
use up germanium, which now appears to be essential for full
metabolic function.

of Candida infection, and in all indicated cases of Candida infection, lithium was low. Lithium is absolutely essential for thyroid function, and it is absolutely essential for the function of the immune system. Perhaps Candida directly impairs the body by depleting the lithium. We do not know, but lithium supplements can sometimes bring a rapid improvement in health, and are sometimes necessary before thyroid supplements become effective.

Mineral tests are made by atomic absorption spectroscopy on any substance from moon rocks to biological materials. Hair is readily available biological material, and head hair is therefore usually used. Body hair, nails, and tissue samples can also be used.

A good mineral test will be by computer printout. Mineral tests are commonly supplied with a nutritional evaluation. There are now quite a large number of labs. supplying mineral tests. Your doctor can get mineral tests from:

Anamol Laboratories Ltd. 105 Scarsdale rd. Don Mills, Ontario M3B 2R5 (416) 449-8988.

Quanta trace laboratories inc. 401-3700 Gilmore Way Burnaby, B.C. Canada. V5G 4M1 (604)438-5226.

Doctor's Data, P.O.box 111, 30-W-101 Roosevelt Road. West Chicago, Illinois. U.S.A. 60185.

LAB. TESTS:

In all of the foregoing the suspicion of Candida can be confirmed by sending fresh scrapings to the lab. Candida yeast is very translucent and is difficult to see under the microscope, unless treated with DMSO to darken the keratin. Most lab. tests are therefore "live" tests, made by growing the yeast on a suitable material, usually Nickersons medium. NIckersons medium is available from the Drug store, with instructions, if anyone wishes to make their own tests. Maintaining the proper temperature during growth is highly important.

With the lab. tests dependent upon both maintaining the exact temperature and the sample being "alive", and with the yeast so difficult to see under the microscope, positive tests should be considered as proof of Candida infection, but if Candida is suspected tests that fail to show Candida should not be construed as proof that Candida is absent. This is particularly to be considered in testicular infection, and in the testing of ejaculate, because prostatic fluids have the ability to kill Candida, which makes infected fluids appear to be free from infection.

ANTIGEN SKIN TESTS:

Skin scratch tests show the amount of yeast infection through the immune system. The tests are always positive, showing that Candida infection is universally present in all humans. The antigen skin test is basically an allergy test, where a small amount of dead Candida is introduced under the skin. The usual test is for four different varieties of Candida yeast. The extent of yeast infection is judged by the color and diameter of the weal (bump) that has developed 10 minutes after the injection.If active yeast infection is indicated the Candida program should be initiated and diligently persued.

It should be emphasized that the antigen skin tests are frequently confusing because they depend upon the reaction of the immune system, while the immune system may of itself be impaired by the infective. Therefore an active positive test is certainly indicative of infection, but a test that shows very little infection may actually be showing a high infection with a non-reactive, badly impaired, immune system.

Antigen skin tests for yeast infection are highly technical and must be properly administered as there is a possibility of irreversible damage in some cases. Doctors should attend a three day course from:
Dr.L.D.Dickey, Director of Continuing Education. 109 West Olive, Fort Collins, Colorado, U.S.A. 80524.
This course includes a manual outlining the test procedures.

CANDIDAL CAPACITY TEST. (Candicidal Capacity Test).

The Candidal Capacity Test is a highly complex medical test that determines the total capability of the body to deal with Candida infection. Although this test seems to be very enlightening, it may be of very little practical value because illness, of any kind, is invariably accompanied by an increase in total chronic infectives, many of which are Candida related.Since they are not Candida, they would not show up on the Candicidal test. The Ketoconazole challange test seems to be an easier and better test of the total ability of the body to deal with the total infection that is present.

BLOOD TESTS.

Blood tests for white cell count and immune globulins may show impaired immune systen function, indicative of possible yeast infection.

FINGERNAILS.

Candida yeast and other fungii show up as white encrustations on the cuticle, and on or under the nails. Thumbs and little fingers may show more than others. Yeast also shows as crosswise bumps or hollows, sometimes with the ends of the nails turned upward, and sometimes with the last joint or whole finger turned upward, caused by the high lactic acid from the infective creating muscle spasm in the muscles and tendons that run down to the finger tips. Nails may also have many longitudinal ridges, sometimes like very fine lines, caused by yeast infection at the base of the nail, under the nailbed. Larger infections make larger ridges, sometimes making a long bend in the nail that can result in ingrown nails.

TOENAILS:

The indications of Candida infection of the toenails are similar to the fingernails. Ingrown nails are much more common and severe. Badly infected large toenails may affect the nervous system, and like Black Toe in runners,(which may also result from Candida infection), there may be consequent frigidity, impotence, sexual failure, or other sexual problems. The stomach and digestive system, and the rectal sphincter may also be affected. The small toenail is very frequently infected, and may be very small, little larger than a matchhead, perhaps embedded in the callus material, or perhaps loose and flaky, with turned up edges. Any abnormal condition is suspect because some doctors think that, due to the position of the toes at birth, the small toenail is the body part that is always infected at birth.

CALLUSES:

Calluses on the feet are caused by many infections. Frequently the infective is trichophyton (ringworm) which will respond to povidone iodine (vaginal douche). Long term calluses usually have a high Candida component. Several varieties may be involved. Candida albicans shows as a fluorescent rosy pink, that is very noticeable under infra-red light, or under the electric light bulb, when compared to fluorescent lighting. Other varieties of Candida may show as smooth areas of very yellowish thickened skin, or even shades of brown. Candida may also show as the fluorescent rosy pink even without calluses, and sometimes with very few other signs of Candida infection.

"BURNING FEET".

"Burning feet", when tired or after a long walk, or after working on a hard floor all day, are an almost certain sign of Candida infection, with the "burning" resulting from the invading Candida attacking each of the nerve endings. "Burning" may also be present in infected heels, and in the area above the heel. The "burning" also may start or increase with even mild sexual arousal. Sexual arousal increases blood sugar levels, which feeds the yeast. Sugar, white flour, caffeine, and niacin also raise blood sugar levels and increase the "burning".

EARS:
Candida infection appears as white scaly encrustations. If there is any response to miconazole lotion,(Micatin) applied daily, fungal infection is certain.

NOSE and SINUSES:
Continuing scaly or scaby material, of any color, in the nose, may have a fungal component. Response to miconazole lotion or to liquid nystatin (mycostatin) is a clear indication of fungus, usually Candida yeast. If miconazole lotion or liquid nystatin alter sinusitis, fungal infection is certain.

MOUTH and CANKER SORES:
Candida infection in the mouth may show as small bits of white stuff particularly at the gum line, or as white canker sores. It is thought that the canker sores are a composite infection because they seem to respond best to iodine. Most dentists are well aquainted with Candida yeast and they use special anti-fungals to deal with the Candida infection. The opinion of your dentist is of value.

ESOPHAGUS and HIATUS HERNIA.
Many cases of Hiatus Hernia are mis-diagonsed and are actually a Candida yeast infection. If the hiatus hernia or other esophagus problems respond to nystatin (chewed tablets or liquid) Candida infection is certain because nystatin is specific against Candida.

DIGESTIVE:
Chronic indigestion is a common indicator of chronic yeast infection of the digestive tract. Honey, sugar, white flour and other highly refined carbohydrates will feed the yeast, producing gas and flatulence in about twenty minutes. Bananas, white rice, potatoes, grapes, peaches, peach and pear juice, and dried fruits may also produce gas. Yeasts grow best in a 2% solution of glucose. Gas from yeast infection is rapidly produced about 20 minutes after intake of refined nutrients, after which the increasing density of the solution inhibits rapid yeast growth, but when the density of the solution falls naturally about two or three hours after the meal, gas and indigestion may re-appear. Gas and indigestion may also follow about 10 minutes after taking a drink of water, which reduces the density of the digestive solution to levels conducive to rapid yeast growth. If nystatin tablets alter the digestive problems in any way, intestinal yeast infection is certain.

COLON and ANUS.

Hemorrhoids (piles) are frequently Candida yeast calluses, with other infectives, but this may be difficult to prove unless they respond to miconazole lotion and Vit.E oil. A "tightened" rectal sphincter, that impedes normal bowel function, may also be caused by Candida infection, but again this may be difficult to prove. "Leaky bowel" and other colon problems are also frequently caused by Candida yeast. The stool can be checked at the lab for dead yeast forms. Yeast infection increases acidity and a stool pH below 8 may indicate yeast infection. Enemas and colonics reduce the protection of the bowel mucosa, and increase invasion and colonization by Candida yeast. Colon problems may result in psychosis and mental problems.

SEXUAL.

Candida yeast infection is certainly known to almost every female. Recurring vaginitis, particularly after intercourse, usually results from stirring up a resident chronic infection. Infection of the cervix may be painless and almost undetectable, and is a frequent source of recurring vaginitis. All vaginal infections are increased with intercourse through the physical abrasive sexual activity, and because the seminal plasma feeds the invasive mycelial phase of the yeast.

Candida yeast infection in the male all too frequently goes unnoticed. Infection of the vessels in the penis results in a "burning" sensation (balanitis) that may last for only a few minutes. Soft calluses in the urethra may cause urine "spray or difficult ejaculation. The tip of the penis may become less sensitive, and may become covered with a softy whitish callus with a rough leathery appearance, very difficult to detect because the changes are so slow. The whitish appearance, instead of flesh pink, is a distinguishing feature. Curdled ejaculate, tender testicles, spermatocelles, hydroceles, and enlarged prostate may indicate Candida infection in the male. Yeast infection is certainly transferred between sexual partners, but sexual fluids are usually free from live yeast due to the inhibiting action of prostatic fluids.

With Candida infection both male and female may experience reduced sexual desire and reduced sexual capabilities. Hormone levels are linked to sexual levels, which are linked to histamine levels, which are linked to basophil cell count. Basophil cell count should be about .6% to.8%. If basophil cell count is below .2% hormone levels will be low, health will be low, and Candida infection may be indicated.

In the male, soft Candida calluses may form in the spermatic ducts, and this, together with thick curdled ejaculate, may make ejaculation extremely difficult or impossible. Difficult or impossible orgasm in the female is thought to have a similar cause but due to anatomy this is very difficult to establish and it can only be assumed. Nonetheless, difficult or impossible orgasm in the female may indicate serious Candida yeast infection. Orgasmic failure, in both the male and the female results in resorption of hormones and other sexual fluids, which usually produces extreme depression, fault finding, and other mental problems. The severity and type of mental problem may increase with the effects from spores, filaments, hyphae, and other toxins from the disturbed yeast infection. Extreme sexual and mental difficulties of this type, together with severe loss of libido, may lead either partner in a marriage to sexual abstinence, or to sexual hate, that grows to personal hate, frequently ending in seperation or divorce. Dr. Orion Truss points out that antibiotics increase Candida infection through the yeast moving into the injured tissues, and that the sharp rise in social problems and in drug and alcohol abuse coincides with the introduction of antibiotics. The "pill" reduces estrogen levels and thus promotes Candida overgrowth. The sharp rise in seperation and divorce also coincides with the introduction of antibiotics and the "pill", with the increased incidence and severity of Candida infection perhaps being the real cause.

BLUE and RED SPOTS and COLD AREAS.

Inexplicable blue to deep purple irregular spots, bright red irregular spots, or mysterious "cold" areas may also indicate Candida infection. The possible etiology of these areas is not known, but there are a number of reports that they reduce or disappear when Candida infection is reduced elsewhere.

ENDOTHALMITIS and DISSEMINATED CANDIDA INFECTION.

Candida yeast, entering the bloodstream through injury, ulcers, surgery, intravenous feedings, drug abuse, or any other source can produce Candida infection in any part of the body, with the infection then perhaps continually seeding the bloodstream, resulting in disseminated Candida infection. Prime targets for infection are heart valves, the meninges in the mind, and the eyes. The liver may become infected and become the principal source of seeding. Scientific American Medical Library explains: "Repeated examination of the fundi is mandatory in any patient with suspected disseminated candidiasis or in any patient on hyperalimentation (intravenous feeding). The lesion consists of white, cotton-ball like areas of chorio-retinitis(the retina of the eye) extending out into the vitreous (of the eye). Other sites of metastatic (disseminated) infection that have been emphasized include the meninges (of the mind), bones and joints, and myocardium (heart). Present in some patients (but not in all) with disseminated infection is a skin condition that is of particular diagnostic help. It is the development, due to metastatic candidal infection, of macronodular (small nodules) erythmatous,(red), occasionally hemorrhagic (bleeding) skin lesions that are 0.5 to 1 cm. in size. Such lesions should be quickly biopsied for early diagnosis soon after they appear."Red bumps about $\frac{1}{4}$ inch in diameter! Check them immediately if they appear. Disseminated candida infection can be rapidly fatal if the immune function is impaired. Health professionals and health "addicts" should read all of the material in Scientific American Medical library on Candida yeast and other mycotic infections. It is very enlightening after you learn to somewhat decode all of the obscure medical jargon.

URINARY:
Blocked urinary passages may indicate Candida infection, and the passage of "cotton balls" makes this certain. The yeast does not invade and colonize the urinary tract, but it does float around in the fluid.

LUNGS and AIR TRACT:
Candida infection of the lungs is said to be very rare, probably because the high amounts of oxygen do not favor growth but the large number of medical papers indicates lung infections may be very common. Air infection will show up in the sputum. Sputum must be lab.-tested, or tested with Nickersons medium. Infection in sputum can come from the nasal area, esophagus, or air tract.

PROBABILITY FACTORS:
The following conditions increase the probability of Candida infections:

Diabetes.	Hyperglycemia.	Cysts.
Arthritis.	Sinusitis.	Ulcers.
Allergies.	Colitis.	Indigestion.
Adrenal Depletion.	Constipation.	Promiscuity.
Pancreatic Failure.	Cortisone.	Vaccinations.
Genital Herpes.	Antibiotics.	Contraceptives.
Intravenous feedings.	Catheters.	Surgery.
Tampons.	Homosexuality.	Aspirin.
Injected Drugs.	Alcohol	Caffeine
Rubber Soles.	Plastic Shoes	Chillblains.

PROBABILITY FACTORS.(Cont.):

Bacterial Infections.	Viral infections.
High carbohydrate diet.	Drugs.
Refined carbohydrate diet.	Tobacco.
Adrenal depletion in mother.	Frozen feet.
Diabetes in mother.	Injured feet.
Difficult delivery.	High shoes.
Injury during delivery.	

Opiates, paralyze the digestive process, and set the stage for infection of all kinds.

The greatest "probability factor" is the finding of serious Candida infection in any area. If there is a large focal infection anywhere, the probability is very high that infection will be almost everywhere, because the focal infection will impair the immune system, and unknowing hands will spread the yeast. Candida infection is a family affair. If one member has a high infection, all other members will be infected to some degree.

ASSESSING CANDIDA YEAST INFECTION.

From the foregoing tests and information some general assessment of total Candida infection in any particular person can be judged. Hidden infections are the rule and are not the exception. The most important and the most practical test is the Ketoconazole challange test, because it reveals the challange to the body, in terms of the total infection available to the bloodstream, and the body's total capability to detoxify and eliminate the dead bodies of the infective. It therefore reveals the total infective situation "as the body sees it". Tests for liver and urinary function will assist in the total evaluation. Size, and total area, of visible Candida calluses will assist in assessing the time that might be required to eliminate most of the infection and return the body to normal. The extent of arthritis and arthritic deposits should also be considered. It should be remembered that new healthy tissue must be built to replace the damaged tissues while the infection is being reduced. Extensive serious infection, with large callused areas and impaired immune function may require three or four years to resolve, but the increasing good health makes the effort constantly rewarding.

THE INFECTIVE CALLUS MATRIX.

Candida yeast has two particular characteristics that combine to make it the most insidious of the chronic infectives. These two characteristics are the ability of the yeast to impair the B, and T lymphocytes, and thus cripple the ability of the body to cope with the infective; together with the peculiar way the yeast colony forms a protective "skin" of its own. The forming of the protective "skin", is described in the medical paper "Magnesium Stimulated Resynthesis of Osmoresistant Layer by Candida Albicans Spheroblasts", and it is the formation of this protective layer that makes the yeast so pernicious and difficult to eliminate.

The actual formation of a typical callus matrix is best seen in the calluses on the feet. Here, usually, tight or ill fitting shoes will wear a blister on the feet. The raw exposed flesh is then colonized by Candida yeast, which is frequently present on the skin of the feet. The yeast infection is then joined by other infectives, to form an infective matrix. As the infection progresses the yeast breaks down body materials and re-forms them into the protective Osmoresistant layer on the outside of the callus, a layer that is highly resistant to penetration by anti-fungals and other agents. The yeast, and associated infectives, continue to invade the tissues, with the infectives becoming intermixed with living and dying cells. Blood and lymph still flow to the area, but in reduced amounts. The infectives induce inflammation, but lymph flow is slow, so the inflammation is followed by calcinosis.

The callus matrix now consists of the many infectives intermixed with many dead and dying cells, calcium and other minerals, reduced lymph, blood, and nerve function, and the entire callused area protected by the Osmoresistant layer. The yeasts and associated infectives are therefore effectively protected against typical anti-infectives by the Osmoresistant layer, while the calcinosis and reduced blood and lymph flow, together with the ability of the yeast to impair the immune system, protects the infectives in the callus matrix from the body's defence mechanism. Thus the callus colony matrix will continue to grow, despite all efforts of the body to reduce it, and as it grows the active tissue will slowly be reduced, to the point that the callus matrix may be only 10% or less normal cells. The amount of calcinosis in the mix appears to determine the hardness of the callus, with soft calluses having less calcinosis. A typical callus is shown in Fig.2.

In looking at Fig.2. it can be seen that although the infectives within the matrix are protected from the immune system, the inner part of the matrix is embedded in live tissue, and it is across the full inner surface of the callus that the battle between the infectives and the host constantly rages. If blood sugar levels are high, the body is well fed, but the yeast is even better fed than the body, so the infectives will advance, and it is their attack on the nerve endings that produces the "burning" feeling

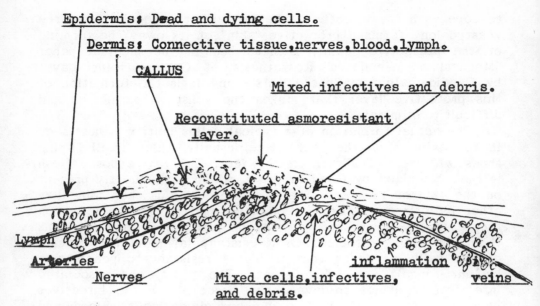

Epidermis: Dead and dying cells.

Dermis: Connective tissue,nerves,blood,lymph.

CALLUS

Mixed infectives and debris.

Reconstituted asmoresistant layer.

Lymph

Arteries

Nerves

Mixed cells,infectives, and debris.

inflammation

veins

Fig. 2. The Candida Callus Matrix.

The reconstituted asmoresistant layer protects the infectives from topical anti-fungals, and it is difficult for the immune system to reach the infectives that are locked into the half dead callus structure. The infectives then live on body nutrients and attack and destroy body cells, while the body is forced to take away the toxins and metabolites made by the infectives. The callus structure, thin or thick and hard or soft, is always present at the site of Candida infection.

* * * * * * * * *

in the feet. This is the reason that diabetics are almost certain to have yeast infection. Near-diabetic hyperglycemics have a similar problem. High carbohydrate diets, and diets high in refined carbohydrate and caffiene also raise the blood sugar levels, promoting growth of the infective yeasts. Similarly stress, lack of sleep, lack of nutrients, or colds or other infections, reduce the defences of the body and again the infective yeasts will advance across the entire inner surface of the callus matrix. The total area of all of the yeast calluses therefore can determine the state of health. Quite obviously, it is across this infective boundary that the infectives dispose of their wastes and toxins and metabolites into the bloodstream and into the lymphatic system of the host. Quite obviously also the greater the total infected area, the greater the amounts of toxins. Further, the greater the area and the larger the amount of toxins, the greater will be the impairment of the immune system. This, at the very time that the immune function is needed most!

68.

Although this is the typical form of the infective callus matrix where the infective has invaded through abrasion to the skin, the actual appearance of infected areas may differ greatly, but the mixed nature of the matrix is a constant feature. Changes in appearance come from:

1. The mixture of infectives. The color is frequently determined by the predominant infective. The infected area may be whitish, pinkish, fluorescent pink, red, brownish, or a sallow yellow. The re-synthesized skin may be rough, pocked, pimpled (sometimes very small) or smooth.

2. Depth of infection. The infective matrix may be very thin if only the first layer of skin has been penetrated, or the callus may be as thick as 3/8 inch, where the infectives have penetrated through all three layers of skin.

3. Injury. Deep thick calluses may follow frostbite or mechanical injury.

4. Blood supply. Where the blood flow has been reduced within the callus matrix the area may be very white.

5. Calcinosis. The amount of calcinosis determines the hardness of the callus, and increases the white appearance.

The infective matrix can therefore be very thin and soft, or it may be thick, with any degree of hardness. If the callus matrix is inside one of the "tubes" of the body, as in the vagina or in the tip of the penis, the callus will usually be very thin and soft, whereas callus forms below the skin are usually attached to bone or cartilage structures, and appear as arthritic bumps. Many such arthritic growths do not appear to be yeast related, yet they frequently disappear when Candida infection is reduced.

The fluorescent pink associated with Candida infections may not appear in the callus matrix if the blood flow is restricted, but it usually shows as a line around the infected area. The line may be very narrow, or it may be quite wide, depending upon the amount of penetration of infectives and toxins into the surrounding flesh. Occasionally, particularly on the feet or hands, serious fluorescent pink infection may develop, together with swelling,but with only one or two small calluses showing. The fluorescent pink shows up under infra-red light, or the light bulb, when compared with fluorescent lighting.

When one considers the formation and makeup of the infective matrix, the true insidious nature of Candida infection is revealed. Any trauma to the body anywhere, by any infection, by any injury, or by any weakness, or by prolonged contact with Candida, at any time at or after birth, can give the waiting Candida yeast an opportunity to invade. Because the Candida yeast is able to sequester itself (along with its associated infectives), it is therefore always present and growing and spreading and, due to the nature of the callus matrix, the body cannot eradicate it. As it grows and spreads, it slowly impairs the immune system, and constantly year after year, it slowly and relentlessly overloads the body's adrenals and detoxification system, while at the same time it keeps pouring in ever more toxins and metabolites that slowly alter the function of all of the organs, glands, and body systems. The total effects depend upon the mixture of the infectives, the total area of the interface between the infective matrix and the living flesh, and the diet and the ability of the body to feed both the infectives and the body itself.

As the total infection increases, you grow old, and it is little wonder that you grow old. If infection starts early, and progresses rapidly, you grow old before your time. That is the fact of life,- and death. Our life-span then is largely happenstance. If we happen to inherit a good immune system, and if we happen to avoid contagious diseases and chronic infectives, degenerative disease and old age will come late. But, if we happen to inherit a poorly functioning immune system, and if we happen to acquire a large amount of chronic infectives, then degenerative disease and old age will come early. Oh Yes!, diet, exercise, drugs, caffiene, and alcohol will play their part, but happenstance will be the major factor. Happenstance, yes, yet the effects of happenstance can be altered.

Fortunately, we do have technology that can reduce the basic chronic infective matrix. Because of the infective mix and the nature of the matrix it is immediately obvious that many different anti-fungal agents will have to be used along with diverse antibiotics, and wherever possible, the anti-infectives will have to be used on both sides of the infective matrix,- on the skin side (topical) and on the blood side (systemic), and even at best the reduction of the infection will be a long and difficult job, because with the reduction of the infectives, the body must not only clear out the dead bodies of the infectives together with their toxins, but the body must also clear out the dead and dying body tissues, and then rebuild everything with healthy tissue. The entire rebuilding is even more difficult because blood and lymph flow are poor, nerves are damaged, calcium deposits must be broken down and eliminated, the immune system is impaired, and usually digestion and assimilation are faulty and the adrenals are depleted. A long difficult job, yes, but very, very rewarding, particularily when the toxins are reduced and body functions start to return to normal. We should therefore understand toxins, and to understand toxins and metabolites we must first understand metabolic processes.

70

TOXINS and THEIR ROLE in METABOLIC PROCESSES.

METABOLIC PROCESSES.
There are many, many, ill people in this world. All are seeking help, all are begging for help, yet help is usually slow and fleeting. Most of these people say that they seek help, but help must be simple and easy, or they do not have the time. Any who do not have the time, or the interest, should put away this book now, and go back to the "boob-tube", because life is not a simple matter; death is not a simple matter; and the living death of severe ill health is never a simple matter. All living processes are extremely complex, more complex by far than all of man's technology combined, so life and health cannot be simple, and therefore there are not, and there cannot be, any simple instant cures. Renewing health is very complex, it is not as simple as drinking tahebo tea, or eating grapefruit, or inserting a few needles, or pushing on a vertebra, or rubbing the feet or hands. There never are, and there cannot be, simple instant repairs for complex machinery, and there never are, and there cannot be, simple instant cures for malfunction of the myriad of even more complex metabolic processes that finally determine the state of Health. We can try to make health technology logical and lucid, but complex technology can never be simple.

Broadly stated, metabolic processes are the complex electro-chemical interactions that occur in the body that finally change food, water and oxygen to (a) energy for movement and thought, and to (b) muscle, skin, cartilage, bone, and other structures of which the body is composed. We are, in fact, a walking, talking heat machine, and metabolic processes keep the machine operating and they also make all of the repairs.

All metabolic processes in the body are discreet complex chemical reactions between various nutrients, but they all occur by happenstance,- they occur because the proper chemicals happen to be at the right place at the right moment in time, and the metabolic reactions cannot take place unless all necessary chemicals are present in the right form. The only control that the body has over the immensely large number of different chemical processes so necessary for full body function is that many of the metabolic processes are dependent upon enzymes or hormones, or other chemical elements produced by the body. Nonetheless, all such enzymes, hormones, etc; are themselves produced by happenstance;- by the reaction of chemical nutrients that happen to be at the right place at the right moment under the right conditions. Thus normal good health, good function, and good thinking, is really a matter of happenstance.

Ch.3. Chronic Infection.

We happened to eat the right things, that happened to provide the right nutrients necessary for good digestion, for good assimilation, and for good delivery of the right chemical nutrients to all of the right places at the right time. All of the right chemical reactions then happened,- all by happenstance.

Although all metabolic processes in the body are by happenstance, they are still always discreet complex electro-chemical reactions between various nutrients. If all nutrients are in place the metabolic process takes place. If the nutrients are not in place, the metabolic process cannot proceed and must await the arrival of suitable nutrients. Such metabolic processes may have more than one healthy route, for instance, in sugar metabolism (which supplies our heat and energy) there are five different paths that the metabolic process can take, with each path dependent upon the chemical nutrients present, and dependent upon body demands. Obviously if metabolic nutrients are not available, or if abnormal metabolic substances are present that happen to work into the electro-chemical reaction, the required body process will be diverted to a different metabolic process, sometimes with less than desirable results. The presence of stray bits of biological material from other organisms can therefore pose a hazard. If the stray waste products from other organisms happen to be useful to the body, as with acidophilus, we call the organism benign flora. If the stray waste products have no effects, we ignore the organism. But if the stray waste products happen to be so similar to normal body nutrients, hormones, or enzymes, that they enter into metabolic processes and produce major alterations and disasterous results, we call the organism an infective, and we call the offending metabolic waste products toxins. Toxins then can affect any body part or metabolic process anywhere in the body, at sites completely remote from the site of the chronic infection.

The total number of fungii, bacteria, viruses and other micro-organisms living on planet earth is astronomical. The number of different bacteria alone number into the millions, while sub-species of each bacteria may be over one thousand. Each living organism, large or small, consumes bilogical food, and each excretes biological material as wastes. The waste of one, becomes food for another. Man too consumes bacterial and fungal wastes as sauerkraut, cheese, yogurt, alcohol, etc. A short list of some of these "foods" is shown in Fig.3. From Fig.3. it should be noted that many micro-organisms used by man for food production are different sub-species (i.e. first cousins) of organisms that infect man, notably Candida yeast, aspergillus, torula, actinomycetales, trichoma, etc. Where an infective matrix already contains infective organisms, others of the same specie that normally do not infect man, may join into the infective colony. This is substantiated by the frequent reports of alcoholics with resident infections that continuously produce alcohol in the intestinal tract.

Further insight into the role of toxins is produced by the following brief article from Healthology member magazine:-

TOXINS:

Almost every book or pamphlet on health talks about "Toxins" and "Cleansing", yet always fails to tell exactly what "toxins" are or just what items are being removed, or are trying to be removed, by the "cleansing".

Adelle Davis is probably the only "popular writer" that has written about "toxins" from "putrefactive bacteria", so the "cleansing" must be intended to remove colonies of infection. The other "health" writers seem to ignore infection, as if it was not present, and as if it did not exist.

Man may think that he is the center of the world, but he is never alone. Biology is an endless scene of eating and being eaten. Just as there are millions of different organisms eating at the fish in the oceans, the trees in the forests and the vegetables in the garden, there are also millions of organisms living with and eating at man. Some organisms (like acidophilus) are beneficial, some are innocuous, and some (like Candida yeast) are deadly. Their effects on man depend solely upon the nature of their waste by-products, the location of the infection, and the nutrients used. Acidophilus happens to make B vitamins so an acidophilus "infection" is encouraged, while the waste products from Candida happen to be biological bits that slowly impair the immune system and allow the yeast to slowly overgrow everything and impair so many processes that death finally results. There are a great many "biological bits" in the waste by-products of the many different organisms. If the "bits" are beneficial and are used by the body, they are "food" (Fig.3.) but if the "bits" have an adverse effect on the body we call them TOXINS.

All biological processes are electro-chemical, and therefore they are mathematical and predictable. Thus, this molecule, with that molecule, produces a specfic effect. Most of the interactions of these complex molecules are by way of electro-chemical "bonds"(shared electrons). Thus hormones bond to appropriate "receptors" at various "bonding sites" on the cell. Other biological processes involve enzymes, with strong "bonding sites", that may pick a specific atom out of a molecule, or a chain of molecules, and thus cleave the chain into shorter chains.

ORGANISM	TYPE	PRODUCT
FOODS AND BEVERAGES		
Saccharomyces cerevisiae	YEAST	BAKER'S YEAST, WINE, ALE, SAKE
Saccharomyces carlsbergensis	YEAST	LAGER BEER
Saccharomyces rouxii	YEAST	SOY SAUCE
Candida milleri	YEAST	SOUR FRENCH BREAD
Lactobacillus sanfrancisco	BACTERIUM	SOUR FRENCH BREAD
Streptococcus thermophilus	BACTERIUM	YOGURT
Lactobacillus bulgaricus	BACTERIUM	YOGURT
Propionibacterium shermanii	BACTERIUM	SWISS CHEESE
Gluconobacter suboxidans	BACTERIUM	VINEGAR
Penicillium roquefortii	MOLD	BLUE-VEINED CHEESES
Penicillium camembertii	MOLD	CAMEMBERT AND BRIE CHEESES
Aspergillus oryzae	MOLD	SAKE (RICE-STARCH HYDROLYSIS)
Rhizopus	MOLD	TEMPEH
Mucor	MOLD	SUFU (SOYBEAN CURD)
Monascus purpurea	MOLD	ANG-KAK (RED RICE)
AMINO ACIDS AND FLAVOR-ENHANCING NUCLEOTIDES		
Corynebacterium glutamicum	BACTERIUM	L-LYSINE
Corynebacterium glutamicum	BACTERIUM	5'-INOSINIC ACID AND 5'-GUANYLIC ACID
SINGLE-CELL PROTEINS		
Candida utilis	YEAST	MICROBIAL PROTEIN FROM PAPER-PULP WASTE
Saccharomycopsis lipolytica	YEAST	MICROBIAL PROTEIN FROM PETROLEUM ALKANES
Methylophilus methylotrophus	BACTERIUM	MICROBIAL PROTEIN FROM GROWTH ON METHANE OR METHANOL
VITAMINS		
Eremothecium ashbyi	YEAST	RIBOFLAVIN
Pseudomonas denitrificans	BACTERIUM	VITAMIN B_{12}
Propionibacterium	BACTERIUM	VITAMIN B_{12}
ENZYMES		
Aspergillus oryzae	MOLD	AMYLASES
Aspergillus niger	MOLD	GLUCAMYLASE
Trichoderma reesii	MOLD	CELLULASE
Saccharomyces cerevisiae	YEAST	INVERTASE
Kluyveromyces fragilis	YEAST	LACTASE
Saccharomycopsis lipolytica	YEAST	LIPASE
Aspergillus	MOLD	PECTINASES AND PROTEASES
Bacillus	BACTERIUM	PROTEASES
Endothia parasitica	MOLD	MICROBIAL RENNET
POLYSACCHARIDES		
Leuconostoc mesenteroides	BACTERIUM	DEXTRAN
Xanthomonas campestris	BACTERIUM	XANTHAN GUM
PHARMACEUTICALS		
Penicillum chrysogenum	MOLD	PENICILLINS
Cephalosporium acremonium	MOLD	CEPHALOSPORINS
Streptomyces	BACTERIUM	AMPHOTERICIN B, KANAMYCINS, NEOMYCINS, STREPTOMYCIN, TETRACYCLINES AND OTHERS
Bacillus brevis	BACTERIUM	GRAMICIDIN S
Bacillus subtilis	BACTERIUM	BACITRACIN
Bacillus polymyxa	BACTERIUM	POLYMYXIN B
Rhizopus nigricans	MOLD	STEROID TRANSFORMATION
Arthrobacter simplex	BACTERIUM	STEROID TRANSFORMATION
Mycobacterium	BACTERIUM	STEROID TRANSFORMATION
HYBRIDOMAS	—	IMMUNOGLOBULINS AND MONOCLONAL ANTIBODIES
MAMMALIAN CELL LINES	—	INTERFERON
Escherichia coli (via recombinant-DNA technology)	BACTERIUM	INSULIN, HUMAN GROWTH HORMONE, SOMATOSTATIN, INTERFERON
CAROTENOIDS		
Blakeslea trispora	MOLD	BETA-CAROTENE
Phaffia rhodozyma	YEAST	ASTAXANTHIN

Fig. 3. Useful Products From Micro-organisms.

Ch.3. Chronic Infection.

In the haphazard nutrition of the cells that make up the various body parts there are millions of different molecules that ebb and flow with the salty fluid around the cells, with each cell taking and utilizing the nutrients that it needs, and expelling its altered unwanted chemicals back into the salty fluid. The fluid therefore contains many molecules that are utilized (nutrients), many molecules that have already been used (wastes), many molecules that do not have appropriate bonding sites, and are therefore inert, and a few "toxins",- molecules that have similar bonding sites to normal biological molecules, but are actually different and that therefore produce different biological processes.

Throughout all living matter, "waste" from one organism is food for another. We have seen (from Fig.3.) that in biological manufacturing we eat the waste from bacteria, yeast, and mold as liquor, cheese, tufu, soya sauce, yogurt, enzymes, or amino acids. But biological activity is not confined to the lab. and industrial plants. Biology is constantly active within us. Therefore the same or similar infectives may alter our foods and give us their good nutritious wastes, or they may give us their toxins, made from the very food that was supposed to nourish our cells. In this way a serious Candida yeast infection can use up iron to the point of anemia, use B vitamins to the point of pellegra, use chromium and selenium to the point of cancer, and use methionine to the point of malnutrition, while at the same time it will change phenalanine, tyracine and tryptophane into lactate and toxic ethanol. The total effects from the infective and it's toxins is to produce a shortage of nutrients, (in spite of good nutrition), place seratonin in excess, produce intoxication from the ethanol, and produce hyperactivity from the lactic acid. This condition produces many sleepless nights for many adults and is even worse for children. Further, taking L-tryptophan to promote sleep increases the elements that prevent sleep.

In cholera, the exact toxin from the infective is known to bind like a water excretion hormone, and the victim dies of nutrient loss and dehydration. The toxic process is also known in cancer, where infectives change nitrates to nitrites, and finally to nitrosamines. Even Adelle Davis describes how "putrefactive bacteria" change the amino acid histidine into the neuro-transmitter histamine.

When we knowingly use micro-organisms to produce all of the "by-products" shown in Fig.3. we must also know and realize that some of the millions of other different micro-organisms in the world might, again by happenstance, produce as by-products many toxins that could be very harmful to man.

Many of these harmful toxins will then unavoidably come to us in our food and in the air that we breathe. Other organisms, capable of living in our bodies, will invade, live on our food, and give us their toxins, and some, like Candida, will not only eat our food, they will also eat at us, and will use us for food.

Eat and be eaten is the natural order of biology and man cannot escape unharmed. But man, and man alone, through science and Technology, can at least reduce the number of little "devils" that are slowly consuming him.

Now look back at List 4. These are some of the metabolic products known to be produced by Candida yeast. But of course the yeast is never alone, it is always part of an infective mix, so the total number of metabolic products excreted into the host from the infective matrix will be a much longer list. After all, the infective matrix could contain all of the infectives shown in List 3, so the total number of toxins and metabolites produced by the infective colony might well number into thousands, with each toxin or metabolite affecting some body process, someway.

It is little wonder then that with high yeast infection many body systems fail, or the mind becomes warped or lost altogether, and degenerative disease and old age, come much too soon.

Candida yeast infection can be acquired at any time, and the infection may grow very slowly, or, if conditions are more favorable the infectives may overtake their unwilling host much sooner. But some unfortunate people acquire such a massive infection at birth that it affects their entire lives, so we call these infortunate victims of continuous yeast infection "Yeast People". If you have been ill as long as you can remember, or if you have had some strange affliction since birth, perhaps you too are one of these "Yeast People".

YEAST PEOPLE:

There can be nothing more beautiful in life than the event of the first born, healthy, baby child. The proud father; the tender young mother, and the helpless little bundle itself. The New LIfe is beautiful, and wondrous;- wondrous because it is the renewing of life;- life with a fresh clean start. Like the first tender shoots of grass in spring; new life has started. Everything is new, everything is clean, everything is beautiful, and yet, everything is hopeful,for even the new born babe is not alone. Even in the moments before birth the many, many organisms that live with man;- the bacteria, the yeasts, the molds, and the cocci, had already joined the new host, some for the better, and yet some for the worse. One of the first, and one of the worst, was Candida yeast, so with the beginning of the new life also began the very first chronic infection; Candida yeast, which is endemic in man and is present in all humans. Candida yeast, lying as always on the mucous of the birth canal, was picked up by the new born babe, and even before the first breath was drawn the yeast was already starting to invade and colonize someplace, somewhere. Then, even before the babe's very first cry, the immune defences were already started on the lifelong struggle between the unwanted yeast and the unwilling host, with the outcome of the struggle largely determining the final capabilities and sometimes the total life of the newborn baby child.

The amount of Candida infection acquired by the newborn infant will depend upon the amount of Candida yeast present in the birth canal at the time of delivery; it will depend upon the length of time for delivery; and it will depend upon the health and strength of the baby's skin and the amount of abrasion and damage incurred with delivery. Thus if previous births or other trauma has abraded the birth canal and has created a high yeast infection in the mother; if nutrition is poor and the tissue strength of the baby is low; and if delivery is difficult, slow, and prolonged; the baby may be born completely covered with a white film of Candida yeast. Typically, and commonly the baby will be swabbed and cleaned up, and during the following weeks nystatin cream will be used to clear up any thrush that is seen to persist. But this is a yeast baby, and this baby will become one of the "yeast People".

After birth, the yeast was cleaned off the outside of the baby, and any further visible infections were cleared up with nystatin. A noble gesture, but most certainly if there is yeast on the outside, the yeast will also infect the inside. The nose, the sinuses, the mouth, the intestinal tract, the rectum, the sexual tract, and probably the toenails, fingernails, ears, and perhaps even the eyes. The immune system will immediately fight the yeast, imposing continuous stress on the growing child, and the yeast will continue to grow, with the growing child, impairing the immune system and interfering with body system and every aspect of health.

This is one of the yeast people; never completely ill; and never well. Usually adrenal depleted from the continous stress; usually a coffee addict; and always a candidate for something to make them feel just a little better,- chemicals, alcohol, drugs. Then if the "yeast person" is female, she may become a "yeast mother", giving birth to more "yeast people", who will be even more adrenal depleted, because adrenal depletion in the mother usually induces adrenal depletion in the unborn child.

Ch.3. Chronic Infection.

"Yeast People" take many forms, depending upon the amount and location of infections. The infections, together with the adrenal depletion, usually alters carbohydrate metabolism. They may be small and thin, or big and overweight. They may be hyperactive, or slow and lethargic. They are frequently "odd" or appear retarded. Where the yeast has disseminated throughout the body and has depleted the minerals, the heart and organs may be affected, sexual development may be slow, the hands and fingers may be short and stubby, and the feet may be stubby and they may walk with a swaying stumpy gait. Nails, and particularly small toenails, may be deformed and almost absent. Usually "yeast People" are "never well", and have never known how it feels to be healthy, full of life, and free from being "tired".For them life is an unending struggle, a constant battle between the yeast and the host, a battle that impairs all of their body functions and saps all of their energy, with nothing left for "living". Allergies, arthritis, heart problems, and hypoglycemia are common, together with a susceptability to colds, flu, and everything that comes.

Already you may have thought of someone, or perhaps a family of several generations, that are probably "Yeast People". So who are the other "yeast people"? The other "yeast people" are many of us, to some degree, depending upon our luck. Extreme yeast infection, and its consequences are very visible, but the lesser infections, with the various complications, may go almost unnoticed to anyone except the victim. Low energy, low capability, and low sexual levels without detectable cause are common indicators. Unless you are extremely healthy you too may be in between,- somewhere.

The difficulty is, that, like calluses and corns, (which are usually yeast infections) visible Candida yeast infections at birth have not been regarded as a significant problem."just a little thrush, and it will go away" or "We will get the baby cleaned up and it will be alright". The baby will survive, yes, and the baby may appear normal, but the baby will not be "alright". Then later, when multiple health problems appear, the child will "outgrow them".Yes? Certainly, as the child grows and as the sex hormones increase, the yeast will be opposed by the increasing sex hormones, so the child, temporarily relieved of the heavy yeast burden, will suddenly blossom, through puberty and past. But then, as the years pass and the yeast continues to grow, it will start to again subdue the sexual system, because with time the sex hormones fall, allowing the yeast to increase. A tragedy for the male, a tragedy for the female, and a catastrophe for the marriage, because yeast infection reduces libido.

Health, happiness, and vitality are intrinsically linked to libido. Sex is life, and life is sex. Marriage is sex. Marriage vows are made to fulfill the need for a continuing sexual partner. Marriage vows are made without thought or fear that sexual function may be reduced, or vanish. So with the changing sexual levels, what happens to those promises, those vows, those hopes, and to life itself, when Candida reduces the male to impotence or sexual failure? Or when Candida reduces the female to complete frigidity? The formerly beautiful marriage turns sour, into a continuing unbearable frustration, with each blaming the other because ill or well, the re-absorbed hormones from incompleted orgasm produce their own psychosis, with depression, blues, imaginings, unreasonable anger, and perhaps violence, while all of the problems are intensified because the hapless victims do not know or understand the cause of their problems, they have nowhere to turn, and their doctor and psychiatrist usually only complicate the problems with drugs and tranquilizers, because they too usually fail to understand the role of Candida yeast infection in health, and in disease.

Part of the"yeast people" problem is that in the past the obvious yeast infection of the newborn was simply dismissed as being of little importance, so records were not kept, and, since memories fade and mothers die, many people do not know if they may be a "yeast victim". Some indication of the yeast infection status of each individual can usually be seen from a mineral test with nutritional evaluation, which can also be used to improve the general health status. As the deep mycoses are completely hidden and obscure, the best Candida test seems to be with a Ketoconazole challange;1/8 tablet, increasing daily by 1/8 tablet, up to 2 tablets, taken at the beginning of the meal with glutamic acid (HCL). Watch for symptoms of any kind, particularly "flu" symptoms that result from the dead bodies of the infective. If the symptoms appear from one tablet or less, serious fungal infection is present somewhere, and ill health will persist until it is reduced.

TRANSMISSION of YEAST INFECTIONS:

Although Candida yeasts are all around us in nature, and although some transmission may occur from airborne droplets from people with lung and throat infections, the principal manner of Candida yeast transmission is through body contact.

1.SEXUAL: Candida yeast is always present in the vagina and birth canal,where it normally lies on the surface of the mucosa and does no harm, yet with every birth there is sufficient infection transmitted to the newborn that every person everywhere has developed antibodies to this universal infective.

Quite obviously Candida yeast is passed freely back and forth between sexual partners, and the larger the number of partners, and the greater the variety of sexual practice, the greater the transmission. But although transmitted, the yeast will not colonize unless the tissues are weak or injured. Herpes and other venereal diseases help the yeasts to colonize.

2.FEET:One of the principal sources of yeast infection is the feet. Candida lives in moist, damp places, and is frequently on the feet. Candida, mixed with other infectives on the feet, does not greatly affect the host, but it serves as a constant infective reservoir; waiting. Waiting for tight shoes or other foot damage so that it can invade and colonize; waiting to be spread by careless and unknowing hands to other parts of the body, where it may live and wait for years before finding an opportunity to colonize; waiting for an opportunity to spread to others where again it may wait for years before chance allows it to colonize.

Candida yeast likes water. Public washrooms, and particularly public swimming pools, gyms. and spas, provide excellent opportunity for transmission. Here debris from the feet of the infected is picked up on the feet of the un-infected. This is not a reflection against anyone except the medical establishment, who refuse to recognize the dangers of Candida yeast and to warn the spa and the public of those dangers. At the spa, both the infector and the infected are innocent. They do not know if they do or do not have Candida infection. They do not know how it might affect their health. Probably they have never even heard of Candida yeast. Yet the peril is there and the peril is real. Shoes should always be worn in moist public areas.

3.HEALTH PROFESSIONALS.(See also List 7.) Yeast infection is transmitted by many health professionals;

(a) Foot reflexologists, who are not warned about the dangers of yeast transmission, and who frequently ignore such warnings when warnings are given.

(b) Massage parlors, where yeast disinfectants are scarce, Candida is transferred from client to masseur, and from masseur to the next client. Thus the client frequently gets more than he bargained for.

(c) Chiropracters and osteopaths, who may be totally unaware of the possible consequences of Candida yeast transfer from their patient to them, and from them to their next patient

(d) Your friendly family physician, who usually disinfects his hands, his instruments and you, against everything except yeast and fungii.

(e) Most other physicians and surgeons, who have all of the information, but fail to use it.

(f) The nursing staff, who are usually uninformed about yeasts and therefore take great care against all infectives except yeasts and other fungii.

CHAPTER 4.

REDUCING CANDIDA YEAST INFECTION.

YOUR DOCTOR and YOU.

Good health is like a tall healthy forest, with each tree proudly doing its part to support the whole. Ill health is like a tall forest blown down by ill winds, with all of the trees that make up the forest criss-crossed over each other in endless confusion, each supporting the others, each depending on the others, and each struggling to survive the smothering weight of all the others.

The body is a forest of biological processes, each of which is highly complex. The normally interdependent biological processes that constitute Health, are certainly very complex. The interdependent biological processes confused by toxins, infectives, extra wastes, and a shortage of nutrients;- as in ill health;- are even more complex because they are so hopelessly confused. Ill health then is always an extremely complex state of biological disarray, with everything failing, and everything functioning wrongly. This is your ill health. This is your extremely complex biological problem. This is your biological confusion. So to start to overcome the extreme confusion that constitutes ill health, you will need to have all of the help that you can get. You will need help from anywhere and everywhere. You will need good technical help that fully recognizes the highly complex nature of all health processes. You will need technology.

Hopefully this book will help you find that technology. Hopefully this book will help you find the physicians and the pharmacists, and the nutritionists and the other health practitioners that you will need. Hopefully it will help you find the tests, and the vitamins and the minerals and all of the other remedies that you will need. And hopefully this book will help you set up your own Health program.

We say YOU, because only you can make Your health program work, and You can make it work only if You fully understand it. It is Your health. It is Your health program. It is You who must be intelligently in charge. Yet the problems of ill health are so complex that you cannot do it all alone. Not even with the help of this book, and many other books, should you try to do it all alone. You must not try to do it all alone. You need all of the wondrous elements of modern technology. You need all of the modern tests, you need all of the modern supplements, you need all of the modern anti-infectives. You also need the knowledgable doctors, and you need full co-operation between yourself and your knowledgable doctors.

This book is therefore written for both you and your physician, so that you can intelligently seek the medical help that you need, and so that you can discuss your problems on a mutually intelligent basis with your doctor. All material in this book is drawn from the best reliable sources the author has been able to find. Therefore, in discussing your problems with your physician, and in seeking his help, do not hesitate to show him your source of information. For your health problems to be reduced, your physician needs your intelligent co-operation, and you need his intelligent expertise. Most good physicians will give you their full intelligent co-operation. If you do not receive that full co-operation you cannot expect to regain your health, so you must part as amicably as possible, but you must part, and seek a different doctor who will co-operate with you. After all, most good physicians realize that their true successes are rare, and their failures many. Most doctors would like to have 100% success, not only for the welfare of their patients, but because real success at any time, and particularly in returning people to health, is itself one of life's greatest rewards. Success also proves that they are indeed a good doctor, and they can be justly proud that they are a good doctor. Further, good successful doctors are always busy, and their high fees are justly earned.

Your doctor can help you with most of your Health program, but he may or may not be able to help you with Nutrition. If your doctor does not have nutritional training, and does not wish to depend upon the outline and suggestions in this book, you may wish to seek the services of a Nutritional Consultant, who will work with both you and your doctor. Some nutritional consultants are also Herbalists. The author does not have an extensive knowledge of herbs, but herbs do contain a very large number of strange chemicals and metabolites, which makes them very effective in some ways. Many of today's drugs are refined herbs, or are synthetic analogues of chemicals found in herbs.(e.g. aspirin, digitalis, etc.) Most drugs, and therefore most herbs, produce their effects by interfering with metabolic processes. Drug therapy is usually referred to as toxi-molecular therapy. The effects of salicylic acid on the body are the same whether the salicylic acid comes from the drug store or comes from willow bark. Clearly, most herbal therapy is also toxi-molecular therapy, with extra effects from other chemicals in the herbs. It would appear to be less than useful to introduce into these programs the myriad of other metabolic factors and unknown side effects associated with herbs. It is therefore suggested that to insure success, the extensive use of drugs and herbs should be avoided.

Ch.4. Reducing Candida Yeast Infection.

Yes, you certainly need your doctor, but if for any reason your doctor fails to co-operate with you, you must part in peace, and seek another. After all, your doctor is a technician. You are paying him for his technical expertise. You are paying him for his time. You are paying him for his co-operation. So if you try, you will find that there are many good doctors that will give you that full co-operation, and will help you to solve your problems. But do not forget, and never forget that the Health problems are Your problems. They are Your life, and co-operation is a double-edged sword that cuts both ways;- you too must co-operate with both the doctor and yourself. Your doctor's greatest frustration is you, and he is entitled to tell you so, if you fail to ask. Usually your greatest problem is You. So if you have not already cleaned up your lifestyle;- cleaned out the liquor, and the aspirin, and the tobacco, and the caffeine, and the etc; then you must go to your doctor fully prepared to do so. It will not be easy, it will not be quick, but it must be done, and then your doctor can help you. But your doctor can help you only if you too, fully co-operate. After all, if he is to sincerely help you, you too must be prepared to sincerely help yourself, without backsliding. "Return to Health" must be your first priority, second to none. Then, with full honest co-operation you can together work out a program of Help Self Management. Although your doctor is an intelligent technician, he cannot think for you, he cannot remember for you, and he cannot act for you. He can watch and help you with your Health Self Management Program, but you and only you can put that program into effect.

Now if your actual health has fallen to the point where you cannot always remember to do everything in the program, you must seek a trusted friend or relative that can be at your side to give you the needed help. They too, then, should read this book, and they too should go with you to discuss your program with your physician. Then, as health returns, you can take charge of your own program. It is your "Return to Health" program. It is you who will benefit from it. It is you who must intelligently follow it, to insure success for both yourself, and your physician.

CANDIDA YEAST SPECIES and ASSOCIATED INFECTIVES.

Yeasts are very primitive organisms that follow mitachondria on the phylogenetic tree for transfer RNA. Mitochondria have their own RNA, and they are still in each of our cells as organelles. Genetically, yeast is a common ancestor to all living organisms, and man is only 22 nucleotide sequence changes away from yeast. Yeasts are therefore very difficult for the body to deal with because their genetic codons are so similar to ours that the body sometimes has difficulty recognizing yeasts as being "foreign", which impairs the ability of the immune system to adequately deal with them. The immune system is further impaired by toxins from Candida, which allows the increased infection to further impair immune system function, sometimes to the point that very little immune response remains, and the infectives then grow very rapidly.

Although Candida yeast species are in fact yeasts, they are very different than other yeasts;- so different that they are frequently referred to as yeast-like fungii. Candida yeasts are dimorphic; (i.e.) like frogs, they have two forms; the juvenile invasive mycelial form, and the mature chlamydospore or blastospore form, that sheds spores to propogate the infection, and sheds connecting filaments that aglutinate blood. Both the filaments and the spores, together with toxins and metabolic by products, alter many of the cellular, intra-cellular, and enzymatic body processes with many wierd and varied effects.

Candida species and the common infectives actinomycetales appear to be the remains of the yeast-to-bacteria genetic division. There is substantial evidence that Candida transforms to actinomycetales, or Candida may be one of the actinomycetales. Candida is known to impair the immune system. Other actinomycetales are tuberculosis and leprosy, (which also impair the immune system), actinomycetes, actinomyces, and nocardia asteroides, (Fig.4.), which are frequently associated with Candida infection, and progenitor cryptocides which is always present in the fulminating state, in cancer. Candida yeast may also fulminate, followed by death. Progenitor also appears to take several forms, both bacterial and yeast;- with crystal bodies, rods, and L forms seen under the darkfield microscope. Candida species also seem to have crystal bodies, rods and L forms. The Candida appears to aglutinate blood cells into crystal bodies that may, or may not be the same as progenitor crystal bodies. Progenitor also seems to have both a bacterial phase, and a yeast phase. Actinomycetes, actinomyces, and nocardia are considered to be bacteria. Basically bacteria are single celled organisms based on bacteriohophane whereas yeasts and other fungii are multi-celled plants, with a cellular system based on ergosterol. Actinomycetes, actinomyces,and nocardia, although considered to be bacteria, are destroyed by ketoconazole which works only on ergosterol, which is basic to plants and fungii.

Candida infection is frequently associated with all of the other infectives shown in Fig.4. It is also associated with the many infectives shown in the medical literature, while the Candida infection itself may be a mixture of different varieties. The worst forms of Candida are Albicans and Krusei.

An Overview of the Incidence and Therapy of Fungal Infections

Incidence

The opportunistic fungi - *Candida*, *Cryptococcus* and *Aspergillus* species - can become pathogenic, and have increasingly done so, as more aggressive or invasive medical techniques have been developed.

The incidence of fungal infections, from the commonplace tinea pedis to the potentially fatal cryptococcosis, is now thought to be greatly underestimated.[1] Most mycoses are not reportable diseases. Many occur in developing areas where accurate reporting has not been possible. In the U.S., it has been estimated that the incidence of even reportable, life-threatening systemic mycoses (as surveyed in at least one state) may be as much as 30 times greater than reports would indicate.[2]

Classification of Fungal Infections

Fungal infections are generally classified as superficial, subcutaneous or systemic, as shown in Table 1. The common superficial infections, caused by dermatophytes, *Candida* species and other yeasts include the tineas, onychomycosis, oral thrush, vaginal candidiasis and *pityriasis versicolor*. These infections have worldwide distribution and can affect half of a tropical area's population, as has been reported since 1950 in the case of *pityriasis versicolor*.[3,4,5] In the U.S., dermatophytosis has been identified as the second most prevalent skin disorder, second only to acne.[6] In 1970, the cost of treating dermatophytoses in the U.S. alone was estimated to be 25 million dollars.[1] Moreover, recent European surveys indicate that from 25 to 30% of gynecological patients have vaginal candidiasis.[7]

The subcutaneous fungal infections, mycetoma, chromomycosis, and sporotrichosis, among others, are seen less frequently, but their chronic nature, potential for local tissue destruction, and occasional resistance to chemotherapy present troublesome clinical problems. Fortunately, they are rarely fatal. In contrast, the systemic mycoses, capable of disseminating via the bloodstream, can produce serious long-term morbidity and, in some cases, mortality.

Systemic Mycoses: Background

Medical interest in the deep mycoses has peaked only in the last 75 years, although archaeological findings suggest that they are an ancient human affliction. The first reported case of disseminated coccidioidomycosis appeared in Argentina in 1892; four years later, the first case in the U.S. was described.[8] Increasingly since that time, the medical, social and economic impact of this varied group of potentially life-threatening disorders has been recognized. We now know that the systemic mycoses are not confined to exotic regions. Coccidioidomycosis, called variously cocci, valley fever and San Joaquin fever, is caused by *C. immitis* found in soil of the southwestern United States. Other systemic mycoses, including histoplasmosis, cryptococcosis, and aspergillosis, are thought to be occupationally incurred in the U.S., where 500,000 *H. capsulatum* infections occur annually.[9] In 1970, *Cryptococcus* accounted for 18 reported fatalities per 100,000 hospitalized patients.[10] Overall, nearly 8,000 patients were hospitalized in the U.S. in 1970 with a primary diagnosis of systemic mycoses at an estimated cost of 9.39 million dollars; 366 deaths were reported.[10]

Aside from the possibility of acquiring a mycotic infection on native soil, the ease with which worldwide travel has been undertaken in recent years makes it more likely than ever before that the physician practicing in the U.S. can be faced with treatment of a mycosis acquired anywhere in the world. Other contemporary practices, such as the use of detergents which remove the skin's fatty acids and bathing in crowded, hot and humid swimming areas, may also promote fungal disorders.

Janssen Pharmaceutica Inc.
New Brunswick
New Jersey 08903
USA

Fig. 4.--A. Human Fungal Infections.

Janssen Pharmaceutica Inc.
New Brunswick
New Jersey 08903
USA

Clinical manifestation	Causative organism

A. Superficial

Mycosis of hair and scalp
Tinea capitis	Dermatophytes
Favus	Dermatophytes
Black piedra	*Piedraia hortai*
White piedra	*Trichosporon cutaneum*
Trichomycosis axillaris	*Corynebacterium tenuis*

Mycoses of the skin
Dermatomycosis	Dermatophytes, yeasts
Tinea imbricate (Tokelau)	*Trichophyton concentricum*
Erythrasma	*Corynebacterium minutissimum*
Pityriasis versicolor	*Malassezia furfur (Pityrosporum orbiculare)*
Tinea nigra palmaris	*Cladosporium werneckii*

Mycosis of the nail
| Onychomycosis | Dermatophytes, yeasts |
| Perionyxis | Yeasts |

Mycoses of the mucous membranes
Oral thrush	*Candida albicans*
Vaginal candidiasis	*Candida*
Gastrointestinal candidiasis	*Candida*
Chronic mucocutaneous candidiasis	*Candida albicans*

B. Subcutaneous

Eumycotic mycetoma (maduromycosis)	*Petriellidium boydii, Cephalosporium* spp. *Madurella* spp., *Phialophora jeanselmi*
Actinomycotic mycetoma[a]	*Actinomycetes*
Chromomycosis (dermatitis verrucosa)	*Phialophora* spp., *Fonsecaea* spp., *Cladosporium carrioni*
Sporotrichosis [b]	*Sporothrix schenckii*
Lobomycosis (keloid blastomycosis)	*Blastomyces loboi*
Rhinosporidiosis	*Rhinosporidium seeberi*

C. Systemic Mycoses

Caused by yeasts
Systemic candidiasis	*Candida* spp.
Cryptococcosis (torulosis)	*Cryptococcus neoformans*
Geotrichosis	*Geotrichum candidum*
Torulopsosis	*Torulopsis glabrata*

Caused by mold fungi
Aspergillosis	*Aspergillus* spp.
Aspergilloma	*Aspergillus* spp.
Phycomycosis (mucormycosis)	*Rhizopus* sp., *Mucor* sp., *Basidiobolus* sp. *Entomophthora* sp., *Absidia* sp.

Caused by actinomycetes
| Actinomycosis [a] | *Actinomyces* spp. |
| Nocardiosis [a] | *Nocardia asteroides* |

Caused by dimorphic fungi
Paracoccidioidomycosis	*Paracoccidioides brasiliensis*
Blastomycosis	*Blastomyces dermatitidis*
Histoplasmosis	*Histoplasma capsulatum*
African histoplasmosis	*Histoplasma duboisii*
Coccidioidomycosis (Valley fever)	*Coccidioides immitis*

[a] At present usually considered bacterial infections.
[b] Can also be systemic, pulmonary, or bone.

Fig. 4.--B. Human Fungal Infections. (Mycoses.)

Note the association with Aspergillus, which is also very high on the phylogentic tree. Fig.4. provides concise information on the potential dangers of some of the mixed infections. The common Candida infectives are Albicans, Krusei, Guilliermondii, Tropicalis, and Parapsilosis.

There is evidence that Candida infection, with associated infectives, may be one of the initiating factors in cancer. Candida infection is always extensive in victims of cancer, but this may simply be an infective invasion of an already weakened body, together with an already impaired immune system, and conversely perhaps the yeast infection precedes the cancer; and the cancer is the end result of Candida infection, that has reduced health to a bare minimum, has impaired the immune system, and has altered all body functions with a massive infusion of toxins. Under the Darkfield microscope blood from cancer victims looks very bad, yet it has many of the same characteristics as blood from victims of yeast infection. Anyone with cancer, or threat or suspicion of cancer, should reduce their yeast infection as rapidly as possible.

EUKARYOTIC CELLS.
The following chart (Fig.5), shows some of the basic differences and similarities between the cells of bacteria, fungii, and man. Note that in both yeasts and man the cells are highly complex eukaryotic cells with similar metabolic processes. Man lives on sugars from the bloodstream. Yeasts thrive in a 2% sugar solution. Yeasts also thrive on Eagles minimum essential medium, the medium commonly used to culture cellular tissues from man. You cannot starve the yeast because you feed the infective whenever you feed yourself, and any rise in blood sugar feeds the yeast better than yourself.

This chart is included to show why it is so difficult to eradicate Candida and other fungal infectives. Bacteria are single-celled prokaryotes that are distinctly different from eukaryotes. Yeasts and fungii, and man, are multi-celled eukaryotes, with many cells that differentiate and grow into the complete multi-celled organism. The single cells of bacteria therefore are not interconnected, and each single cell lives and dies wherever it happens to be, but yeasts and fungii are complete micro-plants each composed of many interconnected cells, and each plant growing while surrounded by the cells of the host. In mammals and all other living creatures the lipids in the eukaryotic cell wall are based on cholesterol. In plants and fungii the lipids in the eukaryotic cell wall are based on ergosterol. Otherwise the basic structures of the eukaryotic cells of yeasts and man are so identical that it becomes extremely

	Organisation.	Reproduction.	Cell wall.	Membrane.
BACTERIA	Prokaryotic	mitosis	present	glycerols
FUNGII	Eukaryotic	meiosis	present	ergosterol
MAN	Eukaryotic	meiosis	absent	cholesterol

Fig.5. BASIC CELLS; -- Bacteria,Fungii, Man.

* * * * * * * * * * * * *

difficult to destroy the yeast without also destroying the cells of the host, and the difficulties become even greater when the yeasts and other fungii are intermingled with the living cells of the host.

Just to make you feel much better towards Nature's wonderful flower gardens, Fig. 6. shows some of the micro "plants within us". These are the approximate shapes of these organisms. Note the great similarity to the larger plants that we know so well. This illustration is from advertising for Econazole cream, (Squibb) which is very effective in reducing these infectives. This illustration is included to show that fungii are entirely different from bacteria, and they are therefore much more difficult to eradicate.

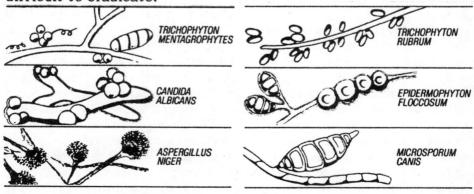

Fig.6. THE PLANTS WITHIN US.

MODERN FACTORS in CANDIDA YEAST INFECTION:
There are a number of factors in to-day's society that greatly increase the rate of Candida infection. Some of these factors are shown in List 6.
1. Sugars.- Yeasts thrive on Sugars.- The extremely high amounts of sugar and refined carbohydrate in to-day's diet therefore contribute to greatly increased yeast infection. Yeasts readily convert glucose and fructose (sugar and honey) and other sugars into ethanol and carbon dioxide. In the lab. Candida thrives on a solution of only 2% glucose. Many fruits are canned in a 10% sugar solution. Thus the yeast grows best when the body slowly dilutes the strong sugar solution. Many people find that a drink of water will produce a stomach-ache. Invariably such people have a yeast infection of the intestinal tract. The water simply dilutes previously consumed starches or sugars to the point where the yeast thrives, and produces the gas that blows up the stomach and produces the stomach ache. You are in fact blown up by the yeast "just like a loaf of bread."
2. Caffiene, tobacco, and drugs.- Caffiene (coffee, tea, chocolate, and cola), tobacco, and most drugs push the adrenals to produce more adrenalin, which pulls sugars out of the liver and into the bloodstream, with the high blood-sugar levels rapidly feeding the infection, wherever it may be.
3. Diabetes and Hyperglycemia.- Refined carbohydrates, caffiene, and yeast infection induce pancreatic failure, leading to a higher incidence of diabetes and hyperglycemia, with the high blood-sugar levels rapidly feeding the Candida infection.
4. Aspirin.- A great many tons of aspirin and other salicylates are consumed every year. Aspirin is very invasive to the tissues (the active ingretient in corn salve) which allows the waiting Candida yeast to invade and colonize.
5. Junk Foods.- Junk foods are so low in nutrients that the body, and particularly the immune system, lacks the nutrition necessary to combat the infection.
6. Shoes.- High shoes, plastic shoes, rubber-soled shoes, and poorly ventilated shoes increase the temperature and the sweating of the feet, and thus create an ideal climate for the growth of Candida yeast.(trench foot).
7.Jogging.- Jogging and running, and some sports, particularly on pavement, damage the lymphatic valves, resulting in reduced lymphatic and blood circulation, sometimes progressing to "Black Toe". The damaged tissues may be rapidly invaded by waiting yeasts, and the poorly ventilated shoes usually worn certainly increase the problem.
8."Athlete's Foot" preparations,although Government approved, kill out other infectives and provide extra nutrients for the Candida.

9. Alcohol.- Distilled liquor kills the bacteria in the digestive tract, and attacks the lining. The Candida yeast, unaffected by the alcohol, has a perfect opportunity to invade, and further alcohol helps it to spread.

In wine and bottled beer, the brewers yeast is killed, but in "tap beer" the brewers yeast is still alive. Although brewers yeast cannot live directly on human tissues, it is thought that the live brewers yeast may join a basic Candida yeast infection, and then grow and produce alcohol within the body, directly from food sugars in the bowel. Indeed, the alcohol levels in some beer drinkers seem to be unaccountably high, and unaccountably constant, and internal production of alcohol has been confirmed in some cases. At one time in England, only ale (grain wine) was used, and there was great opposition to the introduction of beer from Holland, because "Beer doth make men round and fat" and "Beer doth inflate the belly". Nonetheless, beer did invade England, and beer did produce many "Beer bellies". The "beer belly" is real, and the only reasonable explanation is that the brewers yeast does join a basic Candida yeast infection, with the internal fermentation constantly producing gas and with the constantly inflated belly finally taking the shape of a balloon.

In recent years there have been many warnings against yeast infection from the consumption of live bakers yeast. Like brewers yeast, bakers yeast will not live by itself on human tissue, but it is known that bakers yeast will join a basic Candida yeast infection, and increase the total health problems.

There is speculation that there may be some symbiotic relationship between bakers yeast, brewers yeast, and Candida yeast.

10. Antibiotics.- Antibiotics kill out bacterial infectives, and the yeast moves into the damaged tissues and feeds on the dead infectives. Tetracycline is followed by yeast infection at a rate of 90%. Beclomethasone (Vanceril) (anti-Asthmatic) also has a very high rate. All antibiotics increase Candida infection.

11. Steroids. Cortisone and other steroids alter hormone levels and increase yeast infection.

12. The Pill.- Estrogen reduces Candida infection. All female contraceptives except the diaphram reduce estrogen levels with a consequent increase in yeast infection.

15. Sexual.- Vaginal yeast infections are passed to the male and become balanitis (Penisitis) and visa versa. Increased sexual activity, particularly with multiple partners, increases Candida infection. With the new "sexual freedom" infections of herpes and other venreral diseases have increased greatly.

Herpes and veneral diseases damage the tissues, providing an opportunity for Candida to invade and colonize. The increased use of drugs (both medical and social) and / or alcohol, together with junk foods and infections, decreases sexuality and sexual ability. Lack of full sexual gratification increases desire, leading to increased oral and anal sex, multiple partners, sex orgies, and unusual sexual practices, which results in an increased number of mouth and anal infections of Candida yeast, herpes, and venereal diseases.

14. Injected Drugs. Both medical and social. The increased use of hypodermic needles together with lack of disinfectants that are effective against Candida has resulted in a large number of needle induced fungal infections. These infections are particularly difficult and perilous because the Candida is delivered by the bloodstream to the heart, eyes, organs, or other internal body parts.

15. Iatrogenic. Statistically over 60% of hospital admissions are for iatrogenic disease. That is not because iatrogens are contagious. "Iatrogenic"is doctorese jargon for "doctor induced"or "medically induced", disease. Medically injected drugs also induce Candida infections.

Intravenous: Intravenous feedings and medical procedures without adequate yeast disinfectants produces many yeast infections.

Catheters: Catheters without adequate fungal disinfectants produce many yeast infections.

Surgery: The increased use of surgery without effective fungal disinfectants produces many yeast infections, particularly in childbirth and in heart and transplant operations.

Dialasis: Kidney dialasis is another source of Candida infection.

Note:- In 14, and 15, above, infection is disseminated through the bloodstream, and infection may appear at any point in the body. Candida appears to have a particular affinity for the heart, eyes, and brain.

The demands of the general public for instant relief from symptoms encourages the medical profession to give nystatin or miconazole cream to clear up local Candida infections, without clearing up the entire infection, so the Candida goes on to infect the cervix, prostate, intestines, sinuses, etc.

16. Reflexology, Chiropractic, and Massage: The increased use of foot reflexology without effective yeast disinfectants transfers Candida from the feet of infected patients to the feet of non-infected patients, while rubbing firmly implants the infection in the new host. Hard reflexology, foot rollers, and similar reflexology machines may abrade the tissues and increase the infection.

91

Ch.4. Reducing Candida Yeast Infection:

Chiropractors and massage parlors also pass fungal infections from the infected to the innocent through lack of effective disinfectants, and through lackof knowledge and concern.
 The author has repeatedly urged many of these practitioners to use hydrogen peroxide to disinfect their hands, but they only smile and say,"We wash well", while the upturned fingers and ridges and bumps in their fingernails are silent testimony that their "washing" did not prevent the Candida from infecting their fingers, and from their fingers to many parts of the body; both their own bodies, and to the bodies of others.

REDUCING CANDIDA YEAST INFECTION.
Candida yeast infection can never be completely cured because the organism cannot be completely eradicated. Candida yeast infects many other creatures (see List.1.) and it is therefore not confined to man. With a reservoir in nature, small amounts are constantly being re-introduced into the body from the natural reservoir. As these small amounts usually remain on the surface of the mucosa they are beyond the reach of the immune system and the bloodstream. Candida yeast, lying on the surfaces of the mucosa, in itself, does no harm, but it is continuously a constant threat waiting for circumstances; waiting for injury, surgery, or other infection or other trauma to provide an opportunity for the yeast to invade the tissues and set up an over growth colony. Once established, Candida breaks down body tissues and uses the materials, particularly magnesium, to re-synthesize an asmoresistant layer that protects the yeast and associated infectives from disinfectants and other forces outside the colony. In short, the outer layer of the callus itself is synthesized by the Candida, and the "skin" of the callus then protects the colony from outside forces, so the infective colony then becomes a "walled city" living in and off the host. It is this ability of the yeast to protect itself that makes Candida so difficult to reduce.
    It should be noted that Candida usually does not infect internal areas where it is completely surrounded by tissue. It usually forms a callus (soft or hard) on the surface of the skin as shown in Fig.2. The skin may be "internal"(as in the heart valves) or it may be external(as in the calluses on the feet). One side of the callus matrix (composed of many infectives) lies within active tissue, while the other side is "outside" the body and is protected by the re-synthesized asmoresistant layer. Any attempt to reduce the callus matrix with topical applications of anti-fungals is certain to meet with failure becaue the asmoresistant layer reduces the ability of the anti-fungals to reach all of the infectives, while any attempt to destroy the

callus matrix with anti-fungals injected into the bloodstream is certain to meet with failure because of the limited blood supply to the exterior part of the callus matrix. The only fully successful approach must therefore incorporate the use of both topical and systemic anti-fungals, together with improved nutrition, improved immune function, and a large amount of patience and perseverance. In all cases, everything must be done to improve all body functions, because usually, by the time the health has failed to the point of demanding attention, the Candida has invaded and colonized many places, and is probably everywhere.

Reducing Candida infection is a slow tedious process. When yeast and other fungii are killed with anti-fungals, bacteria and other friendly and unfriendly organisms in the infective matrix may thrive on the anti-fungals;- on the dead bodies of the infective; and on the dead and dying tissue of the host. Some of these other infectives will then replace the yeast, and carry on where the yeast left off, with only a change in symptoms for the unfortunate host. Similarly, reducing the bacteria and similar infectives will provide food and a home for increased yeast infection. To overcome this problem many different anti-infectives must be used on a rotational basis, and the infection must be reduced from both inside and outside: from both the bloodstream (systemic) and from direct applications to the callus matrix,(topical).

Candida has now been cultured from the fluid from male sexual cysts. Candida has also been found in a cyst in the elbow. The initiating cause of cysts is not known, but obviously they may be caused by some Candida related process. Again, the Candida, growing in body fluids, has isolated itself from the active body processes that normally destroy it. Candida also is frequently one of the infectives in sinus infection, where again it grows in the fluids, away from the defences of the body.

In setting up a yeast program it is important to assess all possible sites of infection. Any serious attack on the infection with systemic anti-fungals appears to cause the Candida to shed quantities of spores and hyphae, which clog the bloodstream and overload all body systems, with the resulting toxicity ("flu") reducing the ability of the body to resist infective growth, which results in very little final net gain. Topical anti-fungals have a similar, but lesser, effect on the bloodstream, and the program should therefore emphasize the direct application of anti-fungals to all sites of infection wherever possible. Systemic anti-fungals should also be used and the entire program should be adjusted to keep the rate of infective kill just below the toxic threshold, and always within the capacity of the body to re-build the damaged tissues.

Ch.4. Reducing Candida Yeast Infection:

Quite obviously the success of the program will depend largely upon the total health and strength of the body, which in turn is dependent upon nutrition. Many nutritionists will say that if you "Eat right", illness will never overtake you. That is not so. The body has a very limited, finite capacity, to deal with infectives, and if at any time the quantity of infectives exceeds the finite capacity of the immune system, the infective will overtake the body, and when this happens with Candida, a colony is established. The callus colony is then isolated from the immune system, with further spread of the infectives at every opportunity. Nutrition, however, is important to success, because there must be adequate nutrition not only for the normal body processes, but also adequate nutrients for the infectives; for combating the infectives; and for coping with the stress imposed by the infectives. That is a lot of Nutrition! That is a lot of extra nutrition, just to cope with the infective. Digestion requires large amounts of energy, and that is a lot of extra digestion, particularly when the digestion is impaired by infectives growing and living in the intestines. That is also a lot of extra elimination, particularly when the elimination is impaired by infectives growing in the colon. While the toxins being evacuated are particularly noxious.

Here then is the short sighted fallacy of the nutritional adage "We are what we eat". We are not "what we eat". We are "what we and our infectives eat". We are not alone. We will never be alone, and we will never be free from our infectives and their toxins. We can only hope to keep our infectives within the capacity of the body, so the body can deal with them. We can only hope to have a reasonably controlled infective balance, a balance variously referred to as "center of gravity","life force balance", the "ying and the yang" or, more properly, "living balance" or "homeostasis". In short if we can reduce the chronic infectives and improve the effectiveness of the immune system to the point that the body can deal effectively with the ever present infectives, the body itself will maintain homeostasis and health.

There are so many lectures, so many books and so many products devoted to "we are what we eat" and "we are what we do", yet all are so shortsighted that they fail to consider that the body is not pure, it is not alone, and there are and there always will be infectives. If you feed the body better, reduce stress, increase excerise, remove extra weight, etc; etc; the body will certainly respond, and many testimonials have been written on that response. Yet where infection has been firmly established it is only a matter of time until the infectives, also better nourished, will again overtake the host, and this time the extra vitamins and minerals and yoga and jogging will not help, because all systems are already at their maximum. Quite obviously, to start the body on a return path to health the infectives must be subdued and reduced, while at the same time all body functions must be brought up to maximum, and all of those body functions must be supported by maximum nutrition, adjusted to the entire requirement for both the body and the infectives.

There must be adequate protein for the normal operation of the body, and in addition, there must be more protein;- fully digested protein;- to support the immune system in its heroic efforts; and then there must be more good protein for rebuilding the damaged tissues, along with whatever protein the infectives may use. There must be adequate minerals to supply the requirements of the body, to rebuild the body, and yet more to supply the requirements of the infectives. There must be enough vitamins to supply the infectives together with extra vitamins for the immune system and the detoxification system and enough left over to meet normal body demands. There must be enough fatty acids for both the body and the infectives, and there must be enough carbohydrate to run the body with very little left over for the infectives.

The fact is that the total chronic infectives will frequently absorb, use up and tie up many nutrients long before the body has had an opportunity to use them. The awful truth is that whether we like it or not we must feed our unwelcome guests before we can feed ourselves. Still, if we can adjust the total program we can feed both the infectives and ourselves while slowly killing the infectives, and we can thus slowly reduce the total infection, frequently with a dramatic return to health.

An effective anti-fungal program therefore has to be a complete program that covers everything;- lifestyle, sleep, rest, exercise, sexual function, bowel function, urinary function, foods, beverages, digestion, mineral supplements, vitamin supplements, enzyme supplements, antibiotics, antifungals, disinfectants,--- everything! Yes, everything! Candida yeast can infect anything and everything in the body from the hair on the top of the head to the nail on the big toe, so to combat the Candida infection and its effects on the body, we must control everything;- all body systems; from the nail on the big toe to the hair on the top of the head.

Yes, the hair on the top of the head, head hair, is certainly the best place to start, because mineral tests by hair analysis, can be very revealing. Also, blood, good blood, or blood that is not good, circulates throughout the body from the top of the head to the big toe. Health is better if it is good red blood with everything just right, so extensive blood tests can also be very informative.

Ch.4. Reducing Candida Yeast Infection:

MINERAL TESTS with NUTRITIONAL EVALUATION.
Tests for the biological mineral content of the body are usually made by Atomic Absorption Spectroscopy of hair, nails, or other biological material. The tests are extremely technical, and the equipment is essentially the same as is used for testing rocks, soil, and metal alloys. Head hair is usually used because it is non invasive and the sample is easily acquired.

Mineral tests are usually made for calcium, magnesium, phosphorus, sodium, potassium, iron, copper, molybdenum, manganese, zinc, chromium, selenium, lithium, nickel, cobalt, vanadium, lead, mercury, cadmium, aluminum, and arsenic.

Our principal interest is in;-
1. The toxic metals, lead, mercury, cadmium, arsenic, aluminum, and vanadium.
2. Iron and copper, where high levels may be toxic, and where extremely low levels are disasterous.
3. Zinc, chromium, selenium, and manganese, that may be depleted by yeast infection.
4. Calcium and magnesium, and sodium and potassium, that are so essential to metabolic function.
5. Lithium, which controls sodium and the water balance, and is essential to the immune system, and to thyroid function.

The other minerals are important, but much less is known about them. High nickle can be toxic, but high nickle levels are usually associated with the use of tobacco, and the levels usually fall when the source is removed. Nickle can also come from stainless tooth crowns.

The mineral test results provide a computer printout that shows the actual mineral levels, the normal mineral levels, and the symptoms or illnesses associated with the abnormal mineral levels, together with suggestions for increasing or reducing the levels. Except for sodium ans potassium, mineral levels can be altered only very slowly.

The nutritional evaluation computes the total vitamins and minerals in the diet. In filling out the form the quantities and frequency of each food should be as accurate as possible. The usual meal should be dished up, and the actual quantities measured. The form should be filled out on the basis of the usual diet, with the intent of providing a proper measure of the average of foods actually consumed. The resulting computer printout, based on this information, will show the dietary changes and the extra supplements required to bring the metabolism back toward a normal state of health. However, the nutritional evaluation cannot and does not allow for the effects of chronic infection. Specifically then, if yeast infection is present, further adjustments must be made, but these adjustments should be added later, and only the changes shown in the computer printout should be used for an early start on improving metabolic function.

Ch.4. Reducing Candida Yeast Infection.

In addition to the suggestions in the computer printout, the following information may be useful:-

Toxic Minerals:

All toxic minerals, at any level, and all nutritional minerals that have reached toxic levels,impose a severe continuous strain on the adrenals and on all body processes, and they usually also affect the mind, with altered or aberrent behaviour. Health problems will remain until they are reduced.

Much has been written about "natural" chelators. Garlic, grapefruit, bananas, milk, vitamin C, (See Vit.C. Ch.4.), bioflavinoids, and sulphur compounds are commonly mentioned. These may have some chelating effects, but they are slow and largely ineffectual in reducing toxic metal levels. Chelation therapy, with intravenous EDTA is the preferable therapy, and has the further benefit of improving blood circulation. (See chelation therapy Ch.5). Oral EDTA can be used if intravenous infusions cannot be obtained. In all cases the source of the toxic metal should be found and removed.

Lead:-

High lead levels are frequently associated with yeast infection. Yeast infected tissue has much higher levels of lead than normal tissue from the same person. The yeast may have an affinity for lead, and may cause the body to absorb lead.

The Perils of High Mercury.(Ref.27):-

In all cases of high mercury heavy supplements of cysteine and vitamin C, with methionine and selenium, should be used in an effort to reduce the mercury burden. Normally mercury is very slowly excreted by the body, particularly if the diet includes eggs, nuts, or other sources of sulphur bearing amino acids.(Cysteine,methionine). Therefore if mercury is high, the source of the mercury must be diligently sought and removed. The usual sources are game birds, fish, or similar food sources; employment sources in chemical plants, industry or dental offices; or resorption of the mercury from silver amalgam fillings in the teeth. If mercury is high, it would be prudent to replace all amalgam fillings with plastic or cement. Mercury particularly affects the brain and central nervous system, (and therefore every part of the body), the kidneys, the heart and the vascular system, the endocrine system,(pituitary, adrenals, thyroid, etc.); the B and T lymphocytes in the immune system; the mouth tissues; and probably even the unborn fetus. There is now even evidence that mercury may be stored in the body (probably in the nervous system) without high levels showing up in the hair. Anyone with health problems should therefore consider changing their amalgam fillings to plastic or cement. The presence of mercury in the body can usually be proven with 500 mg. Cysteine, followed by urine testing for mercury excretion.

The Perils of Silver Amalgam Tooth Fillings.(Ref.27,28).

In the early days of dentistry the poisonous effects of mercury were well recognized, (The mad hatter), and in some places the use of mercury amalgam fillings, of silver and gold was completely prohibited. Yet mercury amalgam was so simple and effective that dentistry flourished with the use of mercury amalgam. Nonetheless mercury is very poisonous to the body, and should not have been used and still should not be used, because mercury is particulary poisonous to the nervous system. It therefore affects the brain, and through interference with nerve function can affect the function of every other part of the body. It also directly affects the many hormones, including sex hormones. Mercury also now appears to be one of the causitive factors in Addison's disease, Lupus Erthematosis, Hodgkins Disease, Leukemia, and Multiple Sclerosis. There is reason to think that perhaps some of the toxins or metabolites produced by Candida yeast (or associated infectives) induce resorption of the mercury from tooth fillings, and load the body with mercury. If mercury finally proves to be one of the causative factors in M.S. (and similar diseases) it will finally explain the cause of the rapid degeneration of the nervous system, and it will also explain why so many M.S. symptoms are the same as the symptoms of mercury poisoning.

The principal problem in multiple sclerosis now appears to be both the mercury, and the inability of the body to excrete mercury, with the source of the mercury usually being dental fillings. This failure of the body to excrete even small amounts of mercury may result from a dietary lack of eggs or nuts or other sources of methionine or cysteine, or it may be somehow linked to toxins or metabolites from chronic infectives, but without normal mercury excretion the slowly resorbed mercury from the reservoir in the tooth fillings (or other source) slowly builds up in the nervous system, and perhaps also in the other tissues. It now appears that high mercury can exist with only very low levels showing up in the hair.

It has frequently been said that all causes of an affliction should not be judged by a single case. While this is unquestionably true, it is also true that if one single case is cured, then all cases may have a similar basic cause.

In one case of M.S., reducing the Candida component reduced associated allergies and was of great benefit, but problems remained, including very high blood pressure, and high copper. The mineral test showed mercury as being very low, and mercury did not show up in the blood or urine, yet the symptoms still resembled mercury or other metal poisoning.Large amounts of cysteine were then used in an attempt to reduce the copper, but instead of copper, mercury appeared in the urine, indicating that a mercury burden was sequestered somewhere. Cysteine was therefore continued along with large amounts of vitamin C. and other supplements; the amalgam fillings were removed and were replaced with cement; and ketoconazole was continued to reduce the fungal infection. The skin cleared, copper levels dropped, blood pressure returned to normal, menstruation (which had been absent for six years) returned; twenty pounds of overweight vanished, and the multiple sclerosis disappeared. Some Candida calluses on the feet still remain, but they too are rapidly diminishing. The body has been freed from its toxic load, and it is now ahead of its infectives, so health returns.

The point is that amalgam fillings should not have been used, and still should not be used. Mercury is poisonous to most living organisms, and that is why it is used in Mercurichrome. If there are persistent health problems of any kind, have the amalgam fillings changed. They may well be a principal cause of the ill health.

Now of course it is very easy to say "Change the Amalgam fillings", but it may be much easier to be said, than done, so compromises should be explored.

Corrosion of metals occurs through ionic galvanic action. That is to say, any two metals that are not alike will form a battery if immersed in a solution that is alkaline or acid. The solution is called electrolyte. The body fluids are also called electrolytes (the electrolyte balance) because most body processes are electrical in nature. In galvanic action, easily corroded metals will give higher voltages and stronger currents. All batteries work on this principal of dissimilar metals immersed in electrolyte. As you know, when the metal plates of a battery are connected to a light bulb or a radio, an electric current flows and operates the equipment. But current also flows within the battery, where ions are released by the metal and flow into the electrolyte fluid. The flow of ions from the metal into the electrolyte solution is the basic principle of galvanic action and galvanic corrosion. In dry batteries (flashlight batteries), the zinc is consumed and moves into the fluid electrolyte. A steel ship, floating in an electrolyte of sea water, will rust and corrode very rapidly if it is not protected by zinc anodes, which are installed on the sides. Then the zinc moves into the electrolyte, instead of the steel. Also the hot water tank in your house is protected from corrosion in a similar way, by the installation of a magnesium anode, which is slowly consumed by galvanic action, and moves into the electrolyte (water) that you drink.

Now it becomes clear that with the installation of metals in your teeth, your body fluids immediately become the electrolyte of a short-circuited battery, with the metallic ions from the fillings moving into the electrolyte of the body fluids. Candida yeast infection metabolizes sugars to lactic acid. The increased acidity of the electrolyte increases the rate of metallic movement into the body fluids. Easily corroded metals, like mercury, move into the electrolyte fluids more rapidly than "noble" metals like gold or silver, and much more rapidly than "hard" metals like stainless steel, so the mercury moves out of the amalgam by galvanic action and moves into the body fluids to alter nerve function, leaving the unbonded silver particles to fall off and expose more amalgam.

Oh Yes! The mercury moves out of the tooth fillings and into the body fluids to affect nerve functions! So just to make you feel better about your amalgam fillings just note that nerve synapses also function on tiny cycles of galvanic action. When a neuron "fires" it generates enough voltage to overcome the static nerve synapse voltage of about 400 milivolts. Now Dr.Roy Kupsinel,M.D., to his great credit, points out that Dr.Hardy has measured dental amalgams with voltages as high as 600 milivolts, which could certainly send many extraneous shock waves to many parts of the nervous system, particularly with the sharp changes produced by eating.

Removal of the amalgam fillings is therefore highly advisable, yet to be practical some metal may have to remain. If so, to minimize galvanic action all fillings should be made of the same material, and should be as non-corrosive as possible. The first choice would be gold, and the second choice would be hard pressed silver crowns. Hopefully the use of metals could be avoided if your dentist uses some of the new materials like the 3M P-10, or the 3M P-30.

Your dentist of course may be unbelieving and un-coperative. Take him a copy of Reference 2B. If he remains unconvinced, you should certainly see a different dentist. To avoid acute symptoms with removal of amalgam fillings, the suggestions in Reference 2B. should be closely followed.

MERCURY POISONING and CANDIDA INFECTION.

All of the foregoing is based on the research and findings of others, who may not have considered the effects of Candida infection, which appears to increase the density of the electrolyte, and thus increases the voltage and mercury leaching. Amalgam and metal dental filling voltages can be measured with a good sensitive voltmeter, either vacuum tube or FET (Field effect transister), preferably with a needle readout, which is more stable and less confusing than a LED readout.

Ch.4. Reducing Candida Yeast Infection:

A typical voltmeter, is the Sanwa SH-83 TR. Disposable probes can be made from short pieces of plastic insulated wire. (solid core). Present cost in Canada is about $50.00. In our experience so far, after Candida has been reduced and body systems are reasonably stable, amalgam voltages will be very low, and will rarely exceed 10 millivolts, and stainless crowns will seldom exceed 5 millivolts. These very low voltages would have very little effect on the nervous system, and the amount of mercury leaching would also be very low. Many people with a large number of mercury fillings remain healthy, and do not have signs of mercury toxicity.

In general, it appears that if health is low it would be prudent to slowly change all amalgam fillings, but if health and function are reasonably good and if filling voltages are low, there would seem to be little cause for panic, particularly if the diet contains eggs or other sources of cysteine to remove any small amounts of mercury from any source. Future fillings, however, should be plastic or cement, with gold or stainless crowns used as a last resort.

Further to the foregoing, one must of course speculate that perhaps the altered electrolytes associated with Candida infection and with leaching of mercury from amalgam fillings may also be the actual initiating factor in the dental cavities that made the amalgam fillings necessary. In short, perhaps Ketoconazole and other anti-fungals would be much more effective than flouride to make everybody say, "Look Mother, no cavities!" Then, considering that fluoride does in fact reduce cavities, and considering that fluoride is very poisonous to most living organisms, we must further speculate that perhaps the reduction in cavities from the use of fluoride actually derives from the ability of the fluoride to destroy fungii. Perhaps fluoride is just a very potent local anti-fungal that the body incorporates into the tooth enamel.

Mercury and Arsenic Chelation. (Ref.12.):

EDTA, in many forms, including NaEDTA,(which is commonly used for intravenous calcium chelation), will pick up lead and heavy metals, but it will not successfully pick up mercury or arsenic.

British Anti-Lewisite, (B.A.L.), (Dimercaprol, U.S.P.), (2,3 dimercapto proanol) was originally developed for the armed forces to reduce accidental arsenic poisoning. It is also effective against mercury. It is given by intra-muscular (IM) injection. It is not effective against other forms of metal poisoning. Dr.Hardy reports that there is now a new chelator, N.A.P., which is highly effective against mercury. Penicillamine (cuprimine) is an effective mercury chelator.

Chemical chelation of mercury can usually be avoided by using large quantities of vitamin C. with 500 mg. cysteine and 100 mcg. selenium, twice daily.

A very small amount of arsenic is essential for health. If arsenic is high, the source must be sought. The most common sources are poisons for weeds and insects.

Mercury and the Thyroid.

The test for low thyroid is low basal body temperature. (See Low Thyroid Function, Ch.4.). One of the tests for mercury poisoning is also basal temperature. It must then be presumed that the mercury reduces the basal temperature by interfering with the thyroid. Therefore, if basal temperature is low, mercury should be checked and reduced, with appropriate adjustments to thyroid supplements if necessary.

Cadmium.

High cadmium frequently results from low metabolic zinc. Zinc has a very wide range, therefore if cadmium is high zinc should be supplemented. Yeast has a high affinity for zinc, and can produce zinc depletion. Reducing yeast infection will help to restore zinc levels, but, until the yeast infection is reduced, zinc should be appropiately supplemented, particularly in the male.

High Aluminum.

High aluminum can be associated with senility, forgetfulness, and other mental problems. All sources of aluminum must be removed. There is no specific treatment for reducing aluminum levels but heavy supplements of magnesuim, with about $\frac{1}{2}$ as much calcium will slowly reduce the aluminum levels. (See also Alzheimers Disease. Ch.7.)

High Iron.

High yeast infection can use up so much iron that the host becomes anemic, but the altered metabolism from chronic infectives can also induce the body to store iron, with the high tissue levels resembling iron siderosis. Alcoholism, or other liver problems are frequently a contributing factor. Intravenous chelation may help to reduce the high tissue levels. Oral chelation can also be very useful but should be started very cautiously to clear the liver. High iron levels tend to fall toward normal with reduced yeast infection and improved health. All possible sources of metabolic iron should be sought and removed, with particular attention to wine, red wine, or acidic foods or drinks stored in iron or glazed pottery containers.

High blood levels of iron, indicative of iron siderosis, are usually treated by bleeding, but unless hair levels are also high, bleeding should be minimal.

Ch.4. Reducing Candida Yeast Infection:

Low Iron.

Low iron levels may be associated with pernicious anemia and loss of intrinsic factor. B12 levels can be raised with injections. Folic acid should be supplemented, along with niacin and chelated or organically bound iron. Your doctor is well acquainted with pernicious anemia, and he can usually raise iron levels. In desperation iron levels can be raised with a teaspoon, twice daily of red wine kept in a soft iron container. If blood levels of iron are acceptable, tissue levels will usually rise when yeast infection is reduced.

High Copper.

High copper is extremely toxic to many body systems. It can produce severe neurosis and phychosis and other mental effects. Sources of copper should be removed and distilled water should be used. Particular attention should be given to elimination of soya products. All female contraceptives or drugs that alter sex hormones must also be eliminated. High copper levels can be slowly reduced with high supplements of bioflavinoids (particularly rutin) above 250 mg. daily, together with high supplements of manganese and zinc, (even if they are already adequate) and heavy supplements of vitamin C, (8 gm. or more daily). High copper is also involved in low spermine/spermadine ratios. (See Spermine/Spermadine).

High levels of copper also induce high blood pressure and the high blood pressure will persist as long as copper levels remain high.

Sodium and Potassium:-(See also Adrenal Depletion).

Altered levels of sodium and potassium are usually indicative of high levels of stress with consequent adrenal depletion. The stress can come almost entirely from within the body if yeast and chronic infection is high.

Functionally, the body always tends to be short in potassium. Sodium is so plentiful and potassium is so scarce that the sodium overwhelms the potassium. Also the body excretes potassium and retains sodium, while stress, in any form, causes potassium excretion.

It appears that if mineral tests show low potassium or low sodium, the minerals are not there and the levels must be raised. If the tests show sodium or potassium as being high, the minerals are most certainly there, but they may be sequestered in the tissues (and therefore inactive), or they may be part of an obscure aberrant metabolic process. High levels of sodium are frequently associated with lead, yeast infection, and/or calcinosis, and/or low hormone levels. Histamine may therefore have a role in sodium excretion and retention. Histamine is of course linked to the basophil and mast cells, and therefore to the lymphatic system, so the function of the lymphatics may also be linked to sodium retention. Exercise is the only thing that successfully works the lymphatic pump, and exercise must therefore become part of the program to reduce sodium levels. Exercise, with sweating, will also reduce the sodium in the lymphatic system, and tissues. But how can anyone exercise effectively when the adrenals are so depleted that the person is so continuously tired that they can hardly stand? The adrenals are always dependent upon active metabolic potassium, and high potassium levels sometimes seen in the hair may not be biologically active.

Thus the continuous potassium problem is really a viscious circle. To reduce sodium we must always reduce sodium intake, but this is only to prevent excessive sodium overload. Normally the adrenal glands (whose function is dependent on potassium) together with the kidneys, will regulate the sodium balance. Sodium in the food is so much in excess that many healthy people excrete 80% to 90% of the sodium in their diet. Sodium levels, then, are not dietary, they are metabolic, and the metabolism is dependent upon potassium. But if stress is high or continous (as with chronic infection) so much potassium is excreted that every cell in the body becomes filled with sodium, followed by water, and the resulting low metabolic and body function then itself becomes a stress, with even further adrenal depletion, and potassium excretion. With the severe loss of potassium, the adrenals are then unable to restore normal function, and health continues to deteriorate.

Large amounts of potassium would then appear to be the answer, but potassium supplements, supplied under these conditions, will have little effect because, although the potassium is absorbed, the aldosterone is not suppressed, and the loss of potassium with the aldosterone may exceed the amount of potassium that is absorbed. The attempt to raise the potassium levels thus may result in an actual net loss to the body cells. The important point is that sodium, taken simultaneously with the potassium, will suppress the production of aldosterone, and the potassium will then enter and remain in the body cells, and adrenal function will be improved. The extra sodium, that must be taken with the potassium even when sodium levels are very high, is not of consequence because the actual sodium levels are not determined by intake, but by kidney and adrenal function, while the adrenals are dependent upon the potassium that cannot be absorbed and retained without supplementing both sodium and potassium simultaneously.

The altered sodium and/or potassium levels therefore do not result from diet. They are metabolic, and they will return normal with reduction in infection, improved metabolic ly function, and exercise.

Ch.4. Reducing Candida Yeast Infection.

The hair mineral test is therefore very useful for sodium and potassium, because it points to the state of adrenal function, and adrenal function largely determines the state of health.

Potassium is so essential to adrenal function, and is so essential to every cell in the body, and yet is so easily excreted and is so difficult to replace, that potassium can be considered the key to health, and sodium, supplied simultaneously with the potassium can be considered the key to success in raising and maintaining the potassium levels so essential to health.

Sodium and Potassium Supplements:

Altered levels of sodium and potassium are usually indicative of high levels of stress with consequent adrenal depletion, which may produce psychosis, leading to further stress and even more adrenal depletion. The stress may come almost entirely fom within the body if chronic infection is high. Salt should be slowly removed from the diet. Salt substitutes might be used sparingly, but read the labels carefully. A salt substitute of sodium --potassium chloride (as suggested by Adelle Davis) used sparingly will flavor the diet and will help to raise potassium levels. Potassium chloride seems to be invasive to tissues and should therefore be used sparingly.

Bananas: are high in potassium and have sufficient sodium to be helpful in raising potassium levels, but they also contain the poison vanillin (vanilla) which must be detoxified by the body. Bananas are also very high in almost pure carbohydrate that will readily feed yeast and other infectives, and may increase problems for diabetics or hypoglycemics. One half of a banana is usually excellent.

Tomatoes: are excellent if they do not trigger allergies. They are another good source of potassium. They are also high in vitamin C, but they are also one of the nightshades, and as such they contain small amounts of nightshade poison (particularly if they are green). which the body must detoxify, and which may produce allergies in people with a defective or overloaded immune system. The nightshade poison seems to be effective against yeast, so tomatoes are excellent if they do not trigger allergies.

V8 Juice: has about the right ratio of sodium/potassium, It is usually well tolerated although there is still some nightshade poison from the tomato juice. V8 juice is more effective if it is fortified with about 1/3 teaspoon of sodium/potassium tartrate. (From your druggist, if you really insist). Two or three glasses daily will help to raise the potassium levels, but start the tartrate slowly, otherwise water may be eliminated so rapidly that diarrhea may result, and the potassium and all of your B vitamins will leave with the diarrhea.

Sodium Potassium Ascorbate, seems to be the preferred way to raise potassium levels. This can be provided with Energen C with about $\frac{1}{4}$ tablet of Redoxon added, or with Hi KC Fizz. (Ch.4.). A close substitute would be chelated potassium taken with Redoxon or taken with Webber or Stanley chewable vitamin C tablets that contain sodium ascorbate.

Other Principal Adrenal / Immune Nutrients, are pantothenic acid, B6, calcium/magnesium, lipotropics (choline, inositol, methionine) and sunflower oil,(or equal).

With improved adrenal function the hair levels of potassium will return toward normal, and sodium may also return to normal or it may remain high. These high sodium levels seem to be linked to calcinosis, with the sodium somehow being sequestered in the tissues along with the calcium. The high sodium may also be linked to an altered degree of thirst, because people with high sodium levels usually drink far less than the magic 8 glasses of water per day. However, when calcinosis is reduced the desire for fluids will increase, and sodium levels will fall toward normal.

Lithium-Sodium Balance.

Lithium is one of the principal controls of sodium and sodium retention. It appears that Candida uses up large amounts of lithium, so in all cases of edema, or severe adrenal depletion low supplements (150 mg./day or less) of lithium should be tried.

Lithium.

Lithium is absolutely essential for the function of the thyroid, (see Thyroid, Ch.5.) for the immune system, the brain, sodium balance and probably many more body functions.The mineral tests are always ambiguous, because they all seem to be at the low end of what is considered as normal. Lithium should always be tried if thyroid or immune function is low.(See blood test). Lithium must be supplemented slowly and cautiously to avoid extreme mental effects. Lithium orotate is a preferred form.

Zinc.

Zinc is absolutely essential for many metabolic functions, and it is particularly essential in maintaining sex hormone levels. Females need zinc and males need more zinc. Zinc has a very wide margin of safety. Extra supplements of zinc will help to reduce high levels of cadmium, copper,lead,and heavy metals. Adequate zinc will also help to prevent the retention of lead and heavy metals. Zinc is so essential for the function of the eukaryotic cells of which both Candida and man are composed that a high Candida infection will use up and tie up so much zinc that the host becomes zinc depleted. This is one of the reasons that high copper levels and high lead levels are so ntly associated with Candida infection.

Ch.4. Reducing Candida Yeast Infection:

CALCIUM/MAGNESIUM.
(See also Calcium/Magnesium and Calcinosis,and Low Parathyroid)

Calcium and magnesium do have separate roles in human function, but they are so interdependent that they are usually supplemented together.

If calcium or magnesium are high or low, abnormal metabolism should be suspected, and blood levels should be checked. Low blood proteins are usually caused by poor absorption from low blood calcium. (Despite perhaps high tissue levels). Low blood calcium, in turn, is frequently caused by lack of vitamin D.(as in rickets). To raise calcium, magnesium must also be supplemented. For magnesium to be effective, vitamin B6 must be supplied. To raise calcium then, magnesium, B6, and vitamin D must be supplied along with calcium.

Now we again enter a metabolic cycle problem. Yeast infection contributes to calcinosis, with low blood levels of calcium, and calcium stored in the tissues. To reduce the yeast infection, we must use Ketoconazole, which attacks the fungus by blocking the metabolic synthesis of ergosterol. Vitamin D3 is produced in the body by the irradiation of ergosterol in exposed skin. Ergosterol is the sterol that is essential to the function of plant cells, just as cholesterol is essential to the function of animal cells. If Ketoconazole is used to reduce the Candida, it also inactivates the vitamin D, resulting in low absorption of calcium, which reduces absorption of the proteins so essential to immune function and so essential to the rebuilding of body tissues. The low calcium also produces osteoporosis and brittle bones (rickets) and reduces the ability of the bone marrow to produce the precursors of red and white blood cells.

Ketoconazole therefore kills the Candida, but at the same time it also slowly reduces the effectiveness of the immune system. Ketoconazole is completely excreted in about 26 hours. It appears that the most effective way to preserve calcium metabolism while taking ketoconazole would be to take the ketoconazole without calcium and vitamin D for a week, and then supplement the calcium, magnesium, B6, and vitamin D for a week, while off the ketoconazole.

Low levels of magnesium are also frequently seen in people with high Candida infections. The nutritional rule is to always supplement calcium with magnesium, to keep them in balance, but in cases where the magnesium is low and Candida is present, extra magnesium can be supplemented with distinct advantage, because the low magnesium almost certainly results from Candida using the magnesium from the body to form and maintain the asmoresistant layer that appears as thickened skin over the calluses.

Ch.4.Reducing Candida Yeast Infection.

Even when calcium/magnesium appears adequate, every Candida program should include calcium with B6, vitamin D, and extra magnesium.

Nutritional Chelators.

All citrus friuts, and grapefruit in particular are natural chelators, that strip minerals from the body. Anyone on a diet high in grapefruit or other citrus fruits must take a good multi-mineral supplement or they will ultimately suffer the consquences of severely depleted minerals.

Vitamin C, as ascorbic acid, is a natural chelator of minerals, particularly if used in large quantities with bioflavinoids. Anyone requiring high amounts of vitamin C,(above 3 grams per day), should either take multi-mineral supplements, or they should get the extra vitamin C as mineral ascorbates. (See also Ascorbate, Ch.4.)

BLOOD TESTS.

To effectively reduce Candida yeast infection all body systems must be fully functional. Good blood tests, as in Fig.7. will reveal functions that are weak or abnormal.

Appropriate wholistic measures should be taken to slowly correct abnormal functions. Drugs should be used only if absolutely necessary because many of the abnormal functions will be infection related. Do not rush into everything all at once. Make changes one at a time to reduce the risk of hidden problems. The altered functions that you see did not happen overnight. The changes may have taken many years, so you cannot expect to return altered functions to normal in a few days. The object of the tests is to show the various directions that therapy should take, so that the general pattern can be directed back towards health.

The results of these tests may require more tests, e.g.,liver or pancreas scans,etc. The value of your doctor, and the value of these tests should not be under-estimated. You, and he, are looking for the root causes of your ill health. You can attempt to deal with those root causes only if they are identified.

BLOOD MICROSCOPY.

If blood microscopy is available, both darkfield and light field colored photos should be taken. You will recognize poor blood when you see it. People with Candida infection usually have malformed and obviously damaged red blood cells, with large numbers of cells clumped together in rouleaus. Crystal bodies, (as if the cells were embedded in gelatin) rods, and L forms, characteristic of progenitor cryptocides, may be seen with the Darkfield microscope, and are usually associated with Candida infection. The crystal bodies, rods and L forms and rouleaus can be reduced with calcium chelation therapy. Rouleaus can also be reduced with niacin.

XX COMPLETE PARTIAL TEST

CHEMSCAN 25 #:
- GLUCOSE
- SODIUM
- POTASSIUM
- CHLORIDE
- CO2
- ION GAP (NA-(CL+CO2))
- UREA NITROGEN (BUN)
- CREATININE
- BUN/CREAT
- URIC ACID
- CALCIUM
- PHOSPHORUS
- IONIZED CALCIUM,CALCULATE
- TOTAL PROTEIN
- ALBUMIN
- GLOBULIN
- ALBUMIN/GLOBULIN
- ALKALINE PHOSPHATASE
- GAMMA GT
- SGOT(AST)
- SGPT (ALT)
- LACTIC DEHYDROGENASE
- TOTAL BILIRUBIN
- CHOLESTEROL
- TRIGLYCERIDES

THYROID PROFILE I:
- T4 RIA
- T3 UPTAKE
- FTI

CBC:
- WBC
- RBC
- HEMOGLOBIN
- HEMATOCRIT
- MCV
- MCH
- MCHC
- NEUTROPHILS, SEGMENTED
- LYMPHOCYTES
- MONOCYTES
- EOSINOPHILS
- BASOPHILS
- PLATELET ESTIMATION
- SEDIMENTATION RATE

**VALUES ARE ADULT HUMAN UNLESS OTHERWISE

XX COMPLETE PARTIAL TEST OUT

URINALYSIS ADD-ON:
- COLOR/APPEARANCE
  - *YELLOW/HAZY
- SPECIFIC GRAVITY
- UROBILINOGEN
- OCCULT BLOOD
- BILIRUBIN
- KETONES
- GLUCOSE
- PROTEIN
- PH
- WBC, URINE
- RBC, URINE
- EPITHELIAL CELLS
- CRYSTALS
- BACTERIA
- NITRITE
- WBC SCREEN

CORONARY RISK PROFILE:
- SERUM APPEARANCE
- HDL CHOLESTEROL
- LDL CHOLESTEROL
- CORONARY RISK INDICATOR

These are the usual Blood/Urine tests used by Dr. Kimmel, Bellingham,Wash.before intravenous calcium chelation.

Fig.7. BLOOD/URINE TESTS.

**VALUES ARE ADULT HUMAN UNLESS OTHERWISE S

Blood Pressure. (See also Blood Pressure,Ch.7.).
Blood pressure should be taken several days apart, active and resting, standing and lying down. This will give a general average. Blood pressure is never constant, it is always varying up and down.

People with known circulatory problems will have, and should have, slightly elevated blood pressure. Depleted zinc will always raise blood pressure. Zinc is very safe and can always be supplemented. Overweight and edema (see lithium) will raise blood pressure. There are many "normals" for blood pressure. The generally accepted normals are; High--140/80 or higher:Normal--120/80: Low-- 100/60 or less. Some books show; Normal--systolic--120 to 130. Normal diastolic-- 80 to 90. The first number is the systolic or maximum pressure that the heart exerts on the blood and blood vessels. The second number is the diastolic or resting pressure in the blood vessels.

There is great confusion and much controversy about normal blood pressure, how and when it should be measured, the readings that are considered normal, and the significance of abnormal readings for both systolic and diastolic pressure.Some doctors consider the systolic pressure as being of the greatest importance, others consider the diastolic pressure as being of the greatest importance, while some other doctors say that it is the difference between the systolic and diastolic that is of greatest importance, and other doctors pay little attention to the specific pressures unless they are extremely high, or extremely low. In an attempt to establish reference figures that would be of value, the author discussed blood pressure with the Heart Fund, who, of course, have for many years been pleased to accept donations for further "heart research". One might of course be deluded into thinking that some definitive figures had by now been established, but they could not give specific values. Their answers were always vague,--"See your doctor," but when pressed they finally admitted that they spent $70,000.00 on a blood survey at Powell River, and the variations in health and blood pressure were so great that it was impossible to make any conclusions or recommendations of any kind.

Even Scientific American Medical LIbrary recognizes hypertension, and tells how to treat it, yet fails to properly define it, because everything has to be subjectively evaluated with the other problems of the patient. They do say that even small increases in blood pressure carry substantial risk, yet exact figures are so elusive that they finally define blood pressure on the basis of those levels that carry a greater than 50% increase in mortality. Their figures; Men, below age 45,130/90. Men over 45, 140/95. All women, 160/95.

In another view, systolic hypertension exists if the systolic pressure is greater than "the diastolic pressure, minus 15, multiplied by 2. e.g.man over 45,diastolic 95. Maximum systolic is 95-15=80,X2=160, to give 160/95.

Now there are two types of hypertension; primary hypertension for which there is no known cause, and secondary hyperetension for which there are known causes, and which can be "managed" with surgery or drugs. Turned around, this seems to say that if a cause can be found it is termed secondary hypertension, and if a cause is not obvious it becomes primary hypertension.

The fact is that there are so many variables in the control of blood pressure that if the blood pressure remains quite steady at about 140/70, or a little less, good health is indicated, but if blood pressure is abnormally high or very low, malfunction of heart, kidney, renin, adrenals (aldosterone), blood vessels, baroreceptor reflexes, central nervous system, adrenal medulla (catacholamines), and other associated hormones etc; is indicated. These are the interdependent factors, with each affecting the other by neat little chemical feedbacks. So when you or your doctor tinkers with one, you tinker with all. Quite obviously tinkering with drugs or surgery can be dangerous. The effects from caffeine and other self administered poisons are obvious. The toxic effects of mercury (perhaps from tooth fillings), and from high copper and other metals is obvious. The possible role of toxins and metabolites from chronic infectives also becomes very obvious, and the benefits of adrenal nutrients and supernutrition can be clearly seen.

Most certainly, extremely low blood pressure is devastating to adrenal function and to all other body systems, while extremely high blood pressure does present hazards of stroke or herart attack.

The best suggestion seems to be that the present status should be maintained. If drugs are not taken, their use should be avoided if possible. If drugs are being used their use should be continued, blood pressure should be monitored, and the amount of drugs should be reduced to as little as possible. Improvements in blood pressure can then be used to judge improvements in metabolic function. When adrenal function has improved and the effects of Candida infection have been reduced, and when normal mineral levels have been restored, blood pressure too, will probably be back to normal.

It should be particularly reiterated that the entire blood pressure controversy is centered around the old fallacy of seeing the symptoms as the disease. Altered blood pressure is, and always will be, only a symptom; a definite expression of the body that something else is wrong. Obviously, to tinker with the symptom will not alter or correct the cause. The cause can be any one, or any combination, of many things, including hormone disturbances and toxins or toxic substances.

It follows then that blood pressure drugs are entirely wrong because they only tinker with the symptoms, while the cause continues, so the only way to restore normal blood pressure is to correct all of the possible causes;-- specifically by "doing everything".

THE FAITHFUL LIVER.

The following newspaper column shows the importance of full liver function in all health programs.

6 BURNABY TIMES

Return to Health

By RUPERT BEEBE

(All material in this column is taken from apparently reliable sources and is presented as information only. Your physician has the sole and only right to diagnose and prescribe.)

THE LIVER has other functions than just detoxifying poisons and producing bile. It is also a storage depot for blood, a storage depot for vitamins and body starch, and a vital process partner with many other organs and systems.

All nutrients from the intestines are screened by the liver before they reach the circulatory bloodstream. Toxins and poisons are removed by the liver, and appropriate enzymes and co-enzymes are added. Therefore good food may be eaten, digested, and assimilated, yet if the liver enzyme system fails the foods cannot be utilized, body cells will be starved for nutrients, and all body systems will suffer from malnutrition.

Similarly Vitamin E may be well supplied, but the blood may lose its clotting factor if the liver fails to produce prothrombin.

Proteins too may well be supplied, but if the liver fails to break them into amino acids the body will waste away.

The pancreas is always said to be at fault in hypoglycemia, but if the liver fails to produce insulinase the low blood sugar and poor health will continue.

Diet is always used to control weight, but if the liver fails to manufacture the urine production hormones the excess weight may be from an enlarged liver, or from retention of fluid in the tissues or the abdominal cavity, (Ascites).

When the liver fails to inactivate the thyroid hormone, the hormone will accumulate and may force the body into such a frenzy of activity that the stress depletes the adrenals.

Failure of the liver to detoxify the appropriate sex hormones may result in impotence or frigidity, or in partial sex changes, perhaps with homosexuality. Women may grow beards, and men may develop enlarged breasts, and perhaps also the sloping shoulders and wider hips of the female figure.

The principal cause of liver damage is alcohol and the junk food diet of soft drinks, sugar, refined carbohydrate, and saturated fats. Caffeine, (tea, coffee, cola, and chocolate) tobacco, all drugs, and particularly antibiotics contribute to liver damage.

Fortunately the liver can be rebuilt with food supplements and a high protein diet. Liver, as raw as possible, should be eaten daily. Adelle Davis suggests supplements of amino acids, nucleic acids, iodine (8 drops), Vitamin A (up to 100,000 units), brewers yeast (2 tablespoons per meal), eggs or egg yolks (for sulfur), Vit. C (2 gms.), Vit. E, B complex, and particularly ample amounts of lecithin, cholin., panto thenic acid, magnesium and zinc.

Ch.4. Reducing Candida Yeast Infection.

Liver Tests. (See also Ketoconazole).
 Liver tests are of particular importance to the Candida program.
If the tests indicate poor liver function, or if there are any
other liver related problems, an ultrasonic scan of the liver
and bile duct may be of help.
 Ketoconazole is an oral anti-fungal agent that is the
cornerstone of Candida therapy. Many short-term studies have
been made on the effects of ketoconazole, and none of these
studies indicate liver damage, yet long term use of ketoconazole
may reduce liver function if it is not taken on a rotating basis.
People with impaired liver and/or gall bladder function should
use all anti-infectives with caution, and should be retested
peroidically to avoid liver damage.
Liver Injections.
 Liver function can be raised with supernutrition including
ample ascorbate, liver injections, (plexalin) and daily consumption
of liver or liver concentrate. Thin slices of frozen raw liver
are an almost tasteless source for liver supplement. Raw liver
must be from healthy animals only. Do not eat raw pork liver.
The Liver and Feeling Cold and Chilly.
 Body energy reserves are maintained by the storage of
sugars in the liver in the form of glycogen. If liver function
is impaired the amount of stored glycogen is low, which may
result in a drop in blood sugar levels about two hours after the
meal, followed by a drop in body core temperature, perhaps
with impaired digestion and a feeling of being cold and chilly
"in the middle of the back", a feeling that can be only partially
reduced with extra clothes or extra heat. These chilly episodes
can be alleviated by including one ot two slices of whole wheat
bread with all meals to prolong carbohydrate digestion and
thus reduce the need for liver energy storage until liver function
can be improved.
Amino-Acid Tests.
 Tests for low amino acids may also be of value to determine
the state of digestion and assimilation. Amino acid tests are
usually supplied by the labs that supply hair mineral tests. Amino
acids should be appropriately supplemented until digestion and
assimilation are improved. (See also calcium and magnesium).
Citric Acid-Aspartic Acid Supplementation.
 From the Philpott Medical Center.(See Ref.6).
There is evidence from the amino acid profile that
alpha-ketoglutaric acid is likely the most deficient demonstrated
substance in degenerative diseases,either physical or mental.
Alpha-ketoglutaric acid is used as a cofactor in a number of
enzyme steps associated with B6. It is also the precursor to
glutamic acid, which is demonstrated to quite routinely be low.

Ch.4. Reducing Candida Yeast Infection.

Glutamic acid is necessary as a mechanism of detoxifying the brain of ammonia when glutamic acid is turned into glutamine. The net result of low glutamic acid and low alpha-ketoglutaric acid would be that of symptom production, especially weakness. Aspartic acid ties the citric acid cycle to the urea cycle, thus when the function of the citric acid cycle is improved by raising alpha-ketoglutaric acid by giving its citric acid precursor, then it is possible to favorably influence the urea cycle by providing aspartic acid. The net result of increasing urea cycle metabolism is that of the body's increased capacity to detoxify ammonia through the production of urea. Also, stepping up the function of the urea cycle at this junction bypasses the ornithine step. The amino acid profile reveals that ornithine is often high and is the area in which there is a block in urea cycle metabolism. Thus, by providing citric acid and aspartic acid, we help to bypass this disorder of high ornithine with a block between ornithine and citrulline.

A usual satisfactory combination is that of 750 mg. of citric acid and 500 mg. of aspartic acid taken in the morning on arising, with each meal and at bedtime. Occasionally, there are those who feel uncomfortable with this much acid taken, especially with meals, such as in the morning on arising and in the evening on going to bed. This can be handled by taking 10 grains of a combined sodium potassium bicarbonate capsule or $\frac{1}{4}$ teaspoon of sodium bicarbonate.

For those cases in which aspartic acid is already higher than normal on the amino acid profile, the combination of L-aspartic acid and citric acid is not used, but rather citric acid only is used. The adult dose for this is usually $\frac{1}{2}$ teaspoon in the morning on arising, with each meal and at bedtime. This is usuallycombined with sodium bicarbonate, using half as much sodium bicarbonate to citric acid, or if desired, an equal amount. It usually is not necessary to take this alkali, however, with the citric acid taken at mealtime.If it is neutralized in equal amounts with sodium bicarbonate at mealtime, then it is preferred to take it 30 minutes after the meal, so as not to interfere with the acid gastric stage of digestion. If it is taken as an acid without the sodium bicarbonate, then it can be taken at mealtime and will even aid the acid stage of digestion.

The judgement as to a need for citric acid and for aspartic acid in many cases has been drawn from the amino acid profiles of a sizable number of physical and emotional degenerative disease cases as tested by W.H.Philpott, M.D. and Jon Pangborn, PH. D., Chemist. The best judgement can be drawn from an amino acid profile. However, the evidence is strong for a majority having a need for a combination of citric acid and aspartic acid. Therefore, even when an amino acid profile has not been done, this will usually be the correct treatment.

* * * * * * *

The main dietary source of citric acid is of course the citrus fruits. From the foregoing it appears that the effectiveness of the grapefruit in the highly successful grapefruit and egg diet comes from greatly increased levels of citric acid which may be enhanced by the use of bicarbonate to reduce the acidity. Citric acid can also be increased with HiKC Fizz with lemon juice,first thing upon arising in the morning. Aspartic acid can be increased by the judicious use of Aspartame to sweeten the fizz, the grapefruit, or other foods. Aspartame also contains phenylalanine, and it should be avoided by people with PKU (phenylketonuria). It may also induce disorientation or fatigue.

The Spermine Test.

Spermine levels are one of the most important health tests that your doctor can make. One of the most certain and insidious results of the ever present "coffee and doughnuts" diet is hypoglycemia, and hypoglycemics, by test, do have low spermine levels.Low spermine levels are also found in people on estrogen therapy, in premature senility, and in aging.

The first signs of low spermine are memory loss for recent events, and disorientation,(pre-senile dementia), repetition of phrases (unconscious swearing), loss of fine muscle control (poor writing), and finally psychosis.It appears that spermine levels are also associated with lysosome activity. Deranged lysosome function, with abnormal cellular death, and abnormal genetic changes, is now considered to be one of the major causes of cancer. Hence the increased probability of cancer with hypoglycemia and aging.

Spermine normally occurs in large quantities in sexual fluids, (particularly semen), blood, tissues, and the brain. Quite obviously mental, physical, and sexual function will be impaired if levels are low. Spermine levels are also related to levels of spermidine. Normal ratio is about; spermine 1.5 to spermidine .9 mcg %.

Spermine levels can be raised with manganese and zinc. Copper excess may reduce the spermine/spermidine ratio. As hypoglycemics do have low spermine levels it becomes obvious that coffee and junk foods, someway, somehow, reduce manganese and zinc and elevate copper.

The continuing synthesis of RNA in the brain is activated by spermine. Memory of recent events is encoded in RNA. RNA is also involved in the encoding for cellular replication. Where digestion and assimilation of proteins is poor, and spermine levels are low, the mental problems and the high risk of cancer can be reduced, and memory can be improved, with supplements of nucleic acids. (RNA,DNA).However, no amount of supplements will eliminate the problem as long as the hypoglycemia remains. The hypoglycemia will remain if yeast infection is present, or if caffiene, sugar, and white flour remain in the diet.

If spermine and spermadine are low, the tests should be repeated after about six months, to insure that the health program is effective. The inter-relation of minerals, and their relation to Candida is of particular interest. Spermine and spermadine are dependent upon adequate manganese and zinc. If Candida infection uses up the manganese and zinc, copper levels will rise the spermine/spermadine ratio will fall, and health will rapidly deteriorate.

Medical diagnosis is still frequently based on symptoms, even when tests are available. Severe recent memory loss and disorientation are frequently diagnosed as pre-senile dementia, but the same symptoms may also be diagnosed as Alzheimers disease, while these same symptoms can also result from caffeine dehydration, (See Alzheimers disease, Ch.7.) where the diuretic effects from the over-consumption of caffeine induces the excretion of more water than is contained in the cup of coffee. Altered levels of spermine/spermadine may therefore also be associated with cellular dehydration, particularly if caffeine consumption has been high. Extra fluids, particularly in the form of soups, may therefore also be necessary to restore the spermine/spermadine ratio to normal levels.

GETTING BETTER.

This title was not the idea of the author, it comes from one of the people in the audience at an allergy meeting, who, after being told about the difficulties of getting well, looked at the speaker with red swollen eyes, and replied "I don't care if I ever get well, if I can only get a little better" Such is the forever plight of the many desperate people with allergies and other forms of ill health. "Just a little better", is all that they ask, but relief, if it comes, is usually so short and so fleeting. A great many victims accuse the doctors of being heartless and unfeeling, yet the frustrations of the doctors are almost as many as they have patients. A great many alopathic doctors have tried diets and supplements, and wholistic methods, again with almost as many frustrations as they have patients. These doctors are not callous and unfeeling, they know that many of their clients are desperately ill, yet each time they think they have worked out a successful program, they have so many failures and complications that everything becomes uncertain.

Their programs fail because they did not do enough; they did not do everything. They did not consider the whole body ecology. Wholistic doctors seem to have as many failures as alopathic doctors because they insist that everything must come from nature; only "natural" is good, and they too fail to consider the whole body ecology. The orthomolecular doctors too, seem to have as many failures as other doctors. Again they fail to do everything, and they fail to consider the whole ecology;-

they fail to consider the other living creatures--good and bad;-that are in the failing body;- they fail because they do not consider the whole body ecology. They fail to consider the entire living circumstance. They view each system as pure; each body function as pure; each bit of chemistry as pure. But in the real world of "eat and be eaten" no system, function, or bit of chemistry is pure. Everything is contaminated with an endless variety of bits and pieces of biological matter that the body cannot use, and must finally dispose of. The whole body ecology is the body with everything in it; good and bad. The whole body ecology is the body with all of its ever changing infectives, together with all of the toxins and a myriad of stray biological bits and pieces. The whole body ecology is the ecological unit of your body cells, all of the infectives, all of their toxins and metabolites, and all of your own toxins and metabolites as related to your ability to feed all of the infectives; to feed all of your own body cells, and to take away all of the wastes. That is the whole body ecology. That is the real you. The real you is not just your body and what your body is doing, the real you is your body and all of your infectives and everything they are doing. That is the real you. When Sally "Rotating Diet" Rockwell told her audience that a large part of the total volume of the stool was dead bacteria, and that there were more organisms living in the intestinal tract than the total number of cells in the body, the audience gasped. They were totally shocked. "Who, me?", "Not me and my calluses." "Not me and my allergies". "Not me and my constipation". Yet the truth is that every moment from birth unto death you and your infectives are the real you. You cannot escape from them, as they are part of you, so you must learn to deal effectively with them. That is the fact, and you do not have a choice.

The real you, then, can be represented by the Vitality diagram in Fig.8. At (A) you are healthy and have a large Vitality reserve, with well controlled chronic infectives. At (B), chronic infectives have increased. This has impaired digestion and assimilation and other body systems resulting in a reduced total energy, while the increased infection has required extra energy to keep the infectives under control, resulting in a greatly reduced Vitality reserve. Improved lifestyle and better nutrition with supplements of vitamins and minerals will increase the Vitality reserve, resulting in renewed health. But the renewed health was a false cure, and of short duration because the infectives received better nutrition along with the body, and at the dotted line at (C) they have again overtaken the host and they have again reduced the Vitality to constant illness.

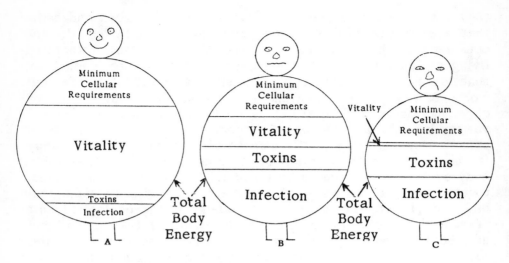

Fig.8. VITALITY DIAGRAM.
"The real YOU is you and your infectives"

A. When infectives are low, toxins are low, and Energy and Vitality are abundant.

B. Increased infection increases toxins. All body systems become overloaded and impaired, which reduces total energy and greatly reduces Vitality.

C. Infection and toxins have reduced body functions and body energy to the point that Vitality has disappeared.

From this diagram it becomes obvious that there are no simple ways to restore health. It does not matter to the ill whether the chronic infectives became established from an overwhelming amount of Candida, or if the chronic infectives became established through tissue injury, or if the chronic infection followed some other illness. The truth is that if ill health has been present for several months, chronic infectives will take advantage of the weakened condition of the host, Candida yeast will be one of the infectives, and the infective colonies will become established. Chronic infection, and Candida yeast, are therefore always an intrinsic part of degenerative disease irrespective of the actual initiating cause. From Fig.8. it is obvious that the only fully effective way to "get better" is to reeduce the total quantity of chronic infectives, wherever they may be, and to rebuild the damaged and altered body functions, whatever they may be. Unfortunately, there are no simple methods. The degenerative process is highly complex and touches upon all body systems. Degeneration is therefore not easily reversed. With everything in the body affected by the infectives and their toxins, health can be renewed only by doing everything, absolutely everything.

THE DEGENERATIVE PROCESS.(Greatly simplified).

In general terms the pathway to degenerative disease is as follows:-1.--The body is overwhelmed by a massive infection, or tissues are physically damaged or abraded, (as in an accident), or the body is weakened by poor nutrition or by drugs.

2.--Candida yeast invades,or it joins other infectives that are already established.

3.--Other infectives join the Candida callus matrix.

4.--All body functions are affected by the toxins and metabolites from the infectives. The variety of infectives is endless. The variety of toxins and metabolites is therefore also endless. Specific toxins and specific metabolites affect particular tissues so the disease is named after the tissues that are infected or affected. Alopathic doctors, herbalists, orthomolecular doctors, chiropractors, and other health practitioners will usually fail to restore health because they are trying to restore health without seeking out and reducing the basic chronic infection.

5.--Impaired body functions together with continuous toxins, results in continuous unrelenting stress. The continuous stress depletes the adrenal glands, depletes vitamin C, and causes continuous excretion of potassium.

6.--Depleted adrenals affect all body systems and particularly the pancreas.

7.--Pancreatic failure results in the hypoglycemia/diabetes condition, with altered levels of blood sugar, which also affects all body systems and all body functions.

8.--Pancreatic failure also results in digestive failure resulting in indigestion and poor assimilation of nutrients, and the pancreatic failure also results in unsuppressed inflammation.

9.--Low vitamin C, as in 5., results in sub-clinical scurvy, with increased porosity of the intestines, colon, blood vessels, lymph vessels, and other body tissues.

10.--Digestive failure, together with increased porosity of the small intestine results in partially digested proteins reaching the bloodstream and tissues, which results in more inflammation and perhaps allergies. The allergies may be severe, sub-clinical, and/or mental, with a further increase in stress.

11.--Increased porosity of the colon results in resorption of toxins from both the body and the infectives. The resorbed toxins affect all body systems, and induce further inflammation and/or allergies.

12.--The basic yeast infection depletes body minerals including selenium while the yeast itself produces lactic acid. Depleted selenium impairs the glucose tolerance factor which increases the diabetes and/or hypoglycemia, which also increases the lactic acid. The lactic acid then increases water retention and edema, and pushes the body to acidosis.

13.--Loss of potassium from the cells as in (5) allows sodium to enter the cells, which is followed by water, further increasing the Edema.

14.--Edema and inflammation reduce blood flow depriving the cells of adequate oxygen. Oxygen starved cells produce more lactic acid, with further increase in edema and inflammation.

15.--The edema and inflammation reduces lymphatic flow at the time that drainage is needed most. The excess water in the lymphatic system impairs the immune system, with increased infection.

16.-- Inflammation and stagnant lymphatic fluids, filled with proteins leaked from the porous blood vessels, permeates the tissues, resulting in a further reduction in the effectiveness of all body functions. The stagnant fluids, filled with proteins, promote fibrosis.

17.--The fibrosis is followed by calcinosis;-- a general hardening of the affected body tissues.

18.--The stagnant lymphatic fluids; with fibrosis, calcinosis, and reduced blood circulation, further impairs immune function, followed by an increase in chronic infection, which takes us back to 4, with the entire process repeating, and repeating and repeating, with an ever increasing certain reduction in Vitality and a gradual certain increase in symptoms.

19.--(a) If the edema and inflammation are focused in the air tract, the symptoms will be called asthma or emphysema,etc.

(b) If the inflammation and calcinosis are centered in the joints, the symptoms will be called arthritis, sometimes with the principal infective added, e.g.,Candida Arthritis.

(c) If the inflammation and cal cinosis are focused in the blood vessels, the symptoms will be called atherosclerosis, or claudication, or heart failure, or stroke.

(d).If the inflammation is focused in the intestines the symptoms will be called colitis or enteritis.

(e).If the inflammation and calcinosis is focused in the tissues the symptoms will be called myositis or synovitis.

(f).When infection and impaired body function have progressed to the point that the liver can no longer detoxify all of the toxins from the infectives; from the body; or leaked into the bloodstream from porous inflamed lungs, intestines or colon, the symptoms will be called allergies.

(g).Etc; and etc; with each afflication named after the affected tissues.

(h).When infection and impaired body systems have deteriorated to the point that the immune function has been greatly impaired, the symptoms will usually be named multiple sclerosis, cancer, or perhaps AIDS.

20.--Each increase in infection reduces body function, and each reduced body function reduces Vitality.
21.--When Vitality drops below (0), infection is unopposed, and death will soon follow. One of the positive signs of certain impending death is the thrush, (Candida) covered tongue, observed and described by Hippocrates over two thousand years ago. Yes, Candida is always with us, unwanted and frequently unoticed, but always with us, from birth even unto death, and even for awhile after death!

THE REAL YOU.
Now the real you is always somewhere between #1, and #20. The closer that you are to #1, the better your life will be, but as you approach #20, life will be only a living death.
So now you can see the real reason that you failed to "get better" under the doctor's program. He failed to consider the real you, so he did not do "everything". Now you understand the failures of the heart specialist, the allergist, and the cancer clinics. Now you can see the reason for the failures of the chiropractors and the naturopaths and the nutritionists and the other "alternate" therapies. They too, failed to see the real you. They failed to make you "better" because they failed to think of you as you and your whole body ecology. Their programs failed because they did not consider your infectives and their far reaching effects. The programs failed because the specialists did not realize the necessity for high technology and therefore failed to make use of all of the technology available to them. Their programs failed because they failed to "do everything'.
You too therefore cannot expect to "get better" unless you plan your program to "do everything", and then follow through to make certain that "everything" is done, because success can come only from a full program that is conscientiously followed. Nothing can be skipped, and "everything" must be done.
"Everything"? What then is "everything"? "Everything" is each and every thing small or large that will increase the function of any body system. "Everything" is each and every thing small or large that will decrease chronic infection. "Everything" is each and every thing small or large that will re-build the body. That is "everything". Short and simple, yes, but the list is long and it will all take time, depending upon where the real You may be. The real You is somewhere between #1 and #20.Your problems may have started with adrenal depletion, or over-active adrenals even before birth, so all of the problems may have had many years to increase. To reverse long standing problems will take both time, and perseverance.

Ch.4. Reducing Candida Yeast Infection.

So now you can look at your mineral test, your blood tests, all of your symptoms, and your present health, and you can probably decide about where you are and how much Vitality the real You now has. But whatever the Vitality, if the health renewal program is complete you will soon start to "feel better". Oh yes! There will certainly be some relapses, but the number of "good days" will increase and the number of "bad days" will decrease, and much of the time you will "feel better". So you must do everything, absolutely everything.

Above all you must do everything possible to improve all body systems even when they seem free from symptoms. When health is low, body defences are low, and if yeast is present anywhere it will probably be everywhere, seen and unseen, so it should be assumed that it is everywhere. It should be assumed that it is in the nose, the mouth and the air-tract. It should be assumed that it has colonized various areas throughout the entire alimentary tract from the mouth to the anus. It should be assumed that it has invaded the sexual tract. It should be assumed that it is on the feet and in the ears, and is perhaps even growing in some internal organs. To improve health, the total infection must be reduced. To reduce the total infection, the yeast and its associated infectives must be attacked wherever it may be. Infection everywhere must be assumed because in some instances the yeast callus may be thin, painless, and almost undetectable, and the lack of symptoms can be very misleading.

DOING "EVERYTHING".

You must do everything possible to break the downward spiral of health degeneration. You must do everything possible to kill out and eliminate the fungus and other infectives while at the same time you must do everything possible to provide super nutrition to restore and rebuild all body systems. All changes must be slow, to allow time for the body to adapt, and all changes should be made one at a time to ensure that each change is compatible. The stress from over-zealous programs can sometimes offset their possible benefits, so wherever possible the program should be kept within the limits of "feeling better". Just keep at each thing, a little at a time, to slowly crowd the body back toward health, and let time make the adjustments.

DIET.

The mineral test and dietary evaluation are excellent, but they assume that you are reasonably healthy and they also assume that you are alone and pure and free from all chronic infectives. The computer printout will therefore have to be adjusted for the real you. The mineral supplements will have to be adjusted upward to provide the extra nutrients stolen by the infectives.

Ch.4. Reducing Candida Yeast Infection.

The unsaturated fatty acids may have to be increased to support the immune system. To starve the yeasts, all refined carbohydrates must be eliminated and total complex carbohydrate must be reduced. Protein must be increased to feed the immune system, to rebuild the body, and to make up for the reduced carbohydrate.

Yes, a low carbohydrate, high protein diet! A "slimming" diet! A hypoglycemic diet! Can it be that people are overweight from the stress from yeast infection? Can it be coincidence that the most successful hypoglycemic diet happens to reduce infection? Or can it be that sugars feed the yeast and the hypoglycemic episodes result from toxins? We do know that everyone with a serious yeast infection is basically hypoglycemic, so the high protein low carbohydrate diet will reduce peak blood sugar levels and will also help to reduce those dreadful episodes of low blood sugar. A snack between meals may also improve general function by helping to stabalize blood sugar levels. Sips of tea , may also help if blood sugar falls too low.

CAFFEINE, TOBACCO and STIMULANTS.

The health perils of stimulants and their total effects on body processes cannot be over-emphasized. Very little progress toward better health can be made as long as stimulants are being used. Tea, chocolate, and cola contain alkaloid poisons that have similar effects to caffeine. These alkaloids are diuretics, and they therefore alter the water balance. Some people who consume large amounts of caffeine (and perhaps smoke) may become so thin and dehydrated that they develop severe mental problems similar to Alzheimers disease. Yet with the removal of the caffeine, together with 8 or 10 glasses of water daily, they return to normal in less than a month. The alkaloids also interfere with nerve control at each and every nerve synapse, which alters each and every body process. The control of the heart is particularly affected, resulting in palpitations, or even in fibrillation. It should be remembered that nicotine is also an alkaloid poison, with very similar effects to caffeine.

Many people seem to think that caffeine is just a very mild drug that is virtually harmless, but one drop of pure caffeine will kill a mouse. For man the lethal dose of caffeine; specifically the quantity that will produce death if taken all at once; is calculated at 10 grams. A cup of coffee contains 200 mg. Not very much, but some people drink as much as 12 or 15 cups per day and they therefore consume as much as 2 grams, or enough to kill one fifth of their body every day. Quite obviously they would die in five days if their body did not manage to somehow detoxify the xanthine poisons of which the alkaloids are composed. The harm fom the caffeine therefore comes not only from dehydration and the effects of the xanthine poisons on the entire nervous system with altered body functions, but the harm also comes from the tremendous load placed on the adrenals, the immune system, and the liver, all of which must struggle valiantly day and night to detoxify and eliminate the poisons, and save the body from death.

Quite obviously, no serious attempt to restore health can be made until these poisons are discontinued.

CAFFEINE THERAPY.

Despite the foregoing, caffeine can have a definite value in therapy. Health, and renewal of health, are largely dependent upon "feeling good". If blood sugar falls too low, the damage from a few sips of tea to raise body function, is less than the damage from the extreme stress of low blood sugar, particularly when adrenal nutrients are taken with the tea, but the quantity of tea should be as little as possible, and never more than $\frac{1}{2}$ cup at a time.

CAFFEINE ENEMAS.

Caffeine is so poisonous to the body that it is very effective in cleansing the colon and intestines when used as an enema. The coffee should be strong, and the enemas should be repeated until the bowels are fully cleared. The caffeine induces high production of bile, and it is the bile that does the cleansing. Vitamin C is essential to the production of bile (from cholesterol) so the best method is to take large amounts of vitamin C, as for the ascorbate flush, together with two or three bile tablets, and followed by the coffee enema. Coffee enemas are particularly used in Cancer therapy.(Ch.7.).

ADRENAL DEPLETION.(adrenocortical insufficiency).

The adrenal glands have two parts:

1.-- The medulla, or inside part, that produces adrenalin and noradrenalin (Epinephrine) which control the amount of sugar released from the liver into the bloodstream. The final metabolism of adrenalin and noradrenalin involves monoamine oxidase, which brings it to vanilic acid, and finally to hydrogen peroxide, (H_2O_2). The hydrogen peroxide then increases the activity of the hexosemonophosphate sugar cycle shunt, producing hyperactivity, and which also increases the production of glucose to fructose. This is important, because the fructose then overloads the bloodstream with sugar that is used directly by the body cells, and is beyond the normal control of insulin, which of course adds to the hyperactive state, increasing the stress, and perpetuating the cycle. The adrenal cortex responds to perceived perils or excitement, and therefore it responds to all forms of stress, and it has the ability to increase in size to meet body requirements. Thus with continuous turmoil, or with the continuous stress of chronic infection, the medulla will increase in size. Adrenalin is so important to the body that some expectant mothers, under severe stress, will have such high requirements for adrenalin that the glands of the unborn fetus will start to also become overactive, and will enlarge dramatically. The baby will then be born with an oversized adrenal medulla, will be born hyperactive, and will usually be born with many health problems, frequently including overweight.

In both cases, the enlarged medulla will stretch the rest of the adrenal gland, the cortex, which will alter its function and will increase or decrease adrenal hormone production.

2.-- The adrenal cortex, or outer part of the adrenal gland which uses methyl groups, hydroxyl groups, and cholesterol esters to make the many corticosteroid hormones that finally control most of the body functions, and include cortisone, mineral balance hormones, and the sex hormones.

Quite obviously health will be affected in a great many ways if adrenal function fails, or if it is increased or altered by an enlarged medulla. Quite obviously also the adrenals cannot function properly without adequate nutrients. The problem is that both the adrenal cortex and the adrenal medulla run on many of the same nutrients. Thus, prolonged stress from any cause can deplete the nutrients, and the body will then start to run on "nervous energy" and will function erratically on whatever meager nutrients that might happen to arrive, with consequent wide swings in blood sugar levels, mood and vitality.

Unfortunately, the immune system and the detoxification system also require many of these same nutrients, and severe continuous stress, as with chronic infection, can therefore use up so many nutrients that all the body systems are grossly affected.

The principal adrenal nutrients are:

1.-- Potassium, which the body excretes under stress.

2.--Vitamin C, which is also required by the liver for detoxification, for the production of bile, and by the entire body for building strong tissues and strong bones.

3.-- B6.

4.-- Pantothenic acid.

5.-- Lipotropics.(Choline, inositol, methionine.)

6.-- Unsaturated fatty acids. (Nuts, sunflower oil etc;)

The principal signs of adrenal depletion are edema, fatigue, extreme exhaustion, and hyperactivity. The final determining symptom of advanced adrenal depletion is the presence of low back pain. Rest, ample adrenal nutrients, a reduction in chronic infection, and reduced stress, with perhaps supplements of glandular extracts or adrenal hormones are the best ways to improve adrenal function.

VITAMIN C. (ASCORBATE)

In addition to the other modifications in the diet you will need large amounts of vitamin C to detoxify all of the toxins from the infectives; to detoxify all of the toxins from the dead bodies of the killed infectives; to detoxify the dead tissues; to provide nutrition for the adrenals; to convert cholesterol from the bloodstream into bile; and to strengthen all of the tissues. Vitamin C is used first by the liver to detoxify poisons. Therefore a good rule to follow would be to add an extra gram of vitamin C to detoxify the poisons in each cup of coffee and for each cigarette, until caffeine and tobacco are eliminated. The vitamin C is used first by the liver, then if there is any left over it is used by the adrenals, and if any ascorbate remains it is used lastly by the body to strengthen the collagen in the tissues. But vitamin C is the tie that binds the chains of protein fibers together. It is collagen that gives strength to bone, cartilage, and tissue, and it is vitamin C that cross-binds the collagen fibers together to give them strength, and bioflavinoids provide a few more cross links. Without adequate vitamin C and bioflavinoids the tissues become weak, porous, and scurvous, now also termed "scorbutic", i.e. ascorbate deprived.

Bioflavinoids and Vitamin C.

Bioflavinoids are a co-factor with vitamin C in the building of strong and healthy tissues. They are particularly essential to blood and lymph vessels. Severe lack of bioflavinoids, even with adequate vitamin C, shows as blue areas of obviously poor blood circulation, with the color ranging down to dark blue or perhaps even dark purple. These areas clear quite rapidly if bioflavinoids are supplied along with the vitamin C.

The bioflavinoids that seem to show the greatest effect on blood vessels and capillaries is quercitin.(Available from Ecological Formulas).

Candida and Vitamin C.

High yeast infection, with the ever present toxins and the ever present stress on the adrenals, will use up so much vitamin C that unless supplements of vitamin C are very high (at least 4 or 5 grams per day) sub-clinical scurvy will be present throughout the cartilage, bones, and tissues of the entire body. Scurvy is disasterous to all body systems but is particularly disasterous to:

1.--Blood vessels that become weak and porous, and leak extra amounts of proteins and fluids into the tissues, which increases lymphatic flow, increases water retention (edema), promotes calcinosis, reduces the effectiveness of the immune system and increases the "protein allergies" to pork etc.

2.-- The digestive tract, that becomes porous and leaks undigested proteins into the bloodstream, resulting in excessive demands on the immune system, and promoting visible and unseen allergies, including affects on the mind.

3.-- The kidneys, where extra porosity fails to strain out body wastes, and leaves toxic elements circulating in the bloodstream.

4.-- The colon, where extra porosity alters the water balance, and increases the resorption of body wastes, together with toxins from the infectives.

5.-- All tissues exposed to infection, where the extra porosity allows infectives to penetrate the tissues and to colonize the weakened area.

To overcome yeast infection, the body will therefore require large amounts of vitamin C. Yes! Yes! Just like Linus Pauling said;--if you are not ill, you need large quantities of vitamin C, and if you are ill you need even more! It has been pointed out that a goat, or a dog, of the same body weight as a man, will produce as much as 15 grams of vitamin C per day. We lack the coding for the enzymes to manufacture our own vitamin C, so we must rely on obtaining it from our food.

However, even when the diet is high in foods rich in vitamin C we seldom obtain more than a few grams per day from the diet. Man is therefore constantly near the point of scurvy, with extra stress or a few more toxins easily driving the body into the scurvous condition.

<u>Vitamin C and the Acid/Alkaline Balance.</u>

Vitamin C must therefore be heavily supplemented. It sometimes seems that it is almost impossible to get too much, but despite the high need, in serious yeast infection most of the vitamin C should not be in the form of ascorbic acid. In serious yeast infection acidity is already too high. When Candida yeast feeds on your sugars; either directly on the sugars in the digestive tract, or indirectly on the sugars in the sexual fluids or from the bloodstream; the final product from the yeast (among many other things) is lactic acid. High yeast infections, anywhere, therefore produce large amounts of lactic acid. The yeast infection also loads the bloodstream with spores and hyphae, and increases blood cell clumping to the point that the oxygen supply to the body is greatly reduced. The low oxygen supply then alters the normal sugar cycle in the cells, resulting in the body metabolizing sugar to lactic acid. The build-up of lactic acid throughout the body increases water retention and calcinosis, which further complicates health problems, and the high amounts of lactic acid also make the entire body highly acidic. Some of the "alternate therapies" are based on restoring the acid-alkaline balance, frequently with limited success, but how could such a half-therapy be reliably effective if the role of yeast infection was not considered? With the body already highly acidic, large amounts of ascorbic acid will only increase the acidity at a time when the body is already much too acid. Indeed, some people with high Candida infection can become very ill with even 100 mg. of ascorbic acid.

The high amounts of vitamin C required to combat yeast infection should therefore be principally in the form of mineral ascorbates, preferably as mixed mineral ascorbate with bioflavinoids, and with emphasis on sodium/potassium ascorbate, which will also help to raise potassium levels.

Cholesterol and Vitamin C.

Vitamin C also has a little known essential role in the processing of cholesterol into bile. Thus if infection is high or if vitamin C is low, all of the cholesterol cannot be changed to bile, so bile will be low (with accompanying indigestion) and blood cholesterol and accompanying triglycerides will be high. Therefore the severe stress from chronic infection can finally result in high blood cholesterol with blood circulatory problems.

Ascorbate.

The following excellent information on ascorbate is from the Philpott Medical Center. Ref.6.

ASCORBIC ACID ULTRA-FINE POWDER.

Ascorbic acid is obtainable as granules, as a powder, and as ultra-fine powder. There are varying degrees of tolerance for these products. One teaspoon equals four grams. Ultrafine powder is used due to its maximum dissolving ability in water and optimum absorption with minimal bowel retention of water. The optimum dose is one tsp. three times per day (12 gms.). This can be taken as ascorbic acid, sodium ascorbate, sodium-potassium ascorbate, potassium ascorbate, or calcium ascorbate.

Optimum Daily Need of Vitamin C.

There is a wide difference in the amount of vitamin C that is sufficient to prevent scurvy and the amount for optimum health including such as its anti-stress value in support of adrenal and other endocrine glands, anti-viral value, and detoxifying value of heavy metals, excessive minerals, and micro-organism toxins. The livers of most animals make their vitamin C out of glucose. The amount made by these animals when stated in terms of body weight ranges from 8 to 13 grams per 24 hours for a human of average weight. When under stress, these animals increase their vitamin C many fold, thus having a ready detoxifying mechanism. Humans should also increase their vitamin

C when under stress, but are dependent on an external source for their Vitamin C. Goats make 13 grams of vitamin C and markedly increase this when under stress. If we are to be as wiry as a goat, we need to approximate an intake of vitamin C to match that produced by a goat. I have not heard of goats being especially prone to urinary tract calculi and reportedly they are not cancer prone.

Optimum Time for Taking Vitamin C.

Ascorbic acid is best taken with the meal by taking swallows along during a meal, at which time the other nutrients are also taken a few at a time. No more than one glass of water with the ascorbic acid should be taken at a time.

If the vitamin C is taken as an alkali salt such as sodium ascorbate, sodium-potassium ascorbate or calcium ascorbate, then it is best to be taken $\frac{1}{2}$ hour to 3/4 hour after the meal and taken with $\frac{1}{2}$ glass to no more than one glass of water. As an alkali salt, vitamin C has a PH of about 7, which helps to provide the proper neutralization for the small intestine after the stomach has done its acid work. This is why it should be taken $\frac{1}{2}$-hour to 3/4-hour after the meal.

Sodium ascorbate can be made by reacting in water equal amounts of ascorbic acid and sodium bicarbonate (baking soda). Sodium-potassium ascorbate can be made by a mixture of sodium bicarbonate and potassium bicarbonate at a ratio of 2:1. This mixture is then in a 1:1 ratio with ascorbic acid powder. Optimum acid-base taste tolerance of vitamin C can be achieved by varying the ratio of ascorbic acid to sodium bicarbonate (or sodium-potassium bicarbonate) all the way from 2:1 to a 1:2 ratio. If potassium is deficient in the hair or serum studies, then sodium-potassium ascorbate is a good source of potassium supplementation. Calcium ascorbate can be made by reacting ascorbic acid with calcium carbonate in a ratio 1:1.

Calcium carbonate and potassium bicarbonate powders can be purchased without prescription at drug stores and/or wholesale chemical supply companies. If potassium bicarbonate combined with ascorbic acid is being used as a supplement for potassium, it would be best to keep the amount of potassium to no more than 1/3 tsp. potassium bicarbonate. $\frac{1}{4}$ tsp. of potassium bicarbonate provides 500 mg. potassium. 1/3 tsp. of potassium bicarbonate provides 700mg. potassium. If more than 500mg. of Potassium per day is being provided, it is best to have a monthly monitoring of serum potassium.

Treatment of Viral Infections with Vitamin C.

(Also all other infections).

The alkali form is best used during acute infections since the infections tend to produce an acid state, and this neutralizes this acid state. It is best to start with one tsp. of the ascorbic acid powder plus one tsp. of sodium bicarbonate each four hours for the first day and increase this by $\frac{1}{2}$ to 1 tsp. with equal amounts of sodium bicarbonate each four hours each day until the stool is uncomfortably loose and then reduce sufficiently (by $\frac{1}{2}$ tsp. each four hours) until there are four to five soft, but manageable stools per day. A cold may take 10 to 20 grams, while the flu may take 50 to 100 grams and viral pneumonia may take 100 to 200 grams before diarrhea results. The bowel absorbs the vitamin C according to the toxic needs and therefore, the amount of vitamin C can be increased as the toxins increase.

Vitamin C in Cancer.

Most of the time, this is taken as an ascorbic acid. Usually, it is divided into five doses, with the first being taken on arising and the last taken as the person goes to bed. The amount taken should be maximum bowel-tolerated doses, which is usually 50 to 60 grams a day in cancer patients.

It should be understood that cancer patients should be under the care of a doctor and preferably be receiving frequent intravenous Vitamin C doses as well as the oral doses of vitamin C and should also be on appropriate supplements and on a diversified rotation diet which has been worked out after discovering the symptom-evoking foods.

Vitamin C as a Bowel Conditioner.

Vitamin C is a natural substance which acts as a bowel conditioner. Sufficient amounts should be taken in to provide a minmum of 2 and a maximum of 4 soft stools per day. This amount of vitamin C also protects against cancer of the colon and the rectum, detoxifies colon bacterial toxin and provides sufficient vitamin C spillage in the urine to protect against urinary tract cancer.

Ascorbate Flush.

Methodology.-One tsp. of ascorbic acid powder to 1 tsp. sodium bicarbonate in a half glass of water taken each 15 minutes fom 2 to 4 hours. For some this may be nauseating, and they may have to sip the sodium ascorbate over a 15 minute period.

Purpose.-To take sufficient sodium ascorbate to produce a colon flush. This is usually preferred to an enema. It provides maximum absorption of vitamin C, a dialysis effect of toxins from the blood through the intestinal mucosa, flushes out food particles to which the person may be reactive, as well as flushing out infectious agents and their toxins.

Use.--1.-- Whenever a purgative is needed.

2.--To flush out foods that are evoking allergic reactions.

3.-- To flush out foods and bacteria when beginning a fast in preparation for deliberate food testing.

Vitamin C as a Chelating Agent.

Vitamin C as ascorbic acid or as ascorbates have chelating value in terms of its ability to remove from the body heavy metals or excesses of minerals. This chelating ability of vitamin C helps in preventing calcium deposits in the arteries. Theoretically, potassium ascorbate is ideal as a chelating agent. The suggested dose is ascorbic acid, $\frac{1}{2}$ to 1 tsp. according to taste tolerance, reacted in a glass of water with potassium bicarbonate, $\frac{1}{2}$ tsp. and taken without food at bedtime, $\frac{1}{2}$ tsp. potassium bicarbonate provides 1000mg. potassium. This chelating treatment should be under a doctor's care. Suggested monitoring while under oral vitamin C chelation is on the order of:

(1) Serum potassium at monthly intervals.

(2) Serum potassium, calcium, magnesium and zinc at three month intervals.

(3) A six months reveiw of the initial demonstrated abnormalities of excessive heavy metals or mineral imbalance by whatever means (hair, urinary spillage or blood levels) it was originally demonstrated.

Vitamin C Problems.

The ability of vitamin C to chelate calcium should be understood. If a patient is symptomatically worse after receiving vitamin C given intravenously or orally, then consider the possibility that calcium metabolism may be disorderd and have a slow recovery phase of serum calcium after receiving the dose of vitamin C such as would be present in hypoparathyroidism or estrogen/testosterone deficiency. If either of these conditions are demonstrated, then treatment specifically for that condition should be given, under which circumstances the vitamin C treatment can be continued.

****

The foregoing information by Dr. Philpott certainly demonstrates the excellent scientific work being done by many people in the field of Health Technology. Dr. Philpott and his associates are to be greatly congratulated for their persistence even when their progressive work is ignored by most of the medical profession.

Vitamin C and the Colon.

Note the foregoing statement under "Viral Infections", "The bowel absorbs the vitamin C according to toxic needs", which means that any extra vitamin C that reaches the colon is absorbed along with the fluids from the colon according to the amount of toxins present. The problem is that many people have not supplemented vitamin C, and many ill people are unable to take vitamin C, which has resulted in a scurvous state throughout the body. So they have developed a porous and leaky colon that permits toxins from the colon to be resorbed with the fluids from the colon, which in turn increases the need for vitamin C and imposes a severe load on the liver and kidneys that are scurvous and impaired from lack of vitamin C. Even some people that can take moderate amounts of vitamin C can develop a scurvous and leaky colon, with allergies and other toxic problems, because it is so difficult to take enough vitamin C to supply the adrenals and to detoxify all of the toxins and still have enough left to reach the colon to strengthen the colon tissues. People with colon problems will therefore always benefit from ascorbate introduced directly to the colon by way of ascorbate retention enemas once or twice a week. The improvement in digestion, colon function, and general health can be surprisingly great and surprisingly rapid.

Ascorbate Retention Enema.

(See also Candida Infections of the Colon, Ch.6.)

The object of the ascorbate retention enema is to provide extra vitamin C directly to the colon in a form that the body can readily assimilate and use, and which will disturb colon function as little as possible. The preferred fluid is therefore the persons own urine which is a natural body fluid that is fully compatible to the body, and which contains anti-bodies to all of the infectives living in the body. If the thought of using urine is highly objectionable, plain salt water, or sea water can be used. Quite obviously the basic concept can be varied and used in many different ways. The following protocol has produced excellent results.

1- 8 oz. Rectal syringe.
1- 8 oz. glass almost full of fluid. (preferrably urine).
 Add slowly:
$\frac{1}{2}$ to 1 tsp. HiKC Fizz (for 2 to 4 gms sodium/potassium ascorbate).
3 Redoxon tablets (3 gms sodium ascorbate).
Contents of 2 capsules calcium ascorbate.
2 droppers full of liquid nystatin.
$\frac{1}{2}$ tsp. sodium bicarbonate. (to increase the alkalinity).
$\frac{1}{2}$ tsp. powdered bioflavinoids. (if they can be found).
The enema should be retained (if possible) for about $\frac{1}{2}$ hour, but not much longer.

These high amounts of ascorbate will not only strengthen and tighten the weak and porous tissues in the colon, but they will also destroy most of the micro-organisms, good and bad. If health is low it may be of benefit to follow the ascorbate enema about 2 hours later, with the introduction of 3 or 4 ounces of acidophilus culture, to which the contents of 2 or 3 acidophilus capsules have been added. Where colon infection is high, caprylic acid, as sodium/potassium caprylate, as the contents of 1 or 2 capsules of Capricin, or in the form of 1 tspn. of MCT Oil (Mead), added to the acidophilus, may be of particular benefit in rebuilding the tissues.

For severe diarrhea, as with "travellers disease", relief can be obtained with the ascorbate flush together with an ascorbate enema made with hot water with 8 tablets of B-Complex Redoxon.

Understanding Vitamin C.

To understand degenerative disease we must understand vitamin C and its many roles in health.

Hominids (man), guinea pigs, and one of the fruit-eating bats are the only mammals that do not produce their own vitamin C. Vitamin C is not plentiful in foods, and the usual diet (for man) contains only about one quarter of the optimum amounts. These low quantities of vitamin C, however, are sufficient to maintain health in the already healthy; hence the notion that if you are healthy you do not need supplements of vitamin C. But if anything;--pregnancy, accident, loss of sleep, overwork, overstress, overindulgence, infectious disease, chronic infection, caffeine, alcohol, drugs, etc; etc; reduces the health levels, a shortage of vitamin C will soon trigger a cascade of health problems. For example: the loss of health may start with a common cold, which depletes the low vitamin C, with the shortage impairing adrenal and immune system function. The cold is then followed by flu, which further depletes the vitamin C, with the adrenals and liver badly impaired. The low adrenal and liver function is followed by low resistance to stress, impaired immune system function, and low bile production with consequent rise in blood cholesterol from the inability of the body to use cholesterol from the blood to make bile. The low bile results in poor digestion, which reduces the amounts of vitamin C available from foods, thus further reducing the total vitamin C, while the poor digestion increases the growth of intestinal infectives living on the poorly digested food. Meanwhile the scurvous condition resulting from the continuing low vitamin C weakens all of the body tissues including the digestive tract and colon. The lowered tissue resistance together with the increased intestinal infectives invites Candida overgrowth, and the Candida infection is then joined by many other infectives, which further impairs digestion and also alters assimilation, with a further decrease in available vitamin C but with increased stress and increased need for vitamin C for adrenal support, while the increased toxic load on the liver caused the liver to use up all available vitamin C, further depleting the adrenals, reducing bile, increasing blood cholesterol, and further weakening all body tissues with scurvy.

Impaired digestion and assimilation, however, reduces all nutrients, including proteins and calcium, while the assimilation of proteins is dependent upon calcium. Thus the shortage of vitamin C finally reduces available proteins, which further weakens the tissues. But proteins are also absolutely essential to the immune system, so the immune system is further impaired with increased infection and toxins. Proteins are also absolutely essential to the pancreas for pancreatic (digestive) enzymes, so low proteins also result in a drastic reduction in digestion and assimilation and a rapid increase in quantity and kind of infectives living on the partly digested food, which of course is followed by constipation, diarrhea and other colon problems, while the colon problems are also greatly increased by the scurvous weakened tissues in the bowel, which leak toxins into the bloodstream setting the environment for allergies and arthritis. Yes, and of course with the extreme shortage of vitamin C the scurvous weakened tissues are throughout the body, including the lymphatic system, so the weakened porous lymphatic system leaks precious proteins rapidly, paralyzing the immune system and promoting calcinosis of all body tissues, with the calcinosis impairing all body functions. The blood vessels also become weakened and scurvous by the lack of vitamin C, while the high levels of blood cholesterol raise blood pressure and promote atherosclerosis. Then the edema that invariably follows adrenal depletion, together with the calcinosis and the inflammation from many infections, also raises blood pressure in the badly weakened blood vessels, followed by increased leakage of proteins into the weak and porous tissues, followed by more calcinosis, and so on, and on.

So now from the lack of vitamin C we have allergies and arthritis from the pancreatic failure, inflammation, and leaked proteins. We have atherosclerosis and high blood pressure, and reduced pancreatic function has resulted in hypoglycemia and diabetic episodes of high blood sugar which has also contributed to vascular problems and to threat of stroke. Then the impaired digestion reduced the absorption of B12, which, together with adrenal failure, has reduced adrenal and sex hormones with perhaps frigidity and impotence. By this time the infectives have used up so many minerals and have altered so many body processes with their toxins and metabolites that thyroid function has been reduced, then body temperatures drop, enzymes work slowly,and nothing is working right and everything is working wrong, and all for the lack of vitamin C.

Need we say more? We have already described the basic causes of everyone else's degenerative disease, and all for a lack of vitamin C. Yet although the lack of vitamin C can bring on a whole cascade of health problems, vitamin C alone cannot repair all of the damaged body systems. Quite obviously repairing the damage will require supernutrition with anti-biotics, anti-fungals, amino acids, nucleic acids, digestive enzymes, etc; along with vitamin C, but ample vitamin C will always be one of the cornerstones for return to health. It would therefore seem to be appropriate to re-read all of the foregoing information on vitamin C, and to refer back to it frequently. Unquestionably Nobel Prize winner Linus Pauling was right about the great need for vitamin C, and he was probably more right than even he had expected. And Linus Pauling's protocol? Fifteen grams of vitamin C per day,-or more!.

To understand vitamin C, is to understand degenerative disease!.

Potassium and Sodium.

Potassium is the working mineral inside the cell and sodium is the working mineral outside the cell. They are inter-dependent. Through a complex pathway, stress, from any source, causes the body to excrete potassium, sodium then enters the cell, and draws water into the cell with it, thus swelling the cell, and frequently swelling the entire body with cellular edema. This condition can be seen in the tight rings and tight shoes so frequently experienced. The sodium/potassium levels can be tested in whole blood, and these tests may sometimes be useful, but the sodium-potassium balance is constantly changing, and the values seen are only momentary values, therefore many tests must be made to develop the average. However, we already know that stress depletes the potassium, so we can assume that everyone with a serious yeast infection is constantly adrenal depleted and potassium depleted, with the only exception being people with nephritis or other kidney problems, who are unable to excrete potassium. The sodium/potassium balance is also affected by low potassium in the diet compared to the high amount of salt that is added to everything we eat.

In high yeast infection, as in any illness, stress is continuously high and potassium should therefore be supplemented. This forever shortage of potassium has long been recognized by the medical profession, and in a vain attempt to raise potassium levels the medical marvel Slow K was developed. Slow K is a potassium tablet that slowly dissolves in the stomach and intestines. An excellent idea perhaps, but if the tablet becomes lodged in one place the high concentration of ionic potassium burns the stomach wall, which may then be followed by ulcers or Candida infection. The health food people have solved this problem with chelated potassium that is readily dissolved and absorbed by the body, but alas, potassium levels still usually remain low. Potassium levels remain low because, although the potassium is absorbed, the potassium triggers the production of aldosterone, which may wash out more potassium than was in the tablet. Sodium suppresses aldostorone, and therefore to effectively raise potassium levels sodium must be supplied simultaneously with the potassium, irrespective of the sodium levels. The sodium levels will then be automatically adjusted by the body as the potassium levels are raised.

With high yeast infection, hair mineral tests usually show sodium/potassium as abnormal. The hair tests do not reflect blood levels. These minerals may be severely depleted, or the tests may show very high, with the minerals sequestered in the tissues. The peculiar metabolism that holds the minerals is yeast related, because sodium and potassium levels, as seen in the hair, return toward normal as the infection is reduced.

Adequate potassium levels are so essential to health that unless there are serious kidney problems, potassium/sodium supplements should be part of every Candida infection program. V8 juice happens to have about the right proportion of sodium to potassium, and can be very useful, particulary when 1/3 tsp. of sodium/potassium tartrate is added to each glass of V8 juice. As always, caution should be used with the tartrate, and the amount should be brought up slowly to avoid diarrhea from rapid water loss.

A superior way to raise potassium levels is with potassium/sodium ascorbate, which provides both potassium and vitamin C in the best form for full utilization. K is the symbol for potassium. Hence the name, Hi KC Fizz.

Hi KC Fizz.

1 part sodium bicarbonate (baking soda).

1 part potassium bicarbonate.(from the drug store or chemical wholesale).

2 parts ascorbic acid crystals. (about 8 grams per tsp.) (adjust quantity if ascorbic acid is only 4 or 5 grams per tsp.)

Mix thoroughly. Mix only about three days supply at a time, because the mix will absorb water from the air. It will get hard and turn yellowish, and it will lose some of its fizz. This will not alter its nutritional value, but it becomes less attractive.

Add about $\frac{1}{4}$ or 1/3 tsp. of powder to $\frac{1}{2}$ glass of tomato, grapefruit, or orange juice (other juices may require different quantities) and stir. Drink either as a fizz, or after the fizz has settled.

Even people with severe allergies who think that they cannot take vitamin C, can usually tolerate Hi KC Fizz. Start slowly and increase.

136

The fizz can be used up to 4 or 5 times per day, pa
for a quick "pick up" if energy runs low. It can als
as an effective substitute for a cocktail, coffee, or a cigar
The effectiveness of the fizz can be increased by adding, once
or twice a day:

1. Protein powder. (slimming powder).
2. I tsp. sunflower oil. (or equal). Do not worry. It will all mix
with the fizz and it makes a very acceptable drink.

Further benefits will result from adding the following adrenal
(stress) and immune nutrients; taken with fizz morning and
evening, or if exceptionally tired; 100 mg. pantothenic acid;
200 mg calcium/magnesium (dolomite); 50 mg B6; 1 capsule,
choline, inositol, methionine. (Quest- Super Lipo. or equal)

The very best way to start the day is with HiKC Fizz, with
supplements, immediately upon arising in the morning. It will
stabalize metabolism and blood sugar levels, and will set up
the body for a good breakfast.

The importance of raising blood sugar levels in the morning
should never be underestimated. In any illness, and particularly
with yeast infection, the adrenals are constantly depleted. With
adrenal depletion potassium is excreted, and without potassium
the normal metabolism of sugar cannot proceed even to the
point of lactic acid.The altered metabolism produces glycerol
instead, and the body then makes the glycerol into the high
levels of cholesterol and triglycerides that contribute so much
to high blood pressure and circulatory problems. To "get better",
everything must be done, and an important part of the
"everything" is to raise and maintain stable levels of potassium,
particularly at the start of each new day.

Some people with high Candida infection may not be able
to use the fizz with juice because the free sugars in the juice
feed the infection. These people also may not be able to eat
bread because the yeast in the bread, although killed in baking,
may trigger allergies. The object of the fizz is to supply potassium
and ascorbate. If juice cannot be used, the fizz can be taken
with water, or with hot water, with lemon or other flavoring.
The fizz powder can also be used as a substitude for baking
powder for making whole wheat pancakes or whole wheat biscuits.
Old fashioned baking powder, made with baking soda and cream
of tartar (potassium tartrate) can also be used for baking, with
benefit to adrenal function.

Salt.

Excess sodium is always a continuing problem. It is greatly
in excess (about 10 times) in all prepared foods, at all restaurants,
and usually at the dinner table.People who do not have health
problems or excess stress can excrete large quantities of excess
sodium, so the excess may not affect their health. Nonetheless,

4. Reducing Candida Yeast Infection.

frequent consumption of high-salt foods should be avoided, and salt in the diet should be restricted.Chelated potassium, taken with high-salt foods will have a beneficial effect when high-salt foods cannot be avoided.

Potassium levels can also be raised by using "No Salt" salt, or "Lo Salt", frequently available at the supermarket. These salt substitutes typically contain potassium (as chloride, etc.) with about half as much sodium. The continuing judicious use of these salt substitutes for family cooking is always of benefit to the entire household. If hair sodium is low, coarse salt or sea salt, used freely, will help to raise sodium levels.

CALCIUM and PROTEIN. (See Also Low Parathyroid).

Calcium is the most abundant mineral in the body, with most of it used in the bones and teeth. It is essential for healthy blood, has a role in sleep, and it helps to regulate the heartbeat. It also serves to regulate the acid/alkaline (pH) balance in the blood. It is active in transporting nutrients through the cell walls, is essential for the utilization of iron, and is necessary for muscle strength, nerve transmission, and many other biological processes. Magnesium is a co-factor of calcium, and calcium chemistry is usually dependent upon the presence of magnesium, while the magnesium itself is also essential to many other biological processes, particularly inside the cells, and in nerve transmission. Magnesium, in turn, is dependent upon B6. Absorption of calcium is dependent upon vitamin D, and excretion of calcium is controlled by parathyroid hormone,(PTH).

A continuing problem faced by every victim of Candida infection is low protein, which will show up on the blood test along with low calcium. It should be thoroughly understood that the white blood cells and all active parts of the immune system are continuously being made up from proteins. This fact is central to health and immune function. The proteins used by the immune system are derived directly from the lymphatic system, which gathers and stores proteins leaked into the tissues from the blood vessels. But the transport of proteins from the digestive tract through the intestinal walls and into the bloodstream is entirely dependent upon adequate calcium in the bloodstream and tissues; i.e.,specifically, the absorption of proteins from the intestines is entirely dependent upon absorbed calcium, while the absorption of calcium is entirely dependent upon vitamin D. Thus even if protein is well supplied and if digestion is complete, or if pre-digested protein, pure amino acids, or nucleic acid supplements are provided, the proteins will remain in the intestinal tract as excellent nutrients for many infectives if absorbed calcium is low. Absorbed calcium is therefore the key to absorbed protein, while absorbed protein is absolutely essential to the immune system, absolutely essential to the pancreas for production of pancreatic enzymes, and absolutely essential to the entire body for the rebuilding of tissues. Absorbed calcium is therefore one of the keys to the restoration of health, and is one of the keys to the entire Candida program.

Everyone talks and everyone writes about proteins. High protein diet, low protein diet, balanced amino acids, pure amino acids, vegetable proteins, avoid red meat, avoid salmon, avoid chicken, etc; and etc. It is all meaningless and misleading without adequate absorbed calcium and any "learned" "scientific studies" on proteins that do not include absorbed calcium as the prime consideration are equally meaningless and misleading. The proteins simply remain in the digestive tract unless adequate absorbed calcium is available for transport into the bloodstream.

So now let us supplement the calcium with lots of good calcium that is biologically active. Let us read the labels and read the advertising, and use calcium orotates, calcium ascorbates, calcium silicates, calcium chelates, oyster calcium, bone calcium, etc. Wonderful! But alas, the effort is useless, because the calcium is not absorbed without adequate vitamin D. So now, with lots of vitamin D and lots of calcium, nutrition has triumphed again! Triumphed, yes, right up until the next blood test, and then, yet again, calcium is low and proteins are low. Oh Yes, proteins are up slightly perhaps, and perhaps body function has improved a little, but with all of those good supplements? Why? Why are the proteins and calcium still low?

The answer is simple. Candida yeast impairs the production of parathyroid hormone, and calcium is retained in proportion to the amount of parathyroid hormone. Note, retained by parathyroid hormone. Low parathyroid hormone therefore equals low calcium retention. Oh! Yes! The calcium did do a little bit of good on its way through, and, because of the large flood of calcium, a little bit more was retained, but most of the calcium came in, and went out, because parathyroid hormone was low, and without PTH the extra calcium simply is not retained. The key to high protein diets, pure amino acids, pancreatic function, immune function, and body rebuilding is therefore not only calcium and vitamin D, but also PTH. So where do we get PTH?

Fortunately or unfortunately, PTH has not yet been synthesized, so at present it is available only as low potency glandulars. The best supplement that the author has been able to find is Seroyal TPA.

CALCIUM MAGNESIUM and CALCINOSIS.
(See also Ref.28.)

Calcium is also involved in the unhealthy aberrant biochemistry known as calcinosis. Calcinosis frequently follows fibrositis or myositis, and is sometimes confused with them.

Blood vessels are very porous (particularly if vitamin C is lacking) and these porous blood vessels continuously leak proteins into the tissues. The leaked proteins are then continuously gathered by the lymphathic system, and returned to the bloodstream, with the immune system using proteins directly from the lymphatic vessels, or from proteins stored in the thymus or other parts of the lymphatic system. Under stress, or under any other condition where water is retained or where inflammation is continuous, the lymphatic flow is reduced, and the leaked proteins stay in the tissues. The stagnant proteins then form long chains of protein fibers, resulting in fibrosis (fibrositis or synovitis if connective tissue is involved, myositis if the muscles are involved) and if the condition is prolonged the fibers become hardened with calcium, resulting in calcinosis. Calcinosis, in all of its many different stages, can frequently be seen in the legs, where the muscles will sometimes harden to the point that the legs feel like they are made of wood. The areas affected by the calcinosis will be the particular areas of inflammation and/or lymphatic retention, and the degree of calcinosis will depend upon the length of time that the calcinosis conditions have been present.

The side effects of calcinosis are severe loss of muscle strength, loss of stamina, increased weight, increased size, impaired lymphatic flow, and impaired blood circulation; all of which contribute to further calcinosis and further loss of health.

Another cause of calcinosis is lactic acid. When body cells are low in oxygen, as with anemia, poor blood circulation, asthma, emphysema, etc; the normal sugar cycle in the cells cannot be completed, and the cycle stops at lactic acid. The lactic acid then builds up in the nerve junctions and muscles where it draws water. But the available water is lymphatic fluids which contain proteins, which then induce fibrosis and calcinosis, with the lactic acid entering the hardening process to form calcium lactate. The most common lactic acid calcinosis occurs in the muscle end plate (nervcite, acupuncture point, reflexology point) which interferes with nerve transmission, resulting in muscle spasm, calcinosis of the muscle, muscle atrophy, or a complete loss of muscle fibers.

The lactic acid problem; and therefore the calcinosis problem; is greatly increased by Candida infection because the carbohydrate metabolized by the yeast is reduced only as far as lactic acid. High Candida infection therefore contributes to calcinosis, and drives the acid-alkaline balance toward acidic.

Lack of magnesium also contributes to calcinosis. Candida yeast has a particular need and affinity for magnesium. The reconstituted asmoresistant layer formed by the Candida yeast, which is the principal part of the callus matrix, is stimulated by magnesium robbed from body processes. A heavy Candida infection of the feet will grow as much as two tablespoons of callus matrix in a single week, which of course requires a high quantity of magnesium, all of which must come from the body. If extra magnesium is not supplied, the entire calcium/magnesium metabolism is altered, resulting perhaps in retention of aluminum, (with Alzheimers disease), or contributing to or resulting in extensive calcinosis.

So here again we clearly must feed the yeast infection extra magnesium (which will help it to thrive) so that the body will get enough magnesium for the proper utilization of calcium.

Many nutritionists speak wisely about the great importance of balancing calcium and magnesium, and nutritional balance of calcium and magnesium is indeed of great importance, but how can we balance calcium and magnesium at the cellular level if the yeast is getting the magnesium before it reaches the body cell? We can see the Candida infection on the feet and hands, but how much exists elsewhere? We can only guess at the quantity and extent of Candida infection, and from this, and from the extent of calcinosis, osteoporosis, and other calcium problems, we can only guess at the amount of magnesium supplements that may be of benefit.

The high levels of calcium sometimes found in the hair are indicative of calcinosis somewhere, but the extent of the calcinosis can be determined only by examination. The high hair calcium therefore does not reflect active calcium levels or active blood levels, and, with so much calcium tied up in the tissues, calcium (always with magnesium) usually should be supplemented, while efforts are directed at reducing the calcinosis and at eliminating the cause of the calcinosis.

The calcinosis can be reduced with massage and neursage, (see Neursage, Ch.5.) as described in "Health Essentials and Basic Nervcite Therapy" ("Return to Health" Book 1.) by Rupert Beebe, and available from the Healthology Association.(Ref.28).

The basic cause of calcinosis is of course linked to adrenal depletion, and particularly to a shortage of potassium, which takes us right back to sodium, potassium, HiKC Fizz, pantothenic acid, B6, and lipotropics.

The difficulties with trying to improve health are many, because all biological processes are so interlocked.Any approach that is taken must be simplified, and the many factors involved in calcinosis are certainly complex and obscure.Two other factors somehow involved in calcinosis are hormones (including sex hormones) and pernicious anemia, which are themselves interlocked. Without proof, and by conjecture, it appears that stress (perhaps with chronic infection) together with inadequate nutrition, depletes the adrenals, which deprives the body of hormones, and which also affects digestion, with the poor digestion reducing absorption of B-12, resulting in anemia, with the shortage of oxygen to the cells producing or increasing the calcinosis. The actual chain of biological events is probably much more complex, but it is degenerative cycles of this kind that defeat the single minded approaches to health renewal so commonly found in the health field. Drugs or herbs may alleviate the symptoms, reflexology, acupressure or neursage may reduce the local calcinosis, but everything must be done before the actual condition can be reversed.

PERNICIOUS ANEMIA and B-12 INJECTIONS.

Vitamin B-12, Cyanacobalamin, is the only use for cobalt in the body. B-12 is absolutely essential to the function of iron in the blood and oxygen transport system, and it is therefore vital to life and health. B-12 can be obtained only from animal matter and it is not found in any plants. Full vegetarians are therefore at peril, and indeed some have died, from lack of B-12. B-12 is picked up in very small quantities by the "intrinsic factor", which is produced in a mysterious area in the stomach, and the intrinsic factor with the B-12 is then re-absorbed by a mysterious area in the small intestine.

When digestive problems, ulcers, surgery, etc; impairs either the intrinsic factor or re-absorption, B-12 is not assimilated, and pernicious anemia follows. The main problem is that the B-12 absorption may be only partly impaired and B-12 may be only continuously low, but the effects on health renewal can be severe. Supplementing the B-12 is very effective if the intrinsic factor is working, but if the intrinsic factor system is impaired, B-12 supplements obviously cannot solve the problem. The problem is best solved with B-12 injections. Your doctor is well acquainted with the mysteries of low B-12, and he will always co-operate with injections.

B-12 tablets are also available for sub-linqual (mouth) absorption, and indeed these tablets may be adequate for healthy vegetarians, but ill health demands and deserves B-12 by injection because folic acid works with B-12, and if folic acid is supplemented over a peroid of time without fully absorbed B-12, permanemt nerve damage may result. The risk is not worthwhile. Anyone with a Candida yeast infection anywhere probably has yeast infection everywhere, so it is probably in the intestinal tract. If yeast infection is in the intestinal tract, intrinsic factor will be affected and sub-clinical pernicious anemia is likely.

Ch.4. Reducing Candida Yeast Infection.

B-12 injections can do no harm, and sometimes the results are spectacular. B-12 injections should be part of every Anti-Candida program. Even if the injections do not appear to be of particular benefit, they should be repeated every two or three months, as the changing metabolic state may make them suddenly very beneficial.

Vitamin B-12 is used in the body only in very small amounts and it has therefore been very difficult to define its full role, but large injections, even up to 1000 U.G.; I.M; daily for 10 days, have had profound therapeutic effects in tiredness, neuralgia, bursitis, Bells palsy, wheezing, asthma, hay-fever, and childhood asthma. (ref.33).

Injectable B-12 is available without prescription and, as with insulin, some doctors and nurses in Canada and the U.S.A. are showing their patients how to give themselves their own injections. Note that vitamin B-12, used in this way, is still only a good crutch that can help until all body functions can be improved.

WATER.
The quality of the water everywhere in the world is usually questionable. Well and spring water should always be checked for toxic minerals. Soft water, in areas of heavy rain, is frequently very high in cadmium. A large number of municipal water systems are quite polluted or are very high in chlorine.

Good hard spring water is the best. If distilled water is used for drinking and cooking, minerals should be supplemented, or multi- minerals should be added to the water. Pure rainwater and distilled water are low in minerals, and they will leach the minerals out of the body, and they will therefore create a mineral shortage.

FREE RADICALS and SOD,DMSO,ETC:
Oxygen is absolutely necessary for cellular function, but in cancer and other degenerative diseases the oxygen may not be completely utilized by the cells, which leads to the formation of "superoxide free radicals" which are oxidative and destructive to healthy cells. Superoxide dismutase (SOD) will reduce the free radicals to hydrogen peroxide, which is less oxidative but is still destructive to healthy cells. However, the hydrogen peroxide can be further reduced and detoxified with DMSO (Dimethyl Sulphoxide) or with selenium methionate. (Note the methyl groups from methionine).

The diseases that produce the most free radicals are cancer, arthritis, atherosclerosis, multiple sclerosis, tuberculosis, and streptococcal infections. People with these afflictions will

143

benefit from the continuing use of SOD and DMSO or selenium methionate,which should also be tried in all other cases of chronic infection. No one could ever guess at the free radicals that could be produced by the different infectives within the Candida Matrix.

Garlic is also high in methyl groups and may have particular benefits in some cases. MSM, is a reduced form of DMSO, that also promises to be very effective in many cases.

Ecological Formulas,(1061-B,Shary Circle,Conord,Ca.) has an anti-oxidant formula that contains ubiquinone (co-enzyme Q), lipoic acid, di-methylglycine, and reduced glutathione, which is very effective in reducing free radicals.

VITAMIN B-15.(Pangamic Acid).

B-15 reduces hypoxia by enhancing the utilization of oxygen in the cells. There do not seem to be any storage sites for B-15 so it should be taken several times per day. Almost any amount can be taken without toxicity, but the benefits from very large amounts seem doubtful.

Every credit and appreciation should be given to Earnest Krebbs (of Laetrile fame) for his dedication in discovering B-15. B-15 is a true vitamin that is of help to all health programs.

VITAMIN B-13, OROTIC ACID.

Vitamin B-13 has a particular role in the metabolism of B-12 and folic acid. It is particularly effective in atherosclerosis and multiple sclerosis. (Note the link). B-13 should be part of every health program. Large amounts of B-13 are found in whey. It is usually found in supplements as orotate. There is therefore extra value in selecting supplements that are put up as orotates; (e.g. calcium orotate) and the orotate form also ensures good assimilation of the supplements.

LOW THYROID FUNCTION.(Hypothyroidism).

Dr.Broda Barnes, in "Hypothyroidism, the Unsuspected Illness", (Harper and Rowe), shows that almost every ailment known to man can be associated with low thyroid function.

Low thyroid function can develop slowly from an altered metabolic state or from inherited deficiency, particularly if the lineage of either or both parents comes from a "goiter zone".

Low thyroid can also be caused by mercury, usually leached from amalgam dental fillings. (See Mercury and the Thyroid. Ch.4.)

The thyroid glands are the two glands that lie on each side of the throat that when enlarged are called goiter. The thyroid glands require iodine for the production of thyroxin, and if iodine is low the glands enlarge in an effort to supply body requirements. The principal source of iodine is the ocean. As late as the 1920's goiter was very common in many areas of the world that were distant from the oceans. Central North America was among these areas and the writer has seen goiters that, when removed, would completely fill a pint sealer, and many goiters were even larger. Large goiters were also common in cattle and other domestic animals. The goiter problem, as such, was solved in both animal and man, by the use of iodized salt, which continues into the present. Reduced use of salt by many people, however, has also reduced the supplemental iodine, in many cases resulting in low thyroid function through lack of iodine, while thyroid deficiencies from the past, together with borderline deficiencies over the last two decades, has led to the low thyroid levels found in many people to-day. Candida yeast depletes lithium, which also reduces thyroid function.

Thyroid hormone from the thyroid, is absolutely essential to life because it controls the "fire" of life itself. Every cell of the body metabolically "burns" the hydrocarbons in blood sugar by combining them with oxygen. It is the heat from this metabolic "fire" that maintains our body temperature. Very small amounts of thyroid hormone control the rate of sugar metabolism; the rate of "burning"; and the thyroid therefore controls both the body temperature and the functional rate of all other body processes. If thyroid hormone is even slightly below normal, metabolism in every cell of the body, including all glands, all organs, and every body process, will be below normal. The list of ailments associated with the low thyroid therefore spans the entire range of diseases that plague mankind. Of particular note are low body temperatures, low energy, impaired blood circulation, impaired sexual and hormone function, overweight and underweight, and a great increase in infections, particularly TB. TB used to be the primary cause of death. It is now suppressed with antibiotics, but the association of TB with low thyroid is of pertinent interest because the TB bacterium is one of the actinomycetales, and it has the ability to impair the function of the immune system. Other members of actinomycetales are leprosy (which also impairs the immune system), actinomyces (considered to be a fungus) and progenitor cryptocides (which is always present in cancer). Some reseachers think that Candida yeast is also a member of actinomycetales and we know that it also impairs the immune system. We know too, that Candida yeast is bi-morphic, with two stages of life, but if it is polymorphic, and does transform into actinomycetales, or perhaps on into progenitor cryptocides, then it may indeed impair the immune system by interfering with thyroid production.

CH.4. Reducing Candida Yeast Infection.

Significantly, actinomycin D is used by some physicians in treating the GD phase,(resting phase) of cancer, and in treating testicular cancer. Actinomycin ia a very potent chemical produced by actinomycetales. Dr. Alslaben says; "The way in which it (actinomycin) works is to arrest the maturation of cells. to inhibit the immune response, to destroy cell integrity, to produce malformation and even death of embryos or conglomeration of cells, (hence its use in cancer) to inhibit and destroy enzymes of all kinds, to prevent synthesis of essential proteins, to decrease thyroid, estrogen, testosterone, and other steroid levels, to tear down cells and poison the host with their products"! Although this information is not exactly heart warming, it does show that low thyroid from inheritance will lead to increased infections of all kinds and Candida will certainly become established, and that the infectives will then probably further reduce thyroid function, or alternately, if Candida infection arrives first, low thyroid function will probably follow. Chapter 3, shows several medical papers that link Candida yeast to altered thyroid function, and indeed, in at least one case knowm to the author, a very small goiter was present for over fifty years, and resisted all efforts to reduce it, but it spontaneously normalized after a heavy Candida infection was reduced.

In consideration of the foregoing, it seems very probable that altered thyroid function will be present in all cases of Candida infection, and some thyroid therapy will therefore be necessary to help reduce the infection. Small quantities of iodine should be supplemented prior to, or along with the thyroxin.

Thyroid Function Test.

Dr.Barnes uses body temperature as a guide to determine thyroid function. Every morning for about a week, a fever thermometer is placed in the armpit for at least ten minutes before getting out of bed in the morning. If the temperature is below 97.8, low thyroid function is indicated.

Lithium and the Thyroid.

The relationship between lithium and thyroid function has already been noted. In about fifty mineral tests that indicated possible Candida infection (and that were later confirmed), lithium was at the very lowest level of normal, with only two tests showing one point higher. This certainly indicates that Candida infection either uses lithium and deprives the host, or some of the metabolites from the yeast infection may tie up or chemically inactivate lithium, thus reducing active lithium levels, resulting in low thyroid function and impaired ability to fight infection. We know that lithium opposes yeast infection, and we know that it is a thyroid nutrient. In all cases of yeast infection lithium should therefore be supplemented until levels reach a high normal. Take it easy. Lithium can have some very potent effects. A successful amount seems to be about $\frac{1}{2}$ of a 300mg capsule, daily.

Thyroid Supplements.

To overcome low thyroid function Dr. Barnes uses thyroid supplements (from your doctor) starting with 1 grain daily for a peroid of a month or more, and increasing by one grain at a time until the basal temperature rises to 98.2. Large amounts should be avoided because they alter the delicate thyroid balance. Sudden spectacular improvement should not be expected, but slow improvement should be evident. The final dose to maintain adequate thyroid levels will probably be a lifelong requirement.

Unfortunately, Dr.Barnes does not say exactly what he is using for thyroid supplement, but presumably he uses thyroxin, although in one place he mentions thyroid extract. Also with therapy centered solely on the thyroid, improvement in thyroid function could not be expected. Our suggestion would be to supplement lithium (if indicated) and iodine, with about $\frac{1}{4}$ tablet of thyroid extract (raw glandular) and check progress by basal temperature. Iodine is available from your doctor or from some health food stores. Raw glandulars are also available from some health food stores, or from your naturopath. Lithium, iodine, and raw glandulars tend to induce the thyroid to produce more hormone, and reduction in Candida infection will also tend to return thyroid function to normal. But take it all very slow and easy, because disturbed thyroid function can produce some very weird effects.

In determining the need for thyroid therapy, or in adjusting the amounts, consideration should be given to the affects of chronic infection on basal temperature. When you take thyroid problems to your doctor, he will probably run thyroid tests to determine thyroid function. If the tests show low thyroid, it is certainly present, but Dr.Barnes has found such tests to be unreliable, with the basal temperature test to be the best. Thyroid certainly controls the "fire of life", and if the temperature is low, the function of every system in the body can be expected to be sub-normal. Basal temperature, therefore, becomes critical.

So the question then becomes, what is a normal basal (or basic) temperature? We know that the normal body temperature is 98.4, and that is the temperature that we must finally seek, but we also know that infection of any kind, anywhere, is always accompanied by inflammation and fever as a natural consequence of the immune response. With chronic continuous infection, as in yeast infection, a chronic continuous low grade fever should therefore be expected, and the "normal" temperature for that person would therefore be above the usual 98.4. Thus a person with a basal temperature of 98.2 without infection would be considered to have a normal thyroid function, while the same temperature in a person with chronic infection might indicate low thyroid and in need for therapy. Transient and chronic infections are one of the principal indicators of low thyroid function. In general, if obvious yeast infection is present, thyroid therapy should be tried, and should be slowly increased until the basal temperature rises beyond the usual 98.4, to probably as high as 99, depending upon the estimated amount of chronic infection.

The amino acid tyrosine is essential to both thyroid and adrenal function. Thyroid therapy should therefore include supplements of tyrosine to insure adequate nutrition.

It should at all times be emphasized that the thyroid gland is very sensitive and that tinkering with thyroid function in any way frequently produces any kind of peculiar reaction. Yet if thyroid function is in any way low, activity must be raised. The basic rule is to take it slow and easy. Start with the tyrosine, lithium, and iodine, and about a week later, after the body has stabilized, start with the glandular substance or the thyroxin, but start with only very small quantities, taken 12 hours away from the other supplements. Aminopyrine, phenylbutazone, and gold preparations affect lithium, and should be avoided. A common prescription thyroid supplement is thyroglobulin (PD) 30 mg.daily.

CYSTEINE, and the PERILS of not EATING EGGS.(see also mercury, CH.4.)

Cysteine and methionine are sulphur bearing (methylated) amino acids, that have many functions in the body, including the scavenging of toxic metals. In the scavenging of toxic metals cysteine appears to be much more agressive than methionine, and cysteine is therefore used for heavy metal therapy. The amounts needed to move heavy metals, are quite high, (500 mg./day), and the amounts removed are very low. Intravenous chelation therefore appears to be a much better way to reduce heavy metals. Mercury, however, is an exception. EDTA will not pick up mercury. Mercury is difficult to chelate, and there are undesirable side effects. Removal of the source of the mercury (usually amalgam fillings in the teeth) with large supplements of cysteine, appears to be the best way to reduce mercury.

It now appears that under some circumstances, and particularly if Candida infection is high, mercury is leached from amalgam tooth fillings by galvanic action, and becomes sequestered in the nervous system, where it induces multiple sclerosis, or where it produces symptoms similar to multiple sclerosis. This sequestered mercury may not show up in the hair test. Normally, mercury is quite rapidly removed from the body by flushing with water, as in calomel laxatives and some "water pills", and through the binding action of cysteine and methionine.

Now we know that mercury greatly affects thyroid function, and we also know that the "grapefruit and eggs" diet (CH.4.) induces effective weight loss in some people. The grapefruit and eggs must be doing something, someway, somehow, so we must postulate that the large amounts of cysteine is scavenging mercury, with the improved thyroid function contributing to weight loss. This could be verified by checking the urine for mercury, and it also infers that the same weight loss might be accomplished with a high protein diet with extra grapefruit and heavy supplements of cysteine.

It should also be noted that Dr.Donsbach's Formula FLW. (Orachel), which has been proven to be effective for improving blood circulation, (in some cases), contains very large amounts of cysteine. (Oral Chelation, CH.6.) Since we also know from the excellent work of Dr. Broda Barnes that atherosclerosis is also linked to thyroid function we must again postulate that it is the cysteine in the formula that is the key active ingredient that is improving thyroid function by removing the interference of mercury.

From the foregoing it appears that perhaps people who eat two eggs per day get enough cysteine that they eliminate mercury and thus avoid mercury retention, with all of its toxic effects, whereas the mercury may slowly accumulate in people who do not eat eggs.

Quite obviously, people with serious health problems should:
1. Replace all amalgam tooth fillings.
2. Eliminate all other possible sources of mercury, like calomel, "water pills", etc.
3. Supplement cysteine.
4. Include eggs in the diet.

As soon as cysteine supplements of more than 250mg./day are started it will be noticed that the breath and body exude a foul odor somewhat like garlic. As with garlic this odor comes from sulphur. Chlorophyl will help to reduce the smell, but unfortunately the odor will remain until a few days after the large amounts of cysteine have been discontinued.

CH.4. Reducing Candida Yeast Infection.

LOW PARATHYROID. (Hypoparathyroidism).
  (See also Osteoporosis and Calcium/Magnesium).
      Parathyroid hormone(PTH) is essential to thyroid function and is also essential to assimilation of calcium, while calcium in turn is essential for the assimilation of proteins so necessary for immune function and for rebuilding tissues.
      One of the principal causes of low parathyroid function is mucocutaneous (skin) Candida infection (Ref.1.). It appears that the Candida impairs parathyroid function by depletion of magnesium and by reduced synthesis of vitamin D. Conversely then, everyone with Candida infection will have, to some degree, low parathyroid function with poor calcium assimilation, and low proteins (blood test) and some osteoporosis, largely in proportion to the extent of the Candida infection. Everyone with serious Candida infection should therefore have supplements of calcium, B-6, vitamin D, extra magnesium, and mixed amino acids.
      Here again it should be stressed that, although the diet may be high in protein, if the proteins are digested, or if they are not assimilated, the body supplies will be inadequate for immune function and tissue re-building, while the proteins remaining in the intestines will become excellent fertilizer for many microrganisms that in turn will fill the intestines with their own biological products, some of which will be toxic. Some naturopaths and nutritionists will "solve" this problem with fasting, or with a low-protein vegetarian diet. At once the victim will feel better, not because of increased calcium and proteins, but because the toxins have been reduced. The health improvement is then mistaken as a cure, despite the low blood values of calcium and proteins. Obviously the change in diet only masked the actual problem of low parathyroid function.
      Where blood tests show low calcium (Hypocalcemia) and low proteins, every effort must be made to improve calcium metabolism. The principal controls of calcium throughout the body are parathyroid hormone (PTH) Vitamin D-3, and calcitonin (from the thyroid). The control is interlocked between blood, bone, and kidney. Usually the defect is in the gut or in the bone, and the leading causative offenders are vitamin D, deficiency and low or ineffective parathyroid hormone(PTH). Calcitonin does not appear to have a significant role, but thyroid function should be improved as much as possible. At present the only way that PTH can be supplemented is with glandulars, but vitamin D-3 has such a similar action that the usual medical treatment is with vitamin D-3 and calcium, while the calcium should be accompanied by magnesium and B-6.

CH.4. Reducing Candida Yeast Infection.

Where calcium/protein levels are very low, every effort must be made to raise thyroid function, to improve the blood [intravenous chelation (if possible), B-12, folic acid, niacin], to improve kidney function (CH.7) and to improve the bone. (See osteoporosis, Ch.7).

Usually and unfortunately the functions of blood, bone, and kidney, and the GI tract, are also being impaired by Candida and associated infectives. Again, everything must be done. Progress then will be positive, even if it may be slow.

Recent research shows that parathyroid hormone controls excretion of calcium, which makes supplements of PTH one of the best ways to increase calcium and protein levels.

LYMPHATIC INFECTIONS.
(See also Travelling Arthritis, and Cancer.Ch.7.)

Lymphatic infections are particularly insidious because the pain and swelling seems to be moving around, (which it is), while the infection itself is walled off by the immune system, of which the lymphatic system is the major part. Various anti-biotics should be tried, starting with metronidazole and sulfamethoxazole. A-E Emulsin may also help.

A-E Emulsin and Lymphatic Infections.(See Cancer Ch.7.)

A-E Emulsin is a highly concentrated form of synthetic vitamin A with vitamin E. It has the peculiar ability to be inversely absorbed backwards through the immune system.

In the normal assimilation of vitamin A the liver monitors vitamin A and allows the body only very restricted amounts of vitamin A, which sometimes are insufficient. The A-E Emulsin gets around this natural liver limitation. Dr.Manner (of cancer fame) has shown that A-E Emulsin will greatly increase the effectiveness of the immune system by increasing lymphocytes, sometimes to almost double.

Start with 1 drop of A-E and work up to 2 or 3 drops. If effects are not obvious do not use for more than two weeks at a time. If signs of toxicity develop, discontinue at once.

A-mulsin is a similar product to A-E Emulsin that does not have the vitamin E and may be less effective.

A-E Emulsin should be part of every Candida program.

A-E Emulsin is perhaps the only substance that is effective in false arthritis (or travelling arthritis) which has all of the symptoms of arthritis except that it seems to move around in the afflicted area. It is caused by infection within the lymphatic system. The infection is reduced by increased effectiveness of the immune system when nourished with the emulsin.

A-E Emulsin will also frequently relieve "deep aches", that feel like the bones are aching (which they may be.) and which is also caused by infection within the lymphatic system.

If signs of toxicity do not develop, A-E emulsin can be continued until the ear-wax (also from the lymphatic system) becomes soft.

It is postulated that the beneficial effects from Dale Alexander's much publicised "cod liver oil/orange juice" therapy comes, not from vitamin D, but from an emulsion of vitamin A, formed by the combination.

Synthetic vitamin A (as in A.E.emulsin) is a retinoid, a form of retinol. It has been particularly effective in cancer, but continued long term use can produce serious side effects. Beta-carotene is suggested as a substitude, that is free from toxic side affects, but does not seem to be as effective.

MUCUS and the MUCOUS MEMBRANE.

Many pages of information, and many more pages of misinformation have been written about mucus. Some writers have referred to mucus as "bad" and "good" mucus, which appears to refer to healthy mucus and perhaps to unhealthy or diseased mucus, and there are even programs for eliminating mucus, and for avoiding so called "mucus forming foods".

The fact is that we cannot live without mucus. Excretion of mucus is an essential part of normal internal skin function. Mucous membranes line passages leading from the surfaces of the body. Mucous membranes are sheets of fibrous connective tissue lined with collumnar secreting cells that secrete the mucus fluid, which is principally dissolved mucins (mucoids) (similar to mucilage). The mucus washes the tissues and carries with it white blood cells, and it is therefore the active substance that prevents infections from developing in the cavities of the body. It is mucus that covers the inside of the mouth and entire digestive tract, and lubricates it so that food and wastes can slide along. It is mucus that prevents harsh acids and alkalis from attacking the intestinal tissues. It is mucus that covers the surfaces of the sexual system and provides sexual lubrication, and it is the layers of mucous membrane (mucosa) covering all internal skin surfaces that prevents infectives from attacking the body.

In all people, healthy or unhealthy, Candida yeast can be found lying harmlessly on the mucous surfaces of the intestinal tract and birth canal. It is only when harsh foods, drugs, spices, virulent infections, continuous enemas, surgery, abrasion, or other trauma that destroys the effectiveness of the mucous membrane that the Candida yeast can attack the body cells and set up a callus matrix. Quite obviously, like all other body tissues, the mucous membranes can be healthy, or not so healthy, and it is also obvious that to effectively combat infection anywhere and everywhere the mucous membranes must be as healthy as possible. Significantly, Candida infection is listed in medical literature as a muco-cutaneous disease, a mucous skin disease. To reduce Candida infection, we must nourish the skin, and the mucous membranes.

The basic skin nutrients are vitamin A, B-complex, C, D, E, B-6, choline, pantothenic acid, and ample fully digested protein. These are required not only to maintain healthy skin and mucous membranes, but also for rebuilding the damaged tissues as Candida infection is reduced. Significantly, these are the same nutrients that are needed to support the adrenals during stress,- to support the adrenals against the high stress of chronic infection,- and these are the same nutrients that the immune system needs to combat and reduce chronic infection. Stress is the greatest single factor in damage to mucous membranes.

Stress and Mucous Membranes.

So much has been written about stress, and the effects of stress on the body, yet the actual physical damage resulting from stress is seldom realized or properly understood.

Under severe stress, as in continous chronic infection, the adrenals produce large amounts of cortisone from the adrenal cortex. Cortisone, either administered, or produced by the adrenals, destroys proteins and particularly damages the mucous membranes. It should be remembered that cortisone is a messenger hormone, that prepares the body for "fight ot flight", and one of the first effects is to draw proteins, from the thymus and lymph glands, which are then broken down for blood sugar for immediate energy. But the thymus and lymph glands are also the storehouse for proteins for immune nutrients, so the final result of stress, added to the continous stress of chronic infection, is to not only destroy proteins and damage the mucous membranes, but also to convert stored proteins to sugars and thus deprive the immune system and the entire body of fully digested proteins at the very time when they are most needed. The lost proteins are particularly needed by the pancreas for the production of digestive enzymes, and they are also needed by the mucous membranes that were damaged by the cortisone. Further, continuing stress, continues to deplete protein reserves, because proteins are constantly being leaked into the tissues, where they are gathered up by the lymphatic system, and are normally returned to the bloodstream. But if the stress is continous, cortisone production will be continuous, and the proteins will be pulled from the thymus and lymph nodes and made into blood sugar, with any excess being stored in the liver as glycogen. Thus, in effect, stress not only destroys proteins throughout the body (by cortisone) but it also converts the proteins into blood sugar and deprives the immune system, and the pancreas and digestive system, and prevents the rebuilding of the damaged tissues.

It is little wonder then, that Adelle Davis's "Anti-stress formula" with fortified milk and dessicated liver, and Dr. Philpott's large quantities of amino acids (as much as 15 grams) have been highly successful for many people.

The other nutrients so essential for adrenal support are potassium and large quantities of vitamin C, perferably as sodium/potassium ascorbate. (Hi KC FIzz).

Total stress should also be reduced. Reducing the total chronic infection will help greatly, but the very use of anti-fungals, anti-biotics, etc; together with toxins from the dead and dying infectives and the rebuilding of damaged tissues increases stress during therapy. Stress from cold and heat, should be avoided. There are countless programs for reducing mental stress, most of which are based on faith and companionship. Peace and tranquilty can be promoted by remembering that nothing can be done about things that are past, and the future will be whatever it becomes,- "whatever must be, must be". and we can live without remorse or recrimination if we do only those things that are honorable. Serenity comes by making molehills out of mountains; serenity comes from looking for the good, and turning a blind eye to evil; serenity comes from faith, faith in tomorrow, faith in life, and faith in your fellow-man. Everyone can find peace, if they seek it.

People with "tight" bowel movements may have low production of mucous fluid. Such people may benefit from supplements of psyllium seed. Psyllim seed contains very large quantities of mucins, that are similar to mucus. Psyllium preparations are available from the drug store. An added benefit from psyllium may be that the body uses the already pre-formed metabolites from the psyllium seed as ready-made nutrients for the production of mucus. Psyllium supplements can usually be discontinued in less than a month.

Intestinal Flora, Caprylic (Octonic) Acid,
   and the Mucous Membrane.

We are never alone. The complete organism is our body with all of its micro-organisms, good and bad, interacting synergistically with us and with each other. There are about 400 different micro-organisms that usually make up the intestinal flora of normally healthy people. The ill health that can follow upon the disruption of the intestinal flora is well documented, and many good doctors avoid the use of anti-biotics and anti-fungals,etc; because they have found that sometimes it is almost impossible to bring the intestinal flora mixture back to normal, and thus avoid continuous chronic digestive problems. The Candida victim however, usually has already had the intestinal flora disturbed to the point of continuing digestive problems, with the anti-biotics and anti-fungals essential to reducing the infection further complicating the difficulties. Mucins, like psyllium seed, will help to restore the damaged mucous membranes, and acidophilus will help to restore one of the flora, but acidophillis is only one, while we really need to restore the other 399 along with their synergistic function, or we need to know what the flora do, so that we can help them.

We have pointed out that Candida is always present in the digestive tract and birth canal, usually harmlessly lying on the surface of the mucosa. With the mucus so thin and with the fungal infectives constantly present, we should expect infection to be constant in everyone, yet many people escape infection throughout their entire lives. They escape infection because the intestinal flora help to protect them from the fungal infectives. The fungal infectives may lie harmlessly on the surface of the mucus on the membrane, but if, or whenever, they try to penetrate the surface of the mucous membrane they encounter many short-chain fatty acids which will inactivate or destroy them. These fatty acids are produced synergystically by "good" bacteria interacting with the cells on the surface of the mucosa, and interacting with each other. Thus it is not just the mucous membrane that protects us against the infectives;- it is the intestinal flora that is our saving;- it is the production of short chain anti-fungal fatty acids by the intestinal flora that is the first line of defence against the hordes of fungal infectives constantly waiting to start growing in us and consuming us. The short chain fatty acid that displays the highest anti-fungal activity is caprylic acid. Caprylic acid can therefore be thought of as an active anti-fungal produced by the mucous membranes with the help of the intestinal flora. Caprylic acid therefore becomes not only our savior, but an anti-fungal agent of choice: specifically the very substance that we need the most to interpose between the fungus and ourselves, until the intestinal flora mix can return to normal.

Caprylic acid, in the form of sodium caprylate, and similar salts, have been effectively used in dentistry since about 1940, with some medical use that was also effective, but, as so frequently happens with the medical attitude of "management", the therapy was unused, lost, and forgotten. However, caprylic acid is still very effective and it is now available in an enteric coated tablet under the name of Caprystatin. Caprystatin, or other forms of caprylic acid should be part of every antifungal program where the intestinsl tract is involved, but here again, we have three different conditions:-

1. The esophagus and upper G.I. tract. Enteric coated tablets will by-pass the upper G.I. tract, so we should break up the tablets, hold them in the mouth, and let them pass down the esophagus slowly.

2. Small intestine. To reach the small intestine, caprylic acid in any form must be enteric coated. With reduced fungal infection of the mucosa a great improvement in digestion and absorption of nutrients, may be seen.

3. Colon. Even with enteric coating and continuing use, it is very difficult for oral caprylic tablets to reach the colon. In cases of colitis, fungal colon infections, or porous "leaky" bowels, the caprylic acid may be much more effective if the caprylic acid is introduced with an enema, or as a suppository. Restoration of normal flora in the colon is the only way that peristalsis can be normalized, because peristalsis depends upon the micro- flora, and the micro-flora depend upon peristalsis.

Caution. -- Despite all of the foregoing the authors experience with caprylic and sorbic acid up until the present time has been very disappointing, as they seem to reduce digestive action and promote constipation without evident benefits. We are still trying.

Changing the Intestinal Flora.

Dr.Pfieffer (ref.5.) to his great credit, points out that in addition to acidophilis, buttermilk, egg yolks, and elemental sulphur are effective in changing and improving the intestinal flora. Saurkraut will also help to normalize the intestinal flora.

Herbs and the Mucous Membrane.

Now here, at the surface of the mucous membrane is another opportunity for the herbalists to display their technology. The short chain fatty acids that show the greatest anti-fungal activity are the fatty acids with 7 to 9 carbons, particularly heptylic, caprylic, and 2, 4-hexadiemoic acid. Sorbic acid is also effective. So which foods contain one or more of these acids in reasonable quantity? Which foods are really the herbs that we need to combat fungal infections? Who knows? Can they be butter? lard? coconut oil? which ones? Oh Technology! Where art thou?

The herbalists do not seem to have the answer, and the nutritionists and the food faddists do not seem to have the answer. Yet nature is grand, so surely mother nature must have caprylic acid stored away in some one of the things we eat. So let us work backwards. Complex compounds are very difficult, and sometimes almost impossible to synthesize, and many complex chemicals are therefore simply extracted from nature's storehouse. Now if we look up caprylic acid, we discover that it is usually extracted from coconut. Coconut then is the new herb that we seek. But we should also realize that coconut is a hard saturated fat that can also raise the levels of cholesterol and triglycerides in people with heart or circulatory problems. So people who may be at risk should monitor their blood pressure and cholesterol if they consume high quantities of coconut. However, atherosclerosis is actually the result of infection that uses up so much vitamin C, that there is insufficient ascorbate to convert the cholesterol in the bloodstream into bile, and providing enough caprylic acid to restore digestive peace seems to take only one small coconut, eaten with all foods, and nibbled at for three or four days, so if large amounts of lecithin and slow release vitamin C, are taken along with the coconut, high levels of blood cholesterol should not become a problem. A tablespoon of shredded coconut, added to the cereal in the morning, can provide a continuing supply of caprylic acid.

OXYGEN.

Adequate oxygen is absolutely essential to good health. Everyone should sleep with windows open to provide higher levels of oxygen during sleep.

Adequate oxygen at the cellular level is necessary for the complete metabolism of sugars. Whenever exercise exceeds the cellular oxygen supply, as with fast or prolonged running, the sugars are burned only to the point of lactic acid, which is stored in the muscles and makes the muscles "stiff". If oxygen is adequate after the over-excerise, the lactic acid will be burned on down to water and carbon dioxide. Thus, if oxygen is adequate sleep will clear up all stored lactic acid, and by morning the tissues will be saturated with oxygen.

In cases of anemia, clumped red cells, high cholesterol and triglycerides, emphesema, or other forms of poor oxygenation, vitamin E, and pangamate (B-15) will be of benefit by increasing oxygen utilization.

Very frequently poor cellular oxygenation reduces total body function, which in turn increases the need for oxygen. Bed rest will always help, but if health is already low, oxygen therapy may be necessary to break this degenerative cycle.

Oxygen Therapy.

Oxygen therapy has been proven to be of great benefit in some cases of multiple sclerosis, cancer, collagen diseases, arteriosclerosis, and emphesema. It is undoubtedly also of benefit in all forms of serious illness.

The simplest form of oxygen therapy is the use of a large circulating fan while sleeping. The fan maintains a moving supply of fresh air, increases the air pressure to the lungs slightly, and it cools the air slightly. Cold air, of course, contains more oxygen per unit volume, and compressed air also has more oxygen per unit volume, i.e. more oxygen in each breath. The benefits from the fan are greater, and of course are more noticeable in hot weather.

In hot weather oxygen therapy can be increased by the use of a large fully circulating air conditioner that cools the fresh air as it brings it into the room. Cracks around doors and windows should be sealed, and the escape vent should be adjusted to raise the air pressure in the room. Air pressure can be measured with a barometer. The increased oxygenation from the system usually promotes deep, sound, restful sleep.

A more expensive form of oxygen therapy is the use of oxygen masks or oxygen tents. These can be used intermittently, are particularly of value after excerise, and can be advantageously used to enable critically ill people to increase their exercise.

Hyperbaric oxygen therapy, as with a decompression chamber, is an expensive form of oxygen therapy that has been of particular benefit in multiple sclerosis, and may be very beneficial in all cases of desperate ill health. It would seem that an oxygenated, pressurized "sleeping chamber", capable of one atmosphere of pressure, could be made of glass or plastic at a reasonable cost.

There are reports that in some of the "Fun Cities", like Les Vegas, the hotel rooms are highly oxygenated to promote customer activity. The writer has been unable to confirm this and has been unable to find out how it may be done, but any system that could increase room oxygen levels by 10% or more would certainly be of great therapeutic help.

SLEEP.

Good restful sleep is absolutely necessary for the maintainence of health, and is essential to the recovery from any health problems. Both the suppression of infectives, and the rebuilding of damaged tissues, occur during sleep. Extra sleep is therefore needed with serious infection, and during recovery. It should be remembered that when anti-fungal agents are used the reduction in infection requires the disposal of the toxic remains of both the dead infective and the anti-fungal agent, together with the disposal of the dead cells in the injured tissues and the rebuilding of the infected tissue, while the reduced yeast infection also reduces stress, followed by rebuilding of the thymus, adrenals, thyroid, liver, and pancreas. Extra sleep is therefore a prime requirement during recovery from serious infections. Whenever possible, respond to the urge to sleep. The body usually knows what it needs. Sometimes it may seem impossible to get enough sleep, with whole days "lost" in bed. But console yourself, the body is rebuilding.

Note that the urge to sleep usually follows about one half hour after taking ketoconazole.

One of the principal sleep nutrients is B-6. Dr.Carl Pfieffer shows that B-6 should be supplemented to the point where dreams can be remembered. (Dream recall). Adelle Davis points out that magnesium should be supplemented in proportion to the supplements of B-6, and calcium should always be supplemented in proportion with magnesium, while vitamin D is essential for the absorption of calcium. Light sleepers, i.e. people who hear everything while asleep, may find that they drift into deep sleep with B-6 supplements. "Dream sleep", is necessary for good rest and health. L-Tryptophane, and the vitamer Deaner will also alter sleep, and may promote better sleep for some people.

Ample oxygen promotes good, deep, healthy sleep. The windows should be wide open, even in cold weather. A large fan will provide extra oxygen in hot weather, and is of particular value to people with circulatory problems. (See oxygen therapy).

Sleeping Problems. (See also Ref.5.)

Most sleeping problems are associated with altered hormone levels, adrenal depletion, and sexual problems. With reduction in yeast infection, hormone and adrenal function will improve, and sleep problems will be reduced. Some of the problems and suggestions are:

A Chilly.-- This is the condition where sleep is poor because the body feels "cold inside", which it is. It is "cold inside" because of low thyroid function or from lack of adequate nutrition; from indigestion, poor diet, or low blood sugar. A night shirt or other close-fitting garment will help. Dense carbohydrate, like a small bowl of granola or a half slice of whole wheat toast, one half hour before bedtime will usually provide enough lasting energy to prevent the "cold" feeling. As liver, pancreas and adrenals improve, the "cold" feeling will disappear. If too much carbohydrate is consumed, or if the carbohydrate is too refined, sweating and hot flashes may occur.

B. Sweating.-- When sleep is disturbed by night sweating, the cause may be fever from rampant infection, excess carbohydrate too close to bedtime, or irregular over-active thyroid. (Hyperthyroidism) Immune nutrients, including A-E emulsin, will help reduce infection. Thyroid function can be improved with Tyrosine, B-6, vitamin C, 300 mg. Vitamin E, and 6 mg. iodine, daily. Thyroxin may also be needed. See thyroid.

C. Wakefulness.-- This is the condition where the person is very tired, yet as soon as they lie down they are wide awake.

It is particularly devastating to health, and recovery, because the person cannot sleep at the very time that sleep is needed so badly.

Many efforts have been made to determine the exact cause of this condition, all without specific answers. However, wakefulness seems to always clear up when chronic infection is reduced. It therefore seems that the wakefulness results from a continuous source of toxins that keeps the adrenals and nervous system constantly active, much like a continuous cup of coffee. The only effective relief therefore comes from a reduction in total toxins; i.e. elimination of all toxic foods and beverages, and reduction of total chronic infection with ketoconazole, resteclin or other ant-infectives, and the re-building of body systems. In the meantime, three other causes can be considered, and various sleep-inducers can be used.

1. <u>Staying up too late.</u> Staying up too late is not a matter of time by the clock, it is a matter of health and energy reserves. If health and energy reserves are low, the natural time for sleep may come only two or three hours after the evening meal. if this "natural time for sleep" is by-passed, the body may respond with excess adrenalin, and the body will then start to run on "nervous energy" with the adrenals running so low on nutrients that they continuously produce whatever adrenalin they can. The continuous adrenalin then acts like a continuous cup of coffee, and keeps the person awake even when they are desperately tired. The wakefulness will then continue until complete exhaustion, or until large amounts of adrenal nutrients are supplied. If the "wide awake" is recognized soon enough, all of the adrenal nutrients including Hi KC Fizz, followed by about one hour of sedentary monotonous activity, (to allow the adrenalin to dissipate) will usually bring natural sleep and the "complete exhaustion" phase can be avoided. Some people get into a state of nightly wakefulness, and almost daily exhaustion, with sleep finally coming at 4 or 5 in the morning. Such severe patterns can sometimes be broken only by the judicious use of a few sleeping pills, together with all appropriate sleep inducers. It should be noted that people who get into the state of "running on nervous energy" usually develop hypertension (from the continuous adrenlin) with consequent high blood pressure, and usually with atherosclerosis and circulatory problems.

Frequently, this wakefulness pattern can be broken by doing up all of the little chores and getting ready for bed early in the evening, then watch for signs of yawning and drowsiness, and respond to them. Bedtime may come early, even one or two hours before the usual bedtime. Note, that if watering the dog and putting out the cat have not already been done before bedtime, the increased activity may stir the adrenals and bring on the wakeful state.

2. The "Too Big" Evening Meal.

Remember the adage- "Breakfast like a King, lunch like a Prince and dine like a Pauper"? Unless there is strenuous physical activity in the evening, the evening meal should be small and appropriate to the amount of exercise, with sufficient dense carbohydrate to last until morning. Without appropriate physical activity, a large evening meal, (and particularly a meal with large amounts of refined carbohydrate) may promote wakefulness. The excess food imposes a large disposal problem on the stomach and digestive system, on the adrenals and on all other systems. Blood sugar soars, and every cell in the body is overloaded with sugars. If the adrenals are already overloaded with the total effects of high infection, they will start running on "nervous energy", and although the body and nervous system are desperately in need of sleep and rest, sleep cannot come until the excess food has been dissipated. The answer is clear; do not overeat!

3. Hypoglycemia. (Low Blood Sugar).

When blood sugar falls below a certain point the adrenals respond with adrenalin, and sleep cannot come until the adrenalin is used up. Again, if adrenal nutrients are already depleted, and if the body is already exhausted, the adrenals may go into the "nervous energy" state, as previously described, followed by wakefulness. The episodes that interfere with sleep are usually caused by stomach dumping (indicated by a soft watery stool), poor digestion and or assimilation, or poor liver storage. As hypoglycemia, digestive problems, and overloaded liver are usually present in serious yeast infection, the episodes of low blood sugar, and perhaps consequent wakefulness, will continue until the infection is reduced. In the meantime life must go on and sleep is essential to recovery, so the following suggestions should be tried:

(A) Include (if possible) dense carbohydrate (a slice of whole grain bread or some whole grain cereal), along with a small quantity of plain carbohydrate (as potatoes, rice, etc;) with evening meal. If the yeast in the bread causes problems try whole wheat biscuits.

(B) Watch the time and the symptoms, and just before the blood sugar drop usually occurs have a small snack, which should contaim some free carbohydrate, (like fruit), some dense carboydrate, and pre-digested protein,(slimming powder).

(C) Change the time of the evening meal. Have it earlier, with a snack about an hour before bedtime.

Sleep Inducers.

1. Go for a walk, or have similar light exercise about $\frac{1}{2}$ hr. before bedtime. This may induce sleep, or it may promote wakefulness, but it should be tried.

2. Avoid "active work" i.e., activities that require even moderate adrenal function, for at least one hour before bedtime. Try a "dull" activity, read a dull book, or mend socks, and try not to think about troubles or problems.

3. Take "sleep nutrients" about $\frac{1}{2}$ hr. before bed.

There are no hard and fast rules for "sleep nutrients" because everyone's mixture of infectives is different, everyone's toxins are different and everyone's adrenal status is different, so the effects on mind and body are different. Various combinations of nutrients should be tried.

Sleep Nutrients.

(Should be taken about $\frac{1}{2}$ hr. before bedtime).

A. Choline, inositol, methionine.(Usually combined) 250 mg. each.

Pantothenic acid --100 mg.

B-6--100 mg. or more. Can be increased to the point where dreams are remembered but are not too vivid. If psychosis or mental problems occur L-cysteine and pyridoxyl -5- phosphate may also be needed. (See also citric acid, Ch. 4.)

Calcium/magnesium--250-500mg. Avoid the lactate forms that may increase build-up of lactic acid.

L-Tryptophane--500mg. Will promote sleep for most people and for people with an L-dopa problem.

B. Vitamin C is another "sleep" nutrient, but some people with adrenal depletion or inadequate vitamin C intake find that it invigorates the adrenals so much that it brings them wide awake. This effect usually lasts only about an hour, followed by relaxation and sleep. Ascorbic acid should be avoided or used sparingly, as it seems to have a waking effect. Sodium/potassium ascorbate, or about 1 gm. of mixed mineral ascorbate is usually helpful. Bioflavinoids can be added to the vitamin C.

C. Nucleic acids, and/or separate amino acids, L-lysine, L-lucine, etc. These should be tried seperately. Wakefulness is the result of an altered metabolic state, usually as a result of toxins or metabolites from some combination of infectives. Each amino acid can alter the metabolic state, but only trial can find the ones that are effective in promoting sleep.

D. Hot milk has been found to be very effective. Although milk does increase lactic acid, sleep is so important that it should be used if effective.

E. B-1 should be tried. If B-1 helps to promote sleep it is probably a relative shortage, where Candida yeast is producing so much B-2 that more B-1 is needed.

4. Slow Breathing and Nervous Release.

Normally, if you are sleepy and lie down, the breathing slows down and increased carbon dioxide remains in the lungs. This slows down oxygenation, metabolism, and body processes, and reduces the number of electrons poised for nerve transmission, with the resulting relaxation inducing the rest of the sleep process. It appears that if nervous activity has been too great, or if nerve function has been altered with caffeine, drugs, toxins from infectives, or other biologically active chemicals, the "nervous energy" may be too high, and sleep becomes impossible. Normally, if nervous activity has been high, the poised electrons may suddenly discharge spontaneously, producing the "jerk" frequently experienced just before sleep, or just at the point of sleep. This pre-sleep jerk has been found in all races of people all over the world and is therefore considered to be natural to man.

Slow breathing, and nervous release can be used to develop relaxation techniques that will promote sleep anywhere at any time.

A. Slow breathing (and preferably deep breathing), at approximately the same rate as sleeping, will promote carbon dioxide retention, which induces deep relaxation and sleep.

B. Slow breathing,-- in for six slow counts; hold for six slow counts; out for six slow counts.

C. Slow breathing as in B, in a massage chair, in a massage vibrator bed, or in bed with a portable vibrator or pad. The massage vibrator seems to promote the dissipation of poised electrons, which reduces nervous tension.

D. Slow breathing as in C, preceeded by neck and back massage, whole body massage, or light neursage of the back and neck.

E. Lie on one side (try both sides) with legs bent at hips and knees. Slow breathing as in B, then on the count of "out six" suddenly tense all of the muscles. With a little practice you will find that you can closely duplicate the natural pre-sleep jerk, with the tension (and consequent relaxation) sometimes running even up into the head. Repeat, and after a few times the jerk will reduce, and may come spontaneously at the count of four or five, with the jerk getting less each time and with sleep usually following immediately

F. Lie on back. While slow breathing as in B, after "in six and hold six" suddenly tense all muscles, pulling the toes up and head and shoulders off the pillow, arms bent up at elbows and fists clenched. Then, on count of six out, suddenly relax, fall back in bed, and keep on relaxing with a feeling of sinking deeper and deeper into the bed. Repeat a few times and sleep will usually follow during the deep relaxation. (This method by the courtesy of Dr. Carlos Mason.)

5. Sexual Release. Sexual activity is a natural integral part of health. Low sexual arousal will usually bring on good restful sleep. With high sexual arousal, without orgasm, the retained hormones are resorbed by the body, and if not completely detoxified, form toxins and metabolites that create and promote nervous tension and sleep then becomes impossible. Full sexual arousal with orgasm, is usually followed by deep sleep, but if sleep is not immediate, may produce wakefulness. If wakefulness is produced, toast and eggs (or cheese) with sleep nutrients, will usually be followed with deep, restful sleep.

6. Wakefulness from aches and pains. The hot water bottle and heating pad will help. Spasmed muscles can be relaxed with neursage. Light spinal neursage is particularly helpful.

7. Restless legs. All adrenal nutrients with particular emphasis on B-6, calcium and magnesium.

8. Midnight Wakefulness. Go to sleep, suddenly wide awake without apparent cause. This is usually a blood-sugar problem. The blood sugar falls to extreme lows, and to save the body from fainting, blackout, or death, the adrenals pump in adrenalin. Every nerve is then active, and sleep is impossible. Every measure must be taken to reduce the hypoglycemic condition; particularly by the elimination of coffee, tea, chocolate, cola, and all stimulants; elimination of alcohol, sugar, white flour and all refined carbohydrates; and the reduction of stress including chronic infectives. The immediate problem however, is that you are extremely tired from the low blood sugar, yet wide awake fom the adrenalin. A snack, with dense carbohydrate, a small amount of refined carbohydrate (like two prunes) and protein (like an egg) together with all adrenal nutrients including potassium ascorbate, will help to reduce the effects of the adrenals and will help to stabilize the blood sugar, and sleep will usually follow in about two hours. Some exercise, followed by relaxation techniques, may help. Digestive aids may be needed with the snack.

Another common cause of midnight wakefulness is sleep induced adrenal depletion. The body fights infection during sleep, and if adrenal and immune nutrients become depleted by excess anti-infectives or by advancing infection from high blood sugar or from lack of anti-infectives the adrenals become alarmed, sleep is impossible, and signs of toxicity may be present, because the quantities of toxins exceed the supply of adrenal and immune system nutrients. All adrenal nutrients should be well supplied together with $\frac{1}{2}$ gm. suckable and 1 gm. slow release C. Then start reading something dull and sleep will probably follow in about $\frac{1}{2}$ hour.

Most ill people, who have trouble going to sleep, or who have trouble going back to sleep, will respond to the following:

1/3 glass of juice, with $\frac{1}{4}$ tsp. Hi KC Fizz, 1 heaping tsp. protein powder, and 1 tsp. sunflower oil, stirred in.

1 tbsp. of granola or muesli.

1 digestive enzyme.

B-15, -50mg.

Bioflavinoids (mixed), 500mg.

B-6, -250mg.

Pantothenic acid, -200mg.

Calcium/magnesium, 200mg.

Choline, inositol, methionine, 250 mg. each.

Tryptophane and/or deaner, if indicated.

Mixed pure amino acids may help if digestion is impaired.

Calcium Sandoz, 1 gm. may help if calcium is low.

Sleepiness and Oversleeping.

Some people certainly seem to require much more sleep than others. The extra sleep requirement, which is very real, can have several causes.

We do not know what priorities the body may have, but we do know that most of the activity of the immune system against infectives, takes place during deep sleep, so the extra sleep requirement of some people results from their need to cope with a high load of chronic infectives. Although wild, vivid dreams can be suppressed with extra B-6 it is thought that these dreams result from the many toxic metabolites that are floating around when the immune system is busy reducing infection. Toxic "morning headaches" frequently result from the inability of the body to detoxify all of the metabolites that have been released from immune system over-activity during sleep. If chronic infection is high, extra sleep will be needed until the chronic infection is reduced.

Extreme sleepiness during the day can also result from the need of the body to fight infectives and eliminate toxins. This is very evident from the sleepiness (which should be heeded) that usually follows about $\frac{1}{2}$ hour after taking Ketoconazole. However, sleepiness during the day can also result from episodes of low blood sugar, (perhaps resulting from chronic infection). If chronic infection is evident, the urge to sleep should be heeded if possible, but if the sleepiness results from low blood sugar Hi KC Fizz, with adrenal nutrients, will quickly relieve the sleepiness.

Sleepiness at all times of the day can result from very low sex hormones, and is very common in men with sexual failure. Adrenal nutrients and supplements of estrogen or testosterone will help, but the sleepiness will persist until sexual levels are raised toward normal.

NEUROSIS PSYCHOSIS and DEPRESSION. (See also REf.5).

The ability to sleep, and the resting quality of sleep, the general health, and the state of happiness are always greatly affected by episodes of neurosis, psychosis, or depression. These episodes may be very subtle, and well hidden, or they may be very obvious to everyone except the victim.

The most significant thing that must be remembered is that, except for tumors, mental problems are always based in altered metabolism; specifically they always have a biological cause. Every female experiences mental effects along with the biological changes from hormones that are constantly changing with the menstrual cycle. Depression, neurosis and psychosis are also very common during the hormone changes associated with menopause. Mental problems therefore cannot be materially improved with psychology, because the aberrant mental function is biological.

The common causes of psychosis, neurosis and depression are the altered biology and altered metabolism from:

1. Toxic minerals: Lead, mercury, arsenic, cadmium, aluminum, and sometimes copper, iron, or selenium.

2. Very low, or very high blood sugar. (Hypoglycemia, hyperglycemia).

3. Allergies. Rotate food and drink on 7 day basis.

4. Body toxins resorbed from constipation or colon problems (See Ascorbte Retention Enema.Ch.4.)

5. Toxins and metabolites from infectives.

6. Toxins and metabolites resorbed from sexual orgasmic failure. These symptoms may not appear for six or eight hours, but they may continue for several days.

7. Lack of nutrients at the cellular level. The best example of this is vitamin B-6, (always so necessary for the female). If the body is unable to make L-cysteine, the breakdown of B-6 is altered and proceeds to methionine enkaphalin, which is more powerful than morphine and is equally addictive. Excess amino acids, or lack of amino acids, combined with toxins and metabolites from the body (or its many infectives) can, in a similar manner, produce many other narcotics that will affect the function of the brain and nerves. Most food addictions (including alcoholism), that affect mental and physical function are based in addictive narcotics produced from within the body.

8. The many variations from inter-reactions from all of these causes.

Psychosis and depression can be very damaging to health, and they have wide reaching family, social, and financial effects and consequences. When episodes cannot be avoided the effects can be reduced or changed by altering the metabolism in the brain. Altering brain metabolism will not effect a cure, but it will help the unfortunate victim to cope with the many difficulties until the basic cause can be altered or eliminated.

Alcohol and similar drugs will affect the mind and will alter the mental state, but in general alcohol and drugs should be avoided.

Pantothenic acid, vitamin C, and niacin may help. Pantothenic acid, B-6, tryptophane, and calcium/magnesium, with sleep, is frequently very effective. If the psychosis remains, the following may be useful. They should be tried one at a time.

1. Tryptophane.
2. B-6. However if B-6 seems to increase the problem L-cysteine and pyridoxyl-5-phosphate may be very effective when used with the B-6.
3. B-15 . If B-15 is effective, vitamin E, circulating air, or oxygen enriched air may be of value.
4. Deaner. (See "mental and Elemental Nutrients) (Ref.5).
5. L-Lysine.
6. L-Glutathione.
7. Lithium. Be careful with lithium. (See thyroid).
8. Gerovital, (GH3) (Novocain).
9. NaEDTA, oral chelator.
10. Resteclin.
11. Ketoconazole.

Further suggestions for reducing the causes of mental problems are included under "Schidsophrenia". (Ch.7.)

ANTI-INFECTIVE FUNCTION.

The eradication of serious Candida yeast colonies from the body is frequently a complex and difficult task because the yeast has usually infected and affected many parts of the body for many years before the total effects of the infectives have reduced health to the point that the yeast infection is discovered.

As with all infections, when any one infective invades the body many other infectives join in. Then if you start to kill out any one of the infectives in the callus matrix, the other infectives will flourish by feeding on the biological material released from the killed infectives, and perhaps by feeding on the anti-infective itself. Effective treatment of yeast infect-ions must therefore include substances that will kill out the other infectives, even when the actual infectives in the callus mixture may all be very different, and cannot be known.

To reduce the infection, the function of all body systems must be improved, with particular attention to the immune system, the liver, the kidneys, and the adrenals. Large amounts of good digested protein must be supplied for rebuilding damaged tissues, and large amounts of vitamin C and bioflavinoids must be supplied to strengthen the tissues against invasion by the infectives, with even more vitamin C to detoxify the anti-infective agents used: to detoxify the dead bodies of the killed infectives; and to detoxify the dead body cells and metabolites released from the callus matrix.

The anti-infectives used should be broad spectrum, to kill as many different infectives as possible, and the anti-infectives must be used on a rotational basis to ensure that all infectives are effectively reduced. The anti-infectives used must also be topical (applied to the skin) and systemic,(working through the bloodstream).

TOPICAL and SYSTEMIC ANTI-INFECTIVES.

Systemic Anti-infectives are anti-infective substances that are carried throughout the body by the bloodstream, and they therefore work simultaneously on all of the tissues of the body except the brain and the gonads, where they may, or may not, cross the tissue barriers. Systemic anti-infectives may be administered as intravenous (injected into the bloodstream) intramuscular (injected into the muscles), pulmonary (absorbed through the lungs), sub lingual (absorbed in the mouth), or oral (absorbed through the digestive system). Although, systemic anti-infectives are effective throughout the body, higher concentrations will usually be found around the site where they are being introduced into the bloodstream. Systemic anti-infectives usually have some side effects, and the side effects from some anti-infectives may be worse than the infection itself.

Side Effects from systemic anti-infectives come from three sources:

1. The effects of the anti-infective itself on all parts of the body. Systemic anti-infectives cannot be selective in scope. They cover all parts of the body equally except the brain, and the gonads.

2. The effects on the body from the killed infectives, together with all resulting toxins and metabolites. These metabolites, although they may be non-toxic, will frequently alter many other metabolic processes and thereby disturb the normal body chemistry.

3. The effects on the body of toxins or metabolites from the

body tissues that were killed or altered by the infective.

Systemic anti-infectives are absolutely essential to the eradication of chronic infections and particularly to the eradication or reduction of Candida yeast, but their use demands great care and attention because the signs of toxicity displayed by the dead bodies of the killed infective are usually identical to the signs of toxicity displayed by the infective itself, while the body, helped in its continuous battle with the infective, may suddenly make further gains against the infectives and load the body with more toxins, or if stress is high, or if other body systems fail, it may be the infective that is increasing. It then becomes extremely difficult to determine the right amount of anti-infective to use because the signs of "too much" are identical to the signs of "too little". The best approach seems to be to set the program with "too little", and thus encourage the immune system to clear up the infection at its own rate. This approach is effective, but it is slow and may be too slow if other health problems are pressing. If higher amounts are used, continuous monitoring is absolutely essential if peroids of extreme toxicity are to be avoided.

Topical Anti-Infectives are anti-infectives that are applied directly to the skin at the site of the infection. It should be particularly noted that the body is composed of several tubes, and that the inside of these tubes is also covered with modified skin, because the inside of the tubes is still the outside of the body. Thus the air tract, the digestive tract, the sexual tract, etc; are in fact tubes that are lined with skin;- although they are "inside" they are still the "outside" of the body, and any anti-infectives applied to the inside of these tracts are still topical applications unless the substances used are absorbed into the bloodstream. Thus Nystatin, which cannot be absorbed into the bloodstream, is always actually a topical anti-infective even when it is used orally, or when it is used "internally" with colon or vaginal suppositories.

Topical anti-infectives usually have less side effects than systemic anti-infectives, but side effects are even more difficult to predict.

Side Effects from topical anti-infectives come from two sources:

1. Direct effects from absorption of the anti-infective through the skin or through the lining of the infected tract. This absorption may be related to the "solidity" of the flesh or the integrity of the cell. Vitamin C, bioflavinoids, and other vitamins and minerals may reduce the absorption of toxins through the tissues.(See Vit.C.)

2. The direct effects of toxins or metabolites from the killed infective, that are absorbed into the bloodstream. Thus nystatin,

169

which cannot be absorbed into the bloodstream, cannot itself have any side effects, but toxins and metabolites from yeast killed by the nystatin can be absorbed into the bloodstream and these toxins and metabolites can affect body function.

Total Side Effects. The total side effects from both topical and systemic anti-infectives are very similar because the total effects on the body come solely from the toxins and metabolites carried by the bloodstream. The actual total side effects however, cannot be predicted and must be dealt with as they appear, because the actual mixture of the different infectives in the infective matrix is constantly changing, and cannot be effectively determined.

All anti-infectives can therefore be used only on the continuing basis of trial, with constant observation and correction.

Disinfectants. Following the discovery that many contagious diseases were caused by micro-organisms that were later called bacteria, many substances were found that would kill the bacteria, and these substances were called disinfectants. Most disinfectants are a very broad spectrum and will "kill anything", but with all infections considered to be coming from bacteria, many disinfectants have no affect whatsoever on yeasts and other fungii, because yeasts and fungii are plants, while bacteria are simple, single-celled organisms. The ability of yeasts, and particularly the ability of Candida yeast, to live and grow despite the use of soap, alcohol, and other common disinfectants is particularly demonstrated by the medical paper,"Survival of Gram Negative Bacilli and Candida Albicans in Hexachlorophene Preparations and Other Disinfectants".Indeed, the overall increase in Candida infection, and particularly the increase in yeast infection in hospitals, in the nursey, and in the doctor's office (chapter 3) has probably come from the low anti-fungal properties of the disinfectants used. Again, this is poor technology, but fact is fact, and the cold, hard fact is that Candida yeast is unaffected by, and may even grow in, many of to-days so called antiseptics and disinfectants.

Anti-biotics, Anti-mycotics, and Disinfectants. The name "Anti-biotics" was originally given to a series of biologically derived substances that would kill bacteria or would inhibit their growth. Some of these, like penicillin, were derived from fungii, and they therefore had very little effect on yeasts. As these substances were systemic, and were effective through the bloodstream, they could not be called disinfectants, so they were named anti-biotics. Since then the name has been misused, and it has now become a general term used for many substances that kill bacteria and viruses, but it does not seem to be used for substances that kill fungii.

Ch.4. Reducing Candida Yeast Infection.

For some strange reason, perhaps to promote the pompous mystery of medical jargon, yet for reasons certainly far beyond the comprehension of this author, fungal infections have been called mycotic infections, or mycoses (Fig.4.) and ant-fungal substances then of course become anti-mycotic.

In todays world then, disinfectants are a class of substances that are supposed to kill all living micro-organisms; anti-biotics are substances that kill bacteria, viros, viruses, and other single-celled organisms; and anti-mycotics are substances that kill yeasts and fungii and other micro-plants.

Everywhere, the rule of nature is eat and be eaten. If anti-biotics are used to reduce infection, the yeasts and other fungii will flourish. If anti-mycotics are used to reduce infection, the bacteria and viruses will flourish. To effectively reduce chronic infection, anti-biotics should be alternated with anti-mycotics and different disinfectants should be rotated, to ensure that each of the many micro-organisms in the callus matrix are effectively reduced.

The ability of micro-organisms to thrive under very strange circumstances should always be remembered. A disinfectant for one may well be food for another. Yeasts, in particular, live in many strange places, and they are spread by air-borne spores that grow wherever they can. These hard facts seem to escape many doctors and other health professionals, sometimes with tragic results. People go to the doctor and hospital to get better, yet active Candida yeast has been found growing in intravenous feeding solutions, dialysis solutions, and in hexachloraphane and other medical disinfectants. Candida yeast also seems to be totally unaffected by alcohol swabs. All infections are multiple infections of many different organisms, so the only way that infections can be effectively reduced is by rotating various broad spectrum anti- infectives.

CHRONIC INFECTION CHEMOTHERAPY.

There seem to be a great many misunderstandings about chemotherapy and therapeutic agents. Yogurt and acidophilus are commonly considered to be the epitome of good natural therapy;- the good guys in nature chasing out the bad guys! Thus yogurt is not a chemical, but a wonderful natural product! It is the very gateway to health! Oh, yes indeed! But penicillin, amphoteracin, and many other anti-biotics and anti-fungals are called nasty man-made chemicals, when in fact they are produced by bacteria, fungii, or other micro-organisms in a manner similar to the production of yogurt, cheese and wine. Thus if the wine, cheese, and yogurt at the natural health food party are natural foods, then penicillin and most other anti-biotics are also natural health foods, with different effects.Thus the chemotherapy normally used to reduce infection is in fact usually accomplished with specific products produced in abundance by Mother Nature. Perhaps to clarify the issue we should really call it Natural Chemotherapy; i.e. the therapeutic use of complex chemicals created by nature.

TOXIC SIDE EFFECTS.

The "flu" is a typical toxic state. The "flu;" that washed out, completely fatigued feeling, perhaps with indigestion, constipation, headache, or other aches and pains, is the result of the inability of the body to detoxify all of the poisons from a transient infection.

The toxic state;- the inability of the body to adequately detoxify toxins,- can result from using too much of an anti-infective that is poisonous to the body, or it can result from killing too many infectives, with the body unable to cope with all of the toxins from the dead infectives.(The Herxheimer reaction).

The toxic state can also be produced by suddenly discontinuing an anti-infective program that has been built up to very high levels. In this case the toxins from the sudden re-growth of the infectives may exceed the detoxification ability of the body, and the toxic state may persist until a low anti-infective program is resumed.

Poor function of the immune system, liver, pancreas and colon will impair the ability of the body to detoxify poisons, which will reduce the level of the toxic threshold, with an increase in headaches, indigestion, constipation and other toxic symptoms. Most migraine headaches are the toxic result of poor colon and body function.

The toxic state, or even the near toxic state, should if possible, be avoided at all times. Thus the total amount of all anti-infectives should always be kept below the toxic level. The high levels of stress associated with the toxic state favor re-growth of yeasts and other infectives, and too much anti-infective can have negative results.

The fine line between "too much" and "too little" anti-infective is very difficult to determine, so it is best to keep the quantities on the low side, but with detoxification ability dependent upon several body systems, (nutrition, rest, total stress, etc;) some toxic episodes seem to be unavoidable.

Toxic symptoms of any kind should be watched, and heeded, and the eposide can usually be reduced or avoided by the following:

1. HiKC fizz with cooking oil and protein powder.
2. Pantothenic acid, B-6, calcium/magnesium, bioflavinoids, lipotropics (choline, inositol, methionine).

3. Try for bowel movement and heed the slightest urge.
4. Hot water bottle for stomach and digestion, and to reduce headaches and other aches and pains.
5. Rest, and sleep if possible.
6. Lithium to raise the PMNs.
7. Mixed amino acids, and nucleic acids, to feed the immune system.
8. Extra good protein, preferably as fish, eggs, or liver. Frozen raw calves liver, thin-sliced, will also help digestion.
9. Ascorbate Retention Enema. (CH.4.)
10. Skin dialysis saltz bath. (As follows).

Skin Dialysis Saltz Bath.

The skin is the largest organ in the body. It is part of the lymphatic system, and when every other system is overloaded the skin will excrete toxins and unusable metabolites. This is evidenced by hives, eczema, and body odor (B.O.). The following formula produces a bath with an alkalinity that is higher than the body fluids. It therefore draws lymphatic fluids, with their toxins, from the skin, by osmotic pressure. It will reduce toxic episodes, and it will reduce the load on the kidneys.

Saltz Bath.
1 cup salt.(Preferably sea salt).
I cup epsom salts.
1 cup baking soda.
1 cup Aloe Vera juice. (wetting factor).

Start with $\frac{1}{2}$ tub of warm water. Add the salt. Get into the tub and add hot water gradually bringing the temperature up to where it is almost uncomfortable. Add the rest of the ingredients. Drink warm or hot water while in the tub. Remain in the tub 20 minutes to one half hour, or longer, if possible. Shower or rinse after bath. Cool down slowly, perhaps by going to an already warm bed for 15 minutes or more.

ANTI-FUNGALS.(Anti-Mycotics).

Although fungal infections in man have been observed for over two thousand years, and despite the trial of a very large number of substances, very little could be done to slow, their growth. During most of those two thousand years the only remedies were herbal remedies, and the only ones that were effective were also toxic to man. Of those two thousand years that man has struggled vainly against fungal infections, it is only in the last thirty-five years that man has been able to develop chemical anti-fungals that are reasonably effective.

The following table shows the progress. (Fig.9.)
Note that Nystatin was the first good chemical that would destroy Candida Yeast.

Year	Anti-fungal.	Year.	Anti-fungal.
1903	Potassium Iodide.	1961	Acrisorcin.
1907	Whitfield"s ointment	1963	Haloprogin.
1940	Undecylenic acid.	1965	Tolnaftate.
1949	Nystatin.	1966	Flucytosine.
1950	Hydroxystilbamidine.	1969	Miconazole.
1955	8-Hydroxyquinoline.	1970	Clotrimazole.
1957	Amphoteracin B.	1974	Econazole.
1958	Griseofulvin.	1980	Ketoconazole.
1959	Pimaricin.		

Fig. 9. DEVELOPMENT OF ANTI-FUNGALS.   Nystatin was the first good chemical that would destroy Candida Yeast.

ANTI-INFECTIVES ACTIVE AGAINST CANDIDA INFECTION.
        The following anti-infectives have been found to be active against Candida infections. They are listed in their general order of effectiveness. Their manner of use, and side effects are also noted.
        This list shows the very best substances and methods that the author has been able to find, but even at best the reduction of Candida infections is slow and tedious. There must be better ways. One of the great hopes of this book is that it might encourage others to find and develop those better substances and better methods.
        1. KETOCONAZOLE (Nizoral).(Fig.10)(Ref.10).
        Ketoconazole is the first good, broad spectrum, systemic, anti-fungal that has been developed. It is taken orally. It is one of the greatest gifts to mankind that the world has known. It is the result of very clever biochemical engineering by Jannsen Pharmaceuticals in Beerse, Belgium, and the scientists who developed it should certainly have a Nobel prize.
        Ketoconazole has been engineered to destroy fungus through the cell wall of the organism. Fungii are plants, with the cell wall based on ergosterol, whereas animals (including man), have a cell wall based on cholesterol. Ketoconazole has little affect on the cell wall of animals, and it therefore does not itself have any direct effects. Any effects that are experienced must therefore come from:
        A. The dead bodies of the infective.
        B. Substances released from the decomposition of the infective matrix.
        C. The rapid growth of bacteria or other infectives feeding on the biological material released from the dying plants.

NIZORAL™
(KETOCONAZOLE)
TABLETS

DESCRIPTION

NIZORAL™ (ketoconazole) is a synthetic broad-spectrum antifungal agent available in scored white tablets, each containing 200 mg ketoconazole. Ketoconazole is cis-1-acetyl-4-[4-[[2-(2,4-dichlorophenyl)-2-(1H-imidazol-1-ylmethyl)-1,3-dioxolan-4-yl] methoxyl]phenyl] piperazine and has the following structural formula:

NIZORAL™ is a white to slightly beige, odorless powder, soluble in acids, with a molecular weight of 531.44.

CLINICAL PHARMACOLOGY

Mean peak plasma levels of approximately 3.5 μg/ml are reached within 1 to 2 hours following oral administration of a single 200 mg dose taken with a meal. Subsequent plasma elimination is biphasic with a half life of 2 hours during the first 10 hours and 8 hours thereafter. Following absorption from the gastrointestinal tract, NIZORAL™ is converted into several inactive metabolites. The major identified metabolic pathways are: oxidation and degradation of the imidazole and piperazine rings, oxidative O-dealkylation and aromatic hydroxylation. About 13% of the dose is excreted in the urine, of which 2 to 4% is unchanged drug. The major route of excretion is through the bile into the intestinal tract. In vitro, the plasma protein binding is about 99%, mainly to the albumin fraction. Only a negligible proportion of NIZORAL™ reaches the cerebral spinal fluid. NIZORAL™ is a weak dibasic agent and thus requires acidity for dissolution and absorption.

NIZORAL™ is active against clinical infections with Candida spp., Coccidioides immitis, Histoplasma capsulatum, Paracoccidioides brasiliensis, and Phialophora spp. Development of resistance to NIZORAL™ has not yet been reported.

The following preclinical data are available; however, their clinical significance is unknown. NIZORAL™ is active in vitro against dermatophytes, dimorphic fungi, eumycetes, yeasts, actinomycetes, phycomycetes and various other fungi. In animal models, activity has been demonstrated against Candida spp., dermatophytes (Trichophyton spp., Microsporum spp., Epidermophyton floccosum), Blastomyces dermatitidis, Histoplasma capsulatum, Malassezia furfur, Coccidioides immitis, and Cryptococcus neoformans.

Mode of Action: In vitro studies suggest that NIZORAL™ impairs the synthesis of ergosterol, which is a vital component of fungal cell membranes. Tests in animals suggest this mechanism is not important in mammalian cells.

INDICATIONS AND USAGE

NIZORAL™ is indicated for the treatment of the following fungal infections: candidiasis, chronic mucocutaneous candidiasis, oral thrush, candiduria, coccidioidomycosis, histoplasmosis, chromomycosis, and paracoccidioidomycosis. NIZORAL™ should not be used for fungal meningitis because it penetrates poorly into the cerebral-spinal fluid.

For the initial diagnosis, the infective organism should be identified; however, therapy may be initiated prior to obtaining laboratory results.

CONTRAINDICATIONS

NIZORAL™ is contraindicated in patients who have shown hypersensitivity to the drug.

WARNINGS

In female rats treated three to six months with ketoconazole at dose levels of 80 mg/kg and higher, increased fragility of long bones, in some cases leading to fracture, was seen. The maximum "no-effect" dose level in these studies was 20 mg/kg (2.5 times the maximum recommended human dose). The mechanism responsible for this phenomenon is obscure. Limited studies in dogs failed to demonstrate such an effect on the metacarpals and ribs.

PRECAUTIONS

General: In four subjects with drug-induced achlorhydria, a marked reduction in NIZORAL™ absorption was observed. NIZORAL™ requires acidity for dissolution. If concomitant antacids, anticholinergics, and H_2-blockers are needed, they should be given at least two hours after NIZORAL™ administration. In cases of achlorhydria, the patients should be instructed to dissolve each tablet in 4 ml aqueous solution of 0.2 N HCl. For ingesting the resulting mixture, they should use a glass or plastic straw so as to avoid contact with the teeth. This administration should be followed with a cup of tap water.

Drug Interactions: There is no evidence for clinically significant interaction with oral anticoagulant or oral hypoglycemic agents.

Carcinogenesis, Mutagenesis, Impairment of Fertility: The dominant lethal mutation test in male and female mice revealed that single oral doses of NIZORAL™ as high as 80 mg/kg produced no mutation in any stage of germ cell development. The Ames' Salmonella microsomal activator assay was also negative.

Pregnancy: Teratogenic effects: Pregnancy Category C. NIZORAL™ has been shown to be teratogenic (syndactylia and oligodactylia) in the rat when given in the diet at 80 mg/kg/day, (10 times the maximum recommended human dose). However, these effects may be related to maternal toxicity, evidence of which also was seen at this and higher dose levels.

Nonteratogenic effects: NIZORAL™ has also been found to be embryotoxic in the rat when given in the diet at doses higher than 80 mg/kg during the first trimester of gestation.

In addition, dystocia (difficult labor) was noted in rats administered NIZORAL™ during the third trimester of gestation. This occurred when NIZORAL™ was administered at doses higher than 10 mg/kg (higher than 1.25 times the maximum human dose).

It is likely that both the malformations and the embryotoxicity resulting from the administration of NIZORAL™ during gestation are a reflection of the particular sensitivity of the female rat to this drug. For example, the oral LD_{50} of NIZORAL™ given by gavage to the female rat is 166 mg/kg, whereas in the male rat the oral LD_{50} is 287 mg/kg.

Nursing Mothers: Since NIZORAL™ is probably excreted in the milk, mothers who are under NIZORAL™ treatment should not breast feed the child.

Pediatric Use: Safety in children under two years of age has been documented in a limited number of cases.

ADVERSE REACTIONS

NIZORAL™ is usually well tolerated. Most adverse reactions reported have been mild and transient and have only rarely required withdrawal of therapy.

The most frequent adverse reactions were nausea and/or vomiting, which occurred in approximately 3% of patients. Abdominal pain was reported in approximately 1.2% of patients; pruritus in approximately 1.5% of patients. The following have been reported in less than 1% of patients: headache, dizziness, somnolence, fever and chills, photophobia, and diarrhea. Infrequent, transient increases in serum liver enzymes have been seen.

OVERDOSAGE

In the event of accidental overdosage, supportive measures, including gastric lavage with sodium bicarbonate, should be employed.

Further information is available from the manufacturer.

Janssen Pharmaceutica Inc.
New Brunswick
New Jersey 08903
USA

Fig. 10. Ketoconazole.

As Ketoconazole destroys fungii through altering the cell wall of the plant it is very broad spectrum, and it will kill most types of fungal infectives,as shown in Fig.4.

Ketoconazole is basically a systemic anti-fungal that is taken orally at the beginning of the meal because it is absorbed during the acid phase of digestion. Absorption can be increased by taking it with betaine HCL or glutamic HCL digestives.

Ketoconazole can also be used topically by chewing the tablet and holding it in the mouth for mouth and throat infections, or it can be taken between meals, with or without bicarbonate, to reduce absoption and increase its topical effectiveness against infectives in the digestive tract. Tablets can also be crushed and added to enemas or to vaginal douches.

Caution-- A full tablet of Ketoconazole should not be taken by an ill person that has not previously had small amounts. Ketoconazole itself does not have any side effects, but a single tablet can kill so many infectives that an impaired immune system or impaired liver function cannot cope, which may result in extreme allergies or an episode of extreme toxicity. There do not seem to be any reports of deaths from such episodes, but one depressed teenager, as part of a suicide attempt, took about ten tablets, and was highly toxic and irrational for two or three days. The good part is that the severe depression cleared and has not returned. This shows that fungal infection was part of the suicidal depression, and that large amounts of ketoconazole can be taken without extreme hazard, but large amounts cannot be considered as the treatment of choice.

Fungal Infection Challenge Test.

Ketoconazole is the only effective agent that can be used for the Fungal Infection Challenge Test. This test indicates the relative amount of fungal infection, as seen by the body; i.e.,the amount of fungal infection relative to the capability of the body to handle the toxins and metabolites.

The test is made by taking 1/8 tablet of Ketoconazole daily (with a meal) increasing by 1/8 tablet daily, until toxic or other effects are seen. Some people cannot take more than $\frac{1}{4}$ tablet,and this would be considered a high total infection, even if infection was not visible, while people that could take two tablets would be considered to be low. Significantly, very few "normally healthy people", as frequently used in "scientific" health "research", can take more than one tablet without experiencing side effects from the killed infectives.

Ketoconazole and B-1.

To be fully effective Ketoconazole should be taken daily in just sufficient amounts to avoid toxic symptoms, yet enough to slowly reduce the yeast. This gives the body an opportunity to rebuild, and avoids excessive stress. Anyone on a steady program of ketoconazole may experience mouth problems from B vitamin imbalance. These problems can usually be avoided by taking 300 mg. daily (or more) of vitamin B-1. The exact cause of this B vitamin imbalance is not known, but it is known that Candida yeast produces vitamin B-2, so it is conjectured that the dead yeast releases large quanties of B-2 into the body, which creates the B vitamin imbalance that affects the mouth tissues.

The amount of B-2 produced by Candida can be quite high. Sometimes the best results seem to be achieved when B-1 is supplemented with 500 mg. tablets once or twice a day.

Ketoconazole and Amphoteracin B.

Ketoconazole and Amphoteracin B are shown by literature to be synergystic, with each more effective when used together. Resteclin(Fig.11) is a combination of amphoteracin B, tetracycline, and vitamin C. A very effective program against fungal infections is the use of ketoconazole with a protein snack about two hours after a meal, (for acid phase absorption) followed by resteclin about one hour later. Resteclin should be used sparingly and intermittently to avoid harm to liver and kidneys.

Medical Literature on Ketoconazole.

The best book on Ketoconazole at present seems to be "Ketoconazole in the Management of Fungal Disease",(H.B.Levine, Medical Microbiology, Dept. Naval Bio-Sciences Lab.,Oakland Cal.)Adis Press, New York.(Ref.10). All dedicated health professionals should have a copy of this book for reference.

This book(1982), seems to be the best that is available, and it contains a large amount of very useful information, but it is still only a half-book, and with to-day's outlook, will probably remain only a half-book despite any number of revisions.

The title of the book reveals the outlook. "The 'Management' of Fungal Disease". The book cannot say the "cure" of fungal disease, because it is principally dedicated to the sale of ketoconazole for use by the medical profession for short term therapy. In general, the book presumes that the infection being dealt with is not ingrown, and has only recently arrived, and it therefore can be reduced with a few days of therapy. Then the book describes in glowing terms the great success story, with "remission" or "improvement" in 80% or 90% of the patients. A wonderful success story for the manufacturers of ketoconazole, and a wonderful success story for the doctor who uses it, yet perhaps a tragedy for you and I, because you and I are not in the success group. You and I are in the group" that did not quite make it"."We do not know why". Then if you gently inquire about the "other 10%", the 10% who did not improve, the answer is clear;"But look at the wonderful success rate!". "Of course, we will have failures"."The doctor will have to look after them as best he can". Yes, the answer is clear. An excellent viewpoint for the manufacturer who thinks largely in terms of black ink on the financial report, and perhaps a good viewpoint for the physician who can point with pride to the 90% relief rate, and who will always try to do the "best he can" anyway. But the viewpoint is certainly not heart-warming for you and I, the unfortunate 10%, who are left out in the cold with our problems and our miseries.

Yes, it is only a half-book, but it is much better than no book at all, and from it much excellent information can be gleaned; information that can be used to help the "easy cases", and information that can also be used to help those unfortunates who have been largely abandoned because they "failed to respond".

In reviewing the book it becomes immediately clear that the doctors and researchers did not have a complete understanding of the ingrown nature of fungal disease. They have not observed the fungus on trees, on plants, and on fruits, and how the fungus invades the tissues of the host, with the cells of the infective intermingled with the cells of the host. They did not and could not have observed or known that Candida Calluses can be over $\frac{1}{2}$ inch thick, with the infectives mingled with the living tissue. Had they known this, or had they considered this, they would not speak of, nor would they expect, "remission" after only three days of therapy, because if all of the infectives were suddenly and miraculously removed by some science-fiction therapy, it would still take the body many long months to repair all of the damaged tissues.

However, despite these shortcomings, the book does contain a wealth of excellent scientific information. In general, it certainly shows the very large number of fungal pathogens that can and do infect man, and it also points out that with to-day's highspeed aircraft any of the many formerly tropical diseases can now appear anywhere on the globe, singly, or in épidemic. Thus the health problems that "failed to respond";i.e. specifically your health problems; may come from pathogens picked up from an innocent "symptom free carrier", that in turn brought the infection from some foreign country half way around the globe. Any people who "fail to respond" to the suggestions outlined in this book should seek diligently for some unusual foreign infective.

Ketoconazole, Sulfamethoxizole and Copiamycin.

Dr.Prato (Page 50) shows that both sulfamethoxizole and copiamycin have a synergistic effect when used with ketoconazole. The infectives that join the Candida callus matrix is always unknown, and in all stubborn cases of Candidiasis these agents should be tried.

Ch.4. Reducing Candida Yeast Infection.

<u>Toxicity. Liver Problems, Vitamin D, Calcium and Proteins.</u>

All of the studies of ketoconazole show that it is not toxic. Yet some patients have reported reactions, and with extensive liver tests so highly recommended, we must assume that there have been some liver problems. The reactions shown probably come from starting with one tablet or more. When one considers that the first thing that keteconazole does is to cause the fungus to shed filaments and spores, (which frequently enter the bloodstream), severe reactions could be expected from one tablet. When the writer enquired about the wisdom of starting with one tablet, the bureaucratic reply was that starting with smaller amounts "might make the food and drug regulators think that the ketoconazole was a homeopathic remedy." Which it is not! Considering some of the extreme allergic reactions that are sometimes experienced if infection is high, this seems to be a very callous and pompous attitude, stemming from an equally callous and pompous government agency.

Despite the medical literature, if toxic episodes are to be avoided, do not start with more than 1/8 tablet, of ketoconazole, increasing daily by 1/8 tablet, up to two tablets, and always stay under the toxic threshold.

There is little question that the combination of ketoconazole with toxins and metabolites from fungii killed by the ketoconazole does place a severe stress on the liver. Whether it is the ketoconazole itself, or the toxins and metabolites from the killed infectives, that affects the liver function is strictly academic, and is of very little importance to the yeast victim, particularly if the yeast victim already has a poor liver function. For the health of the Candida victim to improve they must use ketoconazole as the cornerstone of their therapy to reduce the infection, because they have no other choice. Ketoconazole however imperfect, is the best systemic anti-fungal at the present time, and it certainly has the least side effects. The Candida victim therefore does not have a choice, and must use the ketoconazole within the constraints of their physical function, whatever it may be. Using a quantity of ketoconazole that does not exceed their toxic threshold gives them some therapy, however small, and starts to slowly reduce the total infectives to the point that body systems can improve, and more ketoconazole can be used.

The books of course do not say just what to do if it is found that the liver function is impaired. Presumbably, as with non-responders, such patients are simply hopeless, and should be abandoned. However, there is little reason that ketoconazole therapy cannot be started, if the quantity is kept below the toxic threshold until liver function improves. If haste is required,

1/8 tablet two or three times daily can usually be tolerated, and liver function can sometimes be rapidly improved with calves liver with every meal (preferably thin-sliced frozen raw liver) together with other liver nutrients (see "liver"), particularly lecithin, vitamin A, and other vitamins including vitamin D. Supplementing vitamin D however, opens up a whole new series of limitations and ramifications, that are not described in the books, but come from information from the books.

Now here is the technical catch. Ketoconazole inhibits the formation of both ergosterol and cholesterol, but it is far more active against ergosterol. The vitamin D-3 that you get with your fortified milk is irradiated ergosterol. Thus any substance that blocks the ergosterol will also block the vitamin D. Ketoconazole blocks the synthesis of ergosterol in the plant. It will also block synthesis of cholesterol in the host, but the ratio is 6-1. Specifically, it requires six times as much ketoconazole to block the formation of cholesterol as it does to block the synthesis of ergosterol. At the right dose of ketoconazole, the fungii (plants) die, and the host survives. But in blocking the synthesis of ergosterol, ketoconazole also blocks vitamin D. Thus ketoconazole does not damage the liver, but it does alter liver function by blocking vitamin D. Then with the vitamin D blocked, calcium absorption is reduced (despite supplements) calcium/magnesium ratios are affected, osteoporosis and sub-clinical rickets are engendered, and protein assimilation is inhibited at the very time that proteins are needed so much for immune system function and for cellular re-building. With continuing extended ketoconazole therapy the low protein and low calcium can be seen in a blood test, but the actual cause and metabolic reason is very obscure unless the blocking of vitamin D by ketoconazole is known and is remembered.

Now the books certainly show that ketoconazole does not in any way permanently damage the liver, and this has been confirmed. In one case of severe Candida infection, where even the testis were involved, ketoconazole had been used with success, in various quantities and almost continuously, for two and one half years. Digestive problems were still present so the condition of the liver was important. An ultrasonic scan showed the liver, gall bladder, bile duct, and pancreas to be in perfect condition, yet the yeast victim had watched the color of the stool change from the usual brown to a pale yellowish white, a condition indicative of liver and gall bladder problems and low bile production. The problem was partially offset with supplements of calves liver and bile salts, yet digestive problems persisted. Now the books of course, show that ketoconazole does block cholesterol synthesis, and bile is made from cholesterol largely

Addendum Update.

CLINICAL PHARMACOLOGY

Mysteclin-F Capsules have been designed to provide simultaneous antimicrobial therapy and anticandidal prophylaxis, a concept first developed by Squibb.

The capsules, which contain the broad spectrum antibiotic tetracycline, well known for its pronounced antimicrobial effect against a wide range of pathogenic organisms, produce exceptionally high initial tetracycline blood levels as well as excellent diffusion to tissues and body fluids.

Furthermore, the capsules also contain prophylactic amounts of the antifungal antibiotic, amphotericin B. This antibiotic, first isolated and described by the Squibb Institute for Medical Research, is substantially more active *in vitro* against *Candida* strains than nystatin[1,2,3] and has been widely used by the intravenous route in the treatment of many deep-seated mycotic infections.

Given orally, amphotericin B is extremely well tolerated[1,4] and is virtually nontoxic in prophylactic doses. Although poorly absorbed from the gut, amphotericin B has a high degree of activity against *Candida* species in the intestinal tract and prevents the overgrowth of these organisms commonly associated with broad spectrum antibiotic therapy (amphotericin B has no antibacterial activity). By suppressing overgrowth of *Candida* in the gastrointestinal tract, thereby minimizing a possible reservoir of this organism, Mysteclin-F Capsules provide added protection for the patient against troublesome, or even serious, candidal superinfections, e.g., intestinal (diarrheal) anogenital, vulvovaginal, mucocutaneous candidiasis.

Fig.11. RESTECLIN. (Mysteclin).

This page was reserved for most of the product information on Resteclin, but things have changed! The single sheets have now become several computer pages! The above information is from an old sheet on the U.S. equivalent, Mysteclin-F. Unfortunately the pharmacists say that Mysteclin-F is now no longer used. They do not know the reason. Resteclin is still used in Canada with good results.

Note that oral amphoteracin B is well tolerated and has no known side effects. Amphoteracin B is a very large molecule that cannot be absorbed by the body. It is so effective against fungus that it is still used intravenously under the name of Fungizone for life threatening systemic fungal infections. But given intravenously, and despite being highly effective, the molecule is so large that it is extremely difficult to excrete and it therefore has so many side effects from intravenous use that it was nicknamed Ampho the Terrible. But taken orally it is confined to the intestinal tract where it will destroy only yeasts and fungii. At one time, in the U.S., Amphoteracin B was widely used orally, but with changes in the FDA regulations the manufacturer would have to "prove" its effectiveness even after its effectiveness had already been proven. It seems that the cost of "proof and approval" would be greater than possible profits so it was removed from the market. Therefore the citizens are now fully protected by the FDA from the benefits of the antifungal that they need, while the Amphoteracin B itself is so innoccuous to humans that it should not even be a regulated substance. We understand, however, that it is used as an antifungal in some of the animal and chicken feeds with great success. Perhaps some of us mere humans would be better off if we were chickens!

181.

with the help of vitamin C&D. Further, lecithin, vitamin A, and vitamin E cannot function properly without vitamin D, so the biological function of the liver, and the gall bladder, and consequently the entire digestive system are in fact somewhat impaired by the prolonged use of ketoconazole.

It might appear that this problem could be simply resolved with large supplements of vitamin D, and calcium, but this would only decrease the amount of ketoconazole going to the infective. The best plan for therapy now appears to be a week on ketoconazole, with supplemnents of amino-acids but without calcium/magnesium and vitamin D, followed by a week on calcium/magnesium and vitamin D without the ketoconazole, but with one or two resteclin. As the highest blood levels of ketoconazole are reached with two tablets (400 mg.) taken at the same time, ketoconazole would be started with 1/8 tablet daily and would be worked up in stages of 1/8 tablet to two tablets per day, taken together, but with the quantity always under the toxic threshold. Candida yeast also uses and ties up magnesium (in the callus), so the ratio of magnesium to calcium should be a little higher than normal, or about equal quantities. Protein and calcium levels should be monitored with blood tests, and the progress should be modified if necessary. Bile supplement may need to be continuous, according to the stool. The stool should be a medium to dark brown. It has been observed that the color of the stool may occasionally change to grey. This change is thought to come from the elimination of a colony of Candida yeast. If pale stools persist vitamin C may need to be increased, or the problem may be bacterial infection.

As ketoconazole is almost completely absorbed and used in less than six hours a good alternative to the calcium problem is to take the calcium and vitamin D about 8 hours after the ketoconazole.

Niacin-Ketoconazole Therapy.

The rebuilding of tissues highly infected with Candida yeast is a very long and tedious process because even where exposed, the asmoresistant layer protects the tissues from topical anti-fungals, while it is equally difficult to get enough ketoconazole into the bloodstream to kill the yeast in the Candida callus where the blood vessels are badly damaged and atrophied. It is also very difficult to get effective amounts of ketoconazole into the brain and into the gonads, where the body somehow limits blood and tissue levels to only about 1/6 of the levels found in other parts of the body. Thus,with maximum blood levels reached at about two tablets (taken together) ketoconazole therapy is the only remedy that works at all, yet even it becomes virtually stalled even when high infection is still visible, and it therefore must be equally stalled where it cannot be seen.

At this plateau, health will be good, and the yeast will be a greatly reduced problem, but it will still be affecting many body functions. This limitation can be partly overcome by taking $1\frac{1}{2}$ tablets of ketoconazole, with protein and betain hydrochloride, followed about 1 or 2 hours later with another $\frac{1}{2}$ tablet of ketoconazole and sufficient niacin to produce a heavy flush. Repeat every two or three days, or once a week, and increase the ketoconazole to 2 or $2\frac{1}{2}$ tablets, with 1 tablet reinforcing with the niacin and with massage and neursage at the peak of the flush. A good massage vibrator used on known sites of infection, will help to get more ketoconazole into the infected tissues. Infection can be further reduced by simultaneous application of topical anti-fungals. Micatin, econazole, flagystatin for exposed areas; monistat, phenol, and flagystatin for vaginitis; micatin lotion, phenol, and flagystatin for prostate and balanitis; nystatin for intestinal infections; micatin or phenol for sinus infections, etc. To reduce toxic episodes during niacin-ketoconazole therapy keep quantities below the toxic threshold, and take adequate quantities of all adrenal and immune system nutrients including mixed amino acids, to insure adequate protein.

2. RESTECLIN (MYSTECLIN).(FIG.11).

Resteclin is a combination of tetracycline, amphoteracin B, and vitamin C. It is systemic. It is absorbed into the bloodstream and is effective throughout the body except for the brain. The amphoteracin B will kill some yeast and fungii, while the combination is a strong anti-biotic that will kill most other infectives. Continual use of resteclin can produce severe side effects, particularly on the liver and kidneys.

Throughout nature, everything is "eating and being eaten". This is the rule of nature and that is the reason that we always have something trying to eat at us. Eat and be eaten, cannot be over-emphasized. Ketoconazole is certainly the anti-fungal of choice, and is the main substance for all yeast programs, but as the ketoconazole kills out the yeasts and fungii, the dead bodies of the killed infective become food for bacteria and other infectives that will then flourish and become the principal infective. This change of infectives can usually be avoided if the anti-infective program includes oral resteclin about once a week, with extra taken if indicated. Resteclin should be taken between meals, on an empty stomach.

Oral resteclin should be part of every anti-fungal program, but an allergy test should be made before full use. If resteclin cannot be used, other anti-biotics should be found and used until body systems improve. Note.-Resteclin should be taken four hours away from food or supplements containing calcium.

Topical.

Restecilin cas also be used directly on the yeast by opening the capsules and adding the powder to enemas, douches, mouth wash, glycerine, DMSO, milk of magnesia, etc. Resteclin appears to be compatible with nystatin, and can be taken with nystatin or added to liquid nystatin.

3. MICONAZOLE. (MONISTAT,MICATIN)

Miconazole is a broad spectrum topical anti-fungal that is also effective against some bacilli and some cocii. It destroys the infective by causing peroxides to build up in the cells of the organism. It is available as cream, lotion , and suppositories.

Miconazole should be used as one of the topical treatments for all fungal infections except intestinal infections. Miconazole lotion leaves a very sticky residue and the area treated should be washed daily with a very small amount of mild detergent.

Miconazole suppositories are particularly effective against infections of the uterus and other vaginal infections.

Miconazole (Monistat) IV. In severe and stubborn fungal infections the use of Monistat 1V should be considered according to these indications:

"Monistat IV is indicated for the treatment of the following severe systemic fungal infections:

Coccidioidomycosis, candidiasis, cryptococcosis, paracocci-diodomycosis, and for the treatment of chronic mucocutaneous candidiasis. However,in the treatment of fungal meningitis and urinary bladder infections an intravenous infusion alone is adequate. It must be supplemented with intrathecal administration and bladder irrigation. Appropriate diagnostic procedures should be followed and MIC's should be determined.

Monistat I.V. should not be used to treat common trivial forms of fungal diseases".

A large number of cysts ("bags" of water under the skin) like hydrocelles and spermatocelles, that refill when drained, will respond to miconazole I.V., proving at last that cysts are a result of infection. The castor oil in the intravenous solution will produce a massive inflammation, but the inflammation will clear and the cyst probably will not return. Intravenous ketoconazole, at present not yet manufactured, would probably be a preferable treatment.

4. HYDROGEN PEROXIDE.

Hydrogen Peroxide is a very strong oxidizer. It is very effective against most (and perhaps all) infectives. It seems to be the best of the common disinfectants for ordinary use after washing the areas of infection, and for disinfecting the hands and nails. It should be used by all reflexologists, chiropracters, and other health professionals, between patients, to prevent spreading of infectives. The standard 3% solution seems to be the best. Stronger solutions kill more infectives but they also damage the living tissues, and weaker solutions are not fully effective against the infectives.

Hydrogen peroxide is toxic to the body and some people may have problems with allergies until the basic yeast infection is reduced. Only very small amounts of hydrogen peroxide are normally absorbed through the skin. Larger amounts may, however be absorbed if the skin quality is poor (low Vitamin C) or if the skin has been scraped or abraded. Over use, prolonged use, or high absorption can induce toxic episodes that will usually start in less than an hour after use. Such episodes can be reduced with benzoate, mannitol, thicurea, DMSO, or selenium methionate. If these are not available, some help may come from methionine and selenium. Superoxide dismutase should be avoided during episodes of hydrogen peroxide toxicity, because the S.O.D. reduces free radicals to hydrogen peroxide.

All of those people that are so set against "chemicals" should realize that the common chemicals are also commonly made within the body by biological processes. (e,g. Hydrochloric acid). Hydrogen peroxide is not only a common bleach and disinfectant, it is also produced within the body by phagocytes, where it is the effective agent that is produced by the good friendly Lactobacillus acidophillus that kills yeasts and other infectives.

Now of course if hydrogen peroxide is effective against yeasts when produced by the body, or by acidophillus, it would also be effective if taken in the right amount, and over the years there have been many reports, and there have been a number of medical papers written on, the value of hydrogen peroxide when taken internally. The writer has not tried hydrogen peroxide internally. Food grade hydrogen peroxide is usually used because drug store hydrogen peroxide contains phenol and stabilizers that might trigger allergies. The therapeutic quantities used by some people and described by Dr. Roy Kupsinel are:

Candidiasis-- 1 to 5 drops of 35% hydrogen peroxide in one quart of distilled water. Drink one to three glasses per day,(between meals) taken with bentonite liquid (Sonne 7) or psyllium seed husks in a glass of water.

Bath,-- 16 oz. 35% , in $\frac{1}{2}$ tub of water.

Colonic Irrigation,-- 6 tablespoons, 3% per quart of water.

Douche,-- 3%, with equal quantity of water, to make $1\frac{1}{2}$%.

5. NYSTATIN (MYCOSTATIN).

Nystatin is a selective anti-fungal that is specific against Candida yeast and particularly Candida Albicans. It is strictly a topical agent, as it cannot be absorbed by the body. It is available in pure powder, coated tablets, liquid, cream, and ointment. All forms seem to be very effective except the ointment, where the grease used appears to prevent the nystatin from contacting the infective.

Nystatin powder is particularly effective against infections of the digestive tract, or it can be mixed with other agents for douches, enemas, lotions, etc.

Nystatin tablets are coated, and are effective against digestive tract infections. If the tablets are chewed, they are effective against infections of the esophagus and throat. Mouth infections can be reduced by sucking the tablets, which are slightly unpleasnt but take quite a long time to dissolve.

Liquid nystatin has a high sugar content which poisons the yeast when the yeast assimilates the sugar. The liquid nystatin is very effective against intestinal infections, if all refined sugars and all free sugars are eliminated from the diet, and if liquid nystatin is then added to the weak juice used for fizz drinks. Liquid nystatin can also be used for infections of the mouth and esophagus, with effectiveness increased by the addition of $\frac{1}{4}$ capsule of resteclin added to each tsp. of liquid nystatin. The mixture should be held in the mouth until it disappears. Liquid nystatin can also be added to enemas.

Nystatin cream is quite effective for vaginitis, where it has a soothing effect. It can be used for calluses, but it is less effective than other agents.

Nystatin ointment seems to be less effective than the cream.

The Perils of Nystatin.

Nystatin is a very effective agent against Candida infections, but it should never be used as a single treatment without the alternate use of other anti-infectives. There are many tragic reports where an ill informed doctor has put someone on nystatin, with a rapid dramatic improvement in health, followed by a decline and a relapse, and soon the yeast victim is back to where they were or worse. It is not that the nystatin became less effective. The nystatin killed out the yeast, but it killed only the Candida yeast, and since all infections are multiple mixtures of infectives, other infectives that are not affected by nystatin fed on the dead yeast, increased, and the poor health returned, with perhaps a few changes in symptoms. Another peril is that because nystatin is taken orally (for intestinal infections) it is assumed, even by some doctors (who should be better informed) that it enters the bloodstream and becomes a systemic agent effective against all Candida infections, but this is not so. Nystatin is strictly a topical agent. It is used internally against internal infections of the digestive tract, but this is only an internal topical application because nystatin cannot be absorbed by the body.

Nystatin is an excellent agent against Candida infections, but it must be alternated with other anti-infectives as part of an overall program. Candida yeast is a very unusual micro-organism that readily forms hybrids. One medical paper describes over sixty different transformants when Candida was mixed with actinomycetales. The paper does not show the effects of antifungals on the various Candida hybrids, but some of the actinomycetales are considered to be bacteria. Some Candida hybrids may therefore be unaffected by nystatin and other antifungals, hence the need to rotate broad spectrum anti-fungals and broad spectrum antibiotics.

6. 2% PHENOL in GLYCERINE.

Phenol is an excellent disinfectant that has been used for many years. Phenol is very rapidly absorbed into the skin when mixed with glycerine. Solutions stronger than 2% should be avoided because they are poisonous to the body. The 2% solution can be used for all topical applications except digestive, and it must not be taken internally.

Tampons, soaked in the solution, are effective against vaginitis. Phenol kills a wide spectrum of infectives, and it may be the only fully effective remedy under some circumstances. The phenol-glycerine solution is also effective against balanitis (penisitis) if the solution is forced into the end of the penis. It can also be used for "white penis" where the entire end of the penis is covered with a thin yeast callus.

The phenol-glycerine solution becomes more effective if magnesium hydroxide is used with it.

Chloraseptic mouth wash contains 2% phenol and it is therefore effective against fungal infections.

7. MAGNESIUM HYDROXIDE. (MILK of MAGNESIA).

Candida yeast produces lactic acid and it will grow at a wide range of pH2.2 to pH9.6, but adhesion to body cells reduces above or below pH.6.

Magnesium hydroxide is highly alkaline, with a pH of 9. It does not kill the yeast, but it inhibits the ability of the yeast to spread. Although milk of magnesia is highly alkaline, it does not harm body tissues. Milk of Magnesia is a suspension of magnesium hydroxide that is thicker than a solution would be.

We know that Candida robs magnesium from body cells to form the asmoresistant layer covering the callus matrix. It appears that milk of magnesia supplies magnesium to strengthen the body cells against the infection.

Milk of magnesia can be used directly for mouth infections, in the ears, nose, and other topical applications, and it can be taken internally as it is normally used as a laxative. When taken internally it should be taken about one hour after meals, to insure that it is taken during the alkaline phase of digestion.

Milk of magnesia increases the effectiveness of phenol and glycerine.

8. PHENOL ALKALIZER.

An excellent anti-infective for topical use can be made by adding an equal quantity of milk of magnesia to 4% phenol in glycerine, to make 2% phenol alkalizer. The effectiveness against trychophyton can be increased by adding about 2% providine iodine (Betadine).

Phenol alkalizer can be used for infections of feet, groin, penis, colon, hair, ears, sinuses, and mouth. It should not be swallowed. It is effective against vaginitis when used with tampons, and against balanitis and enlarged prostate, if applied with a catheter. Do not cover too great an area at any one time.

9. DMSO. (DIMETHYLSULPHOXIDE).

DMSO. is a light solvent derived from trees. It has a garlic odor, and it seems to permeate the cells and passes readily through the skin. It has the ability to dissolve keratin, and kills infectives by dissolving the keratin in the skin of the infective. Controversy still rages over DMSO. But, DMSO does not seem to have any side effects even when taken internally or intravenously. It works best against the yeast at 50% solution in water. Taken internally the mixture should not exceed 15%.

At time of writing some doctors are claiming that DMSO affects the eyes and induces cloudiness and cataracts. Caution should be used.

DMSO has been found to be particularly effective against infections in cystitis and arthritis. Intravenous feedings improve circulation in some people.

DMSO can also be used as a solvent carrier. It can be added to other water soluble mixtures to increase the depth of absorption.

10. CHLOROPHYL.

Chlorophyl is a very strong natural oxidizer that will destroy many different infectives. Chlorophyl can be used anywhere, including mouth and digestive tract. It will clear up many mouth infections, but it stains the teeth. Chlorophyl may be the active agent in some of the successful alfalfa and wheat-grass treatments.

Chlorophyl should be included in rotating programs because it has a healing effect and it helps the body to produce healthy new cells.

Chlorophyl works well with DMSO.

As much as a full tsp. of pure chlorophyl has been taken without visible problems, but such a large quantity is certainly not recommended.

11. GARLIC.

Natural garlic oil, with the odor, is invasive to many cells, and it will therefore attack many infectives. It also attacks some of the cells in the intestinal walls, but the host is large and the infectives are small, so the infectives die and the host survives. Garlic oil can also be rubbed into surface infections with varying results

Garlic is one of the oldest herbal remedies. It was used in Egypt for heart problems, headache, bites, worms, and tumors. It was used by the Romans for the expulsion of worms. It was used in China for fever, headache, cholera, and dysentery. It was used in Africa against amoebic dysentery.

Laboratory investigation (Scientific American, March,1985) shows that garlic juice, even in small quantities, is active against staphylococus, streptocoocas, vibrio (cholera), and bacillus (typhus, dysentery, enteritis) and a broad spectrum of zoopathogenic fungii and many strains of yeast including Candida.

The active substances in garlic are diallyl disulfide, allicin, and alliin. Odorless garlic is known to be virtually ineffective against infectives. Allicin is responsible for the odor. Allicin is formed from the alliin in the garlic when it reacts with the sulphur containing amino acid cysteine, which is also a component of garlic. It appears that supplements of cysteine may make garlic more effective.

Garlic also contains an anti-thrombotic agent named ajoene, which is more potent than aspirin. Due to methods of processing, ajoene is found only in fresh garlic, and is not found in dried or prepared garlic.

The continuing problem with garlic is always the continuing odor, which is exuded by all of the pores of the body. Without the odor, the garlic is much less effective. Chlorophyl can be used to reduce the odor, but it also reduces the effectiveness of the garlic. If garlic is used topically (as for calluses on the feet) large supplements of chlorophyl will reduce the odor. If garlic is taken internally, large supplements of chlorophyl, taken a few hours after the garlic, will also reduce the odor.

12. CAPRYSTATIN. (SEE ALSO "HERBS").

Capryatatin is a commercial anti-fungal available from Ecological Formulas,1061,Shary Circle, Concord, Ca.94518. The tablets contain both caprylic acid and fiber. They are intended primarily for fungal infections of the G.I.tract, so they are enteric coated to ensure release far down the intestine. The recommended schedule is:

First week,- One tablet two times daily, between meals.

Second week,- Two tablets, two times daily.

Third week,- three tablets two times daily.

Ch.4. Reducing Candida Yeast Infection.

The tablets can be scored for earlier release, or they can be taken with the meal to reduce indigestion.

Quite probably this schedule should be tried, but many people find it much too much, with burning, digestive arrest, lingering unpleasant taste, or strong unpleasant odor to the gas that must inevitably be passed. Caprystatin may work, but a little seems to go a long way. An alternate slow schedule would be to start with $\frac{1}{2}$ tablet with a meal, and about $\frac{1}{2}$ day later $\frac{1}{2}$ tablet between meals.Then for early release, 1 tablet daily for a few days. Then monitor the results. It seems that it is much better to take too little, than too much.

Caprystatin is a clever formula of caprylic acid where the caprylic acid is incorporated with a timed release fiber, such that the caprylic acid is slowly released by hydrolysis and ion exchange at the surfaces of the mucous membrane. The caprylic acid is therefore released at the very place that it is needed, and since the caprylic acid is bound in an almost insoluble form, it is not absorbed by the body. Excellent engineering. Yet it should be recognized that this arrangement tends to retain the caprystatin, with build-up if too much is used.

Our experience with caprystatin is that the general effectiveness is increased if nystatin and acidophilus tablets, and perhaps psyllium, are taken with the caprystatin.

For infections of the mouth and throat and esophagus, hold small amounts of caprystatin in the mouth so that it will trickle down the throat very slowly.

Caprystatin may be of particular benefit for colitis and "leaky bowel syndrome" as the fiber tends to coat the mucous surfaces. For colon problems large amounts of caprystatin on a continuing basis may be necessary to ensure that there is enough caprystatin to finally reach the colon. The author has attempted to use the tablets for a rectal suppository, with such a quieting of the bowel that it resulted in constipation for a week or more.

Caprystatin should also be tried in every case of alcoholism. With many alcoholics the alcoholism is constantly maintained by the continuing production of alcohol within the intestinal tract by a mixture of chronic yeast infectives. Caprylic acid, as in caprystatin, together with ketoconazole, nystatin, and other anti-fungals, is probably the only way that such infections can finally be reduced and eliminated.

Despite all of the foregoing, and despite some good reports from the use of caprystatin, the author's experience with caprystatin has been very disappointing. It seems to invariably induce constipation that can be cleared only with a Vit.C enema and an ascorbate flush.(Vit.C,Ch.4.).

13. <u>Capricin.</u> is a timed release caprylic acid capsule, with sodium-potassium caprylate as the effective agent. 12 capsules daily for 16 days is recommended. Perhaps this should be tried, but if intestinal infection is high or has been present for many years, it will take much longer than 16 days for the body to break down the callus structures and rebuild the damaged tissues. Therefore, many Candida victims will need two or three capsules daily, with nystatin, for two or three months, or perhaps even longer. In these low amounts, the capricin seems to have very little effect on normal digestive and bowel function.

Capricin capsules can be effectively used as rectal suppositories for colon infections if covered with nystatin or econazole cream and inserted as far as possible.

Capricin is available from "Professional Specialties Inc; Bellevue, Washington. U.S.A. 98005.

14. <u>PBSC.(PENNICILLIN BACITRACIN SODIUM CAPRYLATE).</u>

PBSC. is an anti-infective used in dentistry. It appears that its value has been ignored or forgotten and its use discontinued.

15. <u>SORBIC ACID.(ORITHRUSH, POLYSORBATE).</u>

Orithrush is a buffered solution of sorbic acid. It is a companion product to caprystatin. Sorbic acid is another short chain saturated fatty acid that is effective against yeasts and other fungii. The recommended use of orithrush is for vaginitis and for infections of the mouth, fingernails, and feet. It can also be used for infections of the scalp (dandruff), ears, penis, prostate and rectum, and for exposed infections that sometimes occur anywhere on the body. Very dilute solutions can be used internally.

Sorbic acid is a fine white powder that can be buffered by mixing with bi-carbonate before adding water. Very small amounts, added to Hi Kc fizz may be of benefit but trials indicate that it too may reduce digestive motility and digestive activity.

Polysorbate is an oily liquid particularly recommended for re-growing hair. Oh yes! And for some people it certainly works wonders! It even reduces dandruff! So what is dandruff? Could it be that dandruff is really a Candida infection of the scalp? Could it be that dandruff becomes much worse in wet weather, because the extra water makes the yeast grow better? If dandruff really is a Candida infection of the scalp, why has it been such a well kept secret for so many years? If the polysorbate is not killing and inactivating Candida, what else does it do? Also, if polysorbate reduces dandruff and re-grows hair, would coconut oil, perhaps with aloe-vera as an emulsifier, work even better?

For those who wish to experiment, the stabalizer crystals used at 1 gm. per gallon for making wine are potassium sorbate, and are obtainable from wine-making shops.

16. ECONAZOLE. (SQUIBB, ECOSTATIN).

Econazole is a topical agent that is effective against most yeasts and molds. It should be included as one of the agents in a rotational anti-fungal program. It is usually in the form of a topical cream.

17. NaEDTA (CALCIUM CHELATOR).

NaEDTA is the calcium chelator that is given intravenously to remove the plaques from blood vessels to improve circulation. There is growing evidence that in some people with poor blood circulation the true problem comes from the large amounts of yeast filaments and hyphae in the bloodstream. NaEDTA will pick calcium ions out of anything that contains calcium, and its greatest value in improving blood circulation may be its ability to reduce the amount of debris in the bloodstream, and particularly its ability to reduce the quantity of filaments and hyphae. Most people with yeast infection will therefore benefit from an occasional four hour infusion of NaEDTA.

NaEDTA is also available as a powder. (used as a preservative). Used orally, it will clear many of the infectives from the digestive tract, by picking the calcium out of their thin skin. Oral NaEDTA must always be taken in tablets or capsules because the powder is invasive to the crevices of the mouth and throat. Oral NaEDTA in excess of 3 gm. per day may remove calcium from the lower colon, and produce muscle spasm in the pelvis and upper legs. Oral NaEDTA should be taken on an empty stomach. The usual effective amount is one or two capsules, but only small amounts should be used for initial trials, because it also picks up lead and other minerals with toxic episodes if the liver and kidneys are impaired.

The best oral form of NaEDTA is a common preservative, disodium, dihydrogen ethylene diaminetetra-acetate dihydrate reagent (ACS) made by G. Fredrick Smith (GFS) Chemicals, Columbus, Ohio.

NaEDTA should not be confused with CaNaEDTA, which will pick up metals but will not pick up calcium because it already contains the calcium ion.

NaEDTA, taken orally or intravenously, should always be followed in about 4 hours by at least one multiple mineral tablet to replace lost minerals.

Research has shown that EDTA increases the effectiveness of the immune system, with a reduction in allergies. Reasons are not given but the probable reason is a reduction in yeast infection, filaments, and hyphae.

The full effects of oral NaEDTA are not clear. There seems to be the possibility that although the EDTA kills the infectives it may be sufficiently invasive to the tissues that it may increase the possibility of re-infection. As garlic is also invasive to the tissues,it may present a similar problem. As a precaution against re-infection both EDTA and garlic should be followed, in a few hours, with nystatin, resteclin, yogurt,lactobacilus - acidophilus, caprystatin, capricin, M.C.T. oil (mead) or coconut. Oral NaEDTA should be used for digestive tract infections, but it should be used infrequently, and it should be used with caution.

18. CANDIDA EXTRACT.

Dr.Orion Truss has shown that severe widespread Candida infections are best subdued with anti-fungal agents, but that these agents will not clear up the infection to the point of health, and the immune system must be stimulated before health can be attained. This was the near hopeless situation before ketoconazole was available. Health can now be attained by the use of ketoconazole to reduce infection systemically, and by the use of the other anti-infectives to reduce the infection topically. With the reduction of infection and the return to health, immune function will improve. Nonetheless, when health and function are approaching normal, Candida extract should be used to improve immune system function while the quantities of anti-fungal agents are reduced, so that the body will develop its own capability to overpower the infectives. Although, Candida extract should be part of the anti-fungal program, the immune system should also be stimulated with autogenous vaccine, and should be nourished with all of the immune nutrients including lithium.

19. AUTOGENOUS VACCINE.

Health is largely a matter of energy reserves. Energy reserves are highest when infectives are low. Man harbors a great many infectives in various small pockets in the body, where the immune system has walled the infectives off and has contained them within a small area. This fact is sometimes disputed, yet whenever large numbers of people are killed in a natural disaster, many diseases will break out if the dead are not buried. The diseases then, must be being carried by the living, and the living must be being affected by the diseases that they are constantly carrying and that their bodies are constantly fighting. Any who doubt this, and all who are ill, have only to go on a course of autogenous vaccine, and they will relive, in moments of near diarrhea, many of the illnesses that they have had in the past.

Autogenous vaccines are made from the urine of the patient. Urine contains anti-bodies to all of the infectives in the body. The vaccine therefore stimulates the immune system against all of the infectives in the body. This is the only known way to reduce Progenitor Cryptocides (genus actinomycetales) which is always present in fulminating form in cancer. Unless cancer is present, or is emminent, the use of the autogenous vaccines should be postponed until health has been regained.

While on autogenous vaccine each and every urge to evacuate the bowels or to empty the bladder must be heeded immediately to help the body and to avoid toxic episodes. Extra immune system and adrenal nutrients should be used while on autogenous vaccine.

Autogenous vaccine is available by mail from Bio Med Research Labs.,1115-E- Pike St., Seattle, Wash. 98122 U.S.A. (John Majnarich)

ANTIBIOTICS and ANTI-FUNGALS.

Oral anti-biotics and anti-fungals are easy to take and many are very effective, but all of them, even when rapidly absorbed, alter both the quantity and the quality of the intestinal flora, frequently to the point of continuing indigestion. Acidophilus tablets, together with yogurt and psyllium seed, will help to restore a healthy flora, but the continuing use of broad spectrum antifungals (as is necessary in reducing Candida infections) can lead to extreme overgrowth and superinfection by some single organism that is not affected by the anti-fungals and anti-biotics.

Intestinal superinfection is indicated by indigestion, gas, and diarrhea. Indigestion, gas and diarrhea can also be caused directly by the anti-fungals or anti-biotics, but this will cease soon after therapy has been discontinued. If digestive problems and diarrhea continue, the offending organism must be sought both by biological examination of the stool, and by trial of other anti-biotics or anti-fungals. This problem can sometimes be solved with a few capsules of NaEDTA, taken between meals. Usually the anti-biotics involved in superinfections are the continuing use of tetracycline, chloramphenicol, and neomycin, and the overgrowths usually involved are Candida and other fungii (which we are already dealing with) and staph aureus. Staph aureus will respond to oral vancomycin (5 gm., 4 times daily, but start slowly). In some cases, I.V. Nafcillin may be required. Clostridal difficile, or C.Sorodelli, may also become a principal infective, indicating a trial of vancomycin or metronidaziole.

VANCOMYCIN (VANCOCIN).

Oral vancomycin is so poorly absorbed that vancomycin is usually used intravenously as a last resort for life- threatening infections. Oral vancomycin can therefore be thought of as a topical anti-biotic. Vancomycin is effective against many gram positive bacteria including many strains of streptococci and staphylococci. When used intravenously it is very toxic, and it can further damage failing kidneys. With oral use it is largely confined to the G.I.tract, and any side effects therefore result from toxins from the killed infectives.

Ch.4. Reducing Candida Yeast Infection.

METRONIDAZOLe (FLAGYL) (TRICHOMONACIDE).

Metroniddazole is effective against trichomona, anaerobic bacteria (including B, fragilis) and chlamydia, and it is used for hepatic (kidney) and intestinal amebiasis and giardiasis. It is available in oral tablets, vaginal cream and vaginal inserts. Oral tablets should be started slowly with $\frac{1}{4}$ tablet, to avoid toxicity from a cascade of toxins. If it is found to be effective the sexual partner should also receive therapy, even if indications are negative. Metronidazole is one of the effective remedies in successful programs against both vaginitis and AIDS.

The peculiar interactions of infectives between each other is always obscure, but metronidazole will frequently relieve or alter arthritic pains, weak wrists or ankles or other aches and pains.

Metronidazole is similar to Antabuse and it reacts to alcohol in a similar manner. Alcohol should be avoided if metionidazole is being used.

FLAGYSTATIN.

Flagystatin combines the benefits of nystatin and flagyl, and was developed for therapy where trichomona has also invaded the Candida matrix. It is available in cream and vaginal inserts. The cream should always be used by the male sexual partner, and threapy should usually include oral metronidazole.

SULFAMETHOXAZOLE. (GANTANOL).

Sulfamethoxazole is a broad spectrum anti-biotic that is effective against both gram-positive and gram-negative bacteria. It is particularly effective against E-coli, B.proteus, and B. pycyaneus, and it is therefore particularly useful against urogenital infections. It does affect the liver and kidneys. Use with caution and start slowly and watch for symptoms from the killed infectives.

ERYTHROMYCIN.

Erythromycin is a broad spectrum antibiotic that has been used instead of resteclin to control bacterial infectives while on fungal therapy. Erythromycin, in all forms except estolate, is usually well tolerated and has very few minor side effects.

OTHER ANTI-INFECTIVES.

There are many anti-infectives that reduce Candida yeast infection, but seem to be less effective, or they have side effects or other defects. Use of the foregoing agents seems to at present be the best way to successfully reduce yeast infection and restore body function. It seems certain that there must be other better methods. Time and effort should bring many improvements. Ingenious people, who are interested in developing better methods, should refer to the list of anti-infectives shown in medical papers and listed in Chapter 3. They might also search the alcohol industry, (which is perhaps the largest single industry in the world), for the commercial agents used by industry to maintain pure strains of yeast and prevent contamination with other strains of yeast. Indeed, such a search might well yield a double prize. It might yield other more effective anti-infectives, and it might also yield the sickening knowledge that in fact the breweries and wineries are unable to maintain pure strains of brewing yeast, and that Candida yeasts and other infective yeasts are in fact brewed and sold and consumed along with the great beers, fine ales, and famous wines. Looking back again, at list 1 of Chapter 3, Candida yeast has been found growing on fruit, and it is responsible for "fruit canners disease", so would it not grow on grapes? Would it not thrive on the glucose just as brewers yeast thrives on the glucose? Who would bother to find out if it was there, and how would they separate the Candida yeast from the brewers yeast? Note that chickens, pigs, goats, cattle, and even the farmer himself, are afflicted with yeast infections from the farm, which infers that Candida yeast also grows on grains, so how could the brewery keep Candida yeast from mixing and growing with the brew? Tap beer has live yeast, so perhaps then tap beer also has live Candida yeast. But brewing is big business, so perhaps the breweries have better technology than the doctors who treat the final victims that the breweries so guilelessly exploit.

The following list of anti-infectives is presented, with comments.

1. Potassium Permanganate and Gentian Violet.

These are the old stantard remedies for "Trench Foot". The army found them to be partly successful. They are messy, and they stain everything that they touch. They tend to harden the "skin" on the callus while the yeast continues to grow beneath the "skin".

2. Salicylic Acid (aspirin). (Whitfields Ointment).

Salicylic acid is the effective agent in most corn salves. It is probably the only place that aspirin should be used. Aspirin is very invasive to body cells, and it effectively reduces the calluses and corns, but it either does not kill the yeast, or it is so invasive to body cells that the yeast thrives in the damaged tissues. The author has had very little success with these preparations, but a program where the callus is reduced with aspirin, followed by other anti-infectives might be successful.

Whitfields ointment is a mixture containing 12% benzoic acid and 6% salicylic acid. It may cause irritation, and if used extensively it may be absorbed and cause toxicity.

3. <u>Sodium Bicarbonate (Baking Soda).</u> Baking soda rubbed on the feet and dusted into the shoes will reduce the acidic environment, but the sodium increases the salinity, which favors some of the infectives.

4. Potassium Bicarbonate. (From the drugstore).

This will also reduce the acidic environment and impair the yeast, but it is somewhat invasive to the tissues.

A mixture of sodium and potassium bicarbonate works the best, but even at best does not seem to be very successful.

5. <u>Dettol Disinfectant.</u>

Dettol seems to kill yeasts but when applied in reasonable quantity it is absorbed by the body and may produce a strong toxic reaction.

6. <u>Novacaine (Procaine) Gerovital GH-3.</u>

GH-3 is another controversial remedy that has many testimonials to its effectiveness in renewing health and reducing "aging". GH-3 is somehow very active against yeast infection. It seems to be very active against mouth and throat infections if the tablets are chewed and held in the mouth as long as possible. Novocaine is a synthetic anaesthetic (commonly used in dentistry) and the GH-3 seems to arrest digestion. As it can be seen to be effective in mouth infections it must also be effective throughout the intestinal tract and could be of benefit to people that are not adversely affected by the impaired digestion.

7. <u>Turpentine.</u>

Natural and synthetic turpentine will effectively kill many organisms including yeasts, but it is so rapidly absorbed by the body that toxicity results if reasonable amounts are used. Turpentine is derived (usually) from pitch from pine trees. Pine pitch is also used for making retsin wine. There may possibly be some as yet unknown value for the use of retsin wine as an anti-fungal agent.

8. <u>Desenex, Tolnaftate, Absorbine Jr., and other drugstore Remedies.</u>

These "remedies" seem to have some value against some of the infectives found on the feet, but they do not seem to be fully effective against Candida yeast. They might be included as part of a rotating anti-fungal program. The powders may have an additional value in keeping the feet dry.

9. <u>Infra-Red and Ultra-Violet Radiation.</u>

Infra-red light (the light from a heat lamp) will make areas that are infected with Candida yeast, fluoresce a bright pink. Infra-red radiation will kill some organisms, and it will kill Candida yeast. Ultra-violet light is at the other end of the visible spectrum, and the ability of ultra-violet light to kill infective organisms is well known, but its effect on Candida does not seem to have been established. Radiation with either ultra-violet or infra-red may prove to be an effective treatment for exposed infections, but as with all radiation therapies their use should be approached with caution because there appears to be a definite link between Candida yeast and cancer, while there is also a definite link between cancer and cells damaged by radiation.

10. Alcohol.

Rubbing alcohol has very little effect on Candida yeast, and if applied too liberally it may be absorbed through the skin and produce toxicity. Distilled liquor, like 40% vodka, used externally without dilution, will slowly kill yeast without noticable side effects.

11. Lithium.

Lithium is a little known mineral that is highly involved in mental function. It is usually shown on a good mineral test. Lithium opposes yeast infection. Yeast infection, in turn, may somehow be responible for low lithium levels. If lithium levels are low, lithium should be supplemented to bring levels up to the "high normal".

Lithium is frequently prescribed and is useful in the treatment of schidsophrenia and mental problems, but the possible role of Candida yeast infection in connection with lithium and mental problems is still unknown.

Lithium is essential to the white blood cells (PMN's) and it is also essential to thyroid function. It appears that Candida either depletes or ties up lithium, with cellular depletion finally impairing the immune system, and particularly impairing the B and T cells. It is postulated that yeast mediated lithium depletion is responsible for AIDS.

Low lithium supplements should be part of all yeast programs, unless contra-indicated.

12. Thymus Extract.

Proteins are constantly leaked from the blood vessels into the tissues, and these proteins are being constantly gathered by the lymphatic system where they are stored in the thymus for use by the immune system, with the excess proteins returned to the bloodstream. The thymus uses these proteins to make the T suppressor cells (see lithium, above) so necessary for immune system function, and particularily necessary to combat yeast infections and cancer. Thymus extract will usually improve thymus function. Thymus function is also dependent upon adequate fully digested protein.

13. Yogurt and Acidophilus.

Although yogurt is acidic, and contributes to acidity,(which would seem to favor Candida infection) yogurt is an effective agent against Candida and associated infectives. It is sometimes very effective against mouth infections, if it is held in the mouth until it disappears. There are a number of reports that yogurt has also been successfully used to combat vaginitis, but acidophilus capsules are more effective. Yogurt is usually made with L.Bulgaricus, L.Lactis, or S.Thermophilus, which are not normal human flora. A similar but different bacteria, Lactobacillus acidophilus is normally present in the digestive tract of about 75% of all people, and it is present in the vagina of about 80% of all females. It is active against Candida.

There are now a number of medical reports that show that Candida will overcome yogurt and will use it for food. The use of yogurt should therefore be reduced in favor of acidophilus caspsules, preferably with Bifidus, and preferably so active that refrigeration is required.

14. Coal-oil. (Diesel oil).

Petroleum products are poisonous to both beast and vegetable. Gasoline is rapidly absorbed by the body and is toxic to man while it is killing the yeast. Vaseline and petroleum grease is thick, and will not penetrate the callus. Coal-oil will penetrate the callus and kill some of the yeast, without toxic quantities being absorbed. Coal-oil is useful only for exposed topical applications, like infections of the feet. Coal-oil can be used as a carrier for other oil based anti-infectives like garlic oil, or to carry healing agents like vitamin E or D. Coal-oil is particularly useful in softening calluses, and keeping them soft and pliable, so that other agents can penetrate the reconstituted "skin".

15. Iodine.

Iodine is the most effective agent against trichophyton (ringworm). Trichophyton is commonly associated with yeast infection, particularly in calluses on the feet. Tincture of iodine stains everything it touches, but povidone iodine (Betadine) is water soluble and it can be added to other soluble anti-infective mixtures.

Povidone iodine is also effective against some of the vaginal infectives, and should be part of all Candida programs for the female. Solution strength for douches should not exceed $2\frac{1}{2}$% (25 ml per litre). Povidone iodine can also be added to phenol/glycerine (at $2\frac{1}{2}$%) for use with tampons. In all cases of vaginitis the male sexual partner should use povidone iodine in the urethra and on the tip of the penis, to prevent re-infection and to reduce the possibility of prostate or testicular infections.

16. Herbs.

There are many claims of many kinds for all of the herbs. So very little is known about herbs, and how they scientifically work, that it is difficult to separate science from myth:- or fact from fiction. Indeed there may be hidden values, but then there also may be hidden perils.

Ch.4. Reducing Candida Yeast Infection.

Garlic.

Non-de-odorized natural garlic is invasive to many cells, including infectives and man. It is effective against Candida yeast, as previously described. The active agent in garlic appears to be a plant analogue of DMSO.

Aloe Vera.

Aloe Vera has been reported to be active against yeast infections but trials against known Candida infections have been negative. Many desert plants survive under dry conditions because they have natural saponins, i.e. wetting agents, (that act like detergents) that break down surface tension and promote better use of available water. Some biochemists think that aloe vera promotes more efficient use of water in the body, and helps the large bowel to handle water properly. Aloe vera may be useful to increase the effectiveness of enemas.

Cedar Buds.

The effectiveness of cedar buds against Candida yeast is not known. Cedar buds, and all parts of the cedar tree, are poisonous. We do have several reports of improved health with the careful use of cedar buds. The improvement in health was always accompanied by the clearing of calluses on the feet, which would indicate that cedar is effective against fungal infections. Cedar buds should be used only under the judicious care of a competent herbalist.

Juniper Berries.

Juniper berries are also extremely poisonous. The effectiveness of juniper berries against yeast infection is not known but there are several reports of the clearing of calluses from the feet, together with improved health. Junipers are very poisonous and must be used only under a competent herbalist.

Chaparral (-Creosote Bush),(Greasewood).

The creosote bush is aptly named because of the high quantities of creosote in the stems and branches. The highly effective disinfectant creosol (C-8 H-10 O-2) is derived from creosote. Creosol is widely used by veterinarians. Creosol is a close analogue of carbolic acid, which used to be widely used both as a disinfectant and as a spermicidal. Carbolic acid is a dilute aqueous form of phenol.(C-6. H-5. O-4).

Chaparral, used in appropriate quantities may be effective against fungal infections. There do not seem to be any reports regarding yeast infections, but there are many reports where it has been effective against cancer, arthritis, and other degenerative diseases that are primarily based in fungal infection, so anti-fungal activity is indicated. There are also reports that the creosote bush is entirely free from fungus of all kinds.

Creosote is highly toxic, so chaparral should be used carefully with the help of a good herbalist. Creosol, used directly, would be better.

Ch.4. Reducing Candida Yeast Infection.

Tabeebo (Pau D'Arco) (Ipe Roxo) Tea.

There are many reports of the effectiveness of Taheebo tea against fungal infections. There are reports of its effectiveness for digestive problems, and there are also a number of reports that calluses have fallen off the feet following continued use of the tea. There are also reports of the clearing of skin problems after applying the tea topically. Unfortunately, the author, after repeated trials, has been unable to confirm this effectiveness, nor has the author been able to find anything that will cause the calluses to fall off the feet. Calluses on the feet always seem to be very stubborn and difficult to eradicate, and usually require years of intensive effort. However, taheebo tea is always worth trying, as it may be effective against some specific infectives. Also the tea itself is not too bad, and it is certainly better for health than black tea or coffee. Unfortunately, there are also some reports that some people find tahebo tea to be depressing.

Herbal Formula.

A special herbal formula used by some doctors apparently with some success, is composed of; Aristolochie, Carthamus Tinctorus, Interleukins, Molaleves Alternifolis, Pau D'Arco, Pisum Sativum.

Herbalseptic.(N.F.Factors).

Herbalseptic is a topical anti-infective that is reasonably effective. It contains herbs, with sodium bi-carbonate, potassium iodide, borax, glycerine, phenol, and chlorophyl. Whoever put it together knew what they were doing.

Coconut

Yes, Coconut is now a herb. The herbalists may not know it, because herbalists pay very little attention to science in determining and defining herbs. Probably unknown to the herbalists, coconut does contain quite high amounts of caprylic and other 7 to 9 carbon fatty acids that are fungistatic and fungicidal. Caprylic acid, and similar short-chain fatty acids are normally produced on the surface of the mucous membranes by intestinal flora, and it is these fatty acids that finally stand between the host and his host of fungal infectives that are constantly waiting for a chance to devour him. High infections, anywhere, require anti-fungals and anti-biotics, which not only kill the infectives, but also kill and alter the intestinal flora, reducing the caprylic and other protective acids, followed by intestinal infection, which then requires more anti-biotics and anti-fungals; and on and on. Caprylic acid will help to break the degenerative cycle and will help to restore intestinal flora, but caprylic acid preparations, like caprystatin , seem to alter the water balance and reduce digestive motility and activity. Capricin capsules, which also contain caprylic acid, appear to be a much better alternative than caprystatin. Caprylic acid supplied with coconut is biologically readily available. Most of it will be assimilated, but if coconut is nibbled frequently throughout the day some of the caprylic acid will reach the areas where it is needed. The effects are slow, but coconut makes a good snack, anyway. Yes, a good almost continuous snack for people who do not have heart or circulatory problems, but for people with cholesterol problems extreme care should be used, because coconut can also raise cholesterol and triglycerides. People at risk should therefore monitor blood pressure and cholesterol if they consume large amounts of coconut. The amount of coconut required to restore digestive peace, however is quite small. Usually one small coconut, eaten with all food and nibbled at for three or four days will sometimes provide sufficient caprylic acid to restore the integrity of the mucous surfaces. The coconut should be accompanied by acidophlus tablets to help restore the intestinal flora and large amounts of lecithin and vitamin C to reduce the cholesterol levels. People with hypoglycemia or diabetes should also be careful with coconut and MCT oil, because the short chain fatty acids are so readily converted to glucose.

MCT Oil (Mead Johnson).

MCT oil is a Medium Chain Triglyceride supplement that contains high amounts of caprylic acid derived from coconut. It is more easily digested and absorbed than most food fats and it is therefore used as a supplement for medical conditions where the absorption of fats is impaired. MCT oil is so rapidly absorbed that its use as an anti-fungal agent for intestinal infections seems doubtful. When applied topically to Candida infections on the feet it appears to feed the infectives rather than destroy them, however it may prove to be useful when mixed with garlic oil, phenol, DMSO, or other anti-fungals.

CANDIDA INFECTIONS THROUGHOUT the BODY.

Candida yeast can and does infect and affect every part of the body from the hair on the head to the tip of the big toe. In dealing with specific infections it would therefore seem logical to simply start at the top of the head and work downward, but there are so many interlocking factors in Candida infection that unless the true nature of the infective is clearly visualized success may be limited.

The callus structure of the Candida infective matrix (with the many different infectives harbored therein) cannot be over-emphasized; the inter-relation of infected areas cannot be over-emphasized; the ability of the yeast and its toxins to impair the immune system cannot be over-emphasized; the constant outpouring of filaments and hyphae into the bloodstream cannot be over-emphasized; and the insidious spreading nature of this ever waiting infective cannot be over-emphasized. Candida is very difficult to reduce and eradicate because it is a particularly tough infective that mixes itself with live body tissues, and it will live and grow under extremely adverse conditions, while the total effects from the spreading infective are so slow and subtle that the changes in health go almost unnoticed until the infection is firmly established and has spread to many different parts of the body.

To effectively reduce Candida infection, we must therefore deal with it wherever it may be, and we must assume that it is everywhere, and wherever it is it is in the callus matrix form, perhaps very thick and heavy, perhaps little white dots, or perhaps only the thickness of the epidermus of the skin, but nonetheless in the callus form complete with osmoresistant layer that shields the infectives from attempts to destroy it. The typical callus structure can best be seen in the calluses on the feet.

Wherever yeasts live, they basically live on sugar. Candida yeast lives on directly absorbed sugar; (as in the digestive tract) sugars from the bloodstream; sugars from hormones; and sugars from sexual fluids. Thus the digestive tract becomes a common site for yeast infection; all body parts that are sexually interconnected become particularly vulnerable as sites for Candida infection; hyperglycemia and diabetes, (with episodes of high blood sugar) will increase all yeast infections; and tobacco, caffeine, anger, niacin, or anything else that raises blood -sugar levels, will also increase all yeast infections.

THE SEXUAL INTERCONNECTIONS.

All mammals are sexual creatures, with mankind (or womankind?) probably at the top of the list, even above mice, rabbits, and perhaps baboons. Anything that arouses the adrenals has almost instant sexual effects. A stallion, seeing a mare, will give a snort, and even before the end of the snort the penis has dropped. The hormone reaction from the brain, to adrenals, to sexual system is almost instantaneous, and with the arousal, the adrenals also pumped out adrenalin to raise the blood sugar for instant energy for the occasion. Whenever the adrenals are aroused, whether from excitement, exercise, sexuality, fight or fear, the blood sugar levels are raised and all yeast infectives everywhere in the body will feed and grow on the extra sugars, while yeast infectives in sexually interconnected tissues will also be fed by extra hormones. You will certainly recognize the following hormone interconnections.

The mouth, (kissing), breasts and genitals are obvious sexual organs. But with sexual arousal, digestion stops, and the rectal sphincter tightens, demonstrating that the digestive system, and the rectal area are also sexual tissue. (Which is also well known to homosexuals and to many heterosexuals). Then, at the peak of orgasm, there is spontaneous clenching of the hands and similar movements of the feet, (called corpopedal spasm), demonstrating that the hands and feet are also sexual tissues affected by sex hormones.

Thus the hands, feet, digestive system, rectum, and mouth, are all directly interlinked with the breasts and genitals through the nervous system, and are also indirectly interlinked by sexual hormones. The hands, feet, digestive tract, rectum, mouth, breasts, and genitals, are sexual tissues that are highly susceptible to Candida yeast infection, and if any one of these interconnected parts becomes infected the infection will affect all of the other interconnected parts, and they then also become even more susceptible to infection. Usually, if yeast infection becomes high in any one of these interconnected sexual tissues the influence will be fulfilled and all other interconnected parts will soon also become infected. Therefore heavy calluses on the feet will usually be accompanied by telltale ridges and bumps in the fingernails; digestive problems with perhaps hemorrhoids or a restricted rectal sphincter; together with tooth cavities, canker sores, or other mouth problems; together with cervical infection and/or vaginitis, or balanitis, prostate problems, or tender testicles. The toenails will also usually be infected, with sharp bends, ingrown nails, undulations, and fine or coarse ridges. Toenails and fingernails may be thickened, have growths underneath them, and/or be subject to spontaneous loss. Only the breasts seem to escape, yet here too there may be cysts, or peculiar discharges.

This is the sexual interconnection. There is more food for the yeast in sexual tissues. This is the reason that if Candida yeast is present anywhere it will usually be infecting sexual tissues, and if it has invaded sexual tissues, by the time that it has impaired the health, it will have managed to spread and infect, to some degree, most of the other sexual tissues. Therefore the well justified saying,"If it is anywhere it is everywhere". So how does it spread? Careless or unknowing hands spread it from anus to genitals, to mouth, to feet, (or vice versa) and invariably on to the sexual partner; and frequently on to other members of the family, where again it will be centered in the sexual tissues. It is not that Candida cannot invade and live in other tissues because it does grow in the heart valves; in the sinuses; on the surface of the thalmus behind the eye; under arms, across the abdomen, in the hair, or in scaly patches almost anywhere on the skin; or in little red eruptions with a white center anywhere on the body. But Candida is opportunistic, so the principal infections are usually centered in sexual tissues where the fluids are not only rich in sugars, but where the sex hormones provide an environment rich in vitamins, manganese, zinc, chromium, selenium, and other "yeast nutrients".

It must be remembered that Candida yeast is endemic in the natural world surrounding mankind, and it is therefore endemic in mankind. We cannot escape from it. From our first infection when we draw our first breath our bodies must fight Candida every moment of our lives, with our total health dependent upon how well the battle goes. Some of us start life with very little infection. We escape the trauma of constant ill health, while others of us, starting life with a heavy infection, may never know what it is like to have a truly healthy moment. The battle against the yeast is always constant and that is the reason that people with a high Candida infection are always tired and worn. With all of the body systems impaired by toxins; with all of the infectives stealing many of their body nutrients; with their body having to dispose of all of the extra wastes from the infectives; with their body using large quantities of proteins and other nutrients to fight the infectives; there is simply no energy left to live, and with the quality of life so low, there is usually very little left to live for. Quite obviously, if infection is high the body needs help, so we should not particularly think in terms of killing the yeast; instead we should think in terms of helping the body to contain and destroy the infection. In overcoming all diseases it is the body that finally overwhelms the infective. It is the body that is the Hero. So we must help the body to be the Hero. To help the body to be the Hero we must understand the callus nature of the infective matrix (Fig.2.) and the different ways of approaching the infective matrix, to try to help the body to reduce the infectives. So we should start by looking at the best ways to reduce the calluses on the feet, because here on the feet the callus matrix can be seen in its many different forms.

CANDIDA INFECTIONS of the FEET.

Large calluses on the feet are typical Candida yeast infections, and an examination of these calluses can provide excellent insight into the callus matrix structure involved in all Candida infections. (Fig.2.)

Calluses on the feet may be initiated by a number of infectives that will invade tissues damaged by bruising or rubbing, but if such infections do not clear up quickly, trychophyton (ringworm) and Candida yeast will usually become the principal infectives. Drug-store remedies for athlete's foot may kill out some of the other infectives, but the trychophyton and Candida are immune to most of the drug store remedies and the calluses will usually remain. If started soon enough, iodine (usually as Betadine) will eradicate the trychophyton, but if the calluses have developed to any degree of thickness all of the infectives will remain untouched in the callus matrix, nicely protected from the anti-infective agents by the "skin" on the callus. The "skin" on the callus is not true skin. It is an osmoresistant layer reconstituted by Candida yeast. As the name implies it is an osmosis resistant layer, a magnesium stimulated layer so tightly bound together that fluids pass through it with difficulty even with osmosis. The infectives then, are securely protected beneath the layer and are largely immune to all agents and to all efforts to destroy them. If miconazole lotion and phenolalkalizer are alternately applied to the calluses for a few days, the outer infectives will be killed. Then if the feet are washed, using a very small quantity of detergent, followed by soaking for about 10 minutes, patches of dead skin will show up as a very soft white. The outer layers of the callus can then be scraped off with an "almost sharp" knife. As the scrapings come off you will then see the calluses are actually formed layer after layer, like an onion. It appears that this layer structure is developed by the body continuing to put forth great effort to grow new skin underneath the callus, only to have the infective invade and slowly penetrate the new layer of skin, after which the body puts out another heroic surge of re-building new skin, in another vain effort to protect the nerves and tissues from the invading infective. The quantities of nutrients used in this continuous vain battle are of course enormous, while the continuous constant stress from the fight drains the adrenals and reduces the ability of the body to cope with the slowly invading infectives. But the feet are our means of locomotion. We need to use them, yet with every step our full weight comes down on the infected area, further bruising and irritating the already weakened and inflamed tissues, which are then further attacked by the yeast.

It should be particularly noted that sleep is the time of body rebuilding. During sleep, the body can put all of its energies into clearing out dead cells, killing out infectives, and building new tissues. That is the reason that sleep and bed rest are so essential to recovery from burns and transient infective diseases, including "colds" and "flu". But the body cannot know the difference between chronic and transient infection. All that the body sees is a never ending struggle, where it loses a little during the day, and gains a little during the resting peroid at night, if sleep is long enough. Obviously people with high infection, will rquire more sleep than people with low infections. People with good metabolism will require less sleep than people with poor metabolism. People with low immune function, will require more sleep than people with high immune function. People with good liver and detoxification ability will require less sleep than people with poor detoxification. People with good nutrition will require less sleep than people with poor nutrition. In short, the amount of sleep and rest required to "feel good" can be used as a measure of the ability of the body to cope with its total chronic infectives.

The ability of the body to deal with total infection can also be seen in the feet. The body rebuilds the tissues in the feet at night, then, "toward the end of the day, (and sometimes sooner) as energy levels fall, the feet become tired and start to "burn". The "tired feet" result from the build up of lactic acid, (produced by both the body and the yeast) together with increased numbers of bruised and dying cells from the pressure of the weight of the body on the weak and inflamed tissues, while the "burning" sensation results from the direct attack of the infectives on the large number of nerve endings exposed to the infection. Technically, the greatest pressure on the foot is around the outside perimeter of the foot, and the "burning" is frequently present in this area. Also the "burning" sensation is present in vaginitis, and in balanitis (infection of the tip of the penis) and it is probably part of the many pains from digestive problems. The "tired burning feet" affect all of the other sexual tissues, and the other sexual tissues affect the feet, while all of the stress drains the adrenals. When the feet are tired, the body is tired. When the body is tired, the feet are tired.

Tired burning feet particularly affect the stomach and digestion, reducing cellular nutrition and reducing the ability of the body to cope. The weakened cells in the digestive tract then become targets for infection, and particularly targets for the ever present and ever waiting Candida yeast. Inevitably then extensive foot infections will almost without exception be accompanied by digestive tract infections, probably including hemorrhoids. The foot problems together with the digestive and rectal problems then in a similar way, affect all of the other sexual tissues. With cankers in the mouth, pyorrhea, cavities in the teeth, tonsil infections, and probably sinus infections, together with infections of the vagina and cervix, or infections of the penis and prostate. To reduce foot infections, all other infections must be reduced. To reduce the other infections, the foot infections must be reduced.

Now further examination of the calluses on the feet (where we can see them best) will usually show that the calluses are many different colors. Some will be fluorescent red, some will be pink, some will be white, some will be yellow, some will be almost grey. They will also have different textures. The different colors and textures come from a different infective mix, and probably from different walking pressures. Yeasts and fungii are plants and they grow much like plants. They are very sensitive to the many different growing conditions associated with different tissues and different physical conditions. Heavy white calluses will usually be around the edges of the heels and frequently running up the back of the foot almost to the ankle. Yellowish calluses are usually on the instep, they may not look like calluses, but phenolakalizer, hydrogen peroxide, and persistent scraping will reveal them as a very dense leathery covering that is very difficult to penetrate. Grey calluses will usually be on the ball of the foot, very dense and highly layered with very thin layers. Around the edges of the calluses will usually be a red line, then white skin changing to the natural skin. The red line is the fluorescent inflammation that underlies the callus, but the rest of the inflammation cannot be seen through the callus, and the white skin is not skin. A little water or hydrogen peroxide with a little scraping, will usually reveal this area to be a very thin infection, only as deep as the epidermus of the skin.

Then there are the fluorescent reds and purples. The fluorescent reds (and usually the red around the calluses) show a different color between sunlight, light bulb, and fluorescent light. The fluorescent red is unique to Candida infection, and is a certain indicator of internal Candida infection. The purple comes as usual, from poor circulation, and/or lack of bio-flavinoids.

In some cases, the inflamed fluorescent red, typical of Candida infection, will be seen over the entire feet, without any visible calluses. The red will reduce and disappear with prolonged use of ketoconazole, proving that the infection was definitely fungal. Therefore, the usual foot infection can be seen as being a double infection; an "outside" callus infection above the skin, that sometimes keeps building thicker and thicker, and an "inside" infection below the skin; with each infection penetrating the skin sufficiently to maintain infection on each side of the skin, while the body is vainly trying to interpose and maintain healthy skin between the two infections.

This then can be seen as the typical callus matrix. A callus matrix protected by its own asmoresistant layer. A callus matrix with infection "outside" of the body, but extending through the skin into the "inside" of the body.

Topical anti-infectives, if persistently used almost forever, will sometimes slowly clear up the calluses right down to the real skin, and the skin may heal on the outside, but the infection inside the skin will remain and will present itself as an inflamed fluorescent red, usually with swelling. Indeed, someway, somehow, some people will have feet in this condition when they are first seen by a health practitioner; bright fluorescent swollen and inflamed red feet, without any sign of calluses or other blemishes; and the hapless victim in a state of sexless, desperately ill, ill health.

It becomes obvious then that Candida infection can and does exist within the tissues, without the callus matrix structure, and these infections will now respond to ketoconazole. However, the common infections are always associated with the callus matrix structure, and it seems very probable that all such inflamed infections originated from a callus matrix. Nonetheless, it is certain that for any yeast program to be successful the topical therapy and systemic therapy must be used together, and ketoconazole therefore becomes half of the therapy, because ketoconazole is the only oral systemic anti-fungal that does not have serious side effects.

Trench foot is an extremely heavy growth of Candida yeast (monilia) on the feet. Trench foot was the scourge of all of the armies of World War 1, and certainly also World War 2. Continually wet feet are always part of trench warfare, and Candida yeast grows best under warm, damp conditions; the very conditions continually present in army boots in rain and mud. Further, the infection was also favored by the continuous stress; by poor nutrition, and by endless cigarettes and endless coffee. The standard army remedies were usually gentian violet or potassium permanganate. The army, and the army doctors did their best, but despite their efforts and despite gentian violet and potassium permanganate, trench foot ruined the lives of many soldiers (and their families) with the trench foot becoming also trench mouth, severe indigestion, constipation, enlarged prostate, sexual failure, and mental problems.

From all of the foregoing we must conclude that it is probably impossible to eradicate Candida yeast infection with topical applications. Wherever the infective matrix has been established long enough to penetrate the skin of the host intensive effort with topical anti-infectives can clear the Candida infection down to the skin, but the infection on the lower side of the skin, and the infection below the skin, cannot be reached by the topical anti-fungals so the infection will continue unless it is reduced with systemic anti-fungals to the point that the body can cope with it.

From present experience, and considering that Candida is a parasitic plant that is fed by the body, it seems that ketoconazole alone would finally clear up an infection, but if so it would be a very long and tedious process, because even with the best methods and the best anti-fungal agents it may take several years to clear off most of the calluses. The actual rate of clearing is dependent upon the total chronic infection as compared to the total ability of the body to cope. If total infection is high and the total ability of the body to deal with infectives is very low (as is the usual case) only small amounts of anti-fungal agents can be used, and progress is very slow until the liver, immune system, and other body systems have recovered and larger amounts of anti-fungals can be used. Then, as all body systems improve, the body may become so determined to destroy the infectives that spontaneous episodes of toxicity may result, and anti-fungal agents must be used with care. Alternately, if sufficient anti-fungals are not used, the infectives may advance rapidly and you will then become toxic to the advancing infectives. The principal sources of toxicity are the systemic agents, and the topical agents used in the digestive tract, but the body sees only the total toxic load, and if the load is already high, or if total detoxification ability is low, even the hydrogen peroxide can produce a toxic episode. It is always a problem of too much or too little, but lower amounts over a longer peroid seem to give the least difficulty. The right amount is the amount that makes you "feel good", and if you "feel good" the body will have much less difficulty reducing the infection.

As the calluses are clearing up it will be noticed that in some places around the callused area there will be a thin layer of soft surface yeast that can be scraped off with a knife. This is a non-callus Candida infection that is only one layer of skin deep, not yet deep enough to gain nutrients from live body cells or from the bloodstream, with the yeast living only on the dead skin cells of the epidermus. This thin infection has not yet developed the asmoresistant layer, yet it is very persistent and may remain until there are no other signs of infection. Therapy should therefore be extended for some time after this thin infection has also disappeared.

It should be emphasized that at present there do not seem to be any quick and easy ways to reduce and eliminate Candida yeast, and probably there never will be, although the fortuitous use of ketoconazole very early in life would certainly prevent high infections from developing. Early fortuitous use of ketoconazole would probably also be accompanied by a large reduction in the number of "retarded" and "hyperactive" children in our schools, and an even greater reduction in the number of patients in our mental institutions. But logic, reason, and technology are notably absent from medicine today, so it may yet be many years before any preventive programs are even considered. The very high yeast infections seen today are unquestionably the combined long term effects from anti-biotics, contraceptives, promiscuity, alcohol, caffeine, sugar and surgery, but regardless of cause, extremely high yeast infections are now very common. These high infections may have taken thirty or forty or more years to develop, so in many areas the yeast is living within and among the body tissues, and the percentage of yeast cells to body cells is of course unknown. But if it took thirty years or more for the yeast to invade and mingle with the body cells, one could expect it to take several years to reverse the condition, and with the yeast so intermixed with the body cells elimination of the yeast and rebuilding of the damaged tissues cannot be accomplished in a few days, nor even in a few weeks. Some doctors and other health people may argue that Candida grows only in skin tissues, and does not penetrate other tissues, but if it does not invade deeper tissues why do tissues without exterior calluses show fluorescent "Candida" pink that increases in intensity with elevated levels of blood sugar? The fluorescent "Candida" pink can easily be seen under "dull" light bulbs, like the clear candle-type bulbs used in dining-room fixtures. Examine the feet under fluorescent light (which is very low in infra-red) and then under the candle-type bulb, (which is high in infra-red) and note the fluorescent pink under the candle type bulb. Note also the internal infection, seen under the bulb, involves a much larger area of tissues than just the callused area. Thus the total infection is much greater than the amount indicated by the calluses. Now look at the hands under the candle type bulb, and if infection in the feet is high, the hands will probably also show peculiar fluorescent pink, increasing around the base of the fingernails. The brighter the fluoresent pink, the higher the infection. Now look at the genitals under the bulb, and they too will probably show inflamed fluorescent pink. Now consider the total volume of flesh involved, contemplate and guess at the volume of intestinal and other internal infection that cannot be seen, and wonder how the body can survive.

The Candida content of the tissues that you have just seen and contemplated cannot be known, or even guessed, but most certainly several years may be needed to reduce the Candida and to rebuild the damaged tissues. A tedious task? Yes!, a tedious task, but a tedious task that is highly rewarding! There is certainly a rewarding thrill to see a full sized toenail grow on the little toe, where the only toenail that you remember was only the size of a match head! There is certainly a rewarding amazement when you can again hear a watch tick, after you thought that the ticking of watches had ceased forever! There are very high rewards for vanity when the hair starts to return to the balding scalp, after you had resigned to the certainty that all would be lost! There are rewarding smiles of disbelief, when the skin clears for the first time in memory! There is the reward of a new, quiet, inward joy, when the digestive tract ceases to rumble and bloat with constant gas! There are peaceful, thankful rewards when hiatus-hernia subsides, and lets you eat more than two spoonfuls without feeling that you are bursting! There is just cause for great rejoicing when the nose no longer runs, when the sinuses drain and cease their constant pain, and you can again sleep without two pillows, or miracle of miracles, you can once again sleep on your back if you wish! There is great satisfying relief when you do not have to sit for hours at stool, but can feel the bowels evacuate in one relaxing surge! There is an exhilarating feeling of returning youth to feel the urine pour forth as easily as in childhood! And there is joyous gratification at the return of sexual interest and sexual capabilities! Indeed, the rewards are truly life itself, for life without health is not Life, it is only a living death.

Now some of these rewards may escape you if too much damage has already been done, while other rewards you may not need, but whenever and wherever Candida infection is reduced there will be rewards, wondrous rewards of Life, but it will take both time and continuous, unrelenting, effort.

ALTERNATE HEALTH THERAPIES.

There are constantly blurbs in the media extolling the virtues of alternate health therapies, but unfortunately the media writers usually are at best less than scientific and frequently less than truthful.

Typically the media writer will describe someone who has cured his arthritis or his lumbago with rose petals or with frogs eyes, or someone who has gone to Timbucktoo where the local phalla dowsed away his cancer using only a bent and twisted bunglestick for a divining rod.

Acupuncture, moxibustion, magnets, rays, herbs, pyramids, mineral springs, flowers, magentos, clays, meditation, minerals, seaweed, exposure, blood letting, metals, blood suckers, feasting, fasting, and every part of many animals, birds, fish, reptiles, plants and fungii have all been sold and extolled as wonderful natural remedies. The argument is that our ancestors were wise, they had a "feeling" for what was good; they could tell the good from the bad by "vibrations", so of course experienced natural health practitioners should be encouraged to practice their ancient art in their truly established traditional way.

Yes, yes, and Yes! So the highly qualified experienced traditional acupuncturist, direct from the hinterland of China, came to the fair and sunny province of Alberta where he started practicing the Ancient Art of Acupuncture in the Truly Traditional Manner, and soon everyone was experiencing miraculous great benefits from the Ancient Art!

Oh,Yes! And soon too there was a local outbreak of hepatitis and similar "goodies", which the "dumb Western doctors" had great difficulty to understand. Oh yes, those "dumb western doctors" with all of their white coats, and drugs and disinfectants were indeed baffled at first;- until they discovered that all of the people with hepatitis and etc; had experienced the benefits of the genuine Eastern Traditional Acupuncture. Then those "dumb Western doctors" went out and discovered that the highly trained Traditional Acupuncturist was using nice new factory sterilized needles, which he then re-sterilized in the truly Ancient Traditional Manner, by (of course) passing them through His mouth, before using them! Well;- Oh yes, yes, and Yes! The ancient acupuncturists were certainly wise, indeed!

Then there is the story;- true sad story; of a heart attack. A not-too-old farmer had a "heart condition" and was going to an acupuncturist to relieve the angina. The farmer was just starting to improve, when he lost his acupuncturist, and was greatly agitated because he was having trouble finding another. You see, his acupuncturist died. Yes, died! Very suddenly died; (you guessed it) died of a heart attack!

To try to separate the wheat from the chaff, let us consider the so called "Alternate Therapies"
Herbs.
Herbs are of two classes:
I. Natural substances that are poisonous to infectives. Most of these substances, like Male Fern, Chaparral and Gentian Violet are also very poisonous to man and must be used with great care and caution.
2. Natural substances that contain metabolically active forms of vitamins or minerals.
3. Natural substances that affect or interfere with natural body processes.,e.g. digitalis, which affects the heart.

Most of the chemical drugs used by the alopathic doctors have been derived from herbs, either by direct extraction of the active chemicals, or by synthesis of the chemicals, or by synthesis of analogs of active chemicals. The drugs derived from the herbs usually have less side effects than the herbs, or the side effects may be increased along with a higher potency. Alopathic medicine, with its high use of drugs, can therefore be considered as "refined and modernized" herbal medicine, which of course makes herbal medicine obsolete.

Although some herbs do have high amounts of some nutrients, they cannot cure severe vitamin deficiencies like pellagra, beri-beri or pernicious anemia. They cannot be effective against displaced vertebrae, and they cannot renew atrophied muscles. Herbs are therefore only a supportive form of medicine. They are not an alternate form of medicine.

Vitamins and Supernutrition.

Vitamins, minerals, and supernutrition can be of great value in improving health, but they do not and cannot cure chronic infection, or local infections of the gall bladder or appendix, nor can they alter spinal problems. They are therefore an adjunctive or supportive therapy, but they cannot be called an "alternate" therapy.

Acupuncture.

Acupuncture can be used for anasthesia, for relief of muscle spasm, and pain, and perhaps for the stimulation of body processes, but acupuncture cannot provide extra nutrition and it cannot destroy infectives. It is therefore an adjunctive or supportive therapy, but it is not an "alternate" therapy.

Reflexology, Shiatsu, Neursage and Massage.

These are all adjunctive muscle therapies that can improve body function but they cannot provide extra nutrients or destroy infectives, and they therefore are not an alternate therapy.

Chiropractic.

There is little question that displaced vertebrae can alter nerve function and thereby improve or alter any body processes. Chiropractic is therefore of great value, but it cannot provide extra nutrition and it cannot destroy transient or chronic infectives. It is therefore an adjunctive and supportive therapy but it is not an "alternate" therapy.

Alopathic Medicine.

Alopathic medicine uses drugs, surgery, anti-infectives, some herbs, some vitamins, some electric stimulation and some nutrition, but it usually ignores and sometimes scorns chiropractic, acupuncture and nervcite therapy. Alopathic medicine is therefore incomplete medicine, that needs to improve its technology and needs to recognize and make use of the other supportive therapies, while in turn the supportive therapies need to improve their science and technology and remove the "mystery" from the things that they do.

The fact is clear. There is no such thing as an "alternate" therapy. All of the so called "alternate" therapies are simply adjunctive and supportive therapies, while alopathic medicine is itself very incomplete and lacking in applied science.

The truth is that we can and should do better. Medicine should not talk and write about the "management" of health condition. We have the knowledge to cure. We have adjunctive therapies to assist with cure. We should use the scientific knowledge and the adjunctive therapies to ensure cures for all who intelligently seek health.

SUPPORTIVE THERAPIES
CHIROPRACTIC.

Chiropractic is the manipulation of the spine and other bones to restore them to their proper position, and to thereby reduce pressure on the nerves. Most of the chiropractic adjustments are done on the spine. The spinal cord runs through holes in the center of the spine and it has little bundles of nerves that run out between the vertabrae to all parts of the body. Quite obviously, if any of the vertebra become displaced from any cause, the displaced vertebra can pinch the nerves, altering nerve function to that part of the body. Thus a displaced spine from any cause, can interfere with many body functions, and the health problems will remain until the displaced vertebra is returned to its normal position.

Chiropractic is therefore one of the basic essentials of every health program. There are two types of chiropractor;
1. Chiropractors that work only on the vertebra in the neck. The idea here is to relax or to apply pressure on the nerves to control body processes. These chiropractors can do very little good and they should be avoided.
2. Whole-body chiropractors who work on the entire spine and all of the bones and joints in the body.

Everyone with a health problem should have a full X-ray of the spine from a whole body chiropractor, (with appropriate adjustments if required), to insure that the health problems are not caused or aggravated by pinched nerves.

Most displaced vertebra and other bones, are displaced by falling or similar physical accident, but many bones are pulled out of place by spasmed muscles. The chiropractic adjustments should therefore be accompanied by adequate adrenal nutrients, together with nervcite therapy, to reduce any muscle spasms that may be causing or aggravating spine or other joint problems.

Unfortunately, many chiropractors tend to over-adjust, sometimes to the point that the vertebra may "slip in" and "slip out" by itself. One adjustment per week, for a few weeks, is usually sufficient, if treatment is accompanied by nervcite therapy and adequate adrenal nutrients.

If problems are persistent throughout an area of the body, and if progress is slow, the possibility of lymphatic infection should be considered, and various anti-infectives like flagyl or sulfamethoxazole should be tried. (See Ch 4. Lymphatic Infections. Ch.7, False Arthritis). Chiropractor adjustments should be greatly reduced during therapy for lymphatic infections.

NERVCITE THERAPY.

Acupuncture, reflexology, shiatsu and massage are "mystery" therapies. "We do not know why they work but they are effective", is a common statement that of itself denies the prudent rule that if we do not know what we are doing or why we are doing it, we should use extreme caution. However, there is not any real mystery to acupuncture, or to any other therapy that is based on the so-called acupuncture point.

Anyone can find the acupuncture points. They are very real and you do not need to have any mysterious charts. All that you need is You. They are simply the "ouch" spots or tender spots referred to in reflexology, acupressure, and similar therapies. Doctors however, are unable to find acupuncture points, or to verify them, simply because they are part of well known body structures.

If you look at the broad muscle on the top of the forearm it will seem to be smooth, but in fact it is made up of three rows of muscle segments, each segment about $1\frac{1}{2}$" long, all interconnected to make up the smooth muscle that you see. Starting at the elbow joint, in the center of the width of the muscle, about $1\frac{1}{2}$ inches down from the joint, an "ouch" spot can be found. Try it. This spot, under the pressure of the thumb or knuckle, is more sensitive than the rest of the muscle. It is a nervcite; otherwise called an "ouch" spot, reflexology point, shiatsu point, or acupuncture point. Another spot can be found in the elbow joint immediately above, and more points can be found at intervals of about $1\frac{1}{2}$ inches, running down the center of the muscle, with two more rows of nervcites running down the center of each remaining half of the muscle. These points are really the muscle end plates.

The nervcites (acupuncture points) then are really the muscle end plates, where the nerves are connected to the muscle fibers. The nerves of course, are always well supplied with blood, and wherever there is a blood vessel there is a lymph vessel. The nervcite is therefore a combined nerve junction and lymph node. Commonly, a build up of lactic acid; a shortage of nervous system nutrients; (Vitamin C, pantothenic acid etc;), or interference with nerve transmission, (as with caffeine or nicotine), will cause some of the muscle fibers to become disconnected from the nerves at the muscle end plate, which may cause muscle spasm (with local pain) and which finally results in atrophy of the muscle fibers, with perhaps atrophy of the whole muscle, followed by replacement of the active muscle fibers with fat, water, and connective tissue. This muscle degeneration is then frequently followed by the fibrosis and calcinosis so frequently seen in the legs of older women.

Ch.4. Reducing Candida Yeast Infection.

The muscle spasm and muscle atrophy can be reversed by eliminating drugs and poisons, by supplying adequate nutrition, by reducing chronic infection and other forms of stress, and by using nervcite therapy to re-connect the nerve neurons to the muscle axons so that the muscle fibers can re-generate. Acupuncture, shiatsu, electro-therapy, massage, reflexology, and neursage are all forms of nervcite therapy.

If muscle spasm and muscle atrophy are extensive throughout the body, muscle function can be restored only by whole body nervcite therapy, supported by nutrition and renewal of all failing body systems. The extent of muscle degeneration can be determined by the total amount of atrophy and calcinosis, together with the sensitivity of the nervcites. Highly sensitive nervcites indicate new muscle degeneration, while "dead" insensitive nervcites indicate muscle fibrosis and calcinosis.

For any physicians or others who may doubt the actual existence of the nervcites (acupuncture points)(reflexology points) they can be easily located, as previously described, everywhere on the body. These same points can also be located with a highly sensitive galvanometer (perhaps with a wheatstone bridge) or with a skin resistance meter as used in lie detectors. The reason that the meters show the nervcites is that the nervcites are the muscle end plates, which are a combined nerve center and lymph node. The presence of basophil and mast cells in the lymph nodes increases the local histamine levels, which greatly increases the local electrical conductivity, and the nervcite is then easily located with any skin resistance meter of the type used for lie detectors or for biofeedback. Inexpensive meters of this type are available from Edmund Scientific, or from Efstonscience, Inc. 3500 Bathurst St. Toronto, Ontario, Canada ,M6A 2O6.

If the nerves in the muscle end plate become disconnected from the muscle fibers by lack of nutrients, by synapse interference from caffeine, by build-up of lactic acid, or from any other cause, and the muscle fibers remain disconnected from the nerve supply they will slowly degenerate to a single nucleic chain, with the active muscle tissue being slowly replaced with fat, water, and connective tissue, which is followed by fibrosis and calcinosis. If however the nerve axons become re-connected at the muscle end plate, the muscle fibers will cease to cramp, and atrophied muscles will completely regenerate. The final object of all nervcite therapies is the re-connection of the nerve axons at the muscle end plate to the disconnected muscle fibers. Acupuncture, shiatsu, and reflexology are nervcite therapies. The good that they finally accomplish, not by design but by happenstance, is the reconnection of the disconnected nerves at the muscle end plate. The best nervcite therapy is neursage.

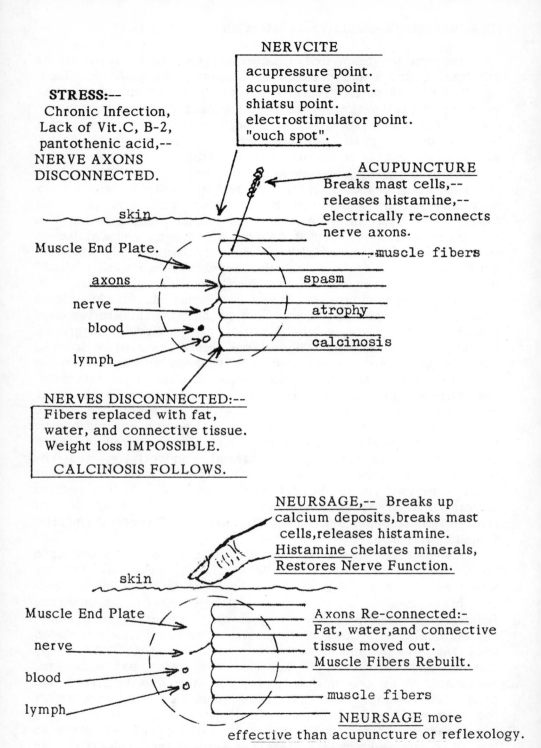

NERVCITE

acupressure point.
acupuncture point.
shiatsu point.
electrostimulator point.
"ouch spot".

STRESS:--
Chronic Infection,
Lack of Vit.C, B-2,
pantothenic acid,--
NERVE AXONS
DISCONNECTED.

ACUPUNCTURE
Breaks mast cells,--
releases histamine,--
electrically re-connects
nerve axons.

skin

Muscle End Plate.

muscle fibers

axons

spasm

nerve

atrophy

blood

calcinosis

lymph

NERVES DISCONNECTED:--
Fibers replaced with fat,
water, and connective tissue.
Weight loss IMPOSSIBLE.

CALCINOSIS FOLLOWS.

NEURSAGE,-- Breaks up
calcium deposits, breaks mast
cells, releases histamine.
Histamine chelates minerals,
Restores Nerve Function.

skin

Muscle End Plate

Axons Re-connected:-
Fat, water, and connective
tissue moved out.
Muscle Fibers Rebuilt.

nerve

blood

muscle fibers

lymph

NEURSAGE more
effective than acupuncture or reflexology.

Fig. 12. BODY REBUILDING WITH NEURSAGE.

Ch.4. Reducing Candida Yeast Infection.

Electro stimulation, auricular medicine, shiatsu, reflexology and acupuncture are less effective forms of nervcite therapy.

All of the nervcite therapies are more effective during the niacin flush, or during the sex flush that follows after sexual orgasm.

Neursage. Fig.12. See also "Basic Nervcite Therapy",Ref.28.

Basic neursage is performed by rubbing the nervcite with a circular motion, with the thumb, finger, knuckle, or with neursage tools. After rubbing, pressure should be held on the nervcite for five or ten seconds. The object of rubbing the nervcite is to mechanically break down and disperse any calcium lactate that may have hardened in the nervcite, and also to mechanically break down mast and basophil cells in the lymph-node part of the nervcite. With the breakdown of these cells histamine is released into the nerve junction and permeates the local tissues producing a bright pink spot. The histamine is quite highly electrically conductive, and the histamine, together with a few seconds of pressure, helps to electrically re-connect some of the nerve axons to some of the spasmed or inactive muscle fibers. With the re-connection of spasmed fibers to nerve axons the spasmed muscle will relax, and it will again become loose and pliable. When inactive or atrophied muscle fibers are reconnected to nerve axons (by any means) the muscle fibers will slowly regenerate according to the type of nerve axon to which they are reconnected (A or B) and the regeneration will be remarkably complete. The histamine released by neursage also travels through the lymphatic system and helps to reconnect disconnected nerve axons in other muscles along the path of the lymphatic flow. Indeed, one of the extra values of the niacin flush (which also releases histamine) is the re-enervation of many spasmed muscle fibers througout the body. The sex flush too, is a histamine flush, and sexual orgasm, with the spontaneous tightening of many muscles at the very time that the histamine levels in the blood are high, is a natural invigorating form of nervcite therapy

Whole Body Reflexology.

Whole body reflexology is very similar to neursage. It was developed many years ago by Dr. Fitzgerald. Foot reflexology was developed from whole body reflexology, and for many years largely displaced whole body reflexology, but whole body reflexology has now been revived. None of the reflexology practitioners seemed to realize that the reflexology points were the muscle end plates so the rubbing motions and methods vary greatly between the different practitioners. Neursage could therefore be considered to be a modern scientific form of whole body reflexology. Dr.Fitzgerald thought that whole body reflexology followed certain meridians (Fig.13). There is some quite

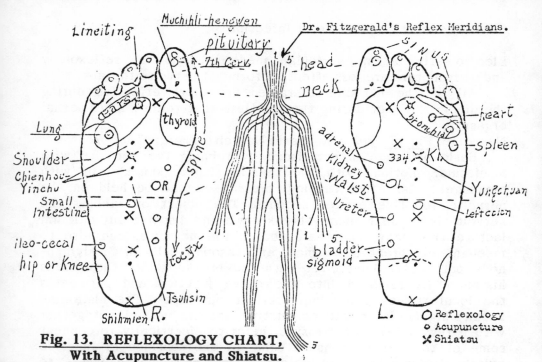

Fig. 13. REFLEXOLOGY CHART,
With Acupuncture and Shiatsu.

Reflexology relates the areas of the feet to corresponding areas of the body, starting with the big toe as representing the head. Either reflexology, or acupuncture, or both, must be wrong, because the same reflex point, (nervcite), is said to have different affects.

Yungchuan, which is between the adrenals and spleen in reflexology, is used in acupuncture for head disorders, vertex pain, infantile convulsions, unconsciousness, heatstroke, cerebral hemmorhage, hysteria, and epilepsy, while this same point in Shiatsu is also used for head disorders; - heatstroke, sunstroke, and fainting, but not epilepsy. For epilepsy Shiatsu uses Lineiting, which is also used for pain in toes, and for infantile tetang, (?). But lineiting in reflexology is about the level of the throat, and pain in toes is down at the bottom of the heel. Muchili-hengwan, is used in acupuncture for Orchitis. (Testicular infection). But this point is at the base of the big toe, while reflexology shows the points for the testicles to be in the heels. Chienhou-yinchu, about the area of the shoulders in reflexology, covers a very wide range in acupuncture, i.e., leg furuncle, lower limb cramps, pain in foot, heart palpitations, high blood pressure, infantile tetang. Tsuhsin, above the waist and about level with the kidneys in reflexology, is used by acupuncture for menorrhagia (menstrual bleeding), headache, and gastroenemius cramp. Shihmien, at the level of the hip or knee in reflexology, is used in acupuncture for insomnia, and pain in the feet.

Quite obviously acupuncture, or reflexology, or both, are wrong, and the claims made for some of the specific effects are questionable.

good evidence for these meridians, because in addition to the lymphatic inter-connections between nervcites there certainly are nerve connections between the many different nervcites. If any of the nervcite therapies do follow meridians, Dr. Fitzgerald's meridians are probably the closest to being correct. However, even if there are meridians, and even if these meridians are correct, use of them does not seem to bring any special benefits even with neursage.

Foot Reflexology.

Foot reflexology is the most publicized form of reflexology. It was developed and promoted by Eunice Dingham Stophel from Dr.Fitzgerald's whole body reflexology. Foot reflexology holds that the nervcites in the feet follow mysterious meridians to all of the organs and other parts of the body in a pattern similar to the body laid out on the soles of the feet, with the big toe as the head and the narrow part of the foot as the waist. There is no evidence whatsoever that these meridians exist, and if there are in fact nerve interconnections directly to other body parts there is very good evidence that the foot reflexology charts are wrong.

Nonetheless, foot reflexology can be quite effective in giving temporary relief to some health problems, particularly if the reflexology is extended to the hands and to the afflicted parts.

Auricular Therapy. (Fig.14.)

If we were scientifically looking for a nervcite network with inter-connections to all other parts of the body we could not expect to find it on our feet, as foot reflexology claims, but we might expect to find it in sensory organs in the head, where fetal development first starts.

Iridology has certainly shown that interconnections between sensory organs and other parts of the body do exist, and that all of the parts of the body do have nerve or other interconnections to the eyes. Because the ears are another major sensing organ, we should expect that they too will have interconnections to all other parts of the body, and indeed the ears do seem to have direct interconnections to all body parts.

Neursage of the ear nervcites is one of the best forms of auricular therapy. Acupuncture and electro-therapy are also used. Information on auricular therapy and associated devices can be obtained from M.E.D. Servi-Systems.Canada Ltd., P.O. Box 1309, Kanata, Ontario. K2K 1X3.

The author does not agree with many of the claims made for auricular therapy, but some benefits can be obtained from neursage of the ear nervcites, particularly when they are tender and sensitive.

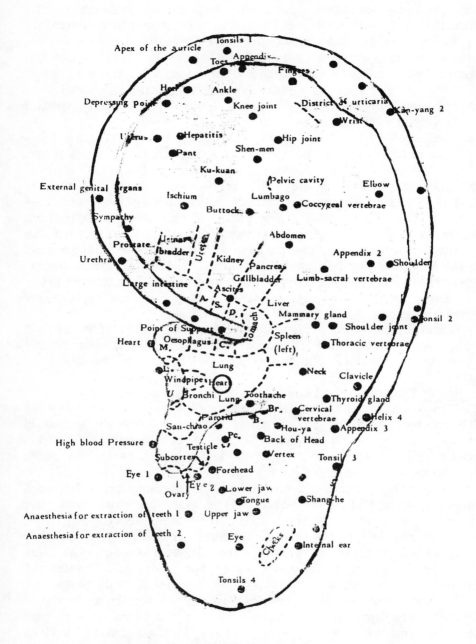

FIG. 14. EAR NERVCITES.
(From "Modern Acupuncture", Tokyo).

Ch.4. Reducing Candida Yeast Infection.

Shiatsu and Acupressure.

Shiatsu is the ancient oriental art of the application of pressure to the acupuncture points. (nervcites). It has been developed over many centuries, and as usually applied it has become very ritualistic, with the sequence of points pressed being the main feature of the therapy.

Shiatsu also uses meridians, but the meridians and the body parts said to be affected are different than acupuncture and they are also different than reflexology. There does not seem to be any scientific reason for any of these charts to be either valid or of value.

Acupressure is a modern form of shiatsu, centered principally on the tenderness of the nervcites. Acupressure can therefore be considered as a form of whole-body reflexology, or as a form of neursage with emphasis on pressure.

Electro Stimulation.

The electrical nature of muscle action and muscle control has been known since the very early days of electricity, when Volta generated small electric currents by moving freshly killed frog's legs, and these muscle experiments later led to the development of the Voltaic Cell; the dry battery that is now in such common use. Also in the early days of electricity it was soon discovered that the application of small currents of electricity to muscles, would make them move, which led to electro-therapy. Today, electro-therapy uses direct current with variable voltage, or alternating current or pulsed direct current, with variable voltage, variable frequency, and variable wave form, which is applied to electrodes placed over the muscle end plates (nervcites), to relax or to improve muscle function.

Electro stimulation may therefore sound like science at its best, but in fact it is incomplete science at its worst. It is incomplete science at its worst because sufficient time has not been taken to investigate the exact role of electricity in nerve and muscle function. For instance, fish also respond to electric currents. Experiments have shown that fish will slowly move to the anode if electric currents are passed through the water, but the exact waveforms and frequencies are difficult to establish because very frequently a little touch on the wave-generator controls will cause all of the fish to almost instantly arrive at the anode;- belly up;- dead! So exactly what do the electric currents do? We just do not know. We do know that electro stimulation seems to work wonders fot relaxing sprained and stiffened muscles, yet when used two or three times per year by some athletes, the athletes may become impotent, and perhaps suffer complete sexual failure; a condition that is apparently brought on by the electro-stimulation, but a condition that certainly is not healthy.

We can therefore only conclude that until science and technology have solved more of the mysteries of muscle function, electro stimulation can hardly be recommended.

Electro stimulators are also now used by many acupuncturists to stimulate the acupuncture needles, so they are now part of auricular therapy. Health practitoners who use electro-therapy almost invariably argue that the electric currents cannot do any damage, because they are so small. But so also are the body cells, very small, and the mitachondria and other structures within the cell are certainly much smaller, so we cannot really know what damage may be done. Perhaps the electric currents do not do any damage, but why take the risk when neursage or whole body reflexology will do the same thing, much better.

Magnetic Therapy, Electro-stimulators, and Pain.

People with unavoidable pain, from chronic infection, accident, life-saving surgery, etc; may be able to relieve the pain with magnetic devices or electro-stimulators. Transcutaneous Electrical Nerve Stimulator (TENS) units have been used by many pain clinics, with varying success. Various types of equipment for both magnetic and electro therapy are available from Med. Servi. Systems. (See auricular Therapy)

Acupuncture.

Acupuncture is a very ancient oriental health therapy. Acupuncture is the insertion of needles into the acupuncture points. Even today most acupuncturists do not realize that the acupuncture points are the nerve junctions at the muscle end plates. Thus acupuncture is an ancient art, developed from trial and error, that still does not have a sound scientific base. As it is practised; acupuncture is sometimes a somewhat effective therapy for some health problems. Like all other nervcite therapies when it is effective it reduces the symptoms, but by itself it seldom effects a cure. Acupuncture appears to work by the electrical conductivity of the needles used, because gold needles are the best, and insulating plastic needles will not work.

Acupuncture is very effective for anaesthesia, pain, and sedation, where the conductive needles appear to short-circuit the electric flows in the nervous system.

One of the principal aims of acupuncture, properly performed, is to alter the pulse. Traditionally there are four different types of pulse, each with about six different categories. Perhaps altering the pulse is of value to health, if somehow acupuncture does alter the pulse, but measuring the pulse is still subjective, as it is judged by finger pressure, and until the alteration in the pulse can be shown on a pulse-volume recorder or similar instrument the factual abi;ity of acupuncture to alter the pulse must remain questionable.

As acupuncture is a form of nervcite therapy it is quite effective when the needle is inserted to the right depth at the right spot. The problem is, that because there is such a great variation in the size and shape of different people, the muscle end plates (acupuncture points) are not always in exactly the same spot. The exact acupuncture point must therefore be found by instrument, or by finding the tender spot by feel. Working the needles and turning the needles seems to increase the conductivity at the muscle end plate sufficiently to relax spasmed muscles and to re-enervate and re-activate atrophied or inactive muscles.

Modern acupuncturists frequently attach electric stimulators to the needles to make the therapy more effective.

Massage.

Massage is one of the oldest therapies known to man. It is so old that it is a natural spontaneous reflex for us to rub some part of the body to make it better. When we rub some part we mechanically break up fibrosis and calcinosis, and we also mechanically break up mast and basophil cells in the lymphatic system, which releases histamine into the area and produces a mild local flush. Hard prolonged massage therefore produces a greater flush. Some masseurs incorporate heat with their practice, some incorporate a little acupressure with their therapy, and some also push a few bones around. Massage therefore takes on as many forms as there are practitioners.

The principal value of massage seems to be to work the lymphatic pump, particularly if the stroking is "toward the heart", i.e. to move the lymphatic fluid out of the limbs. The lymphatic system is composed of many single tubes, with self-closing valves. It is as extensive as the vascular system, but the only pump is movement of the body, which squeezes the tubes and moves the lymph along. If body movements are few, or if the muscles are fibrosed or atrophied, massage moves the stagnating lymphatic fluids along, and muscle and body function improves.

Massage will therefore help many physical problems, particularly if it is combined with neursage. Good massage vibrators and similar equipment increase the effectiveness of massage and they also help the victims of ill health to help themselves.

Massage Chairs.

Massage chairs are particularly effective in promoting relaxation and in improving lymphatic function. The improved lymphatic function then promotes the growth or re-growth of capilliaries. The increased peripheral blood flow together with the improved lymphatic function helps to reduce and stabilize high blood pressure.

A good massage chair will have vibrators on the footrest and seat, together with vibrators, heat, and rollers on the back. These chairs are expensive but they are usually well worth the price. Yet one should remember that without ample good nutrition including emphasis on vitamin E, Vitamin C, and bioflavinoids, the benefits from the very best massage chair may be very fleeting.

Physiotherapy.

Physiotherapy is the manipulation of the body to improve body function. Basically it might be called forced exercise. Over the years many different devices have been developed and used, some with benefit, others without benefit. Heat and cold are also used. Electrostimulation has been added, and many methods and techniques have been borrowed from massage, chiropractic, and other disciplines. Physiotherapy is usually therefore partly scientific, partly guess and as varied as the practitioners. A good physiotherapist is therefore priceless, while a poor one is useless, so be sure to find a good one, and be sure to understand what they are doing and why they are doing it, because some of the useless therapies certainly are not painless, and they are therefore less than beneficial.

HERBAL MEDICINE.

Herbal medicine is the very oldest form of medicine. It has been, and it still is being used and abused by every segment of society from the rich to the destitute, in almost every country, religion, cult and creed.

Many of our drugs come from herbs, yet other herbs have escaped the prying eye of science and we have no factual knowledge about them. Herbs are able to alter body functions because they contain unique highly complex chemical compounds. The problem is that some of these compounds may be beneficial, while the same herb may contain compounds that are very harmful.

Herbs fall into three categories;

1. Herbs that interfere with body systems. (From which drugs are derived. e.g.,digitalis).

2. Herbs that contain special vitamins, mineral, or chemical compounds that assist body systems. (e.g.,garlic, horsetail.)

3. Herbs that are poisonous to chronic infectives. (e.g.,Male fern.)

Some herbalists do have quite good success with herbs, but the fact remains that if herbs were fully effective we would need nothing more.

Some herbs (like garlic) have been scientifically investigated for actual chemical content, and it is the author's view that these herbs can and should be used, but potent herbs of which we know little should be avoided until full knowledge of their chemistry has been gained. After all, tea was a widely prescribed herb until it was discovered that it contained caffeine.

HOMEOPATHIC REMEDIES.

Homeopathic remedies are mixtures of extracts from herbs. They are usually used by starting with very small quantities which are slowly increased. There are many claims for their effectiveness but there is very little scientific evidence to show that they are effective or to show that they should be effective. There is also very little evidence to show that homeopethic remedies do any harm, but they are usually an alcohol extract and they therefore contain small quantities of alcohol.

CALCIUM CHELATION THERAPY.

(See also Ref.12. and Vit.C, Ch.4.)

Intravenous infusion of the calcium chelator NaEDTA (and similar chelating agents) has been found to be a preferred method of reducing the sclerotic blood vessel plaques that produce vascular disease. In short, it reduces the "Hardening" in disorders commonly called "Hardening of the arteries".The Pulse-Volume Recorder Chart (Fig.15) shows the health and life-saving value of chelation therapy. Chelation therapy also removes or reduces lead, and other toxic metals. Chelation therapy was available from Dr.Green's clinic in Toronto, and was given on a limited basis by Dr.Tamms until intervention by the Medical Associations. It is at present available from Dr.Robert Kimmel M.D. 1800 C.St.,C-8 Bellingham,Wash.U.S.A. 734-3250; from Dr.Leo Boles. Bellview Seattle,Wash.-U.S.A.; and from Dr. Harold Harper,11311 Camarillo St. North Hollywood, CA. U.S.A.-985-1103. Additional sources might be obtained from American Association of Medical Preventics, (Los Angeles.) who can also provide a list of technical information. Dr. Garry Gordon is the author of "History and Mechanisms of Action of E.D.T.A. Chelation Therapy", one of the most lucid and complete papers on the subject.

Blood Vessel Plaques.

Scientific American, in "The Origins of Atherosclerosis", shows that blood vessel plaques are formed by the proliferation of a single cell from the middle lining of the blood vessel. As they are a growth from a single displaced cell they are really a form of tumor. In lay terms, they are cancerous by nature, and they will continue to grow until the blood vessel is completely closed unless the growth is arrested. As the cells multiply, they slowly gather materials from the blood stream. The plaques finally consist principally of calcium, cholesterol and triglycerides, and are thought to be initiated by the irritation from high blood levels of cholesterol and triglycerides. NaEDTA,

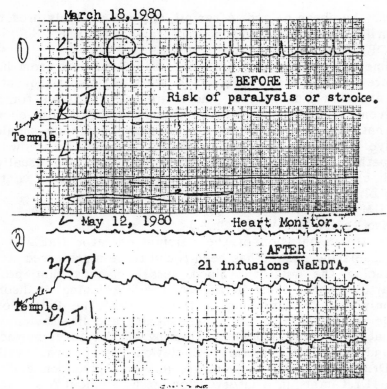

Fig. 15. Intravenous Chelation Therapy, For Hypertension, Arteriosclerosis, Intermittent Claudication. Harper Clinic,L.A., 21 infusions chemo-therapy, continuous I.V. drip.(4 hrs.). 3 gms. Na EDTA, $1\frac{1}{2}$cc 2% Xylocaine, 5,000 units Heparin, in 500 cc Ringers Lactate. Cost,- $87.00 each.

and similar chelators, pick the calcium out of the plaques, and high dietary amounts of lecithin remove the cholesterol and other fats, causing the plaques to disintegrate.

Quite obviously, although chelation therapy is a life and health saving treatment, it is still only a stop-gap therapy because the plaques will surely and slowly again return unless the cause of the high blood levels of cholesterol and triglycerides is found and corrected.

Many years ago Adelle Davis showed that diet has very little effect on blood cholesterol levels because cholesterol is so essential to body function that the body will break down live tissue to manufacture it. Further, high triglyceride levels are found even when it is eliminated from the diet. Dr. Carlos Mason,(Nato Lab.,Box 3944, Vancouver,B.C. Canada, has now shown that the root cause is adrenal depletion,(Ch.4.)

In adrenal depletion, potassium is excreted, and through a complex metabolic process, the cells are filled with excess sugar. Without the potassium, the normal use of sugar cannot even progress to lactic acid, so the excess sugars are made into glycerol, and the glycerol is then made into the excess cholesterol and triglycerides found in the bloodstream. Thus the plaque formation is not dietary, but metabolic. It would seem that to avoid the high cholesterol and triglycerides one would have only to supplement the potassium. But potassium increases the production of aldosterone, which increases edema and excretion of potassium. Sodium decreases production of aldosterone, but excess salt holds water in the tissues. V8 juice contains approximately the correct sodium/potassium balance, and three glasses per day fortified with 1/3 tsp. sodium-potassium tartrate will help raise the potassium levels and reduce the adrenal depletion if all other adrenal nutrients are supplied. The principal other adrenal nutrients are choline, inositol, methionine, B6, pantothenic acid, and ample Vitamin C (ascorbate), together with about 2 tbsp. of sunflower oil, (per day).

High levels of blood cholesterol also result from the depletion of vitamin C, which is essential for the conversion of cholesterol to bile. Hi-KC Fizz (Na K Ascorbate) is therefore an even better sodium/ potassium supplement, because it also supplies large amounts of vitamin C.

Chelation therapy not only improves total blood circulation to all parts of the body, but the chelator also reduces the rods, crystal bodies, L forms, and red-cell clumping that can invariably be seen, with a dark-field microscope, in the blood of victims of Candida infection.

Intravenous chelation therapy should be part of every health program, and should certainly be part of every Candida program. Any doctor and any hospital can give the infusions if they try, because the same intravenous infusions of NaEDTA are routinely given for lead and heavy metal poisoning. If you are too far from a chelation clinic insist that your doctor gives you chelation,(unless prohibited by kidney-liver problems). Do not take no for an answer. Any doctor that does not investigate and respond simply has poor technology. Try another doctor and try another hospital.

The Perils of Niacin.

The use of large quantities of niacin to produce the niacin flush is now very common. The niacin flush reduces red blood cell clumping, and dilates the blood vessels for increased blood circulation. Large quantities of niacin are also used for the treatment of schidsophrenia and alcoholism. Niacin, however also raises blood sugar levels, which feeds any Candida infection that may be present. In those cases where the circulatory, mental, or other health problems are based on Candida infection the niacin may be reducing the symptoms while at the same time it is contributing to an increase in the basic infective problem. Niacin should always be used when necessary, but if Candida infection is present, it should be used with caution, or therapy should be arranged so that ketoconazole is taken about one hour prior to the niacin, then when the fungal infections feed on the high blood sugar they will also get the ketoconazole.

IRIDOLOGY

Iridology is not a therapy but it is a good diagnostic. Anyone who has observed the growth of chickens from eggs, will remember that one of the first things that starts to develop is the eye. The eye is therefore present throughout the fetal development of the entire body, and the connections established by this close association with all of the body parts remains. Therefore, if any body systems fail, they will usually (but not always) show up in the patterns in the eyes. The science, (and it is a science) of reading and interpreting the specific changes in the patterns of the eyes caused by the altered function of various parts of the body is called Iridology. The changes in the eyes that are associated with the malfunction of many of the parts of the body has been charted, and Iridology has now become an excellent scientific diagnostic tool. Iridology, however is not a 100% perfect diagnostic tool, because each and every health problem may not show up as recognizable changes in the patterns, but if eye changes do indicate a specific health problem look closely, because iridology is usually right.

Unfortunately, iridology has now become very interlocked with herbs, and herbs are frequently less than scientific and therefore frequently less than useful, and therefore less than successful, which of course has given iridology a bad name. Nonetheless, if iridology points to a possible health defect do not ignore it, the defect will probably be there. Furthermore, if the actual locus of the principal health problem cannot be found, iridology may pinpoint the defective or infected system.

Extreme care must be exercised when using iridology because so many "kooks" have acquired cameras and have prepared charts with very wild interpretations. Some claim that they can pinpoint Candida infections, then after a week ot two on a herbal concoction, the Candida will be gone! Yes, the Candida vanished, just like that! Yet anyone that is fully acquainted with the insidious nature of the Candida callus matrix will know that after Candida has arrived and colonized, it is not reduced or eradicated that easily ot that quickly. Iridology should be used, but it should be used with care and caution.

KINEISIOLOGY.
Kineisiology started out as the kinetics of muscles, but with time the name has been badly maligned and kineisiology has now become almost anything, fact or fiction, that might have something to do with muscles or body function.

Some kineisiology, as taught in some universities, seems to be quite soundly based, but out in that never-never land of "psychic health" kineisiology has mainly taken the form of "muscle testing", where the need of the body for herbs, vitamins, or minerals is determined by holding the substance tested for in the hand of the outstretched arm, while the need is then determined by the muscular resistance when the arm is pushed down by the person doing the testing. There is no possible scientific reason that the "testing" should work, and on two separate occasions the author has been found to need aluminum, when the "tester" thought that the metal held in the hand was zinc.

It would appear that people legitimately involved with kineisiology should find a new name for their work with muscles.

GLAND and ORGAN SUPPLEMENTS.
From the very early days of medicine it was realized that the organs and glands were composed of special substances and that the best way to nourish a defective organ or gland was to eat the same organ or gland taken from a food animal. Thus to re-build the liver, you eat liver; to rebuild the kidneys, you eat kidneys; etc; etc. The good thing is that it works, and sometimes it works surprisingly well.

Now of course, some people, perhaps with adrenal problems, might object to eating adrenal glands from animals, so to overcome taste and eating predjudices; and to provide a continuous supply, many of the glands have been specially dried and prepared as "pills", with the most common example being desiccated liver. This approach works quite well because the glandular is usually raw, and the re-building of the defective gland or organ is a long process that is dependent upon the long term presence of all nutrients in small quantities, with large quantities being of little extra value.

The best glands and organs are of course fresh, and raw. These are difficult to find and a constant daily source is difficult to maintain. They are also difficult for most people to eat because they usually look terrible, and taste worse.

The next best are fresh frozen, but these have almost as many drawbacks as the fresh raw. However, they are almost tasteless when eaten as thin frozen slices, and they can be purchased in quantity and kept frozen umtil needed.

The next best are the raw, dried and desiccated. These are easy to buy, easy to take, easy to store, and by the pound are very expensive.

The next best are the cooked glands and organs. Cooked, of course, as little as possible, (except pork liver which must be well cooked), because cooking destroys some of the enzymes and alters the food structures. By the pound they are relatively inexpensive.

So there is the quandary, just what is best, a little of the desiccated, or a lot of the cooked?

It really depends upon the particular glandulars that are needed, and your possible sources of supply. Liver, and kidney, and heart, and muscles, and knuckles (joints), and tripe (stomach), and chitlins (intestines), and head-cheese (brains), are easily found at your butcher shop, and if you can find a French delicatessen you may be able to buy many of the glands and organs already prepared at a very good price. The French, you see, are excellent cooks and they use almost every part of food animals. Alternately if you can find a French butcher, or any butcher that will save you the glands that are needed, you can get a French cook-book and probably have a continuing feast on the glandulars that you need the most. To maintain your supply you may have to resort to freezing before or after cooking. Liver, kidney, tripe, and even hamburger can also be used as conveyors for other organs and glands if they are all ground and cooked together to mask the odd flavors.

Glandulars are also available in the form of liquid extracts which are taken as drops and are largely absorbed in the mouth. These have a particular advantage for people with impaired digestion and assimilation. Caution should be used with all glandulars, and extra caution should be exercised with the liquid extracts. Sometimes they can produce very potent reactions.

SPECIAL FOODS.

It is usually difficult for Candida victims to find something to eat that does not somehow create digestive problems, particularly if Candida infection is high throughout the intestinal tract. It appears that Candida cannot effectively feed on the following foods:-

1. Celery. Celery is high in both potassium and sodium. It seems to aid in the digestion of some other foods, particularly nuts.

2. Grapefruit. Grapefruit can usually be eaten when oranges must be avoided. Too many will increase acidity, and too many will chelate out too many minerals. See Pg. 234.

3. Nightshades.(See also "Allergies", Ch.5.). If tomatoes, peppers, and other nightshades do not trigger allergies they can be excellent food for Candida victims, although potatoes may need to be restricted because of their high starch content. It appears that the small amount of nightshade poison in these foods is highly poisonous to the fungus , so the nightshades can be

232

considered as herbal foods if the immune function is good enough to prevent them from triggering allergies.

4. Sardines. Sardines are very high in nucleic acids. They seem to be well tolerated and they can provide protein nutrition even when many digestive and assimilative processes have failed.

5. Papaya. Papaya contains digestive enzymes and a peculiar seven carbon sugar. Papaya seems to be a poor food for fungus and a good food for us. One quarter of a papaya usually makes an excellent snack, or it can be used to assist the digestion of other foods.

6. Pineapple. Pineapple also contains digestive enzymes. It may be trouble for some Candida victims but it is excellent food for many others.

7. Cheese. In the making and curing of cheese, the free enzymes digest some of the proteins, and the final product therefore contains a high percentage of free amino acids. Cheese is excellent food if it does not trigger allergies.

8. Coconut. Coconut contains Caprylic acid, which is effective against fungus, and a teaspoon daily will help to reduce digestive fungal infections. High amounts may result in high levels of blood cholesterol.

BODY WEIGHT.

Body weight is intrinsically controlled by balance between all of the body systems. There are many cases where normally slim and trim people have had accidental injury to internal organs, after which they have become extremely skinny, or continuously obese. The liver, thyroid, and adrenals seem to have the greatest influence on weight. Weight is also greatly influenced by food. Caffeine and tobacco may make people either overweight or underweight, while sugar, white flour, alcohol, and overeating increase obesity. Hyperactivity makes people thin, and lethargy makes people fat.

If weight is abnormal, the thyroid program together with the rest of the entire Candida yeast infection program will probably result in a return to, or in a return toward, natural body weight.

Increase in Body Weight.

The usual causes of low body weight are malnutrition, malabsorption, caffeine, tobacco, and altered thyroid levels. These are covered in the Candida program. Thin skinny people who do not respond to the thyroid and Candida program should consider the possibility of an infestation of worms, amoeba, etc. There are good tests and good remedies available in the doctors office and among the naturopaths and herbalists. Metronidazole (Flagyl) should be tried. A trial of hydroquinones, levamisole (British) or Male fern may be useful but must be carefully supervised. Levamisole is effective against roundworm, but its effectiveness against hookworm, whipworm, and strongyloid are less specific. Male fern (with bi-carbonate) is effective against tapeworm and flukes.

The most common cause of low body weight is caffeine dehydration, sometimes with mental problems and a diagnosis of Alzheimers disease. The symptoms usually disappear with elimination of caffeine and sugar, while increasing the consumption of water. (See Alzheimers Disease. Ch.7.)

Weight Loss.

Overweight all too frequently contributes greatly to ill health. With many people extra pounds are easily put on, but are very difficult to remove, while the effort of dragging around the extra weight imposes further strain on an already overstressed body. Reducing with exercise, however honorable the intent, is seldom effective because the extra exercise demands more food. If the food is supplied, weight reduction will be slow, if at all. If the food is not supplied, the extra stress promotes adrenal depletion, water retention, and extra weight.

Diet and exercise seem to be the most effective method of reducing weight if the weight is not normalized by the Candida program. Reasonable exercise should be included in the weight loss program. Swimming and dancing are preferred forms of exercise. Never over-exercise. Too little is better than too much. The following diets will usually reduce weight in stubborn cases, or they can be used together with the Candida program. Be certain that the entire Candida program is working, that the yeast is being reduced, and that there are ample adrenal nutrients. Do not rush. Dieting imposes extra stress. Be certain that body reserves are adequate before starting.

Grapefruit and Egg Diet.

This is a high protein, low carbohydrate diet. The grapefruit contains hydroquinones and other nutrients that help to release fat, while the eggs provide completely balanced protein. One large grapefruit should be eaten with each meal, or, preferably, $\frac{1}{2}$ grapefruit should be eaten at the beginning of each meal, and $\frac{1}{2}$ glass of grapefruit juice with Hi-KC Fizz should be taken between meals. At least three eggs should be eaten with each meal. Do not restrict the diet. 2% milk can be used conservatively. Nuts can be used. Eat all of the cooked or fresh green vegetables that you wish. Avoid salt and mayonnaise. Use root vegetables, cooked or raw, sparingly. Use cereals sparingly. Avoid all refined carbohydrates. Avoid all free sugars, as in fruits, dried fruits etc. avoid bananas and potatoes. Fish, poultry, and lean meat can be used moderately. Avoid caffeine, tobacco and alcohol. The best fluid to drink is cold or hot water.

De-caffeinated percolated coffee, without sugar or cream, can be used. If the appetite becomes ravenous, eat a few nuts or a piece of cheese $\frac{1}{2}$ hour before dinner to reduce the appetite. Snacks should be nuts, meat, fish or fresh green vegetables. Hi-KC Fizz, made with water and protein powder can be used at any time.

If problems arise, drop the diet for a few days, and then try it again. Continue the diet for about two weeks if possible. The high protein, combined with the large amounts of grapefruit, may require bi-carbonate $\frac{1}{2}$ hour after the meal. Mineral supplements should be used to offset the chelating effects of the citrus fruit. Most people find the diet quite laxative. If bowels become too loose, extra cheese could be added. If problems persist, abandon the diet for a week or two, and try the Onion and Cabbage Soup Diet.

The Onion and Cabbage Soup Diet.
(T-J Miracle Soup Diet).

This diet is presented exactly the way it was received. It is usually very effective in losing weight without undue stress. It appears to work by swinging the PH of the body back and forth between acid and alkaline, with the combination of onions, cabbage, and celery cleaning the intestines while the tomatoes and peppers add extra potassium and vitamin C.

It should be noted that beverages are not mentioned, but it is advisable to stay away from caffeine and chocolate. It should also be noted that all grains, nuts, breads, flour, and sugar are eliminated, along with all dairy products, except for skim milk on banana day. It appears that perhaps calcium should be supplemented while on this diet.

This diet was obviously intended for overweight people who do not have other severe health problems. People with intestinal yeast problems, diabetes, hypoglycemia, high cholesterol, or circulatory or kidney problems may have trouble with all of the free sugars on banana day, and on fruit days. Pears, peaches, grapes, and watermelon may be the principal offenders on fruit days. In addition to the free sugars the vanillin in the bananas on banana day may create problems for some people. People with allergies, arthritis, or other health problems should start with not more than four bananas and work up. The bananas may be of particular value despite their high content of pure carbohydrate. Bananas contain high amounts of vanillin, which is highly poisonous to many organisms, including man. The vanillin, mixed with the free carbohydrate may be very poisonous to yeasts and other infectives when the carbohydrate is assimilated by the infectives. This assumption that the bananas may have a high herbal value is supported by the fact that eating several bananas will frequently result in symptoms of toxicity.

T-J MIRACLE SOUP DIET.

(From Sacred Heart Hospital in Spokane, for overweight heartpatients.)

This 7 day eating plan can be used as often as you like. As a matter of fact, if followed correctly it will clean your system of impurities and give you a feeling of well-being you never thought possible. After only 7 days of this process you will begin to feel lighter, because you will be lighter by at least 10 lbs. (possibly 17 lbs.), and have an abundance of energy. Continue this plan for as long as you wish and feel the difference in both mental and physical disposition.

DAY 1: All fruits except bananas. Your first day is fruit day. For all you melon lovers, this is just the day for you! Two fruits that are lower in calories than most others are watermelon and cantelope. Should you eat melons your chances of losing 3 lbs. the first day, are great.

Day 2: All vegetables. Eat until you are stuffed with all fresh or raw-cooked vegetables of your choice. Try to eat green leafy vegetables and stay away from dry beans, peas, and corn. These vegetables are good for you but not if you are trying to reduce your calorie intake. You may also have a large baked potato, with butter, on your vegetable day.

Day 3: Fruits and vegetables. Same as Day 1 and Day 2, except for no potato.

Day 4: Eat as many as 8 bananas and drink as much as 8 glasses of skim milk on this day, along with T-J Miracle Soup. Bananas are high in carbohydrates and will lessen any craving for sweets.

Day 5: Beef and vegetables. You can have 10 to 20 ounces of beef and 6 tomatoes on day 5. Try and drink at least 8 glasses of water in order to wash away any uric acid in your body.

Day 6: Beef and vegetables. Eat until your heart is content of beef and vegetables. No potato !!!

Day 7. Brown rice, fruit juice (unsweetened) and vegetables. Again, stuff, stuff, stuff!!!

T-J MIRACLE SOUP.

6 LARGE ONIONS (3 is enough)
2 GREEN PEPPERS
WHOLE TOMATOES (Fresh or canned)
1 LARGE HEAD OF CABBAGE.
LARGE STALK OF CELERY.
DRY ONION SOUP MIX.

CUT VEGETABLES AND COVER WITH WATER IN A LARGE POT. ADD THE DRY ONION SOUP MIX. BOIL FOR 10 MINUTES. COVER POT. LOWER HEAT AND SIMMER UNTIL VEGETABLES ARE SOFT.

T-J Miracle Soup can be eaten at any time when you feel hungry during the day. Eat as much as you wish and as often as you like. This soup will not add calories, so eat all you want. The more you eat the more you lose.

Note: T-J Miracle Soup can be eaten each day, along with your food for that day!

These toxic symptoms may of course come directly from the vanillin in the bananas, but the symptoms may also come from killed infectives. The bananas should therefore be included in the diet, but they should be used with caution.

The miracle soup diet has a tendency to be laxative, and will always be a help in cases of constipation, but if constipation persists, saurekraut can be substituted for the cabbage, with the celery and onions eaten raw. Leeks and other members of the onion family could be substituted for the onions, if necessary.

This diet should not be used for periods longer than about two weeks at a time, with intervals of three or four weeks, to allow body function to stabalize.

The most effective weight reduction seem to result when the grapefruit-egg diet is used for about 10 days, and is then followed by the onion-cabbage soup diet.

The Combination Diet.

The basic elements of the two foregoing diets can be combined by substituting the grapefruit-egg diet for any day or days in the miracle-soup diet. Added benefit will come from using Hi-KC Fizz with beverages. Organ meats, fish and fowl can also be substituted for beef.

Special Cases of Overweight.

If the total Candida infection has been reduced, diets have been tried, chelation therapy has been used, and if the overweight or out of shape condition persists, the following may be of help.

1. Liver.

Liver function should be double checked. Abnormal liver function can result in either overweight or underweight and the condition will persist until liver function is restored.

2. High Estrogen.

High estrogen levels frequently result in overweight that will persist despite all other efforts. Your estrogen levels can be measured by your doctor. Estrogen levels are largely controlled by thyroid levels, with low thyroid resulting in high estrogen levels.

3. Low Thyroid.

Low thyroid can result in overweight or underweight. Check thyroid function (See thyroid Ch.5.) with a fever thermometer. Remember that chronic infection should normally result in a low grade fever, with temperatures of 99° or higher. If chronic infection is known, thyroid could be supplemented to 99.2°, with perhaps a spectacular reversal in overweight.

Some nutritionists claim that cabbage, cauliflower, carrots, brussels-sprouts, and turnips are thyroid inhibitors. If thyroid problems are evident their use should be restricted, except for the miracle-soup diet.

Body Type Diets.
(Dr. Abravanel's Body Type Diet. Bantam Press).(Ref.16)

The natural function of the thyroid (T), adrenals (A), pituitary (P), and gonads (G), are intrinsically interlocked, and each influences body weight. Dr.Abravanel shows that genetics, fetal, and early life factors dictate gland dominance, which is reflected in the grown body type. The dominant gland can therefore be determined by assessing the body type, with the types being T,A,P,and G. The overweight problem can then be corrected with a diet designed to correct the glandular imbalance associated with the body type. The diets are quite complex and are beyond the scope of this book. Dr. Abravanels book explains what to do and what not to do, and why it should and should not be done. The book appears to be well founded, and should be of great help to many people in reducing persistent problems of overweight, with a further bonus of also improving general health.

Skinny Legs and Arms.
Small "dried up" legs and arms usually result from the "dried" type of muscular atrophy. Extensive persistent neursage along with the Candida program should start the rejuvenation of the atrophied muscle fibers. Vibrator massage, electro- stimulation, or ultrasonics may also be of help. Good response to neursage during a strong niacin flush and accompanied by mega-doses of amino acids, has been reported.

Oversize Legs and Arms.
The usual cause of oversize legs and arms is calcinosis. Persistent continuing neursage and massage, together with the Candida program and slimming diet may be necessary. Major improvement should not be expected until after most of the yeast infection is eliminated.

Special Cases of Underweight.
(See also Alzheimers Disease. Ch.7.)

Extreme loss of body weight, with shrunken skin that shows the bones and tendons, is caused by lack of cellular nutrition, or lack of water.

If the diet is adequate, low cellular nutrition results from poor digestion or poor assimilation, or both. Protein powders, with digestives should be tried, or high amounts of mixed amino acids can be used until body systems recover. However, even with mixed amino acids improvement may be slow if blood calcium is low, while blood calcium levels, in turn, are dependent upon Vitamin D and parathyropid hormone. (See Low Parathyroid).

The most common cause of extreme underweight is caffeine

dehydration. Caffeine is a strong diuretic, and coffee is so high in caffeine that with each cup of coffee, the coffee addict excretes more water than the amount of water in the cup of coffee. If coffee is the only source of water, the total loss of water is so persistent and continuous that the body suffers extreme dehydration. If the coffee is reinforced with chocolate,the fluid excretion is even greater, while the victim lives on the naked refined sugars associated with the chocolate. Elimination of the caffeine, with extra water, ample nutrition, and lots of vitamins, will usually result in a rapid return to normal body weight, and greatly improved health.

Oversize Bust.

The very large bust is usually the result of altered sex hormones. Several drugs, and particularly Aldoment and Cortisone induce enlargement of the bust, sometimes to extreme proportions. If offending drugs are eliminated as soon as possible, and the condition persists after most of the Candida has been cleared, the entire program should be re-checked for possible hormone effects, and every effort should be made to restore normal sex hormone levels.

Enlarged Hips and Pelvis.

This is usually a female condition resulting from Pelvic Inflammation Syndrome Disease.(P.I.S). (See "Female Sexual Candida Infection".Ch.6.) The sexual infection induces inflammation in surrounding tissues. The inflammation interferes with the lymphatic system and induces increased size by progressive calcinosis. Colon problems are usually a contributing factor. The progressive increase in size is similar to elaphantiasis, which is also caused by an infective. Many females have less pronounced sub-clinical forms. The basic pelvic infection must be reduced before any progress can be made. Ascites may also be a contributing factor, and the possibility of an infestation of worms should not be overlooked. Bacterial and viral infections may also play a role.

This is another case where there are so many variables that everything must be done and every possibility must be explored. Persistent neursage, with perhaps electro-stimulators ot ultrasonic therapy is essential to starting the muscles to rejuvenate. Niacin and chelation therapy may be of particular help.

The Big Belly.

The big belly, and the bulges that are not quite so big, can have several causes;

1. Colon problems. Where the passage time of the stool is too long the colon is continuously overfilled. Charcoal markers

can be used to establish passage time which should be less than two days.(See "Candida Infection of the Colon". Ch.6.)

2. Ascites. Ascites is a condition where the pelvic cavity becomes filled with fluids. Your doctor can give you the tests. (See "Ascites".Ch.7).

3. The "Beer Belly". The "Beer Belly" can form without beer, but is very common in beer drinkers. It is usually the result of intestinal Candida infection together with poor tissue quality from low levels of vitamin C, and bioflavinoids, where the continuous gas from the yeast keeps the weakened tissues continuously stretched and they "grow that way". There is strong evidence that brewers yeast, which is still alive in tap beer, joins the basic Candida infection and continues to brew beer from ingested carbohydrates. Fibrosis and hardening of the muscles and tissues then maintains the enlarged size.

Very little can be done to reduce the size of the enlarged belly until the alcohol is eliminated and the Candida program is well under way. After gas has been reduced and tissue quality has improved, neursage of the internal organs through the skin, while lying on the back, will help to reduce the calcinosis and will initiate rebuilding of normal intestinal muscles. Every effort should be made to pass intestinal gas whenever it is formed. Bending exercises, yoga, and the use of bending exercisers and similar equipment will be helpful. Swimming, dancerise, and bicycling are preferred exercise.

CHAPTER 5.

CANDIDA YEAST INFECTION THERAPY

THE ROOTS OF DEGENERATIVE DISEASE.

Dr. William Phillpott, to his great credit and to the benefit of the world, has brought forward an excellent rationalization of degenerative disease, and has discovered that failure of the pancreas is central to all degenerative health problems. The following quotations from "Proteolitic Enzyme and Amino Acid Therapy", published as a special addendum to "The Physicians Handbook on Orthomlecular Medicine", (Williams and Kalita, Pergammon Press) describes the consequences of pancreatic failure. These passages should be read, and re-read, and all health practitioners should read and re-read the entire article, and the entire book.

Here, in these passages, are the interlocking roots of degenerative disease, cleverly exposed for us to examine. Note the various disease states as they come up, and remember that a disease state can exist in pre-clinical form and can affect all body systems and the entire body long before the disease becomes sufficiently manifest that it can be diagnosed by an M.D. For example, the "diabetic state" is every episode of very high blood sugar (hyperglycemia) whether diabetes has been diagnosed or not, and every "allergic reaction" is every maladaptive reaction to any substance, even when allergic symptoms may not be evident, (hidden allergies). These passages are excellent scientific writing. Each word is significant. Each word means what it says.-----

****

By and large clinical ecology has viewed these maladaptive reactions in terms of the significance of individualized reactions. Recent monitoring of shifts in chemistry comparing the non-reactive state with the reactive state reveals the reactions to be the building blocks of degenerative diseases. Thus an acute arthralgia reaction when evoked numerous times, which damages tissue, becomes arthritis, acute muscle pains become chronic myocitis; acute mental reactions when chronic become named as mental diseases; acute hyperglycemia when it progresses to a chronic state is named as diabetes mellitus. Monitoring of before and after reactions in the areas of blood sugar shifts, pH shifts, porphyric reactions, thyroid reaction, liver function, triglycerides, and cholesterol gives convincing evidence that these acute discrete maladaptive reactions are indeed chronic degenerative diseases in miniature.

CH.5. Candida Yeast Infection Therapy.

The Pancreas as a Primary Shock Organ to Ecologic
Food and Chemical Factors. (Philpott).

The pancreas is the first endocrine-exocrine organ to be influenced by the ecologic contact with ingested foods and chemicals. We can well understand the predisposition of the pancreas as a primary shock organ to ingested foods and chemicals. The pancreas has the monumental task of making useful metabolic products from the ingested foods and chemicals and also buffering against reactions to foods and chemicals. An overstimulated pancreas follows the same general law that other overstimulated tissues and organ systems follow, and that is that overstimulation eventually leads to inhibition of function. Besides the mechanism of inhibition of function by overstimulation, the pancreas has a mechanism of self injury by the mechanism of activation of proteolytic enzymes while still in the pancreas, producing pancreatitis. Pancreatitis states may be severe or mild, but often they are mild attacks which are easily dismissed as mild gastritis attacks.

It is well documented that addiction to alcohol leads to pancreatic insufficiency. What has been little appreciated is that all addictions lead to pancreatic insufficiency of varying degrees. B.M.Frier, et al., made a most pertinent observation about diabetes mellitus observing it to be a state of generalized pancreatic insufficiency. This generalized pancreatic insufficiency occurs in all types of diabetes mellitus whether juvenile, adult onset, or of known pancreatitis origin. Most affected in this pancreatic insufficiency is the bicarbonate production followed by enzyme production and least of all, insulin production.

To understand the significance of pancreatic insufficiency, we need to examine the physiology of pancreatic function especially its exocrine function. Gastric digestion occurs in an acid media (pH of 1.8 to 3 and functions best at a pH of 1.8 to 2) while the small intestine functions in an alkaline medium of pH of 6.8 and higher and most optimum at a pH of 8 to 9). The pancreas produces bicarbonate and the fluids coming from pancreas normally have a pH of 8. Proteolytic enzymes from the panreas function in a neutral to alkali media, and at optimum value at a pH of 8 to 9. These enzymes are destroyed in an acid media. Optimum function of proteolytic enzymes require the presence of the liquid digestive enzyme lipase. Proteolytic enzymes (trypsin, chymotrypsin, carboxypeptidase) digest proteins to amino acids which are then used as building blocks for enzymes, hormones, and tissues. An important systemic function of proteolytic enzymes is a regulatory mechanism for inflammatory reactions from any source and as well as regulatory mechanism over kinins which are tissue hormones.

Ch.5. Candida Yeast Infection Therapy.

Inflammation has two sources:
1. Histamine-mediated inflammation (immunologic).
2. Kinin-mediated inflammation (non-immunologic). Proteolytic enzymes have a regulatory and inflammation resolving control over both types of inflammations,but is of special importance in kinin-mediated reactions since proteolytic enzymes are capable of blocking the rise in kinins thus preventing the kinin-mediated inflammatory reactions from occuring. This fact becomes of special import when we realize there is test information justifying the conclusion that two-thirds of the maladaptive reactions to ecologic substances are kinin-mediated inflammatory reactions and only one-third histamine-mediated inflammatory reactions. The common denominators between histamine and kinin inflammatory reactions, such edema and an acid state, makes these reactions clinically indistinguishable. However, kinin inflammatory reactions are more prone to be painful than histamine inflammatory reactions since kinins evoke pain when in contact with nerve endings.

The consequences of insufficient pancreatic bicarbonate are:
1. Acute metabolic acidosis post meal since the pancreatic bicarbonate has not neutralized the acid from the stomach as it empties from the duodenum.
2. Inactivation of and/or destruction of proteolytic enzymes from the pancreas (trypsin, chymotrypsin, carboxypeptidase) and intestine (prolinase, amino peptidase, cathepsin, A, B, and C).

The consequences of insufficient pancreatic proteolytic enzymes are:
1. Poor digestion of proteins to amino acids.
2. Unusable inflammatory evoking protein molecules absorbed through the intestinal mucosa and circulating in the blood reaching tissue in undigested form, evoking both immunologic (histamine) as well as non-immunologic (kinin) inflammatory reactions.
3. Low systemic proteolytic enzymes allowing:
(a) Allowing inflammatory reactions from any source to go unresolved.
(b) a rise in tissue kinins evoking inflammatory reactions in response to specific substances.
(c) The evoking of severe inflammatory reactions injuring lysosome membranes which start a chain of inflammation, cell degeneration, and carcinogenic potential.

The consequences of amino acid deficiency are:
1. Inability to make emzymes, hormones, tissues, and antibodies against infection in adequate quality or quantity.

2. Excessive demands for vitamins and minerals, especially B6 and its helpers, zinc and magnesium, thus setting up a chain of deficiencies.
3. Infectious invasion due to unhealthy tissues and low immunologic defense which set in motion another chain of inflammation, tissue destruction, and bacterial and viral toxins poisoning vital metabolic processes as well as some of the infectious microbes having carcinogenicity such as <u>Progenitor Cryptocides.</u>

****

Now let us look at these passages, particularly in regard to Candida infection. Note, under "The Consequences of Amino Acid Deficiency" that there will be,- (3) "Infectious invasion" and "bacterial and viral toxins", whereas Candida yeast, ever present and waiting in the digestive tract, will inevitably join the other infectives, invade, establish and protect the infective matrix, and it will then live and thrive on the free sugars in the partly digested food. The Candida then becomes a permanent infective, living on the sugars from the undigested food, and living on the sugars fom the bloodstream, with the end product of the yeast metabolism being lactic acid. The large amount of lactic acid reduces the pH of the entire body, including the digestive tract, with the increased acidity finally leading to increased acidosis and further pancreatic deficiency. Note that the consequences of the increased acidity from the Candida infection are exactly the same as "insufficient pancreatic bicarbonate", because the extra acid has made it impossible for the pancreas to produce sufficient bicarbonate to "neutralize the acid from the stomach as it empties into the duodenum", which is followed by (2) inactivation of digestive enzymes, etc."

Thus alcohol, sugar, white flour, caffeine, or other drugs, singly or in combination, can produce pancreatic failure, followed by degenerative disease and yeast infection, or, Candida infection, from birth, contagious disease, alcohol, aspirin, or other cause, can lead to acidosis and pancreatic failure, followed by degenerative disease.

The point is, that the actual cause of the pancreatic failure is immaterial, because any degenerative disease that has become sufficiently chronic that it is noticed, will have already developed a chronic Candida component with some impairment of the immune system, and despite the re-building of the pancreas and all other efforts with either drugs, nutrition, or megavitamins, the disease will remain, to some degree, until the yeast infection has been reduced to the point where the immune system can again overcome the infection.

The only possible conclusion, then, is that yeast infection and pancreatic failure are synonymous with each other, and are synomymous in some respect with all of the degenerative diseases including cancer. Further, because hyper/hypo-glycemia (high/low blood sugar), absorbed toxins, and altered hormones are invariably part of the pancreatic failure/yeast infection syndrome, all mental disorders, alcoholism, and all drug addictions, should be considered to be in fact different forms of degenerative disease.

To restore health, then, we must not only reduce the yeast infection, but we must also improve the diet, remove all sources of refined carbohydrate, correct other factors involved in high blood sugar, and restore the function of the pancreas, liver, adrenals, thyroid, colon, and other body systems, and to do less will result only in a "half health" program.

Dr. Phillpott, to his great credit, has developed total programs that invariably improve pancreatic function, and the health of victims of degenerative disease. Other doctors have developed programs that are highly effective; to restore adrenal function; for the colon; for the liver; for the thyroid; for the digestive tract; etc; and these programs too almost invariably improve the health of the victim. Sometimes these programs even result in what appears to be a complete cure, yet the old complaint is usually still hanging around in the shadows, waiting only for an opportunity to return. Even when a combination program is used, a cure cannot result unless the total efforts raise the immune system function to the point that the body can subdue the infectives.

One of the most effective, and yet one of the most difficult, of the many health programs, is the acid/alkaline balance program, and this program vividly illustrates the perils and pitfalls if Candida infection is not considered. The outline of pancreatic function should be re-read, and the particular role of changing pH should be noted. Now consider the permanence of a well established Candida matrix. The final metabolism of Candida yeast results in lactic acid, and even if a high yeast infection were confined to the feet (and if it is anywhere it is everywhere) the increased total body acidity would significantly alter the pH of the pancreatic-- gastric process, and pancreatic function would be continuously abnormal as long as the Candida infection remained. Obviously, with the high amounts of lactic acid altering the pH, all pH tests would, in fact, be misleading, because the amount and total effects of the yeast could not be determined. Further, although the pH might be corrected with bi-carbonate, stomach acid and digestion could still be very low.

Of course the real problem is that if serious Candida infection is present anywhere in the body the high increase in lactic acid will alter the pH and therefore the function of all body systems, and will make all pH tests misleading, but the abnormally increased acidity will also make Dr.Philpott's pancreatic program absolutely essential for the successful reduction of Candida infection.

Briefly, Dr.Philpott's work is centered around high blood sugar, (the diabetic state) the resulting pancreatic failure, the ensuing impaired blood circulation, the increased chronic infections, the resultant inflammation and allergies, the altered acid/alkaline balance, and the various combinations of the foregoing that have been named as the different degenerative diseases.

Dr.Philpott's work is well covered in his book,"Victory over Diabetes".(Keats Publishing).

Specifically, high blood sugar, pancreatic failure, etc; etc. are covered later in this chapter under separate headings.

Although Dr.Philpott is very certain that the diabetic state initiates degenerative disease, it is well known that several other conditions can also initiate degenerative disease, with, the diabetic state usually becoming part of the degenerative process.

BASIC ROOT CAUSES of DEGENERATIVE DISEASE:
1. Foreign substances. In general, all drugs (both prescription and social) alcohol, tobacco, caffeine, and many of the herbs.
2. Toxic metals.(Mineral Test, Ch.4.)
3. Inadequate or poorly balanced diet, (Nutritional evaluation, CH.4.)
4. Severe physical injury, or surgery.
5. Pre-natal (before birth) adrenal failure, or abnormal adrenal function, resulting from adrenal depletion of mother during pregnancy. (CH.4.)
6. Infection. Physical damage from contagious disease; from residual chronic infection or from chronic Candida infection from mother at birth, following injury at or near birth, or following an episode of contagious infection.
7. Low thyroid function.
8. Birth defects.
9. Loss of intrinsic factor (low B12).

ANTI-CANDIDA COCKTAIL, with SUPPLEMENTS.
Irrespective of the root causes of ill health, all forms of health problems have two things in common with drugs, caffeine,

tobacco, and alcohol, and those two things are adrenal depletion and impaired immune function resulting from the adrenal depletion. The key nutrients in adrenal depletion are potassium and vitamin C.

Potassium and vitamin C can be considered to be the cornerstone of health.

Potassium,is absolutely essential to adrenal, nerve, and cellular function, yet stress causes potassium excretion, which increases the stress, followed by more potassium excretion. Thus the potassium is easily lost, but potassium levels cannot be restored with potassium supplements alone. Irrespective of sodium levels, potassium supplements must be accompanied by sodium to block production of aldosterone. A very large number of doctors, nutritionists, and "health nuts" miss this scientific reality;- if potassium supplements are not accompanied by sodium the production of aldosterone will not be blocked and the aldosterone will sometimes wash out more potassium than the amount supplemented. There is therefore no net gain in cellular potassium, and sometimes there is even a net loss. In short, to try to supplement potassium without simultaneously supplementing sodium is an excerise in futility and an excerise in folly. Plain potassium supplements, chelated or otherwise, just do not work unless they are taken with steak dinners or other salty foods. Potassium should be remembered as being very easily lost, and very difficult to replace.

Vitamin C, is used by the body for many metabolic processes. The body cannot make vitamin C. and the supply is therefore entirely dietary dependent. Diet alone cannot supply the large quantities needed in ill health. Vitamin C is absolutely essential for:

1. Detoxification of poisons.(toxins).
2. Manufacture of bile (from cholesterol).
3. Adrenal function.
4. Strengthening the collagen in all body tissues.

All forms of ill health are invariably accompanied by increased chronic infection and reduced vitality. The body uses vitamin C first to detoxify toxins. The infection therefore depletes the vitamin C, reducing the amount available for production of bile, for the adrenals, and with usually nothing left for the tissues. Most people try to overcome the reduced vitality with caffeine, tobacco, or alcohol, all of which are poisons that further deplete the vitamin C, and increase the need for supplements. The usual supplement for vitamin C is ascorbic acid, but most forms of ill health, and particularly Candida infection, tend to make the body acidic, and the high supplements of ascorbic acid required to supply sufficient vitamin C push the body toward acidosis. The vitamin C should therefore be taken in the form of non-acidic ascorbate, with sodium-potassium ascorbate being the preferred form because it also supplies the much needed potassium together with sodium to ensure potassium retention. This is the basis for Adrenolift Fizz.(HI-KC Fizz).

The other principal adrenal nutrients are pantothenic acid, B6, lipotropics, and calcium/magnesium (which requires Vit.D.). The immune system requires the same nutrients together with protein and linoleic acid.

Basic Fizz Powder.

2 parts Sodium Bicarbonate.(baking soda).
2 parts Potassium Bicarbonate.
4 parts ascorbic acid.(powder or crystaline. About 5 grams per tsp.)
1 part Calcium Gluconate or Calcium Ascorbate.
1 part magnesium oxide.

Anti-Candida Cocktail.

Use a tall 10 oz. glass.
1/8 glass grapefruit or orange juice.
Fill to 3/4 with water.
1 large tsp. protein powder.(slimming powder).
1 large tsp. Carob powder.
1 dropperful liquid nystatin.
$\frac{1}{2}$ tsp. psyllium seed.
$\frac{1}{2}$ tsp. Fizz powder.
Stir. Add 1 tsp. Sunflower oil.(For linoleic acid).
While drinking the fizz take:-
250 mg. Pantothenic acid.
150 mg. B6.
1 calcium/magnesium tablet.
1 Super lipo. (choline,inositol, methionine).
1000 I.U. Vitamin D. taken sometime every day. (to ensure utilization of calcium.

All quantities can be varied. If there are digestive problems take one nystatin tablet (chewed) and one protein digestive.

This cocktail is excellent if taken the very first thing in the morning, immediately upon arising. It also makes an excellent snack or pick-up during the day.

It can be used to stabalize blood sugar, whenever required, and thus avoid the desperately tired feeling of hypogly-cemia.Continuing use will promote weight loss or gain, back to normal weight. It can be used to reduce sleepiness when driving. It will help to offset the craving for tobacco, caffeine, alcohol or drugs, and it should be part of any program to eliminate them. When used to promote sleep, take one or two tablets of tryptophane and perhaps a tablet of cystine.

Ch.5. Candida Yeast Infection Therapy.

For severe depression or suicidal tendencies, add:-
1 or 2 tsp. tryptophane powder.
150 mg. niacin.
100 mg. cystine.
250 mg. more pantothenic acid.
150 mg. more B6.

A handful of mixed nuts can be substituted for sunflower oil.

The Fizz cocktail, with supplements will give good nutritional support for the adrenals and immune system. It should be used freely throughout the anti-Candida program.

HIGH BLOOD SUGAR.

Candida yeast, with its infective companions, thrives on sugar. In all Candida infections it is therefore of absolute primary importance to remove all sources of refined carbohydrate from the diet, and to carefully regulate many other carbohydrates and thus avoid episodes of high blood sugar that will feed the infectives. It may come as a surprise to many doctors, but for the treatment of serious Candida infections Scientific American Medical Library particularly stresses the importance of reducing the total carbohydrates in the diet, and in removing all refined carbohydrate from the diet. Yeasts feed on sugars, and you cannot expect to reduce the infection if it is multiplying rapidly, so the object is to reduce the blood sugar levels and thus starve the infectives. The role of caffiene, tobacco, and similar drugs is not mentioned in Scientific American Medical LIbrary, but the elimination of everything that increases blood sugar levels is of equal importance.

In one instance, for example, a highly infected person was having digestive problems about five hours after the evening meal, and, in an attempt to get things moving again took a digestive tablet with a glass of water, and ate four large prunes. The indigestion was temporarily relieved, but within a half hour there was gas and bloating, and the badly infected callused feet turned very red and hot and they felt like they were on fire. So also did the hands and wrists, where the only signs of Candida infection were on the ridges on the finger nails. The genitals and ears were also equally affected. What happened? and why?

Yeasts thrive on sugar and Candida grows the best in a weak 2% solution. The water, together with free sugars from the prunes, produced about a 2% solution, which fed the yeasts in the digestive tract, producing the cramps and bloating. The digestive tablet broke down the prunes and released all of the free sugars. At five hours after the last meal the body was ready for more food, so the sugars were rapidly assimilated,

249

pushing up the blood sugar levels and feeding the yeast in all parts of the body, with the visible parts being the interconnected sexual tissues; i.e., the feet, the hands, the genitals, the ears. With the high blood sugars feeding the yeast, the yeast was able to advance, because it was being fed at a rate beyond the ability of the body to suppress it. The advancing yeast, attacking the nerve endings, increased the inflammation, and produced the "burning" sensation.

A similar effect can be produced with sugar and caffeine, chocolate, or tobacco. A similar effect can be produced with sexual arousal. A similar effect can be produced with a fit of anger. A similar effect can be produced by anything that raises blood sugar to high levels. To effectively reduce the infection, we must do everything possible to maintain low stable levels of blood sugar.

Avoiding Episodes of High Blood Sugar.

1. Low carbohydrate high protein diet.
2. Elimination of all refined carbohydrate and other free sugars.
3. Elimination of tea, coffee, chocolate, cola, tobacco, and all similar drugs.
4. Elimination of toxic lead, mercury, arsenic, cadmium, aluminum and reduction of high levels of copper or iron. (Mineral test).
5. Improved adrenal function.
7. Reduced stress.
8. Avoidance of fits of anger. Note that extreme fits of anger may be related to high toxic metals, or to episodes of very low blood sugar.

Exceptions.

Rules can seldom be absolute. Some people reach a state of such low adrenal production that their total body function is impaired unless the adrenals are pushed to raise the blood sugar to functional levels. The golden rule for a return to health is to "feel better". People with low adrenal function may therefore feel better and do better with a little tea, and perhaps a little sugar, first thing in the morning, and perhaps during the day if necessary, until adrenal function can be raised. The object of eliminating caffeine is not to just eliminate caffeine, the object is to reduce episodes of high blood sugar. Drugs (caffeine is a drug) are never good, but the judicious use of a little tea to "feel better" is much healthier than the stress from "feeling worse", and dragging uselessly around all day. Tobacco, coffee, or chocolate could be used in the same way, but tea seems to do the least harm. Like all drugs, the trick is to use just the right amount for the circumstances, and to reduce and eliminate it as soon as possible.

Free Sugars.

Free sugars are rapidly absorbed from refined carbohydrate and many other foods. The suffix "ose" denotes sugar. Thus maltose, lactose, fructose, sucrose, glucose, dextrose, etc; are all sugars. The sweetener sorbitol (with the suffix "ol") is an alcohol, which is the sugar precurser found in green apples. It will not feed yeast. Glucose (grape sugar) is the sugar normally used by the body. All sugars, and even sugars made in the body from protein, are stored in the liver as glycogen, and when used by the body are used as glucose. Glucose is a left-handed molecule, and dextrose (starch) is the same molecule in the right-handed form.

Most flower nectars, and most vegetable, fruit, and free sugars are sucrose. Sucrose (table sugar) is a molecule of glucose with a chemical bond to a molecule of fructose. For the body to use the sugars the chemical bond must be broken by digestive enzymes. Honey is largely sucrose, with the bonds broken and the sucrose and fructose molecules separated by enzymes from the bees, prior to regurgitation. Honey is therefore a mixture of fructose and glucose that is very rapidly absorbed.

Many fruits, vegetables, and grains contain starch, which saliva and other body enzymes rapidly convert to maltose (malt sugar) and maltose to dextrose. Refined starches therefore have the same effect on the body, and will feed yeasts the same way, as refined sugar.

The level of blood sugar is normally controlled by insulin from the pancreas and adrenalin from the adrenals, but unfortunately this control applies only to glucose levels, while the body absorbs and utilizes the fructose half of the sucrose molecule at will. Thus high amounts of table sugar, or the equivalent in syrup, honey, or dried fruit, can elevate the actual active blood levels with fructose, even when the pancreas and adrenals have normal function and regulate the glucose. These high levels of blood fructose will also feed all yeast infections throughout the body.

In reality then, the spoonful of honey, the spoonful of sugar, the slice of white bread, the handful of dried figs, the ripe peaches, the banana, the potato, and the dish of sprouts (malted grains) are equally excellent as yeast nutrients. Each will not only feed an intestinal yeast infection, but each can equally raise actual blood sugar levels to feed all yeast infections throughout the body. Note, that some of these foods might be used with caution, but refined sugars and starches and all dried fruits must be eliminated.

Starchy grains, vegetables, and fruits can be used only by trial, and in small quantities. In general, foods that are slowly digested (and therefore slowly assimilated) will maintain stable blood sugar levels that will feed the body cells and will provide very little nutrition for the yeasts. Thus coarse ground grains, brown rice, and root vegetables can usually be used. Potatoes, sweet potatoes, yams and bananas may give problems, but can usually be used in small quantities with other foods. Grapes and raisins should be avoided. Pears will usually give problems, but cherries, plums, peaches, apricots, nectarines, and citrus fruits can usually be used in moderation. Apples can usually be used, but some varieties may give problems. Canned fruits can usually be used like fresh fruits, but the juice should not be used even if it is pear juice. Berries can usually be used in moderation. Fruit juices can also give problems and each one should be tried. Carrot juice is extremely high in free sugars and should be avoided.

In trying foods for sugar effects, foods that give digestive response, burning, hot flushes, or other indications within the hour after eating, should be avoided. Gas and indigestion two or three hours after the meal is usually indicative of intestinal yeast infection where the yeast multiplies rapidly when the intestinal solutions fall and approach the ideal 2%. The condition may be hastened with a glass of water, and it can occur with any and all carbohydrates. It can be relieved by eating anything, because even protein will make a stronger digestive solution that is less favorable to the infectives.

The importance of maintaining stable levels of blood sugar cannot be over-emphasized. It is folly, and almost impossible, to try to effectively reduce a Candida infection while feeding it with extra sugars from the bloodstream.

High blood sugar, so conducive to maintaining and propagating yeast infection, is always blamed on the food, or on the pancreas, and sometimes on the adrenals, but the liver can also be part of, or perhaps all of the problem. Excess sugar in the body is converted to glycogen and is stored in the liver, but if the liver capability is impaired the extra sugars cannot be stored, so large amounts of glucose rmain in the bloodstream to feed the infectives. High infections, of all kinds, impose an excessive load on the liver, and yeast infection is therefore usually accompanied by impaired liver function. The ability of the body to handle sugars therefore usually improves as the total amount of Candida infection is reduced.

YEAST ALLERGIES.

Bakers yeast is used for baking bread and other foods. Brewers yeast is used for the production of alcohol; is used directly as a food; and is added to vitamins and to many prepared foods.All food yeasts are high in vitamins and minerals and are good for people that do not have a high resident Candida infection. But in people with a high Candida infection the immune system develops a high sensitivity to all yeasts, and even a very small quantity of yeast, like the filler in many vitamin tablets, will trigger an immune response with inflammation and allergies. Such allergies are frequently masked and hidden by allergic addiction.

Allergic addiction to any substance, or to any food (like bread) can be tested by avoiding the substance for seven days and then re-introducing it. Any response of any kind is indicative of allergic addiction , and the substance should be avoided until health improves. All Candida victims should avoid all food yeasts entirely, or they should test each food separately. Live bakers yeast cakes should be particularly avoided at all times because, although the live yeast cannot live within the body itself, it can and will join other yeasts in the resident Candida matrix in the digestive tract, where it will thrive on sugars in the digested food, and where it will then produce copious quantities of gas that will expand the belly like a loaf of bread. Allergic reactions should be avoided if possible because they affect the entire metabolic function while the higher the resident yeast infection the greater the immune response:with the immune response greatly out of proportion to the amount of allergen. The high response to very small quantities of allergens makes life miserable and makes the source difficult to find.

Very small quantities of yeast are a frequent source of allergic episodes. People who appear to be allergic to pears, may not be allergic to peeled pears, because the yeast on the pear skin has been eliminated. People may not be allergic to home-pressed apple juice, but they may be very allergic to canned apple juice where the yeast content may be high because all of the partly fermented apples were not eliminated. Some people may be allergic to wheat or wheat products, yet they may not react to clean wheat that has been scoured and washed to remove all of the rust and smut and other fungii, and which has then been coarse ground and made into baking powder biscuits. The allergic reaction usually does not come from the food; (except for the nightshades), it comes from the fungus and other toxic substances that contaminate the food.

Alcohol.

All alcoholic beverages are a by-product of yeast, and they should be avoided entirely to prevent hidden allergies from being aggravated or induced.

Distilled spirits have a much lower yeast content than "liquor brews" like wine, brandy, ale, and beer, because all of these still have most of the original dead yeast in them. Tap beer is particularly onerous because the yeasts in it are still alive. The brewing of alcoholic beverages poses a further problem because it is always very difficult to maintain a pure yeast culture for brewing, and Candida and other yeasts may sometimes be present in the brew.

OTHER ALLERGIES.

All allergies are the final result of more toxins than the body can handle. All allergies therefore result from excessive amounts of toxins, or from liver, pancreas, immune, or nutritional failure, which reduces the ability of the body to cope; or the allergies can result from leaky, porous tissues in the G.I.tract, or from any combination of these causes.

<u>Vitamin C.</u>

Yeast infection contributes greatly to total body toxins, while it also impairs the B and T lymphocytes and reduces the total capability of the immune system, which results in many victims of yeast infection being plagued by constant allergies.

High total body toxins, however, are also increased by poor colon function, and by leakage of proteins through porous membranes in the digestive tract. Large amounts of vitamin C are therefore necessary to,

(1) supply the extra Vitamin C required by the adrenals to combat the stress;

(2) Supply the liver and the immune system for detoxification;

(3) Convert cholesterol to bile; with enough Vitamin C left to;

(4) strengthen body tissues including the walls of the arteries and veins, and the walls of the colon and digestive tract. The end product of yeast metabolism is lactic acid, and all yeast victims therefore have an acidity from mouth to anus. Use of ascorbic acid to provide the high amounts of vitamin C so necessary to combat yeast infection increases the total acidity so much that most yeast victims find it impossible to take such large amounts. The vitamin C should therefore be"buffered", as an amino acid complex, or as mineral ascorbates (Hi-KC Fizz) and should be accompanied by mixed bioflavinoids which are also necessary to strengthen the weakened and porous tissues (See Quercitin Ch.4). Minimum total vitamin C should be 5 grams, and some yeast victims may "do better" with more. High amounts of ascorbic acid that produce soft stools and wash out water soluble vitamins, should be avoided in favor of mineral ascorbates.

Proteins.

Another cause of allergies is the leakage of large partly digested proteins into the bloodstream and into the tissues. These proteins, because they are not fully digested, are, to the body, the same as transplanted or other "foreign" tissue, and the immune system must break them down and engulf them and dispose of them. These partly digested leaked proteins therefore further overload an already overloaded immune system, increasing the allergies, or perhaps stimulating the immune system into such a high frenetic activity that it will start to attack the body cells, a condition quite frequently associated with cancer.

This protein allergy condition may prompt some people to remove protein from the diet, but protein is absolutely essential to both the function of the immune system, and to the rebuilding of damaged tissues, and total protein should therefore be increased, rather than decreased. The greatest allergy problems seem to come from "red meat"(animal meat), perhaps because animals are much closer to man on the evolutionary genetic tree. Fish, poultry, and cereal proteins are the best choice. Pork should be avoided because pigs do not have a lymphatic system and the meat may therefore be permeated with toxic metabolites.

This "protein allergy" condition rarely occurs if vitamin C has been adequate, and in all cases the vitamin C and bioflavinoids should be increased, but the prime offender is the partly digested protein. In all cases of "protein allergies", in all cases where there are digestive problems, and probably in all cases of serious yeast infection, a protein digestive like Festal should be taken with every meal to insure that the proteins are fully digested, and to further ensure that the body has the adequate fully digested proteins, so necessary for proper function of the pancreas and the immune system, with enough extra for rebuilding the damaged tissues. In severe cases the use of pre-digested protein and/ or nucleic acids may be necessary until body function has been restored. Adequate calcium/ magnesium must be provided to ensure absorption of the proteins, with vitamin D to help the calcium. (See Low Parathyroid.Ch.4.)

Pancreatic Function.

Dr.William Philpott has greatly increased our knowledge of the role of the pancreas in degenerative disease, cardiovascular disease, schizophrenia, diabetes, and allergies, and it is Dr.Philpott that should be thanked fot the now widely used proteolytic enzyme therapy to restore pancreatic function.

Normally we ingest very large quantities of micro-organisms with our food, and most of these are destroyed by the digestive process. Many of the organisms are destroyed during the primary acid phase of digestion, then, one half hour to one hour after the meal the digestive tract is changed from acid to alkaline by bi-carbonate from the pancreas, and the remaining micro-organisms are then destroyed by the secondary alkaline phase of digestion. But if the digestive tract is already highly acidic (as in yeast infection) the bi-carbonate from the pancreas may only shift the pH toward alkaline, without the alkaline phase of digestion ever being reached. Alternately, if protein and other pancreatic nutrients are not available in sufficient quantities, the pancreas may be unable to produce bicarbonate, and again the alkaline phase of digestion may not occur. In either case, many of the micro-organisms will not be immediately destroyed, which may add to the allergies, while digestion and cellular nutrition will also be impaired, and the kinins will not be suppressed.

The kinins are linked to the inflammation phase of immune function and they are normally suppressed by bicarbonate from the pancreas. If acidity is beyond the capacity of the pancreas, or if the pancreas fails, the kinins are not suppressed and inflammation and allergies may run rampant throughout the body.

In all cases of allergies, then, proteolitic digestive enzymes should be taken with the meal, and they should be taken again $\frac{1}{2}$ hour after the meal, along with $\frac{1}{4}$ to $\frac{1}{2}$ tsp. of bicarbonate, perferably sodium/potassium bicarbonate.

Digestion.

Complete digestion, so necessary for providing all body nutrients and so particularly essential to immune system and pancreatic function, is also very dependent upon bile salts and hydrochloric acid.

It should be particularly noted that the pancreas is dependent upon adequate protein while assimilation of protein is dependent upon calcium and the absorption of calcium is dependent upon vitamin D. Blood tests for proteins and calcium will help to identify the problem.

If because of a shortage of vitamin C or poor nutrition, or other factors, adequate bile is not being produced, digestive enzymes with bile salts, taken at the beginning of the meal, may be necessary until bile production is restored. Bile pigments normally give the stool its typical brown or dark brown color, and a yellowish or lighter colored stool is usually an indication of low bile production.

Ch.5. Candida Yeast Infection Therapy.

Yeast infection raises total body acidity, and pH tests may therefore show that stomach acid is normal, or even above normal, when hydrochloric acid, so essential to digestion, may in fact be very low. In all cases of allergies or indigestion, and probably in all cases of chronic yeast infection, supplements of betaine HCL, or glutanic acid HCL, taken at the beginning of the meal with digestive enzymes and followed with digestive enzymes and bicarbonate $\frac{1}{2}$ hour after the meal, should be tried.

In extreme cases of indigestion and/or allergies pancreas substance with duodenum may be needed, and the quantities may need to be increased by taking tablets thirty minutes before meals, with meals, $\frac{1}{4}$ hour after meals with bicarbonate, at bedtime, and at about 2 A.M.

Digestive Enzymes.

There are now many brands of digestive enzymes on the market. Unknown to many people, doctors have been prescribing them for years, so they are available from your drug store or your health food store. Common ingredients in a good tablet are pepsin, bromelain, papian, protease, amylase, lipase, cellulase, trypsin, chymotrypsin, and perhaps bile, and/or HCL, and/or pancreas substance. Protease, pancreas substance, and bile should be enteric coated. Various brands should be tried.

Other Allergy Programs.

The foregoing allergy/enzyme program is only a very small part of a very large number of programs designed to help allergy victims to cope with their allergies. Most of these programs are based on avoidance of "allergens", and avoidance of addictions through rotating diets, etc; etc. These programs have been of great help to a very large number of people but unfortunately it is impossible to remove all toxic substances from our invironment. Toxins from cedar and pine trees, pollen, dust, fungus, etc; are far more prevalent than toxins from man's ever polluting activities. The "sad-bad" part is that if a similar effort had been put into programs for reducing and eliminating the casual chronic infection, "learning to cope" programs would not be necessary. Some insight into the ever changing allergic reactions can be seen when toxic metabolites are considered.

Allergies and Metabolites.

Metabolites are classically substances that are found as part of a chain of chemical reactions within the body. They can be "healthy" (part of a normal metabolic path), they can be inert, (without any effects) or they can be destructive. Metabolites can be part of a normal metabolic process, they can be formed as a result of a lack of some specific nutrients, or they can result from chemical reactions between metabolites and toxins from food and inhalants.

257

The formation and the changing and interchanging of chemical substances within the body and within the cells of the body is the same as it is in the laboratory. The chemical interaction between any two substances depends upon electron bonding sites on the atoms of which they are composed. Very few people even in the medical field have any factual concept of the extremely complex nature of the trillions of complex chemical substances of which we are composed, and the billions and trillions of tiny electron reactions involved in the simplest living tissues. For instance, the formation of collagen starts as pro-collagen, a simple protein chain of about 1,100 amino acids, with every third amino acid being glycine, and with about one third of the intervening amino acids being proline or hydro-proline. The protein chain takes the form of a helix (like a coil spring). Two more similar amino acid helical chains form, and the three strands (which are similar but not identical) then intertwine to form a superhelix, all bonded together with electron bonds. The super helixes then group together to form longer rods, and the rods are then further organized into the longer and thicker rods that we call collagen. To try to get a clear concept, think of the spring-like helixes as being composed of metal chains, with every third link gold, and with one-third of the other links brass or copper, and the remaining links iron, zinc, aluminum etc;. Three chains twist together to form a super coil, and many such super coils twist together to form larger longer strands, and these longer strands then twist together to form fibrils in a way very similar to the way that short fibers of wool and cotton are spun into yarn and string.

One thousand one hundred amino acids electron bonded in each basic helix. Three thousand three hundred amino acids electron bonded together in each tiny rod of pro collagen. Billions of amino acids electron bonded in each bit of collagen fibril. The point is that the electron bonds in the chain are by happenstance, by the fact that suitable amino acids are there, much as if each link in the chain was a small magnet. The magnets might be of many different kinds, yet they would all bond together, end to end in a long chain. Now note that if a different shaped magnet happened to get into the pile of magnets from which the magnetic chain was being formed, it too would become part of the chain, but it could drastically alter the function of the chain. Similarly, if a substance with bonding sites similar to amino acids was present when the pro-collagen nucleic chains were being formed, it too would bond into the chain, but it would alter the final function, and if enough of the stray substance was present, the collagen would not form, and a different metabolite (good or bad) would result. Now if the stray substance had stronger bonding sites than the amino acids, the amino acids would bond to it instead, and the collagen could not form. The stray substance would then be a stray metabolite that interfered with a normal body process to form another different stray metabolite that might similarly go on to further interfere with other normal processes.

Normally, there are billions of different chemical reactions taking place in the body at all times. Many of these reactions are extremely rapid, and billions of different metabolites are formed, with the many chemical constituents of our foods being used or reduced without harm. Normally there are also millions of bacteria, viruses, fungii, and other micro-organisms, each metabolizing hundreds or perhaps thousands of different chemicals, that are also ingested with our food, and normally these bits of chemistry are also used, or are harmlessly reduced. We also have many resident bacteria and other micro-organisms (like E-Coli) that constantly contribute more millions of bits of different chemistry, which normally are also used, or reduced. We say reduced, because all of the millions of metabolites must finally be used or reduced, whether they are good, bad or neutral.

Now the immune system is normally the final scavenger of all metabolites that cannot otherwise be handled by the body, and if immune function is impaired, or if the poisonous metabolites are so numerous that the immune system cannot cope with them, allergic reactions are certain to appear.

With such a very large number of different foods and different micro-organisms involved, and with such a very large number of chemical reactions, we can never know exactly how many noxious chemicals (toxins) may be formed, and we can never know exactly how toxic some of the metabolites may be, nor can we ever know what quantity may be produced. What we do know is that if the immune system is overwhelmed, the body is unable to cope with the toxic metabolites and allergies will result. What we also know is that Candida yeast infection is a very common chronic infective that both overloads the immune system, and impairs the capability of the immune system, usually resulting in allergies that are either evident, or hidden. Hidden allergies result from addiction to the poison (as with tobacco or alcohol) when the poison is continuously supplied. Removal of the poison, or the poison forming substance, for at least four days allows the body to regain some immune system capability, and an allergic reaction will then result from re-exposure to the offending substance.

When chronic yeast infection is present, all unusual reactions to any substance should be regarded as perhaps an allergic response, and all foods etc; should be tested by a four day avoidance, to establish that they are free from allergic reactions.

Most allergies come from toxic metabolites from food and drink. If these are reduced, the overworked immune system will be better able to overcome toxins inhaled or absorbed. The good part is that a comprehensive anti-fungal program will reduce the yeast infection, then as immune function improves and toxins from the infectives are reduced, the total immune capability and immune system reserves will increase, and the allergies will disappear. But in the meantime, foods and drink must be watched closely.

Foods have been correctly described as anything that can be eaten without producing instant death, or immediate severe illness. Some foods are herbs, and some herbs are foods. All foods are like herbs in that they contain a very large number of chemical constituents. Natural foods are never pure, and most foods already contain some toxins, or they contain metabolites that may react with metabolites from infectives or other foods to form toxins. The greatest problem is that any attempt to clear up chronic infectives produces even more metabolites from both the anti-infective agent and from the dead and dying infectives. This problem is increased by the tendency for other infectives to move in as soon as resident infectives are destroyed, thus altering the toxins and metabolites and consequently the allergies. The changing flux of infectives and foods constantly alters the allergies, and the change in allergies is increased by all efforts to destroy the infectives. During therapy, almost any food or drink can produce an allergic reaction, but such reactions are usually transient. Some foods have a greater tendency to produce allergies than other foods, because some foods have quite high amounts of toxic chemicals. Some foods can be grouped according to their toxins, and if allergies result from any one food in a group, all foods in that group should be avoided for about a month.

Toxic Food Groups. (See also special foods. Ch.4.)
1. Deadly Nightshade. All nightshades contain some nightshade poison. The poison is changed and reduced with ripening. Potatoes, tomatoes, and peppers are nightshades.
2. Phytates. (Phytic acid)- cereals and grains.
3. Oxalic Acid. (radiator cleaner) rhubarb, spinach, chocolate. Also made by the body from glycine if B6 is undersupplied. Gelatin is very high in glycine.
4. Vanillin. Vanilla, and bananas.

With the large number of metabolites involved with chronic infection, anti-fungals, and anti-biotics, the opportunity for allergic reactions to develop is constantly changing. If problems of any kind develop, physical or mental, hidden allergies should be suspected, and all foods then become suspect. "Favorite" and "habit" foods are one of the most common causes of hidden allergies, and usually should be avoided until infection is reduced and immune function has improved.

It has been pointed out that allergies are triggered by toxic substances, either in or on the food. Victims of Candida infection are usually very sensitive to yeasts and molds. Therefore apple juice, made from clean washed apples, may be allergy free, but apple juice from a tin may contain enough yeast from spoiled apples and fungal growths on the skin, that it will induce allergic reactions. Thus many allergic reactions do not come from the food itself, but from bacteria and fungus on or mixed with the food.

It is usually necessary for allergy victims to continue with rotating diets, and complete avoidance of yeasts and fungii, until there has been a reduction in total infection, with improved immune system function. Where known allergens cannot be avoided, an allergic eposide can usually be reduced or prevented by taking the digestive enzymes with bicarbonate prior to exposure, or as soon after exposure as possible.

CANDIDA YEAST and SEXUAL TISSUES.

The genus Homo (mankind) has the highest evolutionary development of all of the creatures on earth, and high sexuality and high sexual activity is an intrinsic part of man's extremely complex evolution.

The sexual tissues are distributed throughout much of the body. They respond to sexual hormones, mediated by the sexual neuro-transmitter histamine, and the sexuality and strength of desire and sexual response are related to histamine levels. The sexual tissues are easily identified. The sexuality of the head and mouth, breasts, genitals, and anus are obvious, and are well known. At the beginning of sexual arousal, digestion stops, and the rectual sphincter tightens. At the height of orgasm the hands and feet "clench" in carpopedal spasm. The sexual tissues can therefore be defined as the head and mouth, breasts, genitals digestive tract, anus, hands and feet. These are the tissues that are affected by the sex hormones, and although Candida yeast can and does infect other parts of the body, the high concentrations of nutrients in the sexual tissues makes them the principal target for Candida infection. Unfortunately, if Candida infection becomes noticeable in any of the sexual tissues it will usually have progressed to the point that it will be found, to some degree, in all sexual tissues.

The frequent presence of Candida in sexual tissues is of itself an enigma. Most certainly the sexual tissues are bathed in a high concentration of nutrients on which the yeast can feed, but the sexual tissues also contain high levels of estrogen and testosterone, which oppose yeast, and reduce the amount of Candida in the sexual tissues. We do know that there is a definite relation between sexual levels and histamine levels, and we do know that the production of adrenal hormones falls when sex hormones are low. Perhaps, and probably, high sexual levels keep Candida out of the sexual tissues in the healthy, and the Candida probably does not invade until the basophil cell count has dropped to about .2% or less. It appears that extensive Candida infection is rarely found when histamine levels are high (.8%). Yet we do know that Candida infection is sometimes very high in females with high estrogen levels. Perhaps then it is not the sexual hormones that oppose Candida. Perhaps it is the high histamine that mediates sexual function that opposes Candida. The falling of histamine levels may well be linked to a shortage of naicin, for which yeast has a great affinity. It is therefore suggested that every effort should be made to raise histamine levels with B12 injections, folic acid, a little niacin, and continuing biotin. The results can be monitored with the basophil cell count. Do not be surprised if little effect is seen, but as the Candida program progresses keep trying again every two or three months, then, as biological factors change, the increased histamine and sexual levels will suddenly become very noticeable.

Although infection in each of the sexual tissues will be covered under a separate heading, some infection in all of the sexual tissues should be expected, and considered.

ANTI FUNGALS and ANTI-BIOTICS.

Reduction of Candida infection can rarely be accomplished with diet, vitamins, elimination of coffee and poisons, etc; without using anti-fungal agents and anti-biotics. Topical disinfectants and other agents have been tried for centuries with only limited success because the infectives are constantly shielded by the osmoresistant layer formed by the yeast. For success, treatment must include systemic agents that attack the infective from the bloodstream, but until Ketoconazole was developed all systemic anti-fungal agents were toxic, and all effective herbs were toxic, with potent side effects. Ketoconazole is a systemic anti-fungal that kills the infectives through the sexual system of the plants. Ketoconazole is of itself non-toxic, and any side effects come from the dead bodies of the infectives. In one experiment on a massive infection of the feet, ketoconazole was used together with topical agents but one area was not treated. The treated areas cleared up more rapidly than the untreated areas, but nonetheless the untreated area did slowly improve, which proves that ketoconazole can slowly eliminate the infection, without the topical agents. But this is true only in cases of exposed infection. Fungal infectives feed on nutrients assimilated from the bloodstream, but they also live on fluids within the cavities of the body, away from the bloodstream. To reduce the infection, both topical and systemic anti-fungals and antibiotics must be used. The infectives must be attacked from both sides of the skin. Ketoconazole is the systemic anti-fungal of choice, and should be part of every Candida program. Resteclin, (amphoteracin B and tetracycline) is a preferred systemic antibiotic that is also an anti-fungal, and should be used occasionally unless contra-indicated. Topical anti-fungals and antibiotics will be different for different body parts.

SLOW KETOCONAZOLE THERAPY.
(See Ketoconazole Ch.4.).

Ketoconazole is an excellent anti-fungal that attacks a broad range of fungal infectives with few side effects from the agent itself. Most side effects come from the effects of the killed infective. Ketoconazole is taken orally. Most of it is rapidly absorbed during the acid phase of digestion, and it then attacks the fungal infective systemically through the bloodstream. It is also effective if applied topically.

Ketoconazole should be taken at the beginning of the meal. Start with no more than 1/8 tablet daily, and work up slowly, increasing every 4 or 5 days by 1/8 tablet until ½ tablet is reached. If toxic symptoms appear, drop back 1/8 tablet for about two weeks, then try increasing again. Most people do very well on ½ tablet daily, and ½ tablet daily usually avoids liver depletion. People with low yeast infection can take two or three tablets without visible effects, and as many as twenty tablets have been taken without serious consequences.

The first action of ketoconazole is to cause the Candida yeast to shed its hyphae and filaments, which enter the bloodstreams and produce toxic effects, if the quantity of ketoconazole is too great, the liver and immune system are easily overloaded. Continuing ketoconazole destroys the whole organism, along with all other fungii, and the bodies of the dead infectives are also toxic. Ketoconazole programs should therefore be slow and continuous, and if stopped for a few days, should be started again with reduced amounts.

One capsule of resteclin, or similar antibiotic, should be taken about once a week to prevent bacterial infections from moving in to infect the injured tissues instead of the yeast. If anti-biotics are not used occasionally, the yeast infection will usually be replaced with a bacterial infection, with only a change in symptoms in the unfortunate host. Resteclin should be taken between meals because it is absorbed during the alkaline phase of digestion. Calcium should not be taken with Resteclin.

A slow and easy Ketoconazole program seems to be the most effective, because the liver and the immune system are usually already overloaded by the infection and as soon as you start on the ketoconazole they must also handle all of the dead infectives. Hence the need to start very slowly, particularly if the immune system is already impaired and allergies are rampant.

It should be remembered that Candida infection progresses slowly, and by the time that infection has produced problems it has usually been growing for years. The long standing Candida infection invariably impairs the immune system, despite tests that may show otherwise. Very soon after the Ketoconazole program has started, the reduction in total infection reduces the load on the immune system, and immune system function and capability will increase, followed by increased action against the infectives. The liver must handle all toxins, yet it has no control over the immune system. If the Ketoconoazole program is too much, the liver cannot keep up, a long toxic episode will result, the stress from the toxicity will further decrease body capability, the yeast will again advance, and the net result will be many miserable days for the victim, without a reduction in the infection.

As the Ketoconazole program progresses, toxic symptoms may at any time appear. These can come from an unknown episode of high blood sugar that has fed the yeast, producing very rapid growth and a surge of toxins; it can come from an overloaded liver from eating a large meal containing natural poisons; (like nightshades) or it can come from increased immune system function that has at last been able to get ahead of the infection and is determined to clear out an infected area irrespective of the capability of the liver to handle all of the toxins. Now your health program has become a giant guessing game. Too much, ot too little? Increase or decrease? The toxic symptoms are there, what should you do? only you can guess.

You have to recall what you ate and what you did. Sometimes the answer is very clear. Coffee, tobacco, alcohol, white flour, sugar, anger, sexual arousal, etc. raise the levels of blood sugar, feeding the yeast and indicating more ketoconazole. Toxins from increased immune system function, or from toxic foods like the nightshades overload the liver, indicating less ketoconazole. This may help you to decide. There are also other indicators.

Ch.5. Candida Yeast Infection Therapy.

The body must always divide its total energy between different current necessities. During high physical activity the immune system functions only at very low levels, but when the body is at rest more nutrients and more energy are available to the immune system, with a rapid rise in immune function. The highest immune function, together with the greatest body rebuilding, occurs during deep sleep. This is the reason that bed rest is so necessary to overcome the "contagious diseases" with the least harm. Therefore, during Ketoconazole therapy a "sleepy feeling" will usually occur about $\frac{1}{2}$ hour after taking the ketoconazole, and if possible the urge to sleep should be heeded. Sleep gives the body a chance to recover and heal. Many toxic eposides can be avoided by responding to the urge to sleep, and many toxic eposides can be explained if the urge to sleep is not heeded, or if arousal from deep sleep has prevented the body from bringing infectives under control. Some people call this "listening to the body". You must not only listen, you must also always give the body a chance to heal.

Another indicator of toxicity is total liver function. The liver has such a large number of things to do that many of the tests are really inconclusive. If tests show impaired function, it will be present and Candida therapy must be taken very slow while every effort is made to re-build the liver. But also, an overloaded liver may have excellent function, while still being indequate for the demands of Candida therapy. Bile is produced from Vitamin C and cholesterol, and it is used by the body for many purposes. It is bile pigments that give the stool its characteristic brown color, and liver function, as compared to body needs, can therefore usually be judged by the color of the stool. If the stool is light in color, bile supplements with digestive enzymes may help total liver function, and may help to prevent many toxic episodes. Light stools and impaired liver function may also be caused by liver infection, and metronidazole, sulfamethoxazole, etc; should be tried.

During early Ketoconazole therapy, except for constantly feeling better, it may seem that very little progress is being made for a long time,- as long perhaps as six months or a year, if infection is severe and widespread. But as the infection is reduced and immune system function improves, the body becomes so determined to clear out the infectives that liver over load problems may develop and persist, and the stool may become a yellowish white. Bile supplements will be needed, and the ketoconazole should be cut back to as little as 1/8 tablet daily, or every few days, until liver function improves. If a white stool persists for two months or more, ketoconazole should, be slowly brought up to a lower level.

Liver function is always an ongoing problem during Ketoconazole therapy because the liver must detoxify all of the dead infectives together with a great many metabolites from the reducing callus matrix. The most used nutrient for detoxification is vitamin C, perferably taken as mineral ascorbates.

The most frequent cause of toxic episodes is resorbed toxins from poor colon function, or from delayed bowel movement. (See "Colon Infections in this chapter). It must be remembered that most of the toxic debris in the body is eliminated by way of the stool. Every urge to evacuate the bowels must be heeded promptly if toxic episodes are to be avoided. When highly toxic substances are present in the colon, the body flushes them out with diarrhea. Calomel (mercury) and cascara are highly poisonous laxatives that make use of this natural body response. With the large amounts of toxins released during Candida therapy, small episodes of soft stools and near diarrhea should be expected. Hence the need to respond promptly. Note that extra water is needed to prevent dehydration, and extra water soluble vitamins should be taken after each episode, to replace the vitamins lost with the watery stools.

Another cause of toxic episodes is resorbed toxins from sexual infections in both male and female. (See also "Sexual Infections" in this chapter.) If toxic episodes follow a few hours after sexual activity the toxicity may arise either from a rapid advance of the infectives when fed by the high blood sugar accompanying sexual activity, or the toxicity may arise directly from toxins released from sexual yeast infection or associated infectives when disturbed by the sexual activity; or the toxicity may come from both. This does not mean that sexual activity should cease or be reduced. The body functions best with high levels of sex hormones and sex hormones increase with sexual activity if the activity is kept within total body capability. Toxic episodes from sexual causes will be reduced as total infection is reduced. Toxic episodes from sexual causes can also be reduced by taking the "toxic nutrients" about one hour before, or immediatly after sexual activity. (See "Toxic Side Effects" Ch.4.)

Another cause of toxic episodes is toxins absorbed from topical therapy. Most anti-fungal agents (except ketoconazole) are poisonous to both the yeast and the host, and toxins from the dead infectives can also be absorbed in some areas like the digestive tract, colon, or vagina. For example, too much hydrogen peroxide applied to damaged tissues on the feet can be absorbed to the point of toxicity, and Miconazole vaginal suppositories used daily with high infection can produce toxicity from absorbed toxins.

Ch.5. Candida Yeast Infection Therapy.

Only you can decide the best way to avoid toxic episodes, but the foregoing outline should help to determine the possible causes. A number of uncomfortable hours may have to be spent to find the particular pattern for each individual.

The old saying that "You have to feel worse before you get better" just is not true. The best road back to health is to "feel better". Judicious and careful use of ketoconazole is the best way to reduce Candida infection without "feeling worse".

****

Slow Ketoconazole therapy has been very successful in reducing many health problems including allergies and arthritis. The foregoing description was written before it was doscovered that ketoconazole interferes with vitamin D. (See Ketoconazole, CH.4.) The color of the stool should be watched, light colored stools indicate failure of the gall bladder and liver, which may be corrected with bile supplements and protein digestives. Liver function might also be improved with moderate supplements of vitamin D, calcium, lecithin, and other lipotropics taken 12 hours away from the ketoconazole. If problems persist the ketoconazole may have to be interrupted while levels of calcium and vitamin D are raised. Impaired liver function can also be caused by infectives that are not affected by ketoconazole. Metronidozole, sulfamethoxazole etc; should be tried. (See liver. Ch.4.)

High Ketoconazole Therapy.

Slow Ketoconazole therapy will reduce the total body infection, which will reduce the load on the adrenals, liver, and other body systems, but high blood levels of ketoconazole are necessary before an active quantity reaches the brain, testis, ovaries, and some other areas. Two tablets of ketoconazole, taken together will produce maximum blood levels. Slow therapy should therefore be followed by working up to two tablets a day and then to two tablets twice daily. Niacin, taken to heavy flush 1 hour after the ketoconazole will ensure increased blood circulation and delivery of the ketoconazole to all parts. Start slowly with only one tablet, followed one hour later with niacin, then work up. Therapy can be further enhanced by neursage or with the use of massage chairs and massage equipment during the niacin flush. Ultra-sonic massage may be of extra benefit. Sulfamethoxazole, taken with the niacin, will increase the effectiveness of the ketoconazole.

INFECTION in BODY CAVITIES.

Chronic Candida infection of exterior skin surfaces like feet and hands requires only straight-forward tedious therapy, because topical anti-fungals can be applied to the infected skin, while systemic anti-fungals can be used to attack the infectives from the blood side.

Elimination of infection from cavities in the body, however, becomes much more difficult because the infection can continue to grow away from the skin, floating around in the body fluids within the cavity, completely isolated from both the immune system and systemic anti-fungals, while the cavity itself may be almost totally inaccessable for topical therapy.

Thus vaginal infections are difficult, cervix and birth canal infections are very difficult, sinus infections of the lungs are even more difficult, and infections of the prostate and testicles are almost impossible.

Good health depends upon a minimum of total chronic infection. Infections of body cavities should therefore receive specific constant attention because infected cavities provide a continuing reservoir of high infection that will continuously promote re-infection of all other parts of the body. Therapy for specific Candida infections will be covered in the next chapter.

THE CANDIDA PROGRAM CHECK LIST.

Candida yeast infection has so many biological effects and is so intertwined with all body systems that failure to correct any single problem can drastically reduce the effectiveness of the entire program. The following check list will ensure that your Candida program includes all of the essentials.

1. Complete medical check-up and diagnosis by at least two medical doctors.
2. Mineral test with nutritional evaluation. (If indicated).
3. Chelation therapy to reduce any toxic minerals. Elimination of sources of toxic minerals. Watch for mercury from amalgam tooth fillings. Copper can be reduced with large amounts of rutin and other bioflavinoids with heavy supplements of zinc and manganese. Eliminate contraceptives, soya products, and copper pipes and utensils. Aluminum can be reduced with extra magnesium and B6. Iron can be reduced with special chelators. Avoid wine and red wine.
4. Mineral supplements in the form of oratates or ascorbates (when possible) to raise low minerals. Extra magnesium to offset the magnesium used by the Candida to form calluses.
5. Alterations in diet as suggested by the nutritional evaluation,

with emphasis on elimination of sugar (including honey), free sugars, and free carbohydrates (white flour). Elimination of all self-administered poisons, (tea, coffee, etc.).

6. Vitamin supplements as indicated by nutritional evaluation and medical diagnosis.

7. Adjustments to vitamins to ensure;

　　a. Multiple B vitamins daily. Preferrably broad spectrum, time release, without B2.

　　b. Vitamin E. (Min.200 iu daily),D and A.

　　c. Extra B1 to offset the B2 manufactured by the Candida.

　　d. Extra Biotin, to make up for the biotin used by the infectives.

　　e. B15 to reduce hypoxia.

　　f. A-E Emulsin, two or three times a week to improve immune function. Be careful.

　　g. Continuing Hi-KC Fizz, and all adrenal nutrients, at least once a day.

　　h. Vitamin C, with bioflavinoids, in the form of both ascorbic acid and mineral ascorbates, minimum 3 or 4 grams daily. Perferably time released.

8. Blood tests, and adjustment of diet and supplements. If immune function is low lithium should be supplemented with caution.(PMNs) If calcium and /or proteins are low supplement calcium magnesium, B6, Vitamin D, Parathyroid, and amino acids. If basophil cell count is below .8% raise histamine levels with B12 injections, folic acid, histidine, and a little niacin.

9. Chiropractic check up with full X-rays. Adjustments if necessary. Be careful.

10. Iridology. if possible, to determine possible unknown problem areas.

11. Digestive problems.

　　a. Digestive enzymes, bile tablets, with meals. Bicarbonate, after meals.

　　b. Liver injections.

　　c. Ultrasonic scan.

　　d. Nystatin and ketoconazole.

　　e. Psyllium seed in some form.

　　f. Caprylic acid in some form.

　　g. Acidophilus -Bifidus tablets.

　　h. Metronidazole or vancomycin if indicated.

12. Thyroid test. Iodine, lithium, tyrosine, and thyroxin, if needed.

13. Spermine/spermadine test, if available, with adjustments to supplements.

14. Glandular and organ supplements.

15. Candida challange test with ketoconazole.

16. Ketoconazole as indicated, without calcium or vitamin D, with breaks in therapy for resteclin and supplements of Calcium/magnesium, B6, and vitamin D.

17. Ample sleep and rest. Extra rest if needed.
18. Continuous adrenal support; vitamin C(5 grams), pantothenic acid, B6, lipotropics, Calcium/magnesium, amino acids, nucleic acids.
19. Neursage and massage if needed.
20. Increase or decrease of body weight, if needed.
21. Pulse-Volume Recorder test (blood circulation test). Chelation therapy to reduce blood vessel plaques and improve circulation, and reduce infectives in bloodstream.
22. Avoidance of allergic foods etc. Reduction of allergies with digestive enzymes and bicarbonate if necessary.
23. Disinfecting and vitamin C enemas to improve colon function, if necessary.
24. Autogenous vaccine if cancer may be eminent, and, near end of program, to clean up pockets of infection.
25. Topical anti-fungals and other therapy for each specific infection.
26. Lots of pluck, luck and persistence.

CHAPTER 6.

SPECIFIC CANDIDA INFECTIONS.

CANDIDA INFECTION in SEXUAL TISSUES.

The sexual tissues are the body tissues that receive and respond to sexual hormones. The sexual tissues are the tissues that are most frequently infected by yeast because these tissues have higher quantities of the nutrients that nourish the infectives. This high susceptability to yeast infection occurs despite the fact that both estrogen and testosterone levels are higher in the sexual tissues, and both estrogen and testosterone oppose yeast. The ability of estrogen and testosterone to oppose yeast can be seen at birth. Male babies at birth, have already developed testicles that supply the newborn male with enough testosterone to prevent reversion back to the basic female. If the mother is badly infected with Candida yeast, male babies may be born covered with "thrush" (Candida infection) which may impair them for their entire lives, yet they seldom die. On the other hand, female babies at birth are not sufficiently developed to produce estrogen, and female babies born to infected mothers are at peril, and some do die of overwhelming Candidiasis.

The sexual tissues can be defined as the head and mouth, the entire digestive tract including the colon, the breasts and genitals, and the hands and feet. All of these tissues respond to sex hormones; all of these tissues are involved during sexual activity; all of these tissues are particularly susceptible to yeast infection.

The various body parts will be covered separately. Reference should be made to the appropriate medical papers for further information when required. With 2,300 medical papers on Candida infection the author has been able to read only a few. The full list of medical papers is available from the Healthology Assn. See also Ch.3.

NOTE.

The following information is not necessarily taken from the medical papers. The number of medical papers is provided to show that further medical information is available if needed. The pity is that despite all of our modern technology, and despite the deplorable ill health all around us, everyone is busy cranking out "another paper" that frequently says what someone else has already written. The 2,300 medical papers on Candida could probably be consolidated into 50 papers or less. The information in the papers would then become accessible and useful.

CANDIDA INFECTION and LOSS of HAIR.

In many men (and some women) the hair on the head turns grey and starts to fall out when they are still quite young, yet other men retain their hair color and most of their hair until death at a very old age. The underlying cause of graying hair and loss of hair has been controversial. It has been said for many years that graying hair is the first sign of impotence; a statement that is hotly denied by many young men who have started to turn gray. Yet graying hair and loss of hair does seem to be linked to altered hormone levels, and particularly to reduced levels of testosterone.

Neursage is very effective therapy against calcinosis, and in severe hair loss the entire scalp appears to be severely calcified. Intensive neursage can therefore be used to grow some new hair, but the hair will usually come back only as very fine gray hair, that remains short. If supplements of Paba are added to the hair regrowth program some hair may come back its natural color, and the hair will be longer. This of course indicates that the loss of hair is somehow interconnected with the paba, which is part of the folic acid molecule, and low levels of folic acid may therefore be a contributing factor. Significantly, low levels of folic acid are also linked to low histamine levels and low sexual levels. Folic acid should therefore be supplemented, together with B12 injections and a little niacin, to raise histamine and sex hormone levels. Even with increased histamine levels and Paba supplements, the re-growth of hair by neursage is less than spectacular, and the slow balding will probably return as soon as the program is relaxed.

Research work on hair re-growth in Finland, a few years ago, led to the development of Bioscal. In the Bioscal hair renewal program all soaps and shampoos are avoided, and the hair and scalp are washed daily with bioscal shampoo, which is only a simple pH balanced detergent that cleans the oil out of the hair follicles. The shampoo is followed by special "hair nutrients" rubbed into the scalp. The Bioscal program is very effective in the early stages of balding, and it will assist greatly if added to the Neursage-Paba program. The pH balanced detergent is the effective agent, and the program works almost as well without the "special nutrients" as it does with them. Any simple inexpensive pH balanced detergent seems to be almost as effective as the bioscal shampoo. The Neursage-Paba detergent program is quite effective for many people, but for more severe cases of hair loss the re-growth of hair is still slow and disappointing.

Now note that folic acid is certainly involved in the balding process, but folic acid, or paba alone, will seldom restore hair growth, so there must be other factors. But folic acid (and B12) are nutrients that are used up and tied up by Candida yeast. Thus one of the causes of balding is Candida yeast infection.

Apparently the high lactic acid levels associated with Candida infection also contribute to balding by increasing calcinosis of the scalp. Further, it seems that Candida also directly infects the scalp, probably in a very thin layer that contributes to the many white flakes we call dandruff. Bioscal alone, will reduce dandruff, but so also will phenolalkalizer. If phenoalkalizer is used as a hair dressing (the odor soon dissipates) along with the neursage, paba, and the detergent shampoo, natural colored hair will usually start to re-grow, and the growth will increase as the total Candida infection is reduced with ketoconazole and other anti-fungals. Eyebrows, beard, mustache, and body hair will probably also increase, and change from grey to their natural color. Sorbic acid (orithrush) should be tried, and may be particularly useful to reduce dandruff and other fungal infections of the scalp.

Dr. Lars Engstrand of Sweden, has found that baldness is caused by a thickening and hardening of the galea, which underlies the scalp and covers the crown of the head. In women the galea remains thin and flexible, and it changes very little with age, but in men the galea slowly grows thicker until about age 55. In men, the thickness and flexibility of the galea is related to sex hormone levels. Low levels result in hardening of the galea, which in turn reduces blood flow to the scalp, thus resulting in balding. With reduction in Candida infection, reduced stress, improved nutrition and improved production of sex hormones the hair will start to re-grow. The growth, of course can be stimulated with neursage and massage, and can be further increased with vitamin E and bioflavinoids (particularly Quercitin) to stimulate the growth of capilliaries.

Hair Stimulants.

Hair growth can also be stimulated with Minoxidil (Loniten) dissolved in polysorbate, or similar fatty acids. The author's success rate is very low, perhaps because it seems so difficult to get the tablets to dissolve.

CAUTION,- Minoxidil is a manufactured chemical that somehow stimulates the growth of hair anywhere. Even when small amounts are carefully applied the fluids seem to creep across the skin, which could result in the growth of hair where it is not wanted. Use sparingly and carefully!

Note, the use of sorbic acid (polysorbate) is a short chain fatty acid effective against fungus. Perhaps, continuing use of orithrush would be equally effective.

ENDOTHALMITIS and CANDIDA INFECTION of the EYES.
(20 medical papers, Endothalmitis-8 med.Papers Ch.3.)

The author has not as yet had any direct experience with infections of the eyes, but such infections cannot be uncommon or there would not be so many medical papers. It may well be that many such infections continue to go unnoticed for years, or perhaps for a lifetime. Most people on extended Ketoconazole therapy will experience an improvement in sight, but this improvement may not come directly from a reduction in infectives in the eyes, because it is more likely to result from reduced lactic acid and reduced calcinosis, with a consequent improved function of eye muscles.

People with high yeast infection that also have eye problems might benefit from the medical papers, or they might wish to wait to see what benefits ketoconazole might bring. After all, the eyes do not really lend themselves to the use of topical anti-fungal agents, so it would seem that the best, and perhaps the only treatment, would be with a systemic agent, but weak solutions of sorbic acid (orithrush) could be tried.

Candidal endothalmitis can also be a source of eye infections. Candidal endothalmitis can be seen by looking through the eye with special equipment. The procedure is described in Scientific American Medical Library. Again, systemic agents are the sole therapy,and Monistat IV is the only effective agent.

High Candida infection also frequently affects the eyes with gritty deposits that feel like sand. These deposits seem to be small grains of mixed salts precipitated out of the salty fluids in the eyes. Their formation seems to increase with the use of salt. It appears that Candida infection interferes with sodium utilization with the increased salinity creating super-saturated solutions that precipitate the deposits. People with these deposits experience a very rapid burning of the eyes when they are exposed to water. These people are unable to swim with their eyes open under water, because as soon as the eyes are opened they automatically clamp shut in response to the sharp burning. These deposits are water soluble, and they can be reduced with continuing daily washing with plain water in an eyeglass. Massage of the eyes during washing is helpful. As long as Candida infection is present these gritty deposits will remain and will continue to develop, but the amount and severity will decline along with a reduction of total infection. Reducing these gritty deposits also tends to improve eyesight, and reduces the tendency for the eyes to become tired.

CANDIDA INFECTION OF THE EARS,AND LOSS OF HEARING.
        (5 medical papers,Ch.3.)
Candida infection is frequently present in the ears for a great many years without the knowledge of either the victim or their doctor.A bit of scale is usually all that is seen. But

when the doctor makes an examination he will usually shine a little light through the ear to determine the amount of calcification. Yeast infection of the ears increases the calcification with calcium lactate, and it may be responsible for many cases of loss of hearing.

White scaly debris in the ears is the principal indicator of Candida infection in the ear. Application of miconazole lotion with the tip of the little finger or with a Q-tip swab, for a few days, may loosen more scaly debris, proving fungal infection, in which case the use of miconazole lotion should be continued. For severe infections Phenol Alkalizer, alternated with hydrogen peroxide and ketoconazole dissolved in DMSO should be tried. Sorbic acid (orithrush) may also help, and Flagystatin should be tried.

When hearing is impaired by calcinosis, a 50% solution of DMSO applied daily for about a week, will usually improve hearing ability. Reduction of total Candida infection, together with reduced local infection, will reduce the lactic acid in the tissues and thus eliminate the immediate cause of the calcinosis, after which continuing neursage, or the use of a massage vibrator, togther with DMSO, will help to reduce the calcinosis, which may result in greatly improved hearing.

Auricular medicine (CH.4.) could not be expected to be effective when all of the nerves, lymph vessels, etc; are locked together with hardened calcium deposits. Indeed, different amounts of calcification may be the actual reason that auricular medicine is unpredictable. The success of auricular medicine certainly suggests that the nerves in the ears, like the nerves in the eyes (as evidenced by iridology) are interconnected to all other body systems, and if they are interconnected we could not expect full body function if the nerves in the ears are all locked together with calcinosis.

It has been previously mentioned that Candida yeast seems to have an affinity for lead, or lead poisoning increases the probability of yeast infection, because the two are so frequently found together. One of the first effects of the onset of lead poisoning is tenderness of all "ouch spots" (nervcites) in the ears, followed by calcinosis, and one of the first effects of chelation therapy to remove the lead from the body tissues is tenderness of all of the nervcites in the ears; followed by a reduction in calcinosis.

It takes only a few minutes every three or four days to massage all of the tender nervcites in the ears. As Candida therapy progresses, calcinosis will be reduced and many more nervcites will become unlocked and will again become active. No one can ever know how much good neursage will do for the rest of the body, but for those who seek continuing health, neursage of the ears every few days can provide excellent auricular medicine.

Infections of the inner ear are very difficult to reduce because they are cavity infections. Infections of the inner ear are usually associated with sinus infection, and, like sinus infection will usually be reduced by continuing the use of ketoconazole long after other infections have been reduced and immune system function has been restored. The entire sinus program should be tried.

If inner ear infection is severe, the use of monistat 1V should be considered. Further assistance might be gleaned from medical papers.

CANDIDA INFECTION of the NOSE and SINUSES.

"Sinus Infection" is so very common that it is well known to everyone. There are a number of "drug store remedies" that are available, but most of these only provide temporary relief and do not clear up the underlying infection. The old medical procedure of using probes with silver nitrate seldom helped, and frequently made the condition worse, and should not have been inflicted on anyone. Some of the later medical procedures, where the bone is scraped, appear to have good success. There are a great many types and kinds of sinus infection, and if the infection is severe, a thorough medical examination should be sought because such infections can proceed to meningitis, and perhaps even death.

There are a very large number of infectives involved in sinus infection, and, like all chronic infections, the mixture is constantly changing. The medical literature shows that Staphlococus, pneumoccoci, streptoccoci, haemophilus, mycobacteria, aspergillus, mucor, and mycoplasma are frequently involved. Although Candida is not shown as being a sinus infective, sinusitis will usually be reduced with liquid nystatin, which proves that Candida is usually involved. Miconazole is usually more effective than nystatin, probably because it is also effective against aspergillus, mucor and other fungii.

Sinusitis is frequently referred to, by both the public and much of the medical profession , as "a little sinus infection", but sinus infection should never be treated so lightly. It is always serious. Few people realize that sinusitis is invariably a multiple fungal based infection; that it is a cavity infection and therefore very difficult to eliminate; and it is an infection of the lympathic system.

The nasal sinuses are lymphatic tissue,but they also seem to be sexual tissues because sexual activity will very frequently

276

alter a sinus infection dramatically, either for better, or for worse;- the sinus problem will "disappear", or it will become much worse. This "kill or cure" effect probably depends upon the physical state of the body at the time of the sexual activity. If the body is "on top" of the infection;- if the energy reserve is high enough and if the immune system is functioning properly; the sexual activity will raise the total metabolic rate with a rapid decline in infection, but if energy reserves are low and if nutrients are insufficient the sexual activity depletes all systems; there is nothing to oppose the infectives; and infection makes a very rapid advance.

Here, in the nasal sinuses is one of the most visible interconnections between the immune system and the sexual system, and, in contemplation of the foregoing, one must wonder how many invisible interconnections there may be, and if so, just where such interconnections may be. We do know that sex hormones oppose yeast infection, and we of course know that sexual activity increases sex hormone production. We also know that the entire sexual system and sexual tissues are linked together by the immune system through the histamine bearing lymphatic cells. It may be that sexual activity, with adequate nutrients and within the bounds of the energy reserve, has a cleansing effect on the entire immune and lymphatic system, resulting in increased immune system capability. Sexual activity then becomes anti-infective therapy, which is good news; but it must not be overdone, or it will soon become bad news.

High levels of yeast infection are frequently accompanied by infection of the nasal sinuses, and sinus infection is a constant source of re-infection of the nose, mouth, throat, esophagus, and sometimes the lungs. To clean up one, you must clean them all.

The most effective agent against sinus infection seems to be miconazole lotion with a small amount of resteclin added, and applied as high as possible in the nose, with the tip of the little finger, or carefully applied with a Q-tip. Other effective agents are phenol alkalizer, liquid nystatin, milk of magnesia, and liquid chlorophyl, with resteclin or other antibiotics added. Ketoconazole can also be crushed and powdered, and added to the fluids. Applications of orithrush will help to stablize the local flora.

The first effect of these anti-infective agents will be to loosen the "plugged" nasal passages. When this happens the fluid should be blown out into a handkerchief, always with the mouth open to prevent the pressure from forcing the infection deeper into the tissues. The treatment should be repeated until the nasal passages are reasonably clear.

Sleep is a continuous problem during a "bout of sinus". The nasal passages drain naturally while sitting or standing, but lying down shuts off the drainage, followed by a rapid increase in infection. Raising the head, with two or more pillows will help. Also lying on the side, turned almost to lying on the stomach, with the head turned over the edge of the pillow so that the nose is downward, will help the sinuses to drain. Sleeping on alternate sides, and blowing out the fluid as soon as it starts to "cross over" from one passage to the other, will also help. Oral anti-fungals, held in the mouth, should be used to prevent re-infection to the mouth and throat. The extreme stress, associated with sinus infection should be countered with Hi-KC Fizz and other adrenal nutrients. The immune system should be supported with immune nutrients, and adequate protein (as free amino acids, or, as good protein with digestive aids) should be provided for the immune system, the pancreas, and for the rebuilding of damaged tissues. Sleep and rest are essential, and relief from "pressures' is also helpful.

In severe cases of sinus infection sleeping with a hot water bottle for a pillow, or laying a hot water bottle across the nose and face may help bring some relief. Sinus infection is frequently accompanied by digestive problems, and may sometimes be an allergic reaction. A hot water bottle will help to relieve the indigestion, and digestive aids, with bicarbonate (See Candida infections of the digestive tract) can be used to reduce inflammation throughout the body.

Some people live a lifetime with serious sinus infection and their response to anti-infectives may be poor because of long- standing calcinosis with poor blood and lymph circulation. Progress will therefore be slow until the stagnant congestion is relieved and the sinuses start to drain. Niacin and chelation therapy can be used to improve blood circulation, with (if possible) niacin-ketoconazole therapy.

Ultrasonics, massage, acupuncture, and electrotherapy can also be used either with or without the niacin.-Ketoconazole therapy.

Ultrasonic treatments have been used with excellent success. They should be accompanied by extra ketoconazole (if possible) together with topical agents including phenol alkalizer, or sorbic acid, (Orithrush).

Massage therapy can be used, by hand or with normal or high frequency vibrators. Repeated passes down each side of the nose will usually bring relief.

There are also some reports of excellent success with auricular medicine,i.e. acupressure, acupuncture and electro-therapy of the ears. Acupressure can be used by anyone.The fingers are too large, so stimulation of the tender "ouch spots",(the muscle end plates) is usually done with the blunt end of a chopstick, a large plastic knitting needle, or similar wood or plastic instrument. In acupuncture both needles and electrostimulators are used. See "Nervcite Therapy", Ch.7. for the particular nerve centers on the ears that seem to affect the sinuses. Massage vibrators can also be used on these nerve centers, sometimes with spectacular results.

Another effective method of "breaking" sinus infection is with a vaporizer using Friars Balsam, or by taking deep breaths of extremely hot air as it escapes from a partly opened oven door.

Severe sinus infection will usually reduce quite rapidly along with a reduction in total Candida infection, but infection of the sinuses is a cavity infection and the final eradication of the infectives from their home in the sinus tissues is extremely difficult, if not impossible, with today's anti-infective agents. However, the "Green Aerosol Spray" described in some of the medical papers may be of value. The revival of "lime dust therapy", as used to be used for tuberculosis, may be very effective if resteclin, nystatin powder, or powdered ketoconazole is mixed with the lime dust.

Sinus infection in the young can be serious handicap because extensive infection can affect the mind and retard mental development. With the ability to learn somewhat impaired, the hapless victim at best "grows up late"! All children with any indications of sinus infection should therefore be treated as soon as possible.

Candida infection of the nostrils causes the formation of heavy scaly debris, frequently dark brown or black. It obstructs the nasal passages and it is very persistently annoying to the victim. This is the cause of people "picking their noses" trying to clear out the blocked passages, which is seen by others as a very disgusting habit, but which is seen by the victim as being absolutely essential. The victim usually soon learns to hide their "disgusting habit" behind a handkerchief, and to clear the nostrils daily or oftener, in private. There may be a medical term for this condition, but if so the author has been unable to find it. Most doctors find the problem so trivial that they do not want to discuss it. Fortunately the condition will start to clear up, and will become less of a nuisance with the use of miconazole lotion, miconazole cream, phenol alkalizer, nystatin lotion, chlorophyl, orithrush, flagystatin, and or DMSO. Unfortunately some vestiges of the problem will probably remain long after the high Candida infections have been cleared up.

CANDIDA INFECTIONS of the MOUTH.

(45 medical papers.Ch.3.)

Candida yeast is familiar to your dentist, who can frequently see bits of it laying on the mucous membranes in the mouth. These are small whitish flakes, sometimes almost transparent and difficult to see. Your dentist is very careful with Candida, and if infection of the tissues is evident he may not work on your teeth until the infection is cleared up. He will probably use nystatin or PBSC,(Penicillin- Bacitracin -Sodium -Caprylate). You too are probably familiar with Candida infection in the mouth, where it has penetrated the mucosa and has become the principal infective in canker sores. Sore mouth, where part or all of the tissues of the mouth are infected and inflamed and feel like they are on fire, is also part of a general degeneration of mouth tissues.

It must be remembered that any major imbalance in B vitamins results in poor tissue quality in the mouth, with infection and inflammation. The mouth problem therefore cannot be corrected with anti-infectives or disinfectants. These must be used to control the infection, but the degenerated tissues will immediately become re-infected if the underlying B vitamin imbalance is not corrected.

But first, here, with an infection of the mouth, is an excellent opportunity to observe the relationships between the body and the infectives,- relationships that give insight into all infections, wherever they may be.

Infection causes burning in the mouth. The mouth is washed with a disinfectant.The burning stops and does not return until you get tired. Then it returns with a vengeance because the defences of the body are impaired. This illustrates the need for ample sleep and rest to give the body time and energy to fight the infectives. The "continuous cup of coffee" and the many cigarettes that keep many people going are probably the most dangerous drugs to be found.

The mouth is burning with infection, you chew B vitamins and hold them in your mouth. The burning is reduced. You did not kill the infective. You only supplied nutrients that the body used to improve the tissues. Hence the need at all times to maintain proper and adequate nutrition.

The mouth is burning with infection. You chew vitamin C tablets and hold them in your mouth. The burning is reduced because you supplied vitamin C to strengthen the tissues.

The conclusion must be that the amount of chronic infection in the body is directly related to the quality of nutrition, the effectiveness of the immune system, the amount and quality of rest, and the amount of anti-fungals and antibiotics if they are needed

Ch.6. Specific Candida Infections.

Here, in the mouth, with a mouth infection, is also an excellent opportunity to try the actual effectiveness of anti-fungal agents. Nystatin is specific against Candida, so that if a trial of nystatin reduces the burning then we know that the principal infective is Candida. Chlorophyl, garlic, tahebo tea, etc; can now be tried, and their effectiveness can be noted.

Here in the mouth, with a mouth infection, is also an excellent opportunity to try the effects of the B vitamins, by chewing them and holding them in the mouth. The taste may not be pleasant, but the results are informative. The much talked about B balance is between B1(thiamine), B2 (riboflavin), and B3 (Niacin or niacinamide). In the test, B1 will probably be found to be the only one that has any effect. Looking back over nutritional therapy we find that large quantities of B3, as much as a gram or more per day, are frequently taken without side effects provided the other B vitamins are supplemented by about 35 mg. per day. Thus the actual B balance is between B1 and B2. But we also know that Candida yeast manufactures B2 so quite obviously victims of Candida infection continuously need extra B1 to balance the B2 that is produced by the Candida.

To clear up the mouth infection we must therefore supply vitamin C, (probably about 5 grams or more per day) preferably as mostly mineral ascorbates to prevent increasing the acidity, together with B1. B1 should be taken orally, probably two or three 100 mg. tablets per day, and tablets should also be chewed and held in the mouth to help improve tissue quality. Sodium/potassium bicarbonate, about $\frac{1}{4}$ to $\frac{1}{2}$ tsp. in a little water can be used $\frac{1}{2}$ hour after the meal, to bring the mouth to extreme alkaline. Hold in mouth until it disappears. The most effective topical agent seems to be one dropperful of liquid nystatin in a spoon, with about $\frac{1}{4}$ capsule of resteclin added and stirred in. Swish around in mouth and hold until it disappears. It is best used the very last thing at night. It can be used several times a day. It is also excellent for sore throat. Orithrush is usually also very effective.

A very large number of infectives join in with all Candida infections (See Sinus infections) and no rules can be absolute, because an agent that kills one infective may be good nourishment for some other infective. If the foregoing fails to clear up the infection, mouth washes of hydrogen peroxide, povidone iodine (as mixed for vaginitis or a little stronger), DMSO, and salt. should be tried. Other effective agents are nystatin tablets, chlorophyl tablets, garlic, GH3 (novacaine), a small piece of flagyl or caprystatin, or $\frac{1}{2}$ tablet of ketoconazole, held in the mouth until they disappear.

If a canker sore is extremely persistent, a drop of tincture of iodine, applied directly on the canker once or twice, will usually "burn it out".

Mouth infections can lead to infections of the throat or sinuses, and conversely infections of the nose and sinuses and infections of the throat can lead to infections and re-infections of the mouth.

Where long term therapy with ketoconazole is required frequent mouth infections can be expected. The reason is not clear, but it seems to be difficult to maintain healthy tissues in the mouth even with good nutrition and supplements of B1. It appears that Candida not only manufactures B2, but it also contains large quantities of B2 which is released from the dead infectives and is absorbed by the body. The quantities may be large. Sometimes with ketoconazole therapy of only $\frac{1}{2}$ tablet per day supplements of 500 mg B1 daily are insufficient. There are good reports from the use of B1 injections.

Another common mouth condition associated with Candida infection is enlarged veins at the corners of the lower lips, just inside the mouth. These may at times be almost purple in color, and they may swell or recede with toxic episodes or other changes in the infection. They can even be used to monitor the effectiveness of therapy. They do not seem to create problems, and they will slowly recede as total infection is reduced. These lesions seem to be the mouth equivalent of the enlarged veins that are found at the other end of the alimentary tract,- the lesions that we call hemorrhoids.

CANDIDA INFECTIONS of the THROAT.
(7 Medical papers. CH.3).
Candida infections of the throat will usually respond to the same treatment as infections of the mouth. If infections persists, Sucrets, Strepsils, Chloroseptic (phenol) or other drug store remedies should be tried. As the actual total infectives are unknown, at times it is necessary to try everything. Iodine lozenges are unpleasant, but they are frequently very effective. DMSO, hydrogen peroxide, and phenol alkalizer can be used as a gargle if necessary.

CANDIDA INFECTION of the ESOPHAGUS and HIATUS HERNIA.
(12 medical papers. Ch.3.)
Hiatus hernia has now been found to be very frequently misdiagnosed condition, and anyone diagnosed as having hiatus hernia should suspect that they probably have a Candida infection of the esophagus, probably combined with yeast infection of the stomach and intestines.

Yeast infection of the esophagus is actually a very common condition. In China a large number of people in one particular area developed and died from cancer of the esophagus. Research showed that the carcinogen was a nitrosamine although the diet did not contain nitrosamines. Further research showed that half of the offending molecule came from a common fermented food, and the other half of the nitrosamine molecule was finally found to come from a moldy bread regarded as a delicacy. Note that two metabolites from different sources combined to form the carcinogen. But further investigation showed that a fungal infection of the esophagus with yeasts and molds invariably preceded the cancer, and probably came from one of the foods. Now do not laugh at those Chinese. At least they discovered and eliminated the cause of the problem. Remember, a food is anything that can be eaten that does not result in instant death. Western people too eat some awful fermented foods, and some of our cheeses are made with aspergillus, while other aspergillus specie are known human infectives both on their own and associated with Candida. With all of our great Western technology, do we really know that our hiatus hernia (cum yeast infection) does not come from the very cheese of which we are so fond.

In all cases of yeast infection, and particularly if there is a problem with the esophagus or intestinal tract, it would certainly be prudent to eliminate all of the "exotic fungal foods", for if we insist on eating our favorite infectives they may instead eat us.

Esophagus infections frequently produce a sudden "full" feeling even perhaps at the very start of a meal, together with pressure in the chest. The full feeling comes from gas produced by the yeast from the partly digested foods as they pass by. The pressure from the gas can extend to pressure on the diaphram and heart, perhaps with palpitations or angina.

Esophagus infections will usually respond to chewed ketoconazole. About one hour after the meal, during the alkaline phase of digestion, chew a ketoconazole tablet and hold it in the mouth until it disappears. Ketoconazole is normally taken with the meal so that it will be absorbed during the acid phase of digestion. When taken during the alkaline phase very little of the ketoconazole is absorbed so it will remain in the digestive tract to act as a topical anti-fungal agent throughout the passage. An appropriate amount of ketoconazole should be taken at the beginning of the meal to provide the usual systemic therapy. Other effective agents are liquid nystatin with resteclin, chewed nystatin tablets, nystatin powder, and chlorophyl, all held in the mouth until they disappear. DMSO has been used internally in a strength not greater than 15%, and there are reports that hydrogen peroxide has been used internally, but risk might be very high if used without the full cooperation of a good physician.

Milk of magnesia, with or without resteclin, held in the mouth until it disappears may also be useful, but should be used $\frac{1}{2}$ to 1 hour after the meal, during the alkaline phase of digestion. Orithrush and bits of caprystatin should also be tried.

The effects of the anti-fungal fluids can be increased by adding an appropriate amount of psyllium seed, which makes the fluids cling to the walls of the esophagus.

Rotating the various agents is usually the most effective way to reduce esophagus infection, but many months may pass before improvements can be seen. One very striking feature of success is to suddenly cough up a lot of phlegm, even to the point of almost vomiting,(all without visible cause except the anti-fungal therapy), usually followed by a steady, slow improvement.

A symptomatic whooping cough can also be a factor in "hiatus hernia". If there is a past history of whooping cough, small amounts of Bordetello Pertussis vaccine, or autogenous vaccine, should be tried.

CANDIDA INFECTION of the STOMACH and INTESTINES.
(14 medical papers. Ch.3.)

Candida infection of the stomach and intestines is so very common, and is usually present and part of any digestive tract problems;- chronic indigestion, ulcers, sprue, diverticulitus, chronic constipation, chronic diarrhea, the "beer belly" and chronic gas.

Gas, gas, gas! With some unfortunate people it is a continuous stream, or almost continuous burps. And the ads, the continuous ads in the magazines, on the radio, and on the T.V. show that there are a very large number of people bothered by gas, and there are a very large number of people that buy these remedies in a usually vain attempt to reduce the gas. Gas, gas, gas, a never ending stream, yet the gas is not in the food. The gas comes from the fermentation of food, and yeasts of all kinds are usually the active organisms in fermentation and Candida is the active resident yeast. To effectively reduce the gas, you, must reduce the yeast, and to reduce the yeast you must first stop feeding it refined carbohydrate. Yeasts thrive on free sugars. To bake bread you must add sugar to "activate" the yeast. Sugars, added to the stomach, will also "activate" the yeast, and the stomach will "rise" just like a loaf of bread, with gas, gas, gas.

The refined carbohydrate must therefore be eliminated. This means that you must not only eliminate sugar, honey, and starch, but you must also eliminate all dried fruits, many fresh fruits, melons, and perhaps even potatoes. Milk is high in milk sugar, and should be avoided. Even with the foods with high free sugars eliminated, digestive infections are still very difficult to reduce because the yeasts will continue to live on the sugars from complex carbohydrate as the carbohydrates are digested. However, yeasts grow the best in a weak 2% sugar solution, and a strong solution much less favorable to yeast growth can be maintained by having frequent meals. Many people may have wondered how gas and indigestion could possibly develop three or four hours after the meal, and why the indigestion could be arrested by eating. The strength of the digestive solutions falls as the sugars are absorbed by the body, and three or four hours after the meal, when they approach the weak solutions favorable to the yeast, the yeasts flourish and produce gas and indigestion, which can be reduced by eating and restoring the high fluid concentrarions. Yeast infection usually affects the pancreas and produces hypoglycemia. Perhaps all hypoglycemics have Candida infection. Hypoglycemia eposides can be reduced by eating six small meals per day instead of three. It may be that the hypoglycemia results from feeding the yeast, and the six small meals reduce the effects from the yeast.

Nystatin is the principal topical agent for reducing yeast infections of the digestive system. The small brown tablets (mycostatin) can be chewed for fast action, or swallowed with water for delayed action. Nystatin is a clever anti-infective that is specific against Candida. It destroys the yeast by building up in the sidewall of the plant. It is therefore safe and free from all direct side effects. The only indirect side effects are from resorbed toxins from the dead yeast, and unless there are severe colon problems as many as twenty nystatin tablets can be taken daily without problems. Many doctors suggest taking the tablets with the meal, but nystatin seems to be more effective if the tablets are taken about three or four hours after the meal when the density of the solutions has fallen and the yeasts are feeding rapidly. At least one tablet should be chewed before swallowing. Alternately, the six meal program can be used, with the nystatin taken about 15 minutes before the meal. Better results may be achieved if the between meal snacks are largely protein and are devoid of carbohydrate. Liquid nystatin can also be used instead of the tablets. The effectiveness of liquid nystatin can be increased by adding the nystatin to $\frac{1}{2}$ glass of water with $\frac{1}{2}$ tsp. of psyllium seed, which will cling to the walls of the intestines and will carry the nystatin to the mucous surfaces.

One of the principal factors in initiating and promoting intestinal Candida infection is altered digestive system pH. The swing of the pH from acid to alkaline during the different phases of digestion, together with the different digestive enzymes, normally destroys almost all of the micro-organisms ingested with the food. Intestinal Candida infection produces lactic acid, which alters the pH cycle and prevents the pH from moving to alkaline, producing acidosis and allowing many intestinal organisms to grow, flourish, and add their toxins and metsbolites to the intestinal mix. Digestive enzymes with bi-carbonate, ½ to 1 hour after the meal are therefore essential to the reduction of Candidal infections of the digestive tract. We say digestive enzymes with the bi-carbonate, following the excellent work of Dr.Philpott yet, perhaps digestive enzymes may pose perils of their own.

In a severe case of intestinal Candida infection there is constant indigestion. The constant indigestion may come solely from the yeast, but it would indicate the need for hydrochloric acid, bile salts, vitamin C, and digestive enzymes. A trial of some or all might "prove" their value by reducing the discomfort after the meal. But if the body is already producing sufficient digestive enzymes and the digestive enzyme supplements are over-supplied ("if a little is good, more is better") the complex carbohydrates will be rapidly digested into refined carbohydrates, which will feed the infectives and will encourage the growth and spread of the Candida callus matrix. Although the appropriate digestive enzymes can be ascertained only by trial, the bicarbonate program should be started with protein digestive enzymes only, specifically;-

1. HCL should be tried, despite adequate pH, because the acidity may come from lactic acid. Increased acidity from HCL supplements can be offset with bi-carbonate. The Livingston-Wheeler cancer clinic suggests that you check your urine pH (acidity) in the mornings with Hydrazine strip (available from the drug store) which will indicate your need to supplement with Betaine Hydrochloride. The pH should be between 4.5 and 6.5. If it is 7. or higher they suggest betaine hydrochloride with each meal and increasing until the urine shows the desired value. This will work excellently for people who do not have high lactic acid, but people with high lactic acid; from Candida infection, from high adrenalin, from excess sugars, or from low oxygen or low oxygenation; may show a normal pH when in fact the acidity is all from lactic acid and they may be desperately short of hydrochloric acid. Therefore if there are digestive problems, supplement with Betaine Hydrochloric (HCL) with all meals, use the pH strip, and supplement with bi-carbonate ½ hour after the meal to reduce the acidity to about pH 5.5. If the stool is pale, instead of brown, bile salts will be needed.

2. If tests show bile is low, bile should be supplemented.

3. Digestive aids, pepsin, trypsin, and chymotrypsin. Pancreatin also digests carbohydrates and should be used with caution.

This will provide a good supply of fully digested amino acids for the adrenals, pancreas, and immune system, and for rebuilding the damaged tissues, without increasing the rate of the carbohydrate, while the bicarbonate will induce and ensure the alkaline phase of digestion, which also reduces inflammation, stabalizes weight, and reduces any tendency toward allergies.

Alternately, to start the program the bicarbonate could be used with pure essential amino acids, while the non-essential amino acids are taken with the meal. After a week or ten days, when digestion has improved and pancreatic function has returned, the amino acids should be discontinued but the bicarbonate may need to be used until the yeast infection has been substantially reduced.

The high protein diet is acidic, but this can be offset by a little extra bicarbonate. Supplements of vitamin E, glycine, and lecithin will help the body to handle the extra protein.

The total problems with yeast infection are so all encompassing that sometimes the only possible approach is to just keep reducing it a little, wherever possible, because reducing it anywhere, helps to reduce it everywhere. Many people with high yeast infection are plagued by allergies because of the yeast infection, and some of these people will be allergic to many proteins, which makes a high protein diet almost impossible, in which case the proteins will have to be rotated and restricted until the yeast infection and allergies have been reduced. That is the bad part. The good part is that the bicarbonate will also help to reduce the allergies.

Some of the allergies associated with protein diets, and some of the gas and digestive problems do not come directly from the yeast, but from bacterial infectives harbored in the infective matrix. These must be subdued, or the bacterial infectives will simply replace the fungal infectives, without improvement in health, and with only a change in symptoms. One resteclin capsule, or other appropriate antibiotics, should be taken (between meals) about once a week to keep down these infectives. If problems persist, Metronidazole, Sulfamethoxazole, and Vancomycin should be tried.

All programs to reduce Candida infection are long term programs, and intestinal infection requires long term persistence. Invariably, a program will be developed that works so well that you are certain that you have found the answer. Then indigestion will return and no matter what you do, change digestives, eliminate digestives, eliminate ketoconazole, try garlic, chlorophyl, etc; etc; the indigestion will persist. What happened? What to do?

Ch.6. Specific Candida Infections.

The terrible truth is that there are a very large number of different infectives that are always waiting to eat at you, and somehow some one of these infectives that has not been killed by either the ketoconazole or the resteclin, or anything else, has become dominant, so some other anti-infective agent must be found. Usually the digestive tract can be cleared by using NaEDTA as a general cleanser.

The use of NaEDTA as an anti-infective has been very limited, but it will destroy all micro-organisms that have exposed calcium in their outer membranes, because NaEDTA will chemically pick up calcium from anything that it touches. It is the effective agent used in calcium chelation therapy for atherosclerosis. It will also remove lead and heavy metals. Today it is used intravenously for chelation therapy, but it can also be taken orally. CaNaEDTA will pick up heavy metals only, and should not be confused with NaEDTA, which also picks up calcium. The powder must be taken in a capsule, and is best taken on an empty stomach. Start with not more than ½capsule to avoid toxicity from lead and heavy metals. The amount can then be increased to as much as two or three capsules without toxic effects. Repeat in two or three days if necessary. EDTA should always be followed, a few hours later with multi-minerals and acidophilus.

Acidophilus or yogurt should also be provided continuously as part of the digestive tract program. Acidophilus is an effective agent against Candida, and continuing use will help to establish friendly flora in the digestive tract. Acidophilus and yogurt are more effective if used with psyllium seed.

It has now been established that yogurt may not be as beneficial as it appears because Candida is stronger than yogurt, and, if infection is high, it will overpower the yogurt, kill it out, and use it for food. The best choice seems to be acidophilus-bifidus capsules.

The success of any program can be judged only by the relief it provides. The relief should be continuous, but it will not be. Digestion is linked to colon function, so the colon program, although discussed separately, will have to be integrated with the digestion program. If constipation is a problem, the psyllium seed with nystatin can be increased and/or milk of magnesia can be taken about ¼ hour after the bicarbonate. Milk of magnesia is highly alkaline and should always be taken during the alkaline phase of digestion. It will give the intestinal pH a strong shift to alkaline, and it should not be repeated for four or five days unless absolutely necessary.

The object of all digestive programs is to assist in the development of a natural rhythmic function. Stomach and intestinal problems can be expected if the colon has not emptied.

Bowel training, by consciously picking a suitable time of day for the major bowel movement is essential to rhythmic function of the entire digestive tract.

Loose bowels, diarrhea, and soft mushy stools can be caused by an overloaded liver, by poor liver function, or by "stomach dumping", but the usual cause is high intestinal yeast infection fed by free sugars. The diet must be checked carefully. Free sugars are often well hidden! Single episodes of loose bowels are a good sign that the body has cleared out some infection somewhere, and the body is eliminating the poisons.

One of the most effective methods of reducing intestinal problems is with the ascorbate flush (CH.4.) always followed with acidophilus capsules and capricin or a tsp. of coconut with each meal.

In some cases, where toxicity is almost constant, activated charcoal (CH.4.) may be of particular help until the "leaky bowels" can be improved (vitamin C and bioflavinoids), or until the total toxic load can be reduced. Activated charcoal absorbs nutrients as well as toxins, so the charcoal should be slowly increased until toxicity is relieved, and should then be reduced slowly, and eliminated as soon as possible.

The basic object of a digestive program is to reduce the yeasts and other infectives, restore the integrity of the mucous membranes, and restore the intestinal flora. We cannot know specifically all of the infectives that are involved in the infection, so we must use broad spectrum anti-infectives while at the same time we also know that the use of a number of broad spectrum anti-infectives will destroy the "good" intestinal flora. Although the mucous membrane is said to be the barrier that protects us from invasion by infectives, (CH.4), it is actually the synergistic production of short chain fatty acids (which are both fungustatic and fungicidal) by the mucous membrane reacting with intestinal flora, that is the real barrier to fungal invasion. "Good" natural intestinal flora is composed of about 400 different micro-organisms. If we use broad spectrum anti-infectives most of the good flora will also be destroyed. Thus to restore health we must reduce the toxic infectives with broad spectrum antibiotics and antifungals while knowing that the anti-infectives will also strip the good flora from the mucous membranes, leaving the entire mucosa exposed to any toxic infectives that may survive.

The real trick, of course, is to replace the "good" intestinal flora, but unfortunately we can replace only one of the good flora, out of a total of about 400 micro-organisms. The one flora is lactobacillus acidophilus, and, although lactobacillus has antifungal properties and is highly beneficial,it kills fungii by producing hydrogen peroxide, so Capricin or some other source of caprylic acid should be supplied to renew the protection of the mucosal lining. We do have one report that sauerkraut and/or buttermilk will renew some of the flora, and these should be tried. Potassium sorbate (the stabilizer used for making wine) may also be of benefit.

In stubborn prolonged cases of intestinal infection success seems to come only after extended trials of everything possible. In general the program would start with nystatin, ketoconazole, and resteclin, always followed with lactobacillus capsules, psyllium, caprylic or sorbic acid, and usually with bicarbonate and perhaps digestive enzymes ½ hr. after the meal. Then if problems persist rotate into the general program metronidazole, sulfamethoxazole, and perhaps oral vancomycin. (Ch.4.). Both you and your doctor must watch for possible toxic effects on liver and kidneys. Results may be very spectacular if the anti-infectives clear infection out of the liver or kidneys. Start as always with very small amounts to avoid allergies or severe toxic reactions to dead infectives.

HALITOSIS. (Bad Breath).

Halitosis can always be temporarily reduced with peppermint, or chlorophyl, so the mouth and throat are always blamed for foul odor, but the foul odor originates in the digestive tract and results from infectives feeding on partly digested food. Reduction and elimination of halitosis can therefore be accomplished only by reducing the intestinal infectives, by improving digestion and assimilation, and by cleaning up the colon. Again, halitosis is only an easily recognized foul symptom of major digestive tract problems. See the preceding information on "Stomach and Intestines".

ULCERS.

Ulcers are areas of the stomach or digestive tract where the mucous membrane has failed to protect the lining, and the wall then becomes raw and inflamed, and perhaps infected, with tissue damage sometimes so great that the stomach or intestine will become perforated. (perforated ulcer).

Ulcers can develop in the intestines, but most ulcers develop in the stomach. Duodenal ulcers develop in the duodenum, or first part of the stomach, and peptic ulcers develop in the main part of the stomach.

The basic causes of ulcers are:

1. Highly acidic conditions. (as in Candida infection).

2. Shortage of vitamins and nutrients, particularly pantothenic acid.

3. Cortisone, either supplemented or produced by the body by

overactive adrenal glands. Cortisone depletes the vitamin A, increases the acidity, and destroys the proteins in the mucous membranes thus weakening the membrane and contributing to further ulcers and further intestinal infection. (Mucus and the Mucous Membrane. Ch.4). Stress in any form, induces the adrenals to produce cortisone, and stress is therefore a contributing factor in ulcers.

4.   Aspirin and other salicylates, which attack and destroy body cells.

5.   Porous, weak, and scurvous tissues from lack of Vit. C and bioflavinoids.

6.   Poor tissue quality from imbalance of B-1 and B-2. Note that Candida infection produces large quantities of B-2, and tissue quality throughout the entire alimentary canal from mouth to anus will be poor if B-1 is not heavily supplemented.

Therapy.

Medical therapy for ulcers is now quite successful. The ulcer is examined with instruments using fibre optics, and a drug program is then used, which is usually based on Taganette, a drug that blocks the secretion of acid. But the adage "once an ulcer always an ulcer" still holds true, because the ulcerated state is certain to return if the underlying causes of the ulcer are not altered. If the ulcer returns, it will usually be at the same place, and each episode of damaged tissues increases the risk of multiple infections, altered cellular functions, and perhaps, cancer. However, the medical program can be used to heal the ulcer, while the underlying causes are remedied. Alternately, if all of the underlying causes of the ulcer are reduced, the ulcer will heal if bicarbonate is used after each meal.

Ulcer Program.

1. Nystatin: tablets or liquid, chlorophyl, garlic, ketoconazole, capricin, etc; to reduce Canida infection and reduce total acidity.

2. Bicarbonate $\frac{1}{2}$ hour after all meals to reduce total acidity.

3. Good protein and extra cystine (eggs contain both) and non homogenized whole milk.

4. Supplements of Vitamin A, E, C, B1, B6, Choline, bioflavinoids, pantothenic acid, and lactobacillus.

5. Reduced stress, and elimination of cortisone medication.

6. Elimination of all free sugars and all caffeine from the diet.

This program corrects the basic causes of the ulcers. The taganette program reduces the acidity by reducing the production of stomach acid, promoting poor digestion, and increasing the infectives living on undigested food .

CANDIDA YEAST INFECTION of the COLON.
(8 medical papers. CH.3.)

Constipation and colitis have devastating effects upon all body systems. When bowel movement is delayed, sometimes for even just a few minutes, sweating and headache frequently follow. The sweating and headache are the visible affects from toxins resorbed from body wastes, but the resorbed toxins also affect all other organs and glands, where the effects may be less noticeable but perhaps much more damaging.

The relation between colitis and neurotic and psychotic behavior is well known, with the blame usually being placed on sugar and refined carbohydrate. Yet the exact relationship between sugar and psychosis has not been adequately shown. Most certainly high sugar consumption leads to extreme variations in blood sugar levels, with psychosis from low (and sometimes high) blood sugar. The relationship to colon problems is obscure, but is very certain. We know that alcohol is produced by brewers yeast feeding on sugars, and we know that the alcohol affects the mind. We also know that Candida yeast, feeding on sugars, produces phenethyl alcohol, sterols, tryptophol, ethanol, and similar alcohols that can affect the mind. We know that Candida yeast, and other yeasts and other infectives, infect the colon, so it should not be surprising that free-sugars in the diet would cause colitis with severe mental problems. See Page 370.

Doctors, the media, and the public are astonished at the various reports where non-drinkers with alcoholic symptoms were found to be producing alcohol in their own body. The source of the alcohol is brewers yeast. Brewers yeast is not invasive to the body, but it can and does join colonies of Candida yeast, where it then turns free sugars into alcohol, thus producing the non-drinking alcoholic,(Meiti- Sho disease). Colonies of mixed infectives are frequently found in the stomach and intestines, and are thought by some to be the cause of the "beer belly". Obviously, if Candida infection is found anywhere, it will probably be found throughout the sexual tissues, so it should be expected to be found in the colon, along with other infectives, forcing toxins of many kinds into the bloodstream and producing migraine headaches, mental delusions, or other wierd effects. Yeast infection of the colon is very difficult to identify, but in reducing total Candida infection, infection of the colon should be presumed, and if there are colon problems of any kind anti-infective enemas should be part of the anti-yeast program. If the stool pH is less than 6, Candida infection should be expected.

Anti-Infective Enemas.

Enemas should not be used more frequently than every three or four days unless absolutely necessary. Daily enemas alter the acidity, alkalinity, and density of the fluids in the colon, which interferes with normal colon function and weakens the mucous membranes.

Use of an 8 oz. rectal syringe will reduce the difficulties, and will provide adequate disinfectant. Bottle enemas, where up to a quart of liquid is used, can be used if necessary, but the large quantity of fluids has an adverse effect on normal colon function.

The 8 oz. syringe will hold the contents of a large glass of fluid. To administer the enema lie on the left side with the knees doubled up, head flat. Lubricate the anus and also the tip of the syringe with nystatin cream, and insert the syringe slowly. Squeeze bulb slowly, and keep the bulb squeezed until the syringe has been slowly withdrawn. Use of a rubber sheet and towel is advisable for the first few times to ensure that the enema will be retained.

After receiving the enema lie on the left side 5-10 minutes, lie on back 5-10 minutes, lie on right side 5-10 minutes, lie on stomach 5-10 minutes, rise on knees, head on the floor for five minutes. This sequence will usually get some of the enema into the ascending colon. The enema should be retained for a total time of about $\frac{1}{2}$ hour, but not much longer, as resorption of toxins may occur. If headache or toxic symptoms follow after the enemas, the retained time may have to be reduced or the content of the enema may have to be changed.

Enemas always produce stress while the body re-adjusts the fluids. One half hour or more of bed rest or sleep should follow after discharge of the enema.

Enemas also always disrupt the mucous membrane that protects the intestinal walls from acids, alkalis, infectives etc. The passage of some mucus with one or two bowel movements following the enema, should be expected. To allow full re-building of the mucous lining the use of enemas should be minimised, and if possibe should not be more frequent than ten days or two weeks.

Enema Mixtures.

1. 3/4 glass of warm water with $\frac{1}{4}$ tsp. sea salt. (to provide salinity).
   1 tablespoon milk of magnesia.
   Contents of 1 capsule of resteclin.
   $\frac{1}{2}$ tsp. liquid nystatin or 1 ground up tablet of ketoconazole.
2. Mixture as in 1, with 1 tsp. strong chlorophyl solution.
3. Mixture as in 1, with the milk of magnesia replaced by 1 tbsp. of strong chlorophyl solution.
4. Mixture as in 1 or 2, with the milk of magnesia replaced with phenol alkalizer.

5. Any of the above, with the water and salt replaced with the persons own urine. Some people find this distasteful but there are technical advantages that make urine the preferred fluid.

A. Urine is a body fluid that is always present in the bloodstream and tissues, and the pH and alkalinity etc; are therefore compatible with body tissues.

B. Urine is therefore less disruptive to the mucous membrane which allows more enemas (if necessary) with less mucous membrane damage.

C. Urine contains antibodies to all of the infectives in the body.

Note.- Urine should not be used if there are visible signs of urinary infection.

In considering the use of urine/vs water, it should be remembered that the colon removes water from the body wastes at a very high rate, and the fluids are returned to the bloodstream to be further cleansed by the liver. The total "porosity" of the colon and the density of the fluids determines the amount of fluid and the amount of toxic waste removed with the fluid. Use of water enemas may therefore tend to produce loose bowels, or perhaps constipation, while excess toxic wastes may overload the liver to the point of toxicity.

6. DMSO, about 1 tbsp. can be added to any of the above enemas to increase the anti-fungal action and to increase absorption of the anti-fungals into the infected tissues.

7. Yucca, aloe vera jiuce, or other natural saponins can be added to the enemas. Saponins increase the "wetting factor" by reducing the surface tension of the fluids, which increases the actual intimate contact of the anti-infective agents with the infectives.

Vitamin C, in large quantities, as with the ascorbate flush, or as with the vitamin C retention enema, (CH.4.) is also very effective against colon infections.

Constipation and Colonics.

Constipation and laxatives, headaches, aspirin, and pain killers, are a prominent subject of advertising. Most headaches, and many other pains are indeed induced by colon problems, but neither the laxatives ot the pain killers reach the cause of the constipation. From all of the advertising, and from the total sales of all of these products it seems that most of the population are in fact constipated, or do have colon problems. Also from the total consumption of sugar and white flour one might expect that everyone should have colon problems, and many of these people will also be neurotic, psychotic,"retarded", or have aberrant behavior from the mental effects of toxins and metabolites resorbed from the colon.

In short, and in fact, today's high increase in social problems results largely from the total effects of sugar, caffeine, and impaired colon function. Anyone can themselves observe the effects of resorbed toxins, and particularly the effects on the mind, by noting the mental and physical changes when they have to "put off" a bowel movement. Within minutes, the mind may become sluggish and dull; there is a vague feeling of unease and apprehension, and aches and pains may appear anywhere. With continuous constipation, these changes simply become continuous, and constantly increase into an entirely different miserable life. (See also Ascorbate flush, CH.4.)

Improving Colon Functions.

The following will help to improve colon function:

1. Elimination of all refined carbohydrate, all free sugars, and all caffeine.

2. Yogurt and acidophilus should be used to compete with infectives for free sugars as they are digested. It is more effective if mixed with a small amount of psyllium.

3. Laxatives, if possible, should be avoided. If a laxative is required, milk of magnesia, always taken about an hour after a meal, would be a good choice, because it is highly alkaline and it will help to maintain colon alkalinity.

4. Ascorbic acid, in very large amounts, to the point of diarrhea, is another alternative with the advantage that it supplies large amounts of vitamin C. The ascorbic acid should be followed with bicarbonate $\frac{1}{2}$ to 1 hour after the meal, and all water soluble vitamins and minerals must be supplemented to replace the nutrients lost with the diarrhea.(See also Ascorbate Flush. Ch.4.).

5. Enemas should be used only if necessary, and continuing use should be avoided.

6. Diet should include some bran, flaxseed, and/or psyllium seed, but these should be used with caution if peristalisis (rhythmic movement of the colon) is low, because they tend to hold water and to form "mushy" stools that may form a "plug" in the colon. Pectin and fibrous foods like celery will also help to provide "bulk".

7. Nystatin, used continuously, with the occasional use of NaEDTA (in capsules) together with anti-infective enemas will help to reduce colon infections.

8. Mucous membranes can be improved with the same supplements as used for stomach ulcers.

9. If constipation and colon problems are severe, your doctor can get barium x-rays of the colon, which may show a badly twisted and deformed colon that can be revitalized only with many treatments of colonics. Most people who administer colonics are quite set in their ways, but it would be advantageous if

they could be persuaded to try some of the anti-infective enema mixtures previously described.

10. Vitamin C Retention Enema. (CH.4.).

11. Change of intestinal flora with acidophilus tablets and/or buttermilk, egg yolks, or elemental sulphur.

12. The intestines and colon are sexual tissues. With sexual climax digestion ceases, and the rectual sphincter tightens. There is therefore a direct nerve link between the colon and the sexual organs. The two systems are also linked through sex hormones. Normal colon function is therefore somewhat dependent upon normal sexual function every two or three days or at least once a week, and colon problems may therefore persist if sexual problems are not corrected.

Diarrhea and Vomiting.

(See also Vit.C. Retention Enema ,CH.4.)

Diarrhea and vomiting are the only ways that the body has of quickly eliminating poisonous toxic substances from the digestive tract. All laxatives, from the toxins in cascara to the mercury in calomal through to the excess alkalinity of milk of magnesia work on the principle that the body will always try to flush out poisons.

Warning.

Severe or chronic diarrhea and vomiting can be life threatening. Your doctor must be consulted and every effort must be made to determine the cause. Common causes of sudden severe diarrhea may be botulism, cholera, salmonella, shigella, etc. Do not take chances.

****

Diarrhea and vomiting are certain indications that there are toxic substances in the digestive tract that the body is determined to eliminate.

Single episodes of diarrhea, or short sporadic episodes during the anti-candida program or when using autogenous vaccines are usually good news because they indicate that the body is cleaning out another pocket of chronic infection.

Continuing diarrhea results from serious toxic infections somewhere in the digestive system or colon, which immediately poses a classical conundrum; food is necessary to fight the infection, but every attenpt to eat also feeds the infectives, and every attempt to eat or drink only produces more diarrhea. Function can be rapidly restored only if certain procedures are followed:

At the very start every effort must be made to reduce the infection, but nothing can be effective because everything that is consumed simply rushes straight through. Now the digestive tract is of course a coiled tube. Normally it is filled with semi-solids that move slowly along, but following a severe episode of diarrhea the tube is empty and there is nothing to impede the flow of fluids through the tube. Fluids simply pour through, and solids are flushed through by the fluids. The body rapidly becomes de-hydrated, with an increase in thirst that cannot be satisfied because fluids cannot be retained. Further, the more fluids that are consumed, the greater the loss of vitamins with the diarrhea.

To slow the passage of solids and fluids through the intestinal tract all fluids should be mixed with Mucilose Flakes or similar psyllium preparation. This will help to form a "plug" to prevent everything from rushing straight through. Coarse stringy foods, like celery will also help.

After the very first episode of severe diarrhea, a stalk of celery should be eaten, followed by two capsules of NaEDTA, taken with a little tea and a lot of psyllium, lay down immediately to reduce the forces of expulsion. The NaEDTA will pick calcium out of everything and will usually kill most of the organisms, bad and good, that are in the intestinal tract. About one hour later, more celery should be eaten, with four capsules of garlic, all water soluble vitamins, three or four nystatin tablets, and one tablet of ketoconazole, (if possible) taken with broth, potassium, and psyllium seed. Again lie down for $\frac{1}{2}$ hour, water should be avoided. All fluids should be in the form of solutions, as broth, juice, tea, or coffee. Here even strong coffee may be of value. It will increase assimilation and the caffeine will help to destroy the infectives. Psyllium should be added to all fluids to ensure retention.

Now the real trick is to feed yourself without feeding the infective. Toxic infectives seem to be in two general classes; infectives that thrive on protein, and infectives that thrive on sugars. Infectives that thrive on proteins are less common than infectives that thrive on sugars, so try a little meat. If it makes things worse you know that you will have to avoid proteins, but if it is tolerated you know that you must avoid all sugars, all starches, and all free sugars as are found in fruit and fruit juice. You will have to live on broth, meat, nuts, cheese, and other proteins, complex carbohydrate like whole wheat bread, and fats like peanut butter, but continue with everything possible to destroy the infectives, while adding acidophilus tablets to the diet. Chlorophyl is another effective agent, and resteclin should be taken between meals.

Remember that even when the episodes of diarrhea become less violent, each episode strips out all of the water soluble vitamins and minerals, and these must be replaced after every episode. In addition to replacement of lost vitamins, large amounts of vitamins should be taken, particularly vitamin C, potassium, and all adrenal nutrients.

In severe and persistent cases the NaEDTA may have to be repeated. If the infection appears to be in the colon, anti-infective enemas may be of help, and sometimes a Vitamin C Retention Enema (CH.4.) will give spectacular results.

Hemorrhoids are varicose veins in the rectum. They are very painful, and they can contribute to total stress. They are probably the result of yeast infection that has weakened the tissues, because similar lesions, that rise and reduce with the amount of yeast infection, can sometimes be seen on the inside corners of the mouth. Hemorrhoids, like the lesions in the mouth, are also much worse and much higher, at different times.

Hemorrhoids can usually be reduced with finger massage using a fingerstall and alternately using vitamin E oil (from a capsule), nystatin cream, miconazole lotion, phenol alkalizer, M.C.T. oil, coconut oil, vitamin C retention enemas, and perhaps DMSO or Elase- Chloromycetin (Fibrinolysin- chloramphenical) ointment. As the hemorrhoids start to be resolved they slowly form a hard scab (rectal cag) which then slowly goes away. Success is dependent upon "doing everything else" in the Anti-Candida program.

The Stool.

Digestion, intestine and colon function can be monitored by the appearance of the stool. In the past, some naturopaths have, with success, used the appearance of the stool as their principal guide for health programs. The use of this information should be revived, and a handbook, with colored pictures, would be very useful.

Most people already know the appearance of a healthy stool, and most people with health problems already know that the stool does not look like it used to. A healthy stool will look something like a string of dark fat sausages, about $1\frac{1}{4}$ inches in diameter, with the segments about 4 to 6 inches long, dark to medium brown, porous, so light that it floats, and almost odorless. Bowel movement time should be only a few minutes, and should occur at about the same time once or twice each day.

Very few older people manage to consistently come even close to this ideal.

Color.

Color, (except for foods that color the stool) is largely determined by bile. Light stools are indicative of low bile. Digestion and intestinal function will be improved by the use of bile supplements if needed.

Size

Size is related to density, but is largely determined by the condition of the rectal sphincter. Stress tightens the rectal sphincter, and the adrenal depletion from stress induces muscle spasm and calcinosis, resulting in a highly restricted anus. In extreme cases the tightening of the rectal sphincter will be so great that the passage of the stool becomes almost impossible, and the lower end of the colon will then become weak, stretched, and ballooned from the pressure from trying to force bowel movements. The stool is then larger than the opening, yet it must be squeezed out through the restricted anus, much like icing is squeezed out of a cake decorator, and indeed, the stool itself will be very thin, curled and stringy, and perhaps only $\frac{1}{4}$ inch in diameter.

People with this condition usually reduce their problems with bran, psyllium seed, flax, orange juice, laxatives and enemas, all of which soften the stool and allow it to pass more easily through the severe restriction. But evacuation of the stool is never complete, the intestines and colon become unhealthy, water balance is disturbed, and toxins from the retained stool are constantly being resorbed, reducing health, creating psychosis and mental problems, and greatly increasing the risk of cancer of the colon.

Your doctor may try to solve this problem (sometimes with success) with a rectal operation, by cutting and re-shaping the muscles of the rectal sphincter to create a larger passage. If the restricted anus is not altered, the risk of cancer is high. If the operation is performed, the risk of cancer is lower, but the risk is still high, while the chances of success are low.

The rectal sphincter problem can usually be solved much better without resorting to surgery.
1. Reduce the stress, and use ample adrenal supplements.
2. Improve nutrition, diet, and supplements.
3. Improve digestive and colon function.
4. Vitamin C Retention Enemas. (CH.4.).
5. Daily massage of the rectal sphincter with vitamin E oil, nystatin cream, miconazole lotion, phenol alkalizer, and DMSO, used separately. A fingerstall must be used to prevent cutting the tissues with fingernails. a special rectal vibrator, or a small sexual vibrater will also help.

Passage Time.
Normal passage time for the stool should be about $1\frac{1}{2}$ to 2 days. Passage time can be measured by taking charcoal tablets for markers. If the stool is small, (perhaps only $\frac{1}{2}$ inch in diameter) short ($1\frac{1}{2}$" to 2" long) and hard, the passage time has been too long, and too much water has been removed during the delayed passage. With delayed passage time toxins and metabolites will also be removed from the stool, and psychosis and mental problems can be expected. Passage time is related to digestion and general health and will normalize as health improves. Rate of passage can be increased with a little bran, or psyllium seed, pectin, yogurt, exercise, and if necessary, a tsp. of milk of magnesia 1 hr. after a meal.

Ch.6. Specific Candida Infections.

Floaters and Sinkers.
    If passage time for the stool is not more than 2 days, and
the stool sinks immediately, the density of the stool can be
reduced by the addition of fiber to the diet. Fibrous foods, with
pectin or psyllium seed husks, yogurt and acidophilus are the
best, but bran, flax and other fibers can be used. Some doctors
think that fiber should be increased to the point that the stool
always floats.
Stinkers.
    The human stool should be almost odorless. Odors, and nasty
peculiar odors, are indicative of particular combinations of
infectious organisms. If odors persist, rotate all of the
anti-infectives including chlorophyl, NaEDTA, and DMSO. If
odors still persist, try penicillin and other antibiotics.

COPING with GAS and CRAMPS.
Note.-Sudden severe cramps may indicate appendicitis. See
your doctor immediately. With intestinal yeast infection, gas
and cramps are a constant problem. Simply stated, the yeast
produces gas just like it does when making bread, and the
expanding gas causes the cramps, burps, and discomfort.
Burps.
    Whenever yeast infection is present in the digestive tract,
gas will be produced by the yeast. If the infection is in the
eosphagus and/or stomach, the gas pressure is usually relieved
by burps and belching. Burps and belching can be reduced with
bicarbonate $\frac{1}{2}$ hr.to 1 hr. after the meal.
Rectal Gas.
    If the yeast infection is in the intestines, gas will be produced,
and the gas will either be resorbed by the body (increasing the
acidosis) or the gas must be passed as rectal gas. Relief from
gas pressure is absolutely necessary, yet odor and noise from
passing rectal gas can be extremely embarrassing. The noise
usually results from a tightly spasmed rectal sphincter, which
might be improved by rectal massage with vitamin E oil, taken
fresh from a capsule. A fingerstall must be worn for the massage,
or a rectal or a small sexual vibrator can be used. MCT oil,
coconut oil, and Vitamin C Retention Enemas (Ch.4.) may also
help.
Odor.
    The awful odors accompanying rectal gas do not come from
the yeast, they are produced by other infectives living with
the yeast in the Candida matrix. The odors and the total gas
can be dramatically reduced by avoiding sugars and other
offending foods like beans, and by taking garlic, chlorophyl,
yogurt, and acidophilus, alternately, about 3 hours after the

meal. If foul odors persist, try the occasional use of NaEDTA and alternately ketoconazole about three hours after the meal. Psyllium seed, used with liquid nystatin and acidophilus will help to clear infections from the diverticuli. Yucca and aloe-vera may also help to clear infections from the diverticuli. Try metronidazole, vancomycin, sulfamethoxazole, vitamin C retention enemas and ascorbate flush.

Cramps.

Cramps are caused by expanding gas locked into the intestines between pieces of digesting food, or between segments of forming stool. The main problem is that peristalisis, the rhythmic movement of the intestines that keeps the material in the intestines moving along, is low, causing "pockets" of gas under pressure, which in turn causes the pain and discomfort, and the feeling that everything in the digestive tract has stopped, which it has.

Peristalisis, and consequently digestion, as the mass moves along, can be improved with heat from a stove, heating pad, hot water bottle, or if necessary a tub bath. Although a hot tub bath is the most effective, it is also the most trouble, but hot water bottles, not too hot or equipped with a cover, conform to the body and can be used on the chest, stomach, genitals, rectum and back.

The pressure and dull pain from intestinal gas is always worse at night because the body movements, while awake, help the intestines to keep the digestive mass moving along through the intestines, but at night the movements slow down, and the digestive food mass stops, and becomes a dead weight, slowly expanding from gas pressure creating pain and aches, and sometimes forcing stomach juices backward into the esophagus and throat. This makes the esophagus and throat susceptible to ulcers and infection, deprives the body of sorely needed nutrients, feeds the digestive tract infectives, and interferes with much needed sleep and rest. The lack of sleep then increases the total stress which depletes the adrenals, and the adrenal depletion, together with the pressure from the expanding gas, interferes with the muscular contractions that produce the peristalasis. Nutrition, reducing free sugars, reducing the yeast infection, supplementing the thyroid and parathyroid, and everything else that you are doing, will help to restore peristalisis, but in the meantime you must cope with the intestinal gas.

Moving Intestinal Gas.

When you consider the large number of loops and turns in the small intestine, and when you consider that the colon rises, crosses over, descends, and makes a turn to the rectum, it is mechanically a wonder that you are able to pass any gas at all, because gas will naturally rise to the highest point of the loop. But the fact that gas does not always rise to the highest point, can be used as a means of moving the gas along. It should also be remembered that whereas solids and liquids can be propelled through the intestines by peristalisis, the muscular contractions of the intestines cannot get a "hold" on the gases, and propulsion of the gases is therefore largely dependent upon being carried along with the mass of food and waste.

If persistalisis is high, the intestines may growl and make "stomach noises" but the only real problem will be the large amounts of gas that must be passed, but if movement of the intestines slows down or stops, the aches and cramps may stay for many hours. Then heat and hot water bottles will help, but repeatedly changing position seems to be the only way to restore movement. The principal blockage always seems to be in the colon. The colon is fed from the small intestine on the right side, rises, crosses over, descends on the left side and makes a turn over to the rectum. If you can move the gas through the colon, persistalisis can usually be restored.

Try a hot tub bath, bringing up the temperature as high as possible after you are in the tub. Then;-

1. Lie on the left side for about ten minutes, so that gas in the small intestine will tend to rise into the colon.

2. Sit up for a few minutes, to allow the gas to rise up the ascending colon.

3. Lie on the right side for about ten minutes to allow gas to move through the transverse colon into the descending colon.

4. Lie on left side to allow gas to rise from the descending colon to the anus. If you are lucky much of the gas and all of the pressure will be relieved.

5. If problems persist, lie on the back, pull your stomach in as far as possible, and massage the colon. If you try, you will be able to push the organs around enough that you can feel the hard distended colon. After massage, repeat 1 to 4.

6. If a hot bath is not available, the same sequence of positions can be used together with hot water bottles or other source of heat.

7. A vibrator pad or massage chair may be useful.

8. If the problem is not relieved, get down on your knees, and put your head on the floor so that the gas can rise through the descending colon to the anus.

9. Position seems to be very important in trying to "get hold" so that the stool and gas can be moved along. The following may be of help;-

A. Lie alternately on each side, knees bent as high as possible.

B. Squat above the toilet seat, or perhaps very low.

C. Sit on only one side of the toilet seat (alternately) and rock to and fro and sideways.

D. Stand, with one foot on a chair or stool, as high as possible, and bend and stretch back and forth.

10. Repeat any or all if necessary.

11. Misery usually has company. Do not think that you are alone. Intestinal and bowel gas were a continuous problem long before an 18th century bard sang the following:

> "Oh, I sat with the Duchess at tea,
> In her grand drawing room by the sea.
> Her rumblings abdominal,
> Were simply abominable,
> For everyone thought it was me!"

Coping with Dinners and Parties.

The kind hostess has made you a BIRTHDAY CAKE complete with lots of sweet icing and your name on top! A big surprise, -yes, yes, a beautiful big surprise! The kind hostess too, is a beautiful person, that, without problems herself (or perhaps without perceiving her problems) thinks that anyone should be able to eat anything, and particularly her beautiful baking. What to do ? Offend the hostess and spoil the party? Or should you eat the awful stuff, knowing all of the consequences? Better to just ask for a small piece of the cake, chew a nystatin tablet as discreetly as possible as you eat the cake, and then have a cup of tea, with a few acidophilus tablets, if possible. This is what will happen. The nystatin will be mixed with the sugar that is picked up by the yeast, thus killing the yeast, the acidophilus will compete with the yeast for the free sugars, and the caffeine in the tea will help the body to pull the sugar out of the intestines and into the bloodstream. You will probably survive the party, with very little gas or other effects. But do not try to do it every day. The following list will help you with parties and eating out.

1. Sugars. All sugars, and all free sugars and /or starches, as found in white bread, white rice, pasta, pastry, pies, jams, melons, dried fruits, fresh fruits, fruit juice (and carrot juice) milk, etc; can be offset with nystatin, ketoconazole, acidophilus, garlic, and chlorophyl. The amount of sugars feeding intestinal yeast can be reduced by drinking tea or coffee, which will increase the rate of absorption of the sugars from the intestines. However, the greatly increased blood sugar levels induced by the caffeine will feed the yeast infections wherever they may be, but the total amount reaching the infectives will be reduced.

2. Alcohol. Acohol, if you must have it,— can be somewhat offset with nystatin and very large amounts of vitamin C. The chewable tablets are handy.

3. <u>Salt.</u> Salt, as in soups, meat tenderizer, party nuts, popcorn, etc; can be offset with chelated potassium taken at the same time.

4. <u>Grease.</u> Grease, as in pork, chips, and other fried foods, can be handled better with lecithin.

Coping with Restaurants

The following will help if used in conjunction with coping with dinners.

1. Bring along nystatin tablets, bicarbonate tablets, potassium, vitamin C, lecithin, acidophilus, and digestives if needed.

2. Nystatin, taken just before the meal, will help to offset sugars.

3. "Whole wheat" bread is usually only 60% whole wheat.

4. Bran muffins are usually made with white flour.

5. Soups are always salty. Soups may contain pastas, or they may be thickened with white flour.

6. Gravies are always made with white flour and grease.

7. Pork and fried foods are always greasy, and should be avoided.

8. Always ask for baked potato to avoid otherwise inevitable chips.

9. Food allergies can be reduced by taking digestives with bi-carbonate $\frac{1}{2}$ to 1 hour before the meal and again $\frac{1}{2}$ to 1 hour after the meal.

If foods are selected with care eating out can still be fun!

CANDIDA YEAST INFECTION of the FEET.
(Feet, 1 medical paper, skin, 17 medical papers).
See chapter 4, "Candida Infection of the Feet." The entire passage should be re-read.

Candida infection of the feet (trench foot) is very common, with probably 80% or more of the population infected. Most people, and many doctors, consider the calluses to be "just a little athlete's foot", even when the infection is actually quite high.

Eradication of the Candida from the feet is always a long continuing program, based on ketoconazole to attack the infection systemically from the bloodstream, together with topical anti-infectives rotated every few days. The most effective topical agents seem to be :-

1.Hydrogen Peroxide, 3%. Stronger solutions must be used with care.

2. Miconazole lotion.

3. Resteclin Mixture. 1 tbsp. milk of magnesia with the contents of 1 resteclin capsule. Must be fresh. It will keep only a few days.

4. Phenolalkalizer, with DMSO or 5% aloe vera, if you wish.

5. Econazole.

6. Flagystatin.

7. Antifungal Oil. (Quantities are approximate and can be varied.)
   8 oz. (1 glass) Diesel oil. (Coal oil, stove oil),
   Contents of 5 capsules vitamin A.
   Contents of 5 capsules vitamin E.
   Contents of 5 capsules natural garlic oil, or equivalent.
   2 oz. tincture of iodine.
   I tbsp. MCT.oil.
   Shake well before using.
   Antifungal oil helps to soften the calluses and promotes healing. It should be used alternately to increase foot comfort.

Water and Footwear.

Candida yeast thrives in damp conditions, so keep the feet dry. Wear loose, low, airy shoes, leather only. Avoid waterproof leather and plastic shoes, and avoid plastic and synthetic soles. Shoes must be able to "breathe". Wear light synthetic socks to prevent sweating. Change socks daily.

The importance of keeping the feet dry and well ventilated cannot be over-emphasized because the infectives thrive on the water and nutrients in the sweat, and multiply at the greatest rate at about the usual foot temperatures. Perspiration from the sweat glands (eccrine glands) is part of the normal body control of the conservation of heat, water, and electrolytes. Sweat gland activity is stimulated by acetylcholine, and stress therefore affects the rate of perspiration. Although, the skin of the entire body is involved, the highest concentrations of eccrine sweat glands is on the palms of the hands and on the soles of the feet, where there are over 600 sweat glands per square centimeter. Sweat from these glands is therefore a continuing problem. The feet must therefore be cool and well ventilated to avoid feeding the Candida, and to avoid providing the infectives with the high amounts of moisture on which they thrive.

Removing Calluses.

Soak feet for about 10 minutes in hot water. Some "skin" should turn white, and will be quite loose. Scrape off all loose skin with an "almost sharp knife" but do not scrape too deep. do not draw blood. If an accident happens, (and it will) , apply miconazole lotion or hydrogen peroxide immediately to reduce the risk of disseminating the infection by the bloodstream. After scraping, apply hydrogen peroxide liberally to all calluses and surrounding areas.

If calluses are very heavy, prolonged soaking of feet, as with a long tub bath, may promote more growth than is removed, so if the calluses are thick and heavy, get in the tub, put the feet up, and then run the water, and only let the feet soak about the last ten minutes.

Repeat the foot scraping not oftener than three days, and preferably only once per week. Preferably daily, and/or if the feet hurt, wash the feet quickly with just a very little liquid detergent, dry immediately and apply hydrogen peroxide, then apply the other agents later. A good system seems to be to wash the feet and apply the hydrogen peroxide in the evening, then apply the other antifungals in the morning.

As the treatment is repeated, the osmoresistant (water resistant) layer made by the yeast will be broken down, and very large callused areas, frequently much larger than previously thought, will appear. The hydrogen peroxide will help to bleach the diseased skin, and soon the total infection, with large masses of dead infected skin will be seen.

Now remove only the very loose callused material. Do not be over ambitious or overaggressive. The yeast took many years to grow. It is firmly embedded and firmly established, so it may take a year or two to eradicate it. The yeast is fed from within the skin, and it cannot be eradicated from outside the skin with topical applications. The ketoconazole must start to reduce the total infection, and the immune system must start to improve, before the fluorescent red inflammation starts to subside. Use hydrogen peroxide liberally after scraping the feet. Supplements of selenium and methionine will help to detoxify the free radicals from the hydrogen peroxide, superoxide dismutase (SOD) breaks down to hydrogen peroxide. If SOD is being supplemented, use phenolalkalizer instead of hydrogen peroxide.

Very heavy callused areas can be "thinned down" by softening the thickened areas with hydrogen peroxide, then scraping, followed by more hydrogen peroxide. But again, be careful. The temptation is to overdo; the temptation is to cut out all of the cursed stuff; but if you cut too much you may find yourself very toxic, or you may find yourself walking around with very sore feet.

After a few months you will notice that the feet are becoming fluorescent pink all around the calluses. The pink shows up under the light from a light bulb, but it is not seen under fluorescent light. If you have icecream, cake, candy, or other goodies that raise blood sugar levels, note how much brighter the pink becomes. If you have niacin, note how much brighter the pink becomes. If you look at your feet after intercourse or high sexual arousal, note how much brighter the pink becomes. You are seeing the results of feeding the infection with high blood sugar levels. At times you may also be able to feel the changes as the yeast is advancing and attacking the nerve endings, with a "burning" sensation. So if your feet are "burning", just look at them under the electric light bulb. They will even look like they are on fire!

Now at last you can see the total volume of flesh, and the total area that is infected. You can see how the yeast is living on your body nutrients, and you can see how it is pumping lactic acid and toxins into your lymphatic system and into your bloodstream. You can see the total inflammation, and you can now appreciate the immense load on the immune system and the liver. Oh yes, if you had burns on your feet covering the same area and volume, you would expect to be bedfast and unable to walk. Still, the body must rebuild as much tissue with damage from yeast infection as it would with burns over the same area, so you must help the rebuilding with adequate protein, adequate nutrition, and adequate supplements.

Now it is a matter of persistence, patience, and time. Keep removing the loose dead skin; corns will come out, bunions will subside, big lumps will slowly disappear, and tiny toenails may become full size.

Toenails.

"Black toe,"where the entire toenail becomes black, is frequently a result from running or jogging. The big toenail on one or both feet may be affected. Candida yeast is almost always a major factor. "Black toe" is usually a male condition that is all too frequently associated with impotence and sexual failure. It is certainly a manifestation that the feet are sexual tissue, but the real cause is uncertain. Jogging and running certainly places a heavy strain on the cords and muscles from which the male organs are suspended, while the sudden jar from jogging on pavement may cause lymphatic failure. It has been held that the constant tugging on the sexual cords alters the blood flow, which results in impotence, yet wearing a jock strap does not seem to solve the problem. Some other doctors think that the sexual failure is really a manifestation of severe ill health, and that black toenail and impotence afflicts joggers because so many men take up jogging in a desperate effort to renew the health that they know has deteriorated. Jogging then, becomes an after event, that really had very little to do with either the black toenail or the loss of sexual capability. In any event,"black toe", where most of the toenail is blue or black, is certainly seen in men who do not run or jog.

"Blue Toe" is almost invariably associated with calluses and other manifestations of severe Candida infections. In all cases of black or blue toe, atherosclerosis should be suspected, and chelation therapy, with at least six intravenous infusions should be instituted. If atherosclerosis is severe and chelation therapy is not used immediately, amputation of the toe may be imperative. Thyroid should be checked, and all other measures should be taken to reduce the atherosclerosis. Phenolalkalizer and DMSO will help to check local infections.

Toenail Surgery.

Toenails, and particularly the large toenail, may become so heavily infected and encrusted with fungii that the doctor feels that the toenail must be removed. Usually blue and black toenails must also be removed after local infection has been reduced and blood circulation has improved. These operations are very common but they are usually only partly successful, and frequently have a high risk of disseminated Candida infection. If properly performed, a new toenail will grow, but the operation may have to be repeated every two or three years. If removal of the toenail is necessary it should be preceded by several chelation treatments, and ketoconazole should be started and raised to as high a level as possible. Topical anti-fungals should also be used, and the flesh around the toenail should be cleared of yeast debris several days before the operation. Elase- chloromycetin will help the nail to heal.

There are real perils to any cutting operations where Candida is involved. Damage to infected feet poses the same perils whether the damage comes from blisters, bruises, or the surgeons scalpel. If the skin is broken and Candida enters directly into the bloodstream it can become disseminated and may infect any of the organs or any part of the body. See Ch.3, list 5, "Filaments and Hyphae in the Blood", (12 medical papers). Note that it can infect the brain, eyes, immune system, and all glands and organs, and that it has a particular affinity for the heart and heart valves. Candida can reach these body parts only through the bloodstream. Indeed, Scientific American Medical Library, to their credit, does show that disseminated Candidiasis is frequently induced by unknowing physicians. The peril of disseminated Candida is therefore very real, but if extra quantities of vitamin C and other adrenal nutrients, together with as much ketoconazole as possible are taken prior to the operation; if broad spectrum disinfectants like phenol and hydrogen peroxide are used; and if care is taken to remove as much yeast infected tissue as possible; then surgical removal of the infected toenail can be accomplished with minimum risk. If elase- chloromycetin is then used to help the nail bed to heal, the operation will usually be successful.

Ingrown Nails.

Ingrown toenails can be extremely painful, and very difficult to cure. Cutting the toenails almost straight across will help to prevent ingrown nails. The ridges in both toenails and fingernails are caused by very small bits of Candida infection, under the nail, at the base of the nail. As the nail grows past the infection, the infection alters the metabolic processes that make the nail, resulting in the ridge. The greater the amount of infection, the higher that ridge becomes. If a large bit of infection develops, the ridge becomes very high, which causes the nail to be bent, with the edges turned in. The corners of the nail then irritate the flesh, promoting infection, and the resulting deterioration of the nail at the corners, produces the ingrown nail with its constant pain.

The ingrown nail should be trimmed back as far as possible, which will give it a V cut at the high ridge. Debris will be seen under the ridge and this should be removed if possible without damaging the flesh. Scraping the top of the nail to make it thinner at the ridge will make the nail more flexible, which will reduce the pressure on the corners. Topical agents, applied daily, with careful scraping every three or four days will help to reduce the pain, but an extra effort must be made to avoid damaging the flesh. Lifting the corners of the nail out of the flesh and applying hydrogen peroxide or phenol alkalizer will help. In extreme cases "outgrow" (from the drugstore) should be tried. With increased ascorbate, improved cellular nutrition, and a reduction in total infection, together with the topical antifungals, the nail will slowly return to normal.

CANDIDA YEAST INFECTION of the FINGERNAILS.

Candida infection of the nail bed is the usual cause of deformed fingernails. Depending upon the location and extent of the infection the ridges may be lengthwise or crosswise.

In severe fingernail infections the nails may become thickened, with heavy yeast deposits under the nail. These deposits make the nails very difficult to clean and keep clean, because the deposits seem to absorb dirt and stains. Heavy deposits also occur at the cuticle. These yeast infections will sometimes progress to the point that they can be seen as hairy growths, similar to mold.

Fingernail infections will of course be reduced, along with all of the other infections, by ketoconazole, improved immune function, and the general Anti-Candida program. Topical applications will help, but they become difficult. Frequent brushing of the nails with hydrogen peroxide, and the application of miconazole lotion, phenolalkalizer, DMSO, and/or garlic oil will help reduce the amount of infection. As with the feet, loose infected skin should be scraped off and the debris should be removed from under the fingernails. In severe cases, topical applications should be made at night, with gloves worn until morning.

Upturned Fingers.

In some people the last joint, or the last two joints in some of the fingers become turned upward. If one looks at the back of the hand while opening and closing the hand the tendons that control the top of the fingers can be seen lying under the skin. If these tendons, and/or the muscles that pull on them, become spasmed, fibrous, or calcified, the muscles and tendons will become shorter and the tips of the fingers may be pulled upward. The common causes of muscle spasm are adrenal depletion and build-up of lactic acid. Candida yeast is a common cause of both adrenal depletion and build-up of lactic acid throughout the body. Local Candida infection of the fingernails increases the lactic acid in the hands and wrists, which interferes with blood circulation and increases the already high levels of lactic acid, promoting the muscle spasm that is pulling up the tips of the fingers. Persistent neursage of the wrists, fingers, and lower arms will reduce the muscel spasm and calcinosis if adrenal function is raised and if ketoconazole is used to reduce the total Candida infection.

SEXUAL CANDIDA YEAST INFECTIONS.

Candida yeast is very common in nature; we cannot escape from it, and it is therefore endemic in the human species. It can always be found harmlessly lying on the surface of the mucous lining of the vagina and birth canal. Harmlessly, yes, until trauma and circumstance allow it to invade the tissues. Intercourse is the most common cause of trauma, and intercourse is also the most common mode of transfer of infection to the male. Quite obviously, during intercourse, the male can be infected by the Candida that was lying harmlessly on the vaginal mucosa, in which case the male was infected by a (technically) non infected female. The infected male penis then of course becomes a perfect tool for re-infection of the female, or for passing infection on to other females.

In short, Candida yeast is a very common venereal infection. It is also a conjugal infection, with the sexual partners constantly infecting and re-infecting each other. Sexual practices, being as varied as they are, then spread the infection to many other parts of the body, usually with serious consequences.

Candida yeast is almost always involved in vaginitis. Vaginitis is covered extensively in the medical literature, but penisitis (balanitis) is barely mentioned and very little is even said about treatment. Nonetheless, most males do have infections of the penis and urethra, but the sharp burning sensation frequently lasts less than half an hour, so the event is dismissed as being inconsequential.

The whole issue of human sexuality is constantly clouded by the reluctance of males to even mention actual sexual performance. They all pretend that they are the best "stud", while seldom admitting, even to themselves, that they are anything less. With such extreme reticence by most males, factual male capability is very difficult to assess. The reticence is probably also the reason for the scant medical information on penisitis. Most doctors are male, and they just cannot bring themselves to write about their own lack of sexual capability. The image of the male ego must be preserved at any cost.

The price of preserving the male ego is the price of preserving ignorance, and the price may indeed be very high. There is strong evidence that Candida yeast first infects the urethra in the tip of the penis, then creeps slowly backwards through the male sexual system, first infecting the prostate and causing the well known prostate problems, and then moving on into the testicles themselves, causing varicocelles, tender testicles, curdled ejaculate, and difficult or impossible ejaculation.

Significantly, most females develop severe vaginitis several times during their lifetime, which their immune system may, or may not overcome, while about 80% of all males develop serious prostate problems, and about 75% of all males develop tender tersticles and/or curdled ejaculate.

Perspective.

It should be recognized that sexuality and intercourse are, and always have been the principal driving force throughout all humanity. Many of the religions are actually centered around, or are highly concerned with sex and sexuality, with celibacy being the guardian of virtue in some religions, while in other religions the erect male penis is worshiped as their God. Circumcision, of either male and female, is of great importance in some religions.

Development of personal sexuality usually starts as soon as the new baby discovers their genitals, and continues on, frequently highly visible, through kindergarden and Grade 1. Most people have indeed seen the poor distraut little girl, sucking the thumb on one hand, while holding her genitals with the other. All kindergarden and grade 1 teachers are all too familiar with the "dumb" boy in the class, who almost continuously sucks his thumb on one hand and plays with his genitals with the other. After about grade 1, most children are persuaded to take their sexuality from public view, after which the sexual stimulation becomes privately concealed until a sexual partner is found, which seems to be perhaps as early as grade 1.

It is not the purpose of this book to moralize or to say what is right or wrong. We seek only to present the fact that sex and sexuality does start at a very early age, frequently so early that it is impossible for the young person to know what is happening and to cope with all of the forces.

311

Commonly it is thought that girls reach puberty at about age 13, and boys at about age 15. This is true, but there is a great variation. Some girls may not sexually mature until age 16, and some boys not until 17, while other girls may start menstruating as early as age 9 (grade 3) and some boys may become sexually active as early as age 11 (grade 5). Quite obviously the young people who have reached puberty will be unable to understand the older children who have not yet reached puberty, and "vice versa".

Now let us look at the actual source of sexual drive. In all mammalian males, including humans, sexual drive is normally present at all times after sexual maturity and awaits only opportunity, whether the opportunity is initiated by the male, the female , or both.

In all female mammals except the hominoids, sexual desire (and probably sexual capability) is determined by estrus, the period of ovulation during the reproductive cycle. In humans and other hominoids, female sexuality is determined by histamine levels, with sexual desire and sexual capability continuous, except for a few hours during menstruation. This is the major difference that sets humans and other hominoids apart from all other mammals, and the high continuous sexual levels are also thought to be the underlying reason for the high intelligence levels of humans. The high sexuality of the hominoids is also the reason that baboons are missing from a large number of public zoos. Baboons, (like their human counterparts) are so continuously sexually active that their uninhibited sexual displays, sometimes with a frequency of less than an hour, frequently arouse public outcry, even in a very sexually liberated world.

It is therefore histamine levels (See "Mental and Elemental Nutrients") in both male and female humans that controls sexual response. Histamine levels are related to the basophil cell count, (see Blood Tests) and the basophil count for normally healthy adults should be about 0.8%.We have to say "about" because histamine levels in the female are normally highest just before puberty, reducing after puberty, and reducing further with the birth of each child.These naturally high, then declining, female sexual levels have some very extreme consequences that are seldom realized.

Female Sexuality and the Female Sexuality Test.

This section contains a simple test for female sexual levels. Males should also record their answers. Before reading further get a pencil and a scrap of paper ready for the test. Please do not just read on. Get the pencil and paper now.

Female sexual levels are determined by histamine levels. Some young females may have such high histamine levels prior to puberty that they may experience orgasm riding a bicycle or climbing a tree. This means that some young girls, perhaps only nine years old (grade 3), may experience orgasm while at play. With probably only vague sexual knowledge, the experience would be very confusing, but if the girl was riding on the bicycle with a boy that she liked, however innocently, the effects would be profound, and if perchance the event was not quite so innocent, the effects could be dramatic. Yet whatever the reaction, it would be highly unlikely that the event woulds be discussed with the little girl's mother. Sexual orgasm is very private, and sexual orgasm, however and whenever, is seldom discussed with the parent, while, in this case, the child is trying to cope with events, desires, and feelings far beyond their control. Oh yes, many women will not believe this. "A child of nine, and a child of mine?" "Nonsense". "Nonsense" only because each person instinctively judges and compares the sexuality of others by their qwn sexual levels. If the mother's puberty was late, and if her histamine levels were low, she could not possibly start to understand her little daughter's problems and her little daughter's plight, even if her little daughter tried to tell her.

The natural variation in female sexual levels is very wide, and has several causes. Remember how Adelle Davis describes some intestinal infectives that will change the amino acid histidine into the neurotransmitter histimine? We know that this can create allergies, and it can also raise sexual levels without necessarily causing allergies. We also know that Candida infection can greatly reduce sexual levels. The total variation is therefore very high, with further fluctuations imposed by the menstrual cycle. The wide variation also has many social implications, which are complicated by everyone, male or female, judging others by their own momentary sexual levels.

The great variation in sexual levels, and their implications, is illustrated by the following true incident,---

Here, dear reader, we must pause, apologize, and reflect. We have been pointing out that low histamine people cannot understand people with high sexual levels and high sexual requirements, because sexual forces and sexual behavior normally is assessed according to the sexual levels of the viewer, instead of being assessed by the sexual levels of the viewed. Despite this (hopefully) clear message, when the manuscript for this book was first completed and copies made available to a number of people, so many females found the incident described so very distasteful and it made them so angry, that the incident, although true, and true to life, must be omitted. We do not want to offend. The deleted page is available from the Healthology Association.

It should be noted, that the people who objected so strongly were all ill people. Ill people usually have low histamine levels and low sexual levels, and because they themselves have never experienced high sexual compulsion they are totally unable to understand the actions of other people who are well and are under extreme sexual pressures.

The true incident that was described showed too, that sexual morals are also altered by the actual histamine and sexual levels of the viewer, and it was the "immoral" aspects of the incident that so greatly offended the readers. Now of course, we are in fact mammals. For other female mammals like a cow or a mare, or a female dog in heat, to seek the attention of as many males as possible is not considered immoral. It is considered to be natural and understandable and the altered wild behavior is also considered to be natural and understandable, while similar behavior in the female of the genus homo sapiens may be labelled immoral. From this it may seem that we are attempting to loosen morality, which we are not. Mankind can and should exercise reasonable control over sexual activity. Each person therefore must develop their own ethics, so we seek to provide insight into the problem of morality by showing that morals too are linked to the basic sexual levels of the viewer.

Now let us consider the plight of the nurse, in her thirties, who became so ill with intestinal and vaginal Candida infection that she had to quit work. Her basophil cell count was below .2%. During the interview she said, "I used to do the awfulest things. Sometimes I would have two or three men in a single day. Now I don't care if I ever see a man." Note, how she judges her past actions by her present sexual levels. Then, with the intestinal and vaginal infection reduced she was soon back at work and her basophil cell climbed to 2.4% and with these very high histamine and sexual levels she can again see nothing wrong or immoral about having two or three men each day.

Such high sexual pressures (with sometimes astonishing capabilities) are not confined to the female. Virilent young men are frequently admired as desirable sexual objects. Usually it is not considered particularly immoral for men to seek sexual gratification whenever and wherever they can find it, and very frequently the high histamine male devotes much of his life trying to satisfy his desires. To illustrate:-   A young woman in her thirties came to Canada from Switzerland. She had had a very virile male friend in Switzerland with whom she had intercourse two or three times a day for several years. He did not live with her, but she was in love, until she happened to discover that her virile male companion was also having sexy affairs with several other women.

Immorality (whatever it may be) is of course, also tempered by the sex of the viewer. Males judge male promiscuity and infidelity much more harshly than females, while females judge female promiscuity and infidelity much more harshly than males.

Promiscous sexy matters are of course almost incomprehensible to people with low histamine levels, so note your reactions to the foregoing true accounts, and compare your reaction to the reactions of others. You just cannot believe that anyone could have a different reaction. Your viewpoint is locked into your own sexual levels as they are today, at this moment. If you look back, you may wonder just why you did some of the things that you did in the past, things that quite probably you would do much differently today. Today you may call them foolish or naive, without realizing that if your histamine levels were still the same as they used to be, then the things you did would seem normal and would not be foolish or naive.

Normal Sexual Levels.(Histamine Levels).

Although histamine levels are directly related to basophil cell count, to attain accuracy the basophil cells must be counted as soon as the blood is drawn, or the procedure outlined in Ref.35 must be used. Alternately, histamine levels can be medically measured, (Ref.5) in nanograms/ml. Male, normal, 46.3 high schizophrenic 127.2, low schizophenic 9.8. Female, normal 41.7, high schizophrenic 131.7, low schizophrenic, 15.5. Note the relation between sexual levels and schizophrenia, which shows the continuing affects of sex hormones on all mental processes, including psychosis, neurosis and depression. In the limited experience of the author it appears that extremely high histamine levels may result from bacterial infections that feed on proteins and thus change histidine to histamine (just as Adelle Davis said) while Candida infection invariably reduces histamine levels and basophil cell count. The question should then be asked is schizophrenia actually caused by an infection?

Determination of Sex.

Sex in humans is determined soon after conception. At conception, the egg and the sperm have the capability to become either male or female, but the hormonal environment will swing the sex to either male or female. This results in normal females having two X chromasomes (XX), one from each parent. The female is therefore a mosiac; a combination of the two parents. The normal male however, will have a chromasome pattern (xy), with either the father or mother dominant. The cellular structure of the male is therefore homogenous, following closely one parent or the other. The chromasome pattern, of XX or XY then influences the production of sex hormones, with XX inducing the production of estrogen and XY inducing the production of testosterone.

In birds, the basic creature is male, with the female being a hormonal conversion from the basic male. Those people who are acquainted with chickens will know that very frequently a hen will stop laying, start to develop spurs and a high comb, and will even attempt to crow like a rooster. These hens have lost their ability to produce female sex hormones, and they are partially reverting back to the basic creature, which is male.

In mammals, and therefore in humans, the sexual conversion is opposite. In all mammals, including the genus Homo, the basic creature is female, and the male is a hormonal conversion of the basic female. In females the female hormone estrogen makes the basic female more feminine, and loss of estrogen therefore reduces the femininity, but the female can never regress into being less than the basic female.

Male Sexuality.

In males the male hormone testosterone converts the basic female to male. Any loss of testosterone production, for any reason, reduces the masculinity which further reduces the production of testosterone. Then any further loss of testosterone pushes the male to the point where they are less than male, and they start to revert back to the basic female, usually with severe physical and psychological consequences. These effects are frequently seen in the "Onery old man", who, although in earlier years was always a "wonderful person", yet now fights with everyone about anything and displays violent fits of temper, all in a high pitched voice that is itself certain testimony to female reversion.

The prime cause of a great many marital and family problems lies right here in male to female reversion. All males at times experience sexual inadequacy, a simple fact that is seldom fully forgiven by an aroused female. Anything that affects the health, from diet and alcohol to indigestion or overwork reduces testosterone production, with loss of masculinity, poor erection, and a vague uneasy feeling that "something is wrong";-- which it is. The male is therefore fighting a constant battle to maintain hormone production; a battle that all too frequently, is slowly lost.

As soon as testosterone levels start to fall, the unfortunate male usually senses it and seeks to restore hormone production with increased sexual activity. The real problem may be tobacco, or coffee, or sugar, or alcohol, or anything else that is reducing the level of health and the level of sexual capability, but the lower that the sexual levels fall the greater will be the interest in sexual activity. This is a natural reaction, for under conditions of good health and good nutrition, increased sexual activity will increase sex hormone levels. The dilemma of greatly increased sexual complusion with reduced capability is frequently exaggerated by high histamine levels that increase both desire and compulsion, despite the failing performance. The many problems are then increased even further by the mental effects from toxins and altered hormones produced by badly delayed or frustrated ejaculation. Then as sexual levels fall even lower, and ejaculation becomes extremely difficult, the unfortunate male, plagued by a certain feeling of impending doom, may become a pervert and resort to any act that has any remote possibility of achieving the almost impossible. Yet having found some way to finally accomplish ejaculation, it is only a few hours, or at most a few days, before there is another inescapable compulsion for the entire scene, however bizarre, to be repeated. The male plight is desperate. Life becomes a constant fight to preserve life, in the face of diminishing sanity. A desperate fight, that is continuously centered on sexual activity of any kind, in the vain hope that something can bring relief.

Some males cope with the faltering sexual capabilities as best they can, with masturbation, memory, fantasy, girlie magazines, pornography, vibrators, and other measures usually known only to them. They may linger and survive for years, in a gray gloomy world, suspended between male and female, then when sexual capabilities cease, the health declines rapidly and then comes the miserable ornery old bag of bones, the old man with the squeaky voice that is constantly complaining--- dissatisfied with everything and quarrelling with everyone. Then as health fails further, the transition back to the basic female is almost complete. The mind fails and memory slips away, the fight is gone, and all that is left is an expressionless zombie, a pasty- faced shuffling skeleton, draped with the skin of an eunuch, waiting for the grim reaper.

Perhaps, there beside him is his wife. Her femininity too, has slipped away, the vigor has vanished, and only the bones and skin remain. A compatible couple, yes, for the dead faces never smile or frown, or express emotion, and they seldom even speak, while the striking thing is that except for clothes and hairstyle it is difficult to tell male from female.

You have seen these people many times, and perhaps you have wondered at the cause. The basic cause of course is ill health -- ill health that frequently has been hastened by junk food, self administered poisons, late nights, and usually Candida infection and degenerative disease. All of us are somewhere along the road down. For some the road down starts very early, as can be seen among the young homosexuals and lesbians, while others, by luck or by pluck, defer their loss of sexuality for over a hundred years. Fortunately, most females escape severe loss of femininity, but many males do suffer severe loss of masculinity, so much so that someone was led into inventing the male menopause.

The Male Menopause.

Science, to be real science, must always be meticulously executed. Many "studies" made in the name of science are less than scientific and are therefore less than useful. There are a number of such "studies" (?) that have concluded that 60% to 80% of all males suffer loss of testicular function at about age 60, which prompted the idea of the male climacteric. But these less than scientific "studies" failed to assess the health or the Candida status of the subjects studied. If the average doctor is asked about curdled, thick ejaculate he will usually say that it is very common, do not worry about it, 60% or 80% of the older men have the condition. Yes, and 60% to 80% of the older men also develop prostate problems, so quite probably it is the same 60% to 80% of the older men that have all three conditions;-- the enlarged prostate, the thickened ejaculate, and the decline in testicular function, all of which are indicative of sexual Candida infection.

The male position should probably be expressed in a different way. Because Candida is so omnipresent, most females develop a vaginal Candida infection at some time during their lives. With sexual activity being what it is, most males therefore contract a Candida infection of the penis. In about 20% of the males the Candida infection is subdued and it does not materially affect their lives, but in about 60% to 80% of the males the infection advances and creates problems in the prostate and testicles, which finally leads to complete sexual failure. In short, Candida infection in the male probably results in sexual failure in about 60% to 80% of the older males, which has been interpreted as being the male climacteric. Starvation, malnutrition, and other health problems can also cause, or contribute to sexual failure, and this could reinforce the idea of a male climacteric. Statistically however, all females past age 65 years have ceased to ovulate. The female climacteric is therfore fact. Some males however, remain fertile to age 100 or more, with the oldest known father being 108 years old. The male climacteric is therefore fiction.

Conjugal Bliss.

Most people find weddings to be wonderful events. The beautiful bride and the handsome groom, flushed with excitement, embarking upon a new life together. Usually the sexual union has already occurred, everything is wonderful, everything is beautiful, and these two honest dedicated young people cannot foresee any problems. The vows are made, the vows are sacred, and the vows should be kept. Conjugal bliss, yes, with each finding satisfaction in the other. A beautiful continuation of a wonderful romance.

Indeed the beautiful romance may continue and last for years. Still, with the coming of children, with the many changes in family fortunes and finances, and with the inevitable little problems imposed by parents, in-laws, fools and friends, strains are put on the marriage, yet love and common sense prevail, and the conjugal bliss survives.

The conjugal bliss survives, yes, but it does not survive unchanged. Time, coffee, late nights, and perhaps alcohol or drugs, together with the effects of the first child, have reduced health levels, and little conflicts, particularly over children and relatives, have increased the stress. Whereas at marriage many of these little conflicts were resolved with intercourse at least once every night, the frequency of intercourse may now have dropped to once or twice a week. Still, all is well.

All is well, yes, but not quite the same as it was. Then, after another child or two some of the conjugal bliss may remain, but it has somehow become warped and strained. Reduced vigor, together with the birth of each child, has reduced the sexual levels of the female, frequency of intercourse has reduced to perhaps once a week, and even then it may at times have lost its joy and become a chore, while the male, confused by the slowly changing sexual pattern, must console himself with considerate excuses. She is probably"just too tired".

Solace himself? Of course! Love can conquer all! Yet how can love conquer all when the reduced sexuality of the female has deprived the male of the sexual activity so necessary to maintain both his sexual levels and his health, and peace. This was not the promise of marriage. The unwritten and unspoken promise of marriage was conjugal bliss;-- the promise of con-tinuing sexual availability and desire.

At the time of the marriage, and perhaps before the marriage, intercourse was probably at all times a first priority, but now everything else comes first, and strife over time and frequency will usually only increase the problem. The number one promise and the number one priority at marriage may now have become a number one bone of contention between the two partners.

Frequently, the reduced sexual release, together with the inevitable disappointment and dissatisfaction, will make the male irritable and restless. He will have a constant urge to be on the move. He may have an inner feeling that the marriage has become a fraud; an immense gyp. He can feel his manhood slipping away so he may seek sexual relief elsewhere, or he may plunge himself into some all consuming work; into some all consuming folly; or perhaps into all consuming alcohol.

But love and consideration do conquer many obstacles. If the early conjugal bliss was well founded and if the strains are not too great, the marriage usually survives. But with increasing age, work, alcohol, or loss of health, the male may lose sexual capability and become impotent. He may be able to maintain some sense of sanity through masturbation, but erection and intercourse may be impossible. Now the conjugal bliss has become complete conjugal frustration. Although the female sexual levels have dropped, they are still there, and they are still demanding satisfaction. There may even be moments of extreme desire, all now without possibility or hope of relief, or, if an attempt at intercourse is made, with the almost certain result of frustrated orgasm for both.

Interrupted coitus in the young has extreme physical effects, with perhaps flushing, nausea, weakness, or disorientation as the body resorbs, reprocesses and detoxifies the hormonal fluids, but frustrated orgasm when health and sexual levels are low grossly affects the liver and adrenals, while the resorbed hormones, toxins and metabolites affect the mind, producing neurosis, psychosis, crying, anger, and perhaps violence, with a tendency to criticise and lay blame anywhere and everywhere. The complete dissatisfaction with everything and anything may last for days; nothing is right, everything is wrong, and it is all everyone elses fault!

Oh Yes! Conjugal bliss! All of those wonderful hopes! All of those wonderful promises. All of the loyalty, all of the consideration. All of the sacrifice, and now this! Conjugal bliss? It is not even conjugal peace. It is conjugal Hell!

Yet in those many long hours of soul searching that honest people spend when confronted with an impossible conjugal problem, the answers are never easy. A compromise must be reached, so the answers are as varied as the sexual capabilities of the couples involved, but all too frequently the answers can be seen as twin beds, separate rooms, separate lives under the same roof, or even complete separation.

The sexual separation, slowly forced by declining normal sexual levels in both parties, has finally separated the couple, not for lack of dedication, not by lack of effort, but by lack of understanding. The male cannot understand the lack of desire and availabiity in his sexual mate, and the female cannot understand the desperate plight of her sexual mate. She cannot understand his constant desire when he has such frustrating incapability. The conjugal promises have failed, and all of the wonderful memories have turned to tears and bitterness. A rueful tragedy, yet a tragedy that affects, in greater or lesser degree, almost every couple. A tragedy that almost invariably has a component of Candida infection, because Candida infection reduces sexuality in the female, and drastically reduces sexual function in the male.

In the male, Candida infection of the urethra and prostate reduces the size of the passages, while Candida infection of the testicles curdles the ejaculate, making it thick and heavy. The total infection also reduces adrenal and pituitary function. The combination can make ejaculation so difficult that it becomes impossible with normal intercourse, and it can be brought on only by high stimulation from masturbation, vibrators or other extreme measures.

In the female the results of orgasm are not as readily visible as they are in the male, and even in our high- tech society the exact physical process still is not known. However, it is well known that following self stimulated orgasm the vaginal cavity is filled with copious amounts of fluid. It must therefore be assumed that orgasm in the female is very similar to ejaculation in the male. Under sexual stimulation glands (somewhere) fill with fluids, with orgasm being the spontaneous spasmodic release of the fluids from the overfilled glands.

Now we know that Candida infection and the Candida callus matrix are the usual cause of blockage of the fallopian tubes, so it seems reasonable to suppose that vaginal candidiasis would frequently result in partial blockage of the orgasmic passages. in the female, and perhaps some alteration of the ejected fluids. We must conclude then, that vaginal Candida infection is probably a very common cause of difficult orgasm, or perhaps complete frigidity, in the female. This assumption is well supported by improved sexual function in many females following the use of oral ketoconazole and miconazole suppositories.

The total effects of time on health and sexual capability cannot be denied. We cannot turn back the clock, but we can turn back Candida infection, and we can improve health and sexual function. Then, with a little more attention and a lot of understanding we can restore some of the conjugal pleasures and promises that may have been slipping away.

Sexual Deviation.

Sexual deviation is particularly difficult to define because in some societies, and in some of almost every society, anything and everything is considered normal.

Sexual experimentation in the young, at almost any age, is very common. All too frequently such experimentation takes the forms alluded to in dirty jokes, overheard and passed around among the young. Occasionally homosexual practices may develop between two younger males, and quite commonly a lesbian relationship may develop between two adolescent females, but these deviations usually disappear with the seeking and finding of a heterosexual mate.

Some young females of course, are led into prostitution, where anything can happen and usually does, and some young males are also led into homosexual prostitution, where even more of anything can happen and usually does.

Many books have now been written on sexual function and sexual practices, but all of these books seem to take the attitude that everyone is healthy and free from such things as Candida infection and that everyone therefore has normal sexual function with sexual practices a matter of preference. Indeed, some sexual deviation is learned by otherwise normal people, but the basic hard core of sexual deviation comes from ill people who are not sexually normal and their sexual deviation is forced upon them by impending sexual failure, or by physical defects that demand sexual relief by abnormal means.

We should remember that people in different societies and people from different ethnic backgrounds have different mores. In some societies it is considered to be the father's duty to train his daughters to be good sexual mates, and it is the duty of the mother to train the sons. We think of this as sexual deviation, name it incest, and make it highly illegal. While at the same time we honor and marvel at the great civilization of ancient Egypt where the King's family could not marry outside the family. All of the Pharaohs were therefore inbred, with sexual activity confined to sons and daughters, brothers, sisters, cousins and other relatives.

We should also remember that sexual activity is the most all consuming universal sport and pastime in the world, and that many heterosexual couples do engage in a great variety of experiments in erotica, some of which between other people, would certainly be deviant.

The high interest in obtaining sexual relief at any cost and by any means is older than history. The women in the harems of the past, (or are they still with us?), deprived of all contact with males except for the occasional attentions of the "King", devised an immense array of sexual devices. But these sexual devices were being used by normally sexually active women as a substitute for males that they could not have, so can we really call this sexual deviation? Yet when these same devices are used by females that could have a heterosexual mate we must consider their use as sexual deviation. Animals too, were pressed into service by the deprived females in the harems. Male animals are always sexually active and usually sexually willing.

Small dogs were frequently used because they were so easily trained. The sexual use of small dogs was still quite common in North America even in the 30's and probably still persists in some areas.

Most certainly the training and use of small dogs for female sexual relief is sexual deviation. To people with normal sexual function it certainly seems to be kinky, but dear reader, you can be assured that there are other readers who will say,"Oh my Gosh!,I will have to try that". These are the desperate females that have the dilemma of high sexual desire, with low sexual ability. To clarify:-

In humans, both male and female, the sexual neurotransmitter is histamine. Histamine levels in general, determine sexual desire, and histamine alerts the sexual tissues. But orgasm is the spasmodic discharge of fluids from overfilled glands. If the passages from the glands are partly blocked by Candida overgrowth, desire may be extremely high, but orgasm may be almost impossible. Thus if histamine levels are low, desire is low, and the female is frigid even to the most arduous and experienced male. She is frigid. She can hardly get any response even by herself, and there is no need for response because sexual desire is absent. But if histamine levels are high and sexual capability is low, the plight of the female is almost as desperate as the plight of the impotent male. With unresolved sexual arousal, the mind feels like it will explode if something, anything, is not done. Relief, someway, somehow must be found and indeed, if relief is not found the neurological, psychological and physical effects from repeated episodes can be devastating. This is the desperate plight that leads people to sexual deviation. This is the plight that forces people to do anything at any cost. Orgasmic relief now becomes an overiding constant obsession, supplanting all else.

The plight of the impotent male on the verge of sexual failure is worse. With the sex hormone levels falling and with sexual capability diminishing, desire is increasing and so is a feeling of impending doom, if sexual relief is not accomplished, someway, somehow. Thus the driving force to sexual deviation is the compulsion from impending sexual failure, and with the male as with the female, sexual relief now becomes an overiding constant primary obsession, supplanting all else.

Is it little wonder then, that some females may be driven into using carrots, sausages, dogs, and vibrators, or oral sex with other females, or anything else, in a desperate attempt to try to accomplish the almost impossible?

Is it any wonder then, that some desperate males are driven into trying to use goats, or pigs, or other animals, or into anal or oral sex with other males or females, or anything else, that might possibly help to accomplish the almost impossible?

These people, these unfortunate desperate people, are certainly more to be pitied than censored. Yet somehow it seems that some of the readers can be heard saying "Nonesense. All they have to do is forget about it". Yes! Forget about it! But how? If the reader with such a reaction looks at their own basophil cell count they will probably find that it is below 0.1%, or perhaps totally non existent. They cannot understand the plight of someone with physical sexual failure and a basophil cell count of .3%, and they will continue to be unable to understand the plight of others until their own basophil cell count rises to at least .3%. Forget it? How do you forget it?

Yes, forget it! Forget those sexual urges. Do not eye anyone of the opposite sex, or of the same sex, to see if perchance someway somehow they might play a part in a solution to the problem. Just forget it! It does not bother you. It cannot bother you, although it is constantly on your mind. Forget it! Put it out of your mind, and when you put it out of your mind, it is gone, yet somehow that nagging thought pops right back.

Forget it! Yes, forget it! After all there is so much more to life than just desperate sex. So forget it. Forget it during the day perhaps, but at night, how do you get to sleep? The sexual urge is nagging and demanding, while the capability is lacking. Then completely worn out, if sleep does come, it is only a few hours until awakening with extreme sexual compulsion, complusion that demands an attempt at relief. With each day, and each night the complusion becomes worse, the mental effects stronger, the mental abberations and misperceptions greater, the imaginings more bizzare. With the failing health, and with consequent increased infectives, the resorbed toxins and metabolites further sway the mind and alter other body processes with further altered chemistry. In search for sexual answers, and perhaps to reduce the mental torture, tobacco, caffeine, sugar, alcohol and drugs, if not already a problem, may be added, each increasing and altering the mental chemistry in their own way, and all contributing to adrenal depletion and episodes of low and high blood sugar. The low blood sugar warps the mind through lack of nutrients, while the high blood sugar produces moments of extreme energy, extreme hyperactivity, and another complete set of misperceptions, imaginings, and other mental effects. With the altered health, Candida infection invariably advances, and the altered metabolism may induce the retention of lead, copper, mercury, cadmium, arsenic, aluminum or selenium, any or all of which will exert other influences on the already warped and possibly deranged mind.

The resulting illness may be named Schizophrenia, or maniac depressive, or alcoholism, or drug abuse, or something, and the victim will be censored as unfit for society. Indeed these desperate people may be unfit for society, but it is clearly not entirely their fault.They are the victims of the failure of society to use the science and technology that it already has. They are the hapless victims of a society that gives lip service to great and noble thoughts, but a society that does little to help where help is needed most. These are in fact the people who have been abandoned by society, for they have nowhere to turn.

We do not know if any, or how many cases of rape may be related to the effects of sexual failure. We do not know how many children may be molested because some mad male imagines that "the little girl will enjoy it". We do not know if the extreme violence that culminates in sexual murder also somehow culminates in simultaneous ejaculation for the murderer. If so, is this not a logical explanation for tragic illogical acts, acts that may be repeated fifteen or twenty times? The point is that we should know, and we do not. We know only that sexual murders do occur, and we know that the male on the brink of sexual failure is under extreme strange complusions. If we are to brag about our great technical society we should at least be trying to find out. We should at least be doing a mineral test, and a blood test, and a Candida test, and a lot of other tests, to find the cause of such bizarre irrational acts. Sexual murder is all too common. It is highly probable that it is linked to sexual failure, male sexual failure, because females are exempt.

Then of course there are the peeping toms. Why do toms want to peep? Why do they wait for hours, just to see a female undress for bed? Can it be that the excitement from the illicit sight of the naked female arouses them just a little more and they can then finally reach orgasm? Is the peeping tom really another male regressing back to the basic female?

There are of course, many more male sexual aberrations. Are these too, linked to sexual failure? There is a great possibility and probability that sexual failure does play a role, just as it is highly probable that sexual failure plays a role in hard core pornography. Virile males may well appreciate a display of the body beautiful of naked young women, either real or in pictures. But to most virile males pictures of sexual vaginal arousal, (usually complete with the masturbating fingers) are both unnecessary and degrading. Such pictures then must be for the sexual titillation of males that are less than virile. Indeed, the use of such pictures is advised by most sexual therapy clinics, to provide extra arousal and thus bring results from masturbation.

With the high interest in girlie magazines, the high interest in "strip joints", the high interest in pornography, and the highly aberrant interest in "animal" pornography it is almost certain that all of these things are manifestations of widespread male sexual failure, (in various stages) toward female reversion. If sexual failure is not the reason for all of these things, why do they exist?

Why does hard core violent pornography exsist? Why are pictures of violent sex so interesting? To whom do they appeal? Does violence some how raise sexual levels and sexual capability? Does the thought of conquest, real or fancied, add impetus to the male sexual drive? Certainly it does. It has been proven by every war. In all societies the conquering army has always raped the women of the conquered. It is called the "lust of conquest" and the increased sexual compulsion is so great that many normal males who participated in the rape of the vanquished, with tender wives and famlies at home,"do not understand why they did it."

Undoubtedly the "lust of conquest" is aroused by violent hard porn, and just as undoubtedly the main interest in hard porn comes from males with faltering sexual prowess. Unquestionably then, the whole pornographic scene, from the "dirty old man" to the girlie magazines, to the strip tease, to the flesh market itself is largely supported by males in various stages of faltering sexual capability.

The pornographic material, so avidly purchased and viewed by many males, is also filled with children, young children, and particularly young girls. What can be so very sexually interesting about young girls, very young girls? Do they have some special appeal?

Let us be frank. Sexual ciriosty and sexual interest start at a very early age, and the natural observations of very young boys are usually frustrated by clothes, particularly if the home is Baptist and supposed to be almost sexless. By the time this boy was six, and in grade 1, he still was not sure just what the female genitals looked like, because he had never seen them. The curiosity kept building, until finally he paid one of the other boys ten cents, so that he could see his friends little sister, who was about three. There was nothing to see. There was not even one cents worth to see. So why all of the fuss about clothes and closed doors? About a year later, however, while pasturing the cow near a neighbor's house, a young girl about six years, came over and asked him if he would like to come play with her for awhile. He left the cow contentedly grazing, and soon the two children were happily "playing house" in one corner

326.

of the granary. Then suddenly the little girl, just starting school, said "I know! You be the daddy and I'll be the mummy, and you can play with me like daddy plays with mummy." Where upon she quickly pulled off her panties, pulled up her dress, and threw herself back on the edge of the cot, legs spraddled, ready for "daddy" to play with her. Completely unprepared, and completely surprised, a million emotions assailed the young boy. How things had changed! Now there was really something to see! It was confusing. It was tempting. It was beautiful. It was scary. It was scary because the little girl knew just what she wanted him to do, but he did not know just what to do. He wanted to stay, and he wanted to run. His head whirled. He could not assess his strange emotions, so he left and went back to the cow. Back to the cow, yes, but back to the cow with many mixed haunting emotions, emotions that would become memories, memories that have remained for over sixty years and still produce an immediate strong sexual arousal whenever they are recalled.

Now the average virile male, at any age, does not think of young girls as sexual objects. They may be thought of as beautiful, but not as sexual objects, and that same virile male is ready to defend the young girls against any who do. But does the very young innocent female have a special attraction for males with impending sexual failure? Does the male sense the rapidly increasing histamine and sexual levels, or does the helplessness of the child trigger the "lust of conquest" and predator response. Again we do not know, but we do know that there are a very large number of tragedies involving sexually abused young girls and it is highly likely that the real cause of the tragedies is impending sexual failure in the predator.

The point is that the problem of male sex aberrations is very real, it is ever present, and it will not go away without great effort. It is the cause of untold suffering and misery, and untold misfortune. Some desperate men will pay almost anything, or will do almost anything for any opportunity for possible sexual relief. The "flesh trade" is present in almost every country. White slavery, with all of its degrading variations, is still with us. In a current report in "India Today" a girl of thirteen was kidnapped and sold into Bombay's "flesh market". In eight months she was sold to three different brothels and was forced to cater to the "perverted demands" of up to 2,000 men. She finally became so diseased that she was hospitalized and thus escaped her captors. The incident led to the arrest of 28 people. Yet the "flesh markets" continue. (report from Awake). Wherever you go in the world there are similar reports of male perversion, and wherever you go you find it, to some extent, even in the homes, even in the schools, even in the church, and even in the prison. Significantly, sexual deviation becomes much more common among poor populations where nutrition is poor, health is low, and sexual performance is low.

Although male sexual deviation is very common, it is seldom accepted. To a great many people these men are beasts, yet they are worse than beasts because beasts do not do these things. But are these men "beasts", or are they you or I, in different clothes and different circumstance? A criminal is a criminal, and a sex deviate is a sex deviate. We cannot condone their actions, nor can we be seen to condone their actions, but all sexual deviates are more to be pitied and helped, than censored. Each who censors would be better to say,"there, but by the grace of God and good fortune, go I." Then they would do well to add "and I hope that my good fortune continues", because all of us, and particularly all males, are at all times subject to the same plight, while all too frequently we are unknowingly already on the way to the brink of disaster.

Certainly these people with extreme sexual problems are more to be pitied, (and helped) than censored, yet in a way, censor them we must, because in their sexual plight, with all of their mental aberrations, imaginations, and wanderings, they are constantly seeking sexual relief somehow, and therefore they seek and find weak people with normal sexual function to whom they introduce homosexual practices, and these weak people, following the path of least resistance, then frequently also become homosexuals, but without an underlying need. These weak people may then introduce homosexual practices to other ill or weak people, and soon the homosexuality spreads and becomes a cult, largely composed of basically normal people. But if they were normal when they joined the cult, they will not remain normal for long. Homosexuals are constantly changing partners in an attempt to attain fuller satisfaction or to increase erotic response, and disease in any one soon spreads to disease in all. Severe Candida infection of the mouth, anus, genitals and fingernails is very common, and is soon joined by herpes, gonorrhea, etc; right down to AIDS. The reduced health is soon followed by reduced income, followed by junk food which further reduces the health and contributes greatly to reversion back to the basic female.

In all homosexual populations partial reversion of the male back toward the basic female is highly visible. Many young "junk food junkies" develop high pitched voices, lose most of their body hair, and develop the rounded hips and sloping shoulders of the female figure, while lace and fancy panties become favorite apparel.

Ch.6. Specific Candida Yeast Infections.

We say here homosexuals, which refers to male sexual deviation, but the creation of lesbians and the lesbian cult is little different, except that the females are more fortunate: females can never revert to being less than female and the forces that drive females to sexual deviation are therefore much less pressing.

The causes of sexual deviation are now clear, or are they? If normal intercourse cannot induce orgasm, or if masturbation cannot succeed, how can homosexual or lesbian practices succeed? Let us remember that there are many sexual tissues in the body, and all sexual tissues release histamine and contribute to sexual arousal. For instance, one of the oriental methods of sexual arousal is to caress the feet, while the effects of a long sweet kiss are known to all. Both the mouth and the anus are very sexually stimulating, so it is probably the willingness of both parties to "do anything" that finally brings success, and if success is achieved, repeat episodes become a certainty.

Sexual deviation then is not new, and its victims need help. These are desperately ill people, people who need everything in the Anti-Candida program, and they need time and dedication, and they will need a good and understanding physician.

Where sexual deviation, or where elements of sexual deviation have touched upon or have soured former conjugal bliss, a frank discussion between the conjugal partners will usually help, if the full health rejuvenation program is being followed. The discussion must be totally frank and complete, and the needs and plight of both the male and female must be recognized. Many couples have already solved some of the problems of failing sexual ability by frank discussion, and by making certain that all full attempts at intercourse are always climaxed by orgasm for both partners, even if masturbation, vibrators or other means must be used, or if unusual or kinky practices must be resorted to. The prospect of some of these practices may seem somewhat distasteful, but there are many advantages to keeping all sexual problems within the home, where they can eventually be resolved. The most needed element is understanding, and the least needed thing is criticism. By keeping the sexual problems within the home and by ensuring sexual release, however inconvenient, mutual love, trust, and contentment will return, and with the continuing reduction of the ever present Candida infection, together with the return of health, many of the desperate sexual problems will slowly depart. Success depends upon raising histamine levels, and upon doing everything else in the entire Candida program.

Reviving Conjugal Bliss.

There are many factors that contribute to sexual problems between conjugal partners, but the greatest problem is frustrated orgasm, with impotence, early loss of erection, or early ejaculation being the most common causes of frustration. Thus the female is deprived, resulting in extreme contempt and resentment, and a frequently stated opinion that her mate "could do better". Then the frustrated orgasm, in either or both, unless resolved, will alter the hormone balance and the body chemistry resulting in extreme depression, psychosis, and a dissatisfaction with mate, everyone, and everything, that may last for weeks. Thus the male is blamed, while the female is blameless, yet things are not always exactly as they may at first appear.

In general the sexual anatomy of the female is the inverse of the male, and vice versa, with each having a counterpart of the other, just like the hand fits the glove. Still, there are differences, with the most confounding difference being sexual arousal time. Sexual build up in the male is rapid, orgasm is rapid, and detumescence is rapid. Some females, in disgust, call it "Slap, bang and he's gone". Females on the other hand, have a much slower arousal, a longer orgasm (frequently with four or five spasms), and a much slower detumescence.

Young females, with high histamine levels, have a much shorter arousal time than older females with lower histamine levels. All males, have a very fast arousal time, but they can prolong their arousal time much longer when they are young and virile with ample reserve energy, than they can when they are older, less virile, and have much less reserve energy.

The young conjugal couple therefore has very few sexual problems. Each complements the other, all is well, all is beautiful, everything is so wonderful that they think that it could never be different. Several years and several children later, however, things have greatly changed. In the female the histamine levels have fallen, vaginal tissues have thickened and have become less sensitive, vaginal lubrication has reduced, and arousal time has become much longer, while in the male the desire has increased, arousal time has decreased, erection time has diminished, and total energy reserves have dwindled. Things have indeed changed. If the conjugal couple go away together for the weekend (despite all else) they may indeed have wonderfully successful intercourse sometime while away. All is relaxed, nothing is rushed, and no-one is tired. But if intercourse is attempted some night after all of the work is almost finished, when both partners are tired and nerves are badly frayed, frustration is almost certain. The female is slowly aroused, while the male must make haste if he is to reach orgasm before the almost erect penis subsides into a useless nothing. If he hurries enough to reach orgasm soon enough, his conjugal mate may be only over-aroused, and is left totally unsatisfied and totally dis-satisfied. If he hurries less, his conjugal mate may be ready for orgasm just when his energy has failed and his penis has softened and subsided, leaving both conjugal partners totally frustrated and totally dissatisfied, with he blaming she for being too slow, and she blaming he for not being man enough to satisfy her. They both feel gypped, and think that the other "could do better if they tried!" The conjugal effort has become less than bliss. Try as they will, unless circumstances are perfect, the results are usually the same, and unless there is unusual mutual consideration and understanding the recrimination, blame, and dissatisfaction may last for weeks and may sadly affect other attempts to bring back the conjugal bliss that they so fondly need, and which they so fondly remember.

If an honest attempt is now made to discuss the conjugal problems, the usual conclusion is that through no specific fault of his own, male failure is the basic problem. Yet this is not quite true. There are other factors.

Humans are highly sexual creatures. the ebb and flow of sex hormones is an intrinsic part of our physiology. Active, resting, or asleep, the genitals are constantly changing with the changing hormones. Males are usually unaware of genital changes, but there are changes in size and texture of the testicles and testicular sac from one hour to the next, and there are similar changes in the penis, from completely retracted flatulence to semi-erection, and sometimes, completely without apparent provocation, to a perhaps highly embarrassing full hard erection that does not want to subside. The female genitals undergo similar changes, from a full bulging "vaginal erection" to completely flat relaxation. This too, can sometimes be a great embarrassment, because under some circumstances, when histamine levels are high, the vaginal (horny) erection can become so pronounced that the female can hardly walk, and if she does walk she displays very distinguishing features well recognized and reacted to by the male.

Very little seems to be known about erection in the male, except that the penis becomes engorged with blood; and so much less seems to be known about vaginal erection that it is seldom mentioned beyond the common term of "horny". However, with so many other similarities between the male and female sexual systems we must assume that vaginal erection also results from tissues becoming engorged with blood. Although histamine is probably the neurotransmitter that initiates erection, the erection itself seems to be maintained by other body systems, particularly the adrenals and total energy reserves, which indicates that glycogen (sugar) reserves, stored in the liver, would also be involved. The impaired liver function in alcoholics and Candida victims (from acetaldehyde) would certainly help to explain their frequent high sexual desire, with low capability and impotence. On the other hand, Dr.Pfieffer shows that the principal energy source for sexual orgasm is fructose. But there is no known storage site in the body for fructose, so how could it be the principal energy source for sexual activity that may last for hours? We do know very postively however, that erection in the male lasts much longer and is much fuller after resting. We do know that the male on the verge of impotence requires much more sleep. It would seem logical then, that the female would also be more responsive after resting, and indeed, it is almost impossible to sexually arouse a tired, adrenal depleted female. The resting of course, improves adrenal function, and it is the high production of adrenalin during sexual activity that not only pulls sugars from the liver but also converts proteins and other nutrients into fructose and thus provides energy for the emergency. Sexual function is therefore highly dependent upon the function of both the liver and the adrenals.

It is unfortunate that we do not know the exact role of histamine in sexual performance. Although histamine triggers erection, and probably maintains sexual desire, lack of nutrients or other causes may let the erection slip away unnoticed, while the desire remains. The great problem is that the male may feel that the erection is still good, full and strong, when in fact it has shrunk to only a tiny soft finger, a fact that is of great disappointment and frustration to his conjugal mate, and a fact that is of great surprise to the male, when he unaccountably slips out and he verifies the sad disappointing fact with his own hands. Thus with the male, sexual desire is one thing, while capability and performance are quite something else.

Now what about the female? Oh, the joys of having a ravenous horny female for a conjugal mate! Yes! With vaginal erection the muscles are certainly much tighter on the penis, with the increased traction, full contact, and increased pressure increasing the arousal. Then, as excitement mounts pressure and traction are further increased and increase so much that sometimes, with almost imperceptable movement, the very tightness and traction of the engorged vaginal muscles on the greatly engorged penis raises sexual excitement to an explosion of simultaneous orgasm! A wondrous gratifying experience for both conjugal partners! Oh, yes! For the young and healthy! But you see, if erection in the male slips away so easily without the male really knowing that it has somehow vanished, would not the vaginal erection also perhaps slip away unnoticed? With the vaginal erection gone, and with the traction and pressure on the penis reduced, how could the male possibly maintain an erection? Indeed, although the female usually blames the male for being "useless", the male just as frequently blames the female as being "worn out". Then, to prove the point, the male may seek a younger,"tighter" sexual partner with whom he may have normal intercourse, and then perhaps the "worn out" female, to prove her point, may seek a younger male with whom she may have normal sexual function.

The fact is that many females do lose their vaginal erection in just a few minutes, so the conjugal problems are mutual, and they usually do not become completely frustrating until both partners lose their erection capabilities. There is therefore no true fault with either partner, they are simply victims of time, health, and usually either a little or a lot of Candida infection.

The entire Candida program will help greatly. Candida infections of the vagina tend to thicken the surfaces, reducing sensitivity, and Candida infections of the penis thickens the skin on the tip of the penis, which also reduces the sensitivity. Sexual capability is also very dependent upon energy reserves, and energy reserves are invariably low when chronic infection is high. Sexual lubricants, companionship, and individual therapy will also help to restore conjugal bliss.

Sexual Lubricants.

Everyone with sexual problems of any kind will recognize that the lack of sexual lubrication is definitely a major difficulty. The copious quantities of vaginal sexual fluids diminish greatly with time, and many males lose their capability to produce sexual lubricant by the time that they have reached middle age. The problem is increased by Candida infection, through the yeast itself producing some type of sticky substance that is difficult to wash off. Production of this sticky substance seems to be centered in the genitals, but it is not confined to them. Vaginal fluids may be very sticky, and the penis may be very sticky. Miconazole lotion, miconazole suppositories, and the anti-fungal creams make the condition worse. The sticky condition may appear quite heavy on the testicle sac, and on the area around the anus. Sometimes it also appears on badly infected feet, which proves that it is Candida related. It will also increase with the use of high amounts of Vitamin E, which proves it is vitamin E related, but it still remains if Vit. E.

is discontinued. Vaseline and face and body lotions, and medical lubricants increase the problem. The sticky substance seems to be unaffected by vegetable oils, alcohol, glycerine, urine, or water. Saliva will instantly change the sticky residue to an exceptionally slippery coating, indicating that it is some form of water based mucins, but the effects of the saliva are fleeting, and have vasnished within minutes. Cleansing with mucin from animal joint oil and psyllium seed have been tried without success. Mild soap and water will reduce it somewhat and is the only thing that seems to work at all.

Choice of sexual lubricants has never been easy, because nothing seems to work successfully. The many potions and lotions in the "love" shops do not seem to be any better than creams from the drugstore, particularly when Candida is present. If the creams and lotions that are tried are not pH balanced, libido may be reduced. The author would like to have better suggestions, because a good sexual lubricant is so badly needed. At present good old fashioned saliva may help. The problem with lots of good old fashioned saliva is the peril of mouth infections, but this peril can be minimised with a chewed nystatin, a little chewed ketoconazole, or a little liquid nystatin with resteclin, as soon as it is convenient.

Now surely somewhere there must be a lubricant that works, and indeed there is a recent report that MCT Oil is somewhat effective, which indicates that perhaps the "sticky substance" is a long chain fatty acid that is partly diluted by the medium chain triglycerides. Normal vaginal fluids are mucins, and saliva contains mucins. The chemists. the curious, and the desperate might try mixtures of MCT oil, Joint oil (Neatsfoot oil), (mucins), and aloe vera (emulsifier). Good Luck.

Time of Day. (or night).

It has frequently been said that the best time for intercourse is anytime and the best place is anywhere. Although this maxim seems to be true, there are peroids of heightened sexuality.

The "best time" for females seems to be about three o'clock in the afternoon, which happily, by design or circumstance, falls within the usual "siesta time" for the Latin nations. This is also a good time for the male. Siesta has been held to be one of the reasons for the high birth rate in latin countries. Perhaps it is also a reason for a high rate of good health and contentment.

The "best time" for the male is after two or three hours sleep, or about the time of the "midnight train". This "best time" is certain, because it is at this time that spontaneous ejaculation, (the so-called wet dream) occurs in virile young males. This is also a good time for the female because there are similar reports of spontaneous nocturnal orgasm in young females, but except for copious quantities of vaginal fluids, anatomy prevents positive proof. Another good time for the male is the very first thing in the morning, when fully refreshed, before breakfast or anything else.

Anyone seeking to improve sexual function should consciously try to arrange for opportunity at "The best time of day! (or night).

Companionship.

Remember the heady days of early conjugal union, when it was "just us"! Two people! Only two people! "Just us", the only two people in the world, and nothing else mattered! "Just us" can be a weekend in a motel. Away from telephones and children. "Just us" can be an evening at home, reading a good love story together in bed, or perhaps watching a "blue movie" on the bedroom T.V. "Just us" can be a time when many little conflicts are resolved, and disappear with the return of conjugal bliss. "Just us" can be a wonderful revival of romance and companionship, because successful fulfilling coitus is engendered by love and companionship. "Just us" is the spice of life. You should "do it more often."

Maintaining Sexual Happiness.

The most important element in reviving conjugal bliss is maintaining sexual function until long term Candida therapy can improve the failing biological processes. Despite the foregoing suggestions there will probably be many times when one or both partners may fail to reach normal climax. It should be reiterated that if either partner fails to reach climax every effort should be made to complete orgasm so that the glands are emptied and the mental and physical effects from the resorbed sexual hormones are avoided. Some of the effective measures may at first seem distasteful, but should be used when necessary until health and capability improve. Although intercourse is certainly a conjugal matter, personal sexual relief is strictly a private matter, and the unsatisfied partner should be immediately left in the room by themselves. They can then cope with their problems by themselves in their own way without inhibitions and without explanations. They should be left alone immediately, so that the high levels of sexual excitement can be maintained. Orgasm can then usually be brought on by masturbation or other sexual stimulation.

It should be remembered that sexual function is largely controlled by histamine release. If histamine levels are low, sexuality and sexual capability are low. If histamine levels are high, sexual capability will usually be high. All of the sexual tissues will release histamine when sexually stimulated, whether the stimulus comes from mental suggestions or from physical touch. Quite obviously, to bring on frustrated orgasm everything should be done to promote further histamine release while maintaining or increasing excitement levels with masturbation.

The following suggstions come from many sources, and have been found useful to others:

1. Thoughts should be sexually exciting. These thoughts differ widely, and are usually known only to the person themselves. Sexually explicit pictures may be of help.

2. Massage of the inner thighs, genitals and rectal area.

3. Hot water bottle, applied to the stomach, genitals and rectal area.

4. Massage of the rectal area and masturbation of the sensitive areas in the rectum. Lubrication will help. Fingerstalls can be used to prevent abrasion of the tissues. This is a very sexually sensitive area and some individuals can reach climax with rectal masturbation alone.

5. Sucking of thumb, fingers or hands.

6. Use of vibrators or "sex shop" devices.

7. Use of rectal vibrators.

If climax still cannot be reached take the adrenal nutrients described under "Aphrodisaics" and try again within the hour.

If climax still cannot be reached and the effort must be abandoned take more adrenal nutrients and try to do something that is physically active for at least one hour to give the body time to resorb and detoxify the sexual fluids, and then try again as soon as the sexual urge returns, which will probably be the following night, or at most two nights later. The first urge must be heeded, and will probably be successful with masturbation, but may not be successful with intercourse. If the first urge is not heeded, sexual reversion may start, with the genitals shrinking and becoming flabby. If this is allowed to happen sexual drive and desire may not return for a week or ten days, and sexual capability may be further reduced.

Accurate medical literature on sexual function is very sketchy, but all writers are agreed on one thing, and that is the adage of "Use it or lose it". The more that the genitals are used (within reason) the greater the sexual capacity and the greater the normal capabilities will be. Although intercourse is considered "normal" if it occurs as infrequently as once or twice a month, better health will result if it occurs every two or three days, or perhaps even daily, as normal time for recuperation of the sex glands seems to be only a few hours.

People with genital yeast infection however, do not have normal genital function, and orgasm every two or three days may impose severe extra stress. Nonethless, if Candida yeast is growing within the glands that produce the sexual fluids, the fluids become very thick and sticky, and retention of the fluids makes them even thicker, which of course requires a much greater pressure and effort for orgasmic explusion. It therefore seems that people with Candida infection of the orgasmic glands should have extra adrenal nutrients and get extra rest so that the orgasmic glands can be emptied at least every two or three days. This will increase the body throughput of cholesterol and other sexual nutrients; it will reduce the viscosity of the sexual fluids and thus promote less difficult orgasm; and it will directly dispel some of the infection and its toxins. The extra stress from frequent sexual function may be quite severe, but the increased health and sexuality with the reduced sexual difficulties make the extra effort very worthwhile.

The sticky fluids from sexual Candida infection are always a continuing problem. The male will benefit from daily washing with mild detergent followed by pH balanced soap. The female may benefit from a pH balanced douche. As previously mentioned the only thing that seems to relieve the sticky condition is saliva, which is only a fleeting relief. Some benefit may come from using phenol alkalizer, followed by washing several hours later.

Where both partners experience sexual failure and neither is sufficiently stimulated by the other to reach a climax, they will probably benefit from masturbating together. The results are certainly not as fulfilling as full intercourse, but sexual function, sanity, and companionship will be maintained.

The mental links between conjugal couples are much greater than they appear. There is a silent hidden coupling of the minds. Some people may call it mind reading, but it is much more like mutual mental response. This response is well displayed by couples that are close to each other when they are dancing, particularly in a romantic dance like the waltz, or the slow fox trot. Two bodies moving together, each responding to the other,- two bodies moving to the music, as one. The reason that these dances are romantic is that they are partially sexual. Two bodies moving to a mutual stimulus; a stimulus that is mutually recognized and responded to in unison. This mental bond also plays an important part in coitus. Without this bond of mutual coitus, intercourse is little better than private masturbation, but with the conjugal bond, mutual arousal and mutual orgasm becomes one of the most wonderfully gratifying experiences of life. Candida infection and ill health may deny a bonded couple the satisfaction of mutual orgasm with intercourse, but if the frust-rated intercourse is followed immediately by extra lubrication and masturbation, mutual climax can frequently be achieved. Mutual climax achieved in this way is a poor substitute for mutually successful intercourse, yet it is the closest thing to it, and it certainly reduces the complaint and acrimony that so often creeps into the peaceful homes of older couples.

Aphrodisiacs.

In every human society many real he-men seem to develop impotence, or experience reduced sexual capabilities. Hence the need, real or imagined, for an aphrodisiac.

Powders and compounds containing narwhal tusk, rhino horn, buffalo horn, dried lizards, ginseng, cantherides, monkey brains, sparrow tongues, deer tails, rabbit hair, licorice, gold, spanish fly, tiger penises, and many other substances are used, both internally and as lotions and creams applied to the penis. Note, applied to the penis, because aphrodisiacs are sold principally to males. They are sold principally to males because in many parts of the world female sexual satisfaction is not considered.

Frequently female sexuality is relegated to being only a receptacle for the gratification of the male, on demand. A purely male attitude that is certain to make the female less responsive, and thus greatly increase the need for an aphrodisiac.

Unfortunately there does not seem to be any solid evidence that any of these substances work, nor does there seem to be any scientific reason that they should work. Yet they are rec-ommended and sold by "natural" health practitioners all over the world.

The prime cause of impotence (and frigidity) is ill health, usually resulting from caffeine, alcohol, drugs, or chronic infection. With good health, aphrodisiacs are never needed. With poor health their use, (even if they were effective) would only increase the total stress, which would further decrease the actual sexual and health levels, and thus increase the need for sexual help.

The only true aphrodisiac seems to be a small amount of niacin, probably about 50 to 200 mg. depending upon the histamine response of the individual. Niacin releases histamine into the bloodstream throughout the body, thus increasing the sexual response to stimulation and it also raises the levels of blood sugar at the very time that extra energy is needed. Niacin is also part of the therapy for increasing histamine and sexual levels, so its use as an aphrodisiac is also sexually beneficial.

For those who seek a prolonged event, sufficient niacin can be taken to produce a flush, at which time the nervcites will become very sensitive. Sexual response may be low during the flush, but mutual whole body neursage and massage during the flush may result in a true "loving event" with very high levels of sexual arousal, as the flush subsides.

Sexual function can also be improved and supported with a half a glass of Hi KC Fizz, together with all of the adrenal nutrients.

The foregoing sexual assistance may not sound as sexually compulsive or as titillating as tiger penises or narwhal tusk, but they will certainly produce a more satisfactory result.

For those who are not totally opposed to drugs Yohimbine (an Alpha blocker) could be tried.

Vasectomies.

The male vasectomy is a means of contraception where the spermatic tubes are cut, doubled back, and sewn, to prevent the flow of spermatic fluids. When first introduced vasectomies were lauded as being the final answer for contraception, but many good doctors with better scientific concepts had grave doubts. It has been known for many years that monks and others who practice celibacy will develop premature senility, with other changes indicative of female reversion. Invariably, upon autopsy, a strange brown pigment is found in the testes. The strange brown pigment, which is never found in normal males, is the residue from glandular secretions that have not been discharged, with the remainder of the secretions resorbed by the body. The good doctors that doubted the value of vasectomies expected that this same brown pigment would start to form in the testes of males who had vasectomies. A large enough number of males who have had vasectomies have now died, and autopsies have shown that the same brown pigment does form in the testes of males with vasectomies. This illustrates the folly of trying to shut off a normal body process. The vasectomy forces the body to resorb the contents of the glands after they have filled. The consequences are altered hormone production and altered body function, resulting in reduced maleness and a tendency to revert back to the basic female.

Laudable as the idea of a vasectomy may be, the actual affect of a vasectomy is to produce progressively increasing neurosis and psychosis, with sufficient changes in sexuality, mental attitude, and philosophy that a formerly compatible marriage may fall apart.

· Males who are considering vasectomies should consider these certain consequences and should avoid the vasectomy, perhaps in favor of an operation developed in the Toronto area that diverts the testicular fluids into the urinary system in a manner similar to retrograde ejaculation.

Males who have had vasectomies should have the vasectomy reversed with micro-surgery or altered to the retrograde operation. Large quantities of vitamin E, both taken orally and applied to the genitals, will help the body to resorb the scar tissue and heal the damaged tubes.

Males who have had vasectomies and are now experiencing sexual, mental, or health problems will also have to do everything in the Candida program, and also everything in the program for "Revival of Male Sexual Function", including perhaps supplements of testosterone.

FEMALE SEXUAL PROBLEMS.

It is the author's belief that this entire section should have been written by a female, but the author has been unable to find a female who was willing and capable to frankly undertake the task. However, the following information has been reviewed and approved by two female "sex counsellors" and a registered nurse, and some additions to the original material were added as they suggested.

Female Contraceptives.

The Diaphragm.

The diaphragm is the only female contraceptive that does not have severe side effects. Unfortunately the diaphragm is not a positive contraceptive and pregnancies do sometimes occur.

The "Pill".

The pill was supposed to be the emancipation of all females from the perils of pregnancy. Unfortunately the pill has not ended all of the unwanted pregnancies, and it also has a very large number of serious side effects. These side effects include altered hormones, liver damage, and retention of copper. If copper plumbing is being used, or if the diet is high in soya products, copper levels can occasionally reach the point of psychosis or even insanity. These are long term effects of the pill, that can be reduced with large quantities of all adrenal nutrients, zinc, bioflavinoids (minimum 1,500 mg. daily) and liver, and by reducing the time to peroids not longer than six months. This will make the side effects of the pill much more subtle, yet they will still be frequently seen as bits of indigestion, increased irritability, reduced libido, and perhaps signs of masculinity.

The masculinizing effect of the pill has been rightly credited with the increased number of young females that have become involved in murder, crime, terrorism, car racing, and motorcycle gangs. This may seem a little crazy, but it is true. For instance a young happily married woman, with three young children, decided to take a night school course to become an auto mechanic. When told about it by the husband, the writer remarked, "Oh!, she must be on the pill, it does that, you know". Surprised, the husband replied, "I will tell her". About six months later the writer asked the husband if his wife had become an auto-mechanic. "Oh no. I told her what you said, She went off the pill, and now she cannot understand why she ever wanted to take the course." Oh yes, the changes in thought and personality brought by the pill are slow and subtle, but they are very real.

The altered hormones and reduced estrogen resulting from the use of the pill may also reduce libido and increase irritability to the point of hostility and complete dissatisfaction with any or all "boyfriends"; to the point of disruption of marital bliss; or to complete destruction of a formerly happy marriage.

Estrogen always opposes Candida infection, and the reduced levels of estrogen resulting from the use of the pill therefore increase the opportunity for Candida to invade. If the pill is used, constant vigil must be maintained for any signs of vaginitis.
The IUD.

The IUD was also hailed as a great advance in contraceptives. The IUD is made of copper, and it alters the sexual hormones and the menstrual cycle by copper chemistry. It too, increases the tissue copper levels throughout the body, sometimes with severe mental effects. It also reduces estrogen levels, with psychological changes and reduced resistance to Candida infection. The IUD is a constant irritant to the delicate sexual tissues which make it a continuing cause of vaginal infection, and particularly vaginal yeast infection. It is therefore a common cause of fallopian tube infection, resulting in menstrual problems or perhaps complete sterility from blockage of the fallopian tubes by a Candida callus. Candida infection resulting from the IUD may progress to the point where the entire pelvic area becomes swollen and inflamed, (PID, Pelvic Inflammatory Disease) with the inflammation sometimes extending to the hips and upper thighs; sometimes greatly increasing the size of the hips and thighs by lymphatic interference and calcinosis, in a manner similar to elephantiasis.

If the IUD has been used for more than six months, examination should be made for blockage of the fallopian tubes or indications of other severe vaginal infection. The examination must be particularly complete and thorough because Candida infection of the uterus can be both painless and almost undetectable.

If the IUD is used, it should not be used for peroids longer than six months. All nutrients described under the "Pill" will help to reduce the side effects. Constant vigil must also be maintained for any signs of vaginitis.

Tubal Ligation.

Tubal ligation was also hailed as a new wondrous way to limit the size of families. It certainly limits the size of families, but its final results are frequently less than wondrous. With some women, (probably women with good nutrition and good adrenal function), the effects from tubal ligation seem to be minimal, but to many other women tubal ligation is a hormonal disaster that drastically reduces their femininity to the point where it may alter their entire life.

Vaginal Candida Infection.

(Candidosis),(Candidiasis),(Moniliasis).

Vaginal Candida infection can be very irritating and distressing, but it can also be insidious and painless. Indeed, some medical literature shows that Candida infections of the uterus can be both painless and almost undetectable.

One if the symptoms of hidden Candidosis (or Candidiasis) is toxicity on the day following intercourse. The physical trauma of intercourse releases toxins from the infective, and the toxins are then absorbed by the body with the symptoms appearing in about eight hours. Hidden infections will also usually (but not always) induce some vaginitis, following intercourse.

Hidden Canidida infections can cause infertility if the yeast calluses block the fallopian tubes. Similar Candida calluses, partially blocking the orgasmic glands, frequently result in high sexual desire with difficult orgasm, or with complete orgasmic failure. Pelvic infections- (PID) (Pelvic Inflammation Disease) with perhaps greatly enlarged hips, are also associated with severe chronic vaginitis. These conditions will slowly respond to the entire Candida program, but time, diligence and persistance will also be needed.

Candida infections of deep cavities are always difficult to reduce. Most medical treatments are for only very short periods, sometimes only three days, and they then consider the condition to be cured if tests show absence of Candida four days after the end of treatment. Most certainly treatment of this kind will clear up many superficial Candida infections, but a long standing Candida infection that has invaded the tissues and has formed a callus matrix may be sufficiently subdued that the tests show negative, but it will be far from dead and not really dying. Also, with a three day treatment, and tests four days later, the normal reproduction rate of Candida has been neatly circumvented, because the yeast takes about ten days to complete its life cycle. Thus the treatment may kill the active organisms, but the spores will remain to start the infection all over again. This might be very good for people who are in the business of selling anti-candida agents, because it ensures a continuous business, but it is certainly less than helpful to the victim of severe Candidiasis, who may be even fighting for their very life.

Vaginal infections, including deep infections of the uterus, can be reduced with everything in the Candida program, including continuing ketoconazole, (which helps to reduce the infection from the blood side) and several courses of Monistat 7 (miconazole suppositories) and flagystatin, perhaps even once a month for six months. The suppositories should be inserted as deep as possible. Betadine may also be useful. Tampons, soaked in a solution of 2% phenol in glycerine have been very effective. Miconazole lotion, nystatin cream, and liquid ketoconazole are effective and will increase comfort.

To avoid re-infection the male sexual partner should also be treated with ketoconazole and topical applications of miconazole and phenol alkalizer, both applied to the tip of the penis and also instilled in the upper part of the urethra. If re-infection persists, the possibility of infection of the prostate or testes should also be considered.

Recurrent Vaginitis.

It is always very difficult for the victim of recurring vaginitis to distinquish between re-infection and recurring infection. Biological influences are frequently very subtle, and Candida infection anywhere in the body seems to make all of the sexual tissues much more subject to Candida infection. High Candida infection therefore tends to increase vaginal re-infection particularly from the colon, hands, and the male sexual consort. On the other hand, the recurring infection may result from thick calluses that shelter the infectives from the anti-fungals. Unfortunately for the victim of recurring vaginitis all of the companies that are marketing anti-fungals show the effectiveness of their products by test results, and they are then justly proud if their product shows an 80% or 90% effectiveness. But all of this mass of medical literature does not say what measures can be taken to help the non-responders;- to help the 10% to 20% of victims that fail to respond. So if you are a female reader seeking help you are probably another one of those "20% non-responders". If so, you will certainly have to do " everything in the book" with care, diligence and persistence.

As usual, the medical literature on vaginitis is confusing. Ref.1. shows that the usual infectives are T(Trichomona) Vaginalis, Candida species, C (Corynebacterium) Vaginale, herpes simplex, and rarely N Gonorrhoeae. Metronidazole is suggested for Trichomona, but again the cure rate is only 80%, and again suggestions are lacking for the non-responders. Ref.32, however, shows that although trichomona used to be the principal infective, by 1964 one third of all women of child bearing age had vulvovaginitis, with one quarter of the infections being trichomona and the other 3/4 of the infections being Candida. The increased rate of Candida infection is usually attributed to the widespread use of antibiotics, and hormonal contraceptives. The vaginal fluid is an excellent culture medium for micro-organisms, and it therefore appears that many vaginal infections are multiple infections, and many different anti-infective agents will have to be tried. The following information may be of particular benefit to non-responders;

1. Normal vaginal pH is 3.8 to 4.2 before menopause. After menopause 4.5 to 5.

2. Vaginal pH does not affect the rate of growth of Candida, but it does affect adhesion. Adhesion is much greater at pH 6 than it is at pH 3,4,7, or 8.

3. Although Candida produces lactic acid, Candida infection raises the normal pH toward the pH 6 where adhesion is greatest.

4. Unlike other parts of the body vaginal skin cells are constantly being sloughed off, and the vagina is therefore in a way, self cleansing, if the rate of infection is less than the rate of cellular loss. Reducing the pH to a normal 3.8 would therefore reduce adhesion and would promote self-cleansing.

5. Vaginal pH can be reduced with the use of ortho-acigel or similar preparations.

6. Various studies show that about 90% of Candida free females have a very high vaginal lactobacillus flora. Acidophilus could also be used to reduce vaginal pH to reduce Candida adhesion and promote cleansing.

7. Although some medical information shows Candida vaginitis to be only superficial infection, other authorities show that Candida infection of the cervix can be painless and almost undetectable, and Candida infections of the fallopian tubes are known to be a common cause of infertility. Although the vaginal walls may be self-cleansing, Candida infections of the cervix or fallopian tubes may be a continuous source of vaginal re-infection.

8. Long standing vaginal infection dvelops a thick, leathery callus matrix that shields the infectives from topical anti-fungals. Both systemic and topical anti-fungals must be used.

9. Anti-fungals containing Caprylic acid may be of particular benefit.

10. The male consort is a very frequent cause of re-infection.

11. Chlamydia infections of the cervix may have a Candida component that maintains re-infection. Chlamydia will respond to tetracycline (see Resteclin), Erythromycin or Metronidazole.

12. Non-specific vaginitis is usually treated with ampicillin, which is frequently ineffective. Metronidazole is usually effective. but possible side effects should be considered. (Ref.1.)

Pelvic Inflammatory Disease.(PID).

Acute PID is well known. In the past it has been considered to be a gonococcal disease, but it is also caused by C Trachomatis, mycoplasma, and other micro-organisms. Treatment for acute PID is well described in Ref.1. but, as usual, the sub-climical forms are completely ignored.

In sub-clinical PID the entire pelvic area becomes swollen with inflammation. The inflammation frequently involves the lymphatic system, and spreads to the hips and upper thighs, with the pelvis, hips, and thighs becoming enlarged and calcified in a manner similar to elephantiasis.

The usual underlying cause of PID is deep vaginal and cervical infection, with Candida yeast calluses harboring the many infectives.

PID will slowly respond to the entire Candida program with particular attention to reducing the vaginitis and to improving the function of the immune system and pancreas, both of which influence inflammation. Allergies may also play a role. Massage and deep neursage will help to reduce the calcinosis and the enlarged hips.

It may be six or eight months before the pelvic inflammation is reduced, after which it may be another six months before the size of the hips and thighs start to diminish.

In stubborn cases, bi-carbonate after the meals may help (see pancreatic failure), and the Grapefruit, egg and the cabbage and onion soup diets may also help. Chelation therapy may also be necessary before the enlarged hips and thighs start to reduce in size.

See also "Enlarged Hips and Thighs", Ch.4.

Female Sexual Therapy.

There must be a very large number of females who have severe to extreme sexual problems. The many different types of sexual devices in the "love" shops, and the many variations, is very surprising, and most of these devices are made for the female. There are dozens of different vibrators, in all shapes and sizes, small plastic penises, large plastic penises, and immense plastic penises, some complete with testicles, and some complete with vibrators, while others may be water filled. There are also a myriad of other devices, together with many lotions, potions and perfumes, all mute testimony that many females do have extreme sexual problems, because all of these devices would not be in the stores if they were not being purchased by females in need.

Although some of these devices may be useful, and may help some unfortunate female to "get by" for another day, another week, or another month, they do not alter the basic sexual problems, which are centered in poor health, Candida yeast infection, vaginal infections of all kinds, histamine levels, and thyroid, adrenal, and estrogen levels. These factors are all interlinked. To improve sexual function and reduce the need for these sexual devices, everything in the Candida program must be done, with particular attention to:

1. All adrenal nutrients, particularly potassium ascorbate, (Hi KC Fizz), B6, and extra zinc. Ample adrenal nutrients are necessary for support for the nervous system and for the production of estrogen and other hormones.

2. Adrenal and pituitary substance, (or extracts).

3. Estrogen supplements if needed. Estrogen levels can be medically measured. Estrogen is particularly necessary for the maintainence of healthy sexual tissues, and to combat Candida infections. Estrogen supplements must be minimal, for short periods only, until adrenal functions improve.

4. Liver function, which is important in providing ample energy reserves. Alcohol, in any amount, impairs the liver, and continuing alcohol will destroy it. Liver injections, liver supplements, or a diet high in liver, will help to increase liver function.

5. Histamine levels, which control sexual desire and orgasm.

Female Orgasmic Failure.
   (Frigidity).

Although the female can never become less than female, failure to reach orgasm after high sexual arousal is still a health, happiness, and mental disaster, because the body is forced to resorb hormones and other fluids produced by the glands during stimulation. Female anatomy makes observation of orgasmic discharge almost impossible, and even Master and Johnson have been unable to identify the exact glands and the exact process of female orgasm, but the copious fluids produced by most females during orgasm certainly shows that, as with the male, sexual orgasm is the rapid spasmodic discharge of the contents of glands that have slowly filled during sexual stimulation.

Orgasmic failure can result from four interlocking factors:

1. Social and religious implications. The mind is highly involved in sexual stimulation. It is so much involved that spontaneous emission (the wet dream) is common in all healthy young males, while similar nocturnal "sexual relief" appears to be present in many young females. It is also reported that some high histamine females can bring on orgasm just by thinking about males. Further, the swooning ecstacy" of many young girls at

"Elvis Prestly"[1] concerts and similar "sexy' events is highly sexual with some young girls admitting that they experience multiple orgasms during the concerts.

With the mind so highly involved in sexual stimulation, social and religious inhibitions are very difficult to alter or erase, even when the frigid female realizes that the inhibitions are destroying her life. Although these inhibitions are frequently very deeply ingrained, they are also related to histamine levels, while histamine levels are themselves partly stimulated by the mind. Females with basophil cell counts above .3% are seldom frigid, and many females have a normal sexual life with levels of only .2%. Every effort should therefore be made to raise histamine levels, and each increase will help to reduce the inhibitions.

Just as sexual inhibitions are fostered by deliberately thinking of something else, sexual inhibitions can be reduced by deliberately thinking almost continuously about sex, sexuality, and sexual relief in every way and in every form. Night clothes should be discarded, and going without panties at appropriate times may help. Reading should be changed to sexually oriented romance, or to "sexy" magazines, with deliberate stimulation of the genitals at every opportunity. A trip to the "love shop" to see the many sexual devices may also help. Frank sexual discussions with others is usually of assistance because you are not the only one that has such problems. To overcome the inhibitions it is necessary to become sexually normal, specifically, where the genitals are regarded simply as a necessary part of the body. No less, and no more. Some people report that they have lost their inhibitions and have become sexually normal only after they have joined a nudist colony long enough to become accustomed to and uninhibited by other naked people.

2. Low energy levels. With low energy levels (poor health) the body cannot sustain sexual arousal long enough to fill the glands. Desire rapidly fades, and orgasm becomes impossible. The entire Candida program will help. A short rest before or after dinner may also help. Adrenal nutrients, with juice, before going to bed should be tried. Stimulation should be slow and progressive but rush to climax should not be too long delayed. Some couples solve many of their problems by going back to bed after breakfast.

3. Frustrated orgasm. If intercourse has been interrupted close to climax, by doorbells, telephones, or etc; the resorbed hormones will reduce sexuality, possibly to the point of frigidity. This will occur only if histamine levels are low, and already close to frigidity. Function can usually be restored by reaching orgasm by masturbation, vibrators, etc. But the physical function must also be restored and improved or the frigidity will most certainly return.

4. Candida Yeast Infection. Infertility from blockage of the fallopian tubes is quite common and is well known. The usual cause of the blockage is their embedment in a soft Candida callus matrix. X-rays will frequently show how the callus completely surrounds the tubes, with the tubes becoming so twisted and compressed that passage of the ovum becomes impossible. Soft Candida calluses in the lining of the vagina are also well known. It appears that these Candida calluses frequently also partially block the passages from the orgasmic glands in a similar manner to the blockage of the fallopian tubes, and in a similar way to the partial blockage of the ejaculatory passages in the male. With partial blockage of the orgasmic passages in the female, sexual desire may be very high, and very high levels of sexual excitement may be reached, yet orgasm may be very difficult or almost impossible. Ejaculatory problems in the male are usually also associated with Candida infection of the testicles, together with thickened, heavy ejaculate. Perhaps a similar condition is present in the female. Perhaps the "orgasmic glands" wherever they are, also become infected, with the orgasmic fluids also becoming heavy and sticky. We do not know for certain, because science and medical knowledge are lacking, but we do know that some females with vaginal calluses have great difficulty in reaching orgasm, and we do know that these females usually do have abnormal, thick, sticky, vaginal fluids. We also do know that these females will slowly respond and improve with Candida infection therapy, which should include:
A. Oral ketoconazole.
B. Miconazole suppositories (Monistat 7), and flagyststin, alternated with tampons soaked in a solution of 2% phenol in glycerine, together with an occasional Betadine (iodine) douche.
C. The rest of the entire Candida infection program.
     Although the entire Candida program is essential to improving orgasmic function, it is a long term program that does very little to solve or alleviate the immediate orgasmic difficulties. To preserve health and sanity every effort should be made to maintain regular sexual function and to avoid resorption of sexual fluids from frustrated orgasm, even if the necessary methods may seem bizarre. Accurate information of this kind is very difficult to obtain. Literature is scant. Some females are reticent, while others are misleading. Orgasmic difficulties, although reluctantly discussed are very commonplace, and many females have worked out many different solutions. Some of these suggestions are included in "Reviving Female Sexual Function"

Reviving Female Sexual Function.
     Reviving sexual function in the female is much less difficult

than reviving sexual function in the male because the female can never revert to becoming less than female. The reduced sexuality from loss of sexual ability is, however, reflected in reduced femininity and a loss of vivaciousness and sex appeal. With time the sexless female becomes completely disinterested in sexual matters. Although they themselves have become neutered, they usually demand that their husbands remain faithful; a demand that rapidly and justly becomes a very strong point of contention for a still sexually capable husband.

The only way to effectively solve the problem is to restore female sexual function and the only way to restore female sexual function is to do everything in the entire Candida program;-- Absolutely everything;-- which of course includes "sexual therapy", to get the sexual hormones flowing again, because the sexual hormones are also an essential part of good health.

The program should not be rushed. The body cannot rebuild overnight. After the Candida program is under way, deliberate sexual thoughts, with a little masturbation every two or three hours will help to increase sexual interest while health improves and while adrenal nutrients, together with the hormones released by the masturbation, start to increase the production of sex hormones. A little niacin, at low flush level will help. Small amounts of estrogen will also help. Zinc should be moderately supplemented, with lots of calcium- magnesium, VItamin D, and lots of Vitamin B6.

Response may be very slow at first, but as health and hormone function improve the response will also improve. The rate of improvement will depend upon the amount of Candida infection and the functional level of body systems. Sexual revival may take only a few weeks, or it may take many months.

Revival of sexual function is largely a matter of persistance. Extra stimualtion should be tried at a "good time of day", probably in the morning when well rested, or in the afternoon, before or after an afternoon nap. A sexual partner will help with arousal, and revived sexual function will probably follow sometime after an attempt at intercourse. Everything should be tried. A visit to one of the "Love shops" is an experience and an education. A visit to the "Love shop" will convince anyone that many females do have extreme difficulties, and it will also provide an opportunity to obtain some of the many devices that are sold. As always, some of these are not very effective, but other devices may be very useful. Unfortunately trial may be the only method of selection. Many books are also available, some pornographic, some playful, and some serious. These books can be useful both for possible suggestions, and for mental stimulation. The "Love

Shops" also sometimes have the names of female "sex groups', groups of women with admitted sexual problems, (not lesbians) and attending some of their little meetings with perhaps, a frank discussion with some of the members, may be of great help. No female should ever think that she is alone, and that she is the only female with sexual problems. The truth is sadly the opposite. Probably 60% of all females have sexual problems early in life, and the percentage may even be higher. The usual cause is vaginal infection and reduced levels of health. This is the reason for, and the necessity for the "Love shops" and this is the reason for the "love" groups. They should not be considered pornographic (although some are) they should instead be thought of as groups of people trying desperately to solve a severe mutual problem that should have been resolved by their doctors long before the real problems arose.

It may be that many females would shun these "Love shops" and " Love groups" because they are "coarse" or "pornographic" or "dirty". This may well be true of some, yet others are very realistic and refined. The best approach seems to be to try to separate the sexual fact from all of its social and religious influences and consider sexual function as a usually pleasant necessity of life, like eating, breathing, sweating, menstruating and defecating. These are facts of life that are not always pleasant and refined, yet they are facts. One should not refuse to purchase toilet paper, or deodorant, or sanitary napkins, just because they thought the store was "dirty". One should not avoid discussing the need for a laxative, if a laxative is needed. One should not avoid discussing the need and benefits of sexual devices; because they may be a necessity. They are a necessity much like the need to use a toilet,- very pleasant if clean and tidy, unpleasant yet still necessary even if the toilet is dirty and the walls are covered with pornographic filth.

The following suggestions for restoring sexual orgasm come from several groups where some of the people have had success. The suggestions are not meant to be specific, they are simply a general pattern. If the attempt ends in failure, be certain to reduce the side effects with ample adrenal nutrients. If the attempt ends in success, the adrenal nutrients should still be taken, and the restored function should be maintained by repeating the success on either the second or third day.

Some females have found that going around without panties maintains a constant sexual awareness, which whets the sexual appetite, while others go a little farther and wear a plastic penis to provide a constant awareness, or they may deliberately look at sexual pictures (to taste) to maintain a constant sexual awareness, perhaps spiced with short episodes of masturbation.

Each female will develop her own way of raising sexual interest, and various other alternatives should be tried including "blue movies", sexy magazines, heat, cold, water stimulation as with a portable shower head, etc.

When sexual awareness and sexual interest have increased to the point that an attempt at orgasm becomes irresistable, the following suggestions may be of help. Be certain that it is a "good time of day" when the body is well rested, and allow for at least two hours of uninterrupted time. Unfortunately normal intercourse with a male, however considerate or however avid, does not seem to bring success. Artificial stimulation seems to be the only way that high enough levels of sexual excitement can be attained. Start with relaxation. Then, as interest mounts, change to stronger sexual reading, perhaps a book like "A hundred things to do with your Pussy". Then try some of the suggestions, or anything else that you may think of. Do not be inhibited. You are alone, so you can try anything, and no one else will ever know the things that you have tried. You are fighting a battle to restore the most vital part of your life, and as with all battles, you must resort to "anything that works." Try everything. Many things in the home have been pressed into service. Weiners, sausage, carrots and small smooth cucumbers; with unsalted butter, lard or corn oil for lubrication, have all been used with success. Or try a large plastic penis, perhaps of the type that is filled with warm water. Stimulate all other sexual areas, upper legs, rectal area, breasts and mouth. Sucking the thumb during stimulation may help greatly. Do not rush. Enjoy everything and let the sexual tension build up slowly, then as the need to increase becomes unbearable, rush to climax with as much stimulation as possible. This may take the form of using both the plastic penis (or other) simultaneously with masturbation of the clitoris, or alternately, perhaps a vibrator or vibrator penis might be used together with a small rectal vibrator. The attempts can be as varied as the sexual material that you have been reading. Do not expect success on the first try. There may be many frustrated attempts, pleasant, but frustrated attempts before orgasm is reached. Each attempt may be followed by a day or two of "feeling awful", complete perhaps with neurosis and psychosis, while the body detoxifies the resorbed hormones, but if the side effects from the frustrated orgasm are reduced with large quantities of vitamin C and other adrenal nutrients, and if everything else in the Candida program is being done, each attempt will increase sexual levels with an increasing higher plateau that finally culminates in sexual success, a success that must then be repeated every two or three days until normal sexual function, with easy orgasm has returned.

It must be repeated that females with high sexual desire and the ability to reach high sexual plateaus, yet are still unable to reach orgasm, may have sexual glands blocked by Candida calluses. As much ketoconazole as possible, miconazole suppositosies, and the use of tampons soaked in a 2% solution of phenol in glycerine, together with time for the body to reduce the calluses, is the only way to resolve the problem. The total time required may be six months or more. In the meantime sexual activity should be maintained despite the "bad days" that invariably follow each episode of sexual failure.

Females with an understanding sexual partner will of course have a better opportunity for sexual revival than females without a partner. Do not forget that there are many males that are also in need of an understanding partner. People should never live alone, so if needed, a compatible understanding partner should be sought. It will make revival of sexual function much easier, and it will make life much more worthwhile.

Successful sexual function is always determined by total available energy. If energy levels are low, even at the "best time of day" the sexual effort must be rushed to climax before the energy fails; yet if the sexual attempt is rushed too much the build up of sexual tension will be too rapid to encompass all of the sexual tissues, and orgasm will again fail. When health levels are low and energy is low the balance between too slow and too fast is crucial to success, yet is difficult to attain.

MALE SEXUAL CANDIDA INFECTIONS.
Infections of the Penis.
It is well known that every female may contract vaginal infection at any time, but except for venereal disease, infections of the penis are almost totally unknown and most certainly are very seldom discussed. Yet with all of the great sexual activity that is supposed to represent real manhood, together with the many vaginal infections, how can all of those overactive penises escape from an equal amount of the same infections? The truth is that they do not escape. Penisitis (balanitis) is just as common, and is perhaps more common, than vaginitis. Penisitis usually is not recognized, and if it is recognized the great male ego blocks discussion.

The usual symptom of penisitis is a burning sensation in the tip of the penis. It may be very persistent and return every few hours, or it may last only a few minutes. It may be caused by any of the vaginal infectives, but the usual cause is Candida infection. The Candida usually forms a soft callus in the urethra at the tip of the penis, which makes urination much slower and which usually also results in urinary spray, a condition very frequently present in older men. The internal infection may then spread to the tip of the penis, where it may continue to spread and it may finally cover the entire sensitive end. The tip of the penis may then become almost white, instead of the usual flesh pink. The thick leathery callus reduces the sensitivity of the penis, resulting in difficult or impossible sexual climax.

The Candida infection in the penis may also creep backwards through the urethra, to the prostate, causing enlarged prostate (of which we do hear much) with extreme urinary problems. The Candida infection may then creep on backwards through the spermatic ducts into the testicles, where it causes tender testicles, thick sticky ejaculate, and varicoceles (hydroceles and spermatoceles) with reduced fertility, reduced production of testosterone, and impaired sexual ability to the point of complete sexual failure. Sexual Candida infection is therefore a severe tragedy to every male that happens to become badly infected, and he is also a peril to every female with whom he has intercourse because he will probably pass along many active yeast spores.

Candida infections of the tip of the penis can be reduced by improving total health with everything in the Candida program, together with oral ketoconazole and with miconazole lotion, flagystatin and phenolalkalizer applied to the tip of the penis and to the upper part of the urethra. A small plastic oil can, as used for oiling sewing machines, makes a good applicator for infections of the urethra. The final clearing of the infection is largely dependent upon immune system function. Improvement will be steady but slow, and may take six months or longer, depending upon how much other Candida infection is present. Ketoconazole tablets, crushed and added to 50% DMSO, are particularly effective, topical agents.

Enlarged Prostate.

Candida infections of the prostate are usually very difficult to reduce. The obvious problem is to get topical antifungals to the site. A small plastic oilcan attached to a small "old fashioned" metal catheter, or similar small plastic tube, can be used for the application of miconazole lotion, phenolakalizer, or liquid ketoconazole. Miconazole cream can be used as a lubricant. Some doctors and some naturopaths have some success with prostate massage. Prostate massage, through the rectum, with fingers or a small vibrator will usually help the topical agents to be more effective. There are a number of reports that reflexology and neursage have been helpful, and this possibility should not be overlooked. Progress may be slow if the prostate has become badly enlarged, and sometimes an operation cannot be avoided.

CH.6. Specific Candida Yeast Infections.

One of the progressive doctors in Alaska has found that all prostate problems respond to oral ketoconazole, working up to two tablets, three times a day, with crushed ketoconazole tablets in 50% DMSO, forced down a brass catheter, and also applied to the testicles and penis.

Varicoceles. (Hydroceles, Spermatoceles).

Varicoceles are actually cysts. They are enlargements or "bags" of fluid in the testicular pouch, spermatic tubes, or other male sexual parts. Females seem to be less affected by these conditions than males, but similar cysts are sometimes found. Varicoceles reduce sperm count, and frequently reduce levels of testosterone. The cause of varicoceles is said to be unknown, but they are known to be frequently associated with Candida infection, and Candida yeast has now been positively found in male sexual fluids. Candida yeast is highly transparent under the microscope, and it may easily escape detection unless DMSO or other special techniques are used. With positive finding of Candida yeast in varicocele fluids we must now assume that all varicoceles, and perhaps all cysts, are caused by Candida infection. It therefore appears that varicoceles result from Candida yeast infection that has managed to creep from an infected penis backwards down the spermatic tubes to the testicles, because varicoceles are usually associated with the tender testicles and curdled ejaculate that is typical of Candida infection of the testicles.

Varicoceles vary in size and effects. They may become so large that they affect the legs, and they may hold as much as a liter or more of fluid, or they may be very small and barely detectable. The "tender testicles" appear to result from a number of very small, perhaps microscopic varicoceles, but this has not as yet been medically established. Varicoceles invariably affect sexual function, reduce fertility, and reduce the levels of testosterone. From this then, we know that early Candida infection of the testes, before adolescence, can impair sexual development, reduce the size and capacity of the male genitals, and reduce the total "manliness" of the individual. How many males may be affected in this way is not known, but some older males do have an increase in the size of the genitals and of the chest with ketoconazole and extra zinc.

The usual medical treatment for varicoceles is surgical removal. If the varicocele is in the testicular pouch (hydrocele) where the operation can be "clean", it is usually very successful, but if the varicocele is located in the spermatic tubes (spermatocele) where surgery is more difficult, the varicocele will frequently return.

Quite obviously the surgical operation does not reduce the testicular infection, and therefore does not remove the basic cause of the varicocele. In many cases the varicocele surgery may be fully successful, with the return of the varicocele simply the formation of another one near the same place.

In one instance of a returned spermatocele, where the tender testicles and thick, curdled ejaculate were present, the anti-Candida program, including ketoconazole arrested the growth of the spermatocele, after which the spermatocele was drained, the hypodermic needle was left in place, and the spermatocele was partially re-filled with surgical disinfectant. The spermatocele fluids were then tested, and found to be "normal spermatic fluid" with slight growth of Candida yeast. But in about six months the spermatocele slowly re-filled. The spermatocele was again drained, but was re-filled with an equal quantity of miconazole I.V. (Monistat I.V.)-intravenous. This resulted in a massive inflammation of the testicles, triggered by the castor oil in the intravenous solution. In about a week the inflammation had subsided, and the spermatocele has not returned. This shows that the spermatocele was caused by fungal infection, and it also shows a method of eliminating spermatoceles that is far better than surgery. There must be better antifungals that could be used, and the presence of the castor oil in the monistat I.V. was discussed with the manufacturers, but they assured us that the castor oil was almost the only choice because the imidazole ring is incompatible with most solvents including the master solvent, DMSO. The doctor in Alaska (see prostate) who uses DMSO, does not know that it will not work, so he uses it with good success.

It should be re-iterated that health is largely dependent upon normal sexual function and sexual function cannot be normal as long as varicoceles are present. The problem is that varicoceles frequently do not increase in size, and they may remain so small that they are impossible to drain. This appears to be the true cause of the tender testicles. Oral ketoconazole helps, but there is a real need for a better intravenous antifungal.

Candida Infection of the Testicles. (Eunuchization).

Candida infection of the testicles results in thick, curdled ejaculate; low sperm counts; low sperm motility; reduced levels of testosterone; and impaired or impossible sexual function.

Aside from the problems of infertility and difficult ejaculation, loss of ptoduction of testosterone is tragedy for the male. The cause and the effects of this tragedy are not commonly known.

In all mammals (including mankind) the male is a hormonal (testosterone) conversion of the basic female. Specifically, the female is the basic creature. In the female the production of estrogen by the ovaries and by the adrenal glands, makes the female more feminine. Thus loss of ovarian estrogen, as with hysterectomy, menopause, or perhaps tubal ligation, reduces the female femininity, but the adrenal estrogen will still maintain greater femininity than the basic female. The male however, is also basically female, and also produces adrenal estrogen, which must be countered by production of extra testosterone by the testes. Any loss of testosterone production in the male therefore results in rapid tragedy. He does not just lose maleness, he immediately starts to become feminized;- to become eunuchoid;- because the adrenals continue to produce estrogen. Stress from loss of the testosterone therefore severely strains the adrenals. If adrenal nutrients are then not available in copious quantities, all body systems, including the production of testosterone, will be impaired, and the spiral of rapid health failure and eunuchization will increase. If adrenal nutrients are highly supplemented, the body will respond and counter the stress with increased hormone production, including of course estrogen, which will then increase both the eunuchization and total health problems. It would seem that the problem could be solved by supplementing testosterone, and indeed the eunuchization can be arrested and reversed with testosterone, but alas, when testosterone is supplied in adequate quantities the testicles may cease the production of testosterone, which leaves the male entirely medically dependent.

Although supplementing testosterone in adequate quantities is better than eunuchization, no really satisfactory method of supplying just the right quantities of testosterone at just the right time has as yet been developed, even for the unfortunate males who suffer accidental castration. Life with testosterone supplements is of course much better than female reversion, but even at best it is a rough life, with health, physical capability, mental attitude and emotions going up and down like a yo-yo, suspended alternately between the forces of male and female.

To try to understand the tragedy of eunuchization, we should consider the total affects of castration. We all know how dangerous bulls, boars, rams and stallions can be. If these animals are castrated when very young, as soon as the testicles have started to develop, they grow into docile creatures, usually less dangerous than the female. They are sexless. Although they are male, they have completely reverted back to the basic female. They do not have a flow of hormones to stir the mind. They are creatures that simply exist. If boys are castrated (to preserve the high voice) the same thing happens. They become a vegetable, a eunuch, a "nothing".

Now if a boar, or a bull, or a stallion is castrated after sexual development, they become extremely dangerous and unpredictable creatures that may do anything, and the dangerous condition may be present for several years before the hormone levels drop and they become manageable. Castration of a man, has a similar affect. They become highly unpredictable and very dangerous, and it may be five years or more before hormone levels fall to the point that they become fully eunuchoid. This is the reason that castration has not been widely used as a penalty for rape. It makes the already aberrant male even more dangerous.

These are the affects of complete castration, where the testicles are completely removed and the flow of all testicular hormones cease. But Candida infection of the testicles is the equivalent of only partial castration. Hormone flow is not completely stopped, it is only reduced, and the hormones and hormone flow are altered. The Candida infection victim is therefore suspended between male and eunuch;- he is suspended in the same grey world as the newly castrated male, he is neither male, female, or eunuch. The ebb and flow of altered and reduced hormones makes him extremely unpredictable, perhaps extremely vicious and vindictive, perhaps extremely nasty and critical, and perhaps highly dangerous. This is the "nasty, dirty old man" syndrome. This is the final tragedy of many males, and they may remain eunuchoid, neither man nor eunuch for many years, until overtaken by a usually miserable death.

If however, the Candida infection increases, and the decline in testicular function is quite rapid, the rate of eunuchization will be faster, and the nasty old man may become fully eunuchoid;- a docile creature that just exists, with very little thought or emotion. This is the forgetful doddering old man that exists, yet really seems to have nothing to exist for.

These are the results of testicular Candida infection. So what can be done to reduce the testicular infection and reverse the eunuchization? Your urologist will probably tell you that nothing can be done for testicular infections. Absolutely nothing. Unfortunately he is almost right. Testicular Candida infection is indeed difficult to reduce, and the rate of progress will largely depend upon the total amount of Candida infection in the body, the number of years that the infection has been growing, the amount of testicular deterioration, and the amount of eunuchization. Everything in the Candida program must be done, including ketoconazole/DMSO as in prostate problems. Testosterone must be supplemented according to the amount of eunuchization. Perhaps quite heavily at first, then tapering off to $\frac{1}{2}$ tablet per day as testicular function increases. Your doctor can test for levels of testosterone. Note that it must be slightly under-supplied to renew testicular function.

Varicoceles must also be sought and treated. It appears that perhaps the tender testicles actually come from many very small varicoceles, but this has not as yet been proven. The very small varicoceles may be difficult to treat, but improvement will be seen after each one is eliminated.

Testicular infection is almost a cavity infection, because the spongy tissues provide small cavities where the infective cannot be reached by the immune system. Ketoconazole, reduction of infection in all other parts of the body, improved immune function, and renewal of sexual function will be the main parts of the program, but everything else in the Candida program must also be covered. In the meantime, if eunuchization has started, family and friends should be warned that there are hormone problems and that to forestall the possibility of tragic violence, extreme controversy should be avoided. This may at times be difficult, because the worst psychotic problem is a tendency to pick a quarrel with anyone over anything. Avoidance of all stimulants, avoidance of all refined carbohydrates, small supplements of testosterone, frequent adrenal nutrients, and large quantities of pantothenic acid, perhaps as much as 800 mg. per day, with extra if disturbed, will make life much more bearable for both the victim and everyone else around him.

Reviving Male Sexual Function.

Revival of sexual function in the male is always difficult, usually extremely difficult, and sometimes impossible. With loss of sexual function the male starts to revert back to the basic female. Mental problems with neurosis and phychosis may be severe, and the formation of brown pigment in the testicles will have already started. Revival then is dependent upon the general health, and upon the extent of sexual degeneration and reversion. In general, if there are times when there is some erection, there is good hope for revival of sexual function.

To start, everything in the Candida program must be done. Small amounts of testosterone should be taken daily, together with about 25 mg. of zinc. A little niacin will help and chelation therapy should be included if possible. Adrenal nutrients should be taken at least twice daily. There should be massage of the thighs, anus, and genitals two or three times a day, particularly if there is a partial erection. Do not rush, and do not particularly try for sexual function. It will require time to get things going again. Each little bit of sexual activity, either thought or act, will contribute to revival. Pictures and sexual reading, to taste, will help, and an understanding sexual partner will be of great assistance. It takes many years of health degeneration to bring on complete sexual failure, so it may take as long as six months or a year for revival. A return of total health is the most important factor, together with eradication of Candida yeast from the testes and sexual system. Each improvement in erection and sexual interest will improve health, and each improvement in health will help to improve sexual interest and capability.

The actual rate of sexual improvement is very dependent upon the amount of sexual reversion that has taken place, irrespective of the length of time that it has taken for the changes to occur. One of the greatest problems is that each person considers themselves to be sexually "normal", when in fact they perhaps have really never been "normal", and may have always been very sub-normal.

Some males may not be fully sexually developed through a shortage of zinc in youth (as with the Egyptian dwarfs), or their sexual development may have been suppressed by a high Candida infection that has interfered with sexual development and has used up the zinc and other nutrients that their bodies should have had. These males will frequently have very little pubic hair, and very little chest hair, or the pubic and chest hair may not arrive until they are in their twenties. These people will usually improve only with reduction in the Candida infection and long term zinc supplements, but the improvement may include an increase in chest size, greatly increased pubic hair, and an increase in the size of the genitals even at age sixty or more.

Some males may also have genetic problems, which usually are evident at an early age. These problems can only be sorted out by a highly competent doctor, and the following medical advice illustrates the importance of obtaining a proper diagnosis if sexual function has never really been normal. The reference is to male gonadal disorders. Note the technical complexity of the problems;

1. "Competitive protein binding, immunoassay, or radioreceptor assay, are specific and sensitive and, unlike gonadotropin assays, they provide unambiguous differentiation between male and female, between child and adult, and between normal and abnormal. Thus, assay of plasma testosterone should be the first step in evaluation of any male suspected of hypogonadism.

Semen analysis is required in the investigation of male infertility. Normal examination results (volume, count, motility and morphology) establish the normality of the entire endocrine and duct system. An abnormal result can provide a major clue to the site of the pathologic condition."

2. "The buccal smear for Barr bodies and a karyotype analysis identify Klinefelter's syndrome, the most common gonadal defect. Both tests are useful in providing a definitive guide to prognosis and management. Standard cytogenetic techniques should be adequate most of the time, specialized banding studies are rarely needed." "(The Barr body is a clump of chromatin found in the nucleus of any cell with two x chromosomes. It is present in normal females (XX) and in patients with Klinefelter's syndrome (XXY), but it is not present in normal males (XY). It represents one of the X chromosomes in a genetically inert form.")

3. "Klinefelter's syndrome remains the best defined of the gonadal disorders. In pure form, it is due to a chromosomal defect in which the patient has 47 chromosomes with two X chromosomes and one Y (XXY). As a consequence, the tubules remain small and collapsed, there is postpubertal hyalinization, and there is almost no spermatogenesis. The testes are small, providing the one constant feature of the disorder. Testosterone levels are extremely variable (see figure 5), causing patients to differ greatly in symptoms and appearance, from severely eunuchoid individuals to men who are entirely normal except for small testes and infertility. A chromatin-positive buccal smear, a reduction in testosterone, and a high level of FSH allow definitive diagnosis."

4. "Initiation or restoration of spermatogenesis is far more difficult than replacement of testosterone. If the defect is in the testis, as revealed by elevated levels of gonadotropins, no therapy will restore gametogenic activity; testosterone replacement should be undertaken as necessary. If varicocele is accompanied by hypospermatogenesis, surgical correction is indicated. If testicular deficiency results from a lack of gonadotropin, replacement with FSH and LH-like preparations has a significant chance of restoring both sperm and hormone production."

These short medical descriptions are included to show the extent and complexity of gonadal problems and eunuchization. Scientific American Medical Library, and similar medical publications deal extensively with gonadal problems and your doctor should refer to them for specific information. Other gonadal problems of particular concern are the affects of mumps, varicocele and the anti-cancer drug cyclophoshamide.

To revive sexual function everything in the Candida program must be done, and your doctor will have to give you as much help as possible with testosterone and perhaps other hormones. The penis will probably be small, flabby and retracted, and if uncircumcized, may be continuously within the sheath. Massage of the penis, testicles, and upper legs at any and every opportune time will help to get some erection started again. Although an impotent male can sometimes induce ejaculation without full erection, erection is paramount to re-establishing full orgasm. Try to be patient, and give the program time to start renewal of hormone production. If marital problems have resulted in twin beds, move them together again, or otherwise if possible, seek the help and assistance of a very understanding female, or if absolutely necessary, a capable prostitute. Do not forget that male sexual problems are very common, and older experienced prostitutes are well acquainted with them. In fact, most young people arrange their own ways of fulfilling their sexual needs, so the fact of, and the need for prostitutes is largely based on the older men with failing sexual ability. If necessary, prostitutes may therefore be useful. Close, understanding female presence and female attention, is the best way to get erection to return. Oriental baths and massage may be of great help. If eunuchization has been severe, it may take some time before even small signs of erection return.

When erection starts to return, it should be nurtured. Not constantly, and not too much, but frequently. Reading sexy books and looking at sexy pictures, with slow masturbation will help, but do not overdo. If stimulation is too great, the resorbed hormones will increase the reversion toward female. If stimulation is not great enough, production of testosterone will fall. Extra adrenal nutrients should be taken four or five times a day, with extra pantothenic acid to curb vindictive or violent outbursts. Sleep should be reduced if possible, to not more than eight hours a night, with several short naps during the day if needed. Lethargy, inactivity, and excess sleep seem to somehow contribute to female reversion. Emphasis should be placed on continuing activity, to keep the adrenals active. Skating, dancing, square dancing and swimming are good evening activities. Get up early in the morning, at least before 7 o'clock and go for a walk or a short run before breakfast, and then maintain the physicxal activity (with short rests if necessary) throughout the day.

To re-activate the testes, the whole body and lifestyle must be re-activated. Eunuchization invariably promotes lethargy, with a tendency to sleep many extra hours, and the lethargic cycle must be deliberately broken. Be sure to get enough rest, but the peroids between should be physically active, preferably with physical outdoor exercise like swimming, sawing wood, clearing land, building fences, gardening or perhaps even making a stone folly like a minature of the Taj Mahal. Get extra sleep if you must, but avoid long peroids with books and T.V. Make all activities, active activities.

Do not rush, but as health and sexual capability start to return, attempts should be made to reach ejaculation. If possible these attempts should be preceded by adrenal nutrients, including a little niacin. Male arousal time is usually quite short, so the attempt should not be slow and prolonged. The "best time of day" may be sometime during the night, particularly if there is a spontaneous erection, or it may be sometime early in the morning. Massage of the legs, testicles, and anus, with slow masturbation aided by sexy pictures or sexual reading, together with hot water bottles and sexual lubricants, will help with arousal, then rush to climax. Anything and everything should be done to reach ejaculation. Sucking on thumbs and hands may help, anal masturbation or anal vibrators may help, or success may finally be achieved with both an anal vibrator and a vibrator on the tip of the penis. A willing female may be of great assistance, and in desperate cases oral sex may accomplish the almost impossible. This is a critical peroid. All different lubricants, all devices, and all different methods should be tried. There will be many failures, but with each failure something will be learned. Each failure may be followed by psychosis, headaches, and other signs of reversion, but the effects of the resorbed hormones can be offset and reduced with more adrenal nutrients, together with physical activity, either immediately, or if necessary after a short rest.

Sexual function is so dependent upon so many factors that we must repeat that everything must be done, absolutely everything. Thyroid, parathyroid, B12, folic acid, niacin, zinc, and reduction of chronic infectives are of particular importance. Sexual orgasm in both male and female is dependent upon adequate histamine levels and upon histamine release, so the body must be capable of producing the large number of basophil cells, mast cells and eosinophil cells that are broken down for histamine release. Each sexual attempt will induce the body to produce more histamine release cells, if high hormone resorption can be avoided.

After a frustrated sexual attempt has been made, another quite strong sexual urge may occur in a few hours, or perhaps the next day. This urge comes from the re-building of the histamine cell reserve. However, this urge should be responded to only mildly, because it is short lived and because the other physical capabilities have not had time to be restored. Do not make the next active attempt sooner than two days, but do not leave it longer than four days, or signs of reversion may return.

These are only general suggestions. Persistent trial will usually determine the best course. Everything should be tried, and the health and sexual therapy must be given priority over everything else. Time for return of sexual function cannot even be guessed, because so many other body functions must first be restored. However, each person will sense their own progress, and finally the day will come when ejaculation is again achieved.

Oh wonderful day; and what a relief, as so many parts of life seem to come together again. Rejoice yes, but rejoice with caution. Again this is a very critical peroid. Every attention and every priority must be given to maintaining the restored sexual function. Again, a high sexual urge may come in a few hours, or next day, but again this must be subdued to allow the body time to recuperate. However, a strong urge on the second or third day will probably bring another success, with further improvement in sexual function, but do not let more than four days pass, or there may be risk of reversion.

After sexual function has been restored there may be a quite strong sexual urge every day, as the body tries to re-adjust. Daily sexual relief may then be of great benefit if there is sufficient physical capability, that frustrated orgasm can be avoided.

CHAPTER 7.

DEGENERATIVE DISEASES.

DEGENERATIVE DISEASE.
Degenerative disease is the manifestation of the compound failure of many body systems. Candida yeast infection is invariably a contributing factor. If Candida infection did not contribute to the start of the disease, it will surely follow when the failure of other body systems has weakened the immune system and other body defences. Then when the Candida matrix has been established, many other infectives join the colony with all of the toxins and all of the metabolites from the infectives altering many different body functions.

A close examination of modern orthomolecular methods of successfully combating the different degenerative diseases will soon show that all of the degenerative diseases are interlocked, and that they all respond to similar therapy. The problem is that the orthomolecular therapies do not always work. The macrobiotic diet will always help cancer, and arthritis, and allergies etc; but it will only sometimes cure. Megavitamins will always help high blood pressure, atherosclerosis, etc; but they will only sometimes cure. So the list goes on and on, with many cures with B6, niacin, B12, chelation therapy, autogenous vaccine, Vitamin E, thyroxin, proteolitic enzymes, A-E emulsion, diet, fasting, etc; and etc. Each therapy will have a book, or perhaps sveral books. Each therapy will have its successes. Each therapy will have its failures.

Each therapy will have its failures because all of the degenerative diseases are interlocked by partial impairment and partial alteration of all body systems. The disease is not named after its cause, it could not be named after its cause, because there is no single cause. The causes are multiple, so the disease is named after the symptoms. The ailment then is not a single ailment, like a broken leg, where there is only one thing to heal, instead the ailment is the total of the symptoms from the impairment and failure of all interlocking body systems, with the predominant failure creating the name of the disease by producing the most symptoms. Thus for example, it is folly to medically consider, or to even suggest that arthritis is a "pure" disease, (like smallpox) and that it does not have a component of poor blood circulation, a component of poor nerve function, a component of pancreatic failure, a component of chronic infection, a component of colon failure, etc, and etc. Of course it has these components, and many more, because by the time that the build up of the arthritic deposits is great enough to be aware of the problem there will already be sub-clinical deposits throughout the body, and these deposits will create unnatural pressure on nerves, blood vessels, and lymph nodes, which will further alter all body systems. So alternately, can we have allergies, or diabetes, or colitis without also having a little arthritis? And can we have any of these without impairing body functions and immune function to the point where ever-present chronic infection will advance, and with the advance will impair all body systems, either a little, or perhaps a lot?

Most certainly then, all of the degenerative diseases are interlocked. If we have one, we have them all, or we have the precursors of them all, to some degree. Therefore, again, to gain remission from any named degenerative disease we must do everything, everything in the Candida program, and a little bit more.

To confirm this point of view, and to gain insight into the diseased state, let us consider the basic roots of degenerative disease.

THE ROOTS OF DEGENERATIVE DISEASE.

Consider the body as a whole. The body as a whole is a wondrous electro-chemical-mechanical mobile heat machine, complete with intake and exhaust systems, fuel systems, fuel storage, internal scavenging and cleansing, sewage and waste disposal systems, and continuous renewal and repair.

To accomplish and maintain the wondrous workings of this heat machine, all working parts are enclosed in a dustproof, waterproof skin. Fuel and air are brought in with tubes, and the fuel and oxygen are very finely filtered before they reach any of the parts of the machine. Waste disposal is also through tubes, with the waste finely filtered before disposal. The body is therefore an encapsulated mechanism, complete unto itself, dependent only on an adequate supply of fuel and air. A complete capsule. A capsule free from exterior forces.

If this capsule, this wondrous self-contained design, is free from exterior forces, while it also has its own internal means of rebuilding and repair, what can possibly go wrong with it? Quite obviously, the only way that anything can go wrong is by grossly improper supplies of fuel and air, or by invasion of something from outside of the capsule, into the mechanism inside of the capsule. Something that can cross the fine filter between the outside and the inside. Disease of this wondrous heat machine can therefore come only from improper foods, from contaminants taken in through the filters of the fuel and air systems, or from invasive organisms that make their way through the barriers.

The roots of degenerative disease must therefore be accidental metal poisons, self administrered poisons, or invasive organisms. There can be no other.

Yet there are exceptions. The exceptions are genetic and pre-natal defects, and growth problems;-- problems that are already within the capsule at birth. Indeed, if health problems occur early in life, genetic and pre-natal growth defects should be suspected and diligently sought. Particularly, chromasome tests should be made, to ensure that sexual development matches the chromasome pattern for male or female. Problems with growth can also be genetic, or they may result from transient infectious diseases like chicken pox or mumps, or from early chronic infections like Candida yeast, that sometimes results in the newborn being covered with thrush. Early health problems can also result from toxins imposed upon the fetus during pregnancy. Caffeine, tobacco, alcohol and other drugs can definitely affect the unborn fetus, and adrenal depletion in the mother can result in the baby being born with adrenal problems, either adrenal depleted, or with warped oversize adrenals that constantly produce too much adrenalin. Fortunately, these problems can usually be identified by test, X-ray, and questioning, and your doctor should have good methods to deal with these defects, except perhaps the adrenal depletion, or warped oversize adrenals. Inherited adrenal depletion may require special adrenal supplements for many years, while the oversize warped adrenals may require extra insulin. (See "Diabetes".)

Aside from the early health problems, if there has been reasonably good health for even a few years after adolescence, ill health can be caused by only four things:
1. Grossly improper nutrition.
2. Toxic minerals.
3. Self administered poisons.
4. Infection.

These then are the basic roots of degenerative disease. These are the roots of atherosclerosis, nephritis, high blood pressure, diabetes, etc; right on to multiple sclerosis and cancer. Only four basic roots;-- there can be no others. But yes! Of course there can still be one more! The one more is called "Behavior". And Yes! It is Your Behavior. Behavior is frequently overlooked as being a major cause of ill health, but behavior is responsible for postponed bowel movements, for overeating, for missed meals, missed rest, overwork and overplay and many other things that reduce health. So most certainly behavior, Your behavior, can be a root cause of ill health. But behavior, Your behavior can be changed, and of course you are the only one that can change it, and since you are always a very reasonable person you will of course make those changes, so now we are back at only four root causes of degenerative disease.

The first is nutrition. Nutrition of course can be changed. You and only you can make the changes. You have always known that good nutrition is not junk food and sugar. You have always known that good nutrition is wholesome simple food, without too much cooking, (except meat) without too much refining, without too much salt, without too much baking, and without too many spices and additives. Good wholesome food. You know what it is. You know that it is not what you have been having, you know very well that the food you have been having helped to creat your affliction. But you can change all of that, so now we are down to three basic causes of degenerative disease.

The next on the list is toxic minerals. These insidious chemicals can certainly sneak in unnoticed. Usually they are not your fault, but your bad luck. Fortunately you can get a hair mineral test, and if you need it you can get chelation therapy to remove the metals. It is simple. It should have been done years ago. It is up to you. But be sure to check for mercury poisoning from silver amalgam fillings in the teeth, or slowly have the fillings changed to cement.

So now what about these self administered poisons? Yes, the coffee and the tea, and the cola, and the chocolate, and perhaps tobacco and alcohol or other drugs. You have known all along that they were called stimulants and drugs, and that they acted by altering biological processes. You have known that they were destroying you. So now you have a choice. You can continue with them and suffer with their cumulative effects, or you can eliminate them. Or stated more bluntly, if you do not eliminate them they will help to eliminate you, and they already have a head start. After all, you know within you that they have contributed to your present condition. You have known it for years. The choice is yours. The path you take is up to you.

So now we are down to only one basic cause of degenerative disease, the ever present, ever active, ever inescapable scourge of man;- Chronic Infection. Down to only one cause? No! We still have two causes, Chronic infection and You. You will remain forever as the other cause, and only You can reduce your role. So now we are down to only you, and the compound effects of Chronic Infection, and particularly Candida yeast infection, because Candida yeast is so pervasive that it is almost everywhere, and Candida yeast is so invasive that it will grow almost anywhere if the skin has been cut or abraded, and because Candida yeast forms its own waterproof skin where it harbors hundreds of other infectives within its own little shelter;-- the Candida Callus Matrix. These invasive plants that we call

Candida yeast, together with their associated infectives, then live on Your nutrients, and dump their toxins back into Your body and into Your bloodstream.

So what can You do about all of those nasty little invasive plants? The answer lies in all of the preceding pages of this book.

To reduce and hopefully to overcome your degenerative disease, whatever the particular combination of symptoms or whatever particular name it may have, you will have to do everything in the Candida program. Yes everything, and with particular attention to just a little more than "everything".

In considering the various specific diseases, as diagnosed, we must also look at their interlocking influences on total health, which takes us back to the term "as diagnosed".

Now the very best way to confirm medical diagnosis is with autopsy after death. Unfortunately, autopsies show only the immediate cause of death, and not the underlying degeneration. Also again unfortunately, in North America, only about 10% of all deaths are followed by autopsy. Statistically however, in only about 10% of the cases where autopsies are performed the medical diagnosis and the death certificate are correct, and the death actually resulted from the diagnosed disease. Only 10%. Truly a dismal record, that inverted, says that in 90% of the cases the medical diagnosis was actually incorrect, and the medical practitioner had been treating for the wrong ailment. Now please remember that this is You, that your medical diagnosis is probably wrong, and that there is only a 10% chance that it is right. Of course, any diagnosis is better than none, but the diagnosis should not be considered as fact; it should be considered only as a hopefully accurate probability.

Ninety percent wrong and only 10% correct, a dismal record, yes and certainly a record that casts great doubt upon the wisdom of giving the alopathic doctors a legal monopoly on medical matters, but a record that is nonetheless understandable. It is understandable if we remember that the doctor is relying on the accuracy of tests performed by many other people, and that he particularly depends upon the pathologist, who may or may not have complete medical training, and who is looking at tests and tissues with only slight differences between the different diseases. In other words, even to the pathologist the differences between many of the degnerative diseases is difficult to detect with accuracy.

In considering the various specific degenerative diseases, as diagnosed, we must also look at their interlocking influences on total health. In considering the various degenerative diseases an attempt will therefore be made to consider each of the degenerative diseases in the order of their influence on other body systems, but the person with the affliction should remember that their specific condition is not a single disease, but a combination of many symptoms. They should also remember that their diagnosis is probably wrong, and therefore to regain health they will have to alter and correct all of the underlying causes of degenerative disease, even if the causes do not appear to be related to the diagnosis.

CANDIDA YEAST INFECTION.

Candida yeast infection is the most pervasive degenerative disease with the earliest and most widespread effects on all other body systems. It can mimic each of the degenerative diseases, (creating a false diagnosis). (See medical papers on Candida Yeast Infection, Ch.3.). It can be the sole cause of some of the degenerative diseases, and it is invariably a component of all of the degenerative diseases. Therapy for each and all of the degenerative diseases must therefore include the entire Candida program, which covers all of the basic causes of health degeneration.

THE FOCAL POINT in DEGENERATIVE DISEASE.

We have already shown that degenerative disease invariably has multiple causes. The entire Candida program will certainly help to reduce those multiple causes, and as body systems start to respond and some body functions are returned to normal, the various factors of which the degenerative disease is composed will become much more visible. Sometimes the focal point of the degenerative disease will be revealed by a rapid change in symptoms, but in other cases the health may be slowly improving, but the focal point may be obscure. An assessment of all factors must then be carefully made to try to determine the actual focal point of the disease, so that the therapy can be concentrated on the focal point. Do not be misled by the obvious, because the true focal point may be well hidden. For instance, let us suppose that the medical diagnosis is kidney failure, and the kidney function is badly impaired. It would seem that the kidneys are the focal point of the problem, and of course they may indeed be the focal point, but the true focal point may not be the kidney, because severe kidney overload will have the same symptoms as impaired kidney function. The true focal point of the degenerative disease therefore might not be kidney failure, it might be chronic infection elsewhere that is overloading the kidney, or perhaps the kidney becomes overloaded from partly digested food, metabolites and toxins, absorbed by the body from a loose, porous, leaky bowel. In this case, although there would be health improvement from vitamins, minerals, and anti-infectives. Vitamin C enemas would provide the most spectacular benefits, and it is obvious that good health could not be restored until bowel function was improved.

The focal point of degenerative disease is frequently very obscure, so seek diligently, and when you have found the focal point you will usually be rewarded by a definite rapid improvement in symptoms.

METABOLIC DEGENERATION by CANDIDA and ALCOHOL.

The following information is derived principally from "Metabolic Abnormalities in Patients with Chronic Candidiasis." by C.Orian Truss, M.D. published in the Journal of Orthomolecular Psychiatry. Reprints are available from C.S.F., 2229 Broad St. Regina Sask. Dr. Truss is one of the true pioneers in Candida infection research, for which the writer gives him great credit and personal thanks.

Acetaldehyde

Every thinking person surely must have observed and noted the severe health degeneration resulting from the continuous consumption of alcohol, and every thinking person must have wondered why some severely degenerated continuous drinkers are alcoholic while others ar not. The answers to these two questions are Acetaldehyde and Candida yeast.

Let us first establish some simple facts. Ethyl alcohol (ethanol) is a drug, and it is a poison. After alcohol has been consumed the body must break it down and detoxify it. In the first metabolic step the body robs Acet-(yl-) from any source, and changes the alcohol to acetaldehyde, (the first cousin of formaldehyde), and it is the toxic effects of the acetaldehyde that further affects the mind and damages the body.

Now let us establish a few more facts. Yeasts are composed of eukaryotic cells, like our own, and they thrive on the same sugars that we live on. Yeast fermentation invariably produces alcohol or similar substances. If we look back at the many medical papers on Candida yeast (CH.3.) and the list of substances that Candida produces we find such good things as indole ethanol, sterols, phenethyl alcohol, and tryptophol. Some strains of Candida produce methyl (rubbing) alcohol or ethyl(drinking) alcohol, and all strains of Candida produce acetaldehyde. Although Candida also produces many other toxins, it is the acetaldehyde produced directly by the Candida, or resulting from the alcohols produced by the Candida, that produces most of the lasting damage to the body.

Acetaldehyde degeneration in the victim of chronic Candida infection is therefore almost identical to the acetaldehyde degeneration so visible in alcoholics. The chronic alcoholic however, usually suffers from greater acetaldehyde degeneration because, they are not just alcoholic. With continuing tissue degeneration from acetaldehyde from alcohol they soon become Candida victims with increased acetaldehyde damage from the Candida, or perchance, the Candida infection that they acquire may be a strain that produces alcohol and then, they then become alcoholic because even if they manage to stop drinking their infectives will continue their drunken state by producing alcohol internally from sugars from the food they eat, or from sugars from their bloodstream. Internal alcohol,-- alcohol from which they cannot escape long enough to dry out. There is also evidence that brewers yeast will join the Candida yeast in the callus matrix, which increases the amount of alcohol and increases the problem. The internal production of alcohol within the digestive tract has been known in Japan for many years and has been named Mieti Sho disease.

Acetaldehyde has many effects on the body systems, but one of the most extensive damaging effects is membrane damage to red blood cells. Just put some blood from a Candida victim under a 1,000 X microscope and look at the red blood cells. You do not need to be a doctor or a scientist to be immediately shocked by all of the malformed red cells. Cells that are damaged on one side, on both sides, or perhaps even appear to be square. Your doctor may have just told you how healthy you are, but if you are a Candida victim you will instantly recognize that there are grave problems and the grave problems that you see results from acetaldehyde from the Candida infection, from alcohol or both. Then if you also put your blood under a darkfield microscope you will get a further shock when you see all of the rods, L forms, crystal bodies and clumped red cells, where in each clump ten or twenty red blood cells may be uselessly stuck together like a stack of checkers. All of this can be reduced with I.V. calcium chelation therapy, but it cannot be eliminated because the Candida continues to produce the filaments and hyphae that work their way into the bloodstream, the jelly that engulfs the red cells into crystal bodies continues to come from somewhere, and the red cell clumping is continuously promoted by acetaldehyde damage to the red cell membranes.

All skeptics, all health professionals, all Candida victims and all alcoholics should see the blood under the microscope. It is extremely enlightening, and it is extremely convincing that Candida is the master, nasty infective that reduces health to the point of degenerative disease, and the active agent is acetaldehyde.

Many people, including many health professionals are not fully aware of the life-saving arrangement of our vascular plumbing where everything absorbed from the intestines must pass through the liver before it reaches the general circulation. Thus if alcohol is consumed it must pass through the liver before it reaches the rest of the body. Then small amounts are simply detoxified by the liver, but larger amounts overwhelm the liver and go on to other parts of the body where the alcohol is metabolized to acetaldehyde and carbon dioxide, and the acetaldehyde and carbon dioxide then affect that particular body part. Thus the greater the amount of alcohol, the more extensive the cellular damage. If an intestinal Candida infection produces acetaldehyde, the acetaldehyde will affect the villa and cells lining the digestive tract, and some will be absorbed by the bloodstream, but this will be immediately detoxified by the liver before it can reach the rest of the body. If the Candida infection is in the feet, fingers, genitals or other body part all of the acetaldehyde and carbon dioxide are forced into the bloodstream, with devastating effects on the entire body.

Now let us look at this sequence again:-Beverage alcohol is ethyl alcohol or ethanol, and in the first step in the metabolic reduction of alcohol the alcohol is converted to acetaldehyde. All strains of Candida yeast produce alcohols or acetaldehyde or both. The acetaldehyde is the principal toxin that destroys and alters body tissues, and it also affects the mind. As some of the normal intestinal flora also produce acetaldehyde, the total internal production can be quite high if Candida infection is high, and each and every drink of alcohol will increase the problem. If the Candida infection happens to be a strain that produces alcohol, it becomes obvious that despite abstinence and despite all other efforts the alcoholic thinking, the alcoholic ways, and the alcoholism will remain until the internal production of alcohol is reduced by reducing the total Candida infection. It can now readily be seen that the difference between the non-alcoholic heavy drinker and the alcoholic who drinks much less, is chronic infection by a strain of Candida that happens to produce alcohol. Non-alcoholics that drink therefore should not criticize the alcoholic, because "except fot the Grace of God, there go I".

Acetaldehyde Damage.

The visible damage to the body in alcoholism is testimony to the severe affects of acetaldehyde on all body systems. Production of acetaldehyde (and/or alcohol) by Candida, finally explains the role of Candida infection in degenerative disease. Candida therefore not only initiates and maintains the callus matrix that shelters both itself and its associated infectives from the immune system and from topical anti-fungal agents, but it also produces the acetaldehyde that initiates or increases degenerative disease.

Acetaldehyde has a particular affinity for sulfhydryl and amine groups, and its presence in the intestine and bloodstream therefore affects and alters intestinal function, liver cells (reducing the ability of the body to reduce infection), blood, nutrients, enzymes, vitamins and polypeptides, and where excessive production of acetaldehyde is continuous, as in Candida infection or alcoholism, the buildup of acetaldehyde in susceptible body elements is cumulative.

The principal known toxic affects of acetaldehyde are:- (Just note how it affects the entire body)-

1. Binding to amine groups in neurotransmitters, with "alcoholic effects" on the mind, thought perhaps to be part of alcoholic addiction.

2. Dose dependent suppression of CoEnzyme A.,(CoA) which alters the metabolism of carbohydrate, fats, and some amino acids, and thus alters the citric acid cycle. Supression of Acetyl CoA affects the formation of fatty acids, ketones, cholesterol, steroid hormones, and acetylcholine, and it reduces the ability of the brain and liver to utilize oxygen. Note the reduced liver and mental function. Suppression of acetyl CoA and acetylcholine is directly by the acetaldehyde, and it also occurs indirectly by the body robbing the acet-(yl) to change alcohol into acetaldehyde.

3. Alteration of the ratio of NADA to NAD, which affects lactate, pyruvate, hydroxysteroids, galactose, serotonin, and tryptophol. It too alters the citric acid cycle, resulting in reduced fatty acid oxidation, reduced conversion of excess amino acids to glycogen, and a further reduction in pyruvate. The high lactate raises blood uric acid, which affects the kidney tubules, porphyrin metabolism is altered, phosphorylation is inhibited, and protein synthesis is reduced. This is undoubtedly another reason that Candida victims usually have low levels of blood proteins that are almost impossible to raise. Amino acids that are particularly suppressed by acetaldehyde are glutamate, glutamine, and asparagine.

4. Reduced glutathione in the liver, resulting in reduced removal of free radicals, with consequent damage to many cells. The need for, and the development of, SOD and other "free radical quenchers" is based on reduced glutathione in the liver.

5. Increased deposition of collagen (fibrosis) in the liver which further impairs liver function.

6. Altered fat metabolism which results in altered outer membranes of every cell in the body, making the cells more rigid and less pliable and altering all metabolic and physiological

function. The increased cell membrane (the outer membrane or "skin" of the cell) rigidity has a particularly devastating effect on the red blood cells (erythrocytes), on red blood filtration, on blood circulation, and consequently on the entire body. Truth is often stranger than fiction, and Nature frequently displays amazing mechanical feats in strange places. The diameter of the human red blood cell is about 7 microns, yet the cells pass through capillaries of only 2 microns, and in the spleen they must pass through capillaries as small as one micron. This is equivalent to pushing a 20 inch balloon through a long tube the size of a teacup, all without damage. Quite obviously the cell must be very flexible and easily deformed or it will be stuck in the tubes. So with the reduced cell membrane flexibility and the red cell clumping, alcoholics and Candida victims do have reduced blood circulation and reduced function of the spleen. As normal function of the spleen is essential to both the lymphatic system and the immune system Candida/alcohol victims are subject to increased infections including of course, Candida, aids, and cancer. Further the reduced blood flow through capillaries throughout the body results in a further reduction in oxygenation with reduced function of all body systems and is particularly devastating to the brain and the central nervous system.

7. Altered cell membranes throughout the body affects final cellular nutrition. So much has been written about diet, digestion, and absorption (and rightly so) but the final value of nutrients to the body is determined by the amounts accepted and utilized by the cells. All changes in the outer membrane of each cell alters the transport of nutrients and wastes into and out of the cell and into and out of the compartments of the cell, producing abnormal function of the cell and ultimately abnormal function of the entire organ or body system.

Numerous membrane pumps and shunts function in cell membrane metabolic pathways and any of these can be affected by changes in the cell membrane, while each in turn may affect many others. Metabolic pathways are very complex and technical readers should refer to the medical paper. Suffice it here to say that NAD, NADH, ATP, Adp, carnitine, gluconeogenesis, glycolysis, electrical conductunce, NaK pump, Krebs cycle, glutamate carriers, etc may all be affected.

8. Acetaldehyde has an opposite effect on the intestinal microvilla membranes, and increases their fluidity, with altered sodium gradient, reduced carrier function, and increased permeability, with the increased permeability producing all of the consequences of the leaky bowel syndrome;-- migraine headache, allergies, arthritis, etc., and etc.

9. Changes in cell membranes of lymphocytes impairs their function and alters the effectiveness of the entire immune system with increased total infection and perchance the development of auto-immune disease. Then one must wonder if the presence of Candida is the true cause of AIDs, Cancer, etc.

10. Changes in the cell membranes of some body tissues may alter their immune markers and trigger the immune system to attack and destroy the tissues as though they were "foreign".

11. Changes in red blood cell membranes can reduce the transport of carbon dioxide out of the body, which not only reduces cellular oxygenation but also affects many other metabolic processes by the increased carbon dioxide and carbonic acid. This effect is greatly increased if the Candida infection produces alcohols that are broken down to carbon dioxide and acetaldehyde.

12. Mitral heart valve prolapse is very frequent in Candida victims and may be linked to acetaldehyde changes in cell membranes. Significantly, disseminated Candida infection has a particular affinity for heart valves.

13. Carpal Tunnel Syndrome (which usually responds to B6) is also very frequent in Candida victims and may result from the devastating effects of acetaldehyde on collagen formation. Reduced and altered collagen will also affect many other body parts and systems and may well be true cause of osteoporosis.

14. Formaldehyde sensitivity (as with urea formaldehyde insulation) resulting from high amounts of acetaldehyde which deplete liver stores of aldehyde dehydrogenase, with the body then unable to detoxify the formaldehyde. Alternately, continuous exposure to formaldehyde will impair lymphocyte function with increased growth of ever present Candida, resulting in increasing amounts of acetaldehyde.

15. Acetaldehyde is a very potent blocking agent at the nerve synapses. It therefore alters nerve function throughout the body and it may alter the balance between the sympathetic and parasympathetic nervous systems.

16. It appears that the acet-(yl)- robbed by either Candida or the body to produce acetaldehyde is usually stolen from acetylcholine, which in turn impairs and alters the central nervous system, followed by defective short term memory, impaired concentration, depression, anxiety and mental aberrations from false neurotransmitters and amplified by diminished delivery of oxygen to the brain.

17. It appears that acetaldehyde, by altering leukocyte and lymphocyte cell membranes, induces severe allergies including urticaria (hives) because these symptoms frequently disappear with a reduction in Candida infection.

Yes, all of these effects can result from acetaldehyde from alcohol, or from alcohol or acetaldehyde produced by Candida yeast infection within the body. Many doctors and other health professionals have been unable to understand how Candida infection can affect so many body systems remote from the site of the infection. Candida has been thought of principally as a nuisance, while in fact it is lethal, producing slow death by degenerative disease. Note how every part of the body and every physical and mental process is affected, and each of the foregoing changes in physical function alters the function of all of the others while the entire metabolic mess is further affected by toxins and metabolites from the other infectives that invariably join the basic Candida infection sheltered in the Candida callus matrix, with the total chronic infection increasing and spreading to the weak and damaged tissues largely unopposed by the weak and altered immune system.

These are the affects of acetaldehyde!

These are the affects of alcohol!

These are the affects of Candida yeast infection!

These are the complex scientific biological roots of degenerative disease where nothing is right and everything is wrong, with the disease itself simply named after the predominant symptoms. If we are, or if we are not alcoholic, the only effective remedy must start by reducing the Candida yeast infection, and that is the reason that we must publish this book.

So now, with the typesetting for the book nearing completion, we have discovered (with many more thanks to Dr. Orion Truss) that it is the production of alcohols and acetaldehyde by Candida within the body that makes Candida infection so devastating to all body systems. This opens the door to new possibilities. This opens the door to finally finding real help for alcoholics, and it increases the possibility of reducing the effects of Candida infection. Acetaldehyde (and formaldehyde) are detoxified in the liver by aldehyde dehydrogenase. We should be able to rapidly reduce the effects of acetaldehyde (from both alcohol and Candida) with supplements of aldehyde dehydrogenase. It is available, and we have acquired some,- but alas, we do not as yet know exactly how it can be administered. Yet time waits for no man and typesetting must proceed. With luck, perhaps information on the use of aldehyde dehydrogenase can yet be included in the last chapter. "The Brave New World".

DIABETES, HYPOGLYCEMIA, and ATHEROSCLEROSIS.
    (Sugar and Caffeine disease) (see also ref.6,7 and 29).
    Diabetes is a continuous state of hyperglycemia or high blood sugar. Hypoglycemia is the state of very low blood sugar.

Both hypoglycemia and diabetes (hyperglycemia) can be initiated by the over consumption of sugar, honey, alcohol, or other refined carbohydrate, which at first overworks the pancreas, producing rapid wide swings in the blood sugar, ranging from extreme hyperactivity and the diabetic state to extremely low hypoglycemic levels that produce psychosis, mental wanderings, or perhaps even fainting or blackout. Classically, diabetes and hypoglycemia are considered as diseases of an overactive pancreas and pancreatic failure. However, heavy metal poisons, self administered poisons, allergies, Candida infection, and enlarged overactive adrenals (which produce too much adrenalin) can also raise blood sugar levels to the high diabetic state, and then, by reaction of the pancreas, also produce hypoglycemia, while the much maligned pancreas may be normal and dealing with the high levels of blood sugar as best it can.

Then of course, the thyroid is master of many hormones, and low thyroid, (hypothyroidism) can also produce high blood sugar, and the diabetic state, with sometimes a hypoglycemic reaction.

Normally blood sugar levels keep changing every minute of the day and night, but swings are within reasonable limits. With diabetes and hypoglycemia these levels are greatly changed, so all diabetics are sometimes hypoglycemics, and all hypoglycemics are sometimes diabetic.

Irrespective of the causes of high blood sugar, when there is excess sugar in the blood (the diabetic state) the body is forced to deal with the excess sugar as best it can. The blood can carry only a finite amount of oxygen, and this amount is reduced when blood sugar levels are high. If the oxygen supply to the body cells is insufficient to completely oxidize all of the sugar delivered by the bloodstream the normal sugar metabolism is shunted through the lactic acid cycle. If within a few minutes, or even if within a few hours, sufficient oxygen is delivered to the cells, the lactic acid will be metabolized on down to energy and water. But if sufficient oxygen is not delivered to the cells, or if it is not delivered soon enough, the lactic acid will draw water, overload the lymphatic system (interfering with immune function) and produce the edema that is so frequently seen in diabetes. The tissue pressures from the edema then reduces blood circulation, further reducing the available oxygen and compounding the problem, while the excess lactic acid will also enter the nerve synapses interfering with the function of every gland, every organ, and every muscle. The lactic acid thus leads to muscle spasm, resulting in the many aches and pains that are a common complaint among hypoglycemics and diabetics. If this state continues, calcium joins the stagnating lymphatic fluids, resulting in the fibrosis and calcinosis that is so frequently seen in people with "sugar" problems. Now potassium is absolutely necessary for complete sugar metabolism. But potassium is easily lost with stress, and the diabetic or hypoglycemic state greatly increases stress, which depletes the potassium at the very time that it is needed. If the levels of sugar in the blood exceed the amount of oxygen available for complete oxidation (the usual situation in the diabetic) and if potassium is low, sugar metabolism cannot even proceed to lactic acid, so the metabolism is altered and proceeds to glycerol, with the glycerol then being altered to the abnormally high levels of cholesterol and triglycerides associated with the development of atherosclerosis and circulatory disease.

It can therefore be rightly said that circulatory disease is based in sugar disease;- is based in diabetes and hypoglycemia. It can also then rightly be said that all diabetics and hypoglycemics have circulatory problems, either visible or sub-clinical. It follows then, that the circulatory problems must contribute to the diabetes and hypoglycemia.

It must again be pointed out that Candida yeast thrives on sugars, and high levels of blood sugar makes diabetics and hypoglycemics highly susceptible to Candida infection, which will grow rapidly because the high blood sugar also impairs the lymphatic-immune system, while the presence of the yeast infection, with its toxins and metabolites, contributes to further episodes of high blood sugar, which further feeds the yeast. But that is not all. Candida infection feeds on many body nutrients. It has a high affinity for chromium, which is part of the glucose tolerance factor, it has a high affinity for selenium, which is necessary for carbohydrate metabolism, and it has a high affinity for lithium which is necessary for immune function. Lithium is also essential to thyroid function, and depletion of lithium therefore results in low, or intermittent thyroid function. Circulatory problems, of course, result from low thyroid, but it is not enough to simply say that the victim is hypothyroid and put them on maintainence therapy. Some thyroid tablets may be necessary, but lithium supplements and reduction of the Candida infection is the only path to reducing the causative factors.

To reduce the diabetic-hypoglycemic state we must do everything in the Candida program, with particular attention to:

1. Mineral test,- to check for toxic metals, and to determine the mineral supplements that may be needed. Chromium and selenium are particularly important.

2. Check for low thyroid, and supplement if needed.

3. Check calcium. If calcium is low, supplement calcium, vitamin D, and PTH (parathyroid hormone).
4. Eliminate all tobacco, caffeine, alcohol and drugs.
5. Eliminate all sugar, honey, white starch, dried fruits and reduce fruits that are high in "free sugars".
6. Eliminate slt and substitute with potassium salts. ("No Salt").
7. Supply all adrenal nutrients, with particular attention to potassium. (HiKC Fizz) and to choline, inositol and methionine.
8. Supplement pancreatic enzymes and pancreatic bi-carbonate, with digestive enzymes if necessary.
9. Avoid stress and avoid emotional stress (including movies), which raise adrenalin and promote surges in blood sugar levels.
10. Restore normal sexual function if sexual ability is failing. this may come as a surprise. This is particularly important for the male. The symptoms from resorbed sexual fluids following frustrated orgasm are so similar to the agitation and neurosis of high/low blood sugar that this aspect of hypoglycemia/diabetes therapy should not be overlooked.
11. Chelation therapy. Intravenous infusions of EDTA will improve blood circulation. Chelation will also remove toxic metals, and it will clean some of the infectives out of the bloodstream. See chelation therapy. Ch.4.
12. Neursage and massage to reduce calcinosis and to restore lymphatic and muscle function throughout the body.
13. Regular meals and particularly a good breakfast.
14. Perhaps the judicious use of small amounts of tea to raise blood sugar levels, if they fall too low. (As in the morning).

To reduce the atherosclerosis, everything in the Candida and diabetic programs must be done, together with extra attention to:
1. Increased active exercise to improve blood circulation.
2. Vitamin E supplements to prevent blood clots. About 400 IU daily seems to be adequate, and more than 400 IU daily seems to be of little extra benefit.
3. Extra lecithin, preferably "Super Lecithin" (phosphatydal choline).
4. Extra lipotropics, choline, inositol, methionine, preferably in the same tablet. The methionine is effective in reducing cholesterol and triglycerides.
5. Vitamin B15 -Pangamic acid. B15 increases the utilization of oxygen, which is equal to increasing the oxygen in the blood.
6. Vitamin B13 -Orotic acid. B13 binds with calcium and will help to reduce the plaques. It is usually available as an orotate, e.g. Calcium Orotate.
7. Niacin. Niacin releases histamine and heparin into the bloodstream, which dilates the blood vessels and increases the blood

circulation. Niacin also increases histamine levels, with improved sexual and adrenal hormone function.

One of the greatest problems in blood circulation is the sticking together of the blood corpuscles on their active ends, in roulette formation, like a pile of checkers. If you can persuade your doctor to put some of your blood under the microscope you will see the clumped red blood corpuscles. When stuck together, they are inactive. After seeing them under the microscope, along with many damaged cells, rods, and other junk, you and your doctor may wonder if you will make it from his office back to the car. Candida yeast seems to be a major factor in the forming of the roulettes. Niacin alters the electric charge on the ends of the red corpucles, which helps to break up the roulettes, and reduces their tendency to form. Chelation therapy also helps to reduce the clumping of red corpuscles. The progress of therapy can be checked every two or three months by examing blood samples.

8. A full program of chelation therapy of at least twenty infusions.

ALLERGIES.

Allergies are always based in chronic infection somewhere, and they cannot be cleared up until the chronic infection is found and reduced. The allergies appear when the body is unable to detoxify all of the poisons from the chronic infective together with the poisons from the allergen. The allergy therefore can come equally from;-

(a) High chronic infection.

(b) Low immune function.

(c) Failure of the pancreas to supply enough bicarbonate to suppress the kinens and thus prevent excessive inflammation.

Allergies are also aggravated and increased by the leakage of large undigested proteins through scurvous porous walls of the intestines. Allergies usually result from all four basic causes.

Now of course the diabetic state is also associated with pancreatic failure. We should therefore assume that all diabetics and all hypoglycemics have some allergies, either hidden and obscure, or highly visible. Conversely, we should also assume that all people with allergies must have some diabetes, some hypoglycemia and therefore some atherosclerosis.

Irrespective of all else, the principal initiating factor in allergies is chronic infection, someplace, somewhere. The one single infective that is always present in allergies is Candida yeast. It is the most important chronic infective because it forms a callus matrix that harbors, protects and nurtures many other infectives that the body could otherwise destroy.

The other infectives that may be involved are any or all of the infectives frequently associated with Candida yeast, (Ch.3.) and/or any of the infectives associated with arthritis.

To reduce allergies we must do everything in the Candida program, with particular attention to:-

1. Ketoconazole. Ketoconazole is the single most important anti-infective, but it must be used with caution. Do not start with more than 1/8 tablet daily even if the 1/8 tablet seems so little that it could not do any good. Ketoconazole is a sytemic anti-fungal that attacks the infectives from the bloodstream, and all of the infectives that it kills must be removed by the bloodstream and detoxified by the immune system and the liver, along with all of the toxins from the infective. If too much ketoconazole is taken when infection is high, the immune system and/or liver may become overloaded, the toxins will remain in the bloodstream and tissues, and a severe toxic episode, like severe "flu", may follow. After taking the 1/8 tablet for a few days, slowly increase, 1/8 tablet at a time and watch for signs of toxicity. If toxic symptoms appear, reduce the quantity and try to increase again in another week. It usually takes 8 to 12 hours for killed infectives to clear the body, so 1/8 tablet could be taken night and morning. Try to get the total amount up to at least 1/2 tablet daily. Allergies will frequently start to subside within a few days after starting with the ketoconazole. Ketoconazole should be taken at the start of the meal for better absorption for systemic infections, and should be taken between meals for infections of the digestive tract.

2. Resteclin (Mysteclin) or equivalent anti-biotics. One capsule of resteclin, (or equal) should be taken every two or three days at the beginning of the ketoconazole program. Start with caution and take only 1/4 capsule and then work up. Resteclin should be taken between meals. If resteclin or equal anti-biotics are not taken with the ketoconazole program the ketoconazole will kill out the fungal (plant) infectives and the bacterial infectives will increase and feed on the dead and dying fungal infectives, which will not greatly reduce the total amount of chronic infection. It will only change the infectives from plants to bacteria. After the program is under way the resteclin can be reduced to about one capsule per week. To effectively reduce the allergies all infections in and on the body must be reduced. Special anti-biotics may be necessary for some of the infections shown under "Arthritis".

3. Pancreatic enzymes and bi-carbonate. Allergies can always be suppressed with pancreatic enzymes and bi-carbonate. (Ch.5.) Allergic episodes can also be avoided or reduced if pancreatic

enzymes and bi-carbonate are taken prior to the allergic exposure, or immediately after the allergic exposure.

4. Avoid all self administered poisons (caffeine, tobacco, alcohol, etc.) and try to avoid foods that contain poisons, (e.g., the nightshades,- tomatoes, peppers etc.). If necessary peel and remove stems and blossom ends from fruits and vegetables to reduce the amount of surface poisons.

5. The true source of allergies is usually Candida yeast infection, and particularly infections of the digestive tract. If high Candida infection is present it may be necessary to avoid all sources of yeast. Avoid alcohol, and particularly tap beer. Avoid all leavened bread, and watch for brewers yeast in prepared foods and vitamins. Allergies are frequently another "sugar disease" because the yeast thrives on free sugars. Starve the Candida yeast by avoiding all refined carbohydrate and by reducing total carbohydrate. Avoid all sources of high blood sugar, (the diabetic state). Some people can trigger allergies with a simple fit of anger. The anger forces the adrenals to produce adrenalin. This depletes the already overworked adrenals, and the adrenalin raises the blood sugar, which feeds the yeast and increases the toxins that produce the allergy.

6. Avoid all known sources of allergies, and rotate all foods on a 5 to 7 day basis, until the allergies start to subside.

7. Take large amounts of adrenal nutrients. These are also immune system nutrients. A high protein diet, with digestives, or pre-digested protein, or supplements of nucleic acids or amino acids, should be used to supply extra protein for the immune system.

8. Ample ascorbate and bio-flavinoids and perhaps vitamin C retention enemas to ensure that the intestines, colon, and blood vessels will have normally strong tight walls.

Many health and mental problems are rooted in allergies, and any disease can be imitated. Allergies can be obvious, or well hidden. Food rotation on a 7 day basis will usually reduce allergies, and it will make the offending substances and the ailment that they provoke highly obvious.

ARTHRITIS.

Both osteo arthritis and rheumatoid arthritis are caused by chronic infection, invariably with a high Candida component. Arthritis is a very broad term applied to a wide variety of symptoms, with many variations in cause. Some arthritis is caused by direct Candida infection of the joints. Again we do not know how many such causes there are, but we do know that Candida yeast has a particular affinity for joints and joint tissues because the joint fluids provide a highly nutritious environment for the yeast and its associated infectives.

Quite obviously, if the arthritis is caused by Candida infection, (Candidal Arthritis) the arthritis will remain despite all efforts to "cure" it, or to "manage" it with aspirin, cortisone or DMSO.

The role of infection is well known. You should insist that your doctor take sufficient time to have the necessary tests to find out which infective is causing most of the problems, so that it can be eradicated. It must be remembered that many infectives are harbored within the Candida callus matrix, and that some micro-organisms also directly infect the Candida yeast and its associated infectives. Quite obviously it would be difficult indeed to reduce the arthritis if it was caused by the secondary infectives, unless we destroyed their secure home in the Candida. Significantly, arthritis will frequently respond very rapidly to metronidazole, indicating a secondary infection.

The following list of "arthritic infectives" is compiled from the index of Scientific American Medical Library.

<u>Arthritis Index</u>   Chronic Infectives Are Underlined.

Arthritis, *see also* Osteoarthritis
acute,
  <u>brucellosis</u> and, 7:II:22
  chronic renal failure and, 15:IX:17
  disseminated <u>gonococcal</u> disease and, 7:XXII:5
acute <u>bacterial,</u>
  antimicrobial therapy for, 7:XV:4, 6
  arthrodesis in treating, 7:XV:6
  clinical features of, 7:XV:2–3
<u>acute septic,</u> 7:XV:1
agents used for, in treating renal
    disease,10:II:34–36
<u>bacterial,</u> 15:I:8
Crohn's disease and, 4:IV:10
<u>coccidioidal,</u> treatment of, 7:XV:7
<u>coccidioidomycosis</u> and, 7:IX:8
corticosteroid intra-articular injection causing
    suppurative, 7:XV:1–2
diseases associated with, 15:I:8
<u>erythema infectiosum</u> and, 7:XXX:6
<u>fungal,</u> 15:I:8, 7:XV:7
  synovial fluid findings in, 7:XV:3
<u>genital tract infections</u> causing, 7:XXII:1
in giant cell arteritis, 15:VIII:3
gouty, 9:IV:4
  leukemia and, 5:VIII:3
<u>hematogenous gonococcal,</u> in neonates, 7:XXII:3
heroin use and, 7:XV:1, 2
<u>infectious,</u> 7:XV:1–8, 15:I:8
  synovial fluid findings in, 7:XV:3
in infective endocarditis, 7:XVIII:6
Jaccoud's, in <u>rheumatic fever,</u> 15:VII:3
Lyme, 7:XV:8, 15:I:8
<u>meningococcal bacteremia</u> causing, 7:III:4
<u>meningococcal disease</u> causing, 7:III:4, 5
migratory, chronic <u>active hepatitis</u> causing,
    4:VIII:5
<u>mumps and,</u> 7:XXIX:1
mutilans, *see* Arthritis mutilans
<u>parasitic,</u> 15:I:8
polymyositis and, 15:VI:1
<u>poststreptococcal,</u> 15:VII:2, 4

disseminated <u>gonococcal</u> disease causing,
    7:XXII:4
  treatment of, 7:XXII:7
quinidine therapy and, 1:V:5
reactive, HLA antigen correlation, 6:XVI:6
Reiter's syndrome and, 7:XXII:5
rheumatoid, *see* Rheumatoid arthritis
rickettsial, 15:I:8
<u>rubella</u> and, 7:XXX:3
in scleroderma, 15:V:2
septic, 7:XV:1, *see also* Arthritis, <u>acute bacterial</u>
  antibiotic therapy for, 7:XV:5
  <u>bacterial</u> causes of, 7:XV:2
  <u>gram-negative bacillary,</u> 7:II:20
  <u>Haemophilus influenzae</u> causing, 7:II:21
  <u>meningococcal</u> disease causing, 7:III:1
  <u>pneumococcal</u> bacteremia causing, 7:I:5
  pneumococcal, 7:I:5
  <u>staphylococcal,</u> 7:I:17
    treatment of, 7:I:20
  <u>streptococcal</u> bacteremia causing, 7:I:10
  treatment of, 7:XIV:6, 7:XXII:7
sickle cell disease and, 7:XV:3, 4
<u>sporotrichosis,</u> 7:XV:7
suppurative, *Salmonella* infection and, 7:II:6
<u>syphilitic,</u> 7:XV:7–8
  treatment of, 7:XV:8
systemic lupus erythematosus and, 15:IV:1
traumatic, 15:I:8
<u>tuberculous,</u> 7:VIII:9–10
  clinical manifestations of, 7:XV:6
  diagnosis of, 7:XV:7
  predisposing factors in, 7:XV:6
  surgery for, 7:XV:7
  synovial fluid findings in, 7:XV:7
  treatment of, 7:XV:7
ulcerative colitis complicated by, 4:IV:10
<u>viral,</u> 7:XV:8–9, 15:I:8
<u>viral infection</u> and, 6:XI:1
Arthritis-dermatitis syndrome, 7:XXII:4–5
  <u>gonococcal infection</u> and, 7:XXII:6

Arthritis can usually be reduced by using the hypoglycemia diet coupled with colon therapy, to ensure elimination of body wastes. Several books have been written on the reduction and control of arthritis by diet, exercise, and colon therapy. From this we can deduce that the arthritic can be considered as being a constipated hypoglycemic:- which tells us that the build up of arthritic deposits, or the environment that destroys joint cartilage, comes from the inability of the body to eliminate toxins, metabolites, and other body wastes. We can also deduce that arthritis is another "sugar disease", coupled with colon problems.

To reduce arthritis, everything in the Candida program must be done, with particular attention in the Diabetes- hypoglycemia program, together with particular attention to:

1. Cleaning and restoring colon function, with perhaps colon X-rays, colonics, anti-candidal colonics, ascorbate flush, and vitamin retention enemas.

2. Mineral test and reduction of heavy metal poisoning if present. High levels of copper increases the arthritic condition.

3. Extra potassium (always with sodium) and ascorbate, and other adrenal nutrients, to induce the adrenals to produce more cortisone.

4. Extra supplements of calcium-magnesium orotate and vitamin D, which will increase the rate of calcium excretion and renewal (turnover).

5. Silicon supplements, usually from herbal horsetail, which will improve calcium utilization.

6. Chelation therapy, which will improve blood circulation, reduce heavy metals, and increase the rate of calcium excretion and turnover. Chelation therapy will also clear the bloodstream of many infectives. DMSO mixed with the chelator increases the effectiveness.

7. Intravenous infusions of DMSO, are frequently used by some arthritic clinics. Relief is immediate, but the arthritis will surely return if the underlying causes are not corrected.

8. Elimination of cortisone, aspirin and other "management" drugs as soon as possible.

9. Massage and neursage of the whole body with extra attention to afflicated limbs and joints.

10. Continuing manipulation of stiff joints, with heat, pushing them just a little farther each time.

11. Osteo-arthritis will respond better with extra attention to:-

A. Ascorbate and bio-flavinoids to improve the strength of the cartilage.

B. Extra water and fluids. Cartilage is pliable and spongy because water is locked in between the cells. Avoid all caffeine etc., and avoid diuretics.

C. Digestive supplements, amino acids and nucleic acids, to ensure adequate protein for building collagen and proteoglycans.

D. B12 injections (see Bursitis).

12.Most arthritics also have false arthritis. (as follows).

False Arthritis (Travelling Arthritis).

False arthritis has most of the symptoms of arthritis except it seems to move around in the afflicted area. When checked by anyone that is familiar with neursage the afflicted area seems to be beset by multiple muscle spasms. The pain from the multiple muscle spasms will slowly respond to mild neursage, but will get worse with hard neursage. Neursage is usually very difficult because the nervcites affected are usually very sensitive and are deep between the bones. False arthritis is very frustrating to reflexologists or others who practice neursage because the muscle spasm is so obvious, yet very difficult to relieve, and when relieved moves over to a different spot. All of this is really very understandable because the actual cause of the muscle spasm and the arthritis- like symptoms is infection within the lymphatic system. Neursage then, only increases the trauma within the lymphatics, which increases the infection, and the neursage makes the victim worse.

Fortunately false arthritis can usually be relieved with great benefit to health by the use of A-E Emulsin (Ch.4) which increases the effectiveness of the immune system by supplying extra vitamin A directly to the lymphatics.

All arthritics will benefit from A-E Emulsin, and some aches and pains may disappear within a few hours.

Therapy should include daily active exercise, perferably swimming, to operate the lymphatic pump.

False arthritis is usually part of extensive health degeneration. The A-E Emulsin should therefore be only part of the full Candida program, and the problems are certain to return if the other infections are not reduced.

If symptoms persist metronidazole, sulphamethoxazole, and vancomycin should be tried. It seems that some cases of false arthritis may be caused by infection within the nervous system. If problems still persist, other antibiotics should be tried. Any change in symptoms indicates that you should try other anti-infectives that are effective against the same micro-organisms.

Arthritic pains can also be aggravated by pressure on nerves, as with sciatica. Inflammation can then also play a role, but the inflammation can be reduced with bi-carbonate and pancreatic enzymes after the meal. A good chiropractor can also be very helpful.

385.

BURSITIS.

Bursitis is an associate form of arthritis which will slowly respond to the arthritic program. Excellent relief, with slow dissolution of the calcium deposits has been achieved with large amounts of injected B12:-1cc (1000 micrograms) daily for 7 to 10 days, three times a week for two weeks, then 1 or 2 per week for 2 or 3 weeks. (ref.33.)

BELL'S PALSY. (and other Palsies).

Bell's Palsy is caused by muscle spasm and erratic nerve function. It may be associated with mercury poisoning, usually from amalgam fillings. It will usually respond to the program for Bursitis. The twitching can usually be relieved with electro-stimulation with a TENS unit, or with a "galvanic pack", consisting of a 9 volt battery connected to salty electrodes taped to each side of the afflicted area. The niacin flush may also be of particular benefit.

NEURALGIA.

The neuralgias can be considered as forms of neuritis so they will respond to the neuritis program. Relief can usually be attained with heavy injections of B12, (see Bursitis).

HEART and BLOOD CIRCULATION.

These problems are really a variation of atherosclerosis. The principal causative factors in heart and circulatory problems are low thyroid, tobacco, caffeine, high levels of cholesterol and triglycerides, and direct Candida infection of the heart or heart valves.

The whole truth about the role of Candida infection in circulatory disease is not clear. The plaques that develop and block the blood vessels are the result of the proliferation of a single cell from the middle lining of the blood vessel. These plaques are not cancerous, yet their uncontrolled growth from a single displaced cell is the same type of growth as cancer,i.e., they are a type of tumor. How the single cell from the middle lining of the blood vessel gets through the inner lining into the inside of the blood vessel, and how it attaches itself to the inner lining of the blood vessel is not known. We also do not know why or how it leaves the control of the body and multiplies and proliferates on its own. We do know that as the years pass everyone develops some plaques in their blood vessels. That is, we know that the condition is not normal, yet no one is totally free from the condition. We also know that both tobacco (and perhaps caffeine) and high levels of cholesterol and triglycerides increase the number of plaques and their rate of growth.

Now we also know that people with atherosclerosis have changes in the blood as seen under the darkfield microscope. There are far more damaged red blood cells and there are also many more filaments and L-forms and crystal bodies. Some scientific people say that these are different forms of the infective Progenitor Cryptocides,(Genus actinomycetales) while others say that they are filaments and pieces from Candida yeast, while others say that Candida yeast is really one of the actinomycetales and that Candida is a five phase organism that under certain circumstances transforms into progenitor cryptocides. We do know that plague locusts are three phase insects that under certain conditions become four phase insects, and a five phase micro organism therefore seems not only possible but highly probable. It has frequently been said that exploration is over, and that there are no new frontiers to explore, yet here, (literally), at the very vital heart of man, are many questions to which there are at present no clear definite answers. Man is not always wise, even in his use of information that is readily available. Candida yeast has an affinity for infecting heart tissues, particularly the heart valves and the myocardium. There are 21 medical papers on the reference list, with one paper showing 91 cases of Candidal endocarditis. Until medical doctors improve their technology and until the use of autopsies is increased, we will never know how many heart problems are in fact directly due to Candida infection.

Fortunately the Candida program with chelation therapy, ketoconazole, and perhaps monistat I.V., will help to restore the function of heart valves, and as health improves, autogenous vaccine can be used to reduce the possibility that progenitor cryptocides will initate further plaques.

There are now at least two vitamin-mineral- herbal formulas that seem to be very beneficial for heart and circulatory problems. If they are used, appropriate adjustments to total supplements should be made.

1. <u>Cardioguard Lipotropic Supplement.</u>

Two tablets provide: Lecithin - 400mg, mucopolysacharides 390mg, elastmucoprotease 50mg., Lethicon (choline) 50mg, silicon dioxide 50mg, papain 50mg, niacin 10mg.

Ingredients: The natural lipotropic substances in Cardioguard include lechithin granules, providing phosphatidylcholine (24%), phosphatidyl ethenolamine (22%), and phosphatidyl inositol (18%), plant mucopolysaccharides from red seaweed and Irish moss; elastomucoprotease (from animal sources); additional choline, silicon dioxide; papian from papaya; and niacin.

Suggested use: 2 tablets 2 times daily, or as recommended by your doctor. Initially, higher doses may be required.

Cardioguard is supplied only to healthcare professionals. Your doctor can obtain Cardioguard from: Professional Health Products, 3501 Breakwater ave; Hayward California.94545.

2. Oral Chelation (Orachel).

Oral chelation, using a vitamin-mineral complex with the misleading name of "Orachel" has been heralded by Kurt W. Donsbach,PhD; as a wonderful god send for reducing blood vessel plaques. Now perhaps it is, but however well it may work cannot be justification to call it something that it is not. In his writing, Dr.Donsbach goes on to admit that oral chelation "is a misnomer, since the formulation does not attach itself to, or eliminate via the urine, the calcium in the bloodstream as does the EDTA form of intravenous chelation" In short, the title "oral chelation"is not just a happenstance misnomer, but a completely misleading term designed solely to sell the "orachel" to people considering intravenous chelation, when in fact it is not a calcium chelator. The use of this product, still called an"oral chelator " is also extolled by Glen Mahoney M.D. and by Keith Kenyob M.D.

The fact is that many of the EDTA chelators can be taken orally. Chelation therapy started with oral products, and CaNaEDTA (Versanate) was used for oral calcium chelation of blood vessel plaques with reasonable success. Information on factual EDTA oral chelation is given in "Chelation Therapy", by Dr.Alfred Soffer. (Chas. C. Thomas,Publ.). In general NaEDTA oral chelation can be quite successful if the amount used is kept below 3 grams per day. We have found it very useful for clearing organisms from the intestinal tract. Whenever it is used it should always be followed by supplements of multi-minerals and acidophillus.

The so-called "oral chelator", "Orachel", which does not directly chelate calcium, is composed of:

	1 tablet		
Vitamin A (fish liver oil)	3,333 I.U.	Iron (ferrous fumarate)	1.34 mg.
Vitamin D (fish liver oil)	67 I.U.	Iodine (potassium iodide)	0.03 mg.
Vitamin E (D-alpha)	60 I.U.	Manganese (gluconate)	0.8 mg.
Vitamin C (ascorbic acid)	400 mg.	Zinc (gluconate)	2.5 mg.
Vitamin B-1 (thiamin HCl)	18 mg.	Chromium (acetate)	13 mcg.
Vitamin B-2 (riboflavin)	3 mg.	Selenium (dioxide)	20 mcg.
Vitamin B-6 (pyridoxine HCl)	15 mg.	Choline (bitartrate)	66 mg.
Vitamin B-12 (cobalamin)	16 mcg.	Inositol	4 mg.
Niacin	7 mg.	P.A.B.A.	19 mg.
Niacinamide	2 mg.	Betaine Hydrochloride	13 mg.
Pantothenic acid (d-calc.)	33 mg.	Lemon Bioflavanoids	10 mg.
Folic acid	0.06 mg.	dl-Methionine	16 mg.
Biotin	5 mcg.	l-Cysteine HCl	66 mg.
Calcium (carbonate)	42 mg.	Thymus concentrate	6 mg.
Magnesium (oxide)	42 mg.	Spleen concentrate	6 mg.
Potassium (chloride)	42 mg.	Adrenal concentrate	4 mg.

In Canada Orachel is sold as "Donsbach's Formula F.L.W."

The claims for this supplement appear to be well backed up by tests by both Plethysmograph (Pulse-Volume Recorder) (PVR), and by Thermograph (temperature) of hands and feet. Average time of treatment was 5 weeks. Average age of patients was 62. The failure rate was not stated.

Note the great similarity of this formula to the nutrients in the Candida program:

1. All of the minerals that Candida usually depletes.
2. All of the vitamins, with very low B2.
3. Biotin. (which Candida consumes).
4. B12 and folic acid.
5. Choline, inositol, methionine. (mega lipotropic).
6. Adrenal and thymus glandulars.

The only substance in the Orachel that is not in the Candida program, is relatively high amounts of cystiene hydrochloride, added (they say) to reduce free radicals, and to reduce lead. The literature on cysteine however, does not mention an ability to bind with lead, but cysteine does bind with copper and will reduce copper levels. The mineral test will show if copper supplements would be needed. Both cysteine and methionine contain sulphur, which ultimately becomes sulphuric acid, which aids in detoxification of toxins. The questions should then be asked, "Free radicals from what?" "Toxins from what"? If there are toxins and free radicals they must come from infectives someplace. The supernutrition will improve the host, and will provide a period of better health, until these infectives again catch up.

It should be noted that if lead is a problem it can be reduced with oral CaNaEDTA, but the only effective way to eliminate lead is with NaEDTA intravenous chelation therapy.

The author has not as yet had a good opportunity to try Orachel, and the misleading name certainly creates doubt and skepticism. Nonetheless, it should be tried, and it may be very useful when incorporated into the Candida program along with intravenous chelation therapy every two weeks.

Anyone using Orachel, or otherwise regularly taking large amounts of cysteine should look at their mineral test to see if they will deplete the copper which is so necessary fot the transport of oxygen, and they should remember that large amounts of cysteine without adequate B6 can produce homocysteinuria, with schizophrenia and other mental affects.

The normal body requirement for sulphur (usually from cysteine or methionine) is 850mg per day. Two eggs, (the best source of cysteine) will provide about 150 mg. So the Orachel formula (or extra cysteine) may be of benefit, particularly for people who do not eat eggs.

It should be noted that cysteine does bind mercury, so the blood-vessel problems may in fact be a side effect from amalgam tooth fillings. Changing amalgam fillings to cement or plastic may then be of help.

There is now some evidence that the formation of blood vessel plaques may result from sub-clinical scurvy of the blood vessels which allows "loose" cells to pass through to the inner lining of the blood vessel. In all cases of poor blood circulation very large amounts of vitamin C are therfore indicated.

Now in another view of poor circulation, high levels of cholesterol and triglycerides are considered to be the cause. These high levels come from high levels of blood sugar that the body cannot process in the normal manner, and when oxygen and potassium are low in comparison to the blood sugar levels, the body makes the excess blood sugar into glycerol, and then the glycerol is changed to cholesterol and triglycerides. The usual cause of the high blood sugar is low thyroid which results in high adrenalin that pulls sugar from the liver storage. Yet another factor is low ascorbate. If the diet is low in vitamin C, or if stress, chronic infection, drugs, self administered poisons etc., uses up the available vitamin C, there will be insufficient ascorbate to change cholesterol from the bloodstream into bile. The body then has high levels of cholesterol, and the shortage of bile impairs the digestion and assimilation and promotes constipation, all of which complicate the problems. High triglycerides can be reduced with supplements of vanadium, which also obviously has a metabolic role. Both Candida toxins and cholesterol contribute to blood-cell clumping which not only impairs circulation but drastically reduces the ability of the red cells to transport oxygen at a time when it is needed the most. Blood cell clumping can be reduced with both niacin and manganese.

Another factor in blood-cell clumping is mucopolysaccharides, (M.P.s), (Cardioguard) that also react with collagen and elastin to maintain the integrity of the blood vessels. The M.P.s form extra cross-links that further strengthen and tighten the walls of the blood vessels. M.P. metabolism reduces with age, so supplements are of value in all degenerative diseases.

Supplements of M.P.s along with further information are available from Cardiovascular Research, 1061 B, Shary Circle, Concord Cal. 94518. U.S.A.

Quite obviously there are so many causes and so many factors in poor blood circulation that by using chelation therapy together with doing "everything else", blood circulation can always be greatly improved.

ANGINA and CORONARY OCCLUSION. (HEART ATTACK).

Coronary occlusion is the blockage of the coronary arteries that supply blood to the heart muscles. Slow blockage produces angina, with sharp pains usually accompanied by pain in the left arm, but if a blood clot lodges in the restricted coronary artery the heart will fail, or it will almost fail, hence the name, "Heart Attack".

Angina

Anyone with angina should immediately start taking vitamin E, 100 IU daily, slowly increasing to 400 IU daily, to reduce the risk of formation of blood clots. They should also have a complete medical examination including Pulse Volume Recorder (PVR) tests to establish the extent of the atherosclerosis. Here it should be remembered that large quantities of gas in the stomach and intestines can put so much pressure on the heart that false angina can be produced. The PVR is the very best method of establishing the actual flow of blood in the arteries.

If the arteries are reasonably clear, and if there are gas forming conditions in the stomach and digestive tract, the angina is probably false angina, and the Candida infection and other infectives in the digestive tract will have to be reduced. (CH.6.)

If the arteries are partly closed with plaque, chelation therapy should be started as soon as possible, along with the entire atherosclerosis program.

If the medical tests show that the coronary artery has deteriorated to the point that time is running out and a by-pass operation is absolutely necessary, the Vineberg Heart Operation seems to be a better choice.

In reversing atherosclerosis and heart problems there is an immediate need for a reduction in angina and risk of heart attack. The usual medical treatment is with "calcium channel blocker" drugs, that also have potent side effects. Magnesium however, is a natural "channel blocker" that can be used safely and without serious side effects. The following information for its use is by Dr.Roy Kupsinel, (ref.33)

Orals.

Magnesium ascorbate or magnesium aspartate, 500 mg daily, with potassium and without calcium, until improvement is evident. The only side effects have been a few cases of dose-dependent diarrhea. Note that the amount can be increased by taking 200 mg four times daily.

I.M.(Intramuscular)

.5 to 1 gram every 5 days for 12 injections, followed by 1 gram every two weeks for maintainence. In clinical trials these amounts reduced myocardial infarction (heart attack) by 50%. They were also effective against intractable ventricular tachycardia. Side effects were transient and few, except for a beneficial increase in HDL cholesterol. In severe cases 1 gram or more twice weekly may be needed.

I.V. (Intravenous).

In some cases intravenous injection may be necessary. As much as 10 grams in 24 hours have been successfully admininistered to some eclamptic mothers. Broad spectrum multi-minerals should always be taken to reduce possible side effects. Dr. Kupsinel also shows that, for angina and cardiovascular disease, the following items have been used with success, singly and in combination;- Vitamin C, E, B3, B6, selenium, garlic, mucopolysaccharides, eicosapentaenoic acid, intravenous chelation. It should be noted that Candida infection uses up large quantities of magnesium. The great value of magnesium supplements in cardiovascular disease therefore raises the possibility that atherosclerosis is really a side effect of high Candida infection.

The Coronary By-Pass.

Although the coronary by-pass was widely acclaimed and has been credited with saving many lives, a recent survey reported in Scientific American, shows that in fact it has not on an average increased the length of life, nor has it on an average increased the usefulness of life, but it has decreased the pain from angina. From this report it is obvious that chelation therapy would have been a much better treatment, because chelation will always relieve or reduce the pain from angina, and it will improve circulation with much less risk.

Usually the coronary by-pass is in place for only two to five years before it too becomes filled with atherosclerotic plaque. The problem is that the doctors that perform the operation are good mechanics, but they are much less than scientific. Anyone with any technical capability should realize that if the basic cause of coronary occlusion is not altered or reduced before or after the by-pass, then it is only a matter of time until the new artery will also become filled with plaque. People who have already had a coronary by-pass will benefit from chelation therapy, but the response is much slower. They will also require the entire Candida - atherosclerosis program to reduce the causes of artery occulsion.

If another heart operation has become absolutely inevitable, the Vineberg Heart Operation is a better choice than re-doing the coronary by-pass.

The Vineberg Heart Operation.
By Eugene Maurey. 4555 W. 60 Chicago Il. 60629.
An alternative to the Aortocoronary Vein Bypass Procedure.

Victims of coronary arteriosclerosis, who are not candidates for an arotocoronary vein bypass, have an alternative procedure available to them. This procedure is called the "Vineberg Operation" as conceived and perfected by Dr. Arthur Vineberg, research and consultant surgeon at the Royal Victoria Hospital in Montreal, Canada.

In layman's terms, I will describe my personal experience with this procedure. About four years ago I was suffering from angina pectoris, pains in the chest radiating down my left arm. My doctor suggested an angiogram to determine the cause of the problem. This test revealed that the right and left descending coronary arteries of the heart were 100% blocked. My immediate family and friends urged me to have a vein bypass operation. I refused. As a graduate engineer, I felt that the bypass procedure is poor mechanical engineering! In this procedure, the surgeon makes an 18 inch incision in your leg and then removes a section of vein. Now we have tampered with a perfectly good leg. Next the chest is opened to expose the problem area. The vein from the leg is sewn in as a bridge or aqueduct from the great aorta to the coronary artery beyond its blockage. These sewn joints cannot be made without rough edges. The blood would have a turbulence at these points such as one would find in house plumbing, where the joints are the first to plug up. I also learned that the national average for a bypass operation indicated that for every four bypass veins installed, one will fail within three years.

My condition was deteriorating, the angina pain became more frequent and my physical energy was reduced. I kept searching for a better way.

One day at a book counter I picked a book entitled, "How To Live With Your Heart." by Arthur Vineberg. I read it carefully and then with enthusiasm phoned Dr. Vineberg and scheduled the operation! I had found exactly what I was looking for! Let me briefly describe the operation.

Under the chest wall there are 2 mammary arteries which start approximately near the lower part of the neck and extend downward some 10 to 12 inches. These arteries are about 4 inches apart and supply the chest wall. The arteries are removed by carefully teasing them away from the chest wall. The small arterial branches extending from the arteries are carefully tied and cut to free the artery from the chest.

A hole is made in the left wall of the heart using a forcep at a place undamaged by scar tissue. The left mammary is then inserted in the hole after its arterial side branches 4, 5, and

6 have been opened. In like manner, if deemed necessary, the right mammary is inserted in the wall of the right section of the heart. In about 3 to 6 weeks the small arterial branches of the mammary artery in the heart begin to grow and reach out to connect with other small arterioles in the heart muscle wall. The diseased surface coronary arteries are thereby bypassed and the fresh blood is supplied to the nondiseased heart muscle arterioles. Since the right section of the heart has low pressure, the wall is somewhat like a sponge and the effect of the right mammary is immediate, and the patient feels better at once. It should be noted that the small arterioles grow slowly, particularly where the heart muscle is dense, such as it is in the left side.

Perhaps the limitation to the Vineberg operation is that if a patient has all three main arteries 80% to 100% plugged, with impending heart attack, only an immediate vein bypass is recommended. When a surgeon knows there are large blockages through the entire length of the surface arteries, he becomes reluctant to use the aortocoronary vein bypass because the chances of survival are small. When the surgeons exposed my heart, they found that a vein bypass would not be possible.

We all know of persons who have had 2 bypass operations and are thinking of a third. This is because the ongoing disease has closed the substitute vein arteries. In the case of the Vineberg operation, the mammary arteries are not subject to filling with the usual cholesterol, platelets and calcium. This artery is primarily a female artery and like all women's arteries have a thin inner lining of the wall which resists the accumulation of the obstructing material. This is why a woman, comparatively, rarely suffers from atherosclerosis disease. On the other hand, a normal man's artery has a thick inner lining which is readily susceptible to the accumulation of the obstructing materials. Why isn't the Vineberg operation more prevalent? The main reason is economic. The vein bypass operation is simpler and gives immediate relief. In the U.S. the usual surgeon's fee is $25,000 for the bypass operation. For a 3 hour operation, this is an attractive incentive to a surgeon, especially since in 5 to 10 years another operation will most likely be needed. On the other hand, the Vineberg operation takes 4 to 5 hours, is much more difficult to perform and the surgeon's fee in Montreal is but $8,000. For further information you may write or phone Dr. Arthur Vineberg, Royal Victoria Hospital, 687 Pine Avenue West, Montreal, H3A 1A1, Canada, Tel. 514-288-9337.

Coronary Occlusion.

Anyone who has survived a heart attack will benefit from intravenous vitamins, large amounts of adrenal nutrients, pure amino acids, nucleic acids, and as soon as possible chelation therapy, starting with infusions not longer than one hour. Vitamin E immediately is of particular value to prevent further blood clots from forming. Niacin in small quantities, probably 20mg four times a day, will reduce the blood sludge. Cardioguard or pantethine (Cardiovascular Research) may be of value. Thyroid and parathyroid should be checked immediately and supplemented if low. As soon as possible the entire Candida and atherosclerosis programs should be slowly and cautiously started.

Recovery from heart attack requires much patience and understanding from everyone associated with the victim. The greatest problem is the psychology of the victim who is usually badly depressed and confused. They should be reassured that most people who survive heart attacks regain most of their faculties and function in less than six months. If possible something useful should be found for them to do. Most victims of heart attack are busy doing things that are useful, and if the heart attack suddenly plunges them into a vacuum where they are doing nothing useful, the helplessness and the feeling of uselessness is frequently worse than the heart attack itself. Pantothenic acid, up to 800mg daily, will promote stability and will reduce the severe depression.

It should be particularly remembered that although bed rest is essential for the first few days, excerise, even in the form of moving the fingers, hands and arms is highly essential to prevent serious loss of calcium and nitrogen. (See Ref.5. Page 271).

Stroke.

"Stroke" is the name usually given to occlusion of arteries to the brain. The artery becomes blocked (occluded) by a blood clot. If the artery that is blocked is only a small arteriole, the event will pass unnoticed, but with blockage of larger arteries small areas of the brain will be damaged. If large arteries become blocked, brain damage will be extensive and immediate death will follow.

Vitamin E is the most important nutrient that prevents blood clots from forming, 200 to 400 IU of vitamin E per day will prevent blood clots from forming.

Many people survive small strokes. If brain damage is not extensive the lost abilities or lost faculties usually return. The entire Candida program will aid recovery, and will reduce the many factors that initiated the stroke.

Stroke is really "mental occlusion", so the therapy for stroke is the same as therapy for coronary occlusion. The victim of stroke may also require the almost constant services of an understanding person to help them re-gain mental function, and to help them to re-learn many things that they are now unable to remember.

CALCIFIED HEART VALVES.

Heart murmers and many heart and circulatory problems are caused by hardened and calcified heart valves. A number of surgical procedures and various mechanical valves have been developed to solve the problem. Some of these devices and procedures work quite well, but the fact is that nothing can work as well as a healthy living heart valve.

It is medically well known that Candida yeast has a particular affinity for infecting heart valves, with the infection forming the usual callus matrix, where it shelters and protects other infectives, with everything being well nourished by the blood supply to the heart valves, and by the nutrients in the blood stream. Quite obviously, heart valve infection is particularly insidious because the infectives are continuously seeding the bloodstream, and the rest of the body, with constant infection. Then, as the well nourished callus matrix increases in size, the heart valve slowly becomes stiffer and less pliable, and is soon unable to close completely, producing the gurgles and murmurs that your doctor hears in his stethoscope. Just how many of these murmurs and gurgles are based in Candida yeast infection we do not know, but we do know that calcium is also involved in the hardening of heart valves, so anyone with gurgles or murmurs, or other heart valve problems, will usually benefit from the entire Candida-atherosclerosis program, including chelation therapy.

HEART PALPITATIONS.

Heart palpitations and missed heart-beats (missed systoles) are very common, but they are also very unhealthy. If episodes of palpitations become prolonged extreme weakness follows, and if the palpitations become faster and the heart goes into fibrillation (rapid completely irregular beats), death may follow. Therefore if palpitations become severe, your doctor will probably have to install a pacemaker to avoid the possibility of fibrillation.

Most cases of heart palpitation can be directly attributed to caffeine and tobacco, which contain an alkaloid poison that blocks noradrenalin in the nerve synapses, causing the nervous system to run at full speed and out of control. The heart nerves are then trying to make the heart beat faster, while the electric-electronic heart control loop keeps telling the heart to slow down. The heart cannot obey two masters at the same time, but it tries. It tries to speed up, and it tries to slow down, producing the palpitation. Caffeine and tobacco also greatly increase stress, and this stress, together with the stress from the heart palpitations, causes potassium excretion. Potassium of course, is absolutely essential to muscle function, and particularly to heart function. It is so very essential, that heart palpitations may also occur if potassium becomes depleted. Allergies and chronic infection can also cause heart palpitations. Heart flutter is therefore usually caused by a combination of chronic infection. caffeine, and adrenal depletion, perhaps aggravated by tobacco or allergies.

The Candida program, with emphasis on adequate potassium (always with sodium) will usually restore normal heart function, and it will also reduce the number of missed beats, (missed systoles). If drugs are being used to reduce the palpitations they should be slowly phased out as normal heart function returns.

BLOOD PRESSURE. (See also Ch.4.)

For many years blood pressure has been used to diagnose the state of health, but just how much help it has been to the doctor and to the patient is at best questionable. Most certainly continuing high blood pressure is dangerous and contributes to many health problems. The difficulty is to determine what is normal, what is too high, what is too low, and the significance of minimum, resting (diastolic) and maximum (systolic) pressure.

For many years the maximum (systolic) pressure developed by the heart was used as a guideline, but today the diastolic (resting) pressure is considered to be of greatest significance, while another view is that the difference between the diastolic and the systolic pressures is the best indicator of health.

There are also differing opinions about just what "normal" blood pressure may be, and when and how it should be measured. It is the authors view that too much significance has been placed on high blood pressure, and that pressures anywhere between 180/80 and 130/55, may be normal for many people. Blood pressure varies greatly from minute to minute, and many factors can raise or lower it. Even a cup of tea, or the slight anxiety over a trip to the doctor's office can raise an otherwise normal blood pressure up into the high range. Further, at least 80% of the population are hypoglycemic, with extreme swings in blood sugar and energy levels, and these people will have wide variations in blood pressure along with their changing levels of blood sugar, so how can their actual average blood pressure ever be determined?

There are a large number of factors that alter blood pressure. Inflammation, edema, fibrosis and calcinosis increase internal tissue pressure, and the body must respond with higher blood pressure. Nervous tension, atherosclerotic plaque, and hardened arteries reduce blood flow, so the body responds with increased blood pressure in a usually vain attempt to supply adequate nutrients to the cells. High cholesterol, high triglycerides, clumped red cells, anemia, high blood sugar, toxins in the bloodstream, and poor lung function all reduce the amount of oxygen reaching the cells, and the body again responds with high blood pressure. Caffeine, tobacco, alcohol, excitement, frustration, or anticipation of reward, glory, or doom; or anything else that increases adrenalin, forces up the blood pressure, while allergies, colon, liver and kidney problems, or even a shortage of zinc, will also raise the blood pressure.

So just what is your doctor looking for? If he does find high blood pressure is it momentary, or is it continuous? Which factor, or which combination of factors caused it?

It would seem, that with so many possible causes, that unless blood pressure is extremely high, it should be watched but largely ignored in favor of improving total health;-- in favor of improving all body functions;-- in favor of the entire Candida program. Then the blood pressure will usually return to about 140/80, which may be slightly high by some standards, but is certainly very acceptable.

The point is that high blood pressure is not an illness in itself. It is invariably the result of some other malfunction, and monitoring blood pressure can therefore be used to determine the effectiveness of other therapies. Mercury, cadmium, birth control pills, kidney infections and altered calcium metabolism are common causes and all should be investigated.

Restoring the potassium/sodium balance with HiKC Fizz, large amounts of vitamin C and all adrenal nutrients will help to normalize the blood pressure. Salt should be avoided, chromium and zinc should be supplemented to high normal, and chelation therapy will help in cases of atherosclerosis.

Low Blood Pressure.

Low blood pressure is thought to be uncommon, but many people experience episodes of low blood sugar when adrenal nutrients are low. Low blood pressure is almost invariably caused by adrenal depletion, and can be corrected with full adrenal support with particular attention to supplements of sodium/ potassium ascorbate (HiKC Fizz), calcium/magnesium, vitamin D, B6, pantothenic acid, vitamin E, and B15.

If low blood sugar persists, adrenal substance, or adrenal glandulars may be of particular benefit. In all cases of low blood pressure the elimination of chronic infection with other efforts to reduce stress and thus reduce the load on the adrenals, is of prime importance. Blood pressure can be temporily raised with 1/2 cup of tea, or a little bakers chocolate.

CATARACTS. (Scurvy of the eyes).

The presence of cataracts, or even the presence of cloudiness of the lens of the eyes, is a definite symptom of a long standing cellular malnutrition. To reverse cataracts, everything in the Candida program should be started, including chelation therapy if possible. Particular attention should be given to very large supplements of vitamin C, because here again in the eyes, vitamin C is absolutely essential in lens metabolism, where it protects the lens from photo (light) oxidative damage. Vitamin C concentrations in the lens are usually forty times the levels found in the circulating blood. These high levels of vitamin C are initiated and maintained by glutathione, which of course is equally essential. The other nutrients highly essential to clear lens are argenine, inositol, cysteine, with calcium, magnesium, and vitamin D, which are essential to the absorption of amino acids. Supplements of potassium, (always with sodium) will help to reduce the swelling.

Dr.Alex Duarte has written a book on the nutritional therapy for cataracts. It is available from; Cataract Break Through, Box 2235, Wrightwood, California, 92397.

A special supplement to reduce cataracts is available from; D and B Enterprises, 19400 Beach Blvd., Suite 21, Huntington Beach California, 92647.

KIDNEY DISEASE. (Nephritis, nephrosis) (Pyelitis).

Kidney problems are frequently associated with, and or are confused with bladder problems. Bladder infections are called cystitis, and can usually be reduced with ketoconazole, or resteclin or other antibiotics, together with large quantities of ascorbic acid, sufficient to overflow into the urinary system. Lack of bladder control is usually caused by low magnesium (perhaps being metabolically tied up with calcium), while urinary retention can usually be relieved with potassium, B2, and/or pantothenic acid. Be careful with potassium when kidney function is abnormal.

Causes of Kidney Failure.
1. Lead, mercury, and toxic metals. (Care must be used during intravenous chelation).
2. Drugs of all kinds. (Reduce and eliminate or use intermittently).
3. Infections, (called pyelitis), particularly Candida Yeast.
4. Low protein or low fat diets.
5. Stress.
6. Excess toxins from a leaky porous bowel.

The pathway to kidney failure is usually a combination of the above, with the actual failure precipitated by stress. Infection is always a factor.

Infections. (See also vitamin C, ch.4.)

The medically listed infections are; infective endocarditis, streptococcal, pneumococcal, staphlycoccous, viral, bacterial, typhoid, parasitis disease, low immune complex, low complement levels, yeasts and fungii.

It should be noted that the infection does not have to be in the kidneys. High infections elsewhere in the body place a severe continuing drain on the adrenals and the immune system, alter nutritional and metabolic processes, and overload the kidneys with damaging toxins. SOD, and other "free radical" agents may be of particular value.

Reversing Kidney Failure.

In general, if the kidneys are large, or are enlarged, the condition is considered to be reversible, but if the kidneys are small and wasted, the condition is considered to be irreversible. The problem is that kidney failure leads to kidney damage, with more kidney failure. The condition is therefore difficult to reverse, but when it is reversed even severely damaged kidneys can be rebuilt.

In the usual case, there is an underlying condition of poor cellular nutrition, coupled with infection somewhere, that depletes the body reserves of protein stored in the lymphatic system. Stress from the chronic infection, coupled with stress from overwork or traumatic event, then depletes vitamin C, glycogen and other body reserves. This causes the adrenals to panic and produce large amounts of adrenalin, which calls upon the body to break down body tissues for proteins to change to sugar for energy. The body is now running on adrenalin and protein, taken from the body itself. This is a close equivalent to an all protein diet, with the protein being taken from body tissues. It is an aberrant cycle that is difficult to interrupt. The body must have sugar for energy, but if glucose is supplied it will trigger the production of insulin and adrenalin, which will increase the problem. Fructose however, does not have an insulin response, so fructose and pre-digested protein can be used to break the aberrant nephritic cycle.

Kidney Program.

We should here give special credit to Dr.Carlos Mason (Biochemist) who developed Methyl-Pro Powder for Mato labs. Methyl-Pro Powder is a well balanced complete food powder (you can live on it) developed to overcome hypoglycemia, that is also useful for kidney failure. The carbohydrate in the powder is fructose, and the powder contains adequate vitamins and minerals. Start with the following for one week; This is the program suggested by Mato Labs.

5 tablespoons Methyl-Pro Powder, with water, 4 times a day. 4 large glasses of V/8 juice, with 1 teaspoon sunflower oil added to the juice, 4 times a day. Watch for potassium problems and reduce if necessary.

Uva Ursi,-2, ten grain tablets, per day as a Beta Blocker. Watch this. It too may give problems.

1/8 to 1/4 tablet ketoconazole per day ,(with the powder).

Every second day, 1/4 capsule resteclin at some time between "meals".

Extra lecithin, up to 3 tablespoons granules (or equal in capsules) daily.

If there is gas, 1 tablet of nystatin, with the powder may help. If there is indigestion, 1 tablet Festal, with the "meal" may help.

In cases of kidney failure that do not respond to the foregoing, the focal point of all health problems must be sought, and everything must be done to improve all health factors. A thorough chiropractic examination should be made to ensure that the problem does not result from pinched nerves. Metronidazole, sulfamethoxazole, vancomycin, and other antibiotics should be carefully tried. Ascorbate should be increased to the point that it overflows into the urinary system, and the ascorbate flush and Vitamin C Retention Enemas should be used to ensure that the kidneys are not simply being overloaded with toxins from a porous and leaky colon. The Skin Dialysis Saltz Bath, (Ch.4) will help to maintain physical function until the kidney problems can be reduced.

OSTEOPOROSIS.

Osteoporosis is another degenerative disease that is principally caused by toxins from chronic infectives that are not subdued by a failing immune system. In osteoporosis the bones lose calcium and become very weak, porous and brittle, are very easily broken and are very slow to heal. Osteoporosis is very similar to rheumatoid arthritis. Reducing osteoporosis will therefore require the entire Candida program together with the suggestions for arthritis.

It has been suggested that the bone deterioration of osteoporosis may be linked to free radicals. The Candida program with time, will reduce the free radicals, but in the meantime the free radicals should be reduced with superoxide dismutase, together with selenium methionate, (or equal).

Faulty calcium metabolism is the obvious problem in osteoporosis, but this may be linked to poor collagen formation in the bones. Heavy supplements of ascorbate, with adequate bioflavinoids, will help to strengthen the collagen; calcium-magnesium orotate, with vitamin D will provide the best form of calcium; and supplements of silicon (usually from herbal "horsetail") will help to improve bone structure and will increase the ability of the body to repair broken bones. Supplements of parathyroid hormone are essential to raising calcium levels because parathyroid hormone determines the amount of calcium retained by the body. Low thyroid and Candida infection impair parathyroid hormone production. The entire Candida program will therefore continue to improve calcium levels.

After the program is under way and the basic causes of the deteriorating bones are being reduced, it will become necessary to get the calcium moving so that the old bone calcium is being replaced with the new bone structure. This can be accomplished with "spurts" of 4 or 5 infusions of calcium chelation taken three times a week, followed by several weeks of heavy calcium orotate supplements, with (vitamin D), preferably rotating between natural forms and chemical types, e.g. bone calcium, oyster calcium, calcium-magnesium orotate, chelated forms, etc. Fluoride is also essential to the formation of strong bones and small amounts should be supplemented daily throughout the program.

ALZHEIMERS DISEASE. (Aluminum disease) (Caffeine disease). Some people do develop Alzheimers Disease, but many other people diagnosed as having Alzheimers disease are simply de-hydrated from high continuous consumption of caffeine. The symptoms for both conditions are very similar, but people with Alzheimers disease will have high levels of aluminum. People with caffeine induced "Alzheimers disease" will respond quite quickly to elimination of tobacco and all caffeine (coffee, tea, chocolate, cola), together with the consumption of 8 or 10 glasses of distilled water per day and one chelated multi-mineral tablet per day. The distilled water will extract minerals from the tissues, which are then replaced with fresh minerals from the supplements.

The ill health that always accompanies caffeine dehydration usually induces chronic infection, which increases and perpetuates all of the other health problems. Most people will therefore benefit from the entire Candida program.

People with true Alzheimers disease will have high levels of aluminum which will show up on the Mineral Test. Caffeine dehydration is usually also present. They will respond to the foregoing program, together with the elimination of all possible sources of aluminum (including foil and baking powder) with extra suplements of chelated magnesium and zinc to help the body replace the aluminum with magnesium, i.e. to reverse the process of aluminum retention. Aluminum is the next element to magnesium on the atomic periodic table of elements. If the body is short on magnesium for an internal chemical reaction, it can use the next element (aluminum) as a substitute, which eventually results in the high aluminum retention associated with Alzheimers Disease.

MYOSITIS,SYNOVITIS AND FIBROSITIS. (Inflammatory Disease). (Collagen disease).

These are "muscle diseases", that can be thought of as "arthritis of the muscles". They develop from either inflammation or edema, and usually from both. Pancreatic failure, or chronic infection can initiate either the inflammation or the edema (or both), or the edema may be caused by lymphatic failure, a high salt diet, loss of potassium, by overstressed adrenals, or by caffeine or other stimulants. Low ascorbate with sub-clinical scurvy and weak tissues, will contribute to the problem.

It should be remembered that all of the tissue fluids are connected to the lymphatic system, which then drains into the bloodstream. Normally all of the arteries leak proteins into the tissues. These proteins are then soon gathered by the lympathic system, which uses them and returns any extra proteins to the bloodstream. Low ascorbate results in porous arteries that leak high amounts of protein into the tissues. If then the tissues are filled with fluids, as with inflammation and edema, (from any cause) the fluids stagnate, and the proteins in the fluids will then develop fibers (fibrosis). The fibrosis then interferes with normal muscle function, resulting in the formation of excess amounts of lactic acid, which attracts calcium and results in calcinosis. Poor blood circulation with decreased oxygen, increases the problem.

All of these inflammation diseases will respond to nutrition and nervcite therapy, but the benefits will be minimal and fleeting, unless there is ample, exercise, (to work the lymphatic pump) together with everything in the Candida program.

BRONCHITIS and EMPHYSEMA.

Bronchitis and emphysema are infections of the lungs and air tracts. They are so closely related that it is doubtful if one exists without the other. Candida yeast is invariably one of the infectives and is usually the key infective because it harbors the other infectives within the Candida callus matrix. Bronchitis and emphysema are cavity infections, and they are therefore very slow to respond and very difficult to eliminate. Asbestos emphysema, where the aviola are pierced with asbestos fibers, is a particularly difficult condition that can be improved, but response may be very slow.

Everything in the Candida program must be done with persistence, diligence and care. Clearing up Candida infections of the sinuses and throat are of particular importance. Chelation therapy, vitamin E, and B15 will help improve oxygen utilization. Sleeping with fresh air supplied with a fan, or sleeping in an oxygen enriched atmosphere can be very helpful. Green aerosol spray, 2% phenol sprays (chloraseptic), sprays made with liquid ketoconazole and 15% DMSO or lime dust therapy (as was once used for tuberculosis) will be very helpful. If lime dust therapy is used, additional benefit may come from adding crushed and powdered ketoconazole tablets to the lime dust.

It should be remembered that inflammation and excess fluids in the lungs are a serious part of this condition, and pancreatic function must be improved, including supplements of bi-carbonate. Reducing the excess fluids is an essential cornerstone of the program. Ultrasonic massage of the chest may help in the elimination of the excess fluids. Some people obtain relief and benefit from breathing very hot dry air from a partly open oven.

In addition to the Candida program, and at the very start of the program, lab tests should be made to try to determine the principal infectives so that appropriate antibiotics can be used.

Bronchitis and emphysema are true degenerative diseases that follow after degeneration of many other body systems. Allergies should be considered as a possible hidden factor.

LOW BACK PAIN, SLIPPED DISC, SCIATICA and SPINAL PROBLEMS.
(See also Ch.6. Chiropractic, Nervcite Therapy and Vitamin C.) Contrary to common belief, low back pain and slipped disc are true degenerative conditions because they are the cumulative effect of adrenal depletion and failure of other body systems. The slipped disc is not a slipped disc as such. Depletion of Vitamin C contributes to adrenal depletion and muscle spasm, while the shortage of vitamin C also produces sub-clinical scurvy that weakens the collagen in the spinal discs, causing the disc to deform under the body weight. The disc degeneration can invariably be seen in "slipped disc".

Now there are always many strange things happen in biological processes. We could expect adrenal depletion to cause muscle spasm somewhere in the body, but we would not expect the muscles in the lower back to be the most vulnerable. Yet it is muscle spasm from adrenal depletion that causes the low back pain, and if the muscle cramps are severe and if the collagen in the spinal discs is soft, the spasmed muscles, now without nerve control, simply pull the vertebra out of place, creating the so-called slipped disc. Most certainly the disc may have finally "slipped" when using the back, but how else could the disc "slip" when bending to pick up a piece of paper? Quite obviously it was not the weight of the paper. It was a degenerative process simply waiting for a minor event to trigger the muscle spasm.

If adrenal depletion and muscle spasm are severe, other vertebrae in the spine may also be pulled out of place, pinching the nerves and creating sciatica and the other "pinched nerve" disorders that your chiropractor sometimes "cures" with spinal manipulation. But how long will the spinal adjustments last if caffeine, alcohol, chronic infection, or other stress continues to deplete the ascorbate and the adrenals?

Quite obviously, low back pain, slipped disc, sciatica and displaced vertebrae (called subluxation) are all manifestations of the same degenerative condition; scurvy and adrenal depletion. To improve adrenal function we must do everything in the Candida program, with particular attention;
1. All adrenal nutrients, with emphasis on ascorbate and potassium. (Hi KC Fizz).
2. Elimination of all self administered poisons.
3. Reduction of all other sources of stress.
5. Nervcite therapy, preferably neursage.
6. Niacin flush.
7. Chiropractic adjustment following after the neursage, if indicated by X-ray.
8. B12 injections.(see Bursitis).
9. Calcium, vitamin D, and PTA (parathyroid hormone).

Low back pain usually strikes without warning. Immediate relief can be obtained by taking large amounts of adrenal nutrients, neursage of the affected areas, application of DMSO to the spasmed muscles, application of heat to the area with heat lamp or hot water bottle, and perhaps acupuncture or electrostimulator if pain continues to be severe.

Common contributing factors to low back pain are kidney infection, Pelvic Inflammatory Disease (PID) and/or a porous leaky bowel. The sharp pain itself is caused by muscle spasm, but the muscles that are cramped are frequently some distance from the actual pain, because the lower back has a very large number of tender anchors associated with the legs. The information on neursage should be reviewed. The muscle end plates (nervcites) involved can be easily located because they are so tender and sensitive. Sensitive nervcites can usually be found in the low spot in the center of the upper hip, and in the center and inside of the thigh above the knee. Usually many more very sensitive nervcites can be found along the inside of the hip bones by laying on the back with the legs spraddled. The tender nervcites will be along the edges of the bones, between the genitals and the anus, and continuing on up in the groove between the genitals and the leg.

Nervcite therapy is effective because it mechanically breaks up calcium lactate deposits in the muscle end plates, re-connects some of the nerve axons, and releases histamine and heparin which also re-connects more nerve axons. A heavy niacin flush, following nervcite massage, will increase the histamine and heparin, sometimes to the point where so many spasmed muscles are relaxed that the back pain vanishes.

It should be noted that the kidneys are located very close to the areas affected by low back pain, and muscle spasm in the back may therefore also affect kidney function. It may well be that low back pain contributes to nephritis and alternately it may well be that kidney problems contribute to low back pain, particularly if the kidneys are the site of chronic infection.

Low back pain is also frequently associated with difficult sexual orgasm, or orgasmic failure. This association may only be from the increased stress, or it may be from a direct nerve connection to the ovaries or to the testicle chord anchors. Alternately then, infection of ovaries or testicles may contribute directly to low back pain.

Slipped Disc.

For many years slipped disc has been treated by surgically removing the defective disc and allowing the two vertebrae to grow together. This operation is complete folly. It is usually unsuccessful because it does nothing to cure the cause, and frequently it produces lesions and other side effects. The best approach seems to be many treatments of neursage and many trips to the chiropractor to relieve pain and discomfort until the underlying scurvy and adrenal depletion can be reduced.

Although the chiropractor may be essential until tissue strength and body systems improve, chiropractors, and sometimes very good chiropractors, frequently tend to over-treat. The spinal disc grows in the proper form to hold the vertebrae in place. Chiropractic adjustments that are too frequent alter the shape of the disc, and the vertebra will then sometimes fall out, or fall back in, without apparent cause. If possible, chiropractic adjustments should be limited to once a week.

It should be noted that a modern form of surgical removal of damaged discs seems to be quite successful if adequate rest and ample excerise are included in the program.

Sciatica.

Sciatica is caused by pressure on the sciatic nerve, from either a displaced vertebra or from degeneration of the spinal disc. Therapy is the same as for slipped disc. Sleeping on a solid flat bed, with foam mattress may help.

HAND, WRIST PROBLEMS and CARPAL TUNNEL SYNDROME.
(See also Page 375.)

Dr.Ellis (ref.34) has used B6 (Pyridoxine) to relieve a very large number of problems with the hands. Carpal Tunnel Syndrome will also respond to B6. The effective quantities start at a very low 200mg daily, and may run as high as 1200mg daily in divided amounts. Note that Ref.5, considers B6 to be so important to total health that the advice is that everyone should supplement B6 up to "dream recall", and then reduce a little if dreams become too vivid. Some people may take 500mg or more four times daily. If B6 fails to relieve hand or carpal problems pyridoxal-5-phosphate, 50mg, three times daily, by itself between meals, should be tried. In a few cases relief may come only with periodic injections of B6,- 300 mg.

The reasons that the hands are sensitive to a lack of B6 is not clear, but the improvement with B6 may be linked to magnesium/calcium processes, or just to a shortage of magnesium. It should be noted that Candida infection uses up large quantities of magnesium, which alters the calcium/magnesium balance. The hand problems, including carpal problems, may therefore be a side effect from Candida or other infectives. Magnesium supplements, with the B6 should be tried, and if magnesium is effective Candida infection is a probable factor. An examination of the hands, including people with carpal problems, will always show tender nervcites and extensive muscle spasm. It is the pulling of the spasmed muscles that frequently deforms the hands and creates the carpal problems. Adrenal nutrients and neursage of the hands and wrists will usually be of further help, but if the hands are particularly painful or if they are tender between nervcites, local infection may be involved.

We can never know the subtle reasons that specific infections are found in specific parts of the body, but weak and painful wrists frequently result from the infectives that are subject to Metronidazole. If some problems remain, Sulfamethoxazole and Erythromycin should be tried. Infections that affect the wrists will of course also affect the hands. All of the foregoing suggestions however, should be considered as only temporary "band-aid" treatments. The prime causes of hand problems are the same as for all degenerative diseases. To effectively reduce problems with the hands and wrists the entire Candida program will be needed, with particular attention to chronic infection, neursage, and adrenal support.

BROWN "AGE SPOTS".

Brown "age spots" are simply areas of degenerative skin necrosis, where the outer skin has become almost dead. Fungii and other infectives are then able to feed on the dead and dying tissues, with their toxins and metabolites increasing the necrosis.

Age spots usually start as a few small spots on the hands and arms; and sometimes on the legs, throat and face; these slowly increase in size and number to the point that the entire skin may be almost covered.

As "age spots" are a truly degenerative condition they can be reduced and eliminated only by reversing the entire degenerative environment, as with the entire Candida program, together with the application of anti-fungals and healing agents to the affected areas. The brown spots may appear to be unaffected by the program for several months, but after the body starts to recuperate they will start to loosen, after which their removal can be accellerated by light scraping with a knife before each application of phenol alkalizer, and before each application of Elase-Chloromycetin. Supplements of zinc and large amounts of vitamin C and bioflavinoids are essential to the rebuilding of healthy skin.

PSORIASIS and SKIN PROBLEMS.

Psoriasis is an eruption of the skin that takes almost as many different forms as there are doctors who diagnose it. In other words, if there is a skin eruption that is not a boil, it may be called psoriasis, simply because the good doctor did not know what caused it and he had to give it a name.

The body has six main elimination systems; the lungs, the kidneys, the colon, the sexual organs, the hair, and the skin. The skin has the greatest exposed area, it is very active in waste disposal, and it is used by the body as a last resort. Specifically, if any of the other waste disposal systems fail, within a few hours, and sometimes within a few minutes, the body will try to eliminate the toxins through the skin, sometimes so successfully that the failed elimination system can be identified by the strong body odor. If the toxins are many, and if detoxification and elimination by other systems is poor, the body will be forced to try to eliminate all of the toxic substances through the skin, resulting in the necrosis and rash that is called psoriasis.

Psoriasis then, is easily "cured". Improve colon and kidney function, get a little more rest, apply a little disinfecting cream, take a few vitamins, and it will all disappear, only to return, months, weeks, or days later. It was not cured. It could not be cured because the psoriasis was only a skin manifestation of much underlying ill health. Psoriasis is just as much a degenerative disease as allergies or arthritis. So the only real cure is the entire Candida program, together with the phenol alkalizer applied to the rash, followed perhaps with vitamin E and or/Elase-Chloromycetin to promote healing. Particular emphasis should be placed on improving colon and digestive function.

SCHIZOPHRENIA, NEUROSIS, PSYCHOSIS and DEPRESSION.
(see also "Colitis" Ch.6, Ref.5.)

Schizophrenia is a broad and nebulous name given, rightly or wrongly, to many different aberrant mental states.

Anyone who really thinks about mental aberrations and remembers even a few of their dreams and nightmares must conclude that all mental aberrations must come from within. Specifically, although we can and do control some thought processes, any serious mental problems, are biological and they are not psychological. To understand that mental problems come from altered brain chemistry is the most important part of dealing with mental problems. We must remember that psychology is indeed mixed with the altered brain chemistry, but we must also remember that the basic cause is biological. To attempt to deal with mental problems with psychology is like trying to rationalize dreams, or like trying to rationalize and understand the terrifying nightmares and delerium associated with many infectious diseases;- nightmares and delerium that obviously result directly from toxins from the infectious disease. Following these observations, if mental problems occur we must expect them to come from within the brain itself; we must expect them to come from metabolically altered brain chemistry;-- we must expect them to come from brain starvation, as in the delerium that sometimes precedes death; from toxic metals, as with mercury poisoning, (The mad hatter); or from toxins and metabolites produced by infectives, as in the delerium of malaria. Logically, we should really expect that mental problems finally result from some strange mixture of all three basic causes;-- we should really expect schizophrenia and mental problems to be just what they are;--a truly degenerative condition with multiple causes.

The most common causes of schizophrenis and mental problems are;

1. Nutritional shortage, usually dietary related;- pellagra, beri-beri, scurvy, etc. Look closely. Beri-beri can be produced by continuous over-consumption of alcohol. Sub-clinical and obvious scurvy is very common, pellagra is frequently seen in orientals who have changed from eating brown rice to eating white rice, (which is devoid of vitamins). Pellagra can usually be seen as a thin bright red line along the gum-line.
2. Hypoglycemia, diabetes and "sugar disease".
3. Caffeine dehydration.
4. Toxic metal poisoning,- lead, mercury, cadmium, arsenic, aluminum (Alzheimers disease), copper, iron (iron siderosis) and sometimes selenium.
5. Pyrolluria, Histapenia, (See "Mental and Elemental Nutrients", Ref.5.)
6. Colon and/or sexual toxins.
7. Allergies.
8. Toxins and metabolites from Candida yeast and other chronic infectives. These include sterols, indoles, ethanols, phenethyl alcohol, etc. (See list ch.3. and page 370).

The schizophrenic state is usually produced by some weird combination of these basic factors that finally results in an equally weird pattern of mental symptoms.

To reduce mental problems everything in the Candida program must be done, with particular attention to everything in the foregoing list. Until the basic program can reduce the symptoms, the mental state can usually be temporarily altered with one of the following tried separately, or in combination: HiKC Fizz, with all adrenal nutrients; niacin (to flush level), pantothenic acid, (to 600mg); tryptophan with B6 (to 1 or 2 grams) (Magnesium and pyridoxyl-5-phosphate may be needed with the B6); Deaner (to 200mg); L-lysine; L-cystine; L-tyrosine; all with ample fresh air and exercise. The fresh air and exercise are very important as they are required for the body to oxidise the metabolites. If low blood sugar is suspected, a few sips of tea, up to 1/2 cup, with protein or complex carbohydrate may help.

Every effort must be made to determine any other chronic infectives that may be involved, such as pinworms, flukes, etc. with many tests and/or trial treatments. Levamisole may help.

Altered sexual levels are always present in schizophrenia and they are one of the most important features. Particular attention should be given to histamine levels, and to levels of spermine and spermadine. (Ch.5.). If histamine levels (sexual levels) are very high (120 nanograms/ml) temporary relief may come from the judicious use of estrogen or testosterone.

The entire Candida program will always alter and improve schizophrenia and mental problems. People who do not fully respond to the program may benefit from reading "Mental and Elemental Nutrients" (see reference list), or from additional information from;

"The Canadian Schizophrenic Foundation", (CSF)

2229 Broad St. Regina, Saskatchewan, Canada. S4P-1Y7. CSF have local chapters across Canada. There may be a chapter in your community.

MULTIPLE SCLEROSIS.

Multiple Sclerosis is another true degenerative disease that is the final result of multiple causes. The principal feature of multiple sclerosis is the degeneration of the nerve sheaths, which leaves the nerves exposed to other body processes. It is said that the exposed nerves produce the mental and other symptoms of multiple sclerosis, but none of us develop nerve sheaths for several years after we start life, so if lack of nerve sheaths produces multiple sclerosis then all babies and very young children should have the same symptoms, which they do not. The extreme depression and other mental problems associated with multiple sclerosis therefore do not come from the exposed nerves; quite obviously they come from some altered body chemistry that causes the deterioration of the nerve sheaths, and altered chenistry similar to schizophrenia that expresses itself in a slightly different way. In short, we should think of people with multiple sclerosis as being schizophrenics who also have exposed nerves. (See schizophrnia). The causes of multiple sclerosis are then so diverse and so interlocked that to reduce multiple sclerosis we simply must do everything in the entire Candida program, and we must do it well, together with all of the suggestions for schizophrenia.

Now there is quite good evidence that allergies are always part of multiple sclerosis, and there is further evidence that the allergies are always based in Candida infection. Thus ketoconazole, starting with very small amounts, becomes the cornerstone for improvement.

In the case of one young mother, where everything that could medically be done had been tried, and where everything in the health food store (including the macrobiotic diet) had also been tried, without success, then ketoconazole 1/2 tablet daily was started. Within a few hours allergic symptoms and depression started to clear, and within two weeks the complexion started to clear, causing the young woman to exclaim; "Just look, I have never before seen my skin so clear." In other words,

411.

she had lived all of her life and she had raised a family under the constant shadow of Candida infection. Within a month she was back at work, and within a few months most of the symptoms of multiple sclerosis had vanished. Vanished yes, which caused her doctor to simply cop-out by saying that the multiple sclerosis must have been mis-diagnosed, "because multiple sclerosis cannot be cured".

Not all cases of multiple sclerosis will respond so quickly, but the entire Candida program with ketoconazole will always reduce the many symptoms.

One of the erosive factors in multiple sclerosis may be free radicals, which can be reduced with superoxide dismutase to bring the free radicals down to less toxic hydrogen peroxide; and selenium methionate to reduce the hydrogen peroxide to water.

Particular attention should be given to adequate lipotropics to assist in re-building the nerve sheaths. The diet should include lecithin with supplements of choline, inositol and methionine, alternated with phosphatydal choline. Pure free amino acids, and raw cabbage to promote healing, may also be of value. Whenever possible supplements should be in the form of orotates to provide the B13 that is so necessary for cellular function and for the utilization of folic acid and vitamin B12. B13 is particularly helpful for multiple sclerosis and atherosclerosis, indicating a close link between the two conditions. Heavy injections of B12, (see Bursitis) will frequently improve nerve function. Note that lack of B12 results in pernicious anemia, indicating that low oxygenation is part of the problem. Supplements of vitamin E, and B15 (Pangamic acid) will also help, and there are many reports of good response from "oxygen therapy", from fans, oxygen masks, oxgenated rooms, and the decompression chamber. It is also well known that the methyl groups are effective against multiple sclerosis, indicating poor glucose metabolism (oxidation) or heavy metal toxicity, or both. Supplements of betain, cysteine (lots of eggs), methionine or elemental sulphur will be useful.

Now note the possibility that heavy metals are involved. In one case, good progress was made by reducing chronic infection and upgrading all body systems, yet serious problems remained. The patient's doctor said it was not multiple sclerosis, it was mercury poisoning. The hair mineral test showed mercury as low. High supplements of cysteine were given, and mercury showed up in the urine. The amalgam tooth fillings were changed, and the multiple sclerosis disappeared. Perhaps, amalgam fillings, or other sources of mercury are always part of the basic problem. (See Mercury, Ch.4.).

PARTIAL PARALYSIS. (See also Travelling Arthritis).

Partial paralysis of one side of the body, or of limbs or other body parts is frequently a degenerative condition even when it appears to result from injury or other nerve damage.

The principal causes of partial paralysis are displaced vertebra, muscle spasm and chronic infection of the cords and tendons, the lymphatic system, or possibly even the nerves themselves. Chiropractic examination, with X-rays is essential, all body systems should be improved, toxic minerals and particularly mercury must be eliminated, and the various anti-fungals and antibiotics must be tried including anthmentics. Watch carefully for any changes. Any changes indicate that the body systems are still functional, and any changes also indicate that you have touched upon the problem. Then you must make a careful and diligent search with trials of similar antibiotics and antifungals to find others that also make changes, and from the overlapping of these anti-infectives you may be able to deduce the micro-organisms that are the focal point of the problems.

The entire program should be accompanied by neursage, and perhaps by ultrasonic massage of the afflicted areas including the adjacent spine, and the same "reflex" parts on the opposite side of the body. Electrostimulators and galvanic pads should be tried.

Pure amino acids, mixed nucleic acids and lecithin will help the body to repair nerve damage. Sardines are high in nucleic acids. Partial paralysis will usually affect many body systems, and any improvement in the afflicted area will help the other body systems to recover.

CANCER.

Cancer is the malignant growth of body cells independently from the body and beyond the control of the body, yet with the cells being nourished by normal body processes. Cancer cells are malignant because they not only multiply on their own, but they are also invasive and destructive to normal body cells.

Tumors are similar growths to cancer, but in benign (?) tumors the cells are not invasive, while in cancerous tumors (the start of cancer) some of the cells have become invasive. We do not know exactly what causes normal body cells to form tumors, but from varicocelles we do know that Candida yeast can be one of the causes. We also do not know exactly what causes "benign" tumor cells to become invasive and cancerous, but we do know, from the admirable work of Dr.Virginia Livingstone and her associates (San Diego) that the chronic infective Progenitor Cryptocides is always present in the fulminating form in every case of cancer.

We always know that Candida yeast infection is always present in cancer. Although cancer may appear to strike without warning, we do know that the immune system and many other body systems have already become badly degenerated long before the cancer appears. From all of this we must assume that cancer is a true degenerative disease that finally results from the failure of many body systems and particularly the failure of the immune system to;-

1. Destroy Candida yeast.

2. To destroy Progenitor Cryptocides.

3. To destroy the aberrant cancerous cells as soon as they appear.

Dr.Krebbs Jr. has dedicated a lifetime of exceptionally admirable and lucid work in developing a scientific understanding of cancer, and in developing laetrile to destroy it. It was also Dr.Krebbs who revived the admirable work of Beard, who had carefully noted the actual complex development of the embryo from the fertilized cells, and who also showed that it was chorionic gonadatrophin, produced by the female only during pregnancy, that prevented the immune system from destroying the foreign proteins of which the growing fetus is composed.

Yes, chorionic gonadatrophin indeed does inhibit the immune system, and of course, if cancerous cells started to grow anywhere in the body they could continue to multiply as long as chorionic gonadatrophin was present. But pregnancy has a finite time, and whith the end of pregnancy the chorionic gonadatrophin is no longer produced so the immune system of the young mother can again destroy any cancerous cells that may have started to grow. But what would happen to cancerous cells if some infective, by chance, happened to produce chorionic gonadatrophin as a waste metabolite? Would not the chorionic gonadatrophin prevent the immune system from destroying the foreign proteins of cancer, just as it does during pregnancy? Oh Yes! and Dr. Livingstone has shown that Progenitor Cryptocides does indeed have the capability to produce choroionic gonadatrophin, so Progenitor does not initiate cancer, but it allows the cancer to grow, completely free from the immune system, just as the unborn fetus grows free from the immune system.

The development of cancer therefore briefly becomes:-

1. Failure of body systems, perhaps initiated by Candida yeast infection, reduces the effectiveness of the immune system.

2. The failing immune system however caused, is unable to control Progenitor Cryptocides. Progenitor then multiplies and produces chorionic gonadatrophin, or a close analogue.

3. The chorionic gonadatrophin then prevents the immune system from destroying the invasive cancerous cells, irrespective of their source, which may be embryonic, or which may be mutated biologically, chemically, or by radiation or by some as yet unknown process.

4. The invasive cancerous cells, protected by the chorionic gonadatrophin then multiply unchecked, to form the cancer.

Cancer then results principally from chronic infection, immune system failure, and progenitor infection.

Arresting Cancer.

One of the greatest problems in dealing with cancer is that so many body systems have failed before the cancer appears. Time is required to rebuild failed body systems, but with cancer, the time for action is short because the rate of cancer growth will usually be greater than the rate at which body systems can be improved when under the severe stress imposed by the cancer. Thus the war may be lost while the battle is being won. Dr.Gold's hydrazine sulphate however, can be used to arrest the invasive action of the cancer. This will reduce the stress and pain and will give time for body systems to be re-built.

Hydrazine Sulphate.

Hydrazine sulphate does not cure cancer. It only arrests the cancer, and prevents it from consuming the body. Body systems can then be renewed and improved, and laetrile can then be used to reduce the cancer.

Hydrazine sulfate is a common and widely available chemical compound, NOT to be confused with the methylhydrazines or methylhydrazine derivatives such as Procarbazine (Matulane series), from which it differs both pharmacologically and toxicologically. Hydrazine sulfate functions to inhibit gluconeogenesis in the liver and kidney cortex at the phosphornolpyruvate carboxykinase reaction -- and as such represents a new means to limit host energy wasting as a result of malignancy, and thus to retard or attenuate cancer cachexia while at the same time exerting indirect anti-tumor effect. Its lack of direct cytotoxicity may account for its relatively low incidence of side effects.

(A) one 60mg. capsule, q.d.- for first three days. With or before breakfast.

(B) One 60mg. capsule, b.i.d. for next 3 days. Before breakfast and before dinner.

(C) One 60mg capsule. t.i.d. thereafter. Approximately every 8 hours beginning with breakfast. The above protocol is based on a patient weight of 55kg and above; for a patient weight of 50kg and below, half-dosages (i.e.,30mg capsules) have been reported as effective.

Generally it is reported that hydrazine sulfate is most effective when administered by itself (no other medications given one-half hour before or after administration of hydrazine sulfate) before meals. If adequate response is made on 2 capsules daily (60mg, b.i.d), patients have been reported maintained on this dosage schedule and not increased. Hydrazine sulphate as used in cancer, was developed by Dr.Gold at the Syracuse Cancer Research Institute, Presidential Plaza, 600 East Genesee St., Syracuse, New York 13202. U.S.A. Send $5.00 or more for their big package of information.
LAETRILE .
Physician's Protocol.
　　Dr.H.Manner, Loyola University ,Chicago, U.S.A.
　　The following is given in response to the many requests received from practicing physicians. It is presented only as a guide with the full realization that modifications will undoubtedly be mandated by the condition of specific patients. It should in no way be considered a "do-it-yourself" cancer therapy. Professional diagnosis and regular check-ups are absolutely essential. Specific names are given for the therapeutic components. This is only because I am most familiar with these brands and the companies producing them. Others may be available, and a check of labels will certainly allow substitutions.
Pre-Treatment.
　　The mineral balance of cancer patients is usually out of balance. It is essential that the body be brought back to normal as rapidly as possible. A hair analysis or a blood elemental analysis should be done. Once the mineral deficiencies and surpluses are known, supplementation measures should be taken to correct the imbalances.
First 21 days.
1. Diet.-- This is one of the most important components of the treatment plan. A vegetable juice extracter should be purchased by the patient and most of the vegetables in the diet should be juiced. In this way all the naturally occurring enzymes, minerals, and vitamins will be present. The complete diet is given at the end of this protocol.
2. Detoxification. --Each day a coffee retention enema should be administered. In cases of extreme toxemia, this should be repeated twice a day. One cup of coffee (not instant) mixed with 1 tablespoon lactose sugar should be retained for 30 minutes. The caffeine stimulated secretion of bile is an important part of the detoxification plan.
3. Digestive Enzymes.-- To decrease the stress placed on the gastric glands and the pancreas, 1 or 2 Hydrozyme tablets should be taken with each meal. This compound contains hydrochloric

acid, pepsin and enterically coated pancreatic enzymes. This will insure the proper digestion of ingested food. The patient should be given a graded litmus paper and instructed to test the first urine in the morning. it should have a pH of about 5.5.

4. Anti-neoplastic enzymes. -- Three Retenzyme and one Intenzyme tablet taken together 3 times daily. These enzymes must be taken when the digestive tract is the most empty. They should be administered mid-way between breakfast and lunch; lunch and dinner; and again at bedtime.

A- if tumor is palpable, 1 ml of Wobe-mucos intratumoral enzyme is injected directly into and around the tumor mass on alternate days. This enzyme has been found to be very effective in breast adenocarcinomas.

B. If there is a problem with oral administration of the enzyme, or if it is felt that additional enzyme therapy is required, a rectal form of the enzyme (Retenzyme 5X) is available. Two tablets are given as a daily retention enema.

5. Vitamin A.-- This should be given in an emulsified form to prevent liver involment. Twenty drops of Bio-Ae Mulsion (Forte) are given in morning juice and another 20 drops in the evening juice. This will give the patient 500,000 I.U. daily. The skin should be watched. When drying or scaling occurs, discontinue Vitamin A for one week. Return after one week with a two-week on, one-week off routine.

6. Vitamin C. -- Fifteen grams of ascorbic acid should be the minimum given daily. This amount of ascorbic acid may cause gastric disturbances. For this reason, it is suggested that mineral ascorbates be substituted. Super-gram 11 is a good compound for this. Spread the 15 grams throughout the day. The dosage may be increased at the discretion of the physcian. Some have recommended dosages as high as 50 - 75 grams daily.

7. Vitamin B 15. The salts of pangamic acid will increase the efficiency of cellular oxidation. Pangamic 15 is a calcium pangamate. True 15 is also available as the zinc and magnesium pangamates. Two of the B-15 tablets should be given with each meal.

8. Amygdalin.-- Three 3-gram vials should be administered intravenously daily.

9. A therapeutic vitamin mineral preparation such as Plus 198 should be given morning and evening.

10. Other Supplements. Other nutritional supplements can be considered for individual cases. Selenium, zinc, RNA-DNA and vitamin E have been used by physicians.

After 21 days.

1. All dietary and therapeutic modalities remain the same excepting amygdalin.

2. <u>Amygdalin</u> --Two 3-gram vials are administered intravenously twice a week. On non-injection days, two 500mg. tablets are given in the morning and two again in the evening for a total of 2 grams per day.

Addendum

For the name of the supplier nearest to you, the following manufacturers should be contacted:

Alacer Corp; Buena Park, California 90622, USA. --Super-Gram 11.

Biotics Laboratories, Houston, Texas 77038 USA. --Hydrozyme, Retenzyme, Intenzyme, Retenzyme 5X, True-15, Bio Ae-Mulsion.

Graham Pharmaceuticals, Graham, Texas 76046 USA. -Amygdalin (Mexican manufacture).

Laetrile Corp., Burlington, Vermont 05401, USA. - Pangamik-15. Amygdalin (European manufacture).

Mucus Corporation, Woodland Hills, California 91367, USA. -Intra-tumoral enzyme.

Plus Products, Irvine, California 92714, USA. -Plus 198

For further information on the chemistry and biochemistry of Laetrile (Amygdalin) See Ref.31.

Curing Cancer.

There are a great many ways that cancer has been cured. These cures range from cobalt and chemotherapy through herbs like juniper and chaparral, to meditation, prayer, vitamin C, the macrobiotic diet, intravenous chelation, laetrile, DMSO, etc. and etc. Unquestionably, many of the cures were real. Yet there have been problems. Not always, but frequently, and unfortunately, a few years after the cancer is cured the victim dies, -- of cancer.

The reason for this is clear. Yes, the cancer was cured, with the cure sometimes proven by X-rays. The therapy used either destroyed the cancer, or it helped the immune system to destroy the cancer, or to destroy or reduce Progenitor. So the cancer was gone. But the underlying causes of cancer, specifically the degenerated body systems, did not disappear. The cancer simply re-grew, perhaps somewhere else, but usually in the tissues already weakened by the former cancerous growth. To cure the cancer then, we must do everything in the Candida program and more. While the hydrazine sulphate holds the cancer arrested and reduces the pain, the Candida program will improve all of the body systems, and will reduce the Candida infection, which is invariably a major part of the physical degeneration and a major factor in the failure of the immune system.

We do not know the exact role of Candida yeast in the development of cancer. Yeasts are very ancient plants that appear at the very first evolutionary division between plants and animals. Progenitor cryptocides, the infective that is always present in cancer, is a member of the genus Actinomycetales, which is also an ancient micro-organism that appeared about the same time as the yeasts. Other members of the genus actinomycetales are also very damaging to man, with names like Tuberculosis, Leprosy, Actinomyces and Actinomycetes. Actino- mycetales are fungal plants, yet actinomyces is at present thought to be a bacterium, although it can be killed with ketoconazole like a fungal plant. There is also a very strong indication that Candida yeast may not be a yeast, it may also be a member of actinomycetales, becaues there is a medical paper that infers that Candida yeast transforms into the rods and L forms of progenitor cryptocides, and also transforms into progenitor itself. This means that the cancerous environment will remain as long as the immune system is not keeping the Candida yeast and/or the progenitor crytocides subdued.

The Candida program will therefore help to reduce the progenitor component either directly or indirectly by reducing the Candidal demands on the immune system so that the immune energy can be devoted to subduing progenitor.

The Cancer program should therefore include the entire Candida program with hydrazine sulphate, and:

1. Intravenous chelation, probably once a week, to improve blood circulation and to kill infectives present in the bloodstream. Stress must be reduced at all times, so the chelation could start with daily hypodermic injections, perhaps with a little DMSO added one day, or a little Monistat 1V added on another day. To reduce possible complications it might be advisable to skip the hydrazine sulphate before the DMSO or Monistat are used. Vitamins should be added to the chelator to improve cellular nutrition.

2. Large quantities of vitamin C, as both ascorbic acid and as mineral ascorbates, and by injection if indicated. (See also Vit.C, Ch.4.).

The "alcoholic" (See alcoholism) cell rebuilding program should be followed. 30grams vit.C daily principally as sodium ascorbate plus 8 grams mixed amino acids with 500 gm B6, three times daily for one month. Vitamin C can be reduced to 15 gms after 3 or 4 days.

4. Laetrile.

5. Abcissic Acid. (to counter the chorionic gonadatrophin).

Abcissic acid is part of the vitamin A molecule. Vitamin A is protective against cancer and carcinogens. Abcissic acid is the plant dormin that suppresses plant growth in the fall and causes the plant to"go to sleep" for the winter. It has a similar effect on progenitor cryptocides, which of course infers that progenitor is a plant type infective similar to yeast. Abcissic acid is very expensive, but it is easily made (thanks to Dr.Virginia Livingston) (Ref.30). by adding one heaping teaspoon of liver powder to an 8 oz. glass of carrot juice. The liver powder (or blended raw liver) will digest the carotene and produce abcissic acid. The actual yield is about 7 gms. of abcissic acid per quart of carrot juice.

The author is unable to find a recommended daily amount, but some health practitioners have success with one eight-ounce glass of liver-digested carrot juice per day, taken four hours away from A-E Emulsin, which is another retinoid.

6.Superoxide Dismutase and selenium methionate, or equal.

7. Improved colon function with;

    A. Vitamin C. Retention enemas.

    B. Coffee enemas to clean out the bowels. (Ch.4.).

    C. Acidophilus, buttermilk, egg yolks, sauerkraut, coconut, capricin, NaEDTA to change the intestinal flora.

8. Particular attention must be given to improving immune function:

    a. Thyroid, if indicated.

    b. Emulsified Vitamin A (A/E emulsin).

    c. Proteolytic enzymes.

    d. Lithium. if indicated.

    Then as the victim improves;-

    e. Occasionally, bee pollen, royal jelly, or Spirulina. These contain very small amounts of a great many very complex proteins which serve as a multiple oral vaccine.

    f. Small amounts of Bordetella Purtussis vaccine.

    g. Levamisole, Metronidazole, Sulfamethoxazole.

    h. Progenitor vaccine, or preferrably autogenous vaccine.

9. Other non-invasive Cancer therapies. These would be principally herbs and homeopathic procedures, like Essaic. Information on Essaic can be obtained from:

Mrs.Diamond, 416-985-2363.

The Resterin Corp. 280 Cochrane St. Port Perry, Ontario, Canada.

There are about forty more cancer therapies that have been successful. About twenty metabolic therapies are described in "Metabolic Cancer Therapies" Donsbach/Walker,

International Institute Health Sciences. 7422 Mount Joy Drive. Huntington Beach, California 92648. USA.

<u>Eliminating the Cancer.</u>

The foregoing combined cancer program should slowly reduce and eliminate the cancer, but the circumstances of location of the growth and how far it may have progressed may force other choices. Radiation, surgery and chemotherapy should always be considered.

Chemotherapy.

Chemotherapy is sometimes successful, and might be undertaken after general health starts to improve. Chemotherapy is a very clever technical procedure, but it places very high stress on the victim. Extra support with vitamins and minerals will reduce the stress. In general, chemotherapy is a poor choice that should be considered only as a last resort.

Radiation.

Radiation is an excellent therapy where the cancer is exposed. It should certainly be considered for skin cancers or other cancers where there is a good opportunity for success. Radiation for deep cancers should be avoided because the damage frequently exceeds the benefits.

Surgery

Surgery is also excellent where all conditions are favorable to clean and complete removal of the cancer. Unless the operation is very small and easy, surgery should be postponed (if possible) until the health has improved and stabilized. Breast surgery is usually very successful, but complete mastectomies have now been shown to have no greater value than simple surgery, so they should be avoided.

One of the peculiarities pf cancer is the ability of the growth to develop its own blood supply, usually from a single artery. This artery can usually be found with radioactive scanning, following radioactive injection. If the artery is located, a single injection of the right quantity of silicone will block the entire blood supply right down to the arterioles. After which the cancerous cells will die, and the entire cancer can then be safely removed.

Mercury.

Mercury poisoning may be a primary factor in cancer, particularly in Leukemia.

Combined Therapy.

One of the greatest perils of man is not a disease or an infective, it is a simple stupidity called predjudice. The excellent chemical engineering in chelation therapy, which was originally developed by the armed forces, has been savaged by ignorant medical predjudice, to the point that some doctors are persecuted for using it, even when it saves lives and is effective against cancer. The equally brilliant chemistry involved in the development of Laetrile has been equally savaged and suppressed by ignorant medical predjudice. Even Linus Pauling's work with vitamin C, has been savaged by ignorant medical predjudice. This same medical predjudice has almost completely prevented the medical profession from combining the many non- invasive cancer therapies with radiation, surgery and chemotherapy.

In this ignorant predjudice there is no thought or consideration for science, and there is even less consideration for the hapless victim. Yet in a society that prides itself so much on the welfare state it seems impossible and incongruous that the physicians do not think in terms of combined therapy. For, most certainly, the chances for the survival and happiness of the hapless victims would be greatly increased by combined therapy. If radiation, surgery or chemotherapy must be used, why not follow it with laetrile, or Essaic? Why are not proteolytic enzymes used? Why not use Vitamin C? We do not know what benefits may be derived from combined therapy. Ignorant medical predjudice prevents us from finding out. But anyone who has had, or who feels that they have to have surgery, or radiation, or chemotherapy, might well consider doing everything else that they can, because all too frequently only a few years after a medical cure, cancer makes a very final return.

Preventing Cancer.

Cancer does not strike the healthy. Many signs of ill health appear long before the body systems have degenerated to the point of cancer. Very few people have ever even heard of a dark-field microscope, and many doctors have not even seen one, but the dark-field microscope should be in every health clinic. One drop of fresh blood can be better than many tests, because progenitor cryptocides, and the degeneration of red blood cells, can be seen under the dark-field microscope long before any other signs of cancer appear. The degeneration seen in the microscope forms definite patterns that are typical of cancer and are well known to science. The cancerous environment in the body is therefore not difficult to detect, and with early warning, the cancerous environment can be reversed with the Candida and cancer programs.

Cancer however, should really be prevented before the body is damaged. After all, we do not have to eat meat preserved with nitrates. We do not have to use tobacco, caffeine or alcohol. We do not have to consume large quantities of sugar. We do not have to use strong spices. We do not have to consume large quantities of salt. We do not have to eat smoked meat and fish. We can avoid strong sources of radiation. We can avoid urea formaldehyde foam. We can have our houses checked for natural radiatiom (radon gas). We can also improve our diet. We can have a few injections of autogenous vaccine. We can take a little nystatin and ketoconazole once in a while, and we can also even have a few apricot kernels once a month; --- just in case.

In short, if we did not do the things we should not do, and if we did do the things that we should do, cancer would be very rare. Prevention is certainly the very best cure, for cancer.

Other Cancer Therapies.
There are a very large number of Cancer therapies that have had limited to good success. Some may sound queer, but if they worked, there must be merit. IACVF have information on these. Write them.

The International Association of Cancer Victims and Friends Inc; Playa del Rey, Ca. USA. (1-213-822-5032). or-- 9634-28 th. N.W. Seattle, Wa.98117. USA.

OTHER DEGENERATIVE DISEASES.
There are so many other degenerative diseases that to discuss them at all would be far beyond the scope of this book. However, all degenerative diseases are named after their symptoms, while their basic causes have already been shown in the foregoing pages. As all degenerative diseases are different symptoms from different combinations of the common causes already described, all degenerative diseases will start to respond to the entire Candida program. Then, as health and body systems start to improve, the various causes of which the disease is composed will become quite clear and definite, and appropriate therapy for each component can then be worked out.

To illustrate how one factor can be common to many different diseases, Addison's Disease, Lupus Erythematosis, Hodgkins Disease, Leukemia, Multiple Sclerosis, Eczema, and psoriasis can all have a component of, or be founded in, mercury poisoning. (See Mercury, Ch.4.) usually from silver amalgam tooth fillings. Quite obviously, despite anything else that might be done, serious symptoms will remain until the fillings are changed and penecillamine or cysteine is used to chelate the remaining mercury. Then after the mercury was removed, the remaining symptoms would clearly indicate the adrenal failure and other components that produced the combined symptoms after which the disease was named.

DEGENERATIVE DISEASE CONSOLIDATED REVIEW.
Basic Causes of Health Degeneration.
The body is a truly wondrous, extremely complex, self contained and self propelled electro-chemical heat machine. If we are fortunate enough to be born healthy, with full normal function of all body parts, it becomes obvious that exterior forces only can alter the intrinsic state of good health. These exterior forces are:
1. Alcohol. Alcohol affects the mind and nervous system, depletes the adrenals, and damages the liver and the digestive tract, leading to intestinal yeast infection and ulcers.

2. Caffeine and tobacco, -- deplete the adrenals and alter nerve function leading to diabetes, hypoglycemia, increased digestive acidity and heart palpitations. Caffeine is also a diuretic that frequently leads to serious dehydration, with mental problems and failure of all body parts.

3. "Social drugs", barbiturates, sedatives, "downers and uppers" herbs and herbal teas, have individual specific effects on various parts of the body.

4. Sugar and other refined carbohydrates produce high levels of blood sugar, resulting in pancreatic failure, diabetes, hypoglycemia, edema, muscle spasm, impaired immune function and increased Candida infection.

5. Severe malnutrition, and/or continuous use of some single food (e.g. corn,soya) weakens the tissues, alters metabolism, or deprives normal metabolic processes.

6. Overwork or lack of sleep and rest, leading to, or contributing to adrenal depletion.

7. Toxic metals,- Lead, mercury, cadmium, arsenic, aluminum, copper, iron, fluorine.

8. Destruction of body functions and weakening of tissues by contagious infection.

9. Impaired body function by chronic infection following consumption of invasive substances (spices, herbs, alcohol, aspirin, drugs, etc.), or following contagious infection, surgery, vaccinations, intravenous procedures, burns, bruises, broken bones, abrasion (tight shoes, sexual practices etc.) or from overwhelming exposure. It should be noted that Chronic Infection invariably follows as a consequence of 1,2,3,4,5,6,7, and 8, and chronic infection thus becomes part of, and a major contributing factor to, degenerative disease.

In the case of birth defects, the defect itself may come directly from Candida yeast or similar infection, or from adrenal depletion, and any other defects will increase the stress and reduce resistance, which will again be followed by chronic infection.

The chronic infective that always enters and increases with every episode of body failure, from any cause whatsoever, is Candida yeast, and it is the Candida yeast which continues to grow and to shelter the other infectives within the callus matrix, that maintains the continuous chronic infection. This is the insidious role of Candida yeast in degenerative disease. This is the Candida Factor.

The Candida Yeast Factor in Degenerative Disease.

Candida yeast is endemic in man, and it is endemic in our environment. It is on us, it is within us, it is on the food we eat, and it is in the air we breathe. Anything that abrades the

the tissues in any way, allows the Candida to invade the tissues and form a callus matrix that harbors many other infectives, and thus continually maintains an ever expanding multiple chronic infection, based in Candida yeast. Candida yeast has many effects on the body:-

1. It produces large quantities of vitamin B2 which alters the much discussed B vitamin balance, which is followed by altered and impaired metabolism.

2. It induces the absorption of lead, and perhaps also the absorption of cadmium, mercury, and aluminum, with "toxic metal effects" on the nervous system, glands and organs.

3. It uses up and ties up zinc, iron, manganese, chromium, selenium and lithium, thus producing trace mineral deficiency, which alters and impairs all body functions.

4. Depleted zinc particularly alters sex hormone levels and induces high blood pressure.

5. Depleted selenium affects all body systems and leads to Cancer.

6. Depleted lithium reduces the number of PMN leucocytes resulting in an impaired immune system, which permits the Candida and other infectives to flourish, and to further reduce the health of the victim. Depleted lithium also reduces thyroid function, leading to increased infection, lower body temperature, lower metabolic rates, and atherosclerosis, with the reduced blood circulation affecting the function of the body.

7.Candida infection also impairs the para-thyroids, which reduces thyroid function, and the reduced parathyroid hormone increases calcium excretion, with the low calcium reducing the absorption of proteins so essential for pancreatic enzymes, immune function and body-rebuilding.

8. The impaired immune system, and/or the low thyroid, encourages the Candida and other infectives to multiply, resulting in inflammation, allergies, edema and calcinosis.

9. Depleted chromium reduces the Glucose Tolerance Factor, resulting in episodes of diabetes and hypoglycemia, leading to adrenal depletion, pancreatic failure, mental problems, failure of all body systems, atherosclerosis, and addiction to alcohol, caffeine, tobacco and drugs.

10. The stress from the chronic infection depletes the adrenals, resulting in increased lactic acid, with aches and pains, edema, muscle spasm, calcinosis, arthritis, and impaired function of all body systems. The increased lactic acid increases the total acidity, leading to acidosis, indigestion, and pancreatic failure. The increased stress also results in excretion and depletion of potassium, resulting in increased cholesterol and triglyceride.

11. The high stress from fighting the infectives, together with

further stress from impaired body function, causes the adrenal cortex to produce excess cortisone, which destroys proteins, and which particularly impairs the immune system and damages the mucous membranes resulting in increased intestinal chronic infection and peptic and duodenal ulcers.

12. Intestinal infection, ulcers, altered digestive pH, and alcohol or spices leads to loss of intrinsic factor, followed by depletion of B12 resulting in pernicious anemia and altered function of folic acid. Pernicious anemia impairs every cell in the body and thus impairs all body functions. Altered folate function impairs the nervous system and reduces histamine levels, with reduced sexuality, reduced sexual ability, and reduced sex hormones, which also affects every cell of the body.

13. Yeast infection, anywhere in the body, produces lactic acid which alters total body pH toward acidic, with episodes of acidosis, and increased water retention throughout the body which impairs the lymphatic system and the immune system, with the edema followed by muscle spasm, fibrosis, calcinosis, and arthritis, anywhere. The acidic pH in the digestive tract leads to increased intestinal infection, ulcers, pancreatic overload and pancreatic failure, which in turn leads to inflammation, allergies, loss of intrinsic factor, impaired digestion, diabetes, hypoglycemia, and further pancreatic failure, which in turn further increases the pH toward acidic, throughout the body and throughout the entire alimentary canal from mouth to anus.

14. Acidic pH in the digestive tract results in reduced alkalinity in the colon, which favors the growth of Candida yeast in the colon, which further reduces the alkalinity, with colitis, altered bowel movement, loose or hard stools, constipation, hemorrhoids, spasmed rectal sphincter, and resorbed toxins that overload the liver and overload the immune system, producing allergies, arthritis, migraine headache, neurosis, psychosis, and schizophrenia.

15. Acidic pH in the vagina and birth canal alters the vaginal flora and favors the further growth of Candida infection resulting in tubal infection with loss of fertility, reduced libido, altered sexual lubricants, difficult or impossible orgasm, and infections of the uterus, which are painless and almost undetectable.

16. Vaginal infections in the female are transferred to the male by sexual intercourse (and vice versa) resulting in infections of the tip of the penis (balanitis), enlarged prostate, tender testicles, curdled ejaculate, infertility, and increased sexual desire and sexual need, despite reduced sexual capability, impotence, or complete sexual failure.

17. Yeast infection in the sinuses increases stress, <u>interferes</u> <u>with sleep and rest</u>, overloads and <u>impairs the immune system,</u> and <u>continuously "seeds" the mouth air tract</u>, and <u>alimentary</u> <u>canal with spores and filaments</u>, thus maintaining and increasing the total Candida infection.

18. Candida yeast infection, established anywhere, will spread to the sexual tissues, and when established in the sexual tissues, usually spreads to the other sexual tissues,- namely ---

1. Head (mouth, sinuses, ears,).

2. Digestive tract. 3. Colon. 4. Breasts. 5. Genitals. 6. Hands. 7. Feet.

19. Severe Candida infection overloads the adrenals and the liver, with a greatly increrased need for vitamin C, usually resulting in <u>weakened tissues</u> and perhaps <u>scurvy</u>. Without vitamin C. cholesterol cannot be changed to bile, resulting in <u>high blood</u> <u>cholesterol</u>, and digestive problems.

20. All or any of the foregoing, in various combinations, lead to the highly complex "total body" diseases like <u>Multiple Sclerosis</u>.

21. High yeast infection, together with various combinations of the foregoing factors severely impairs the immune system, which allows <u>Progenitor Cryptocides</u> to flourish, resulting in <u>Cancer</u>. or perhaps resulting in <u>Aids</u>, if there has been close personal contact with anyone already infected with Aids.

These are the multiple interlocking causes of degenerative disease. The true problem is that the multiple causes are so interlocked that to correct any one you must correct them all.

The true problem with present medical practice is that physicians recognize each part singly, and usually attempt to correct each set of symptoms with "interference drugs" or with irreversible surgery, without recognizing the interlocking factors and without recognizing that the causes are multiple and that to cure any single set of symptoms all interlocking factors must be reviewed.

Indeed, a review of all of the foregoing symptoms and afflictions underlined will soon show that these are indeed the root causes of degenerative disease because all of the basic health problems are repeated several times from different causes. Obviously, any attempt to correct any single one of these interlocking casual factors is almost certain to adversely affect several other factors, thus increasing "side effects", and these adverse side effects will be further increased if the treatment itself induces its own particular set of adverse symptoms. This then is the reason that under drug oriented allopathic medicine as practiced in North America today, 60% of the hospital beds are occupied by iotrogenic (physician induced) cases. A truly horrible statistic, and a terribly damning statement against the use and abuse of our technical expertise. But there are good and effective remedies,-- drugless remedies,-- for all of these basic causal factors. Therefore to cure. Yes, to actually cure the degenerative diseases, each and all causal factors must be scientifically reduced while at the same time every effort must be made to reduce the symptoms, all with a very minimum of side effects.

The cure for degenerative diseases is therefore essentially the same for all degenerative diseases because they all have common root causes. The cure must be a carefully planned and carefully executed medical program, a highly technical preferably drugless program aimed at both the symptoms and at the basic root of degenerative disease.

THE HEALTH RENEWAL PROGRAM.

To be effective the health renewal program must cover all of the foregoing factors and thus start to unravel all of the interlocking causes and symptoms. A review of the foregoing causal factors will soon reveal that most symptoms can have several different roots, with everything being held together and the ill health being maintained by Candida yeast and other chronic infectives living in and sheltered by the Candida matrix. The program should therefore be a double program,-- a program aimed at the Candida yeast and other chronic infectives,-- and a program aimed at cleaning up the diet and lifestyle and eliminating all toxic factors. The program should also be aimed at reducing and eliminating medical drugs in favor of nutritional and substitute supplements. The program should include the following. Check each item carefully.

1. Medical diagnosis from at least two physicians.
2. Elimination of self administered poisons; alcohol, tea, coffee, chocolate, cola, tobacco, social drugs, amphetamines, barbiturates, sedatives, and if possible, (with the help of your doctor) reduce and eliminate all medical drugs. This program should be taken slowly, and the offending substances should be eliminated one at a time because each one in turn may present problems with withdrawal.
3. Give full adrenal support with mineral ascorbates, sodium/ potassium supplements, pantothenic acid, B6, calcium/ magnesium, Vitamin D., and lipotrophics. (Choline, inositol, methionine). These can be used several times per day throughout the program. Vitamin C should be a minimum of 5 grams per day. The Anti-Candida cocktail, with supplements and with or without niacin, will usually offset the effects of withdrawal from alcohol, caffeine and other drugs.

4. Mineral tests with Nutritional Evaluation. This must be adjusted for all supplements that may be taken. It will reveal toxic metals and it will show major deficiencies and excesses. Diet and supplements can then be adjusted. If lithium is in the low range, it should be cautiously supplemented.

5. Chelation therapy with intravenous NaEDTA if toxic metals are revealed or if poor blood circulation is diagnosed or suspected.

6. Eliminate all refined sugar and white starch. Eliminate white rice and perhaps potatoes. If there are digestive or colon problems or if diabetes or hypoglycemia are suspected, eliminate all sources of free sugars, e.g., honey, melons, fruit, dried fruit, milk, etc.

7. Adjust the diet, for high protein, low carbohydrate. Extra supplements of Calcium/ magnesium, Vitamin D, PTH, digestives, Vitamin E, glycine and lecithin will help the body to handle the extra protein.

8. Candida yeast challenge test with ketoconazole, and general Candida assessment. Start slow anti-fungal program with keto-conazole and resteclin, together with topical anti-fungals wherever indicated. Supplement biotin, B1, and magnesium.

9. Complete blood test, including basophil cell count to determine sexual and sex hormone levels and immune globilins to determine immune system function. If protein and/or calcium are low supplements of amino acids, calcium, vitamin D, and parathyroid hormone.

10. Blood microscopy. If red blood cells are damaged, if there is a history of alcohol or drugs, if Candida is obvious, or if illness is severe as with cancer or multiple sclerosis, cellular integrity can be improved with the Alcoholism program, 30 gms Vitamin C daily, principally sodium ascorbate, and 8 gms mixed amino acids with 500 mg. B6, three times daily with meals for 4 weeks. After 3 or 4 days, reduce the vitamin C to 15 gms daily. (See Alcoholism, Ch.8.).

11. A-E Emulsion to improve immune system.

12. Lithium if PMN's are low.

13. B12 injections, supplemented with folic acid and niacin should be repeated at intervals throughout the program. Supplements of histidine should be added cautiously if basophil cell count is low, if sexual levels are low, or if there are sexual problems.

14. Thyroid Function Test. Fever thermometer under arm for ten minutes before arising in morning. If temperature is low, supplement thyroid cautiously. Also supplement iodine and or lithium cautiously. Continue to check thyroid function about once a month.

15. Ensure adequate daily excerise. Excerise is the only thing that works the lymphatic pump. Paraplegics and others with

physical handicaps will benefit from the use of a massage chair, or equivalent. Swimming is the best form of exercise.

16. Full body examination to determine extent of muscle spasm and calcinosis, with neursage and massage to reduce calcinosis and improve muscle function. If muscle spasm is extensive or if arthritis is present, increase Vitamin C and sodium/potassium supplements. Intravenous calcium chelation and/ or niacin may be of help. In stubborn areas electrotherapy or electro- acupuncture might be used with caution. Whole body chiropractic treatments with X-rays should be used if bones are out of place.

17. Adequate sleep and rest, with extra sleep if extreme sleepiness occurrs, to give the body an opportunity to fight the infection and rebuild damaged tissues. Stress must be reduced as much as possible.

18. Glucose tolerance test and /or other tests or assessment to determine hypoglycemia and /or diabetes. Alter diet and eating habits if suspected. Use digestive aids with meals and again with bicarbonate 1/2 hour after meals. Use pre-digested protein.

19. Allergy Test. Avoid each common food group (i.e. foods with similar poisons), in turn, for one week, and watch for symptoms when each food is returned to the diet. Any foods that produce symptoms should be avoided for at least one month and should be returned to the diet with caution. Avoid all known allergens, if possible. If allergies persist, reduce symptoms with digestive aids and bicarbonate. (Dr.Philpott).

20. Digestive problems and gas. Completely eliminate all sugars and white starches, and eliminate all foods containing free sugars from the diet. Use ketoconazole with bicarbonate, or nystatin, chlorophyl, garlic, and/or resteclin 1 hour before meals or if gas and indigestion are severe. Use NaEDTA, by itself between meals. Use pre-digested protein or pure amino acids, with lots of yogurt and acidophilus.

21. Colon. Use psyllium seed and/or cracked flax seed (linoseed) and/or bran and/or coconut and/or pectin with ample yogurt and acidophilus to restore bowel function. Use milk of magnesia for laxative occasionally if necessary. Use disinfecting enemas, not oftener than every three days, with phenol alkaizer, milk of magnesia, nystatin, resteclin, chlorophyl, garlic and/or DMSO. If problems are severe and persistent get colon X-ray and use colonics to restore bowel function. Use vitamin C enemas.

22.Rectum. Spasmed rectal sphincter and/or hemorrhoids will usually respond to strong massage with vitamin E, every second day. A fingerstall should be used to avoid cuts from fingernails. If problems persist phenol alkalizerchair may be useful. Special massage vibrators, or sexual vibrators, with vitamin E, can also be used for severe cases.

23. Chest and Lungs. Increase ketoconazole to as much as possible. Reduce sinus infection with miconazole lotion, milk of magnesia, liquid nystatin, resteclin, chlorophyl, and/or DMSO. Reduce mouth infection with liquid nystatin, chewed nystatin tablets, resteclin, chlorophyl, and/or chewed ketoconazole. the hot water bottle on chest and breathe hot air from oven to relieve symptoms. Vapors of Friar's Balsam, and mustard plasters on back and chest help. Lime dust therapy, as formerly used for tuberculosis, with nystatin powder or powdered tablets of ketoconazole can be used for severe cases.

24. Sexual. Low basophil cell count, loss of libido, and sexual function problems,-- raise histamine levels with B12 injections, folic acid, niacin, and histidine. Use testosterone or estrogen with extreme caution.

A. Female. Females should repeat several courses of Monistat 7, and should be very conscious of symptoms. Candida infections of the uterus can be painless and almost undetectable. If vaginitis is present and persists, tests and treatment for other infections should be persued. Micatin cream can be used to reduce discomfort but should not be used to mask serious infection. Long term treatment, with every different agent including phenol alkalizer and DMSO may be necessary if severe Candida infection has followed from surgery or pregnancy problems. The sexual partner must also receive treatment to avoid reinfection.

B. Male. Male Candida infection is frequently very well hidden but the consequences may be severe. Urinary spray, enlarged prostate, impotence, tender testicles, thick curdled ejaculate and the presence of male cysts (hydrocelles and spermatocelles) may indicate Candida infection. Cysts can be drained and re-filled with Monistat IV, with or without intravenous tetracycline and amphoteracin B, added. (Severe inflammation can be expected). Ketoconazole should be increased to maximum. The tip of the penis may be white and leathery (insensative) which can be slowly reduced with the continuing use of miconazole cream and phenol alkalizer. Balanitis (burning of the tip of the penis) indicates infection and can be reduced with miconazole lotion and phenol alkalizer forced backward through the urethral tube. Enlarged prostate can be caused by Candida infection, and some improvement can be achieved by the use of miconazole lotion and phenol alkalizer introduced by a catheter. Prostate massage (from your doctor or naturopath) may help. Tender testicles and curdled ejaculate are very difficult and pose a further threat of perhaps inducing testicular cancer. Despite all other reassurances, removal of the infected testicles is castration, which is invariably followed by many of the neutering effects of castration, despite supplements of testosterone. Removal of the testicles should be avoided if possible. Infection can be reduced if testicles are emptied frequently, at least every two or three days if possible. Small amounts of testosterone may be of help. Autogenous vaccine (see cancer) may also be of help. The total condition will improve slowly as total health and total immune function improves. In all cases of male infection the sexual partner must also receive treatments to avoid re-infection.

25. Ears. White scaly material. Use miconazole lotion, phenol alkalizer, or DMSO. Calcinosis can be reduced with neursage. DMSO may also improve the hearing.

26. Dandruff and loss of hair. Wash hair with mild detergent only. Do not use oils, soaps or shampoos. Use phenol alkalizer for a hair dressing and rub into scalp.Extensive neursage of the head and neck will reduce underlying calcinosis. Gray hair may return to natural color by the addition of supplements of biotin or Paba.

27. Disseminated Candida infection (carried in the bloodstream) is usually (but not always) characterized by small round red spots with a spongy yeast-like core, that may appear anywhere on the body. A very difficult condition. Raise ketoconazole to maximum, and improve immune system. Intravenous calcium chelation may help. Monistat IV should be tried. Autogenous vaccine may help. A long term program can be expected. Disseminated Candida infection is indicated if problems persist in any organ or area. Infection should be suspected and all medical papers on Candida that pertain to that particular condition should be examined for help. Candida yeast has a particular affinity for the heart valves where it causes malformation, hardening and calcinosis. Intravenous calcium chelation, high amounts of ketoconazole, and perhaps the use of monistat 1V, over time, will greatly improve the heart valves and may restore full function.

28. Birthmarks and Blue Spots. These are frequently caused by deep Candida infectiom at birth. After the body is reasonably clear of Candida infection in other areas, miconazole lotion and/or phenol alkalizer, followed by DMSO to carry the anti-infectives through the skin may be effective. Abrading the skin by scraping with a knife may also help. A courageous doctor might try injections of monistat 1V into the surrounding area, followed by injections directly into the lesion.

29. Iridology. Iridology is an excellent diagnostic indicator, but it does not provide a positive diagnosis. However any problems

that are indicated should be thoroughly investigated. Iridology is sometimes very useful for complex problems.

30. Five day Candida Infection Test. After all visible signs of Candida infection have disappeared, try 1 tablet of ketoconazole per day, increasing by 1 tablet per day for 5 days. If toxic signs do not appear the body can be considered to be essentially free from fungal infection.

31. Autogenous Vaccine. If resteclin and/or other antibiotics have been used to keep bacterial infections down, the body will now be essentially free from the common chronic infectives, but there will still be small areas of chronic infection. Autogenous vaccine is made from the person's own urine, which contains anti-bodies to all of the infectives in the body. The autogenous vaccine will stimulate the body to reduce these small pockets of infection.

CANDIDA INFECTION PROGRAM PROBLEMS.

The development of an effective Candida infection program is definitely a science, but the application of the program is just as definitely an art. The art is to continuously monitor and balance the quantities and timing of all of the components so that the victim is constantly and steadily improving.

Both the victim, and the health practitoner, should expect that the health rebuilding program may take years, but with a steady improvement in health the time and difficulties are always worthwhile. The real trick,-- the real art,-- is to take just enough of the anti-infectives to ensure improvement without overloading the body systems, and to improve all body functions together, with each other. The constant problem is that the body response can be very erratic. There indeed seems to be a hidden interlocking unpredictable role between biotin, thyroid, lithium, B12 (injections), niacin and sex hormone levels. Niacin itself is a separate enigma because, while it does improve blood circulation and while it does reduce blood cell clumping and while it does stablize histamine and sex hormone levels, it also raises blood sugar levels, which tends to feed the yeast. It is significant that the Candida fluorescent pink increases greatly during a niacin flush, sometimes as much as the increase from a heavy feeding of glucose, which in turn makes one wonder if the diabetic state is not one of the principal causes of high Candida infection. Lithium and thyroid seem to be key factors in the Candida battle. Lithium of course, is essential to thyroid function but lithium also increases the immune system leucocytes. (PMNs).

The real art in the application of the Candida program centers around allergies and toxic symptoms. The body can be very aggressive if it has the opportunity, and as the immune system improves the body may at any time start to clear out large pockets of infection. Then the victim will suddenly become very tired and sleepy, because the body is using all available energy to kill out the infection and to rebuild the damaged tissues. The urge to sleep, should be heeded, because the entire program is aimed at restoring the ability of the body to cope with infection. Sleep may be normal, but if the body is aggressively attacking the infectives, sleep will be very deep, with a feeling of being drugged, or perhaps a feeling that a battle is raging, which is what is happening. If sleep is interrupted, there may be a feeling of extreme depletion or extreme weakness, perhaps with dis-orientation. If possible, just go back to sleep and let the body finish what it had started. This is a good sign that the program is working. It is also a time when full nutritional support is needed. Load on all of the adrenal and detoxifying nutrients, which will also support the immune system, with lots of pre-digested protein for body rebuilding. If ample nutrients are present, all may go well, but if nutrients are lacking, or if the immune system is too aggressive, then allergies or a toxic episode may result from the excess toxins, perhaps even with a sharp rise in arthritis or muscle spasm if the toxins build up in the tissues. Then if the hapless victim has not been previously informed of this possibility, they will feel that they have been betrayed because they are getting worse instead of getting better.

If all or any of this happens (and it always does) lots of adrenal nutrients, rest, and light exercise outside in the fresh air will help. Allergic symptoms can be reduced with digestive enzymes and bi-carbonate, but the muscle spasm and increased arthritis will require extensive massage and neursage, with extra attention to colon problems.

Now the question is, too much, or too little? Too much of what? Too little of which? We are dealing with multiple infections. The same symptoms, the allergies, the headaches, the toxicity, the muscle spasm, and the increased arthritis can also result from an upsurge in infection,-- an upsurge of either fungus (plants) or bacteria or virus infection. So is it too much anti-fungal, or not enough anti-fungal, or is it too much or too little anti-biotic? You can only review what has been done, and try to guess what went wrong. Remember, that excess stress, that reduces body capability, will produce the same symptoms. So also will a toxic food. So also will free sugars that feed the yeast. So also will coffee, or anger, or niacin, or anything else that raises blood-sugar levels. Frequently the cause can be found, and in future avoided, but if the cause cannot be found and if the program is not too aggressive, the best thing is to treat the incident as an isolated episode, get lots of rest, take lots of nutrients, and carry on.

Free sugars in foods, and toxic (allergic) foods are the most common causes of toxic episodes. Restaurant foods and prepared foods can be very deceiving both in allergens, and in sugars, e.g. "whole wheat" bread in a restaurant is usually only 60% whole wheat.

An ongoing problem that cannot be fully resolved, is sexual activity, which raises the blood sugar levels; and the burning in ankles, wrists, or other infected areas (from the advancing yeast) can frequently be felt. The problem may be further increased, in both male and female, by the resorption of infected (toxic) sexual fluids. Yet sexual activity should not be avoided, because life without sexual relief is a very poor life filled with psychosis; and sexual relief is certainly an essential part of good health. However, if ketoconazole and adrenal nutrients are taken with the evening meal, or at bedtime, or otherwise sometime before sexual activity might occur, the body will be better able to clear the toxins, and the anti-fungal will be high in the bloodstream at the same time that the blood sugar is high, so the infectives will be poisoned as they feed on the high blood sugar.

Another frequent continuing problem is poor quality in the mucous membranes. This usually appears in the mouth first, with sore mouth and mouth infections. The common cause is B vitamin imbalance. The Candida infection produces B2, and as the yeast is killed, more B2 is released from the dead yeast. The high amounts of B2 therefore produce a relative shortage of B1. B1 should therefore be supplemented (250mg 2 or three times) in all Candida programs to preserve mucous membrane quality. If mouth problems develop, B1 tablets can be held in the mouth for local absorption, while topical anti-fungals and resteclin are used to eliminate the mouth infection.

CHAPTER 8.

VIRAL INFECTIONS and OTHER HEALTH PROBLEMS.

The role of Candida yeast (and its associated infectives) in viral infections is not clear, but it should be remembered that the viruses are very small micro-organisms, and there are several medical papers that describe viral infections of larger micro-organisms like Candida yeast. Quite obviously if the virus infects the yeast while the yeast infects man, the viral infection cannot be eliminated or reduced until the yeast is reduced or eliminated.

HERPES VIRUS INFECTIONS.

Herpes infection is a viral infection, and like all viral infections all strains of Herpes are impossible to eliminate and are very difficult to reduce.

At present there are no known agents that are directly effective against Herpes virus, but it is known that trehelose sugar will build up in the side-wall of the organism and finally destroy it. A diet high in trehelose sygar, or ointments made with trehelose sugar and DMSO may be of value. As always, the best defence is the body's own immune system. For all viral infections everything should be done to eliminate Candida infection (which may be playing host to the virus) and to improve the immune system. The program should particularly include thyroid (if needed), lithium (if needed), autogenous vaccine and A-E Emulsin. If viral infection still persists levamisole, metronidazole, sulfamethoxazole or Bordetello Purtussis vaccine may be of further help. Heavy injections of B12 (See Bursitis, Ch.7.) with extra folic acid, will usually help the body to reduce Herpes infections. Although Herpes infections are definitely viral, herpes usually becomes serious only when the body is weakened. Herpes is therefore really a disease of degeneration.

Herpes Zoster. (Chicken Pox and Shingles).

Most children get chicken pox early in life, are ill for a few days, recover, and do not realize that they have acquired a chronic infection that will continue to live within them until they die. It was an infection of Herpes Zoster that caused the chicken pox, and indeed the immune system responded and killed most of the virus, but some viral particles immediately escape into the nervous system where it is very difficult for the immune system to reach them, and it is within the nerves themselves that the virus continues to live for the entire life of the host. Just what the viral particles may be doing within the nervous system for thirty, fifty, sixty years or more we do not know and we cannot guess. We do not know how many headaches or other pains the virus may have caused; we do not know if the virus gave us the jitters; we do not know if it made us forget, or if it gave us heart palpitations, or if it affected the function of the pancreas, liver, or limbs. The truth is that anything that affects the nervous system can affect any part of the body and any body function, and micro-organisms living within the nerves certainly must at times affect nerve function. So the herpes virus lives within the nerves themselves, doing we know not what, and then, after half a lifetime or more, if body and immune defenses are low, the herpes virus will move to the nerve endings just below the skin, where it produces the many knife-like pains and the blistery red rash that is known as shingles. Shingles can affect any part of the body, but it commonly appears in the lower back and sides, just below the ribs.

In all cases of shingles everything in the Candida program should be done to improve all body functions. In the meantime the pain and discomfort can be reduced with local applications of phenol alkalizer, DMSO, flagystatin and perhaps trehelose sugar. Lipotropics, pantothenic acid, ascorbate, and all adrenal nutrients are particularly important. Heavy injections of B12, with extra folic acid should be tried. Stress must be kept at an absolute minimum. Your doctor will also have ointments that may, or may not reduce the pain, and itching. (See sciatica. Ch.8.)

Herpes E.B.(Epstein Barr). (Mononucleosis)(Kissing Disease).

Mononucleosis starts as a sore throat that gets progressively worse, followed by weakness and a general inability to function. It may take a month or more before the body can resolve the infection, and it may be several months before reasonable health returns.

The problem is that quite frequently the body does not fully overcome the virus, then months or years after the original infection some infected cells from the throat will shed into the mouth, and the infection may then be spread to others by kissing, hence the name,"kissing disease".

To reduce the effects of mononucleosis everything must be done to support and improve the immune system. A-E Emulsin, Phosphatydal choline and pure amino acids are of particular value. Gargles of phenol alkalizer, or 2% phenol in a 15% solution of DMSO may help. Bits of Redoxon left to dissolve in the mouth will help to strengthen the throat tissues. Iodine lozenges, bits of ketoconazole, or a mixture of liquid ketoconazole and resteclin, held in the mouth while lying down, and held until they disappear will give the immune system extra help. Sucking candies, made from trehelose sugar (from the chemical wholesaler) may help to destroy the virus.

There may be many cases of chronic or recurring laryngitis that are actually Herpes E.B. locked into the matrix of a Candida throat infection. At present we know that herpes may be sequestered somewhere in the body for years, and the Candida matrix is an excellent place for it to hide. People with chronic throat problems will need the entire Candida program, with special attention to topical anti-infectives, and autogenous vaccine.

Herpes Simplex. (Cold Sores) (Genital Herpes).

Herpes Simplex is the common infective that produces cold sores. LIke all viral infections, the cold sores come and go in proportion to immune system function. Genital herpes is said to be the same herpes simplex virus, with the "cold sores" transferred into a genital infection, which then becomes a venereal disease that is sexually transferred. With sexual practices of men and women being what they are, severe infections of fingers, mouth, and anus are now quite common.

There are now said to be several virulent strains of genital herpes, dubbed "King Herpes", or "Queen Herpes", etc. It is thought that these virulent forms may in fact be herpes mixtures, where the herpes is mixed with other herpes viruses, or is mixed with other synergystic infectives.

Again everything in the Candida and immune system programs must be done, because Candida infection may be the "holding" infective that is sheltering the herpes and other infectives from the immune system.

The same topical anti-infectives that are used for other herpes infections will promote comfort, and will also help to reduce the infection.

LARYNGITIS.

(See also Candida Infections of the Mouth and Throat).

(See also Herpes E.B. Mononucleosis).

Laryngitis will usually clear up with liquid nystatin, liquid ketoconazole, and resteclin, mixed and held in the mouth until it disappears. Phenol alkalizer can also be used as a gargle. If infection persists embark on the entire Candida program, with emphasis on improving immune system function. Autogenous vaccine may be of particular benefit. Bordetello Pertussis vaccine may be the final answer.

AIDS.

Aids is said to be a "new" disease, but there is ample evidence that it is something like "legionaires disease", simply an old well established micro-organism that has found a fertile environment in people that are already ill. Aids strikes only those with an already badly compromised immune system; people who in former years would probably have already succumbed to polio, tuberculosis, or pneumonia. Most certainly Aids is largely confined to homosexuals, which is quite understandable because the simple fact of homosexuality is evidence of low sex hormone levels, resulting from poor health, while lengthy exposure to the infectives through sexual contact floods the victims with such high quantities of the infective that the already weakened immune system is completely overwhelmed. Significantly, perhaps, the first person with Aids that died, did not die from Aids, they died from Candidiasis. Most, and perhaps all, active homosexuals have high Candida infection. There are a large number of reports and photomicrographs that show that viruses and other micro-organisms infect amoeba, yeasts, and other larger microrganisms. Doctors and scientists who are acquainted with Candida therefore postulate that the Aids virus infects both the Candida and the host, and because Candida has already impaired the immune system and many other body processes the Aids continues to increase to the fateful end. Quite obviously everyone with a high Candida infection should avoid the Aids environment because they are certainly at risk. Quite obviously also, to overcome the viral infection we must first reduce any infectives that may be playing host to it.

Now the many newspaper reports on Aids all say that everyone that contracts Aids dies from the disease. For anyone, and particularly for a doctor, to make such a statement is both ignorant and irresponsible, because the very same doctors say many people who do not have Aids have antibodies to Aids, which is ample proof that at some time that particular person had contracted Aids, and the body did overcome the infection;- hence the antibodies. Therefore anyone with Aids can certainly overcome the infection if they do the right things, and contrary to most reports some Aids victims are at present overcoming the infection:--

One of the IACVF newsletters, (see cancer) reports that Dr.Gerber, of Wellcorp, Reno, Nevada, USA, claims that 18 out of 18 Aids patients at his clinic have now survived for over 2 years. His program includes:

Flagyl for amoebas and small colonic parasites.

Ginseng, Procaine,(novocaine,GH3) and lots of Garlic.

Intravenous Vitamin C.

Nystatin for some patients with Candida.

Now note the successful use of flagyl , garlic, and nystatin to reduce the chronic infectives. Nystatin of course is excellent against Candida, but the use of nystatin without ketoconazole and other anti-fungals indicates that the clinic does not have a good understanding of Candida and nystatin, because nystatin is strictly topical and cannot reach infections through the bloodstream.

CH.8. Viral Infections and Other Health Problems.

Quite obviously, to avoid becoming another Aids statistic, all Aids victims should do everything in the Candida program, with particular emphasis on improving immune and sexual function and on reducing all infections with antifungals, antibiotics, and autogenous vaccine.

The following information from another IACV. Newsletter (June 1986), certainly shows that Aids is not a single infective, it is the result of extensive degeneration of all body systems.

AIDS, ARC and STATISTICS.

Aids -- often called a tip-of-the-iceberg phenomenon, is causing far more illness than the official figure of 21,000. The low figure is due to (a) a too narrow definition historically because of lack of similiarity of the spectrum of diseases involved, (b) the syndrome is evolving many more diseases, (c) under-reporting by physicians out of sympathy or discretion.

The first narrow definition made 5 years ago by the center for Disease Control identified only immune disturbances with infections such as PCP pneumonia or certain malignancies such as Kaposi sarcoma, a capillary cancer. But now the list has grown to include a complex of diseases called Aids Related Complex or Arc. These embrace tuberculosis, regular pneumonia,meningitis, Hodgkins disease, squamous cell carcinoma of the mouth (the lining), adenocarcinoma, lymphodenopathy, Candidiasis, diarrhea, fever, and a number of neurological diseases such as psychosis seizures, paralysis, neuropathy, and dementia. With this list the number grows to 200,000 cases.

There is a reluctance to expand the narrow definition because this would confuse the statistical case already established. Further it is estimated that there are nearly 2,000,000 people infected with Aids virus. About 5-20% of these will progress to Aids and 25% more to Arc. (WSJ 5-30-86). (Are we now reaping the harvest from additives, processed foods, chemical agriculture, and environment pollution? Ed).***

Other recent information shows that a resurgence of a new type of Tuberculosis (See cancer) that does not show up on the patch test, is also frequently associated with Aids.

WARTS.(Verruca).

Warts are caused by a papovirus, which produces both the knobby type seen on the hands, and the flat type seen on the face, and against which there is no known effective drug or other substance. Normally warts can be reduced with application of Salicylic acid (aspirin) as used in corn salve, or with trichloracetic acid, both of which are very invasive. Warts can also be surgically removed (usually with scars) but they also frequently return.

Warts usually return because surgery and chemicals cannot remove all of the infectives, which are finally controlled by the immune system. Warts therefore increase with any deficiency in the immune system, and particularly if immune-suppressing drugs are used. Again, "The Body is the Hero". If the immune system is not impaired or overloaded, it will take care of the papovirus and you will never know that you have had it. Note that if you take a holiday, stress is reduced, the adrenals are not so depleted, the immune system functions a little better, and it reduces the warts. Then after the holiday, when a little extra stress returns, the warts return.

The presence of these so-called benign growths is therefore proper cause for alarm. Although they can usually be physically reduced with applications of vitamin E, and supplements of manganese, methionine, choline, inositol, sunflower oil, vitamin A, all B vitamins, and large amounts of tomatoes and vitamin C, warts are a definite indicator of so much infection elsewhere that the immune system is greatly overloaded and impaired, and almost totally incapable of controlling any additional infection. The usual infective that harbors and shelters the other chronic infectives, and that also impairs the immune system, is Candida Yeast. If the Candida program is initiated the warts will usually just fade away, particularly if the diet is high in fresh tomatoes.

CAFFEINE DISEASE. (Dehydration).
See also Alzheimers Disease,Ch.7.

Caffeine is a very strong diuretic that induces the excretion of more water than is consumed with the caffeine. When used continuously in large quantities it slowly produces dehydration, with physical and mental effects similar to Alzheimers Disease. The dehydration may be highly visible, or it may be masked by fatty tissue from the conversion of sugars consumed with the caffeine. The dehydration can be reversed with vitamins, good nutrition, and elimination of caffeine, tobacco, and sugar, together with 6 or 8 glasses of water per day. If the dehydration results from many years of excess caffeine, hypoglycemia will also be part of the problem and the entire Candida program will be necessary to help rebuild all of the degenerated body systems. The lethal dose of caffeine is 10 grams. A strong cup of coffee contains about 150mg, or about 1.5% of the lethal dose; or 67 cups of coffee contain enough caffeine to produce death if consumed all at once.

PHOBIAS. (Imagined Fears).

Today, with the extremely high consumption of sugar, refined carbohydrate, and caffeine, phobias of all kinds abound. There are fears of snakes, fears of water, fears of heights, fears of crowds, fears of everything. They are real fears. They are hysterical fears. They are imagined fears.

The basic cause of phobias is hypoglycemia;--usually continuing episodes of very low blood sugar that produces mental wanderings not unlike dreams. The basic hypoglycemia is usually aggravated by poisons from caffeine or other drugs, by heavy metals, or by toxins from chronic infectives. The entire Candida program is usually necessary to ensure the re-building of body systems to the point that the phobias will vanish.

NAUSEA and VOMITING.

Nausea and vomiting are the normal body response to toxic substances in the digestive tract. Continuing nausea will usually respond to supplements of magnesium and B6, but the underlying chronic intestinal infection should be reduced. Usually Na EDTA, followed by Lactobacillus is effective.

Air sickness and motion sickness will also usually be reduced or prevented with lots of B6 and vitamin C.

The nausea and vomiting of pregnancy can usually be reduced with B6 and vitamin C, with vitamin K added if necessary. The nausea appears to originate from toxins and metabolites resorbed from the fetus. The vitamin C strengthens the tissues, while the vitamin K thickens the blood and reduces the uptake of toxins through the porous placenta.

BIRTHMARKS and MOLES.

Birthmarks may appear anywhere on the body, in many different forms, the commonest forms being moles (frequently with a single hair in the center), red or purple splotches, raised rough bumps, and "skin spindles", where a bit of skin extends outward like a large hair.

It now appears that all such birthmarks are caused by a local infection, acquired at birth, that the immune system has walled off from the rest of the body. This concept is supported by the fact that birthmarks are usually tender, and they always get worse if they are rubbed or disturbed. There are a growing number of reports that birthmarks have miracukously disappeared during or following Candida therapy, so it becomes obvious that at least some of the birthmarks are bits of Candida infection picked up at birth.

The "skin spindles" seem to definitely be bits of Candida infection because they usually dry up and fall off quite early in the Candida program if ketoconazole is being used.

The raised rough bumps and moles may also change with the use of ketoconazole. If changes are noticed phenol alkalizer applied daily, with perhaps DMSO and massage will help the body to eliminate the lumps, which will then start to scale away. As the bumps start to change there may be a temptation to pick at them, but just massage them, and if you do pick at them, pick carefully, removing only material that is loose. After the bump is gone there may be little hard particles, like grains of sand, embedded in the scaly skin. Pick them out when they come loose, and remove any loose or scaly skin. If the area is irritating, rub in phenol alkalizer, DMSO, or flagystatin.

Experience with the red and purple splotches is limited, but there are several reports of them changing or disappearing after extensive Candida therapy. After a few months on ketoconazole, phenol alkalizer and DMSO can be applied to the birthmark. If the area is not tender, scraping with a knife will reduce the thickness of the skin, which will help the anti-infectives to penetrate.

If your doctor is courageous he might try injections of monistat IV around, (but not into) the birthmark. The results can be surprising.

ULCERS and OPEN SORES.

Many people develop ulcers and other open sores on different parts of the body. Women are particularly afflicted with leg ulcers following difficulty with childbirth. Frequently such ulcers do not heal; they remain open, or only partially healed, and they may give continuous problems for many years.

The usual medical practice with open ulcers is to clean them out and then graft new skin over the area, but such operations are usually unsatisfactory. The skin graft may take, and it may grow and cover the ulcer, but the area usually remains tender and frequently takes on a blue, purple, or reddish hue, not unlike the red and purple birthmarks. (See "Birthmarks"). Sometimes, with extra stress, the ulcer will again open out into an open sore.

The truth is that all parts of the body will heal readily unless something interferes with the healing process. A cut or a bruise the same size as the ulcer will normally heal without any difficulty. Something then must be interfering with the healing process, and the something usually is Candida yeast, and/or other fungii. If ulcers or open sores do not heal, or do not heal properly, the patient should go on the Candida program with as much ketoconazole as possible. The ulcer should be cleaned and disinfected with anti-biotics and anti-fungals, and Elase Chloromycetin should be used to promote healing. If the ulcer area is very large, skin can be grafted over the entire area after the fungal infection has been cleared up.

BAD BREATH.

Bad breath results from infectives in the digestive tract. Mouth washes therefore provide only a fleeting temporary relief. Chlorophyl will reduce the symptoms, and it will help to reduce the infection, but the basic problem will remain until the intestinal infection is reduced and normal digestion and elimination are restored. Oral NaEDTA, followed by a vitamin C flush, together with ascorbate enemas should be tried.

BODY ODOR.(B.O).

B.O. can be a very unpleasant affliction. The principal causes of B.O. are poor colon function, intestinal infection, or both, which forces the body to use the skin to eliminate the toxic wastes. Another cause of B.O. is a shortage of zinc.

SCIATICA, NEURITIS, NEURALGIA, and SHINGLES.

Neurobion is used successfully in Central and South America but must somehow be ineffective in the USA and Canada, where many vitamin combinations are strictly prohibited.

Merk and Co. Rahway,N.J., and other manufacturers must have many more nutritional therapies that are effectively used in other countries.

Your doctor can give you equal vitamin injections and you can take equal amounts of vitamins orally.

DISABILITIES, MENTALLY RETARDED, and "ODD PEOPLE".

In recent years much publicity has been given to the many sincere efforts to help people with mental handicaps, yet very little attention has been given to what the mentally handicapped really need. What they really need is therapy to improve their mental function and thus reduce their handicap. The less that they are handicapped, the less help they will need, and much of their problem is their frustration when they realize and recognize the many things that they should be able to do, and yet are unable to do them like others.

There are many basic causes of mental retardation. Some of the causes, like oxygen starvation in the newborn, destroy so many brain cells that mental ability is impaired. But brain cells are also destroyed by stroke, and we know from stroke that although some of the brain cells are destroyed, the remainder are not impaired and the victim can usually re-learn that which has been lost. Further, although people with stroke do have mental difficulties, they cannot be considered as, and they do not have the same characteristics as people who are considered to be mentally retarded. The difficulties then must come from lack of nutrition to the brain cells, or from lack of communication between the brain cells or both. The mind also fails and is badly affected by caffeine dehydration, by high aluminum as in Alzheimers disease, and by the senility that results from the build up of brown pigment in the testicles of males with sexual failure. Yet again, the characteristics of these people are not the same as the characteristics of the mentally retarded.

Also, many people who are considered to be mentally retarded find great solace in alcohol. Therefore, it seems unlikely that the problems of mental retardation come from a lack of active brain cells. A lack of active brain cells could certainly limit the total abilities of people, but if the remaining cells were functioning normally the total mental capability would be low, but whatever function was left would be normal.

The point is that in most of the mentally retarded the mental processes are slow and confused, instead of limited, as with a shortage of active brain cells. In fact, many "retarded people" exhibit exceptionally high mental capabilities in some things, yet are incapable of doing other things.

So from all of the foregoing it appears that the mental retardation comes from a lack of communication between the brain cells, or from a lack of nutrients reaching the brain cells, or from interference in the nervous system, rather than from a lack of active brain cells.

The real cause of most mental difficulties therefore appears to be foreign substances that alter the communication between brain cells and between the brain cells and the nervous system, or foreign substances that interfere with the nutrition of the brain cells, or both.

Now we do know that there are "yeast people", people who have had so much Candida infection since birth that they have been "half dead" with continuous health problems all of their lives. We also know that many of these "yeast people" are hyperactive, or slow, or have other mental handicaps that may reduce and disappear when Candida infection is reduced. We also know that Candida yeast seems to have the ability to alter metabolism enough that the body will store lead and heavy metals, which also greatly affect mental function. We know too, that the mental disabilities could come directly from Candida infection because people with high Candida infection frequently have trembling hands, or slow or delayed speech, which improves or disappears when the Candida infection is reduced.

What we do not at present know is how many of the people with stuttering or mental disabilities, or how many of the people that are simply "odd" are really "yeast people", or are really early victims of Candida yeast. Certainly, all of these people with mental problems could be Candida victims, with the mental difficulties coming from a continuous supply of toxins and metabolites, with perhaps heavy metals, that interfere and alter brain cell communication.

People with stuttering, impaired muscular control, or learning or mental disabilities of any kind, should therefore try the entire Candida program together with the schizophrenia program, which will reduce the interference of foreign substances in the brain, and which will promote a continuing supply of normal mental nutrients.

Particular attention should be given to:-

1. Nucleic acids, as from supplements, or from foods like sardines.
2. Pure crystalline amino acids.
3. Glandulars, liver and "head cheese" daily. Rotate supplements of other glandulars.
4. Elimination of refined sugars, free sugars, and white starch. (See diabetes).
5. Ample vitamin C and pantothenic acid. (Ascorbate, 8 - 10 grams, pantothenic acid 600 - 800 mg.).
6. Oxygen therapy (if possible) where the patient sleeps, or spends several hours per day in an oxygen tent or oxygen enriched room.
7. Trials of anti-infectives, levamisole, metronidazole, etc.

8. Continuing explanatory and psychological counselling.
9. They must have something that they want to do that is useful and worthwhile, with definite goals to be reached so that they can see and know their own progress.

The entire program should be slow and progressive, with each component introduced separately so that the effects can be assessed. Mental and health problems arise from many failed systems, but most of the problems usually come from only one or two sources which are much easier to improve if they can be identified. Any rapid improvements should therefore be noted, and extra effort and attention should be given to that particular therapy. When a plateau is reached where there is continuing constant progress, the entire program should be continued, but at a slower rate, to let the body make its own improvements, in its own way.

STUTTERING and DISLEXIA, (lack of muscular control).
Stuttering and dislexia are a form of mental disability, where the lack of communication in the nervous system, or between brain cells, is very obvious. The program is therefore the same as for mental disabilities. Watch for heavy metals, particularly mercury.

DEEP ACHES, (bone aches).
Deep aches, frequently described as "even the bones are aching" (and perhaps they are),are frequently caused by infection within the lymphatic system. The symptoms may resemble arthritis, but the aches may move around. Infection within the lymphatic system is almost impossible to reach, even with systemic antibiotics and anti-fungals. Fortunately however, A-E Emulsin (ch.4.) which supplies vitamin A and E directly to the lymphatic system, will usually give the immune system sufficient extra support that the body can reduce the lymphatic infection.

Therapy should include all adrenal and immune system nutrients, and probably the entire Candida program, together with active exercise (preferably swimming) to operate the lymphatic pump. Abissic acid (see cancer) may be of value. See also Travelling Arthritis (ch.7.).

ALCOHOLISM.
This material was written before obtaining information on the role of acetaldehyde in alcoholism. Acetaldehyde and the internal production of alcohol by Candida infection are definitely a factor in alcoholism, but at present the extent of the acetaldehyde factor is not known and probably will not

be known until after extensive trials with the use of aldehyde dehydrogenase, in the rebuilding of damaged tissues. See page 370.

Alcoholism is one of the world's most widespread degenerative diseases, yet it is fully preventable, and it is therefore fully curable with complete abstinence, and a reduction in Candida infection. Alcoholism is very difficult to deal with, because the addiction is highly complex, while the psychology that induces the alcoholic to return to the bottle is even more complex. Addiction to any drug is understandable, but many alcoholics may be away from the alcohol for weeks, then suddenly they are back to the bottle. The first drink after a peroid of abstinence cannot come from addiction. It is a deliberate act, probably linked to an episode of low blood sugar, with the psychology and rationale known only to the alcoholic. Nonetheless, the "return" drink is a deliberate act, and as long as the alcoholic does not really want a cure all efforts at reducing the alcoholism will be fruitless. Because alcoholism is both metabolic and psychological, a cure cannot be achieved without the full co-operation of the alcoholic including an honest desire for cure. Where such a desire does not exist, the only hope is to improve the health and reduce the chronic infection (with the full Candida program), and then hope that the improved biology will lead to an honest desire for cure.

Alcoholism is undoubtedly the most difficult of the degenerative diseases to deal with because everything in the body has degenerated, and the alcoholic syndrome is therefore composed of a very large number of interlocking components, both biological and psychological. In an attempt to simplify these components, we can consider them as:

1. Metabolic problems from exterior sources. Specifically, sugars, diet, caffeine, tobacco, lead and heavy metals, chronic infection, and alcohol. (See List 4, Ch.3.).
2. Metabolic problems from internal sources, e.g., impaired liver, pancreas, colon, etc.
3. Altered metabolism and altered systemic function resulting from the foregoing.
4. Sexual problems, either genetic, or resulting from the foregoing.
5. Psychological and mental problems resulting from the foregoing, including aberrant philosophy and aberrant self image.
6. Marital and family attitudes and acts, resulting from:
   a. The ill health of others. (as with hypoglycenia).
   b. Unresolved disagreements.
   c. Alcoholic acts.
7. Financial problems resulting from all of the foregoing.

8. The intertwining of all of the foregoing into locked self-perpetuating cycles. (e.g., liver failure, causes digestive failure, causes pancreatic failure, causes episodes of low blood sugar, causes need for alcoholic lift, causes alcoholism, causes liver failure.) are the most important feature of the alcoholic problem and are central to it. In some cases all that is required is the breaking of only one or two of these self-perpetuating cycles, but usually the total alcoholic problem is much more complex and requires not only the breaking of the aberrant cycles but also the re-building of all body systems together with the alteration of exterior influences.

The very core problem in alcoholism is the seeming inability of the alcoholic to "take it ot leave it". It is a problem of the total amount of addiction. The ability to "take it or leave it" is the true test of alcoholism, and unfortunately it is the test that is also imposed by the alcoholic on themselves, usually with at least a short return to alcoholism. This basic addiction is real, it is metabolic, and it is created by a weird combination of biological products from chronic infectives and the alcohol. It too is therefore a self-perpetuating cycle that can be broken only by a reduction in the chronic infectives, or abstinence, or both. But note that abstinence alone cannot cure the basic problem. Abstinence can at any time shut off the alcoholism, but the alcoholism can return at any time with a single drink, unless the shutting off of the alcohol has allowed the body to rebuild and reduce the chronic infection.

Very little seems to be known about the actual chemistry of the alcoholic sugar cycle, beyond the fact that the alcoholic stops eating and starts to use the alcohol exclusively as a source of food. Thus the aberrant alcoholic sugar cycle is a hunger cycle, and the addiction is a hunger addiction from low blood sugar when the basic alcoholic food is shut off. The problem is therefore increased by the aberrant function that is always associated with low blood sugar; with the common symptoms of neurosis, psychosis, sly cheating and lying, and a tendency to live from one day to the next, one hour to the next, or one minute to the next, while the mental effects of the alcohol keep everything mixed in an irrational mental fog. yet for the alcoholic the only relief is more alcohol because the body has largely ceased the utilization of any other foods.

The closed, locked, metabolic cycle of alcoholism is somewhat similar to, and has a well known parallel in the altered chemistry of nephritis. In nephritis the body produces so much adrenalin that it develops a protein-to-sugar cycle that progresses to the point that it breaks down live body tissue for food, despite any amount of good food that may be eaten. Thus the body starts to consume itself even when food is plentiful. In the alcoholic the normal sugar metabolism is altered in a similar way to nephritis, but in alcoholism the sugar cycle is switched from normal foods to alcohol. So the body "starves" unless alcohol is supplied. In severe alcoholism the body will continue to starve almost to the point of death before it will switch back to normal foods. Thus the alcoholic "feels normal" only when the metabolism is running on carbohydrate supplied by alcohol, any kind of alcohol, including rubbing alcohol, canned heat, shaving lotion, etc. The alcoholic withdrawal is therefore very real, it is a manifestation of cellular starvation, and the addiction is a starvation addiction caused by the total dependence upon alcohol. The degree of alcoholism therefore is related to the amount of alcohol consumed. It is well known that there are many light drinkers that are alcoholic, and there are also many heavy drinkers that are not alcoholic and can drink, as they choose. The degree of alcoholism is therefore related solely to the degree that the body processes the alcohol on the alcoholic cycle, with the alcoholism increasing gradually as normal body systems fail and as chronic infection increases.

We do not know, and we probably never will know, all of the factors in alcoholism, but we do know enough that we can alter the metabolic path sufficiently to break the aberrant cycle. We do know that glutamine (not glutamic acid) will reduce alcoholism, presumably because the alcoholic sugar cycle will use the glutamine as a food substitute for alcohol. We do know that all alcoholics have a degenerated fatty liver, and that they will benefit from liver injections and other liver therapy. We do know that all alcoholics are hypoglycemic, with episodes of very low blood sugar, and they will therefore benefit from a full hypoglycemic program. We do know that all alcoholics have some allergies, and we do know that all alcoholics have a high basic Candida infection, which would contribute to the allergies, and which apparently supplies some of the metabolites used by the body to awitch to the alcoholic sugar cycle.

The brain allergy component in alcoholism is well known. Dr.Philpott describes how he was able to induce a full alcoholic binge with only two drops of sherry placed under the tongue of an alcoholic who was allergic to sherry. Thus the mental effects do not necessarily come from the alcohol, but may at times come mostly from brain allergies induced by the alcohol. As allergies always result from chronic infection, and with Candida infection always present in all alcoholics, Candida must be presumed to be the prime cause of the allergies. Further, Candida therapy will invariably reduce and alter alcoholism, but it will not always cure alcoholism.

Clinically the continuous consumption of alcohol, as in alcoholism and heavy drinking, depletes the ascorbate throughout the body so badly that the tissues become weak and scurvous, while the degeneration of body systems from loss of B vitamins presents a clinical picture with all of the symptoms of severe beri-beri.

One of the most noticable features of alcoholism, and one of the symptoms that always precedes full alcoholism, is the almost schizophrenic definite changes in personality that appear after only one or two drinks. With these personality changes there is usually a tendency to become belligerent and violent and there is also a tendency to become a "loner", with separate ideas even when seeking the company of others. This tendency to become a "loner" results in the alcoholic drinking alone, from hidden bottles, while basking in the euphoria of their own separate world, created by their own alcoholic mental meanderings.

To reduce the alcoholic syndrome, therapy should start with abstinence. A.A. and many religious and other groups have had many cures with abstinence alone. Abstinence cures can be expected if degeneration from alcohol was the root cause, but if the root cause is allergies, or metal poisoning, or chronic infection etc., or if any of these things have crept in along with the alcoholism, abstinence will help, but cure will not come until the root cause has been found and reduced. Many alcoholics have been cured along with their allergies, others have been cured when their hypoglycemia improved, others have found a cure with improved liver function. One alcoholic did everything possible to reduce her alcoholism, including ketoconazole to reduce a severe Candida infection. The skin cleared, mental capabilities returned, and the alcoholism abated for about a month, then returned, reduced, but still present. More ketoconazole, nystatin, and resteclin were tried, without visible change. Then, in an attempt to improve immune function, some heavy doses of levamisole were tried. The alcoholism cleared almost overnight, and has not returned, despite continuing malnutrition and continuing psychosis and neurosis. Levamisole and other anthelimintics are said to be effective in improving immune function, but they have been developed as a poison to eradicate roundworm, hookworm, and flukes. Was then the alcoholism caused by a chronic infection that was destroyed by improved immune function, or was the alcoholism caused by worms or flukes, or similar infectives. We will never know, but this certainly points out the complex nature of the alcoholic problem with its continuing cycles of degeneration, that degenerate not only the body, but also behaviour, to the point of living in unsanitary conditions, and eating irresponsibly, right down to the point of eating other's garbage straight from the garbage can. This also points out that to cure alcoholism everything must be done, absolutely everything, with emphasis on abstinence, to give the many body systems a chance to improve, because the liver and other organs cannot be rebuilt if they are being continuously destroyed by alcohol.

The immediate rehabilitation program should therefore start with the entire Candida program, with emphasis on:

1. Early rising, (at least before 7 P.M.) with 1/3 glass of grapefruit juice, with HiKC Fizz immediately upon arising, followed by a good high protein breakfast, low in sugars and without coffee. Preferably without tea, but with a half a cup of tea if blood sugar remains low. Most of the support vitamins should be taken with breakfast. Early morning exercise is of great benefit, and will frequently clear the morning "fog", making the tea unnecessary.

2. Low carbohydrate, high protein diet, with 2 eggs per day and a little bit of liver 2 or 3 times a day and liver injections once a week.

3. Nystatin, resteclin, and oral EDTA to reduce chronic intestinal infection.

4. A complete break away from old alcoholic "friends", preferably by moving to an entirely new environment.

5. New interesting hobbies or social activities that are not alcohol related, perferably including active exercise, for example swimming, hiking, skiing, or square dancing. An interesting hobby should be taken up to fill every moment of the day and thus eliminate idle time.

6. Confession is good for the soul, so peace should be made with the family, together with appropriate apologies, and their full help and support should be sought. It will be needed.

7. A.A. or similar group should be joined, preferably with counselling or brotherhood activities. Alcoholism always has some psychological roots, with the build up of mental pressures contributing to the alcoholism.

To help with abstinence, the following should be tried:

A. At the usual "drinking time", work, business, or special activity may help to reduce the craving for alcohol.

B. If there is a craving for alcohol, HiKC Fizz or Redoxon and potassium- with root beer, Nescafe instant coffee, cold tea, egg nog, or grapefruit, tomato, or V8 juice, or water, should be tried.

C. If the craving for alcohol persists, or is very strong, the following should be tried separately, and in various combinations, with and without the fizz: Glutamine (not glutamic acid), sorbitol candies, niacin (not niacinamide), GH3 (novocaine), tryptophan, magnesium, B6, L cystine, L Lysine, deaner, B1, adrenal nutrients, nystatin, ketoconazole (chewed), sardines, salmon, sauerkraut, Miracle Soup (see weight loss), liver, kidney and other unusual foods. B1., Glutamine, and niacin should be taken two or more times a day.

The blood chemistries of alcoholics are grossly abnormal, but they can be normalized with large amounts of vitamin C. (See "Abnormal Blood and Urine Chemistries in an Alcohol and Drug Population" Ref.4.). An orthomolecular approach would be:

1. 100 mg. niacin every hour until a heavy flush is produced. The alcoholic must have someone present at all times until after the flush has subsided. Followed by enough niacin to produce a heavy flush each day.

2. 30gms vitamin C daily, principally as sodium ascorbate, for 3 days, plus sufficient vitamin C at the beginning of the program to produce diarrhea for 3 or 4 hours. This is essential for early detoxification. After 3 days 10 to 15 gms daily. The sodium remains bound to the ascorbate. It does not react like salt and it does not alter the Na/K balance. If sugar and other refined carbohydrates are removed from the diet the large amounts of vitamin C will reduce the cholesterol and triglycerides, and increase blood circulation.

3. About 8 gms of mixed amino acids with 500 mg. B6 , 3 times daily with meals for about 4 weeks.

Note that cellular nutrition for both sugar and protein depends upon sodium and B6, as supplied by this program.

We really do not know enough about the altered chemistry of the alcoholic syndrome but at present it appears that the adrenals become completely depleted and unable to produce sufficient adrenalin to pull enough sugar into the bloodstream to supply the body, resulting in very low levels of blood sugar at the cellular level. To survive, the body cells then start using the carbohydrate from the alcohol in the blood stream. Thus blood sugar is no longer the energy carrier, because the energy is being carried to the cells in the form of alcohol. Therefore alcoholism appears to be a form of hypoglycemia, where the cells start using the alcohol in the bloodstream as a direct source of energy, and the addictive force that forces the alcoholic to seek more alcohol, is the force of cellular starvation. This concept is supported by the extreme craving for alcohol, and it is also supported by the fact that alcoholics when drinking, eat very little, and of course they would not need to eat if the alcohol was supplying substitute sugars directly to the body cells. Thus a reduction in eating leads to increased alcoholism, while ample good food reduces alcoholism.

Quite obviously the mental effects from lack of alcohol, the "hangover" or withdrawal symptoms that can be relieved with alcohol, result from starvation of brain cells. This is the basic core of alcoholism. Yet we do not know the exact cause although it must be one of the following:

1. Degeneration of all metabolic systems finally reduces the production of adrenalin to the point that blood sugars are reduced to starvation levels, and the body cells then start using alcohol directly for energy. In this case adrenalin (epinephrin), perhaps as supplied by Nephron for asthma, together with food, would relieve the addictive craving for alcohol.

2. Degeneration of all metabolic systems reduces the ability of the body to digest and assimilate carbohydrate, but the body is still able to convert alcohol to blood sugar, thus creating the dependence on alcohol. In this case fructose (which the body uses directly) and digestive enzymes would reduce the craving for alcohol.

3. Toxins and metabolites from chronic infectives interfers with the normal sugar cycle, producing cellular starvation, but the body is still able to use alcohol as a substitute for sugars. In this case the only way to reduce the alcoholism would be to reduce the chronic infectives.

4. Alcoholic interference with the adrenals and other degenerated metabolic systems reduces blood sugar levels and results in cellular starvation. The body cells then start to use the alcohol in the bloodstream for metabolic sugars. In this case abstinence with feedings of glucose (glucosade) and fructose would reduce the alcoholism.

5. Alcohol interference with the adrenals and other body systems, together with toxins and metabolites from chronic infectives, interfere with the normal sugar cycle, and the body cells then start to use alcohol directly for energy. In this case the only way to reduce the alcoholism is to reduce the chronic infectives and improve health and metabolic function.

Among these different possibilities only the last one seems to have all of the unpredictable complications of alcoholism. Number 5 is full of variables, each with different consequences, but three things are paramount to success:

A. Complete abstinence.

B.Reduction in chronic infection.

C.Improved nutrition which must extend to the cellular level.

Quite obviously, continuing large quantities of adrenal nutrients will be required, and the thyroid must also be checked. It seems that all alcoholics are low on thyroid, whether basically low, or low as a result of the alcohol. Low thyroid is usually associated with low lithium levels and both low thyroid and low lithium impair immune function, with increased chronic infection.

Some of the mental effects from alcohol also resemble oxygen starvation. It could be that alcohol and/or toxins create a temporary anemia, which may be part of the altered sugar cycle, or perhaps the electrical charge on the red corpuscles is altered, which would create the red cell clumping and blood sludge seen in alcoholics. Niacin, in continuing large quantities, seems to be the only way to normalize the electric charge on the red corpuscles and thus reduce the clumping and blood sludge and improve normal sugar metabolism, and thereby improve all body functions. Niacin therefore becomes one of the cornerstones of all alcoholic programs.

The full role of iron in alcoholism is still not known, but it is known that impaired liver function, (usually from alcohol) leads to iron storage and iron siderosis. Iron siderosis has extreme mental effects with many symptoms similar to alcoholism, and some alcoholics who have developed iron siderosis claim that their alcoholism; specifically their change in personality and their dependence on and their addiction to alcohol, arrived at the same time as the high blood levels of iron. Perhaps high levels of iron in the blood are part of the altered metabolism of the alcoholic. We do not know, but we do know that high levels of iron in the blood increase the tissue levels of iron, so the iron levels in the blood can be measured by your doctor, and the tissue levels will be shown on the mineral test. The high iron levels can be reduced with chelation therapy, particularly if special iron chelators are used, but the high iron will return until liver function is restored, and liver function cannot be restored in the presence of continuing alcohol, which of course takes us back to abstinence.

Despite all of the foregoing at present the only known way of switching the body from the alcoholic metabolic cycle (however created) back to the normal sugar cycle, is by abstinence. Cutting down on the quantity of alcohol, i.e. "I am drinking less these days", cannot slowly reduce the alcoholism because each drop of alcohol not only destroys brain cells and liver cells and depletes ascorbate levels, and impairs and alters almost every body system, but each drop also perpetuates the alcohol food cycle, and prevents the body from switching back to the normal sugar cycle. Thus until we know more about the intricacies of the alcoholic-metabolic cycle, the only way to reduce alcoholism is by complete abstinence, which of course has been the only method known for many years, and is the method still employed by the rehabilitation centers, that usually fail to rehabilitate. In the rehabilitation center all sources of alcohol are immediately cut off, after which the body goes into a state of cellular starvation despite any food that is consumed. The cellular starvation then produces "the hell of withdrawal", with all of the aches and pains and hallucinations. Then the "hell of withdrawal and detoxification" remains until the body, faced with cellular death, finally switches back to normal sugar metabolism. The "hell of withdrawal" therefore comes with approaching death, and the hallucinations and mental wanderings and feelings of loss of reality come from the cellular starvation of an almost dying mind,- a mind and body that are finally saved from complete death only at the very last moment, when the body switches back to the normal sugar cycle. With cellular nutrition restored by the normal sugar cycle all systemic functions can slowly return to normal, and when they have returned to close to normal and a measure of health has returned, the alcoholic can be discharged from the rehabilitation center,-- because he is normal.

But the alcoholic is not normal. He has not had sufficient special nutrition, and he has not had a reduction in chronic infectives, and he has not had sufficient time to become normal. And unless and until the function of the damaged body systems has been restored and the chronic infection has been reduced, the pathway back to alcoholism is still there, and to the alcoholic strangely inviting. So with the alcoholic metabolic pathways, that have been so firmly established still open, it takes only one drink, only one little bit of alcohol and the body will switch back to using alcohol directly for food. Then the alcoholic, in just a few moments, has slipped back into alcoholism and is again almost irreversibly forced back into the alcoholic world with all of its alcoholic ways.

You see, there are two worlds. There is the real world, where problems must be faced and where rules of conduct must be obeyed; and there is the alcoholic world, a different world, a false world, a world of fuzzy dreams, a world of euphoria, a world of hate, and a world of irresponsibility, where alcohol is an excuse for doing or for saying anything. The inhabitants of the alcoholic world live in both worlds, moving from the alcoholic world back into the real world only long enough to acquire more alcohol.

So to the alcoholic, the alcoholic world is quite a good world, despite the tremors and the chills and the aches and the pains. It is quite a good world because it is a world where responsibilities and rules can be pushed aside without immediate penalty; it is a world where spite and hate can be expressed without immediate retribution; it is a world of euphoria where the unfettered ego can soar to any fancied height; it is a pleasant world of escape, and it is therefore populated by people who have, or who think that they have, so many insoluble problems, in the real world that the alcoholic world appears like paradise;-- and it is so pleasant to cross the threshold;-- all it takes is a few drinks;--

This then is the basic driving force that starts people across the threshold to the alcoholic world. The real world seems so harsh, while there, only a few drinks away, is Utopia and euphoria! So why not cross the threshold? There is time for a little beer, or a little wine, and it can do no harm among friends! So with the first peek inside the alcoholic world there are more friends, beckoning and saying, "Come on and join the party". "A party"? "Well, perhaps there is time!" Then, with another cocktail or another hot toddy, and one more step into the alcoholic world, what a pleasant surprise! Why, the place is full of friends, in fact they are all friends, so why not drink up and join the fun? Why not? After all, the rent and the groceries can wait until tomorrow. The fuel and the electricity can wait until tomorrow. The car payment and the license can wait until tomorrow. The painting, and the chopping of wood and the cutting of grass can wait until tomorrow. The nagging wife or the grumbling husband can wait until tomorrow. The family can wait until tomorrow. In fact, the whole damn world , including the boss can wait until tomorrow, or they can all wait forever, because tonight now here, I am King! Tonight, now here, I am free! Free! All of my troubles are gone. Everything can wait, because here now I can do what I wish, think what I wish, be what I dream! At last I am free! I have escaped!

Escaped? Yes, escaped! Escaped from the world! At last I have shed the fetters and escaped from the world! Escaped from the real world into the wonderful world of euphoria! How Wonderful! How wonderful!-- But tomorrow waits, and when tomorrow comes, all of the fetters of life are back in place, and they are screwed down tighter. The rent is due, car payments are due, the lights are out, the stove is cold, the spouse and children are hungry and crying, and all of the money is gone. Yes, all of the money is gone! What a hell of a thing to see! What a hell of a thing to face! What a hell of a life! The fetters of life have tightened again, and there is no escape. No escape except, perhaps,-- well-there is that other world.-- and it beckons,-- and it was pleasant there among good friends, really good friends,-- so if there was only some money, just a little money, like perhaps a loan from a friend, or perhaps pawning a watch, or maybe what is left of the grocery money,or perhaps from the children's piggy bank,-- and then, in only a pleasant quick gulp or two it is back to freedom! Back to Euphoria! Who the hell cares about tomorrow! Everything can wait! It has waited before, and it can wait again! It is for today that we live! Let tomorrow take care of itself!

This is the escape world of the alcoholic. So alcoholism is not entirely metabolic. In the early stages there is always a driving force, a force to which many weak people succumb, and a driving force to which many strong people succumb. So there is always a driving force, and the development of alcoholism invariably reinforces and increases the driving force, so to overcome the alcoholism the driving forces must be found, altered, and rationalized with counselling. Otherwise, the program will fail. The alcoholic therefore has to be willing to "give up the other world," before they can be helped, and this is the central reason that all re-habilitated alcoholics invariably insist that the alcoholic has to really and honestly want to stop his alcoholism before any program can help. This is also the reason that so many alcoholics descend to the horrors of skid row before they honestly try to change. Of course the alcoholic world is not all euphoria, because the alcohol does wear off and to-morrow does come, with headaches, with tears and trauma, with hunger and thirst, and cold stone floors for a bed, the wife or husband gone, friends gone, and nothing left except remorse and alcohol,-- alcohol of any kind,-- cheap wine, rubbing alcohol, canned heat, vanilla extract, shaving lotion,-- anything. And anything for clothes, anything for a bed, and perhaps only garbage for food. Everything is always cold and chilly, and there is a constant maddening unsatisfied thirst, and always a hangover, a hangover that slowly and certainly becomes worse, with shaking hands, shaky body, and perhaps even the dreaded delerium tremens. Oh yes, the DTs, the bottom of the alcoholic pit, the worse Hell of all! Yes, these are the horrors of the alcoholic world. They are always there, but so also is the euphoria, so it is not until the horrors of the alcoholic world become greater than the horrors of the real world that the alcoholic really seeks a solution, but by then the job is gone, the money is gone, the family is gone, and the alcoholic is helplessly sinking in a stinky sea of cheap alcohol. So this is the necessity for counselling if the alcoholism is to be reversed before the bottom of the pit is reached. This is the necessity for the rationalization. It is all a matter of perception,-- a matter of point of view,-- because the horrors of the real world are never really as great as they seem, and they are certainly never as great as the alcoholic sees them, because the alcoholic is constantly comparing the real world with their own euphoric dream world. We cannot effectively help the alcoholic until they honestly want to be helped, and the alcoholic will not honestly want and seek help until the horrors of the alcoholic world seem to be greater than the horrors of the real world. We need to greatly alter the perception. We can, of course, increase the horrors of the alcoholic world with the drug called Antabuse, yet Antabuse does little to solve the problem, because it increases the stress and it also increases the depths of despair, forcing the alcoholic deeper into alcohol. It increases the depths of despair because, although the alcoholic agrees to take the antabus, they still have not reached the point where they honestly desire change, so they view the extra horror of the antabuse not as an extra horror of alcohol, but as an extra horror imposed upon them by the outside world,-- it is a real world horror, so they must sink even deeper into the alcoholic mire before they honestly seek change. The only value of antabuse is possibly as a deterrant when they are sober, or if it is given to them secretly by others, who may be in real peril if the secret is uncovered.

So we cannot effectively help the alcoholic until they honestly want help, and the desire for help comes only when the perceived horrors of the alcoholic world become greater than the perceived horrors of the real world. The turning point is therefore in the balance between the perceived horrors. It is largely a matter of perception. To achieve an early turn around we cannot increase the perceived horrors of the alcoholic world because the alcoholic will then twist the effort and view it as another imposition of the real world, so we must reduce the perceived horrors of the real world. You know, really "This old world is not such a bad world after all!" That is the message that the helping hand of counselling must somehow instill in the mind of the alcoholic. We say somehow, because the problem is psychological, and it is complicated by alcohol. Camaraderie, fellowship, friendship, religion, hobbies, music, art, theater, travel, new acquaintances, new friends, with a stern but understanding family, may help. There are no rules or magic formulas, but information and rationalizing are the only way that counselling can show the fact that the perceived horrors of the real world are few, and can be diminished. After all, the mountains of despair are really only molehills that all of us must take in our stride. Actually, there are no real horrors in the real world, they are only perceived. Every cloud has its silver lining, and every disaster has its comic side,-- if we really look. If we look back, yesterday's horrors have faded, yesterday's gloom is only a faint memory. It really is a bright world, it really is a good world, and the little pitfalls are few, and they are easily dodged.

Rehabilitation of the alcoholic then, is in two basic parts, psychological and biological, but the two parts are definitely interlocked and intertwined. They are intertwined by euphoria and hypoglycemia. All alcoholics are hypoglycemic, and when the blood sugar is low the mind drops into a state of unreality, where the victim is unable to distinguish between fact and fancy.

Fact then, may be seen as fancy, and fancy may be seen as fact. Thus as with all cases of severe hypoglycemia, the alcoholic may have exaggerated fears, or fears of things and situations that do not in fact exist. Both the euphoria and the horrors may be exaggerated, warped and twisted; with counselling the only method of correcting the misperceptions.

These hypoglycemic fears and fancies may be further complicated by dehydration. The fact of alcoholism makes adrenal depletion certain. The alcoholic, in a vain attempt to maintain reasonable levels of blood sugar, therefore almost invariably uses large quantities of caffeine and tobacco. Alcohol, caffeine, and tobacco are all strong diuretics that cause the excretion of more water than is consumed, usually to the point of severe de-hydration. In some alcoholics the "dried and shrunken" dehydration can be plainly seen, but in other alcoholics the build up of fatty tissue may mask the actual dehydration. Dehydration by itself, has extreme mental effects resembling Alzheimer's disease. (Ch.7.). In the alcoholic, the forgetfulness and the imaginings from the dehydration superimposed on, and mixed with the fantasies of hypoglycemia, and the mental effects of the alcohol, create the completely aberrant mentality so visible in the alcoholic.

These severe mental effects are further complicated by sub-clinical scurvy, sub-clinical beri-beri, sub-clinical pellagra, and toxins and metabolites from Candida yeast and other chronic infectives; all of which invariably result from alcoholism.

But all of these things, the liver failure, the adrenal failure, the pancreatic failure, the dehydration, the hypoglycemia, the scurvy, the beri-beri, the pellagra, the Candida and chronic infection, etc., are all biological, so even with the very best counselling, many more psychological problems are constantly being created than can ever be resolved. The counselling must therefore be started as soon as possible, but it cannot start to be effective until the many health problems are reduced, which will require the entire Candida program, and then with complete abstinence and lots of glutamine and lots of niacin, the alcoholism will slowly fade into memory.

Note now, that the alcoholic program consists of three principal interlocking factors; biological, counselling, and an honest desire for change. The alcoholism cannot be fully cured without all three. The entire Candida program will slowly start to improve the biological factors, and counselling will help with the psychological factors, but the honest desire to change is frequently the greatest problem. The desire to change is a balance between the perceived horrors of the real world and the perceived horrors of the alcoholic world. If the honest desire for change has already arrived, the biological program with counselling is all that will be needed, but if the honest desire for change has not yet arrived the problems can become very complex. Counselling can help with all of the perceived horrors of the real world, but it cannot help with some of the real horrors of the home. Usually the same junk food, the same delinquent lifestyle, and the same shared infectives that produced the hypoglycemic- alcoholic also produced hypoglycemic neurosis and psychosis in the spouse and in the rest of the family. Thus the horrors of the home are very real and very fixed, with very little room for rationalization with counselling. To all social workers, the typical alcoholic household is well known.

The typical alcoholic household is not a home. It is only a household where everyone fends for themselves and makes a life as best they can. It is usually a hypoglycemic household, where each day starts with everyone getting up late, grumbling, grouching, and fighting with each other. Everyone else is to blame for everything. Clothes are everywhere, washed and unwashed. Dishes are everywhere, washed and unwashed. Both children and adults grab what they can, and fight over what they want. Each gets their own sugar breakfast, if they bother with breakfast at all. Younger children usually have sugar-cereal and milk for breakfast, older children perhaps only a cup of tea or coffee, with lots of sugar. There is little to make lunches from, so the children do not take a lunch, or they take a poor lunch, or they take a few cents to buy a chocolate bar or other junk food. After the children, the parents will come dragging out of bed, shouting sharp instructions to the children. Up much too late, aggravated by the chaos of the children leaving for school, and lost among the unwashed clothes and unwashed dishes, they find something to wear,-- anything to wear,-- they hurry off to work, gulping a cup of coffee as best they can while they are finding clothes and gettimg ready. One or both will have a hangover. One or both will be constantly carping about something, real or imagined. Both will have more coffee and cigarettes as soon as possible, probably with more sugar and a jellied doughnut. Lunch will be more coffee and more sugar, and perhaps a start on the alcohol. Once or twice in the afternoon there will be more coffee and more sugar and probably more alcohol. There will probably be alcohol after work, and more before dinner. Dinner will be late, perhaps sporadic, with each one more or less fending for themselves and eating by themselves; or dinner may be more or less together, with the alcoholic growling and lashing out at everyone, and everyone lashing out at each other. The alcoholic, finding the house an unpleasant place to be, will find some lame excuse to escape to the alcoholic world, while the household sighs with relief,-- and goes right back to watching T.V. and to fighting over the spaghetti and jam. Then off to bed late, with the clothes unwashed and the dishes unwashed, and with no thought for tomorrow,-- because, like the alcoholic, today is now, and tomorrow will have to look after itself,-- somehow.

Then very late, the alcoholic will return. They always do,- raising hell, or just passing out on the couch, bottle in hand. This is a typical scenario, there will be variations, yet the basic elements are always the same. One parent, or the other may struggle valiantly to cope with all of the problems. Love, or duty, often has no bounds and the fruitless struggle may go on for years, with all of the money slipping away, and with all of the debts and other troubles piling up on each other; piling up so high that no one person could possibly cope with them.

Now with a scene like this, how could any alcoholic ever honestly want to give up their alcoholic escape world? How could any counsellor ever change the perception of the alcoholic so that they would want to give up their alcoholic escape world, when the cold hard fact is that the house is not a home, it is only a bickering household that is so bad that "it would drive anyone to drink." The fact also is that it is a neurotic household, a household filled with hyperactivity, psychosis and neurosis. It is a hypoglycemic household, where everyone is snapping at everyone else because everyone is frequently at least partly schizophrenic and half crazy with episodes of very high or low blood sugar;it is a sugar and coffee household, and the inevitable truth is that the alcoholic cannot be brought back from the alcoholic world until the household is changed into a home,-- a home that is more attractive than the euphoria of the alcoholic world.

Quite obviously we can start to reduce the alcoholism with the Candida program, but before we can hope to cure the alcoholic we must first cure the hypoglycemic - alcoholic household. We must reduce the hypoglycemia. We must put the whole household on the Candida program, and they will all have to change their lifestyle. They will all have to eliminate the tobacco, and the caffeine, and the sugar and the white starch, and they will all have to get up early enough that they can do all of the things that they know that they should do, and still have time to have a good breakfast together. In short, the household must be cleaned up, and made into a home. A home that is pleasant. A home that is largely free from strife. Oh yes, amd making the household into a home is perhaps the most difficult part of the task, because all too frequently, even with

462.

the hypoglycemia reduced, the spouse may continue to create battles, or will have so many complaints or will make so many unreasonable demands that the horrors of the real world have not been reduced, or alternately, if the spouse does not insist upon responsibility and fails to make sufficient appropriate and reasonable demands, the alcoholic atmosphere will remain, and the perceived horrors of the real world will still be greater than the horrors of the alcoholic world, so again there will not be a real desire for change.

The inescapable truth is that some women will make several husbands into alcoholics and some men will make several wives into alcoholics. The alcoholism therefore is not just a matter of alcohol, it is the product of alcohol together with an irresponsible and frustrating alcoholic environment, so it becomes obvious that the counselling, and the health program, and the changes in habits and lifestyle cannot be confined to the alcoholic, but must include the entire household, so that the alcoholic will have good reason for a desire for change. The real root problem in alcoholism therefore frequently becomes not the alcoholic, but the neurotic and psychotic spouse of the alcoholic, who holds the alcoholic like a slave, and may not wish to relinquish that power. However, if some arrangement can be made to start the whole family on the Candida program the hypoglycemia will improve, relations within the family will improve, and the household may then become a home, a considerate and responsible home where everyone is living together, eating together, and sharing everything together, including the chores and the responsibilities, and the joys and the sorrows, and where the improved levels of blood sugar have quenched the explosive fires of spite and hate. Then, and then only, is there real hope for the alcoholic because the real underlying cause of the alcoholism will have been eliminated. Abstinence? "Why bother with alcohol, who needs it? It's just boring".

JAPANESE DRUNKEN DISEASE. (Meitei-Sho).
Time magazine, July 20,1959, told the story of a man who had been on a 25 year alcoholic binge without drinking, with the alcohol produced internally by yeast infection. The problem was cleared up with trichomycin, a Japanese anti-fungal. Since then several Japanese medical papers have detailed 30 more similar cases of internal Candida produced alcoholism, involving Japanese from age 3 to 74. The anti-fungal successfully used was Ancobon, (Ancotil) (Flucytosine) which is active against both Candida and Cryptococcus. (See Flucytosine Ch.4.) There are now a very large number of similar reports from all over the world. It appears that perhaps the high alcoholism results from a combined infection where other infectives join the basic Candida matrix.

Every alcohlic should suspect that perhaps most of their continuing problems are centered in intestinal Candida yeast infection, because high Candida infection is invariably present in alcoholism. (See page 370).

DRUG ADDICTION.

Dr. Libby and Associates, in their paper on the blood chemistries of alcoholics and drug addicts, do not differentiate between the metabolic damage of drugs or alcohol. Candida is invariably involved in alcoholism, and is usually also part of drug addiction, so cellular damage from acedaldehyde is part of the problem with both drugs and alcohol. The Libby institute has demonstrated that the Vitamin C /amino acid /B6 program used for alcoholics is equally effective in restoring cellular function in drug addicts. Drugs usually harden the veins so a daily niacin flush will also help to increase blood circulation. As drug addicts also have similar episodes of low blood sugar and similar "alcoholic" behavior, the program for drug addiction is largely the same as the program for alcoholism.

* * * * * * * * * * * * * *

Lessons From The Past.

"For some years past a decided inclination has been apparent all over the country to give up the use of whiskey and other strong alcohols, using as a substitute beer and bitters and other compounds. This is evidently founded on the idea that beer is not harmful and contains a large amount of nutriment; also that bitters may have some medicinal quality, which will neutralize the alcohol it conceals, etc. These theories are without confirmation in the observations of physicians and chemists where either beverage has been used for any length of time. The constant use of beer is found to produce a species of degeneration of all the organism, profound and deceptive. Fatty deposits, diminished circulation, conditions of congestion, perversion of functional activities, local inflammation of both the liver and the kidneys—all are constantly present. Intellectually a stupor amounting almost to paralysis arrests the reason, precipitating all the higher faculties into a mere animalism. The most dangerous class of tramps and ruffians in our large cities are beer drinkers. If these facts are well founded, the recourse to beer as a substitute for alcohol merely increases the danger and fatality following."

APRIL, 1879:

THE BRAVE NEW WORLD.

NEW CONCEPTS for BETTER HEALTH.

The Ultimate Contraceptive.

A great many different contraceptive devices, operations, and methods have now been tried, but as yet even the best have serious side effects and other drawbacks.

The concept of the vasectomy was perhaps one of the best methods of contraception, but the technology was poor because escape for the sexual fluids was blocked, which leads to the formation of brown pigment in the testicles:- the same brown pigment that is associated with premature senility. Infertility from natural retrograde ejaculation, where the semen flow is reversed and goes into the urinary system and bladder, is quite common among older men. Logically, a surgical operation that re-routed the spermatic duct to duplicate retrograde ejaculation would provide a 100% effective means of contraception, without side effects, but it would still require invasive medical surgery, and the operation might also be difficult to reverse. Surely there must be an even better way!

The ultimate contraceptive would, of course, be a non-invasive contraceptive that would be triggered by the fact of conception. Preferably it would be something that was 100% effective and would be used after intercourse. It could be used either oral or topical. Such a contraceptive would give the female the right that she really deserves;- it would give her the right to decide if she would or would not have a pregnancy after possible fertilization, but long before the fetus started to develop. A fully effective oral or topical contraceptive, used sometime after possible fertilization, without detectable side effects, would then be the ideal ultimate contraceptive, that could be used, or not used at the complete discretion of the female.

Now from Dr.Beard's work we know that very soon after the ovum is fertilized, and while the very first cellular divisions and replications have started, the chorion starts to produce chorionic gonadatrophin, which prevents the immune system from destroying the newly formed cells that are actually "foreign" to the body. These are not yet the newly formed cells of the fetus, they are only the cells that will lead to the development of the fetus.

So here, at the crossroads of Dr.Beard, Dr.Krebbs, and Dr. Virginia Livingstone, here where all three meet at the very heart of Cancer; is the place for the ultimate contraceptive. All that is needed at this point is a chemical substance, from herbs or the laboratory, that will selectively, without side effects, inhibit or interfere with the production of chorionic gonadatrophin. This would be the ultimate contraceptive, that is triggered by the start of conception, and uses the body forces to prevent conception. Simple and effective. So simple and effective that doubtless there are women with chorionic gonadatrophin defects that cannot bear children. Simple, so very simple. All that is needed is straight forward chemical engineering. Yet chemistry is never really simple, so perhaps instead it is an immense task in chemical engineering, but a very worthwhile task because such a substance would finally emancipate women, and would provide all of womankind with full control of their lives.

Many people have said that all of the new frontiers have been crossed, and that anything that is worth knowing is already known. That just is not true. Here is a real challenge in chemical engineering. A challenge that can at last free all of the women in the world. A challenge to both male chauvinism, and to women's lib. So who will it be that sets women free? Will it be Male, or Female?

So the challange is there. Whoever solves the little problem in chemistry and produces the ultimate contraceptive will deserve a Nobel prize; and they would also make a lot of money and gain a lot of fame. So let us hope that they will not forget that the basic concept came from these pages, and that they will share some of the credit with the Healthology Association. We cannot work out the chemistry although it may be centered around absissic acid.. Hopefully we have pointed the way toward female freedom.

<u>Improving Blood Circulation.</u>

It has been said that hardening of the arteries is natural to man because everyone in every society develops some atherosclerotic plaques if they live for fifty years or more. Impaired blood circulation certainly is not natural, but it is certainly so pervasive that despite improved nutrition and reduction in chronic infectives, and despite all other health measures, everyone will benefit from intravenous chelation therapy as the years pass and as the blood vessel plaques increase.

Now intravenous chelation therapy, with NaEDTA, heperin, and vitamins, followed by calcium, minerals, lecithin and niacin is an excellent way to improve blood circulation, but there are also other ways. Massage chairs are noted for their ability to improve the growth and function of capilliaries, and local blood circulation can also be improved with massage vibrators and ultrasonic massage. Vitamin E and bioflavinoids are also noted for their ability to promote the growth of capilliaries, and thus improve blood circulation.

Niacin is also known to have ability to expand the blood vessels, and to alter the electrical charge on the red blood corpuscles and thus reduce red cell clumping.

The greatest circulatory benefit should come with combined therapy, as follows:

1. Avoidance of sugars and refined carbohydrate. Sugar overload increases blood cell clumping by changing the electrical charge on the red cells.

2. Reduced chronic infection and reduced stress, to reduce the production of adrenalin, which not only pulls sugar from the liver into the bloodstream, but which also converts glucose to fructose. The fructose then overloads the cells with sugar that is beyond the normal control of insulin.

3. Continuing supplements of niacin, to normalize the electrical charge on the red cells to reduce clumping. Manganese also reduces blood cell clumping.

4. Continuing supplements of Vitamin E to promote growth of new capilliaries, and to prevent the formation of blood clots.

5. Supplements of ketoconazole to reduce the amount of Candida hyphae and filaments in the bloodstream.

6. Continuing supplements of lecithin to move cholesterol and fats out of the bloodstream.

7. Larger amounts of vitamin C, sufficient to ensure that there is enough for the body to manufacture bile from the blood cholesterol.

8. Intravenous chelation in a special massage chair with the feet elevated almost as high as the head.

9. At intervals during the chelation, the use of massage vibrators and ultrasonic massage of feet, hands, and other afflicted parts, so that the chelator could help the massage, and the massage could help the chelator.

The only objection to giving chelation with massage has been the remote possibility of loosening a blood clot or other debris. This objection can be eliminated by the use of vitamin E supplements and the massage chair for about a month prior to the combined therapy, and by having three or four intravenous infusions prior to the combined therapy.

Scientific people, who are interested in circulatory problems should note that they can watch Candida cause spermatic fluid to clump, while under the microscope. Clumped, curdled spermatic fluid from males with testicular Candida infection is always associated with a very sticky substance that seems to be insoluble in water, oils, mucins and everything else. It seems to be a type of glue or adhesive. Many of the new adhesives have been developed around the alteration of electric charge in the molecules of the adhesive, which makes the adhesive "stick" to most surfaces. It appears very likely that Candida produces a sticky adhesive substance by similar alteration of electric charge. The scientific question then becomes; Does the Candida produce the adhesive that causes blood cell cumping, which we know to be an alteration of electric charge? If so, which again is highly likely, blood circulatory problems are actually a long term result of Candida infection. Only scientific investigation can answer these vital questions.

Vaccinations and Intra Muscular (I.M.) Injections.

There can be no question about the great value of vaccinations and intra muscular injections, but their present use and administration can only be described as dumb. The value of vaccinations, and the ability of the body to make effective use of the vaccinations is entirely dependent upon the state of the immune system. If the immune system is fully functional and if it is not overloaded, and if immune nutrients are well supplied, vaccination will be without risk and without complications, but if the immune function is impaired, or overloaded, or if immune nutrients are low, perils and complications should be expected. Everyone, and particularly children, the aged, and the obviously ill, should either have a blood test to determine the state of the immune system before vaccination, or the vaccine should be attenuated and extremely weak for the first vaccination, and the vaccination should be placed so that it is as far as possible from lymph nodes and nerve centers.

At present, vaccinations and I.M. injections are usually placed willy nilly, helter skelter, right into the center of the muscle, and therefore all too frequently right into a muscle end plate, which we call a nervcite, and which is also called an electro-stimulator point or an acupuncture point. The muscle end plate is of course a combined nerve center and lymph node, so the nervous system and the lymphatic system are immediately shocked by the sudden massive overload of strange chemistry forced upon them by the vaccination, and complications should be expected. In all muscles there is a row of nervcites about $1\frac{1}{2}$ inches apart, down the center of the muscle. Each nervcite can be easily detected because they are sensitive to pressure from the thumb or finger. (Ouch spots) (See ref.28.). Quite obviously if the vaccination or I.M. injection is placed slightly off center, between the nervcites, the injection will be of full biological value and many unnecessary complications will be completely avoided.

CANDIDA INFECTION and the NEWBORN CHILD.

When each and every baby comes into the world its tissues are very soft, the skin is soft, and infectives of any kind can easily invade. Candida yeast, which is always present in the birth canal, invariably does invade the newborn child. If infection in the mother is low, and if the birth is quick and clean, the Candida infection in the baby will be low and the only sign of Candidiasis may be a little fluorescent pink on the infected parts, appearing two or three days after birth, and disappearing in a few more days as the immune system subdues the infection. Alternately however, if Candida infection in the mother is high, and if the birth is prolonged and complicated, the new baby may be born covered with "thrush"; completely covered with a thin film of white, active, growing Candida yeast which of course is wiped off the outside, but which may continue to grow wherever it has managed to invade the openings; the eyes, the ears, the mouth, the anus, the vagina, the penis; and from which it can spread to many other internal parts of the body. The final health of all newborn babies, and the continuing health of the growing child and final adult, is therefore largely dependent upon the amount of infection picked up at birth; how well visible infections were cleaned up inside and outside; and how well the immune system cleared up any Candida that did invade the tissues. Thus the health, and consequently the ensuing life, of every individual is largely determined by circumstance and happenstance at birth. The female is infected and affected more than the males, because sex hormones oppose Candida, so the male babies are partly protected by the already present testosterone: while the female babies are at much greater risk because production of estrogen does not start until long after birth. Indeed the pattern of Candidiasis and consequent adrenal depletion and ill health can be seen on the female side of many families, passed down from generation to generation.

Yet health and life should never be, and need not be, a matter of maternal health, circumstance, and happenstance. We do not need to have Candidiasis in the mother, in the infant, in the aged, or in anyone else. Indeed we would have much less if nystatin, ketoconazole etc; were common words and common substances, found in every home and used to help every infant.

It is amazing how rapidly an apparently healthy fussy baby settles down with just a little liquid ketoconazole to help it with its struggle against fungal infection. It is amazing how quickly diaper rash clears up completely with a little Flagystatin. It is amazing how quickly infections of little ears and tiny runny noses can respond to Micatin and Nizeral. It is amazing to watch skin blemishes and developing birthmarks disappear with Econazole and Nizeral. It is amazing that all mothers and all babies are not nurtured and protected by the use of all of the new anti-fungals. The technology is here and it has been here for several years. It is amazing how few doctors know about all of these new anti-fungals, and it is amazing how so few doctors use them. Babies deserve the very best. They do not need to have Candida infection.

HELPING ALL OF THOSE PROBLEM CHILDREN.
Special information and suggestions for all Teachers, Professors, Principals, School Boards and all others concerned with improving education.

****

"When Father was a boy" every school had its dummy, who was called a dunce, sometimes even by the teacher, complete with a "dunce cap". These were usually oversize young people who just seemed to be unable to learn as fast as the others, and some almost unable to learn at all. Their classmates called them stupid, yet they were not stupid, they were different and some things were difficult for them to learn, while in other things they might be brilliant.

Today these children are labelled "learning disabled". Today we find these people in a special class complete with special equipment, special teachers, and special methods of teaching, all provided at very high cost just to teach these "slow learners". A noble costly thought, and a noble costly gesture, that unfortunately, does very little for the basic problems of the young person, and provides an atmosphere of perpetuating the problems, with increasing costs to the taxpayers.

Now, if these young people are slow learners, or are hyperactive, the real problem must be biological; a problem that we know is associated with sugar, caffeine, diet, metal poisoning or chronic infection. A problem that science can solve, with many of the solutions already provided in the foregoing pages. It appears that school boards, principals, teachers, and other educators fail to realize and to recognize that the cost of perpetuating student mental handicaps is very high.

Let us hope then, that the educators will think about all of the money and frustrations that would be saved if each child starting school had a few more tests, other than just the eye and the hearing tests, which have already saved school boards so much money, and have saved so many children from being classed as retarded. Let us hope that all schools will start to test all children for minerals, so that those children with hypoglycemia or nerve disorders from lead and heavy metal poisoning could have chelation therapy so that there would be greater peace and more learning for everyone in the classroom. Let us hope that the tests would include a dietary evaluation to be used with the mineral test, to reduce the number of children who disrupt the classes with hyperactivity induced by sugar, chocolate and coke. Let us hope that children with learning problems would be further tested for hypoglycemia and Candida yeast infection so that they could have normal function restored, and they would then no longer need to be in a special class. Then if there are a few children who still have learning or behavioral problems, let us hope that they would be checked for worms, or flukes, and tested for pyrroles, and other less common conditions.

Let us also hope that the educators will also teach all of the students that all illness, including mental problems, is biological, and is usually correctable. Then everyone will fully understand that to be slow or "dumb" is an illness, that is not the fault of the victim.

This is not just a plea for effective help for the mentally handicapped:- it is also a plea for the educators to use a little science and to use a lot of common sense.

PRESCRIPTION DRUGS and ANTI-INFECTIVES.

One of the greatest problems in combating Candida yeast infection is that some of the effective substances are locked away from the public as "prescription items". The reasoning of the beauracracy in placing some of these items on "prescription only" is very obscure and probably highly illegal and a violition of the new "Consitution".

For instance, let us consider nystatin. The nystatin molecule is a very large molecule that cannot be absorbed by the body, and if it was absorbed the only thing that it could do would be to kill Candida yeast. In Canada nystatin cream can be purchased without a prescription if for external use, yet the same cream cannot be purchased without a prescription if it is to be used for vaginitis. All other forms of nystatin are on prescription only, because beauracracy calls nystatin a drug, which it is not.

What then can be the rationale? Nystatin can kill only one fungus (a plant). It can be taken internally, or it can be applied externally with reckless abandon because it cannot be absorbed by the body, and yet it is available by prescription only, while aspirin (which is very invasive), lye, carbolic acid, phenol, ether and a hundred other lethel substances can be freely purchased without prescription and without signature.

Ketoconazole, which kills only fungus (plants) and which does not injure the body even if taken over long peroids, is also classed as a drug, which it is not. Yet alcohol, which is highly toxic to the liver and which is in fact a drug, certainly is not restricted and is consumed freely without prescription. So what is the rationale? Or is it completely irrational?

The real problem seems to be a great confusion about drugs. Drugs are substances that alter the physical and mental state of man (and perhaps animals). They are substances that interact directly with mammalian tissues and mammalian physiology. Nystatin and ketoconazole react only with fungii, which are plants. Nystatin and ketoconazole therefore cannot be drugs, and they should be on the open market for people to use as freely as they use lye, carbolic acid, or alcohol.

DMSO is a solvent that is extracted from wood, and is similar to turpentine. DMSO is absorbed through the skin very rapidly, at about the same rate as garlic oil, gasoline, turpentine and carbon-tetrachloride and a little more rapidly than rubbing alcohol, but it is not toxic like gasoline, turpentine, carbon-tetrachloride, or rubbing alcohol. If rubbing alcohol can be used so freely without prescription, and if carbon-tetrachloride can be used freely for the production of stainless steel parts, and if turpentine can be used freely as paint thinner, and if everyone pumps their own gasoline (with many spills), why cannot DMSO be purchased as freely? Afterall DMSO is not a drug, and it is not injurious to the body, but it does have the ability to destroy plants like Candida yeast.

The use of Ecostatin, Flagystatin, and many more antibiotics and antifungals is also limited by prescription. Perhaps it is now time to remove all safe pharmaceuticals from the prescription list.

ANTIFUNGALS, OLD and NEW.
Medical people have known for many years that fungal infections both caused and aggravated many diseases, but they were powerless to reduce the fungal infections because they did not have a good and effective antifungal. They did not have a good antifungal because although fungii are in fact plants, they are composed of highly complex eukaryotic cells. Man is also composed of eukaryotic cells. It was, and still is therefore almost impossible to find or to make a compound that will selectively kill the fungus without also killing the mammalian tissue with which the fungal cells are interlocked.

In developing the imidazole antifungals (clotrimazole, myconazole, ketoconazole) the problem of selectivity was solved by the use of chemicals that attach to the ergesterol of the plant, and have a much lower affinity for the cholesterol of animal cells, thus killing the fungus without directly affecting the host. The imidazoles however, are not water soluble, and they therefore present problems with absorption. The latest improvement is the new liquid ketoconazole, which is absorbed in the mouth, and another imidazole with one more active chemical bond that is under testing.

Although the imidazoles have been a wonderful godsend to many people, they still create liver problems when taken in quantity over a long peroid of time. Still at present, ketoconazole and miconazole are the very best of the modern antifungals.

So for the present. But what about the past? Do we have any hang-overs from the past? We probably do.

Now in the making of sour dough bread the greatest problem is to keep the starter pure and free from other organisms that want to join the feast. The problem is the same when making wine, or beer, or bakers yeast, or yogurt, or anything else that is cultured. So when you drink wine, or tap beer, or eat yogurt, how do you really know that in fact it does not have a little Candida yeast, or a little Torulopsis Glabbrata, or other active human infective mixed with it? When you inquire about the purity of cultured food and drink, everyone immediately reassures you that every precaution is taken to keep the culture pure; and indeed every precaution may be being taken, but hospitals too, take every precaution with their many solutions, yet Candida has been found actively growing in hexachloraphane solutions, intravenous solutions and dialysis solutions. So just how good are the precautions taken by the food industry?

Certainly, the baking of bread and bread products is supposed to kill both the bakers yeast and any other organisms that may inadvertently be growing with it. However, if the bread is just a little doughy, are all of the yeast spores killed, or do a few active spores remain? Candida is a very hardy organism that can survive where least expected. If Candida is so hardy and so sneaky that it readily invades the hospital where precautions are very stringent, how do we really know that we do not buy a little Candida with our bakers yeast? How do we know that it does not escape into many areas of the food industry where precautions against its entry would be much less than at the hospital? How do we really know that we do not get a little, or a lot of Candida and other infectives with our healthy whole wheat bread, with our yogurt, or with our cheese? Even with the current food terchnology, if Candida has invaded and has mixed with the food culture, could it readily be detected, and if found could it be readily eliminated?

One must at once wonder that if Candida is so difficult to selectively eliminate from the body, how is it eliminated from our foods? Or is it in fact in many of our prepared foods? Quite understandably the manufacturers of food cultures are reluctant to discuss the matter, or to tell what substances are used to keep the cultures pure, while Health authorities only reiterate that they are assured that the culture manufacturers are doing their best to keep the products free from other organisms.

Perhaps the future will tell us that the cultures are kept pure by the use of certain substances. If so, the same or similar products might be very useful in eliminating Candida from man. If however, the future shows us that the cultures are not really pure, and are not really being purified, then we might suddenly discover that contaminated bakers and brewers yeast, and other food cultures are contributing to continuing and increasing degenerative disease.

The brewing industry is of course one of the largest industries in the world, and brewers and wine makers have certainly developed many substances for disinfecting their tanks, barrels, bottles, pipes, tubes and other manufacturing and bottling equipment. People who are interested in developing improved methods for destroying Candida and fungal infections might therefore look to the brewing industry for better antifungals than we now use. They must be there. If they are not there, everyone who consumes alcohol in any form other than distilled spirits is certainly at high risk of getting much more than a temporary lift from their next drink.

PANDORA'S HOPE for a BRAVE NEW WORLD.

Remember how Epimetheus helped Pandora open her mysterious box, and how all of the ugly little troubles escaped into the world? Remember how the Good Fairy then came out of the box, and with her wand cured all of the aches and pains left by the troubles? Would it not be nice if we could persuade the good fairies to help us put all of the troubles back into the box, where they could stay locked up forever?

Many of the troubles you know, do not just have names like Ache, and Pain, and Misery, but they also have names like Greed, Avarice, Pride and Jealousy. Then of course, there are other troubles called Depression, Neurosis, Psychosis, and Schizophrenia. While the parents of most of these troubles are much older troubles called Nicotine, Caffeine, Marijuana, Heroin, Sugar, Salt and Alcohol.

Perhaps, if the Good Fairy could persuade all of the mothers and fathers and teachers and other educators to put caffeine and sugar back into Pandora's Box, they would then stop drinking coffee, stop eating sugar foods, and perhaps the children would follow their example. Then they would soon see that many of the little troubles like Anger, and Obstinacy, and Jealousy, and Neurosis, would also be back in Pandora's box.

Would it not be nice if everyone that grew and prepared and sold tobacco would put Greed back into Pandora's Box, and start growing and selling blueberries or tomatoes, or potatoes, or anything useful. Certainly the air would be cleaner, the minds would be clearer, and many of the Aches and Pains and Heart Attacks, would simply vanish.

Would it not be nice, if all of the people that engage in the dark dealings of Marijuana and Heroin put avarice back into Pandora's box, and put their money and efforts into solar energy or space programs? They would probably make more money, and many of the troubles like Woe and Despair would also disappear.

Would it not be nice if the millions of people who spend their entire lives producing the alcohol that ruins the lives of millions of other people also put Folly and Greed and Avarice back into Pandora's box, and fed all of the rice and the grain to the starving world.

Would it not be even nicer if the Good Fairy helped all of us to put Bacchus himself back into Pandora's box (where he rightfully belongs), because Bacchus really is the Devil that persuades people that the ellusive little creature called Happiness always comes from a bottle or an upturned glass. Neither Joy or Happiness ever came from a bottle or a glass, even if it appears that they might. Bottles and glasses contain only Woe, Misery, and Sloth, but never Joy and never Happiness. If Bacchus were put back into Pandora's box a great many Woes and Miseries and Sloths would disappear and Joy and Happiness would appear in much greater numbers.

These are Pandora's hopes. These are some of Pandora's dreams. Forlorn hopes and forlorn dreams perhaps, because Bacchus is not in Pandora's box; Bacchus is still free, and it is not man, but Bacchus, that rules the world. Bacchus of course, is the Devil himself, cloaked in a pleasant misleading garb, yet it is the smiling and laughing Bacchus that rules the world with a tortuous twisted hand driven by a warped and twisted mind, for it is Bacchus that also forces Deceit and Flattery to do his evil deeds.

Oh yes, the smiling jovial Bacchus does not look like the ruler of the world, nor does he look like the Devil himself, and that is the great evil of the deception, because throughout the world, wherever people gather to plan the affairs of man, Bacchus is there. Bacchus is always there, pouring the wine, filling the cocktail glasses, and presenting the toasts. Bacchus, the Devil himself is ever present. With Nicotine and Caffeine always helping with equally sinister and twisted hands, everything seems so pleasant, while the mind slowly becomes fogged and thoughts become fuzzy, and the poisonous Acetaldehyde creeps in to slowly but surely destroy both mind and body. Then unnoticed, Hypoglycemia creeps into both thought and action, accompanied by Candida, and more Acetaldehydes to assist with further silent destruction of both mind and body. Thus it is not the pure mind of man that shapes man's destiny. Man's destiny is influenced by Bacchus, by the continuous cup of coffee, by the endless chain of cigarettes, by the constant wine and cocktails and by the ever delicious cookies and cake. Even the stalwart and the wary seldom escape the effects of Bacchus, because Bacchus always helps Candida and Candida always helps Bacchus, while both help Neurosis and Phychosis and Violence and Depression.

And Pandora's hopes for a Brave New World? How can her hopes ever be fulfilled when the jovial Bacchus blinds the eyes and dulls the mind. Still, the good fairy Hope is always with us. Many years ago she nudged the politicians and Cocaine was finally removed from Coca Cola. A few years ago she pushed the doctors and tobacco advertising was reduced. The Wand of Hope has also touched a few teachers and some nutrition is now taught in the schools. Despite Bacchus, Hope, whispering in the ears of perceptive physicians has brought Vitamins to both drug stores and medical clinics, and she has even persuaded some physicians to perceive and eliminate Candida.

Oh yes! Pandora's Brave New World could perhaps still come with a little more perception. So let us all help Pandora put all of the troubles back into the box, and let us all hope for a little more perception. Knowledge comes from the teachings of others, but Perception is a gift from Hope and the Almighty. We trust that these pages will help the Good Fairy Hope to provide just a little more perception and a little more help for Pandora!

> "Oh childhood days of Zest and Glee,
> What made'st thou flee so rapidly?
> So full of bloom,so full of Life;
> To romp and play from morn 'till night,
> In boistrous noise and child delight!
>   Why hast thou gone?- -
>   Why? - - Why? - -
> "Oh childhood days! - -
> Come Back! - - COME BACK!.

476.

ADDENDUM UPDATE.

Publishing a large book on a new subject is always difficult, and the publishing of this book has been greatly delayed by lack of funds. Time invariably brings change, as shown by the progress and new information in this update.

CHRONIC INFECTION.

The insidious role of hidden chronic infection in ill health is being recognized by progressive doctors with clever new products. Two of these new products are Primaxin and Vitek, which illustrate two different approaches to the problem. Primaxin uses the shotgun approach, where synergistic antibiotics are combined to cover a very wide range of infectives. In contrast, the Vitek computerized system pinpoints the specific infectives involved so that specific anti-infectives can be used.

Primaxin. (Merck).

Primaxin is a very wide spectrum antibiotic with low toxicity and very few side effects. Start slowly to avoid toxic reactions from the killed infectives. Primaxin may prove to be the antibiotic of choice to prevent the overgrowth of other infectives during anti-fungal therapy.

Primaxin is effective against,-

Achromobacter spp.	*Haemophilus influenzae*	*S. liquefaciens*
Acinetobacter spp.	*Haemophilus*	*S. marcescens*
Actinomyces spp.	*parainfluenzae*	*Shigella* spp.
Aeromonas hydrophila	*Hafnia* spp., including	*Staphylococcus aureus*
Alcaligenes spp.	*H. alvei*	(PCNase ±)
Bacteroides spp.,	*Klebsiella* spp., including	*Staphylococcus epider-*
including	*K. oxytoca*	*midis*
B. asaccharolyticus	*K. pneumoniae*	(PCNase ±)
B. bivius	*Listeria monocytogenes*	*Streptococcus* spp.,
B. disiens	*Moraxella* spp.	including
B. distasonis	*Morganella morganii*	Group A streptococci
B. fragilis	*Neisseria gonorrhoeae*	(*S. pyogenes*)
B. melaninogenicus	(PCNase ±)	Group B streptococci
B. ovatus	*Nocardia* spp.	(*S. agalactiae*)
B. thetaiotaomicron	*Pasteurella multocida*	Group C streptococci
B. vulgatus	*Peptococcus* spp.	Group G streptococci
Bordetella bronchiseptica	*Peptostreptococcus* spp.	Group D streptococci,
Campylobacter spp.	*Plesiomonas shigelloides*	including entero-
Citrobacter spp.	*Propionibacterium* spp.,	cocci (*S. faecalis*)
Clostridium spp.,	including *P. acnes*	*Streptococcus*
including	*Proteus mirabilis*	*pneumoniae*
C. perfringens	*Proteus vulgaris*	Viridans streptococci
Enterobacter spp.	*Providencia rettgeri*	*Veillonella* spp.
Escherichia coli	*Providencia stuartii*	*Yersinia* spp., including
Eubacterium spp.	*Pseudomonas aeruginosa*	*Y. enterocolitica*
Fusobacterium spp.	*Salmonella* spp.	*Y. pseudotuberculosis*
Gardnerella vaginalis	*Serratia* spp., including	

Vitek.

From McDonnell Douglas. (Aircraft). 595 Anglum Dr., Hazelwood, Mo 63042.

The Vitek system is a highly technical computerized infective detection system that is easy to use to determine the specific infectives present. In the Vitek system the biological sample

Addendum Update.

is added to a container type card, sealed, and loaded into the incubator-reader, which uses light to measure the activity of different materials against the sample. Container cards are available for different tests. The Vitek system is much faster than manual tests, with results available in a few hours. The Vitek system covers Urine I.D., Gram-Positive I.D., Gram-Negative I.D., Yeast I.D., Gram-Positive Susceptibility, Gram Negative Susceptibility, Gram Negative Urine Susceptibility, Supplemental Susceptibility, Enteric Pathogen Screen, Anaerobe Identification, Neisseria/Haemophilus I.D., Bacillus, and Bioburden.

This system is certainly a giant stride in the right direction and it should be used in all cases of serious illness to determine the full amount of hidden chronic infection, and it should be used even when chronic infection does not appear to be central to the health problem. It is particularly of value in identifying remaining overgrowth infectives if broad spectrum antibiotics like Primaxin are not fully successful.

CHELATION THERAPY.
(Atherosclerosis, stroke, coronary by-pass.)

Several people who were faced with a coronary by-pass have found the Donsbach Formula F.L.W. (Orachel) to be of so much help that their doctors have told them that the by-pass is no longer needed. The Donsbach F.L.W. can also be alternated with intravenous EDTA chelation therapy to rapidly improve blood circulation. Everyone with serious health problems, and particularly people with lead or heavy metal poisoning, diabetes, cancer, or high Candida infection will benefit from EDTA chelation therapy. Chelation is now available from Dr. Roland Watson Memorial Chelation Clinic, #302- 582 Goldstream Ave., Victoria, B.C. V9B 2W7. Cost is $50.00 per treatment, for 20 treatments or more.

Blood Cleansing with Intravenous Chelation.

It should always be remembered that NaEDTA will pick calcium, zinc, lead, and other minerals out of anything with which it comes in direct contact. That is the reason that it is so effective in reducing vascular plaques. That is the reason that it is the best method to clear up lead poisoning. That is the reason that mineral supplements must be taken after each infusion of EDTA. That is the reason that I.V. chelation is very effective in reducing any infectives that are in the bloodstream. That is the reason that it also reduces the indefinite and nebulous condition called "blood sludge".

Blood samples from victims of both cancer and Candida, when placed under the Darkfield Microscope, show rods, L forms, and jellied crystal bodies. Some doctors say that the rods and L forms are Progenitor Cryptocides, while other doctors say that they are Candida hyphae, but whatever they are they clog the bloodstream and greatly reduce blood flow through the capillaries. They can be reduced by as much as 50% with chelation. EDTA will also reduce the "jellied crystal bodies", (whatever they are), which appear to be another root cause of blood cell clumping and blood sludge. Thus the total benefits brought to circulatory victims by I.V.EDTA are much greater than just the reduction of blood vessel plaques, because ill health invariably has a Candidal component, and about 80% of the population also harbour Progenitor, and therefore risk of cancer. Intravenous EDTA chelation is therefore of particular benefit to victims of both Cancer and Candida, but it could probably be of much greater benefit if some of the vast amount of cancer research funds were devoted to a full scientific investigation of the mysterious forms that can be so clearly seen in the blood of Cancer and Candida victims, with the aid of the Darkfield microscope.

ALZHEIMER'S DISEASE AND CANDIDA.

There are several constants in Alzheimer's disease;-
1. Abnormal deposits of amyloid beta protein in the brain, the exact cause of which is unknown but may be genetic.
2. High levels of aluminum, even when common sources of aluminum have been avoided.
3. Very low levels of acetylcholine. Acetylcholine in the nervous system is opposed by cholinesterase. A new drug for Alzheimer's disease, called THA, has now been developed. THA blocks cholinesterase, thus making more of the low levels of acetylcholine available to the body, producing a marked improvement in the function of the patient. Note the exasperatingly blind scientific folly. The discovery of the low levels of acetylcholine is science at its best. But to block cholinesterase instead of raising acetylcholine is certainly warped psuedo science, which, like many other drugs, is certain to also produce profound side effects.
4. Candida Infection.

From all of the forgoing it certainly appears that Alzheimer's disease is actually a Candidal disease, where;--
1.--The Candida depletes the magnesium, followed by retention of aluminum by the body when the body tries to use aluminum as a substitute for the depleted magnesium. (Magnesium and aluminum are chemically very similar and they differ by only one atomic number).
2.---The Candida robs the acetyl-- from the acetylcholine to make acetaldehyde (Page 372.), or, if the Candida produces alcohol, or if the victim consumes alcohol, the body robs the

acetyl-- from the acetylcholine in the nervous system to make, acetaldhyde in the first heroic chemical step of alcohol detox-ification. Therefore it is the Candida infection that reduces the levels of acetylcholine. Note that the very low levels of acetylcholine not only impairs mental function, it also impairs the entire nervous system, which also alters the function of muscles, glands, organs, and each and every body process.

3.--- The acetaldehyde attacks all body cells, which further alters all body processes including brain, nerves, and blood.

4.--- The reduced acetylcholine in the nervous system reduces nerve transmission to the brain, and within the brain, and the nerve transmission is then further blocked and reduced by the high levels of aluminum, resulting in the erratic and fluctuating episodes of mental and physical dysfunction displayed in Alzheimer's disease.

5.--- The further detoxification of the acetaldehyde, together with the extremely high stress from the Candida infection and the impaired physical function and mental disorientation, depletes the vitamin C, resulting in increased infection and sub-clinical scurvy, which further impairs all body systems and all body parts including the mind.

6.--- The reduced state of health together with the depleted vitamin C results in adrenal depletion with muscle spasm, aches and pains, and episodes of low blood sugar, which usually drives the victim to alcohol, tobacco, and/or caffeine. The alcohol increases the problem directly when the body robs the acetyl-- from the acetylcholine as in 2. above. The caffeine and/or tobacco momentarily improves body function by inactivating cholinesterase at every nerve synapse in the body and allows the nervous system to run wide open and uncontrolled, until of course the acetylcholine is fully depleted and the victim is in a state of extreme exhaustion, which of course calls for a little more caffeine. But caffeine, and particularly coffee, is a diuretic, so the high consumption of caffeine, (including cola and chocolate) finally results in cellular dehydration, and the dehydration then further impairs all body systems including the brain and the nervous system.

7.--- With the vitamin C already depleted the body is unable to detoxify all of the caffeine, and the alkaloid poisons and any metabolites formed by the caffeine through side reactions, remain in the tissues, perhaps resulting in the strange deposits of amyloid beta protein.

It should be noted that the new drug, THA, has the same effect as caffeine, specifically it blocks the cholinesterase, so the new drug is the equivalent of administering just a little more coffee, but perhaps and hopefully without the diuretic effects of caffeine.

Addendum Update.

Another recent discovery on the possible cause of Alzheimer's, however, shows that the amyloid deposits in the brain may be caused by a slow virus, very similar to scrapie in goats and sheep. Many infectives of course do cross natural specie barriers, so one must immediatly speculate that perhaps Alzheimer's IS scrapie from undercooked mutton. In either case, autogenous vaccine would improve the immune response and reduce the infection.

From all of the foregoing it appears that the new knowledge and new therapies will bring very little actual help for today's Alzheimer's victim, but these new findings do reinforce the notion that Alzheimer's is principally a social disorder of lifestyle, caffeine, and alcohol, complicated by Candida and perhaps "scrapie" infection, and its many victims cannot hope to improve without doing everything, absolutely everything, outlined in the foregoing pages of this book.

PROTEIN ALLERGIES AND CANDIDA.

Dr. Jeffrey Bland has rightly pointed out that high intestinal Candida infection produces allergies when the Candida infection breaks down the membrane of the intestinal wall, which allows large incompletely digested protein molecules to enter the bloodstream, which in turn both triggers and overloads the immune system and results in extensive protein allergies. Unfortunately all of this occurs at the very time that the pancreas needs amino acids from fully digested protein to manufacture pancreatic enzymes for protein digestion, and it also occurs at the very time that the immune system itself requires very large amounts of amino acids to fight the Candida infection and to clear up the undigested proteins leaked into the bloodstream and tissues.

Most of the protein allergies are centered around large molecules of animal protein, but the fact remains that animal proteins are largely complete and they do provide excellent nutrition for people with normal digestion and assimilation. The problem is not the kind of protein, but protein allergies have caused many people to condemn animal protein as being allergenic and carcinogenic, when the real culprit is candidiasis, and when the health so avidly sought could not return as long as the Candida infection remained.

Inversely, of course, protein allergies should be considered as almost certain evidence of intestinal candidiasis, and protein allergy victims can therefore be equally certain that most of their health problems will remain until the total Candida infection is reduced and the tissues are strengthened with large amounts of vitamin C, bioflavinoids, and good complete protein.

481.

Addendum Update.

COENZYME Q-10 and CANDIDA.

ATP (Adenosine Triphosphate) is the basic reactive molecule that is essential to conversion of food to energy within the mitochondria of every cell. In turn, Coenzyme Q-10 is the active molecule necessary for the production of ATP, and shortage of Q-10 will therefore limit ATP and total body function. But Q-10 is reduced by the effects of infection, resulting in health decline and aging. Supplements of 20-60 mg. of Q-10 daily should therefore be part of every health recovery program.

AMINO ACID THERAPY.
(Ref."The Healing Nutrients Within", Drs. Eric Braverman and Carl Pfeiffer, Keats.)

To their great credit Drs. Braverman and Pfeiffer and ass- ociates, with this book, have now opened the way to the intelligent use of a wide range of substances that are highly effective in improving body function.

Unfortunately the Health Protection Branch and the FDA have taken it upon themselves to call all substances that directly affect health, "drugs". Thus amino acids, chelators, antibiotics, and antifungals become drugs, which they are not. Most true drugs are complex chemicals that are unnatural to the body and work by a negative mechanism of inhibiting some specific body process that may be out of control, or to unnaturally stimulate a body function at great cost to other body functions. Drugs therefore can have side effects that are all too familiar, and frequently are severe and dangerous.

Amino Acid therapy, in contrast, is obviously superior to drug therapy because it is a positive method of directly stimulating and improving failing body processes with substances that are natural to the process and are natural to the body. Body function is therefore improved directly with a minimum of side effects.

There are about 22 principal amino acids, with perhaps a few more yet to be isolated. They are the building blocks of cells. They are useful only when incorporated into cells. Each amino acid has a specific function in each of the cells of the organs, tissues, glands, muscles, or other body parts in which it is incorporated, and function of that body part can therefore be limited if the required amino acids are not fully supplied.

At present nine of the amino acids are thought to be essential, because the body cannot make them and they must therefore be obtained from food. Hence the need for balanced protein in the diet. The other amino acids are therefore considered to be non-essential because the body can make them.

Addendum Update.

Most certainly a healthy body can make them, but here we are considering bodies that are not healthy, instead they are worn and torn and ill. We should not expect that people who are ill, or who have been ill from various infections of many kinds, to have body processes that are intact and capable of making these other amino acids in sufficient quantity. Therefore to these ill people the non essential amino acids become essential, and health cannot return until they are fully supplied. Then, with body processes restored the body may be able to again make the non-essential amino acids in sufficient quantities to maintain health. This further illustrates the reasons that the sick get sicker, but if the illness can be turned around it also shows the reasons that the healthy get healthier. Amino acid therapy can therefore be seen as yet another scientific opportunity to turn the state of ill health into the state of returning health.

Here perhaps we should review protein. Normally the protein that we eat is digested into the amino acids of which it is composed. The amino acids are then assimilated into the bloodstream and delivered to all of the cells of the body where the cells accept or reject the nutrients that are surrounding them in the interstitial fluid. A grand and simple design that normally produces abundant health. Yet this normal path is in fact complex and filled with perils. If the protein is not fully digested by pancreatic enzymes that themselves require specific amino acids, the proteins simply continue on through the digestive tract to become food for usually gas producing bacteria that may also produce various toxins, while the body still remains starved for protein and the immune system is impaired by the lack of protein. If digestion is complete, and the protein is digested into amino acids, it still requires calcium in adequate quantities to act as a carrier for the amino acids into the bloodstream. If calcium is inadequate, again, the protein remains in the intestinal tract to become food for intestinal flora, -good or bad. To ensure that amino acid supplements are assimilated, calcium levels should be determined. If levels are low, they can usually be raised with calcium, magnesium, and Vit.D. The retention of calcium, however, depends upon parathyroid hormone (PTA), which may have to be supplemented if calcium levels remain low.

All health professionals will benefit from reading "The Healing Nutrients Within", which opens new vistas for better physical function. The following is not a substitute for the use of this excellent book, but it is included as being pertinent to the subject of Candida infection and illustrative of the great value and potential of amino acid therapy.

Addendum Update.

VITAMINS and AMINO ACIDS.

Nutritionists should note that vitamins and amino acids are constantly interacting with each other. Vitamin C is pure carbohydrate and our bodies should be able to make it but we cannot because all hominids lack the genetic coding. All of the B vitamins contain nitrogen like an amino acid group. They are also acidic. In a sense then the B vitamins are amino acids that are not incorporated into protein.

B-6 is a particularly important vitamin that is a co-factor for the transaminases that metabolize the amino acids, and most of the spectacular health improvements arising from the use of B-6 therefore do not come directly from the B-6, but result from the improved amino acid metabolism.

B-2 and B-3 are the next important vitamins, but it should be noted that B-3, (Niacin) is not really a vitamin,-- instead it is actually made by the body from tryptophan,-- and many of the spectacular results from niacin therefore do not come directly from the niacin but result instead from the sparing effect of the extra niacin which increases total metabolic levels of tryptophan.

AMINO ACIDS IN HEALTH AND DISEASE.

This is only a brief consolidated list. There are many more.

Note, GABA is Gamma-aminobutyric acid.

Growth--Arginine, Carnitine, Glycine, Taurine, Methionine.

Muscles--Arginine, Glycine, Tryptophan, Valine, Ornithine.

Stamina--Carnitine, Dimethylglycine (DMG).

Healing-- Arginine, Cysteine, Glycine, Proline, Methionine.

Pain--Methionine, Tryptophan.

Insomnia-- GABA, tryptophan, Glycine.

Reduce Appetite--Tryptophan, Phenylalanine, GABA, Carnitine, Arginine.

Reduce Cholesterol and Triglycerides-- Methionine, Taurine, Arginine, Carnitine, Glycine.

Reduce Blood Pressure.-- GABA, Taurine, Tryptophan.

Osteoporosis--Lysine.

Hypoglycemia-- GABA, Alanine.

Diabetes-- Tryptophan, Alanine, Cysteine.

Liver Failure-- Valine, Leucine, Isoleucine.

Gall Bladder-- Glycine, Leucine, Isoleucine, Valine, Taurine, Methionine.

Parkinsons-- GABA, Methionine, Threonine, Tryptophan, Tyrosine, L-Dopa.

Chorea and Tardive Dyskinesia-- GABA, Leucine, Isoleucine, Valine, Taurine, Methionine.

Relieve Aggressiveness--GABA, Taurine, Tryptophan.

Drugs-- Heroin - Methionine, Cocaine --Tyrosine,

Alcohol -- Glutamine (GABA), Cysteine.

Addendum Update.

Tobacco-- Tyrosine, Cysteine.
Detoxification-- Cysteine, Glutamine, Glycine, Methionine,
    Tyrosine, Taurine.
Radiation-- Glycine, Dimethyl Glycine, Cysteine, Methionine,
    Taurine.
Immunostimulants-- Glycine, Lysine, Threonine, Alanine, Aspartic
    Acid, Cysteine.
Diuretic-- Jamieson Slim Down,-- Arginine HCL 300mg, Lysine
    HCL 300mg, Ornithine HCL 225mg. 3 tabs at bedtime.
    Very effective.

These are only a few of the afflictions that can be helped
with amino acids. There are many more. Amino acids are
particularly effective against psychosis and other mental
problems. Dr. Braverman provides many details.

AMINO ACID INTERACTIONS.

Amino acids of the same general structure compete with
each other for absorption and they are therefore antagonistic,
but amino acids with different general structures can complement
each other. Vitamins and minerals can also be complementary
or antagonistic to each other, and to the amino acids.

Complementary:
Taurine-- Glycine, GABA, Alanine.
Arginine-- Ornithine, Citriline, Aspartic acid.
Tryptophan-- Niacin, B-6, Zinc.
Carnitine-- Lysine, Niacin, Taurine.
Phenylalanine-- Tyrosine, Methionine, Copper.
Cysteine-- Methionine, Taurine.
Threonine-- Glycine, Proline, Arginine.

Antagonistic:
Taurine-- Glutamic Acid, Aspartic Acid.
Arginine-- Lysine.
Tryptophan-- Tyrosine, Vanadium.
Phenylalanine-- Tryptophan.
Cysteine-- Lysine, Copper, Zinc.
Threonine-- Copper.

AMINO ACID THERAPY.

Some of the amino acids, like tryptophan, have been used
to improve body function for years, but the knowledge to use
many of the amino acids is quite new. An engineering approach
to their use would be to:
1. List all of the symptoms.
2. List all of the amino acids that would alleviate the symptoms.
3. Determine which amino acids are common to the symptoms.
4. Check for possible interactions.
5. Develop the indicated amino acid program.
6. Add other complementary, synergistic or antagonistic nutrients.

485.

Addendum Update.

Due to their reinforcement and enhancement of body systems amino acid supplements are constantly elevating homeostasis, with the need for the supplements then gradually reducing.

This is only a brief overview of the great value and potential of amino acid therapy. Except for specific amino acids and Candida, greater detail is far beyond the scope of this book, but the foregoing does show the need for a detailed Handbook of Scientific Nutritional Therapy similar to an engineering handbook, which would contain all of the charts and tables for easy and effective reference and determination. Then, following the handbook, one might of course postulate that a complex computer program might provide even greater options.

L-CYSTEINE and CANDIDA.

L-cystine is the oxidized form of L-cysteine and biologically they are almost interchangeable because the body readily converts one into the other. However L-Cysteine is the only form that should be used as a supplement because under certain circumstances large amounts of L-Cystine can build up as crystals in the kidneys. (Cystinosis).

L-Cysteine is abundant in many proteins and it is therefore essential to many life processes. It is necessary in quite large amounts for the production of Coenzyme A, keratin, insulin, digestive enzymes, and glutathione,(GSH), and in lesser quantities for hemoglobin, albumin, carboxypeptidase, and edestin.

L-Cysteine is also the great detoxifier that can bind and remove arsenic, mercury, cadmium, cobalt and other heavy metals, and is also effective against nuclear and X radiation. It works with vitamin B-6 and should be supplemented along with B-6 if a B-6 disorder is suspected.

In addition to the foregoing, Cysteine is effective against acetaldehyde poisoning from drinking or smoking. Yes, drinking or smoking, because smoking also produces acetaldehyde. Candida infection too, produces acetaldehyde. So here, with the amino acid L-Cysteine we have finally found a better therapy against acetaldehyde than aldehyde dehydrogenase. (Pages 376 and 481). Cysteine supplements should therefore be part of all alcohol programs to reduce hangovers and brain and liver damage, and it should be part of all non-smoking programs to reduce emphysema and risk of cancer. Candida victims, who of course have their own built in source of alcohol and acetaldehyde, should almost continuously supplement Cysteine to protect all body processes and thus improve total function. But note also that Cysteine will bind not only mercury and arsenic etc. but many nutritional minerals as well. Cysteine supplements should therefore be accompanied by multi-minerals, taken 12 hours away from the Cysteine.

Addendum Update.

Cysteine is also effective against baldness, psychosis, asthma, bronchitis, bacterial infections, diabetes and seizures, kidney failure, and cancer.

L-Cysteine only should be used for supplements, usually up to 500mg twice daily, but not to exceed 5 grams.

L-Cysteine is the precursor to glutathione (GSH) which has such a large number of functions in metabolic health that it is usually considered as a seperate nutrient.

TYROSINE, ADRENAL DEPLETION, and DEPRESSION.

Tyrosine is an essential amino acid that particularly affects the brain. It is precursor for the catecholamines dopamine, epinephrine, (adrenalin) and norepenephrine. It is also precursor for thyroid, catacholestrogens, the skin pigment melanin, and the enkephalins. (pain relievers).

Candida frequently suppresses thyroid, and the affects of the low thyroid can be catastrophic. (Page 144). Thyroid levels can be raised with thyroxin, but if thyroid is low it is much better to raise thyroid levels with tyrosine, iodine, and perhaps lithium.

It has been pointed out that the unending stress from high Candida infection not only uses up all available Vitamin C, but also results in adrenal depletion with resultant devastation of other body systems. In stress induced adrenal depletion tyrosine becomes depleted, and the body is then unable to make dopamine, epinephrine, and norepinephrine, frequently resulting in biochemical depression. These catecholamines are all neurotransmitters of the sympathetic nervous system, and with their depletion mental fatigue and depression could well be expected. Tyrosine then becomes the key supplement that should be added to B-6 and Vitamin C to reduce and avoid adrenal depletion.

Loss of libido and perhaps even sexual failure are also associated with high Candida infection. The drug Yohimbine has many side effects but it is still used by many doctors to increase sex drive, and it does so by prolonging the effects of tyrosine. Direct supplements of tyrosine are of course much better and more effective, and they are completely safe. Tyrosine supplements will not only increase libido, but erection and duration of excitement in both male and female will also improve, and female health may be further enhanced with the higher catecholestrogens.

With the usually dramatic benefits of tyrosine supplements to the Candida victim, we must wonder if perhaps Candida has a high need for tyrosine or its precursor phenylalanine, with the Candida starving and subdueing the host by bringing down thyroid, adrenal, and sexual levels.

Addendum Update.

There are many more benefits from tyrosine, particularly in Parkinson's disease, depression, hypertension, appetite suppression, and therapy for smoking and cocaine. Some people may also benefit from phenylalanine, the precursor of tyrosine.

Tyrosine is virtually non-toxic, and, although useful in depression, it may aggravate psychosis. Supplements of tyrosine up to 6 gms daily have been used. Normal actual daily requirement is about 1 gm. D-tyrosine is toxic and should be avoided.

Tyrosine is a "brain" nutrient, and some doctors suggest that the "mental" amino acids should be taken between meals so that they will be rapidly absorbed, with the resulting high blood concentrations increasing the amounts that finally reach the brain.

TAURINE and CANDIDA.

Taurine is normally made within the body from Cysteine, but the process is complex and requires many other nutrients, so the body may be continuously deprived unless extra taurine is derived from the diet. Taurine is essential to the normal function of the brain, heart, gallbladder, eyes, vascular system, and the entire body. Its basic function is to stabalize cell membranes and to assist sodium and potassium and calcium and magnesium into, and out of, every cell in the body.

Animal tests have shown high concentrations of taurine in the cortex of the kidney, in the liver, pituitary, thymus, adrenals, eye, heart, and the mucous membranes of the nose and digestive tract. The tests did not include the brain, but taurine is known to be a "brain" nutrient second only to glutamic acid. Quite obviously if taurine synthesis is impaired all of the foregoing parts of the body will be impaired, and function will be improved with adequate supplements. With so many inter-dependent body functions depending on adequate taurine synthesis it becomes easier to understand how a slight change in nutrition, digestion, or body stasis can cause a complete collapse of health, and conversely, it is easy to understand how even small supplements of taurine may sometimes produce spectacular results.

Taurine has particular value in hypertension, skipped heartbeats (arrythmias), weak heartbeat, calcified heart valves, gallstones, epilepsy, retinitis, diabetes, and much more.

Candida victims usually have almost continuous "stomach problems", frequently with a very pale stool indicative of a shortage of bile. Taurine and vitamin C are used by the body to convert cholesterol into bile. Taurine supplements will usually increase bile, with added benefits of improved digestion and a reduction in blood cholesterol. A further additional benefit is improved mucous membranes that are less susceptible to the inroads of Candida yeast.

. Usual supplements are 500 mg. to 5gms. per day.

Addendum Update.

THE ROOTS OF DEGENERATIVE DISEASE.
Free Radicals, Calcium Chelation, Cholesterol, Cancer, Etc.

Man, with his often fumbling but enquiring mind has been seeking the basic causes of illness for years, and now perhaps he is at last zeroing in on the ever elusive basic cellular causes of degenerative disease. Dr. Elmer Cranton, in "Bypassing Bypass" (Sterne and Day) provides excellent insight for both the physician and the victims of degenerative disease. Intravenous calcium chelation (page 227) is the infusion of the man made amino acid NaEDTA into the vascular system where the chelator picks the calcium out of the plaques. This allows the body to dissolve the plaques and the increased blood flow can be measured on a pulse-volume recorder. (Plethysmograph). The wonderful thing is that it works! Yet to some thinking people there has always been a problem,-- not with the results or the method,-- but with reconcilliation of the facts. The fact is that the calcium is the last addition of material to the plaques, and the EDTA is a very large molecule that can remove only one atom of calcium, and each four-hour infusion would then remove only a little more calcium than would normally be excreted each day. Therefore the chelator works, but in some different way. Dr. Cranton shows the different way. EDTA will bind calcium, but the bonds are weak and if metals are present the EDTA will give up the calcium and bind the metal. Free metalic ions are free radicals that are capable of spawning many more free radicals. If it is the free radicals and their cumulative effects that create and maintain the blood vessel plaques, what then are free radicals?

Free Radicals. (Page 143).

Our bodies are a highly organized mass of active chemicals complete with complex electric and electronic reactions. Specifically, a free radical is any element with an unpaired electron in its outer orbit, which causes it to be highly unstable and to react instantaneously with any adjacent substance. Sometimes the reaction can knock loose an electron, or perhaps a single oxygen atom, both of which are unstable and create more free radicals. The principal free radicals generated within the body are hydroxyl radicals, superoxide radicals, and singlet state oxygen, which usually react to produce hydrogen peroxide (hair bleach) and other peroxides that in turn rapidly produce more free radicals. In the great multitude of electro-chemical reactions in living organisms free radicals are constantly being produced as part of the living process, but normally they are neutralized by antioxidants which are frequently coupled to a metal. Superoxide dismutase (SOD) (manganese,zinc,copper), glutathione (selenium), and catalaze and peroxidaze (iron), are examples. Other better known antioxidants are DHEA and estrogen, cysteine, methionine, tyrosine, the B vitamins, beta carotene, vitamin E, vitamin C, and, yes, cholesterol. These antioxidants use interdependent multistep processes that finally transfer the free radical to the Krebs cycle where the extra energy is utilized. Uncontrolled free radicals damage tissues within the cell and also the cell wall itself. They also damage and alter enzymes, induce inflammation, and most importantly, by complex anaerobic electron transport, they can "oxidize" without oxygen (called auto-oxidation) that induces malignant mutation and promotes tumor growth. Whenever free radicals exceed the local antioxidants each uncontrolled free radical multiplies not by only a hundred or a thousand, but by a millionfold, with the damage to tissues liberating metal catalysts and singlet stage oxygen that does even more damage than the free radicals. The extreme damage from uncontrolled free radicals is well illustrated by nuclear radiation, X-rays, ultraviolet light, etc. that knocks photons out of orbiting electron pairs and thus creates free radicals within the living tissues, with the spawning of more free radicals so great that today the Laplanders of northern Scandanavia will die from radiation damage (free radical damage) if they cook and eat the meat from the raindeer that are all slowly dying from the radioactive fallout from Chernoble. We have known for many years that radium induces cancer, and we now know that the radiation simply produces large quantities of free radicals within the living tissues, which causes mutagenic damage to the nucleus of the cells. Then, when a very large number of cells are damaged only one in a million or a billion or more, may become malignant. Altered body function and illness then starts from uncontrolled free radicals, and the greater the number of uncontrolled free radicals the faster the illness will progress. It does not matter if the uncontrolled free radicals come from a shortage of antioxidants, or from high levels of free radicals, it is the total uncontrolled free radicals that produces tissue damage and illness. It also does not matter if the uncontrolled free radicals come from burned hamburger, ultraviolet light, tobacco, bacon, X rays, oxidized cholesterol, acetaldehyde, lipid peroxides, caffeine or anything else,-- the result may be the same,-- any degenerative disease from graying hair to cancer!

Here then, in uncontrolled free radicals at the cellular and subcellular levels, are the true roots of degenerative disease. The real issue is the total free radicals versus the total antioxidants, while the degenerative disease itself will largely be determined by the location of the uncontrolled free radicals. If the excess free radicals were in the brain, we could expect

Addendum Update.

Alzheimer's or Parkinson's disease with damaged brain cells and unusual growth of neurons; if in the nervous system we could expect multiple sclerosis with the lipids in the nerve sheaths altered or destroyed; if in the vascular system we could expect damaged blood cells, blood sludge, and changes to the arteries themselves. So now let us go back to the vascular system and chelation therapy, while remembering that all body cells contain trace metals and that all trace metals (and particularly copper) act as catalysts in the production of free radicals. Catalysts are intermediate substances in chemical reactions that facilitate the chemical reaction without themselves being altered or consumed. If free radicals injure and destroy more cells than the body can detoxify the cellular materials will remain in the tissues and the metallic ions released from the dead cells will then catalyze many more free radicals.

CALCIUM CHELATION THERAPY. (Page 227.)

If for any reason free radicals within the vascular system exceed the antioxidant defences the free radicals will damage the blood, but they will also damage the blood vessels. It has been known for several years that the plaques in blood vessels are initiated by the proliferation of a single cell, not from the inner lining of the blood vessel, but from the middle lining. The question then has always been; how does a single mutating cell from the middle lining of the blood vessel get through to the inside of the inner lining? It now appears that the cells of the inner lining are resistant to mutation, but the cells of the middle lining are susceptible to mutation. Therefore it is free radicals within the vascular system that damage the inner lining and finally penetrate to the middle lining where they damage the cell nucleus and induce mutation of one or more cells, resulting in the tumorous replication of the cells and the ultimate development of the plaques. The chemistry of the development of the plaques is highly complex, but it is scientifically detailed by Dr. Cranton on pages 217-219 in his excellent book. Ultimately, and largely as a result of free radical damage, "the central core of the plaque degenerates into an amorphous fibro-fatty mass which contains varying amounts of calcium, cholesterol, connective tissue, and cellular debris while ongoing free radical activity also promotes arterial spasm which further occludes blood flow". Another effect of free radicals and metallic ions is to promote cross linkages of connective tissues and elastin (the elastic in the blood vessels), which reduces the elasticity of the blood vessels and prevents dilation to accomodate requirements for increased blood flow.

Although chelation therapy does pick some of the calcium out of the blood vessel plaques and thus promotes disintigration of the plaques, its greatest benefit comes from the removal of metallic ions which in turn reduces the total body load of free radicals and allows the blood vessels to heal, while its other, perhaps even greater benefit, is to reduce the "hardening" of the blood vessels by removing the metallic cross linkages. Significantly, although intravenous chelation is of particular benefit to vascular disease, it is also effective against all degenerative diseases because it not only promotes better health through improved calcium utilization and increased blood flow, but it also greatly reduces the total toxic load by removing toxic metals like lead, mercury, and cadmium, and the free metallic ions, which together contribute to the free radicals that induce degenerative disease. The reduction in free radicals, in turn, reduces the need for antioxidants, which allows all body systems to stabalize.

DMSO is well known as an active fluid that readily penetrates living tissues. It has been so successfully used against arthritis that some clinics have been using it intravenously with even greater success. This in turn has led to it being added to the EDTA solution with extra visible benefit to many people. The reason for the benefit is of course that DMSO is an active antioxidant that is highly compatable with the body. Indeed, one must postulate that perhaps intravenous EDTA and DMSO could also be a highly effective therapy against all forms of radiation damage.

FREE RADICALS and CHOLESTEROL PROBLEMS.
Cholesterol levels are an indicator of vascular risk, but they really are not a problem. Cholesterol is essential to the body in many ways including the production of Vitamin D, bile, and sex and other hormones, while its most important role is as an antioxidant in the sidewall of every cell in the body where it protects the vital phospholipids from free radical damage. Cholesterol is so vital to all of these processes that it is made by many parts of the body in response to the various requirements. High blood cholesterol levels have long been associated with vascular disease, but, while the association is fact the cholesterol itself is not the problem. Cholesterol, as found in the blood, is of two types, HDL which is said to be good and LDL which is said to be bad. It is the difference that is significant. Unoxidized "good" cholesterol is selectively bound to HDL (High Density Lipoproteins) while oxidized or "used" cholesterol is selectively bound to LDL (Low Density Lipoproteins). Remember now, that despite diet, the body makes its own "good" cholesterol according to demands. High numbers of free radicals induce the body to make more HDL cholesterol which is "oxidized"

by free radicals to LDL cholesterol. High HDL cholesterol is therefore not the villain, but the savior against free radical attack, while the LDL cholesterol, although toxic, is not the true cause of the plugged arteries. Instead it is plainly just the result of the quenched free radicals. High blood cholesterol is therefore associated with vascular disease because it is a certain indicator of extensive free radical activity, but to reduce blood cholesterol levels with drugs that interfere with the production of HDL cholesterol is utter folly because the result is to reduce body defences against the free radicals and thus promote the vascular destruction that you are trying to reduce. From all of the foregoing it is clear that HDL cholesterol levels could be quite high, but LDL cholesterol levels should be reduced as much as possible.

Cholesterol is not static in the bloodstream. It is removed from the blood by the liver, which, aided by Vit.C and taurine, makes it into bile. It appears that both forms of cholesterol are removed but this point is not clear. If the stool is pale, taurine and/or vitamin C will usually increase bile and reduce blood cholesterol levels. The extra bile will improve digestion of fats and the stool will become darker. If the stool remains pale, bile salts, taken after the meal should be intermittently tried as a means of re-starting the cycle. If this too fails, infection of the liver should be suspected with trials of resteclin, metronidazole, ketoconazole etc. Chiropractic may also be effective.

It may now appear that high blood cholesterol results from impaired formation of bile, and indeed this may be the case, but biological systems are seldom simple. Cholesterol is the basis of animal life, and it is so precious that some of it must be saved, so the cholesterol is retrieved and resorbed from the stool by the colon, and returned to the bloodstream. It appears that both forms of cholesterol are resorbed, although it seems doubtful that any HDL cholesterol would remain unchanged. It also appears that the amount of cholesterol resorbed is dependent upon colon porosity and colon transit time. Dietary fibre will reduce transit time and it may substantially reduce LDL cholesterol levels.

From the forgoing it can be seen that long and delayed stool transit time, or other colon problems could result in high LDL cholesterol levels without producing or indicating serious vascular problems, but the increased density of the blood together with the toxic effects of the LDL cholesterol might raise blood pressure and certainly would not be conducive to good health.

If LDL cholesterol levels remain high despite chelation and the forgoing suggestions, then the drug Questran, taken in small quantities 4 or 5 times daily should be tried. Questran will selectively bind cholesterol in the colon and thus ensures excretion with the stool. Questran is a chemical which may have some adverse side effects if the prescription quantities are used.

Cholesterol therefore is the saviour. It is not the villain. High blood cholesterol is only a symptom,-- an indicator of too many free radicals, and the villain,-- the real villain,-- is the source of those free radicals.

FREE RADICALS AND HARDENING OF TISSUES (CALCINOSIS).

Many things in life are just taken for granted without any thought to their actual formation. We all use leather, and we all wear leather shoes, - shoes that withstand mud, water, abrasion, and untold and unthinking abuse. What then is this peculiar material that we call leather. Leather is animal hide that has been "tanned", i.e. specifically, treated with substances that cause cross linkages of connective tissues and elastin by free radical activity. Some leather is urine tanned, and some leather is manure tanned, which indicates the free radical activity of these two very human substances. Tannin (from hemlock bark) and formaldehyde and similar chemicals have also been used for many years. Formaldehyde is such a successful promoter of free radical cross linkage of connective tissues and elastin that for many centuries it has been used as embalming fluid, - fluid that "tans" the body inside and out with so many free radical cross linkages that no biological organisms can attack the remains. Formaldehyde, added to protein, forms a durable plastic. Now each time that alcohol is consumed it is changed by the body to acetaldehyde, which is another aldehyde that is so similar to formaldehyde that cirrhosis of the liver is, quite factually, a form of ante-mortem embalming. Can anyone think then that free radical activity, from any source, would be confined to the inside of arteries? Free radicals attack and permeate the tissues wherever they are. The arteries are wrapped with sensitive muscles, muscles that contract in a repeated sequence initiated by the heart, which help to squeeeze the blood along and forms the pulse. When free radicals cross link the arteries and associated muscles, the arteries become hard, and almost brittle, a fact observable on autopsy, and a fact that imposes an immeasurable strain on the heart, which, instead of being helped by the squeeze of the pulse is now struggling to push the blood through the entire vascular system. Is it any wonder then that people with vascular disease have high blood pressure and a hard, sharp, pulse?

Now if cross linkage from free radicals so greatly affects the vascular system, will it not also affect the muscles of the heart and other organs, all of the glands, and all of the cords and ligaments? Free radicals then, must be the real cause of the failures and deformities, seen and unseen, that we know as old age. Yet there is more, much more, than just free radicals to hardening of the tissues, because calcium too, plays a role.

Low tissue oxygen, from any cause, forces the body to metabolize glucose only as far as lactic acid. If then extra oxygen is supplied, the body will be able to metabolize the lactic acid to energy, carbon dioxide, and water. If extra oxygen is not supplied, the lactic acid will build up and produce metabolic acidosis. Metabolic acidosis can also result from excess protein and/or excess sulphur. (from protein, junk food etc.), while metabolic acidosis in turn induces the parathyroid to produce excess hormone (PTH) which increases calcium uptake. Calcium is alkaline so the calcium then reacts with the lactic acid and the tissues then become hardened with calcium lactate. Note that all acids carry free radicals that are short one electron but are marked plus +, while all alkalis carry free radicals that have an extra electron but are marked negative -. Therefore any major disturbance to the acid/alkaline balance results in excess free radicals. Lactic acid, then, is the principal active agent in calcinosis, and lactic acid can be produced in several ways:

1. "Oxidation" of glucose without oxygen, by electron transport (free radicals) by mutated cells, or by cells completely starved for oxygen, with the "reduced" glucose then going to lactic acid.
2. Free radicals in the bloodstream attack and perforate the inner lining of the arteries and then attack the middle lining where they initiate mutagenic proliferation of an atheroma. As the atheroma grows the mutagenic cells become starved for oxygen and they too then metabolize glucose only to lactic acid, followed by calcinosis and build up of cholesterol within the plaque. Reduced blood flow and reduced oxygenation to the parts of the body fed by the artery then further increases the internal production of lactic acid, followed by acidosis and calcinosis and on and on.
3. Altered hormones, altered sodium/potassium, (stress), or lack of exercise induces edema and lymphatic failure. Proteins in the stagnant lymph induces fibrosis with reduced blood circulation, followed by increased lactic acid and more calcinosis,-- etc.
4. The diabetic state, where excess adrenalin or shortage of insulin forces more glucose on the cells than the oxygen supply can metabolize, with the glucose then going to lactic acid. As most diabetics are actually adrenalin diabetics the extra insulin usually prescribed increases the lactic acid and multiplies the problems.

Addendum Update.

5. Lactic acid generated by infectives.

Now here we should again note that acidosis and high lactic acid of itself generates free radical activity, while the free radicals from the lactic acid together with other free radicals cross links the hardened tissues and makes them as firm and durable as leather, a simple fact that can be seen in the legs of many people.

REDUCING FREE RADICALS.

Dr. Cranton, Dr. Stephen Levine, and others, to their great credit, have greatly increased our knowledge of free radicals and their disastrous effects, and they have also greatly expanded the list of antioxidants.

The principal antioxidants that can be readily supplemented are: Vitamin C, Vitamin E, beta carotene, cysteine, methionine, tyrosine, selenium, and superoxide dismutase. (SOD). Manganese, copper, zinc, and iron are necessary co-factors that can be supplemented according to hair mineral test. Note that these metals promote free radical activity only when released in ionic form from dead cells within living tissues, and dietary forms do not promote free radicals. DMSO has been used topically, intravenously, and internally in concentrations of less than 15%. Extra oxygen reduces the production of free radicals within the tissues. Hyperbaric oxygen therapy has been used for cancer, multiple sclerosis, and spinal cord injury, and it may be very useful for many other conditions. Sleeping with fresh air from a fan is also beneficial. Several other ways of increasing tissue oxygen are of value, including hydrazine sulphate (cancer), potassium chlorate ($K\ Cl\ O_3$) and the new "stabalized electrolytes of oxygen", which we believe may be $Mg\ Cl\ O_4$ and $Mg_2\ Cl\ O_7$. Intravenous chelation is a preferred therapy that will reduce free radicals and tissue damage throughout the body. It is more effective when DMSO is added to the solution. Oral EDTA (Page 227) in amounts up to 4 gms per day is also effective. Cholesterol is produced by the body as a necessary antioxidant. It cannot be reduced by diet. Reduced dietary cholesterol and drugs that inhibit cholesterol formation (Lovestatin) reduce the bodies defence against free radicals and are counter productive. Taurine increases the removal of cholesterol from the bloodstream and conversion to bile, which allows the body to produce more "good" cholesterol to combat free radicals. With improved colon function the body excretes more oxidized cholesterol, which can be further increased by careful use of Questran. Citric acid is an effective chelator of metals. The grapefruit and egg diet is successful because the citric acid removes the ionic metal cross-links in the hardened tissues and the cysteine and the cholesterol in the eggs reduces free radicals, while the high protein diet promotes rebuilding

496.

of damaged tissues. For success, minerals must be supplemented two hours away from the grapefruit, and bi-carbonate must be taken $\frac{1}{2}$ hr after meals. "Free Radical Quenchers", sold under various names and containing various substances are usually well formulated with EFAs (Essential Fatty Acids) as a base, usually featuring fish oils, Omega 3, Flax oil, and GLA (Gamma Linolenic Acid).

Although the damaging effects of free radicals is well known, the actual source of the free radicals is less certain. Because fats are so easily double oxidized, i.e. changed to the form of peroxide (peroxidized), modern degenerative disease has been blamed on all of the heated and rancid fats from peanut butter and corn oil to lard and chicken skin, and many books and articles have been written on fats and free radicals, and yet, -- now does this not really take us right back to Page 2, and Sam. Yes, remember Sam? Sam, the rotten old fossil that drinks and smokes and drowns himself in coffee and booze, and lives on bacon and rancid fats, -- and yet remains healthy! Can it be that peroxidized fats are not the culprit, and are not quite as lethal as we think?

Now when we eat these dangerous fats they enter the stomach where they are joined by many other dangerous foods. These other foods contain phytates, and salicilates, and nightshade poison, and bromines, and oxylates, and vanillins, and many other poisons along with various acids and alkalis, and the body then pours in more acids and more alkalis. All of these substances have free radical activity, but many are plus + and many are minus - , so the free radicals largely cancel each other out, resulting in relatively few free radicals being absorbed from food unless the system is very badly overloaded. Overloaded? Surely it cannot be overloaded by the alcohol, or the caffeine, or the tannin from tea, or the carbonic acid from pop, all of which may be added to the mix! Overloaded? How greatly overloaded? We all know that yogurt and acidophilus are good for us because they kill the bad organisms by producing -- well-- of course, hydrogen peroxide! Yes, hydrogen peroxide, that same disinfectant and hair bleach that endlessly spawns free radicals.

The real question then is how many free radicals from the digestive tract actually reach body tissues? Will care with fats and oils ensure health? If rancid fats are the cause of arthritis and cancer why is Sam still healthy at 90 while others are deperately ill at 60?

Quite obviously it is not entirely free radicals from food and foolishness that induces degenerative disease. The cause is unquestionably free radicals, but free radicals generated within the living tissues, so the destructive free radicals must come from chronic infection, and Candida Yeast must be the leading infective.

Addendum Update.

CANDIDA YEAST,-- THE LIVING AGENT OF DEATH.

So here we are back again to Candida. Candida, the ancient yeast-like fungus that is in fact a multi-celled plant that grows within us. Candida, with two forms, the juvenile budding form that lies innocently on the surface of the mucosa, and the adult mycellial form that produces both filaments and hyphae; hyphae that penetrate the flesh and lock the infective into the living tissues like the arms of an octopus, while the filaments enter and clog the bloodstream with rods and L forms. Candida, the only infective that produces hyphae so strong that they can grow through the intestinal walls and make the intestine porous. Candida, the infective that is so invasive that it breaks down body cells and uses the magnesium and other nutrients from the plundered body cells to form its own water resistant callus complex that shields it from both the immune system, and from topical anti-fungals. Candida, the sly invader that steals body nutrients and slowly reduces the immune system and subdues the host with arthritis and allergies and other infections. Candida, the stealthy infective that lives within us and uses our food to produce alcohol and acetaldehyde that slowly embalms the living tissues and leaves us a weak and rickety zombie. Yes! That is the Living Agent of Death! That is CANDIDA!

> "Oh childhood days of Zest and Glee,
> What made'st thou flee so rapidly,----
> Where hast thou gone? --
> Where ? -- Where ?"

Where? Oh Yes! You were forced out by CANDIDA. And now you cannot return until CANDIDA is gone, -- gone, --gone ----

AFTERWORD.

Many people are known for their failures,-- only a few are known for their successes. We would like to hear about both. If this book has helped you to regain some of your lost health, please let us know. But alas, if you have tried, and this book has failed to help you to re-gain your health, please also let us know. Perhaps we can still be of assistance.

We believe that all of the material in this book is scientifically well based. Doctors and other scientific health professionals are invited to send us comments of any kind, suggestions of any kind, and further information of any kind.

We sincerely hope that the reader has both learned, and has gained perspective from these pages, because to think is to know, and to know is to be able to do.

****

PRINCIPAL REFERENCES.

1. Scientific American Medical Library. Scientific Anerican Inc. New York.
2. Scientific American monthly magazine.
3. A Physicians Handbook on Orthomolecular Medicine. Kalita. Pergamon Press. New York.
4. Journal of Orthomolecular Psychiatry. Acad. Ortho. Psychiatry, 2229 Broad St. Regina Sask.
5. Mental and Elemental Nutrients. Pfeiffer, Keats Pub. New Canaan, Conn.
6. Victory Over Diabetes. Philpott. Keats Pub. 27 Pine St. New Canaan, Conn.
7. Hypo-thyroidism. Broda Barnes. Harper and Row. New York.
8. Nutrition and Your Body. Colimore. Light Wave Press, Los Angeles.
9. Nutrition Against Disease, Williams. Bantam Books. N.Y.
10. Ketoconazole in the Management of Fungal Disease. Levine. Adis Press, Auckland, New Zealand.
11. How to Survive the New Health Catastrophes. Alslaben. Survival Publications, Anaheim, Ca.
12. Chelation Therapy. Soffer. C.Thomas. Springfield,Illinois.
13. The Science and Practice of Iridology. Jensen. Bernard Jensen. Escondido, Ca.
14. Lets Get Well. Davis. Harcourt, Brace and World. New York.
15. The Body is the Hero. Glasser. Random House. New York.
16. Dr. Abravanal's Body Type Diet. Abravanel. Bantam Books. Toronto Ont.

Principal References.

17. Dr. Kinsey and the Institute for Sex Research. Pomeroy. Signet. New Am. Lib. Bergenfield. N.J.

18. Human Sexual Response. Masters & Johnson. Little, Brown & Co. Boston. Conn.

19. Impotence and Frigidity. Hastings. Little, Brown & Co. Boston.

20. Everything You Always Wanted to Know About Sex. Reuben. Bantam Books. New York.

21. Dr. Wilfrid Shute's Vitamin E. Book. Shute. Keats. New Canaan, Conn.

22. A Doctor's New Home Cure for Arthritis. Campbell-Stone. Parker Pub. West Nyack, New York.

23. Nutrigenetics. Brennan. Evans & Co. New York.

24. Control for Cancer. Kittler. Warner Books. New York.

25. Nutrition Almanac. Kirschmann, McGraw-Hill, New York.

26. Literature Survey on Hair Analysis. Mineralab. 22455 Maple Ct. Hayward, Ca.

27. Silver Dental Fillings.- The Toxic Time Bomb. Sam Ziff. Aurora Press.N.Y.

28. Health Essentials and Basic Nervcite Therapy. R. Beebe. Healthology Assn. Vancouver B.C.

29. The Methyl Approach to Hypoglycemia. C.Mason. Mato Labs. Vancouver. 30. The Conquest of Cancer. Dr.V. Livingston. Watts. New York.

31. The Death of Cancer. Dr.H.Manner. Century Pub. Chicago.

32. Vaginal Candidosis

33. Health Consciousness. R.Kupsinel M.D. Oviedo, Florida.

34. The Doctor that Looked at Hands. J.Ellis M.D. Arc Books N.Y.

35. Basophil Cell Counts. C.Pfeiffe.M.D. Journal of Orthomolecular Psychiatry. Volume 13 Number 3.

36. The Healing Nutrients Within. Drs. Eric Braverman and Carl Pfeiffer. Keats, New Canaan, Conn.